Seventh Edition

❖ THINKING ABOUT WOMEN
Sociological Perspectives on Sex and Gender

Margaret L. Andersen
University of Delaware

PEARSON

Boston   New York   San Francisco
Mexico City   Montreal   Toronto   London   Madrid   Munich   Paris
Hong Kong   Singapore   Tokyo   Cape Town   Sydney

❖ For my grandmother,
Sybil R. Wangberg
(1895–1995)

A woman who always said she was just ordinary
but who was very special to those of us who loved her

Series Editor: Jeffrey Lasser
Series Editorial Assistant: Heather McNally
Marketing Manager: Kelly May
Editorial Production Service: The Book Company
Composition Buyer: Linda Cox
Manufacturing Buyer: JoAnne Sweeney
Cover Administrator: Linda Knowles
Electronic Composition: Omegatype Typography, Inc.

For related titles and support materials, visit our online catalog at www.ablongman.com.

Between the time Website information is gathered and then published, it is not unusual for some sites to have closed. Also, the transcription of URLs can result in unintended typographical errors. The publisher would appreciate notification where these errors occur so that they may be corrected in subsequent editions.

Library of Congress Cataloging-in-Publication Data

Andersen, Margaret L.
    Thinking about women : sociological perspectives on sex and gender / Margaret L. Andersen.—7th ed.
        p. cm.
    Includes bibliographical references and index.
    ISBN 0-205-45647-2
        1. Women—United States—Social conditions.   2. Feminism—United States.
    3. Social institutions—United States.   4. Social change.   5. Feminist theory.   I. Title.

HQ1426.A6825 2005
305.42'0973 2—dc22

                                                                              2005046479

Printed in the United States of America

10   9   8   7   6   5   4   3   2   10   09   08   07   06

❖ Contents

Preface   *ix*

About the Author   *xv*

PART I   *Introduction*

1   Studying Women: Feminist Perspectives   1

Why Study Women?   2

The Sociological Imagination   6

Defining Feminism   9

Women's Studies and the Inclusion of Women   11

The Growth of Men's Studies   13

The Significance of Gender, Race, and Class   14

A Sociological Framework for Thinking about Women   16

Chapter Summary and Themes   16 ❖ Key Terms   17 ❖ Discussion Questions/ Projects for Thought   18 ❖ Internet Resources   18 ❖ Suggested Readings   18

PART II   *Gender, Culture, and Sex*

2   The Social Construction of Gender   21

Biology, Culture, and Society   21

The Biological Basis of Sex Identity   22 ❖ Ambiguous Sexual Identities   22 ❖ Nature/Nurture and Sexually Dimorphic Traits   24 ❖ Biological Determinism   25 ❖ The Difference Culture Makes   27 ❖ The Institutional Basis of Gender   30

Socialization and the Formation of Gender Identity   33

Sanctions and Expectations   33 ❖ Race and Gender Identity   35

Socialization across the Life Course   37

Infancy   37 ❖ Childhood Play and Games   38 ❖ Socialization and the Schools   40 ❖ Adult Socialization and the Aging Process   41

Theoretical Perspectives on the Formation of Gender   43

Identification Theory   43 ❖ Social Learning Theory   44 ❖ Cognitive-Developmental Theory   45 ❖ Symbolic Interaction and "Doing Gender"   46 ❖ Comparing Theoretical Perspectives   47 ❖ Limitations of the Socialization Perspective   48

Chapter Summary and Themes   49 ❖ Key Terms   51 ❖ Discussion Questions/ Projects for Thought   51 ❖ Internet Resources   51 ❖ Suggested Readings   52

3 Gender, Culture, and the Media:
The Social Construction of Knowledge   53

Gender, Language, and Popular Culture   56

Gender and the Media   59

Content Analysis and the Media   59   ❖   Theories about the Media's Influence   64

The Sociology of Knowledge   68

Marx and the Social Construction of Knowledge   69   ❖   Sexism as Ideology   71

Chapter Summary and Themes   72   ❖   Key Terms   73   ❖   Discussion Questions/
Projects for Thought   73   ❖   Internet Resources   73   ❖   Suggested Readings   74

4 Sexuality and Intimate Relationships   76

The Social Construction of Sexuality   77

The History of Sexuality in the United States   77

Contemporary Sexual Attitudes and Behavior   79

Race, Sexuality, and Power   84

Sexual Development over the Life Cycle   85

Menstruation   86   ❖   Menopause   87

Love and Intimate Relationships   88

Interracial Relationships   92   ❖   Friendship   93

Lesbian, Gay, and Bisexual Experiences   95

Chapter Summary and Themes   100   ❖   Key Terms   101   ❖   Discussion Questions/
Projects for Thought   101   ❖   Internet Resources   101   ❖   Suggested Readings   102

PART III   *Gender and Social Institutions*

5 Gender, Work, and the Economy   104

Historical Perspectives on Women's Work   105

*The Family-Based Economy   106   ❖   The Family-Wage Economy   107   ❖   The
Family-Consumer Economy   109   ❖   Ideology and the History of Women's Work   110*

What Is Work?   113

Economic Restructuring, Class, and Gender Stratification   115

The Contemporary Status of Women   119

*Labor Force Participation   119   ❖   Gender Segregation   120
❖   Earnings   130   ❖   Promotions   134*

Poverty and Welfare   136

Work Environments   139
    Tokenism   139 ❖ *Sexual Harassment   141* ❖ *Workplace Culture   142*
Intersections of Family and Work   142
    The Second Shift   143 ❖ *Housework and Care Work   143*
Policies for Gender Equity   147

Chapter Summary and Themes   149 ❖ Key Terms   150 ❖ Discussion Questions/
Projects for Thought   150 ❖ Internet Resources   151 ❖ Suggested Readings   151

6 **Gender and Families   153**

Historical Perspectives on Modern Families   155
Feminist Perspectives on Families   159
    The Social Construction of Families   159 ❖ *Family Diversity   161*
    ❖ *The Influence of Class, Race, and Gender   162* ❖ *Linking Social Structure
and Human Action   163* ❖ *The Family Ideal   164*
The Diversity of Contemporary Families   165
    Measuring Family Status   166 ❖ *Divorce   167* ❖ *Balancing Family
and Work   168* ❖ *Cohabitation   170* ❖ *Gay and Lesbian Families   171*
    ❖ *Motherhood   173* ❖ *Fatherhood   175*
Race, Gender, and Families   176
Families and Social Problems   182
    Family Violence   182 ❖ *Teen Pregnancy   187* ❖ *Child Care   189*

Chapter Summary and Themes   193 ❖ Key Terms   194 ❖ Discussion Questions/
Projects for Thought   194 ❖ Internet Resources   195 ❖ Suggested Readings   195

7 **Women, Health, and Reproduction   197**

The Social Structure of Health   200
    Gender and Health   200 ❖ *Race, Class, and Health   202*
    ❖ *Reproduction and Protective Legislation   203*
Gender, Health, and Social Problems   205
    Gender and the Body: Weight, Food, and Body Image   205 ❖ *Substance Abuse:
Alcohol, Drugs, and Smoking   209* ❖ *Women and AIDS   212*
    ❖ *Disability   213* ❖ *Health Insurance   214*
The Politics of Reproduction   214
    Birth Control   215 ❖ *Abortion   217* ❖ *Racism and Reproduction   218*
    ❖ *The Politics of Birth: Pregnancy and Childbirth   219* ❖ *New
Reproductive Technologies   225*
Gender and the Health Care System   226
    Women as Health Care Workers   226 ❖ *The Women's Health Movement   226*

Chapter Summary and Themes   228 ❖ Key Terms   229 ❖ Discussion Questions/
Projects for Thought   229 ❖ Internet Resources   229 ❖ Suggested Readings   230

8   Women and Religion   232

Sociological Perspectives on Religion   234

Religion and Social Control   235

Religion and the Emergence of Feminism in the United States   237

Women and Religiosity   240

*Images of Women in Religion 240 ❖ Religious Texts as Interpretive Documents 240
❖ Gender and Religious Beliefs 242*

Women's Status in Religious Institutions   244

Gender and Religious Participation 244 ❖ Women as Clergy 246

Religion and Social Change   247

*Race, Religion and Social Justice 248 ❖ Religion and Antifeminism 249
❖ Feminism and the Religious Right in the United States 250 ❖ The Abortion
Debate: A Conflict of World Views 251 ❖ Faith, Feminism, and Spirituality 252*

Chapter Summary and Themes 256 ❖ Key Terms 256 ❖ Discussion Questions/
Projects for Thought 257 ❖ Internet Resources 257 ❖ Suggested Readings 257

9   Women, Crime, and Deviance   259

Sociological Perspectives on Crime and Deviance   260

*Early Traditions 261 ❖ Defining Deviance 263 ❖ Labeling
and Social Deviance 264 ❖ Deviance, Power, and Social Conflict 264
❖ Feminist Perspectives on Deviance 265*

Women as Criminals   267

*The Extent of Criminality among Women 267 ❖ Causes
of Women's Crime 269 ❖ Defining Crime 271*

Women as Victims of Crime   271

Rape 274 ❖ Causes of Rape 276

Women in the Criminal Justice System   279

Gender and the Courts 279 ❖ Women and Prison 280

Chapter Summary and Themes 283 ❖ Key Terms 283 ❖ Discussion Questions/
Projects for Thought 284 ❖ Internet Resources 284 ❖ Suggested Readings 284

10   Gender, Education, and Science   286

Women and the History of Education   288

Gender and Educational Success   290

*Gender and Schooling 291 ❖ Academic Achievement: Is There
a Gender Gap? 295 ❖ Gender and the Curriculum 297
❖ Class and Race Inequality 298*

Women in Higher Education   300

Gender, Science, and Society   304

  *The Status of Women in Science   304   ❖   Science, Feminism,
  and the Social Construction of Knowledge   307*

Chapter Summary and Themes   312   ❖   Key Terms   313   ❖   Discussion Questions/
Projects for Thought   313   ❖   Internet Resources   313   ❖   Suggested Readings   313

11   Women, Power, and Politics   **315**

Defining Power   317

Women and the State   318

Women and the Law   320

Women in Government   323

  The Gender Gap   327   ❖   Do Women Make a Difference?   327

Women and the Military   328

  Lesbians and Gays in the Military   330   ❖   Feminism and Militarism   331

Rethinking the Political   331

The Women's Movement   333

  *American Feminism in the Nineteenth Century   334   ❖   The Emergence of the
  Contemporary Women's Movement   337   ❖   Feminism and Civil Rights   339
  ❖   The Second Wave of Feminism   340   ❖   Feminism for the Twenty-First
  Century: A Third Wave?   342*

Chapter Summary and Themes   344   ❖   Key Terms   345   ❖   Discussion Questions/
Projects for Thought   345   ❖   Internet Resources   346   ❖   Suggested Readings   346

PART IV   *Gender and Social Change: Frameworks of Feminism*

12   Women and Social Reform, Liberal Feminism   **348**

Frameworks of Feminist Theory   350

The Liberal Basis of Modern Feminism   353

Liberalism as a Mode of Social Thought   354

Early Liberal Feminists   358

  *Mary Wollstonecraft   358   ❖   Harriet Martineau   360   ❖   John Stuart Mill
  and Harriet Taylor Mill   362*

The Critique of Liberal Feminism   368

Chapter Summary and Themes   370   ❖   Key Terms   371   ❖   Discussion Questions/
Projects for Thought   371   ❖   Internet Resources   372   ❖   Suggested Readings   372

13 Contemporary Frameworks in Feminist Theory   373

The Radical Origins of Feminist Theory: The Critique
of Liberal Feminism   374

Historical Roots of Radical Feminism   375

Socialist Feminism: The Importance of Class and Capitalism   377

*Karl Marx and Historical Materialism   377   ❖   Class and Capitalism   379
❖   Ideology and Consciousness   380   ❖   The Woman Question   382
❖   The Socialist Feminist Critique of Marx   383*

Radical Feminism: The Power of Patriarchy   386

*The Sex/Gender System   387   ❖   Sexuality and the State   387
❖   Intersections of Capitalism and Patriarchy   388   ❖   Comparing Liberal,
Socialist, and Radical Feminism   389*

Multiracial Feminism   390

Postmodernist Feminism   393

Queer Theory and Sexualities   397

Continuing Questions for Feminist Theory   399

Chapter Summary and Themes   400   ❖   Key Terms   401   ❖   Discussion Questions/
Projects for Thought   401   ❖   Internet Resources   402   ❖   Suggested Readings   402

Glossary   *404*

Bibliography   *409*

Name Index   *439*

Subject Index   *449*

❖ *Preface*

When I first wrote *Thinking about Women* in the late 1970s, feminist scholarship was new and struggling to find a legitimate institutional location in higher education. Now, the study of gender and the field of Women's Studies, along with the growing field of Men's Studies, have become relatively secure within colleges and universities across the country—indeed, around the world. The early editions of *Thinking about Women* reflected the often strident dialogue that feminist scholars had with their home disciplines. Much of the early work criticized the tendency to see everything about women as biologically based. As feminist scholarship developed over the years, more and more work documented the social basis for gender.

That insight about the social construction of gender has produced many volumes of work, more than could ever be reviewed in a single book. Feminist scholarship has flourished—not just in Women's Studies, but in every discipline. Now, thousands of students every year take courses on gender and women's studies and feminist scholars are frequently cited as experts in the media on a wide variety of topics. The growth of feminist scholarship has helped us see how gender influences everything—from the most immediate bodily experiences to large-scale world problems, including war and terrorism.

Thinking about Women is a comprehensive text that reviews how much gender relations have influenced women's lives, as well as men's. Furthermore, it shows how gender is also tangled with systems of race, class, and sexual inequality. From the early years when the feminist movement was largely centered on the lives and experiences of White women, feminist scholars now anchor their work in recognizing the interrelationship among gender, race, and class—and increasingly, sexuality. Although no single book can do justice to this now huge field of study, *Thinking about Women* introduces students to the basic ways that gender operates in society—influencing women's and men's self-concepts, relationships with others, life opportunities, and experiences of inequality. Gender continues to operate in a way that disadvantages women in most settings, even though highly successful women are increasingly visible in public life. But we cannot let the more visible presence of women in positions of leadership and power blind us to the continuing differences that gender makes.

Thinking about Women develops from the empirical research and feminist theory that has taught us how much gender matters in society. It presents the most current scholarship on gender, but in a style that is accessible to those who have never thought much about it before, as well as to those who have been introduced to studying women in other undergraduate courses or life activities. *Thinking about Women* is grounded in a sociological perspective, although it can be used in interdisciplinary courses.

Organization of the Book

Thinking about Women is organized in four parts. Part I, introduces students to the study of gender as it is rooted in feminist analysis. This section introduces the sociological framework that underlies this book and shows how research on women and women's studies has developed from the feminist movement. This section includes discussion of men's studies and its connection to feminist scholarship.

Part II, "Gender, Culture, and Sex," focuses on the social construction of gender and the representation of gender in culture, particularly in the media. Chapter 2, on the social construction of gender, reviews the influence of gender socialization and the role of gender in shaping women's and men's identities. Chapter 3, "Gender, Culture, and the Media," has been significantly rewritten to give more attention to the influence of the media and popular culture on the social construction of gender. Chapter 4, "Sexuality and Intimate Relationships," examines the relationship between gender and sexuality as social constructions. This chapter shows how gender and sexuality reinforce each other.

Part III, "Gender and Social Institutions," examines the institutional structures of work, family, health, religion, criminal justice, education, and politics. Chapter 5, "Gender, Work, and the Economy," includes new research on women's work and economic status. The chapter includes a discussion of poverty and welfare reform, as well as balancing work and family—a theme also picked up in Chapter 6 on gender and families. Chapter 6 includes a discussion of the historic evolution of contemporary family forms and emphasizes the diversity of women's experiences in families. It also includes discussion of various problems for families, including family violence, teen pregnancy, and child care. Chapter 7, on gender and health, looks at the consequences of gender inequality for women's health compared with men's and also includes extensive discussion of reproductive politics. Chapter 8, on women and religion, conceptualizes religion as both a source of women's oppression, but ironically, also a source for women's liberation. Chapter 9 studies women and crime—both as perpetrators and victims. There is an extensive discussion of women's victimization by violence and also discussion of how men's violence is related to gender roles. The chapter on gender, education, and science (Chapter 10) studies gender and schooling, but also shows how the construction of scientific knowledge is influenced by the exclusion of women from positions of scientific leadership. Finally, Chapter 11, on

women, power, and politics, forms a segue from the focus on institutions to the last section on social change. It discusses women's status in political institutions, but also includes an overview of the women's movement and other forms of women's political activism.

The final part of the book, "Gender and Social Change," introduces students to feminist theory and its link to the women's movement. Chapter 12 reviews the evolution of liberal feminism, showing students how the term *liberal*—though widely stigmatized in conservative discourse—is a specific feminist philosophy with important implications for social change. By detailing the historical evolution of liberal feminism, students can examine their own assumptions about the dominant strategy of "equal rights" that has characterized much feminist transformation of society. Chapter 13 reviews more radical perspectives and updates the discussion of theory to include multiracial feminism, postmodernism, and queer theory. Throughout, the presentation of theory emphasizes the need to examine one's underlying assumptions—theoretical or common sense—to understand the different strategies needed to improve women's lives.

New to the Seventh Edition

There are many changes and additions to the seventh edition that both update and improve earlier editions. There is a new introduction in Chapter 1, written to capture the attention of a new generation of students and to make the opening part of the book more "user friendly." The book has been reorganized to put the chapter on politics at the end of the section on institutions, thus linking politics and the women's movement more closely to the section on feminist theory. At the suggestion of reviewers, there is greater attention to violence against women throughout the book, and examples have been updated to reflect the changing context of the time.

In this edition, the chapter summaries have been replaced by something called "Chapter Summary and Themes" at the end of each chapter. This feature highlights the major themes of each chapter so that students will know the major points that frame the data being discussed. This feature is formatted in a way that should help students and faculty review the major objectives of each chapter.

Throughout the new edition, new research has been incorporated, examples revised to appeal to a new generation, and figures and empirical facts updated to reflect the most current information. More material on men is included throughout the book, reflecting the new scholarship on men, as well as reviewers' suggestions. There is new material on a wide array of subjects that now are capturing public attention, including (but not limited to) gay marriage, welfare reform, women and the military, interracial dating and friendship, affirmative action, transgender identities, disability, and the global AIDS epidemic. Specific changes to each chapter are detailed below.

Chapter-by-Chapter Changes

In addition to the updating and incorporation of new research, there are particular changes in every chapter that are noteworthy.

Chapter 1: Studying Women: Feminist Perspectives
- a new introduction to engage the attention of contemporary students
- updated examples and data throughout

Chapter 2: The Social Construction of Gender
- updated material on gender and social interaction
- more focus on gender identity, beauty, and appearance

- inclusion of transgender identity
- new material on retirement, aging, and gender

Chapter 3: Gender, Culture, and the Media: The Social Construction of Knowledge
- an expanded section (and new title) to emphasize the influence of media and popular culture
- inclusion of concept of controlling images
- new material on images of lesbians and gays in the media

Chapter 4: Sexuality and Intimate Relationships
- new research on homophobia
- new material on "hooking up" on college campuses
- inclusion of research on cross-cultural studies of menopause
- stronger section on interracial dating and friendships
- revamped section on gender and friendship

Chapter 5: Gender, Work, and the Economy
- income and poverty updated to 2003
- discussion of phenomenon of "stay-at-home moms"
- more coverage of the consequences of welfare reform
- new material on care work
- more discussion of impact of Title IX

Chapter 6: Gender and Families
- chapter now framed by structural diversity model of families from Baca Zinn and Eitzen
- new material on same-sex marriage debates
- updated discussion of child care

Chapter 7: Women, Health, and Reproduction
- new section on gender and disability
- new material on spread of AIDS among women, including globally

Chapter 8: Women and Religion
- new research on evangelical women
- added material on the Wiccan movement

Chapter 9: Women, Crime, and Deviance
- new research on stalking
- updated discussion of victimization of women by rape and other forms of violence
- new discussion of the characteristics of rape-prone environments
- new research on prostitution

Chapter 10: Gender, Education, and Science
- new data on the status of women in scientific professions
- updated material on women's educational attainment

Chapter 11: Women, Power, and Politics
- enhanced section on women in the military, including material on women in the Iraq war
- new data on women in politics, following the 2004 elections

Chapter 12: Women and Social Reform: Liberal Feminism
- inclusion of the concept of affirmative action and Supreme Court *University of Michigan* cases
- strong historical analysis of the emergence of liberal feminism

Chapter 13: Contemporary Frameworks in Feminist Theory
- added discussion of third-wave feminism and generational differences in support for feminism

Pedagogical Features

Thinking about Women includes several features to make it easy to teach. With the seventh edition comes a new *Instructor's Manual,* developed by Dana Hysock under the supervision of Margaret Andersen. Dana Hysock is a Ph.D. student at the University of Delaware who has been regularly teaching the sociology of women and men in American society, using *Thinking about Women.* The *Instructor's Manual* includes suggested classroom exercises, recommended films, and discussion questions for students.

In addition, students and instructors will find very useful **Chapter Summaries and Themes** at the conclusion of every chapter. These are intended to highlight the major points of each chapter, thus enhancing student learning.

Every chapter also includes a list of **Websites** appropriate to the chapter material. These can help students with course projects, can show them different organizations, and can, in some cases, even suggest places where students may be able to pursue internships and employment opportunities if they want to work on gender or women's issues.

Each chapter also includes—in the text itself—**discussion questions/projects for thought,** which can be used for in-class projects or research assignments and papers. The list of **suggested readings** at the end of each chapter also direct students and faculty to the most current and accessible new scholarship on women and gender.

All **key terms** at the end of each chapter are also defined in a glossary at the end of the book. **Chapter outlines** open each chapter so that students will know what key ideas to look for. **Graphics** are found throughout the book, developed by the author, to help students learn to interpret data; these have been updated to the most recent available.

Acknowledgments

I could never have written any of the editions of *Thinking about Women* were I not fortunate enough to work within a community of scholars, friends, and family who support my work. Although writing the seventh edition meant many hours sitting alone, navigating my way through the new research, it is collective work that produces what we know about women—and the new perspectives on men that feminism has inspired. Thus, there are many people to thank for sharing ideas, providing resources, and encouraging me. I thank Tammy Anderson, Maxine Baca Zinn, Joel Best, Anne Bowler, Patricia Hill Collins, Ben Fleury-Steiner, Arlene Hanerfeld, Valerie Hans, Elizabeth Higginbotham, Carole Marks, Susan Miller, Howard Taylor, and Kathleen Tierney for the many conversations and other forms of support that sustain this work. My undergraduate and graduate students have also strengthened this book through their questions and ideas. I have written this book with them in mind.

Working with Dusty Friedman, my production editor, is always a pleasure and I thank her for her excellent work and good friendship. I also thank Jane Loftus for her expert copyediting; her careful eye and gift for language have improved this book.

Thank you, too, to Jeff Lasser and Heather McNally for their efforts on behalf of this book.

Special thanks also go to Vicky Becker, Linda Keen, and Judy Watson for all they do to keep computers purring, manage correspondence, keep up with students, and handle various accounts. They are dedicated and hardworking—women I can always count on—and I greatly appreciate all they do. Thanks as well to Bethany Brown for having spent part of her summer doing library work that saved me countless hours. And, to the folks in Oxford—Art, Barry, Brett, Claire, J.C., Judy, MJ, Mimi, Rob, Sam, and Tom— you provided support in various ways, but mostly kept life fun even when there was a surge of work. Most especially, Richard Rosenfeld has been with me through every edition, every deadline, and every fit of anxiety about too much to do. No matter what, he stays calm and his support never wavers. Thank you for your love and for keeping me afloat!

About the Author

Margaret L. Andersen (B.A., Georgia State University; M.A., Ph.D., (University of Massachusetts, Amherst) is Professor of sociology and Women's Studies at the University of Delaware. She is the author of *Race, Class, and Gender: An Anthology* (co–edited with Patricia Hill Collins (Wadsworth 2004); *Sociology: Understanding a Diverse Society* (co–authored with Howard F. Taylor); *Sociology: The Essentials* (coauthored with Howard F. Taylor); *Understanding Society: An Introductory Reader* (coedited with Kim Logio and Howard F. Taylor); and *Race and Ethnicity in Society: The Changing Landscape* (co–edited with Elizabeth Higginbotham).

Professor Andersen received the 2004 SWS Feminist Lecturer Award, given annually to someone whose work has improved the lives of women. She is a recipient of two teaching awards: the College of Arts and Science Outstanding Teaching Award and the University of Delaware Excellence in Teaching Award. She currently chairs the National Advisory Board for the Stanford University Center for Comparative Studies in Race and Ethnicity. She is the former editor of *Gender & Society,* past president of the Eastern Sociological Society, and has served on the Council of the American Sociological Association.

STUDYING WOMEN:
Feminist Perspectives

Why Study Women?

The Sociological Imagination

Defining Feminism

Women's Studies and the Inclusion of Women

The Growth of Men's Studies

The Significance of Gender, Race, and Class

A Sociological Framework for Thinking about Women

Chapter Summary and Themes

Key Terms

Discussion Questions/ Projects for Thought

Internet Resources

Suggested Readings

Have you ever asked yourself:

- Why do so many women spend so much time and money on beauty and diet products—even when some of these products are detrimental to their health?
- Why, when there is a visible presence of women in positions of power and influence, do so many still think that women are not getting the same chances as men?
- Why is violence so much more likely to be committed by men—either against other men or against women and girls?
- Why are there not more women in fields such as science and math, even though, when girls are young, they do at least as well, if not better, in these subjects at school?
- When you look at news images of demonstrations in the streets of Iraq or Pakistan—and other countries—why are all the people men?
- Why is there no national sport that routinely draws stadium-filling crowds where the athletes are all women?
- What would happen if every woman in the United States stayed home from a job for just one week?
- How would your life change if you woke up tomorrow morning and were a different sex?

You could ask yourself many such questions—and you will find that such questions guide much of the content of this book. If you find them intriguing—or you want to know the answers—then you already have the kernel of imagination that can sprout the study of gender in society.

Gender refers to the cultural expectations and societal arrangements by which men and women have different experiences in society. As you will learn throughout this book, gender relations in society are complex, variable, and deeply entrenched in society. Gender shapes all facets of our experiences—what we think, how we walk, how we interact with others, and what opportunities are likely to be available to us. There is no simple or single way to think about gender, but how gender affects women and men in society is a fascinating subject—and one that is important to making social changes that will improve people's lives.

❖ Why Study Women?

As you can see from the title of this book, women are the major focus of study here. But when you think about women, you also have to think about men. Why, then, does this book focus on women? The answer is, first, that too many studies simply do not focus on women. Even now, after several decades of the growth of women's studies, much of what is known stems from an exclusive focus on men. Interestingly, men have been such a primary focal point that many people seem to assume (falsely) that a primary focus on women seems out of balance somehow. But focusing on women brings new questions to light and shows how gender shapes everyone's experience, including men's. This book focuses on women because it is mostly the study of women's lives that has built the study of gender and because it is through focusing on women that we can see the influence of gender in society. Moreover, despite the changes that have occurred in women's lives, women remain disadvantaged relative to men, although, as we will see, this depends on other factors, including race, social class, and sexual orientation, among other social factors.

You may think that studying women is no longer as important as it once was, because women seem to have it made—at least compared to the past. Many believe that equity for women has been achieved. Formal barriers to discrimination have been removed. Women have moved into many of the top professional positions, are now the majority of college graduates, and are more visible in positions of power than at any other time in the nation's history. Over the past 30 years (the full life span of many of you reading this book), the position of women in U.S. society has changed dramatically. The majority of women are employed, and they now number close to half of those in the workplace.

Attitudes have changed, too. The majority of women now say they would prefer to combine marriage, children, and a career. Men have also changed. In the early 1970s, nearly half of all men thought that a traditional marriage—in which the husband provided for the family and the wife ran the house and cared for the children—would be the most satisfying lifestyle. Now, half of all men say the most satisfying lifestyle would be a marriage in which the husband and wife share responsibilities—work, housekeeping, and child care (Roper Organization 1995, Hoffnung 2004).

These changes have led many to conclude that women now have it made, that as long as women and men choose a satisfying lifestyle, no further change is needed. Consider the following facts, however:

- Now, women college graduates who work full-time earn, on average, 76 percent of what men college graduates earn working full-time (DeNavas-Walt et al. 2004).
- Despite three decades of policy change to address gender inequality at work, women and minorities are still substantially blocked from senior management positions in most U.S. companies (Glass Ceiling Commission 1995).
- Twenty-eight percent of all households headed by women are poor; the rates are higher for African American women, Latinas, and Native American women and they have been increasing (DeNavas-Walt et al. 2004).
- Each year, one-half million women are raped or sexually assaulted; three-quarters of these violent acts are committed by friends, acquaintances, or intimate partners (Tjaden and Thoennes 2000).
- Despite the fact that they are the most likely to be employed, women of color are concentrated in the least-paid, lowest-status jobs in the labor market (U.S. Department of Labor 2004).
- Married women and men have increased the number of hours they work per year substantially since 1980—men by 4 percent, women by 42 percent (Mishel et al. 2001).

These facts indicate that although women have come a long way, there is still a long way to go. Little wonder that there is a substantial gender gap in women's and men's perception of society's treatment of women: Women are much more likely than men to perceive job discrimination based on gender (see Figure 1.1).

Look around, and you will see many signs of the status of women in society. In the grocery store, for example, women are clustered in those departments (deli and bakery) that are least likely to lead to promotion; men, on the other hand, predominate in departments such as produce and groceries, where the majority of store managers begin (Padavic and Reskin 2002). In schools, women constitute a large majority of elementary school teachers, but through the higher grades and into college, women become a smaller proportion of the faculty. Despite the recent movement of more women into political office, the vast majority of those who make and enforce laws are men, particularly among those holding the most influential positions.

Differences between women and men can also be observed in interpersonal interaction. Watch the behavior of men and women around you—how they act with each other and with those of the same sex. In public places, men touch women more often than women touch men. Men also touch women in more places on the body than women touch men. Despite stereotypes to the contrary, men also talk more than women and interrupt women more than women interrupt men or men interrupt each other. Women are more likely than men to smile when interacting with others (especially with men), even when they are not necessarily happy. Men, in general, are less restricted in their demeanor than women and use more per-

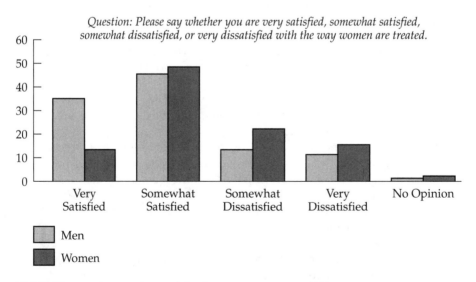

FIGURE 1.1   Perceptions of Society's Treatment of Women

Source: Data from Lydia Saad. 2001. "Women See Room for Improvement in Job Equity." Princeton, NJ: The Gallup Organization. Website: www.gallup.com

sonal space. Although these patterns do not hold for all men and all women, nor necessarily for people from different cultural backgrounds, in general, they reflect the different ways that women and men have learned to interact (Basow 1992).

Many current social problems also call attention to the status of women in society. Violence against women—in the form of rape, sexual harassment, incest, and wife beating—is common. Changes in U.S. families mean that more families are headed by women. Although there is nothing inherently wrong with such arrangements, women's low wages mean that female-headed households have an increased chance of being poor. As a consequence, the rate of poverty among children in such households has increased dramatically in recent years. As a final example, the national controversy over health care also has particular implications for women. Although women live longer than men, they report more ill health than men do, spend their later years with more disabling conditions, and tend to take primary responsibility for the health of others in their families (National Center for Health Statistics 2003).

Thinking about women helps us understand why these things occur. For many years, very few people thought seriously about women. Patterns affecting the lives of women were taken for granted as natural or to be expected. Few people questioned the status of women in society, presuming instead that studying women was trivial, something done only by a radical fringe or by frivolous thinkers. Even now, studying women is often ridiculed or treated with contempt. For example, conservative talk-show hosts portray feminism as "leftist extremism," "out of touch with the mainstream," and "an attempt to transport unpopular liberalism into the mainstream society" (Limbaugh 1992:186–187). Attacks on new multicultural studies, of which women's studies has been a strong part, have accused such studies of only striving for "political correctness" and weakening the traditional "standards" of higher education. Despite these claims, women's studies has opened new areas for questioning, has corrected many of the omissions and distortions of the past, and has generated new knowledge—much of which has important implications for social policy. Moreover, by bringing attention to the study of gender, studying women has opened new ways to think about and study men.

Women's studies, as a field of study, is relatively new, having been established in the late 1960s and early 1970s to correct the inattention given to women in most academic fields. Because of the influence of the feminist movement, scholars in most fields have begun thinking seriously about women. Whereas 30 years ago the study of women's lives and gender relations had barely begun, now women's studies is a thriving field of study. Studying women and men as gendered subjects has often required challenging some of the basic assumptions in existing knowledge—both in popular conceptions and in academic studies. Scholars have found that thinking about women changes how we think about human history and society, and it revises how social institutions are understood. Thinking about women also reveals deep patterns of gender relations in contemporary society. Much of the time, these patterns go unnoticed, but they influence us nonetheless. Often, we take these patterns of everyday life for granted. They are part of the social world that surrounds us and that influences who we are, what we think, and which opportunities are available to us. Women's studies scholarship is transformative; it informs our understanding of women's experiences and changes our thinking about society and the assumptions that different academic fields use to understand the social and cultural world.

The purpose of this book is twofold: to show how the sociological perspective explains women's lives and the structure of gender in society and to show how sociology itself has been transformed through thinking about women. A single book cannot discuss all of the research and theory that has been developed to understand women's experiences, but it can show how knowledge has been reconceptualized as the result of thinking seriously about women's lives.

❖ *The Sociological Imagination*

Patterns in gender relations are found throughout society, although much of the time these patterns remain invisible to us. At some point, however, you may start to notice them. Perhaps at school you see that most of the professors are men and that, among students, men tend to be more outspoken in class, or perhaps at work you notice that women are concentrated in the lowest-level jobs and are sometimes treated as if they were not even there. It may occur to you one night as you are walking through city streets that the bright lights shining in the night skyline represent the thousands of women—many of them African American, Latina, or Asian American—who clean the corporate suites and offices for organizations that are dominated by White men.

Recognizing these events as indications of the status of women helps you see inequities in the experiences of men and women in society. Once you begin to recognize these patterns, you may be astounded at how pervasive they are. As the unequal status of women becomes more apparent, you might feel overwhelmed by the vast extent of a problem most people have never acknowledged. What you see might become troubling, and you may find it difficult to imagine how these long-standing inequities can be changed, but once you start to question the position of women in society, you will want to know more and will begin to ask questions such as: What is the status of women in society? How did things become this way? How does learning about women's experiences change one's thinking about men? How can we change the inequalities that women experience?

Adrienne Rich (1976), a feminist poet, suggests that simply asking "What is life like for women?" will create a new awareness of the situation of women in society and history. This questioning, in part, is what the feminist movement has encouraged in most of the academic disciplines. With whatever question we begin—whether it is "Why is there so much violence against women?" or "Why is it that women clean the offices and men usually manage them?"—by virtue of asking, we are creating new questions and new issues for investigation. It is this process of questioning that gives birth to a sociological and a feminist imagination.

The **sociological imagination** was first described by C. Wright Mills (1916–1962), an eminent sociologist and radical in his time. Mills's radicalism was founded, in part, on his passionate belief that the task of sociology is to understand the relationship between individuals and the society in which they live. He argued that sociological understanding must be used in the reconstruction of more just social institutions. Except for the masculine references in his language, his words still provide a compelling argument that sociology must make sense of the experiences of women and men as they exist in contemporary society. He writes:

> *Nowadays men often feel that their private lives are a series of traps. They sense that within their everyday world, they cannot overcome their troubles, and, in this feeling, they are often quite correct. What ordinary men are directly aware of and what they try to do are bounded by the private orbits in which they live. . . . The sociological imagination enables its possessor to understand the larger historical scene in terms of its meaning for the inner life and external career of a variety of individuals. . . . The first fruit of this imagination—and the first lesson of the social science that embodies it— is the idea that the individual can understand his experience and gauge his fate only by locating himself within his period, that he can know his chances in life only by becoming aware of those of all individuals in his circumstances (Mills 1959:3–5).*

Mills's ideas are strikingly parallel to the feminist argument that women can see how their private experiences are rooted in social conditions by discovering their shared experience with other women. In fact, Mills professes that the central task of sociology is to understand personal biography and social structure and the relations between the two. His argument is best illustrated in the distinction he makes between personal troubles and social issues.

Personal troubles are part of the personal experience of an individual. They are privately felt, and they involve only those persons and events in an individual's immediate surroundings. **Public issues** are events that originate beyond one's immediate experience, even though they are still felt there. Public issues involve the structure of social institutions and their historical development. Mills's own example is that of marriage. He says, "Inside a marriage a man and a woman may experience personal troubles, but when the divorce rate during the first four years of marriage is 250 out of every 1,000 attempts, this is an indication of a structural issue having to do with the institutions of marriage and the family and other institutions that bear upon them" (1959:9). Mills's point is that events felt as personal troubles often have their origins in the public issues that emerge from specific historical and social conditions.

Another example is that of a woman who is beaten by her partner. She experiences deep personal trouble, and perhaps her situation appears to her as unique or as only a private problem. When others in the society have the same experience, then a public issue is found. Common patterns in the experiences of battered women reveal that battering is more than just a private matter. It has its origins in complex social institutions that define women's place as in the home and as subordinate to men. In this sense, battering is both a personal trouble and a public issue. As Mills would conclude, it is then a subject for sociological study. For feminists, this junction between personal experience and the social organization of gender roles is also a starting point for thinking about women.

The relationship between personal troubles and public issues reveals an essential premise of the sociological perspective—that individual life is situated in specific social and historical environments. These environments condition not only what our experience is but also how we think about it. Thinking about women from a sociological perspective asks us to look beyond taken-for-granted ways of seeing the world and, instead, to see how social structures generate the patterns of everyday life.

The concept of social structure is central to sociology. **Social structure** refers to the organization of society that shapes social behavior and social attitudes (see Figure 1.2). This is a broad and abstract concept, one that emphasizes the collective and social basis for behavior, not individual motivations and actions. Of course, abstract realities like social structure ultimately have their origins in how individuals behave, but it is the collective and persistent results of that behavior that make social structures. Social structures shape individual and group choices, opportunities, and experiences. People can feel the effects of social structures in most of what they do. The observation of social structure is the basis for sociological inquiries.

The concept of social structure is aptly described in the feminist philosopher Marilyn Frye's discussion of oppression. Using the metaphor of a bird cage and supposing that you are looking at the cage from the perspective of the bird, Frye observes that if you look only at one wire, you cannot see the other wires; you miss

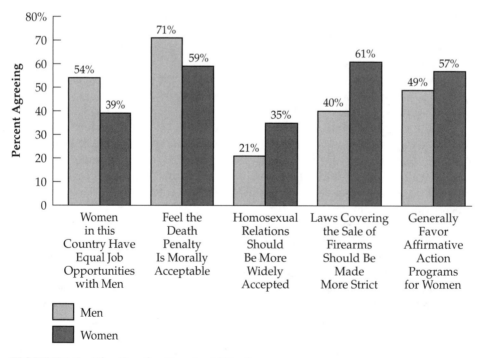

FIGURE 1.2   The Gender Gap in Attitudes

Sources: Data from Lydia Saad. 2003. "Pondering 'Women's Issues,' Part I and Part II." Princeton, NJ: The Gallup Organization. Website: www.gallup.com

seeing the whole, because you are focusing only on one part. Even if you look at each wire, discovering all of its properties, you will still not see the whole. Only when you step back from the cage and look at its structure as a whole—seeing all of the parts in relationship to each other—can you understand why the bird cannot escape the cage. As Frye writes, it is then

> *perfectly obvious that the bird is surrounded by a network of systematically related barriers, no one of which would be the least hindrance to its flight, but all of which, by their relations to each other, are as confining as the solid walls of a dungeon. It is now possible to see and recognize: One can study the elements of an oppressive structure with great care and some good will without seeing or being able to understand that one is looking at a cage and that there are people there who are caged, whose motion and mobility are restricted, whose lives are shaped and reduced (1983:4–5).*

Oppression and social structure are not the same thing. Some social structures are clearly beneficial to some groups. Frye's metaphor, however, helps us understand the meaning of social structure and, in studying oppressed groups, helps us see the social structural basis for group oppression.

As you will see throughout this book, gender is one element of social structure that, along with class and race, shapes the experience of all groups in society. The sociological perspective is fundamentally structural; that is, sociology helps us see the structural origins of individual and group experiences in society. For this reason, it is a critical component of thinking about women.

The study of women requires more than a sociological perspective, however. Much of the current scholarship on women is interdisciplinary. This means that the perspectives of multiple disciplines—whether history, anthropology, psychology, economics, or the humanities—contribute to our understanding of the position of women in society. Although the primary focus of this book is sociological, much of the research on which the book is based is interdisciplinary in character. In addition, contemporary scholarship has been much informed by the women's movement. Feminist thought has stimulated and enriched our understanding of women's lives in society. Feminism shares certain premises with sociology—namely, in understanding that the origins of women's experiences lie beyond individual realities, as Frye's work shows. Feminism, like sociology, points us to understanding the social basis of women's experiences. At the same time, feminism is based on a philosophy of change, particularly that we can build a more just society for women if we consciously understand and seek to transform the social behaviors and institutions that are the basis for women's experiences.

❖ *Defining Feminism*

Feminism is not easy to define because it includes a variety of political perspectives and ideas. As this book will show, there is no single feminist perspective, and feminist theories and programs for social change sometimes differ quite substantially from one another. Still, there are certain common assumptions within feminism.

Feminism begins with the premise that women's and men's positions in society are the result of social, not natural or biological, factors. Although different varieties of feminist thought have developed, feminists generally see social institutions and social attitudes as the basis for women's position in society. Second, because there are structured inequities between women and men; feminists believe in transforming society on behalf of women. Thus, feminism is a way of both thinking and acting; in fact, the union of action and thought is central to feminist programs for social change. Third, feminists believe that women's experiences, concerns, and ideas are as valuable as those of men and should be treated with equal seriousness and respect. This does not mean women have to be like men, but that women's interests should be central in movements for social change.

Public opinion polls indicate that the majority of women in the United States support feminist issues such as equal pay for equal work; improved child care policies; reduced violence against women; and greater opportunities for women regardless of their race, class, or sexual orientation. Why, then, is the label "feminist" so controversial? The word *feminism* conjures up different images to different people. As a result, many who might even agree with feminist ideas and programs for change find it difficult to call themselves feminists. Sometimes not calling oneself a feminist reflects actual disagreement with feminist policies and perspectives, as will be seen in the discussion of antifeminist movements in Chapter 8. Often, people are reluctant to call themselves feminists because of misunderstandings about what it means. Feminism is often equated with being a lesbian, which, in turn, is equated with man hating; thus, for many, rejection of feminism is linked to fears and stereotypes about lesbians. Others feel it is risky to become a feminist, fearing that friends and lovers might reject or tease them. These reactions show how threatened people can be by a movement that advocates change in women's lives. Some have come to think that feminism is no longer necessary, assuming that discrimination has been eliminated by recent reforms and that women and men now stand on relatively equal terms. This book will examine these assumptions, but the point is that many hesitate to call themselves feminists, even when they agree with the ideas of feminism. The negative label associated with feminism is also a serious impediment to improving women's lives.

Why is being a feminist so stigmatized? For some, feminism conjures up images of man-hating and aggressive fanatics, as if to be feminist means one cannot be gentle and kind, be reasonable, or have good relationships with men. This is simply not true, as any careful look at the diverse women and men who are feminists would show. Others will say, "I'm not a feminist; I'm a humanist," reflecting their belief in the betterment of life for all persons—men and women alike—but such a view does not preclude being a feminist. In fact, if one really is in favor of the betterment of all human beings, then it is logical to call oneself humanist, antiracist, *and* feminist. The fact that the label "feminist" carries a stigma to some reflects the deep and continuing devaluation of women throughout U.S. society. Popular stereotypes of feminists as angry, radical, man-hating women encourage this kind of thinking. Some feminists are, indeed, angry—angry about the injustices women face in the workplace, angry about the violence perpetrated against women, angry about persecution of gays and lesbians, and angry about the persistent denigration of women in popular culture. Many feminists are also radical thinkers, particularly if we take *radical* to mean looking at the roots of women's status in society. Feminism includes a wide range of feeling, thought, and ways of being, none of which are so narrow and ugly as the popular stereotype of feminists suggests.

Many feminists are men, although men may find calling themselves feminists especially difficult. Adopting a pro-woman attitude puts men and women at odds with the dominant culture. Men may think that by calling themselves feminists, they will be thought of as gay, itself a stigmatized identity in the dominant culture. As you will see in Chapter 4 on sexuality, this labeling, rooted in the homophobic attitudes of our culture, is a form of social control. It is society's way of trying to force men and women into narrowly proscribed gender roles. Men who call themselves feminists—some of whom are gay, others of whom are not—are men who support women's rights, who do not believe men are superior to women, and who are willing to work for liberating social changes for women and men. This shows another point learned from feminism—that men are subjected to cultural expectations about masculinity that affect their emotions, identities, and social roles.

The fact is that feminism is threatening to those who want to protect the status quo. This has been vividly shown in a global context when in 1994 Taslima Nasrin of Bangladesh was threatened with death by Muslim extremists in her home country. Nasrin is a novelist and poet who, in her writing, has challenged fundamentalist Islamic decrees on the role of women. When religious leaders called for her death, the Bangladesh government sought to arrest her. Islamic radicals renewed their death threat and offered a $5,000 reward to anyone who killed her. She has since been living in exile.

This case is an extreme one, but one need not witness such extremes, nor leave the United States, to see how threatening feminism is for many. Conservative women's groups have targeted women's studies programs, accusing them of being like-minded, distributing misinformation, and brainwashing women. The fact is that becoming a feminist does change the way you think, because it gives you a critical awareness of relationships and social systems that you might have previously taken for granted. And, feminist programs for change would dismantle the privileges that many (though not all) men get simply by virtue of being a man.

Although not everyone who reads this book will be or become a feminist, each reader should at least be willing to examine the questions that feminism raises in order to learn what constitutes feminist thinking. Doing so will help you describe and understand women's and men's experience in contemporary social institutions and make informed judgments about social policies and actions that affect all people's lives.

❖ *Women's Studies and the Inclusion of Women*

Women's studies, with its origins in the women's movement, is grounded in research and theory and in political commitments to improve and transform the status of women in society. Women's studies rests on the premise that changing what we know about women will change women's and men's lives; consequently, developing women's studies as an academic field is seen as part of the process of transforming women's place in society.

Since the resurgence of feminism in the 1960s, women's studies has produced a dramatic outpouring of studies and theories about women in society. These studies have questioned the assumptions and biases of existing work in almost every field, including science, the humanities, and the social sciences. Women working in different fields have discovered that much of what stood for knowledge in their disciplines either was overtly sexist or ignored women altogether. Often, academic women found that they had more in common with each other than they did with the men in their disciplines. As they began to study what their disciplines said about women, they forged new ideas that were critical of preestablished thinking in traditional disciplines. Feminist reconstructions of academic scholarship have now touched every discipline and have resulted in major changes in the assumptions, theoretical frameworks, and research data on which the disciplines rest.

Examples from many disciplines show that when women's experiences are taken seriously, new methods and perspectives must be established. For example, in history, feminist scholars have criticized the "women worthies" approach for recognizing only women who meet the male standards for eminence in history. Although it is important to recognize the contributions of prominent women in history, these women stand out because they are exceptional. They do not represent the experience of the majority of women in their time. In their transformations of historical scholarship, feminist historians have shown how even the periods used to define time frameworks in history are based on men's achievements and men's activities (Lerner 1976). The Renaissance, for example, is typically depicted as a progressive age that encouraged humanism and creativity; yet for women the Renaissance was a time of increased domestication of bourgeois wives and intensified persecution of witches—most of whom were single peasant women. To see the Renaissance from a woman-centered perspective is to see that this was a period marked by increased restriction of the power of women (Kelly-Gadol 1976), not the era of creativity and humanism that male-based studies have defined.

Similarly, in the area of psychological development, feminists have revised models of development that have been based on male experience. Gilligan's (1982) classic work on moral development shows how theories of moral development have taken the male experience as the norm and then measured the female experience against it. In fact, as Gilligan shows, women's moral development follows a different plan from men's, with women's orientation toward morality being more contextual than that of men. In other words, women make moral judgments based on their assessments of conflicting responsibilities in a given situation, whereas men are more likely to make moral decisions based on their judgments of competing rights and abstract principles. Gilligan's point is to show not only that men and women have different conceptions of morality but also that men's experiences have been taken by psychologists to be a universal standard by which both men and women are evaluated.

Women's studies shows how ideas and theories have been derived from the particular experiences of some men and then have been used as the universal standards against which all others have been seen and judged. In any field, whenever men's experience is the standard, women and other subordinated groups (including many men) can only appear incomplete, inadequate, or invisible (McIntosh 1983).

One objective of women's studies scholarship is to see all groups in relationship to one another and to include multiple human groups in the concepts, theories, and content of human knowledge. Including women and people of color in our studies reveals hidden assumptions in what we have learned from more exclusionary studies. This would be a fifth phase of curriculum development and thought: inclusive thinking—that in which women's and men's experiences are seen in relationship to the other and in which multiple human groups are included in the concepts, theories, and content of human knowledge. These different phases are important descriptions of the academic curriculum, not so much because they measure one type of thinking against another, but because they help us identify hidden assumptions in our thinking. Revealing the assumptions embedded in ideas or knowledge helps us envision the process by which knowledge can become genuinely inclusive and take gender, race, and class together as part of the complexity of human experience.

❖ *The Growth of Men's Studies*

The development of more inclusive work on women has spawned the development of another new field: **men's studies.** As scholars have revised their thinking about women, they have likewise reconsidered the lives of men (Kimmel and Messner 2000; Messner 1997). The field of men's studies is different from just studying men. Men's studies specifically challenges the patriarchal bias in traditional scholarship, which has tended to take men as the given universal standard against which others are judged. The debates about using the pronoun *he* as a universal term illustrate this well. Research has found that when *he* is used in the universal sense, those who hear it do tend to presume they are hearing only about men (Henley 1989). Although use of the word *he* may be intended universally, it has a particular effect and that effect is exclusionary. That is, women become invisible and men emerge as a universal standard. Men's studies challenges this kind of thinking.

Men's studies is also explicitly feminist. In fact, men's studies emerged from the women's movement when men, too, began to see how gender and sexism shaped their lives. Men's studies challenges existing sexist norms and, like women's studies, has an activist stance. As a result, it is not just knowing about men that is important, but men's studies encourages using that knowledge to create a more just world.

Like women's studies, men's studies takes gender as a central feature of social life, seeing how gender shapes men's ideas and opportunities; thus, men's studies is not just about men but sees men as gendered beings. Without men's studies, there is a tendency to presume that only women are gendered, as if gender only affects one group. We know, however, that gender affects the experiences of us all, although in different ways, depending on factors such as one's social class, sexual orientation, nationality, or race. Because of this, men's studies also sees diversity among men as important to understanding men's lives. Not all men are sexist in their attitudes and beliefs, although as a group, men benefit from gender privilege; again, however, this varies by social class and race.

Men's studies, like women's studies, also recognizes the importance of sexuality within the matrix of gender, race, and class domination. Heterosexuality is a privileged form of sexual identity; consequently, gays and lesbians suffer oppression because of their sexual orientation. Together, men's studies and women's studies have analyzed the social structures that generate heterosexual privilege, now leading to new areas of inquiry within gay and lesbian studies. Some of this work is examined further in Chapter 4.

❖ *The Significance of Gender, Race, and Class*

The transformation of knowledge through women's studies has shown the inadequacy of generalizing from studies of men to thinking about women. **Faulty generalization** takes knowledge from one experience and incorrectly extends that knowledge to another (Minnich 1990). Women's studies has shown how not to generalize from the experience of men to the experience of women. Similarly, studies by and about women of color have shown the importance of not generalizing from the experiences of White, middle-class women to all women. Doing so only replaces one false universal (White men) with another (White women).

Developing inclusive thinking reminds us that women's experiences vary by race, class, age, and other social factors. Although women as a group share many common experiences, recognizing and understanding the diversity of those experiences are equally important in the construction of descriptions and theories about women's lives.

For example, much is now known about the "second shift" women experience whenever they are employed and also do most of the housework in their own homes, but this is not a new development for African American women, who, since slavery, have worked in the homes and raised the children of White women while also caring for their own families. Analyses of domestic work that ignore the domestic labor of women of color, including the relations with White women such a labor system creates, are faulty and incomplete. One of the major challenges for feminist studies is to create knowledge that penetrates the complex dynamics of race, class, and gender relations in shaping the experience of all persons.

Gender, race, and class are overlapping categories of experience that shape the experiences of all people in the United States. This means that race relations shape the experiences of White people and shape the experiences of people of color but in different ways. In the same vein, gender shapes the experiences of women and shapes the experiences of men; furthermore, class relations affect not just the poor and working class but also the experiences of elites and the middle class.

Each of these categories also overlaps with others. This results in distinct experiences for members of different race, gender, and class groups. Individuals may feel the salience of one or another category at a given time, but their life experiences are shaped by the confluence of all three. As an example, an Asian American woman who hears a derogatory remark about Asian Americans experiences racism, but she may also be stereotyped as a woman. That stereotype, however, is likely to be unique to Asian American women (e.g., that they are submissive and passive), whereas a gender stereotype about another racial group of women may manifest itself differently (e.g., that all blondes are dumb). An Asian American woman's experience will depend not only on her gender and race but also on her class. Her identity at any given time may be centered in any one or more of these experiences, but the point is that her position in society (including the opportunities available to her and what people think of her) is conditioned by her race, class, *and* gender position.

This perspective on the simultaneity of gender, race, and class is different from the additive model that has characterized some thinking about women of color. The term *double jeopardy,* for example, has been used to describe the disadvantage that women of color experience because of their race and their gender. This phrase, however, conjures up images of race and gender as separate experiences, whereas they are integrally related in the experiences of different groups. Race, class, and gender form a **matrix of domination,** meaning that the particular configuration of race, class, and gender relations in society is such that together they establish an interlocking system of domination; no one of them can really be understood without understanding the others, as well (Collins 1990; Andersen and Collins 2004).

Consider the following: White women may be privileged by their race but disadvantaged by their gender and class. Likewise, African American men may be privileged by their gender, but in the context of race and class oppression, this means something different from saying that White men are privileged by their gender. In fact, thinking about race and class oppression in the lives of African American, Native American, and Latino men makes a word like *privilege* even seem out of place. Analyses that are inclusive of race, class, and gender also do not see White men as a monolithic group. Although White men have historically benefited from their gender and race position, class differences among them, not to mention differences in White men's behavior and beliefs, make universal statements about men inaccurate, just as it is incorrect to generalize to all women based on the experiences of some. As you will see throughout this book, studying women requires an understanding of race and class, too. Scholarship about women of color is newly emerging and is an important dimension of women's studies.

❖ *A Sociological Framework for Thinking about Women*

The framework for this book is distinctly sociological. Although much of the research within it comes from other fields or from interdisciplinary work, a sociological perspective forms the core of the book. As you have already seen, the social structural analysis provided by sociological thought is essential to comprehending the situation for women in society. In addition, sociology is an **empirical** discipline, meaning that its method of study is the observation of events in the social world. Sociologists observe social events, discover their patterns, and formulate concepts and theories that interpret relationships among them. An important point about empirical studies is that when the theories that explain observed events no longer make sense of what is observed or when one's observations change, then revisions are necessary. A central point in feminist criticism of sociological work is that conventional theories have not always made sense of women's experiences and therefore must be revised.

Sociology is also a discipline that claims social improvement as part of its goal. Most sociologists believe that sociology should contribute to the improvement of social life. They differ in how to produce this change—some emphasizing gradual improvement through existing governmental and political channels and others believing that only radical social change can solve contemporary social problems. Regardless of their differences, sociologists believe that the purpose of sociological investigation is to generate improved social policies and consequently to generate social change. Sociologists share with feminists the idea that knowledge should provide the basis for improving the lives of women in society.

In sum, sociology is a discipline that purports to give accurate accounts of the social world and its social problems, with the purpose of suggesting policies and possibilities for humanitarian social change. Feminists have argued, however, that sociology has not always made good on its claims. The purpose of feminist scholarship in sociology, as in other fields, is to use the perspective that the discipline offers to develop more complete and accurate understanding of women's and men's lives.

❖ *Chapter Summary and Themes*

Gender refers to the cultural expectations and societal arrangements by which women and men have different experiences in society.

Gender influences all aspects of our lives—our thinking, our interaction, and our life chances. Moreover, it can be seen in the experiences of men, as well as women.

Despite the changes that have been made, women have hardly achieved equality with men.

On numerous indicators, women are disadvantaged relative to men, whether in earnings, the likelihood of poverty, risk of violence, and opportunities for advancement. Furthermore, these patterns are exacerbated for women of color.

Evidence of women's status in society can be found by looking critically at everyday life.

Gender is so pervasive that it can be seen. Once you become attuned to it, you are likely to be surprised by how pervasive gender is in social relations. Thinking critically about gender—and observing its influence in society—is the basis for women's studies.

The sociological imagination links the experiences of individuals in society to the more abstract social structures of which they are a part.

This insight, fundamental to feminist thought, has also been developed by sociologist C. Wright Mills, especially in his distinction between *personal troubles* and *social issues*. Troubles affect a given individual (or individuals), but social issues are found in the structure of society. Seeing this connection requires understand the concept of *social structure*.

There is no single definition of feminism, but it is premised on the belief in social justice for women.

Although the majority of people support feminist values, there is a stigma that many attach to the label feminist. Despite the misunderstandings associated with feminism, it is premised on belief and actions that promote respect, equality, and the value of women's lives.

The scholarship produced by women's studies has transformed knowledge.

Women's studies is a field originating in the feminist movement and committed to the growth of knowledge about and for women. As women's studies has developed, it has also spawned new work in men's studies—scholarship that takes a feminist perspective to interpret how gender influences men.

Because feminism is about the lives of all women, it is important to understand the interrelationships among gender, race, and class.

Generalizing from the experiences of any one group of women leads to false and incomplete conclusions. Developing an inclusive perspective on race, class, and gender helps you see both commonalities and differences among women—and corrects misleading claims that all women are oppressed relative to men.

A sociological framework for thinking about women is marked by a focus on empirical observation, as well as an understanding of the significance of social structures.

❖ *Key Terms*

empirical	matrix of domination	social structure
faulty generalization	men's studies	sociological imagination
feminism	personal troubles	women's studies
gender	public issues	

❖ *Discussion Questions/Projects for Thought*

1. Think about one of the other courses you are currently taking. How are women depicted in this course? If you were to use the phases of curriculum change discussed in this chapter to analyze the presentation of women in this other course, what would you say?

2. Interview your friends and/or family about what feminism means to them. What assumptions do they make about those who call themselves feminists? What does this reveal to you about how feminism is popularly defined?

3. Put yourself in a familiar situation—perhaps at a party or in a classroom or an office. Ask yourself the question similar to what Adrienne Rich has posed: What is life like for women in this situation? What new questions might you ask that would reveal more about women's experiences in this setting than what might be immediately apparent?

❖ *Internet Resources*

Humanists Net Project

http://www.taslimanasrin.com

Following the case of Taslima Nasrin, living in exile because she was threatened for being a feminist in her home nation, Bangladesh, this site provides information about her life and her speeches and written work.

The Feminist Majority

http://www.feminist.org

The Feminist Majority is a private organization dedicated to women's equality. The website provides information on a wide array of subjects, including global issues, reproductive rights, health and safety, careers, and other subjects.

❖ *Suggested Readings*

Baca, Zinn, Maxine, Pierrette Hondagneu-Sotelo, and Michael A. Messner, eds. 2005. *Gender Through the Prism of Difference: Readings on Sex and Gender.* New York: Oxford.
This anthology explores the race, class, and sexual diversity among women and men, both in the United States and in international settings. Through comprehensively examining differences, the editors show how gender is structured in relationship to other social facts.

Baumgardner, Jennifer, and Amy Richards. 2000. *Manifesta: Young Women, Feminism, and the*

Future. New York: Farrar, Straus, and Giroux.
This book is written especially for young women. Baumgardner and Richards explore the implications of feminism for a new generation.

Goetting, Ann, and Sarah Fenstermaker. 1995. *Individual Voices, Collective Visions: Fifty Years of Women in Sociology.* Philadelphia: Temple University Press.
This biographical collection of essays by women sociologists explores their diverse lives and shows how individuals' experi-

ences have led to sociological perspectives on women and society.

Walker, Rebecca. 1995. *To Be Real: Telling the Truth and Changing the Face of Feminism.* New York: Anchor.
This anthology of writings is directed at young women who are examining the meanings of feminism in their own lives. As experiential and analytical essays, these papers help young women understand the multiple currents of identity in their lives.

2

THE SOCIAL CONSTRUCTION OF GENDER

Biology, Culture, and Society

The Biological Basis of Sex Identity
Ambiguous Sexual Identities
Nature/Nurture and Sexually
   Dimorphic Traits
Biological Determinism
The Difference Culture Makes
The Institutional Basis of Gender

Socialization and the Formation of Gender Identity

Sanctions and Expectations
Race and Gender Identity

Socialization across the Life Course

Infancy
Childhood Play and Games
Socialization and the Schools
Adult Socialization and the Aging
   Process

Theoretical Perspectives on the Formation of Gender

Identification Theory
Social Learning Theory
Cognitive-Developmental Theory
Symbolic Interaction and
   "Doing Gender"
Comparing Theoretical Perspectives
Limitations of the Socialization
   Perspective

Chapter Summary and Themes

Key Terms

Discussion Questions/ Projects for Thought

Internet Resources

Suggested Readings

To understand what sociologists mean by the phrase the social construction of gender, watch people when they are with young children. "Oh, he's such a boy!" someone might say as he or she watches a 2-year-old child run around a room or shoot various kinds of play guns. "She's so sweet," someone might say while watching a little girl play with her toys. You can also see the social construction of gender by listening to children themselves or watching them play with each other. Boys are more likely to brag and insult other boys (often in joking ways) than are girls. When playing, girls are more likely than boys to engage in "pretend" play; boys, more likely to engage in physical play (Lindsey and Mize 2001).

To see the social construction of gender in another way, try to buy a gender-neutral present for a child—that is, one not specifically designed with either boys or girls in mind. You may be surprised how hard this is, because the aisles in toy stores are highly stereotyped by concepts of what boys and girls do and like. Even products such as diapers, kids' shampoos, and bicycles are gender stereotyped. Diapers for boys are packaged in blue boxes; girls' diapers are packaged in pink. Boys wear diapers with blue borders and little animals on them; girls wear diapers with pink borders with flowers. You can continue your observations by thinking about how we describe children's toys. Girls are said to play with dolls; boys play with action figures!

When sociologists refer to the **social construction of gender,** they are referring to the many different processes by which the expectations associated with being a boy (and later a man) or being a girl (later a woman) are passed on through society. This process pervades society, and it begins the minute a child is born. The exclamation "It's a boy!" or "It's a girl!" in the delivery room sets a course that from that moment on influences multiple facets of a person's life. Indeed, with the modern technologies now used during pregnancy, the social construction of gender can begin even before one is born. Parents or grandparents may buy expected children gifts that reflect different images, depending on whether the child will be a boy or a girl. They may choose names that embed gendered meanings or talk about the expected child in ways that are based on different social stereotypes about how boys and girls behave and what they will become. All of these expectations—communicated through parents, peers, the media, schools, religious organizations, and numerous other facets of society—create a concept of what it means to be a "woman" or be a "man." They deeply influence who we become, what others think of us, and the opportunities and choices available to us. The idea of the social construction of gender sees society, not biological sex differences, as the basis for gender identity. To understand this fully, we begin with a discussion of biological sex differences.

❖ *Biology, Culture, and Society*

What significance does biology have in shaping the different experiences of women and men in society? Biological explanations of differences between women and men are commonplace and popular. It used to be said that women's status in society was somehow "natural," stemming from the fact that women bear children. Although this is believed less now than in the past, how often have you heard people, perhaps even feminists, say, "Oh, he's just behaving that way because of too much testosterone (the so-called male hormone)," or, referring to some observed difference between women and men, "That's just the way women are." Biological explanations of gender in society have a deep hold in people's thinking, but, as you will see, there is not a fixed relationship between biological features of human life and the social creatures we become. The link between biology and human life is highly mediated by social and cultural influences.

The Biological Basis of Sex Identity

The biological sex of a person is established at the moment of conception and is elaborated during the period of fetal development in the womb. During conception, each parent contributes 23 chromosomes to the fertilized egg, for a total of 46 (or 23 chromosomal pairs). One of these pairs determines the sex of the offspring; they are called the **sex chromosomes.** Under normal conditions, the sex chromosomes consist of an X from the mother's egg and an X or a Y from the father's sperm. The 23 paternal chromosomes (including the X or Y sex chromosome) are selected randomly when the sperm is formed (Hoyenga and Hoyenga, 1979). Genetically normal girls have a pair of X chromosomes (designated 46, XX), and normal boys have the chromosomal pair XY (designated 46, XY). Because the sex chromosome from the ovum is always an X, the chromosome carried by the father's sperm (either an X or a Y) determines the sex of the child. Despite popular belief, there is no evidence that Y chromosomes are stronger than Xs. In fact, the XY male chromosome pair forms a link that is less viable in genetic coding than is the XX female pair. This fact accounts, in part, for the greater vulnerability of male fetuses in the womb and may contribute to higher prenatal and early childhood mortality rates for males (Harrison 1978).

Following fertilization of the egg, a complex process of *fetal sex differentiation* begins. Before the sixth week of development, the XX and XY embryos are identical; the external genitalia of the embryo remain identical until the eighth week of development. During the sixth week of fetal development, the Y chromosome stimulates the production of proteins that assist in the development of fetal gonads (Hoyenga and Hoyenga 1979). Sexual differentiation also involves complex genetic messages encoded on the Y chromosome, the X chromosome, and the non-sex chromosomes.

Ambiguous Sexual Identities

Under normal circumstances, the process of fetal sex differentiation results in unambiguous sex characteristics; however, cases of chromosomal abnormalities sometimes occur, resulting in biologically mixed or incomplete sex characteristics. Studies of such cases reveal the complex relationship between biological sex and the social construction of gender.

Hermaphroditism is "a condition of prenatal origin in which embryonic and/ or fetal differentiation of the reproductive system fails to reach completion as either entirely female or entirely male" (Money and Ehrhardt 1972:5). Normally, during fetal development, fetal gonads produce sex hormones that, in turn, produce the internal and external sex organs. In cases of hermaphroditism, babies are born with their sexual anatomy improperly differentiated; thus, they may be born with both testes and ovaries or will appear ambiguous or incomplete.

Such cases—now referred to as **intersexed persons**—add an important dimension to discussing the relationship between genetic sex, biological appearance, and sex of rearing. True hermaphrodites typically possess the chromosomal patterns characteristic of normal females or normal males. For example, a genetic female who is prenatally androgenized may be born looking like a boy—that is, with a penis (although sometimes incomplete) and no clitoris. On the other hand, a genetic male may be born with the genital appearance of a normal female. Other cases of hermaphroditism may involve mixed genital appearance. Because we typically assign sex according to the appearance of the external genitalia at birth, cases of intersexed persons allow us to look carefully at the role of biology and culture in the development of gender identity.

Such studies reveal the complex interaction of genetic, biological, and cultural factors in the development of a social gender identity. In one case, a genetic male was born with a tiny penis (1 centimeter long) and no urinary canal. At age 17 months, the child was reclassified as a girl. She was given a new name, hairdo, and clothing. Shortly after the sex reassignment, the parents noticed a change in the older brother's treatment of her. Before the sex reassignment, he had treated his "brother" roughly; now he was very protective and gentle toward his new "sister." By age 3, the daughter had developed clearly feminine interests. "For Christmas, she wanted glass slippers, so that she could go to the ball like Cinderella, and a doll. The parents were delighted. The girl continued to receive typically girlish toys from her parents. She continued more and more to show feminine interests, as in helping her mother" (Money and Ehrhardt 1972:125).

In another well-known case of sex reassignment, the reassignment did not follow from hermaphroditism, but from accidental mutilation when a biologically normal male, age 7 months, had his penis burned off during a routine circumcision. The boy was recreated as a girl, using surgical and hormonal treatment. This child had difficulty adjusting to her identity and at age 14 chose to live as a man, undergoing extensive surgery to partially restore his penis and having a mastectomy. At age 25, he married a women and adopted her children. Some have concluded that his case reveals that one's sense of sex identity is innate, but there is another side to this argument. When the child was growing up as a girl, her peers teased her mercilessly and refused to play with her; she also spent much time having her genitals scrutinized by doctors. By the time the child was a teenager, she was miserable, contemplated suicide, and was then told of what had happened earlier in life (Diamond and Sigmundson 1997). Although biological identity may have played some role in the child's difficulties, it is also clear that social factors (such as peer ridicule) strongly contributed to the child's difficult adjustment. Thus, the case is evidence for the strong interplay of culture and biology.

These cases demonstrate that biological sex alone does not determine gender identity. In fact, one's gender identity can be different from one's genetic sex.

Research shows that sex of rearing is the key factor in determining gender identity, even though prenatal hormones can have some effect on behavior (Money and Ehrhardt 1972; Preves 2003; Fausto-Sterling 2000). In other words, gender identity cannot be reduced to biological categories alone.

You can also see the strong influence of culture when you think about transgendered people. **Transgender** refers to those people who deviate from the binary (male or female—one or the other) system of gender. Whereas the binary system of gender tells us we have to be either male or female, transgendered people fall outside of these social norms. Yet, they report that they experience enormous pressure to fit within standard normative. Thus, they hide their cross-dressing in many situations. Similarly, those who undergo a sex change report enormous social pressure, particularly during their transition period. This is because people generally are expected to be one sex or the other. Whatever their biological sex, many transgendered people have to actively manage and negotiate a gender identity that does not fall into just one category (Gagne and Tewksbury 1998).

Nature/Nurture and Sexually Dimorphic Traits

Controversies about the relative effects of nature versus nurture on human social behavior have been plentiful in the scientific and social-scientific literature for years. Although the nature/nurture debate is often posed as an either/or question, human characteristics emerge from the complex interdependence of biological factors and social systems. Indeed, even traits that would seem to be primarily biological, such as body size and strength, hormone levels, and brain development, are affected considerably through environmental influences. Body size provides a good example. Although men are, on average, larger than women, body size is known to be influenced by diet and physical activity, which, in turn, are influenced by class, race, and gender inequality. Explanations of sex differences that ignore such sociological factors are incomplete and misleading.

Genetic research itself shows the strong effect of culture on the expression of genetic traits. Geneticists use the term *genotype* to refer to inherited genetic characteristics; the *phenotype* is the observed expression of the genes as they interact with each other and with the environment in which they appear. This is no simple process, although popular conceptions of genes imagine them as mechanical things that exert a direct influence on human behavior. The expression of genetic codes is, in fact, a complex process, involving the molecular structure of DNA and protein synthesis (Fausto-Sterling 1992). Even the most simple traits involve complex processes of genetic expression. Explaining these traits requires an elaborate and multidimensional analysis. Simple assertions claiming a direct association between genetic structure and social behavior do not match the intricacy of this process.

Sex differences that appear between males and females are known as **sexually dimorphic traits.** These include physical as well as social and cultural differences; they are traits that occur in different frequencies among male and female populations. For example, color blindness is a sexually dimorphic trait that is found more often in men than in women. Although rare, color blindness can be found in women. Most sexually dimorphic traits are distributed in both male and female populations. They are dimorphic usually because there is a significant difference in their distribution between the two populations, not usually because a sexually dimorphic trait appears only in one sex.

Statistical measures of the variation of a trait within a given population represent the degree to which the population deviates from the typical case. Most sex differences are distributed widely throughout the population, leaving a wide range of variation on any given trait appearing among men or among women. Body weight provides a good example. On the average, men weigh more than women, but weight differences among women and among men far exceed the average weight difference between men and women as populations. A sex difference may be found when comparing male and female populations as a whole, but it may not be found when comparing any given male-female pair.

The point is that the *variability within gender is usually larger than the mean difference between genders.* Sexually dimorphic traits are so labeled because they are found in different frequencies in men and women. For any given trait, there may be a substantial degree of overlap between the two populations. Usually, sexually dimorphic traits represent quantitative, not qualitative, differences between the sexes.

Discussions of male-female traits almost always emphasize traits that are different instead of similar in men and women. But the vast majority of human traits are shared by both men and women. Because knowing a person's biological sex does not provide a very accurate prediction of his or her physical characteristics, you have to wonder why biological differences are so often claimed as explaining inequality between the sexes.

Biological Determinism

An argument that reduces a complex event or process (such as social identity) to a single monolithic cause (such as the form of one's genitals) is called **biological reductionism.** A related form of argument is known as **biological determinism.** Determinist arguments are those that assume that a given condition (such as the presence of a penis) inevitably determines a particular event (such as male aggression). Arguments about the biological inferiority of women are usually both reductionist and determinist in that they explain gender differences in the social world as the natural and inevitable consequence of the singular fact of women's biological nature.

Determinist and reductionist arguments are closely related and can be made in any number of forms, including psychological, economic, and cultural contexts. Biological determinism and reductionism have been especially rampant in the discussion of gender and race differences, and they have been the basis for conservative views about the proper role for women and racial-ethnic groups in society.

Biologically determinist arguments often assume that hormonal differences between women and men explain presumed differences in aggressive behavior. This argument should be examined carefully. To begin with, both males and females have measurable quantities of the three major sex hormones—estrogen, progestin, and testosterone. Hormonal sex differences are caused by differences in the levels of production and concentration of each, not in their presence or absence per se. The greater production of testosterone in males is because of stimulation by the testes, whereas in females the ovaries secrete additional estrogens and progestins. Before puberty, however, there are few or no sex differences in the quantity of sex hormones in each sex; at this time, all of the sex hormones are at very low levels. If high levels of testosterone were needed to produce aggression, then we would expect to see little difference in aggressive behavior between prepubescent boys and girls. Much research, however, shows that boys are more aggressive at an early age, thereby contradicting the implications of biologically determinist arguments.

Similarly, following menopause, women actually have lower levels of estradol (the major estrogen) and progesterone (the major progestin) than do men of the same age (Hawkins and Oakey 1974; Hoyenga and Hoyenga 1979; Tea et al. 1975). Because there is no empirical evidence that older men are more feminine than older women, we must doubt the conclusion that hormonal differences explain differences in the behavior of the sexes. Moreover, changes in testosterone levels do not consistently predict changes in aggressive behavior (Hoyenga and Hoyenga 1979). Studies of "chemical castration" show that the procedure is not very effective in reducing violent or aggressive behavior in men; similarly, studies of castrated rhesus monkeys show no straightforward relationship between castration and the lessening of aggression (Fausto-Sterling 1992).

Some studies find small correlations between the level of testosterone and aggressive behavior, but correlations show only association, not cause. Although there may be a slight tendency for aggression and testosterone to vary together, "this does not mean that testosterone caused aggression or dominance; the reverse could just as well be true" (Hoyenga and Hoyenga 1979:139). In fact, much of the research on hormones and aggression shows that experiential factors (such as stress, fatigue, or fear) may have a greater effect on hormonal production than hormones have on behavior (Hoyenga and Hoyenga 1979).

In sum, reductionist arguments do not account for the complexities of patterns of human aggression or for the wide variation in patterns of aggression among and between men and women. No single hormonal state is a good predictor of any form of social behavior. Studies of the relationship between hormones and aggression typically confuse biological and social facts anyhow, because measuring and defining aggression is itself a matter of interpretation.

Biologically reductionist arguments rest on the assumption that differences between the sexes are "natural"; yet, in fact, it is quite difficult, if not impossible, to distinguish so-called natural and social events. Cultural attitudes influence what we think of as natural, since what is deemed natural is typically only that which we believe is unchangeable. Biology itself is neither fixed nor immutable, since biological processes themselves can be modified through cultural conditions. The fact is that human biology sets extremely broad limits for behavior. Most of us vastly underuse our biological capacities, including both motor skills and cognitive ability.

The Difference Culture Makes

If differences between women and men were determined by biological factors alone, we would not find the vast diversity that exists in gender relations from society to society, nor would what it means to be a man or a woman vary from one culture to another. Culture clearly matters, and it matters a lot.

Sociologists and anthropologists define **culture as** "the set of definitions of reality held in common by people who share a distinctive way of life" (Kluckhohn 1962:52). Culture is, in essence, a pattern of expectations about what are appropriate behaviors and beliefs for the members of the society; thus, culture provides prescriptions for social behavior. Culture includes the *norms* that shape everyday life—that is, the expectations about how to act in any given situation. Culture also establishes the *values* and *beliefs* of a society—those commonly held ideas that members of a society broadly share. Culture tells us what we ought to do, what we ought to think, who we ought to be, and what we ought to expect of others.

The concept of culture explains a great deal to us about variation in human lifestyles and human societies. One feature of a culture is that its members come to take cultural patterns for granted. Thus, culture provides its members with tacit knowledge, and much of what members believe as true or what they perceive as real is learned to the point where it is no longer questioned. Culture provides assumptions that often go unexamined but that, nonetheless, fundamentally guide our behavior and our beliefs. Cultural norms vary tremendously from one society to another and, within any given society, from one historical setting to another and among different groups in the society. You can see the influence of gender norms in everyday life, all around you. Just imagine, for example, that tomorrow you woke up and were no longer a woman but a man, or no longer a man, but a woman. What would change? First, your appearance would undergo a great transformation, not just because of physical differences, but also because of the norms we associate with being a man and being a woman (your hair, what you wear, the adornments you put on your body, even the color of the lotions and creams that you likely use). You would likely talk differently, sit differently, even think differently, given what we know about men's and women's differing attitudes about a large array of subjects (see Figure 2.1).

The specific cultural expectations for women and for men vary from society to society, but in every known culture, gender is a major category for the organization of cultural and social relations. In most Western cultures, people think of man and woman as dichotomous categories—that is, separate and opposite, with no overlap between the two. Looking at gender from different cultural viewpoints challenges this assumption, however. Many cultures consider there to be three genders, or even more. Consider the Navaho Indians. In traditional Navaho society, the *berdaches* were those who were anatomically normal men but who were defined as a third gender and were considered to be intersexed. Berdaches married other men. The men they

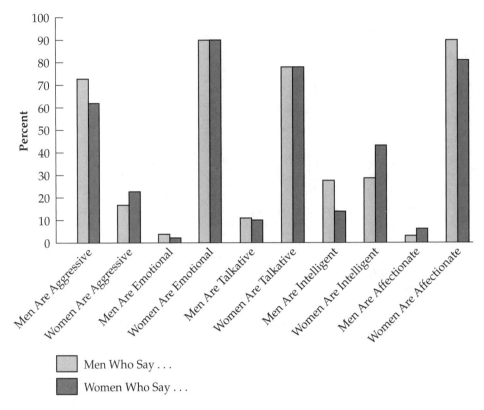

FIGURE 2.1   Gender Stereotypes: What Do Men and Women Believe?

Source: From Frank Newport. 2001. "Americans See Women as Emotional and Affectionate, Men as More Aggressive." Princeton, NJ: The Gallup Organization.

married were not themselves considered to be berdaches; they were defined as ordinary men. Nor were the berdaches or the men they married considered to be homosexuals, as they would be judged by contemporary Western culture. Similarly, in some African and American Indian societies, there are those who are biological females living as men, known as manly hearted women. They are considered "female men," but they do not have to dress or act like men; they only have to have enough money to buy wives (Lorber 1994; Nanda 1998; Amadiume 1987; Blackwood 1984).

Another good example for understanding the cultural basis of gender is the *hijras* of India. Hijras are a religious community of men in India who are born as males, but they come to think of themselves as neither men nor women. Like berdaches, they are considered a third gender. Hijras dress as women and may marry other men; typically, they live within a communal subculture. An important thing to note is that hijras are not born so; they choose this way of life. As male adolescents, they have their penises and testicles cut off in an elaborate and prolonged cultural ritual—a rite of passage marking the transition to becoming a hijra.

Hijras occupy a special place within Indian culture and society, a situation stemming from Hindu religion, which, different from Western culture, values the ambiguity of in-between sexual categories. Hinduism holds that all persons contain both male and female principles within themselves, and Hindu gods are commonly seen as sexually ambiguous. Hijras are believed to represent the power of man and woman combined, although they are impotent themselves. Hijras perceive sexual desire to result in the loss of spiritual energy; their emasculation is seen as proof that they experience no sexual desire. Their special place within Indian society is evidenced at Indian weddings, where hijras often perform rituals to bless the newly married couple's fertility. They also commonly perform at celebrations following the birth of a male child—an event much cherished in Indian society and the cause for much celebration (Nanda 1998).

These examples are good illustrations of the cultural basis of gender. Even within contemporary U.S. society, so-called "gender bending" shows how the dichotomous thinking that defines men and women as "either/or" can be transformed. Cross-dressers, transvestites, and transsexuals illustrate how fluid gender can be and, if one is willing to challenge social convention, how easily gender can be altered. The cultural expectations associated with gender, however, are strong, as one may witness by people's reactions to those who deviate from presumed gender roles. Think, for example, of how you react when you meet someone whom you cannot identify as a man or a woman. Most likely, you feel unsure about how to act. You may even find this somewhat unsettling—evidence of how much we rely on gender categories to guide our interactions with others.

Gender expectations in a culture are sometimes expressed subtly in social interaction, as, for example, in U.S. culture, where men interrupt women more frequently than women interrupt men, where women smile and cry more than do men, and where women have more frequent eye contact with others (Basow 2003; Robinson and Smith-Lovin 2001; LaFrance 2002; Lombardo et al. 2001; Anderson and Leaper 1998). At other times, gender expectations are not so subtle, as in the cultural practices of Chinese foot binding, Indian suttee, European witch-hunts, and the genital mutilation of women documented in some African countries (Blake 1994; Hosken 1979; Jacobson 1974; Stein 1978; Wong 1974). Within U.S. culture, extreme physical practices are also evidenced in the sadistic treatment of women in pornography and in the common surgical practices of face-lifts and silicone implants.

Sociologists use the term **gender** to refer specifically to the social and cultural patterns that we associate with women and men in society. **Sex** refers to the biological identity and is meant to signify the fact that one is either male or female. One's biological sex usually establishes a pattern of gendered expectations, although, as we have seen, biological sex identity is not always the same as gender identity, nor is biological identity always clear as this definition implies. *Gender* is a social, not a biological, concept. Simply put, being "female" and "male" are biological facts; being a woman or a man is a social and cultural process—one that is constructed through the whole array of social, political, economic, and cultural experiences in a given society. But, as we will see, even the distinction between sex and gender is not as clear cut as one might think.

Gender can even construct our concepts of biological sex identity. Anne Fausto-Sterling, a noted feminist biologist, has argued that the fact that we think of there being only two sexes is itself a social construction. Drawing on her knowledge of hermaphroditism, she suggests that if we truly defined the number of sexes in terms of biological possibilities only, we would have not two, but five, sexes: males, females, herms ("true" hermaphrodites, that is, those with the biological sex characteristics of both males and females), merms (male "pseudohermaphrodites," that is, those with mixed sex characteristics, but more male than female), and ferms (female pseudohermaphrodites). Although this probably sounds odd, you might ask why doctors feel compelled to force those born with mixed sex characteristics to be one sex or the other through medical intervention (Fausto-Sterling 2000). Physicians advise parents of those who are given a sex reassignment and genital reconstruction to give the child a new name, a different hairstyle, and new clothes—all intended to provide the child with the social signals judged appropriate to the new gender identity. Human beings make up the system by which we classify bodies; the meaning attached to this is not inherent in the body itself, but in the social meaning our bodies acquire because of culture.

Furthermore, cultural expectations associated with gender can also change how we experience what would otherwise be thought of as purely bodily events. Menopause provides a good example. Menopause is a biological event—the cessation of the menstrual cycle. But how menopause is experienced, indeed whether it is even named, is a cultural phenomenon. In the United States, menopausal women are culturally depicted as cranky, uncontrollably emotional, and irritable. Indeed, as the population bulge known as Baby Boomers has reached middle age, menopause has become a major industry, replete with advice books, products, and a cultural movement. In North America, menopause is viewed in pathological and medical terms, and menopausal women are stereotyped as depressed (even though many women experience this as a happy time of life). Comparatively, in Japan women rarely express menopausal discomfort—a fact explained by anthropologists as resulting from the positive role given Japanese women as they age and the fact that menopause is culturally defined as a social, not a biological, change in life. In other words, how women experience menopause depends not just on physiological changes per se, but on the cultural attitudes that surround this phenomenon (Lock 1993, 1998).

In sum, gender is a social construct that establishes our definitions of self, our relations with others, and our life chances. As a concept, gender emphasizes the social and cultural experience within society. Moreover, gender is not just an individual attribute. Instead, it is part of the social structure of society and thus has an institutional component—to which we now turn.

The Institutional Basis of Gender

Social institutions are established patterns of behavior with a particular and recognized purpose; institutions include specific participants who share expectations and act in specific roles, with rights and duties attached to them. Institutions define reality for us insofar as they exist as objective entities in our experience. They are "experienced as existing over and beyond the individuals who 'happen' to embody them at the moment. In other words, institutions are experienced as a reality of their own, a reality that confronts the individual as an external and coercive fact" (Berger and Luckmann 1966:58). Institutions arise within particular and historic environments and constitute the social structure of society. Although the idea of institutions is an abstract one, the various institutional forms within society form the social structure that guides our collective lives.

Understanding gender in an institutional context means that gender is not just an attribute of individuals; instead, gender is systematically structured in social institutions, meaning that it is deeply embedded in the social structure of society. Gender is created, not just within families or interpersonal relationships (although these are important arenas of gender relations), but also within the structure of all major social institutions, including schools, religion, the economy, and the state (i.e., government and other organized systems of authority such as the police and the military). These institutions shape and mold the experiences of us all.

Think again about the things you thought you would change about yourself were you suddenly to become a member of the other gender. Most likely the things you would list stem from institutional arrangements in society. If you thought of products that you use as a man or a woman, those products are produced, bought, and sold in economic institutions that are organized around lines of gender, class, race, and other social factors (such as age). If you imagined that your attitudes might change, think of how those attitudes are promoted through media institutions or established within families—both of which are institutions organized by gender. Or, perhaps you imagined different religious proscriptions for how women and men are to act and be—again, reflecting the institutional structure of religion. All of these examples show how the institutional structure is the backdrop for gender relations in society.

Furthermore, all of the institutions we will study in this book are themselves gendered, just as you might think of individual people and social groups being gendered. To say that an institution is gendered means that the whole institution is patterned on specific gendered relationships. That is, gender is "present in the processes, practices, images and ideologies, and distribution of power in the various sectors of social life" (Acker 1992: 567). The concept of a *gendered institution* was introduced by Joan Acker, a feminist sociologist. Acker uses this concept to explain not just that gender expectations are passed to men and women within institutions, but that the institutions themselves are structured along gendered lines. **Gendered institutions** are the total pattern of gender relations—stereotypical expectations, interpersonal relationships, and men's and women's different placements in social, economic, and political hierarchies. This is what interests sociologists, and it is what they mean by the social structure of gender relations in society.

Conceptualizing gender in this way is somewhat different from the related concept of gender roles. **Social roles** are the culturally prescribed expectations, duties, and rights that define the relationship between a person in a particular position and the other people with whom she or he interacts. For example, to be a mother is a specific social role with a definable set of expectations, rights, and duties. Persons occupy multiple roles in society; we can think of social roles as linking individuals to social structures. It is through social roles that cultural norms are patterned and learned. **Gender roles** are the expectations for behavior and attitudes that the culture defines as appropriate for women and men.

The concept of gender is broader than the concept of gender roles. Gender refers to the complex social, political, economic, and psychological relations between women and men in society. Gender is part of the social structure—in other words, it is institutionalized in society (Martin 2004, Risman 2004). Gender roles are the patterns through which gender relations are expressed, but our understanding of gender in society cannot be reduced to roles and learned expectations alone.

The distinction between gender, as institutionalized, and gender roles is made most clear perhaps by thinking about analogous cases—specifically, race and class. Race relations in society are seldom, if ever, thought of in terms of "race roles." Likewise, class inequality is not discussed in terms of "class roles." Doing so would make race and class inequality seem like matters of interpersonal interaction. Although race, class, and gender inequalities are experienced within interpersonal interactions, limiting the analysis of race, class, or gender relations to this level of social interaction individualizes more complex systems of inequality; moreover, restricting the analysis of race, class, or gender to social roles hides the power relations that are embedded in race, class, and gender inequality (Lopata and Thorne 1978).

Understanding the institutional basis of gender also underscores the interrelationships of gender, race, and class, since all three are part of the institutional framework of society. As a social category, gender intersects with class and race; thus, gender is manifested in different ways, depending on one's location in the race and class system. For example, African American women are more likely than White women to reject gender stereotypes for women, although they are more accepting than White women of stereotypical gender roles for children. Although this seems contradictory, it can be explained by understanding that African American women may reject the dominant culture's view while also hoping their children can attain some of the privileges of the dominant group (Dugger 1988).

Institutional analyses of gender emphasize that gender, like race and class, is a part of the social experience of us all, not just of women. Gender is just as important in the formation of men's experiences as it is in women's (Messner 1998). From a sociological perspective, class, race, and gender relations are systemically structured in social institutions, meaning that class, race, and gender relations shape the experiences of all. Sociologists do not see gender simply as a psychological attribute, although that is one dimension of gender relations in society. In addition to the psychological significance of gender, gender relations are part of the institutionalized patterns in society. Understanding gender, as well as class and race, is central to the study of any social institution or situation. Understanding gender in terms of social structure indicates that social change is not just a matter of individual will—that if we changed our minds, gender would disappear. Transformation of gender inequality requires change both in consciousness and in social institutions.

❖ *Socialization and the Formation of Gender Identity*

The fact that gender is a social, not a natural, phenomenon means that it is learned. Although rooted in institutions, gender is passed on through social learning and is enacted through what sociologists call gender roles. Gender roles are the patterns of behavior in which women and men engage, based on the cultural expectations associated with their gender. Gender roles are learned through the process of socialization. It is through the socialization process that individuals acquire an identity based on gender. **Gender identity** is an individual's specific definition of self, based on that person's understanding of what it means to be a man or a woman. In other words, it is through the socialization process that gender is socially constructed.

Sanctions and Expectations

Through gender socialization, different behaviors and attitudes are encouraged and discouraged in men and women. That is, social expectations about what is properly masculine and feminine are communicated to us through the **socialization** process. Our family, peers, and teachers, as well as the media and religious groups, act as agents of the socialization process. Although probably none of us becomes exactly what the cultural ideal prescribes, our roles in social institutions are conditioned by the gender relations we learn in our social development.

Some persons become more perfectly socialized than others, and sociologists have warned against the idea of seeing humans as totally passive, overly socialized creatures (Wrong 1961). To some extent, we probably all resist the expectations society has of us. Our uniqueness as individuals stems in part from this resistance, as well as from variations in the social experiences we have. Studying patterns of gender socialization does not deny individual differences, but it does point to the common experiences shared by girls as they become women and boys as they become men. However much we may believe that we were raised in a gender-neutral environment, research and careful observation show how pervasive and generally effective the process of gender-role socialization is. Although some of us conform more than others, socialization acts as a powerful system of social control.

Peter Berger (1963) describes social control as something like a series of concentric circles. At the center is the individual, who is surrounded by different levels of control, ranging from the subtle (such as learned roles, peer pressure, and ridicule) to the overt (such as violence, physical threat, and imprisonment). According to Berger, it is usually not necessary for powerful agents in the society to resort to extreme sanctions, because what we think and believe about ourselves usually keeps us in line. In this sense, socialization acts as a powerful system of social control.

The conflicts we encounter when we try to cross or deny the boundaries between the sexes are good evidence of the strength of gendered expectations in our culture. Although most of us resist the idea that we are controlled, because we like to think we are individuals, the effects of social expectations are easily apparent.

What happens, for example, if you deviate from your expected gender role? Men who do so will likely be presumed to be gay, indicative of the link between gender socialization and expectations about sexual identity, something we will discuss later. Women who deviate from expected roles will be labeled "tomboys" or will be judged as "unladylike."

The pressure to adopt gender-appropriate behavior is evidence that the socialization process controls us in several ways: (1) it gives us a definition of ourselves; (2) it defines the external world and our place within it; (3) it provides our definition of others and our relationships with them; and, (4) the socialization process encourages and discourages the acquisition of certain skills by gender.

Gender socialization is a powerful process involving our individualism, as well as the multiple forms that gender roles can take. Gender expectations confront us everywhere and shape our identities and relationships with others, perhaps even at times when we might wish they did not. Some argue that the pressures of gender socialization are even more restrictive of boys, at least at the early ages, than of girls. Men's roles are more rigidly defined, as witnessed in the more severe social sanctions brought against boys labeled as sissies, compared with girls who are thought of as tomboys. For girls, being a tomboy may be a source of mild ridicule, but it appears to be more acceptable (at least until puberty) than being a sissy is for boys.

Some researchers explain this finding as the result of **homophobia,** defined as the fear and hatred of homosexuals (Pharr 1988). Homophobia acts as a system of social control because it encourages boys and men to act more masculine, as a way of indicating that they are not gay. Homophobia further separates the cultural roles of masculinity and femininity by discouraging men from showing so-called feminine traits such as caring, nurturing, emotional expression, and gentleness.

Researchers conclude that "homophobia thus appears to be functional in the dynamics of maintaining the traditional male role. The fear of being labeled homosexual serves to keep men within the confines of what the culture defines as sex-appropriate behavior, and it interferes with the development of intimacy between men" (Morin and Garfinkle 1978:41). Indeed, both men and women with the most traditional gender-role beliefs exhibit the most homophobia (Burgess 2001; Alden 2001; Basow and Johnson 2000), evidence of how gender socialization is propped up by homophobia.

Conformity to traditional roles takes its toll on both men and women, and research shows that those who conform most fully to gender-role expectations experience a range of negative consequences. For example, higher male mortality rates can be attributed to the stress in masculine roles. The cultural association between masculinity and aggression can also help explain the high rates of violence that encourage behaviors in men that put them at risk in a variety of ways.

For women too much conformity to gender expectations also produces many negative consequences. Women who score as "very feminine" on personality tests tend to exhibit more feelings of depression and say they do not feel in control of their lives (Sayers et al. 1993; Sprock and Yoder 1997). The cultural expectations associated with gender and beauty are known to produce a whole range of negative health consequences. The dominant culture promotes a narrow image of beauty for women. Women and young girls who internalize this ideal—one that is generally impossible to achieve—often end up being disturbed about their body image, feeling they are never adequate. Millions then engage in constant dieting, even when they are well within healthy weight standards. Purging themselves of food via eating disorders or cycling through fad diets can all have serious health consequences. Many young women develop a distorted image of themselves, thinking they are "overweight" when they may actually be dangerously thin. And, despite the known risks of smoking, increasing numbers of young women smoke and do so not only because they think it "looks cool," but because they think it will keep them from gaining weight (Logio 1998; Thompson 1994). Thus, patterns of both physical and mental health are clearly related to the gender expectations that both men and women internalize.

These patterns are confounded by race, class, and sexual orientation. Poor women, regardless of their race, have nearly twice the rate of depression as middle-class women; most researchers associate differences in depression by race to the influence of social class. Lesbian women also face unique problems of mental health, although there is no evidence that they have rates of depression different from heterosexual women. Lesbians face discrimination and homophobic attitudes, contributing to stress; in addition, they have higher rates of poverty and barriers to health care access—both of which contribute to problems with mental health (Bradford et al. 1994; Greene 1994).

Figure 2.2 reports the sources of the changing stress patterns that men and women experience. Note that in the brief 5-year period between 1990 and 1995 (the time of the two surveys), the percentage of women and men reporting certain sources of stress nearly converged, especially stress associated with money and the amount of work in a day. Still, in other areas, women still experience significantly more stress than men—namely, stress from children, spouses, parents, and the chores of shopping and driving people around (Roper Organization 1995). These data suggest that not only is gender an internalized role but it is also a pattern of behaviors and expectations that shapes the daily experience of women and men in different ways.

Race and Gender Identity

Gender socialization does not occur in a vacuum, apart from the other features of our lives that also shape our experiences. As one would expect, given the intersections of gender and race, gender identity is also mediated by the racial identities we acquire. For example, many of the characteristics associated with feminine stereotypes, such as that women are dependent on men or that women are weak and more helpless than men, are simply not typical of many women of color. African American women, for example, like White women, are socialized to place primary emphasis on nurturing their loved ones, but they are also socialized to be self-sufficient, to aspire to an education, to regard employment as part of the role of women, and to be more independent than White women (Collins 1987, 1990; Ladner 1995).

This does not mean that women and men of color are unaffected by gender socialization. It is only to say that gender is manifested differently among different groups. In other words, gender identities intersect with racial identities. African American, Asian, and Latino men, for example, construct concepts of masculinity in the context of negative stereotypes about them that are both race and gender

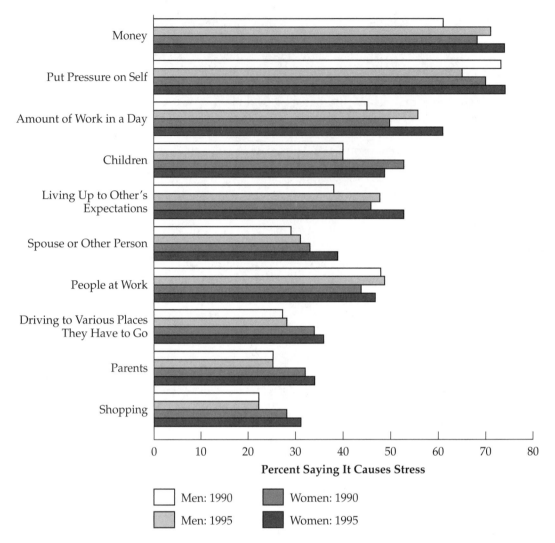

FIGURE 2.2   Gender: The Toll It Takes

Source: Survey by the Roper Organization for Virginia Slims. 1995. *The 1995 Virginia Slims Opinion Poll.* Data provided by the Roper Center at the University of Connecticut.

based (Chen 1999). Women of color likewise develop their gender consciousness in the context of their racial and class status in society (Chow 1987). Together, gender, race, and class influence how all people—including White people—learn and develop their gender identity.

Research regarding Black and White families illustrates this point, showing both similarities and differences in the long-term goals, parenting practices, parental roles, and disciplinary strategies of Black and White parents of boys and girls. But these patterns are influenced both by the gender of the child and the race and class of the family. Thus, both Black and White parents value their child getting a good job and a good education and having a strong and loving family as priorities. But education and a job are more of a priority for Black parents than for Whites; both Black and White parents emphasize this less if they are of higher class status. Thus, among upper middle-class White parents, family is the most important priority, whereas for Black parents, education and jobs are ranked as most important. Furthermore, these priorities do not change according to the gender of the child. White parents, in general, are also more likely to emphasize happiness for their children. White parents also emphasize the importance of obedience for boys, though Black parents are more likely to emphasize discipline by the withdrawal of certain privileges. The researchers use their conclusions to argue that gender is not a monolithic influence since gender patterns in socialization are so strongly shaped by race and class as well (Hill and Sprague 1999). Such conclusions shows the importance of using a multidimensional understanding of socialization—one that examines race and class along with gender, not just gender alone.

New experiences that families face can also change gender expectations within the family. This is especially evident in studies of immigrant groups, a phenomenon of increasing importance in U.S. society. Studying Mexican immigrants to the United States, Hondagneu-Sotelo has found that men's expectations about their roles changed as the result of the migration experience. Because families are often separated during the early phases of migration, men may live in bachelor communities when they first migrate. They learn to cook and clean for themselves. Once the family is reunited, the men do not necessarily discard these newly learned roles (Hondagneu-Sotelo 1992, 1994). Likewise, Chinese women who migrated to the United States found they had to find employment to help support their families. Their earlier-held cultural norms about the desirability of women's employment changed as a result (Geschwender 1992).

Clearly, generalizations about gender role socialization need to be carefully examined in the context of the experiences of different groups. As you read the results of studies, including those related here, you should ask yourself if the same conclusions would be reached depending on the race *and* gender of the research subjects.

❖ Socialization across the Life Course

Socialization begins at birth, and it continues throughout adulthood, even though gender roles are established very early. When we encounter new social experiences, we are socialized to adopt new roles through the expectations others have of us. Socialization patterns can be observed in many individual and group experiences and in the context of all of the institutions of society. This section examines the processes and consequences of gender socialization as it occurs throughout the life course.

Infancy

Beginning in infancy, boys and girls are treated differently. Research on infant socialization shows, in fact, how quickly gender expectations become part of our experience. Studies find that as early as 18 months, toddlers have learned to play mostly with toys judged to be appropriate for their gender (Caldera and Sciaraffa 1998). Parents describe their babies differently, depending on their gender—including descriptions rating their male children as more intelligent than female children (Furnham and Gasson 1998).

Research continues to show that parents treat their infants differently, depending on the infant's sex. How parents act may even be unintentional or subtle, but it has an effect on later life, nonetheless. In one fascinating series of studies, researchers observed fathers and mothers (in couples) walking young children through public places. Both fathers and mothers were more likely to let boy toddlers walk alone than they were to allow girls to do so. These same observers found that even when the child was out of the stroller, mothers were far more likely to push the empty stroller than were the fathers, demonstrating the attachment of mothers to child care roles (Mitchell et al. 1992). Despite the fact that mothers are much more likely than fathers to engage in and manage child care, research also finds that fathers are more likely to gender-type their children (Mitchell et al. 1992). Parents living in nontraditional households, however, do tend to gender-stereotype their children less than parents do in traditional families (Weisner et al. 1994).

Parents are not the only agents of gender socialization, however. Other children have just as important an impact on learning gender roles. Children of all ages notice the sex of infants and use it as a basis for responding to the child. Preschool girls also show more interest in interacting with babies than do preschool boys, a pattern that is most pronounced among children whose parents hold gender-stereotyped attitudes (Blakemore 1998). As children grow, their engagement in gender stereotyping also increases, especially between the ages of 3 and 14 (Vogel et al. 1991). Peers develop expectations and definitions of gender-appropriate behaviors and use those expectations as the basis for their interaction with others.

Childhood Play and Games

Research in child development emphasizes the importance of play and games in the maturation of children. Through play, children learn the skills of social interaction, develop cognitive and analytical abilities, and are taught the values and attitudes of their culture. The games that children play have great significance for the children's intellectual, moral, personal, and social development and for their gender identity.

George Herbert Mead, a social psychologist and major sociological theorist in the early twentieth century, described three stages in which socialization occurs: imitation, play, and game. In the *imitation stage*, an infant simply copies the behavior of significant persons in his or her environment. In the play stage, the child begins "taking the role of the other"—seeing himself or herself from the perspective of another person. Mead argues that taking the role of the other is a cognitive process that permits the child to develop a self-concept. Self-concepts emerge through interacting with other people and from learning to perceive how others see us. The other people most emotionally important to the child (e.g., parents, siblings, or other primary caregivers) are, in Mead's term, significant others. In the *play stage,* children learn to take the role of significant others, primarily by practicing others' social roles—for example, "playing Mommy" or "playing Daddy."

In the *game stage,* children are able to do more. Rather than seeing themselves from the perspective of only one significant other at a time, they can play games requiring them to understand how several other people (including more than just significant others) view them simultaneously. Playing baseball, to use Mead's example, involves the roles and expectations of many more people than does "playing Mommy." Eventually, children in the game stage learn to orient themselves not just to significant others but to a generalized other, as well. The generalized other represents the cultural expectations of the whole social community. Mead's analysis of the emergence of the self emphasizes the importance of interpretative behavior in the way the child relates to others in the social environment. Early activity, especially through play, places children's experiences in a social environment; therefore, meanings communicated through play help the child organize personal experience into an emerging self. Children's play, then, is a very significant part of the socialization process.

Research reveals the pervasiveness of gender stereotyping as it is learned in early childhood play. The toys and play activities that parents select for children are a significant source of gender socialization. Studies of parents find that they gender stereotype toys for boys and girls of all ages, although toys for infants and toddlers are somewhat less stereotyped (Campenni 1999). Children also quickly pick this up. As research on preschoolers has found, given a choice between playing with a tool set or a dish set, boys will pick the tool set, saying that their fathers think playing with the dishes would be "bad" (Raag 1999; Raag and Rackliff 1998). Clearly, parents' values influence the gender play of children. Other studies find that parents, especially fathers, are more likely to be involved in physical play with boys than with girls; not surprisingly, then, boys are more likely to play physically than girls, whereas girls engage in more fantasy or "pretense" play (Lindsey et al. 1997). At the same time, parents are more likely to tolerate cross-gender play in girls than in boys (Sandnabba and Ahlberg 1999).

These patterns are not fixed, however, because changing attitudes among parents are reflected in the values their children learn. Compared to 20 years ago, young girls now express a greater number of occupational aspirations, more so than young boys. Mothers' education and employment also have a significant impact on the gender attitudes of their daughters and sons; in general, there has been some shift in attitudes toward more egalitarian roles—a fact that will influence the gender attitudes of future generations (Harris and Firestone 1998; Helwig 1998; Ex and Janssens 1998).

Even with these changes, however, the world children encounter is laden with gender-stereotypic expectations. Children themselves impart gender expectations to each other. Thus, researchers observing children's activities have found that when girls disregard the ordinary codes for gender behavior and transgress into other activities, higher-status boys react in ways that regulate the transgression (McGuffey and Rich 1999). Aside from the behavior of children and adults, young people are also bombarded with gendered images from literature, video games, and television. Even with a greater awareness of the importance of reducing gender stereotypes, studies of children's literature show that males are still overwhelmingly shown as aggressive, argumentative, and competitive, even though publishers have published guidelines for nonsexist portrayals (Evans and Davies 2000). Female characters are more likely to be depicted using household objects, whereas male characters use nondomestic objects (Crabb and Bielawski 1994). Girls and women are still depicted as less adventurous and more domestic than boys. In general, there are still more males than females in children's picture books, and males are shown as more potent and active, although, interestingly, more positive adjectives are used to describe female characters (Turner-Bowker 1996). Books written by African Americans are more likely to show girls and women as less dependent and more competitive, but they also show them as more nurturing than do books written by White authors (Clark et al. 1993).

In television cartoons, boys are depicted as more violent, girls as more domestic; furthermore, children who watched such cartoons subsequently express more traditional job expectations for themselves and others (Thompson and Zerbinos 1997). Even the Sunday comics communicate these expectations, with researchers finding that, although some stereotypical images have diminished over the last 20 years, there is now a return to earlier levels of stereotyping (Brabant and Mooney 1997). In video games—one of the major outlets for children's play—traditional gender roles and violence are central themes. Using a sample of Nintendo and Sega Genesis games, researchers found that 41 percent of the games had no female characters at all, 28 percent portrayed women as sex objects, and 80 percent included aggression or violence as the strategy. Half the games included violence directed at others; the other half depicted violence toward women (Dietz 1998). All told, these sources of socialization send powerful messages to young boys and girls. The numerous examples that can be found in children's play, literature, and other cultural systems demonstrate how gender is socially constructed.

Socialization and the Schools

Although we tend to think of the family as the primary source of social values and identity, peers, teachers, the media, and additional significant others are important agents of the socialization process. Schools, in particular, exercise much influence on the creation of gendered attitudes and behavior, so much so that some researchers call learning gender the "hidden curriculum" in the schools. In the schools, curriculum materials, teachers' expectations, educational tracking, and peer relations encourage girls and boys to learn gender-related skills and self-concepts.

Within schools, teachers and older children display expectations that encourage children to behave and think in particular ways; moreover, these expectations are strongly influenced by gender. Teachers, for example, respond more often to boys in the classroom. Even when they do so in response to boys' misbehaving, they are calling more attention to the boys (Sadker and Sadker 1994). Differences between boys and girls become exaggerated through practices that divide them into two distinct human groups (Thorne 1993). In schools, children are often seated in separate gender groups or sorted into play groups based on gender; these practices heighten gender differences, making them even more significant in the children's interactions. In school, boys tend to be the center of attention, even when they are getting attention for disruptive behavior; girls are, in general, less visible and more typically praised for passive and acquiescent behavior (Sadker and Sadker 1994; American Association of University Women 1998).

These gender-typical behaviors have consequences for what boys and girls learn in school. Although boys and girls enter schools with roughly equal abilities, and although overall gender differences in such important areas as math and science are no longer pronounced, girls report liking these subjects less than boys and they express little confidence in their math and science abilities. Those who report liking math and science have higher self-esteem and have higher career aspirations than other girls. Moreover, gender expectations influence other course-taking patterns, so that girls are far more likely to take courses in social sciences, foreign languages, and the arts and humanities—suggesting how patterns of thinking become arrayed along gender lines (American Association of University Women 1998; Phillips 1998). These patterns also have profound effects on the extent of gender segregation in the labor market as young men and women become adults.

Families and schools are not the only sources of gender socialization. One of the reasons that gender is so extensive in its influence on our lives is that it is so pervasive throughout all social institutions. Gender expectations are also visible at work, in voluntary organizations, in health care organizations, and in athletics. Religion, as you will see in Chapter 8, also has a significant effect on our concepts of who we are and our consciousness of gender. Families and schools are primary sources for some of the earliest influences of gender socialization, but the process of learning and enacting gender goes on throughout people's lifetimes.

Adult Socialization and the Aging Process

As we encounter new experiences throughout our lives, we learn the role expectations associated with our new statuses. Although our gender identities are established relatively early in life, changes in our status in society—for example, graduation, marriage, or a new job—bring new expectations for our behavior and beliefs.

Aging is perhaps the one thing about our lives that is inevitable; yet, as a social experience, it has different consequences for men and women. Cross-cultural evidence shows that aging is less stressful for women in societies where there is a strong tie to family and kin, not just to a husband; where there are extended, not nuclear, family systems; where there is a positive role for mothers-in-law (rather than the degrading status attached to it in our society); and where there are strong mother–child relationships throughout life. Even within our own society, racial and ethnic groups attach more value to older persons, thereby easing the transition to later life. Although the elderly in African American and Latino communities experience even greater difficulties with poverty and health than do the White elderly (Atchley 2000), their valued role in the extended family seems to alleviate some of the stress associated with growing old.

Gender differences in the social process of aging can be attributed in large part to the emphasis on youth found in this culture and, in particular, to the association of youth and sexuality in women. Cultural stereotypes portray older men as distinguished, older women as less desirable. As a woman ages, unlike a man, she will generally experience a loss of prestige; men gain prestige as they become more established in their careers.

The effects of aging for women and men are, however, strongly influenced by factors such as one's class, race, and other social factors. The cumulated inequities that women experience because of gender, race, and class continue into their older years—both in the social and economic value placed on them. And, as we will see further in the chapter on health, these inequities have consequences for the physical and mental health that different groups experience. Research consistently demonstrates that poor women are less likely to receive good-quality health care. In fact, financial resources are one of the best predictors of health for both women and men. Being in a subordinated race, class, or gender group makes some groups more vulnerable to problems of physical and mental health at all stages in the life course, but these can become more acute in old age (Logue 1991).

For women, the caregiving responsibilities that mark younger years continue as they grow older. Even during so-called "retirement" women most often do the unpaid labor associated with caring for others (Richardson 1999). Researchers have found that there can actually be increased differentiation in the gender roles of men and women in their older years because of women's ongoing caregiving responsibilities (Dentinger and Clarkberg 2002). And one's well-being as an older person depends a great deal on one's level of education and the resources one has—such as during retirement. Because they have generally had lower levels of earnings during their younger adult years, during retirement, women typically have less retirement pension and receive less in Social Security than men do—even though women are also more likely to be dependent on Social Security and other forms of government assistance during retirement than are men (Moen et al. 2001; Warren et al. 2001; Morgan 2000; O'Rand and Genretta 1999; Gregoire et al. 2002).

Despite these problems for older women, aging also relaxes some of the social pressure experienced by younger people. Many women report more satisfaction and personal freedom in their later years than they felt during their earlier lives (Hess and Markson 1991). How positively one experiences the aging process depends to a large extent on the economic and cultural resources one has available, as well as the social supports received from family and friends. One study of retired African American professional women has documented, for example, the satisfaction that these women experience from their achievements, especially in regard to the social supports they both create and rely on over a lifetime of confronting racism (Slevin and Wingrove 1998).

There is little doubt that women experience significant disadvantage during the aging process. At the same time, however, the capacities and strengths that women acquire over their lifetimes also give them certain advantages as they grow old. Older women report higher levels of emotional support than do older men, and they tend to have more extensive social contacts and friendships. In general, the fact that women work throughout their lives to maintain social and emotional networks helps them maintain this connection in their older years, whereas men may experience greater social isolation. Better social support also has a known positive effect on people's ability to withstand stressful life events; thus, this learned ability among women helps them face the difficult problems of death, loss, and, perhaps, poor health in their elder years (Gibson 1996; Stoller and Gibson 2000).

❖ Theoretical Perspectives on the Formation of Gender

Social scientists use different theoretical perspectives to explain gender socialization and the formation of gender. Each carries different assumptions, but all contribute to our understanding of the social construction of gender identity.

Identification Theory

According to **identification theory,** children learn gender-appropriate behaviors by identifying with their same-sex parent. This explanation is based on a Freudian psychoanalytic perspective that assumes that children unconsciously model their identities on the behavior of their parents. Identification theory posits that children learn behaviors, feelings, and attitudes unconsciously; through unconscious learning, children develop motivational systems. The child's identification with the same-sex parent, coupled with the powerful emotion associated with the parent–child relationship, results in an unconscious psychosexual bond that shapes the child's sex-role identity.

Empirical evidence to support the perspective of identification theory is, at best, shaky. Because the focus of this theory is on unconscious states of mind, it is impossible to measure directly the internal motivation of the child. Instead, researchers study motives indirectly by examining characteristics of the parents and associating those characteristics with behaviors and attitudes of the child. Such associations do not show a causal relationship between the parents' characteristics and the personality tendencies of their child. Because there is no direct way to observe the process of identification, this theory remains largely speculative; moreover, evidence that children are oriented to same-sex models is inconclusive, casting further doubt on the validity of identification theory.

Chodorow's (1978) theory of gender identity is related to the perspective of identification theory. Chodorow argues that modern nuclear families are characterized by an "asymmetrical structure of parenting," meaning that parenting is characterized by a division of labor in which women "mother" and men do not and in which women's work is devalued. This creates a dynamic of identification in which only girls adopt the personality characteristics associated with mothering. In Chodorow's theory, called **object relations** theory, as boys and girls develop their own identities, they must become psychologically separate from their parents. Boys, who gender-identify with their fathers, form personalities that are more detached from others, because family structures in this society are based largely on the father's absence. Girls, who gender-identify with their mothers, become less detached because the mother's role in the family is one of close attachment to others. Girls' personalities, then, are more focused on attachment behaviors and on orientation to others. Boys, on the other hand, have personalities characterized by repression of their emotional needs and their commitments to others. Chodorow's work maintains some of the orientation of identification theory in its emphasis on unconscious psychic processes. It is distinguished, though, from traditional psychoanalytic theory by its placing of gender identity clearly in the context of the division of labor by gender in work and in the family.

Because the family form Chodorow analyzes is not universal, critics have questioned whether it holds only for White, middle-class nuclear families. Would this theory, for example, hold in families marked by different cultural traditions and a different family structure? This has been examined in the context of Chicano families (Segura and Pierce 1993). Chicano families are characterized by *familism*— a concept describing the generally large size of Chicano families, the existence of multigenerational households, the value placed on family unity, and the high level of interaction between family and kin (Baca Zinn and Eitzen 2005). Segura and Pierce found that Chodorow's analysis is useful in describing the experiences of Chicana mothers and their daughters. Chicana mothers' identity tends to revolve around family and home, and they tend to identify more with their daughters than their sons; however, Chicanas do not practice exclusive mothering. Mothering figures include other women, such as grandmothers, aunts, or godmothers, just as African American communities often involve the extensive engagement of "othermothers" (Collins 1990) in the care of children and kin. As a result, young Chicanas identify not only with the mother but also with other women in the family system. Segura and Pierce conclude that, especially considering the cultural representation of women within Chicano culture as sacred and self-sacrificing, Chodorow's point about gender identification and attachment is particularly salient for Chicanas.

Chodorow's analysis of families sees them in relationship to particular cultural ideals and social forms. The importance of her work lies in the connection it makes between gender identity and family structure. Her theory also suggests that transformation in family structures is a necessary prerequisite toward creating more gender-balanced personalities.

Social Learning Theory

A second theoretical perspective is **social learning theory.** Whereas identification theory rests on the idea of unconscious learning, social learning theory emphasizes the significance of the environment in explaining gender socialization. Social learning theory is a behaviorist orientation, meaning that it sees social behavior as explained in terms of human responses to the environment. According to behaviorists, appropriate social responses are positively rewarded, whereas inappropriate responses are punished. Social learning, then, occurs through an ongoing process of reinforcement from other people. Like identification theorists, many social learning theorists believe that children model themselves on the behaviors and attitudes of same-sex parents. From a social learning perspective, behavior is not fixed according to early established patterns; rather, behavior and attitudes change as the situations and expectations in the environment change. Learning gender roles, although very significant in childhood, continues throughout life. As a consequence, one's gender identity is not fixed or permanent except when the social environment continues to reinforce it.

Like identification theory, social learning theory rests on the assumption that children model their behavior according to the roles of same-sex significant others, but social learning theorists point out that parents are not the only significant role models. A wide array of images and expectations in the culture serve as reinforcement for gender identity. Empirical evidence to support social learning theory comes from the vast amount of research on variations in parental expectations for children of different sexes, stereotypic responses from teachers and peers, and the influence of institutional practices that reinforce gender stereotypes. One implication of social learning theory is the view expressed by some feminists that women need women as role models in positions of leadership and authority to compensate for the learned sense of self that they acquire through traditional socialization practices.

Cognitive-Developmental Theory

The third theoretical framework used to explain gender-role learning is **cognitive-developmental theory.** This theory is based largely on the work of Swiss psychologist Jean Piaget and, more recently, psychologist Lawrence Kohlberg (1966). Piaget suggested that children create schemata—mental categories that emerge through interactions with the social world. These schemata, in turn, are used in the child's subsequent encounters with his or her environment; thus, the child accommodates and assimilates new information into this existing stock of knowledge. According to Piaget, all children experience distinct stages of cognitive development, so that the developmental process is marked by alternate states of equilibrium and disequilibrium. In other words, as the developing child discovers new information or experiences in the world, he or she must adjust previously existing schemata to fit these new observations. At various points in cognitive development, the child reaches equilibrium because the child's reasoning ability is limited. Most importantly, cognitive-developmental theory emphasizes that the process of social development is one in which the child interacts with the social world through the mediation and active involvement of his or her cognitive abilities.

Kohlberg uses Piaget's perspective to explain the emergence of children's gender identities. According to Kohlberg, children discover early that people are divided into two sexes. They come to know their own sex, and they categorize others as either male or female. As their own gender identity stabilizes, they also begin to categorize behaviors and objects in the social world as appropriate for one sex or the other. At this point, gender has become an organizing scheme for the developing child, and the child attributes value to the traits and attitudes associated with his or her own sex. Children also begin to believe that gender is an unchanging category. As a result, they model their own behavior on the behaviors of those of the same sex, and they develop a strong emotional attachment to the same-sex parent.

Symbolic Interaction and "Doing Gender"

The previous three theoretical perspectives have been developed primarily by psychologists. Both the cognitive-developmental perspective and social learning theory are related to a perspective in sociology called symbolic interaction. According to **symbolic interaction theory,** people act toward things (including objects, abstract ideas, and other people) based on the meaning those things have for them. That meaning evolves from culture. From this perspective, the socialization process develops as people (initially, young children) take on the roles of others around them. In this sense, the concept of *role models,* as in social learning theory, is an important one. Critical to the symbolic interactionist perspective, however, is the idea that people reflect on how others see them and through this reflection form their self-concepts. From this point of view, the self is established as one becomes an object to oneself—something upon which people reflect. Symbolic interaction also emphasizes the ability of humans to form and understand symbols; it is through symbolic interpretation that consciousness and, therefore, the self are formed.

Evolving from symbolic interaction is a new way of conceptualizing how gender is formed. This is called the **doing gender** perspective. This perspective sees gender as an accomplished activity—accomplished through the interactions one has with others (West and Zimmerman 1987; West and Fenstermaker 1995). Stated another way, this perspective analyzes gender not as something essential to men and women nor fixed in biological status or social roles. Instead, it sees people as constantly re-creating gender meanings and gendered social structures whenever they act in gender-typical ways. From this point of view, gender is routinely reproduced in everyday interaction. It is not an individual trait; rather, it is created through social interaction.

From the perspective of "doing gender," whenever someone interacts with another in a way that displays a particular configuration of gender, gender is "done." This perspective conceptualizes social structure as existing only insofar as actors continue to act in ways that reproduce gender relations. Gender is thus constituted through routine social interaction, as individuals (consciously and unconsciously) engage in behaviors identified with specific gender meanings. The woman who smiles at a man (even though she may not like him), the man who opens doors routinely for women (regardless of who is more conveniently able to do so), the woman who dresses in feminine clothes, or the man who takes the lead in dancing are all "doing gender." Harmless though their behavior may seem, it contributes to the social reproduction of gender relations in society.

The perspective of "doing gender" emphasizes the fluid character of gender identity. Rather than seeing gender as a fixed or learned set of roles, this framework interprets gender as an ongoing and fluctuating series of behaviors that is created through social interaction. A good way to illustrate this is the case of Billy Tipton, a famous jazz musician who died in 1989 at age 74. Tipton married five times and had three adopted sons. Not until the day he died did many learn that the man whom everyone thought was such a fabulous musician and loving husband and father was really a woman! Few knew of how he had "done gender." Tipton began his identity as a woman in the 1930s, when he was relatively young—a time when an unwritten code in the jazz world kept women from being hired. One cannot help but marvel at the effort it took to maintain this social identity and to imagine how his life would have been different, including what his career would have been, had it been known that "he" was a woman (D. Smith 1998; Middlebrook 1998).

This is a highly unusual example of doing gender, but understanding gender as an accomplished act helps one see how people create the gender categories that constitute being a man and being a woman. Whether putting on makeup (Dellinger and Williams 1997), asserting oneself in a group, or exercising power in an organization, one may be doing gender in a way that continually re-creates, but also can change, the social definition of gender. The doing gender perspective also suggests that people enact gender to varying degrees and also that socialization into gender roles is not just a passive process whereby people simply internalize others' expectations (Messner 2000).

As an example, think about the experience of being a tomboy. We have already seen that sanctions against tomboys steer young girls into behaviors judged appropriate for their gender. But research on tomboys also shows that young girls actively resist conforming to gender-appropriate roles. Thus, girls who are tomboys are not just trying to "be boys," but are actively constructing a concept of themselves as embodying traits of both genders (Carr 1999).

The doing gender perspective sees people as also engaged in **gender displays**— that is, demonstrations of behavior that communicate gender identities. Gender displays may be subtle, perhaps hardly conscious, but they may also be hypermasculine or hyperfeminine. *Hypermasculinity*, for example, can be defined as gender displays that strongly portray one's presentation of self as aggressive, domineering, and controlling. Hypermasculinity is also associated with militaristic aggression and some forms of sport—showing as well how "doing gender" is promoted by institutional structures.

Comparing Theoretical Perspectives

There are important differences between these four perspectives. Identification theorists assume that imitation of same-sex persons is motivated by fear—the fear of separation from a psychosexual love object. Cognitive-developmental theorists assume a more positive motivational basis for learning, namely, mastery. In the cognitive-developmental framework, children are actively involved in the construction of the social world. In contrast, both social learning and identification theories assume a somewhat more passive view of the child's development.

Both the social learning and cognitive-developmental perspectives emphasize the role of culture in shaping gender identity. Social learning theorists have a more deterministic view, however, in that they see culture as a model and reinforcer for what the child becomes. In the cognitive-developmental framework, the child does more than simply react to the culture. He or she searches for patterns in the culture and actively seeks to structure and organize the concepts of the world that the culture provides.

The perspective of doing gender takes a completely interactionist point of view—that is, seeing gender as real only insofar as people continue to do it. This perspective has been criticized for understating the significance of institutional arrangements in shaping gender relations. It tends to make power differences between men and women less visible and understates the significant economic and political advantages that existing social arrangements give to men. Like the other perspectives, however, it helps us see how gender is constantly reproduced through the behaviors of women and men. Each of these theories shows us how central gender is to the formation of our gender identity. From the day we are born to the day we die, social expectations about our gender confront us in the everyday world. These external social expectations become internalized in our self-concepts, and they become identities through which we experience the social world.

Limitations of the Socialization Perspective

Questions about gender identity and socialization as an origin for gender differences are more than academic matters. Whether women hold the status they do because they choose their positions or whether there are structural obstacles to their well-being lies at the heart of many public policy discussions about the status of women. Of course, socialization and structure are highly interrelated; as this chapter has shown, gender socialization originates in gendered institutions. If men and women become different from each other as the result of socialization and social structures, should social policies treat them differently or the same? This question is the focus of many current debates, affirmative action being one example. The framework of U.S. law, based on the principle of equality, theoretically means that all groups should be treated the same. If men and women are different as the result of their social experiences, should we expect that treating women like men will result in fairness and justice for them? If we develop gender-blind policies, will they assist only women who make choices as men would make them? In a world where policy values sameness, not difference, how do we recognize, value, and support the lives of women and men, regardless of the gender roles they take on? Should women have to become like men to be accorded the privileges men hold?

These questions are well illustrated by the desegregation of two formerly all-male military academics: Virginia Military Institute (VMI) and The Citadel. The U.S. Supreme Court ruled in 1996 that women could not be excluded from state-supported military academies such as The Citadel and VMI. This case followed the public spectacle when Shannon Faulkner had earlier fought for two and a half years to gain admission to The Citadel. Once admitted, she was subjected to extreme humiliation, both by the other cadets and by instructors. After this debacle, which ultimately caused her to leave, two other women left The Citadel after a serious hazing incident in which they were sprinkled with nail polish remover and their clothes set on fire. In the court case that ultimately gave women the constitutional right to attend such academies, attorneys defending VMI argued that women were "not capable of ferocity, are more emotional, and cannot take stress." This was countered by the expert testimony of sociologist Michael Kimmel who argued that the exclusion of women from military academies was based on gender stereotypes that supported their culture of masculinity (Kimmel 2000).

At issue in this case was whether women were so different from men that they could not succeed in rigorous military training or whether there were structural obstacles to their success. In its ruling, the Supreme Court clearly indicated that excluding women was a violation of the equal protection clause of the Fourteenth Amendment to the U.S. Constitution. While the number of women who might choose to attend a military academy may now be small, such cases make us think about how women's capabilities are shaped by the opportunities they have.

This case also shows that matters of gender socialization have serious implications for social policy. Socialization does not occur in a vacuum. It is a process by which human beings adapt to their environment, and in this society that environment is one structured on gender inequality. Socialization does not explain the origins of inequality by itself, but it is a very effective way of explaining how that inequality is reproduced. If we limit ourselves, however, to thinking of gender differences as only a matter of learned choice, we overlook the patterns of institutionalized gender inequity that pervade society. Stated differently, the socialization process shows how individuals become gendered persons, but it does not explain the social-structural origins of gender inequality.

Another caution about seeing gender solely in terms of socialization is that people are not mere receptacles for social life; rather, they actively participate in and create social change. Role-centered perspectives may exaggerate the extent to which we become socialized, leading to an oversocialized view of human life. Focusing on gender roles also tends to exaggerate the differences between the sexes because, by definition, its emphasis tends to be on differences, not similarities. In gender-role research, gender differences typically are built into research designs. The items on questionnaires, for example, or the factors selected for manipulation in experimental studies necessarily reflect the differences that a researcher wants to test. The end result may be that the research literature on gender roles exaggerates and polarizes masculine and feminine differences.

Not all girls and boys grow up in the gender-stereotyped way that the research literature sometimes suggests; nevertheless, research on childhood learning underscores the point that gender socialization is situated within social institutions that tend to value masculine, not feminine, traits. Were values associated with women—such as flexibility, orientation toward others, and cooperation—to be incorporated into dominant social institutions, then we might well produce more gender-balanced boys and girls. As it is, the process of socialization throughout life separates men and women and creates gender differences among children and adults.

❖ Chapter Summary and Themes

Although biological causes of gender differences are commonly believed, culture is more significant in shaping who we become as women and men.

Biology sets very broad limits for human behavior and is a poor predictor of what people become. Cases of those born as biologically intersexed can be used to show the significance of social factors in shaping gender identity. Carefully observing gender differences can also reveal that there are usually greater differences among people within gender categories than across such categories, even though men and women are culturally described as "opposite sexes."

Gender is a social construction, meaning that gender is created through social learning and the structure of social institutions.

Many social scientists distinguish the concepts of sex and gender, *sex* being used to refer to one's biological identity as male/female and *gender* being used to refer to the social and cultural patterns associated with being men and women. Social institutions also guide how gender is constructed in society, with significant variation across diverse cultures.

Gender is embedded in social institutions; social institutions can also take on the characteristics associated with gender.

Gender is not just an individual attribute, but is deeply embedded in social structures. Thus, while gender is a social role—in the sense that people enact the social expectations passed on to them—gender is also a social structure, that is part of the whole structure of society, not just located "within" individuals. Put differently, gender is in society and a gendered society is within us.

The process of gender socialization shapes various aspects of our lives, including gender identity, attitudes, and self-concepts.

Gender is a learned phenomenon, acquired through diverse influences of family, peers, schools, the media, and other socialization agents. Studies of childhood socialization reveal how early gender expectations are passed on to young children. The influences of socialization persist, however, over the life course, resulting in different experiences for women and men as adults, including into one's older years.

Gender does not exist in isolation from other social factors; as a result, one's identity is shaped by the interactive influence of race and gender, along with other social factors.

Gender identity is manifested differently depending on one's race, ethnicity, and other factors. Even when recognizing the influence of gender as a social category, one must be careful not to overly generalize from the experience of any one group.

Different theoretical perspectives on the social construction of gender emphasize different dimensions to this process.

Theories can be used to understand the social processes by which people "become gendered." Some theoretical perspectives emphasize psychodynamic processes, such as same-sex identification. Others, such as social learning theory, emphasize environmental influences. The perspective of *doing gender* interprets gender as activity that is accomplished through everyday interaction. All contribute unique ways of viewing how gender is created and maintained in society.

❖ *Key Terms*

biological determinism	gendered institution	sexually dimorphic traits
biological reductionism	hermaphroditism	social construction of gender
cognitive-developmental theory	homophobia	social institutions
culture	identification theory	social learning theory
doing gender	institution	social roles
gender	intersexed persons	socialization
gender display	object relations theory	symbolic interaction theory
gender identity	sex	transgender
gender roles	sex chromosomes	

❖ *Discussion Questions/Projects for Thought*

1. Describe the play you remember from your childhood. Who did you play with? What did these games communicate about gender? How have they affected your current interests, skills, and aspirations? It would be good to discuss this question in mixed-gender groups.

2. Identify some of the research studies described in this chapter, and develop some experimental observations that let you replicate these studies. You could do this in the same setting as the original research or introduce new conditions or research subjects that let you develop further questions raised by the subject. For example, take a walk through some place where you are likely to see men and women with baby strollers. Who pushes the stroller when the baby is in it or when the stroller is empty? Observe places where you are likely to see toddlers and their mothers and/or fathers. Is there a difference in whether boy toddlers and girl toddlers are allowed to walk on their own? How much distance do the parents let each sex roam before going to get them? Does this vary depending on the sex of the parent?

3. Interview a racially diverse group of men and women, asking them to define what womanhood and manhood means to them. What do their answers tell you about the interplay of race and gender in the construction of people's identities?

❖ *Internet Resources*

American Association of University Women

http://www.aauw.org

This organization promotes education and equity for women and girls. They monitor policy issues and provide extensive research on subjects important to equitable socialization of young girls. They also provide funds for research and for women seeking legal redress in cases of sex discrimination.

The Feminist Press

http://www.feministpress.org

This press is dedicated to "restoring the lost multicultural history and literature of women in the United States and the world." Their list includes books for young readers that reject gender stereotypes and provide important resources for transforming gender socialization.

Women's Studies Database, University of Maryland

http://www.inform.umd.edu/EdRes/Topic/WomensStudies

This extensive database includes numerous links to resources about a variety of gender issues,

as well as film reviews, bibliographies, employment opportunities, and course syllabi. It is one of the most extensive women's studies websites.

❖ Suggested Readings

Abbott, Franklin, ed. 1998. *Boyhood, Growing Up Male: A Multicultural Anthology,* 2nd ed. Madison: University of Wisconsin Press. Using autobiographical accounts, this anthology shows the influence of gender, along with ethnicity, race, class, and sexuality, in shaping men's socialization.

Calasanti, Toni M., and Kathleen F. Slevin. 2001. *Gender, Social Inequalities, and Aging.* Walnut Creek, CA: Alta Mira Press. This book explores the different social processes in aging for women and men, with special attention to ethnicity, race, sexual orientation, and social class.

Due, Linnea. 1995. *Joining the Tribe: Growing Up Gay and Lesbian in the '90s.* New York: Doubleday. Due's work explores, using personal accounts, the experience of growing up lesbian and gay. The book pays particular attention to the interaction of sexuality and gender.

Fausto-Sterling, Anne. 1992. *Myths of Gender,* 2nd ed. New York: Basic Books. In a review of the research on biology and gender, Fausto-Sterling challenges many of the popular myths about the biological basis of gender.

Fausto-Sterling, Anne. 2000. *Sexing the Body: Gender Politics and the Construction of Sexuality.* New York: Basic Books. This noted biologist reviews current research on intersexed persons, indicating the significant role of social expectations in how we define sexual identity.

Findlen, Barbara, ed. 1995. *Listen Up: Voices from the Next Feminist Generation.* Seattle: Seal Press. Based on the accounts of young women, this collection explores many of the feminist issues facing the current generation.

Nanda, Serena. 1998. *Neither Man Nor Woman: The Hijras of India.* Belmont, CA: Wadsworth. This fascinating account of the hijras of India, a group of men with mixed gender/sex identity, probes the meaning of gender in different cultural contexts.

Rothman, Barbara Katz. 1998. *Genetic Maps and Human Imagination: The Limits of Science in Understanding Who We Are.* New York: W. W. Norton. Rothman explores the social beliefs surrounding genetics and argues that politics and ethics shape our understanding of genetics as much as science per se. This book is an important sociological treatment of science, genetics, ethics, and politics.

Stoller, Eleanor Palo, and Rose Campbell Gibson, eds. 2000. *Worlds of Difference: Inequality in the Aging Experience.* Thousand Oaks, CA: Pine Forge Press. Combining social science research with personal narratives, this anthology explores the experience of aging by examining the diverse experiences of women of different class, ethnic, and racial backgrounds.

Thorne, Barrie. 1993. *Gender Play.* New Brunswick, NJ: Rutgers University Press. Thorne examines how gender is constructed in schools, based on observations of boys and girls in school settings. By showing the socially constructed basis of gender, she also makes recommendations for teachers interested in producing greater equity within schools.

3

GENDER, CULTURE, AND THE MEDIA:
The Social Construction of Knowledge

Gender, Language, and Popular Culture

Gender and the Media
> *Content Analysis and the Media*
> *Theories about the Media's Influence*

The Sociology of Knowledge
> *Marx and the Social Construction of Knowledge*
> *Sexism as Ideology*

Chapter Summary and Themes

Key Terms

Discussion Questions/ Projects for Thought

Internet Resources

Suggested Readings

It is said beauty is in the eyes of the beholder. A team of scientists even concluded that beauty can be scientifically determined—or so the headlines promise. Women who have been wondering whether they are sexually attractive can now determine how they measure up against a scientific standard that purports to be the perfect measurement for a woman's body: weight in pounds, divided by 2.205 (to convert to kilograms), multiplied by height in inches times 0.0254 (to get meters), then that number times itself and divided into the weight. Does this sound like a hoax? Not if you think that a sound source of information is one of the world's leading medical journals, *Lancet.* In 1998, a group of scientists from England conducted a study in which they asked a group of 40 male undergraduates to observe pictures from magazines such as *Playboy* and rate the sexiness of 50 naked women of various shapes and sizes, but without faces. The results—that the men's judgments matched the body-mass index described above—were published in *Lancet* and reported throughout the world (Tovée et al. 1998, Tovée et al. 1997, Browne, 1998).

Cultural images of women's beauty—and implicit ratings of their bodies—are replete throughout the culture. One only has to glance at a magazine stand or skim through advertisements to see that we are bombarded with specific ideals for women's appearance—ideals that rarely match what real women actually look like. With scientific experts telling women that to be sexy they should measure up to the norms of 40 male undergraduates in one specific culture, you have to wonder why so much effort is put into establishing such expectations.

Advertisements admonish women to be afraid—afraid of aging, afraid of food, afraid of being alone, afraid of having too small a bust or too big a bust. They promise that with the right products, a woman can be beguiling and seductive, as long as she changes how she looks. Smooth your skin, wear the right scent, change your hair color, color your lips, and, above all, be thin! Why? To attract men. And, if the ads don't work, the articles tell you month after month how to please men: "Touch him this way," "The one word he's dying to hear during sex," "How to make scent your secret weapon" (an article on so-called "man-entrancing elixirs" at the workplace—as if all women needed at work was the sexual attention of men!). Where does feminism fit in this? Advertisements tell it all: "The new movement"— an ad for hair gel or "the new women's movement"—the ad copy for a bra! So not only do advertisements tell women exactly what they have to buy to have the right look, they have also appropriated the women's movement by claiming that new freedoms allow you to buy the right products. These are powerful messages, and though you might think no one takes them seriously, consider the impact that images of thinness have on women's eating disorders—a phenomenon especially common among younger White women who literally starve themselves to try to attain the cultural ideal of thinness.

Images of men in popular culture are also heavily stereotyped, although in different ways than women. Men are most likely to be shown in dominating, self-assured postures, usually more in the foreground than women. But images of men also communicate strong messages about the ideal body—messages that have changed over time and in recent years emphasize more a strongly built, muscled, and larger ideal for men.

Advertisements are only one source for the ideas generated about women in the mass media and popular culture. Popular music, advice columns, television shows, and other cultural materials all carry explicit and implicit suggestions about gender. Cultural icons like "Barbie" and "Ken" teach girls and boys from a young age about gender ideals. Although children may play with such dolls as a fantasy world, they nonetheless communicate strong messages about appearance, body size, and heterosexual relationships.

Each of us sees thousands of advertisements per day. Advertisements not only sell the products we use but they also convey images of how we are to define ourselves, our relationships, and our needs. If men were shown in advertisements as women routinely are, people would probably find it laughable. How often are women displayed in ads in their underwear or lying on beds? Do you see men in such poses? Although the use of men as sex objects in advertisements has increased, it is not nearly so frequent as for women. The demeanor of women in advertising—in the background, on the ground, or looking dreamily into space—makes them appear subordinate and available to men.

Advertisements also portray stereotyped racial images of men and women. Just walk through your local grocery store and look at products carefully. What do you see? Indian chiefs on corn meal, Native American princesses on butter, Black mammies on pancake mix, Mexican banditos on salsa, and "hot" Latinas on margarita mix.

These images merge racial and gender stereotypes, as if Latin men were all rogues, African American women were docile and servile, and Native American women all beguiling. Whites do not escape such stereotyping either. Stereotypes about blonde women as being sexy, but dumb, are common in the dominant culture. Although blondes are only one-quarter of the White population, they are one-third of those shown in women's magazines and half of those depicted in *Playboy*. (Rich and Cash 1993). Studies of magazine ads find that the number of Black models has increased, but Latinos and Asians are still very underrepresented. Black men are still most typically depicted as athletes and musicians (Bowen and Schmid 1997).

You can also observe the pervasive influence of gender images in popular culture by analyzing the content of films, magazines, videos, or music lyrics. Indeed every object of popular culture seems to deeply embed gendered images. Computers for young people are the Barbie model for girls, Hot Wheels for boys. Incredibly, although the hardware for each is identical (though the Barbie model is pink and the Hot Wheels model is blue), each comes with different software packages, including more math-based software for boys and fashion-based software for girls! Music videos usually show women trying to get men's attention (Gow 1996). In some forms of popular music, women are overtly degraded and depicted as deserving violence, such as in some heavy metal and rap music (Sloat 1998). These depictions cannot be taken lightly, because research on college students also shows that exposure to sexualized imagery of women has an effect on students' attitudes about the adversarial character of sexual relationships and on students willingness to accept interpersonal violence and to believe in myths about rape (Kalof 1999).

Magazine covers also focus on how women should make themselves appealing to men. And when women are depicted as victims of crime, such as on the now popular reality crime shows, men usually do the speaking (Cavendar et al. 1999). Even buying a Father's Day card can be a challenge should your father not like to golf or fish. Most Father's Day cards narrowly cast fathers into those two leisure roles. The images of popular culture are not only obvious in mass-produced popular culture. You might even think of how gender images are also apparent in things people name: their pets, their e-mail addresses, or their names and nicknames.

The ideas and images presented to us, whether through advertisements, cyberspace, other cultural media, or labels we choose, exert a powerful influence over our lives and greatly influence how we think about gender. Popular culture conveys an impression about the proper roles of women and men, their sexual and gender identities, and their self-concepts. The ideas we hold about women and men, whether overtly sexist or more subtle in their expression, create social definitions that we use to understand ourselves and the society in which we live. The ideas that people have of one another guide their behavior, even though there is no direct fit between what people believe and say and what they actually do. What is known or believed about women and gender relations, even when it is based on distortions of social realities, influences our mental experiences. These experiences, in turn, become part of the basis for sexist social arrangements.

Ideas, although based in the interpretive realm of thought and subjectivity, direct our behavior and constrain the ways in which we see each other and others see us. Ideas also have a political reality because they affect how society works, who gets rewarded, and how things should and should not be. For example, if we believe that women's proper place is in the home, we are not likely to object to the sexist practices of employer discrimination. If we believe that women are as capable as men, however, we are likely to support policies and changes that would make more opportunities available to them.

This chapter studies the social construction of knowledge about gender. Popular culture, the media, even the language we use exert a powerful influence on how we define reality and men's and women's roles within it. Images of women conveyed by the dominant culture have been based on distortions and stereotypes that legitimate the status quo at the same time that they falsely represent the actual experience of women in the society. As a result, the ideas we acquire regarding gender relations poorly prepare us for the realities we will face.

❖ Gender, Language, and Popular Culture

One of the first ways we see the influence of culture in the construction of gender is in how we speak. As the system by which we generally communicate with each other, language both reflects and reinforces the cultural systems in which it is used. Note that this is a two-way process in that language reflects the values of the dominant culture and therefore can be one means by which stereotypes are communicated and reproduced. However, language can also produce changes in society, since by changing how we think and speak we can communicate new meaning systems to others.

Although it may seem trivial to insist on nonsexist language (e.g., calling women *women* instead of *girls*), changes in what we say can influence how we think, and language can be used to break social stereotypes. For example, it is now commonplace to address women as *Ms.*, but not that many years ago all women were referred to as either *Miss* or *Mrs.*—as if the single-most important feature of a woman's identity were her marital status. Similarly, the practice of using the word *man* to refer generically to all people makes women invisible. The contemporary practice of being more sensitive to the specific inclusion of women has transformed language use throughout society.

These are not trivial issues, because language reflects the social value that is placed on different groups in society. Language also reflects the power dynamics that are embedded in systems of gender, race, and class inequality. Racial epithets provide a good example, because the numerous negative terms that have been used to label racial-ethnic groups hold very negative connotations. Likewise, feminists have pointed out that terms such as *chicks, gals, foxes, hotties,* and *babes* demean women by associating them with animals or little girls or lustful creatures.

Language is contextual—that is, what something means varies depending on the situation in which it is expressed. Thus, women who are good friends might refer to each other as "girl" or "girlfriend" and this can be affirming, not demeaning. On the other hand, a man who refers to his secretary as his "girl," given the power differences in that relationship, is trivializing her status and reaffirming the power relationship that exists between them. Similarly, lesbian women may affectionately refer to each other as "dykes"—as a way of reclaiming a stigmatized status—but this approbation has a highly negative and hateful meaning when used by homophobic persons who use it to demean or insult. The important thing to notice here is that language is used in a context, and, when that context is marked by power differences between people or groups, the meaning of language reflects power relationships.

The gendered nature of language is not only a matter of content but also of *how* people communicate. Much research has been done on this subject and there is no simple way to summarize it, but one of the basic questions has been whether women and men use language in different ways and what this means in terms of power relationships between them (Cameron 1998). Studies have shown, for example, that despite the stereotype of women as talkative, in a variety of settings (including classrooms, meetings, and other social interactions), men take more than their "share" of talk time (Crawford and MacLeod 1990; Sadker and Sadker 1994). In addition, men are more likely to interrupt women in conversation, whereas women are more likely to use hesitancy in speaking—perhaps deferring to others, speaking more softly, laughing, or just being silent in group discussion. Again, context matters, since scholars have also shown that, even though women talk less than men, men also use silence as a way to assert their power. Silence can control interaction by expressing little interest in the other or withholding information. Someone who does not respond may dominate interaction by controlling topic development in conversation or refusing to recognize others' contributions (Anderson and Leaper 1998; Mast 2001).

Studies of gender and language have generally focused on questions of differences between women and men, leading to debate about how significant such differences are. Popular stereotypes suggest that the differences are large and real, such as in the best-seller, *Men Are from Mars, Women Are from Venus* (Gray 1994)—a practical guide for improving communication in marriage, premised on the idea that women and men communicate differently. So popular is the idea that men and women are fundamentally different that this book has sold over ten million copies and spawned an industry of related products, talk shows, workshops, and on-line advice about relationships.

There are two ways to think about gender differences in communication. One, referred to as **essentialism,** is the argument that men and women are basically different and that this shows up in bipolar patterns of language use, along with other social behaviors. The other is **social constructionist theory,** which sees people as constructing gender through their ongoing interaction with others. In this framework, gender is a system of meanings that people enact; moreover, even when "doing gender," people may not internalize what they do. This does not mean that stereotypes and patterns of behavior associated with one gender or the other do not exist, only that gender is a fluid category, one constantly changing and evolving through human interaction. The social constructionist approach, as you saw in the previous chapter, is a less simplistic approach to the study of gender in society than the essentialist framework, which sees gender as more fixed, even if by culture and society. More than seeing gender as a matter of differences, social constructionists see people as having human agency—that is, as actively creating their lives, even if within the context of social structures that supersede them. From this point of view, even when people conform to social stereotypes, they may do so without internalizing a belief in them. Furthermore, enacting gender may even be a form of resistance to traditional gender roles, as when people act "supersterotypically" as a way of mocking dominant expectations.

The focus on differences between men and women, not just in studies of language but in studies of all forms of social behavior, has been so strong that at times it seems the only alternative way of thinking is to deny the significance of gender differences altogether (Crawford 1995). Certainly gender differences do exist and they are reported throughout this book, but it is important to understand that gender is a changing social construct and one that reflects complex patterns of social behavior and social change. At the same time, even in recognizing differences between men and women as a whole, we should also be careful not to overgeneralize about women. On all matters of social behavior, language included, there is significant variation *within* gender and by race, class, ethnicity, as well as social context.

Language is yet one dimension of what can broadly be referred to as **popular culture**—the beliefs, practices, and objects that are part of everyday traditions. Popular culture includes popular music, film, magazines, television, and some forms of the arts that are widely accessible to the public. Popular culture has an enormous influence on the cultural values of a society and is one of the dimensions of life that has been widely examined by feminists because of its significance in the social construction of gender. Take, for example, romance novels—a subject carefully studied by feminist scholars because of its influence on the fantasy lives of millions of women. Such novels portray women as needing men, although feminist critics also point out that women read such novels as an escape from the domestic demands of others (Radway 1984). At the same time, popular culture can provide for millions of women (and men) alternative images—such as in the growing popularity of feminist murder mysteries where independent, savvy, strong, and sometimes armed women work as private investigators, prosecutors, or sleuths of other kinds.

Images from popular culture reveal numerous contradictions with regard to gender. On the one hand, much of popular culture is deeply stereotyped by gender. A quick perusal of a greeting card rack will show you this. Women are ridiculed for aging (as are men, but in different ways), whereas cards presumably for men commonly promise them voluptuous, full-breasted women to make their day! Simultaneously, popular culture can be transformative, as exemplified by some contemporary performance art involving the portrayal of transgendered selves. As you begin to examine one of the most influential sites of popular culture—the media—you should keep in mind that culture is an ever-changing and dynamic process that is not an abstract thing, devoid of people's ability to interpret, resist, and change.

❖ Gender and the Media

One of the most significant influences within U.S. culture is the mass media. The media include television, magazines, films, music, newspapers, radio, and now the Internet, to name just a few of the sources of media in contemporary culture. Although many deny that they are significantly influenced by the media, the influence of the various forms of media is enormous. According to national surveys, Americans spend 73 hours per week exposed to various forms of media, including television, radio, film, music, the Internet, newspapers, books, and magazines, spending in total almost $16 billion to do so (U.S. Census Bureau 2004).

Content Analysis and the Media

What do you see in the media? Even a cursory look at advertising, television, film, or other media forms reveals gendered images of women and men that permeate everyday life. Those who systematically study the media look at what images are projected and how they influence people. To accurately assess what is depicted in the media, social scientists use careful methods of observation, most often what is called content analysis.

Content analysis is a research method whereby one systemically analyzes the actual content of documents, images, or other cultural artifacts. By counting particular items or images within a defined category, researchers are able to systematize their observations of the media's content. Of course, describing the content does not show how people respond, but it does give a report of what is there. Other research methods can then examine people's responses—both conscious and un-intended—to media depictions.

When you examine the media carefully, you might be surprised at how pervasive gender-based images are. In television ads, for example, women are more likely to be seen in service roles than in professional jobs (Coltrane and Adams 1997). Men are less likely to be shown cooking, cleaning, shopping, or washing dishes. When men are shown in the context of family life, they are usually engaged in activities stereotypically associated with men—in cars or mowing the lawn. Moreover, men are usually seen with boys, not girls, and rarely with infants. And, though nurturing images of men are now more frequent in the media, they most often appear in magazines read by women, not by men (Vigorito and Curry 1998; Kaufman 1999). One particular study has systematically examined the portrayal of women and men in prime-time commercials on Spanish-language television. The pattern is clear: Only in a few cases were men seen doing household work; women were most often depicted in the role of homemaker (Fullerton and Kendrick 2000). Such stereotypical images are not confined to U.S. markets, but are common in nations as diverse as Great Britain, Indonesia, Kenya, Mexico, and Portugal (Furnham and Mak 1999).

In some regards, women are more visible in the media than they were years ago, reflecting some change in traditional roles for women. For example, there is increased coverage of women's sports. How are women athletes are depicted in such representations? In 2001, researchers analyzed the representation of women athletes in *Sports Illustrated* and *Sports Illustrated for Women*, finding that women were presented as powerful, strong, fit, and "pro-woman." Indeed, feminist themes were often used in such portrayals, such as by asking, "What if women ruled?" in the ad copy. But, at the same time, the tendency was to show only the most attractive athletes, and the coverage of women athletes emphasized their nurturing character (Gordy 2002). Researchers have also analyzed the cover photographs in media guides for the NCAA (National Collegiate Athletic Association), finding that women are less likely to be portrayed as active participants in sport and more likely to be shown in passive and traditionally feminine poses (Buysse and Embser-Herbert 2004).

On television there has been some change in how women and men are depicted. Women now play strong and intelligent roles in many TV dramas. Yet, in most shows, men are still the major characters and women are cast as glamorous sidekicks—or often scheming villains. Systematic content analyses of prime-time television show that, even with greater respect now given to women on prime time and more women being shown working outside the home, women are much more likely to be shown as sex objects than is true of men (Signorielli and Bacue 1999; Lin 1998). In commercials, women are also underrepresented, except for commercials involving health and beauty products (Ganahl et al. 2003).

Children's television may be one of the most stereotypical sources of gendered images. Considering the number of hours that children spend watching television, this means that such images are a powerful source of gender socialization. Ninety-eight percent of U.S. homes are equipped with at least one television, and these are turned on an average of five hours a day. By the time a child is 15 years old, she or he will have spent more hours watching television than attending school. Moreover, analysts estimate that in nearly half of U.S. households (42 percent) televisions are on most of the time; Black children are even more likely than White or Hispanic children to live in these "constant television households" (Gitlin 2001).

Does this matter in terms of what children learn about gender? Numerous studies find that children's attitudes about gender are influenced by the amount of television they watch. Children report that they want to be like certain television characters when they grow up. And, children who watch the most television are those who hold the most stereotypical, gender-typed values (Signorielli, 1989, 1991). In television, children see more male characters than they do female characters. Although there is some change in the gender stereotypes that children see on television, they are still pervasive in this and other media forms. Children's programming is still more likely to show male characters in more active and individualistic activity and in occupational roles (Davis 2003; Powell and Abels 2002).

Violence in children's media is also associated with gender. Over one-third of children's commercials include acts of aggression. You might expect that this would be associated with commercials that include only boys, but aggression is found more often in commercials that include boys and girls. However, aggression is much more frequently associated with White boys than children of color (Larson 2003). Other research also finds that boys become more desensitized than girls to violent content in the media (Klinger et al. 2001).

Television, as influential as it is, is not the only source of gender images in the media. Music videos, magazines, and film also convey powerful messages about gender possibilities, especially for young people. Even a quick look at the covers of women's magazines shows a cultural obsession with women's appearance. Stand in the line at the grocery store and what do you see? Covers promising quick and easy diets—of course, right next to mouth-watering, rich desserts that women can cook. Next to these promises are admonitions to women to please men—if not through food, through sex. From *Cosmopolitan* to *Ladies' Home Journal*, magazines promise all kinds of sex tips intended for men's satisfaction. And young women's magazines similarly present limited possibilities to young girls. A study of *Seventeen* magazine, for example—one widely read by young women—finds that the overarching message about work to young women is that women work primarily to meet and assist more powerful men (Massoni 2004).

These vast and popular images reinforce gender expectations, as well as those associated with race, class, sexuality, and age. Indeed, the mass media promote narrow definitions of who people are and what they can be. Although aging is inevitable, women and, increasingly, men, are warned to fight the signs of aging. Youth, not age, for women is defined as beautiful. Light skin is promoted as more beautiful than dark skin, regardless of race, although being tan is seen as more beautiful than being pale. Even in magazines targeted for Black women, the models typified as most beautiful are generally those with the lightest skin and straight or wavy hair, resulting in color stratification even within the African American population (Herring et al. 2003). European facial features are also pervasive in the images of Asian and Latino women.

Taken together, these images reinforce gender stereotypes and limit the possibilities that people see for themselves. In this way, the images in the media can be defined as controlling images (Collins 1990). The concept of **controlling images** refers to the power of the media and popular culture to direct our concepts of ourselves and others. It is meant to highlight the power of those running the media to shape our consciousness and self-concept. The images we see in the media are not just neutral, appearing without effect. The media is a source of authority in society, producing what you might think of as "cultural narratives"—frameworks by which people come to understand themselves and their world.

The media provide a common basis for social interaction in society. People talk about the latest episodes of their favorite programs, sing the lyrics of various songs, dress like the models in music videos, desire the bodies that they see in magazines. The very nature of the media makes the images seen less fluid and emergent than they would be in reality. In the media, ideas and characters seem fixed, giving a singular and narrow definition of reality. Rarely does the public get a glimpse of how these images are actually produced. Instead, they appear as objective truths.

Controlling images of gender are compounded when you look at race, social class, sexuality, and age. Although Latinos and African Americans tend to watch more television than White people, they are underrepresented in the media and, when shown, are usually in subordinate and stereotypical roles. Black men are most often portrayed as athletes, criminals, or entertainers. Only occasionally are Black and Hispanic people shown as complex, loving, and intelligent people (Dines and Humez 2003). Asian American and Native Americans are virtually invisible on television and often play "disappearing" roles—in the background or catering to the needs of more dominant groups. If you look at magazines targeted toward young, White women, chances are that most images of African American men will show them with bare chests and gold chains around their neck—an image based on racist images that sexualize Black men.

Women of color are stereotyped in television programs as humorous but dominating characters. And much research has been done analyzing the image of women of color found in popular music. Hip-hop and rap refer to women as "bitches" and "hoes." And in most music videos women of color are turned into commodities—appearing as property, something to be had. Other images in music videos show women of color as vacuous and empty—looking into space with dreamy eyes averted from the camera. Analysts argue that such depictions teach women (and men) a narrow definition of being sexy and beautiful (Perry 2003).

Concepts of social class and its relationship to gender are also taught through these media narratives. In general, working class characters are more likely found in comedies than in dramas, suggesting that there is something funny about their life situations. Working-class women are most often objects of laughter, and rarely do we see realistic portrayals in the media of women in working-class jobs. Working-class men are most likely seen in beer commercials or police shows (Bettie 1995). Instead the media promote a belief that everyone can be middle–class and that the accoutrements of social class are available to anyone who works hard enough. Thus, welfare mothers are depicted as dependent—an image that has increased over time and is most commonly associated in the media with African American women (Misra et al. 2003).

Along with race and class, age and sex stereotypes abound in the media. Women tend to be shown as younger in the media than are men (Ganahl et al. 2003). In films, older men are depicted as vigorous, employed, and involved in adventure, whereas women of the same age are usually peripheral to the main action or are portrayed as rich dowagers, wives and mothers, or lonely spinsters. Furthermore, the roles for women in film have remained remarkably static over time (Markson and Taylor 2000).

In recent years, gays and lesbians have become more visible in the media. Popular shows such as *Queer Eye for the Straight Guy* and *The Ellen Degeneres Show* have provided new visibility to gay and lesbian life and, in some regards, have produced more positive images of lesbian and gay people. Advertisers have sought to expand their commercial markets, so there are now more lesbian and gay characters being shown on television. But many argue that lesbians and gay men are still cast in stereotypical ways, with little realistic portrayal of real gay and lesbian lives. Still, the increased visibility of lesbians and gays in the media can influence public acceptance of gays and lesbians and generate support for equal rights protection (Gamson 1998).

Even the news, something to be taken seriously and as objective truth, is loaded with biases of gender, race, and class. Women, and especially women of color, usually report the "soft "news or human interest stories; men's voices carry the authority of world events. Women of color appear on the news as reports and anchors more often in late night hours, weekends, and holidays when the "senior" staff has time off. Men are the vast majority of political pundits and are far more likely to be interviewed, heard, and seen in news reports. Even in reports of rape women's experiences are often filtered through men's voices; and, in celebrity rape cases, male voices are much more "championed"—that is, the men, not the women, become the story's focus (Moorti 2002).

Many have targeted the controlling images of women that appear in the media as contributing to the high rates of violence against women in society. Some have associated the use and presence of pornography with violence against women, though the conclusions are mixed. Many find no association between exposure to pornography and attitudes toward violence against women or the likelihood of rape (Kimmel and Landers 1996; Barron and Kimmel 2000), but exposure to violent pornography has been shown as related to the likelihood of men's engaging in sexual aggression and being less sympathetic to rape victims (Donnerstein and Linz 1986). In a recent study of Internet pornography, it has been found that it is generally more violent toward women than other forms of pornography. Moreover, content analyses of Internet pornography sites that depict rape seldom show the perpetrator, focusing instead on the rape victim who is most typically shown as young and docile. Asian women are vastly overrepresented on such sites, reproducing sexual and gender stereotypes of Asian women as sex objects. In many other ways, images of rape on the Internet are highly racialized, showing that the sexual politics of pornography are about more than simply gender (Gossett and Byrne 2002).

Do the images found in the media matter? Studies have found that seeing stereotypical sexual imagery in music videos affects college students' attitudes, encouraging them to see sexual relationships as adversarial (Kalof 1999). Even when people think that media images are unrealistic, they think that others find the images appealing. Thus, young girls, even if they are critical of media ideals, think boys will judge them by how well they match the ideal (Milkie 1999). People do not just passively internalize media images, and they can distinguish fantasy and reality (Currie 1997), but media images form cultural ideals that have a huge impact on people's behavior, values, and self-image.

You cannot tell what effect media images have simply by reporting on the content of the media. As the studies cited above indicate, understanding the effect of the media requires understanding how people respond. For example, although music videos have been strongly criticized for their misogynistic (that is, woman-hating) character, the presence of more women in this world can transform the meanings produced therein. In hip-hop, Black women's performances often counter the exploitative and objectifying depictions of women (Emerson 2002). The media creates narratives—that is, frames by which people come to understand the world around them. People react and respond to them, not just passively internalizing the dominant frames. Feminist performers have used their artistic talents—in numerous cultural fields—to challenge and resist the dominant constructions of women that appear in dominant cultural narratives. In other words, people are not without the power to make change.

Theories about the Media's Influence

Several approaches have been developed to explain the depiction of women by the media. These include the reflection hypotheses, role-learning theory, organizational theories of gender inequality, economic explanations of media organization.

The Reflection Hypothesis

The first and theoretically the most simple explanation of the depiction of women by the media is called the **reflection hypothesis** (Tuchman 1979; Tuchman et al. 1978). This hypothesis assumes that the mass media reflect the values of the general population. Images in the media are seen as representing dominant ideals within the population, particularly because the capitalistic structure of the media is dependent on appealing to the largest consumer audience. According to Gerbner (1978), the ideals of the population are incorporated into symbolic representations in the media. The reflection hypothesis asserts that, although media images are make-believe, they do symbolize dominant social beliefs and images.

The volumes of data produced by marketing researchers and ratings scales indicate that popular appeal is significant in decisions about programming content. Observations of shows such as soap operas also reveal that television attempts to incorporate into its programming social issues that reflect, even if in an overblown way, the experiences (or, at least, the wishes) of its viewers. Although viewers may escape into soap operas as a relief from daily life, the fact that they can do so rests on some form of identification (even if fanciful) with the characters and the situations portrayed (Modleski 1980).

The reflection hypothesis leaves several questions unanswered. To begin with, as content analysis studies have shown, much if not most of what the media depict is not synchronized with real conditions in people's lives. In part, this phenomenon is explainable by a time lag between cultural changes and changes in the media (Tuchman et al. 1978). It is also explainable by the fact that the media portray ideals, not truths; furthermore, people may not actually believe what they see in the media, and, if they do, it may be because the media create, not reflect, viewers' beliefs. A causal question is asked in theoretical explanations of media images: Do the media reflect—or create—popular values? The reflection hypothesis makes the first assumption; other explanations begin with the second.

Role-Learning Theory

The values and images of women and men in the media represent some of the most conservative views of women and men. **Role-learning theory** hypothesizes that sexist and racist images in the media (and the absence thereof) encourage role modeling. That is to say, "the media's deleterious role models, when internalized, prevent and impede female accomplishments. They also encourage both women and men to define women in terms of men (as sex objects) or in the context of the family" (Tuchman 1979). The assumption that the media encourage role modeling is the basis for feminist criticisms of the media's depiction of women.

The role-modeling argument assumes that the media should truthfully reproduce social life and that there is some causal connection between the content of the media and its social effects (Tuchman 1979). In other words, the role-modeling argument assumes that media images produce stimuli that have predictable responses from the public. This is an argument that sees human beings as passive receptacles for whatever media inputs are poured into them. People may, in fact, view media images much more critically or even with cynicism, making it unlikely that they would modify their behavior in accordance with the images. This possibility does not deny the fact that people, especially children, do learn from the media; rather, a criticism of role-modeling theory suggests that it is an oversimplified perspective. As you will see in examining postmodernist theory, many recent feminist theorists see role-learning theory as too one-dimensional and simplistic in assuming that images in the media are internalized by viewers.

Organizational Theories of Gender Inequality

Although both the reflection hypothesis and the role-modeling argument alert us to the fit between images and reality, neither adequately explains the reasons for sexism in the media. Other scholars have attempted to explain sexism in media content by studying gender inequality within media organizations. This perspective assumes that the subordinate position of women and people of color in the media influences the ideas produced about them. If women and people of color are absent from the power positions where ideas and images are produced, then their world views and experiences will not be reflected in the images those organizations produce. In addition, because those who occupy power positions come to share a common world view, the ideas they produce tend to reflect the values of the ruling elite.

White women and people of color have made many inroads into media careers, but behind the scenes these appearances are deceiving. Almost half (43 percent) of women in radio news and 48 percent of women in television news have said that discrimination has hurt their careers. At the same time, however, much progress has been made. White women have made substantial progress in the news work force, and the pay gap that continues for women is mostly the result of differences in the years of experience. But, minority women and men have not made the same progress (Stone 2001).

Do the numbers of women and minorities in the media matter, as far as explaining the images of women and racial-ethnic groups that appear? The argument that increasing the number of women and minorities employed by the media will transform the images portrayed of them presumes that men and women and Whites and people of color hold different values; this belief has not been consistently demonstrated in research. Persons who work in an organization become socialized to accept the organization's values. Those who do not conform are less likely to build successful careers; hence, organizational workers more often than not adopt the values of the organizations in which they are employed. Within the media, professional attitudes discourage workers from offending the networks. Professionalism encourages workers to conform to the bureaucratic and capitalist values of their organization (Tuchman 1979). This influence affects how all workers portray gender and racial issues in the media because the organizational culture discourages controversy. That men and women working in the media adopt similar values to each other tells us not so much that men and women think alike, but that all workers' behaviors and attitudes are shaped by the organizations in which they are employed.

Capitalism and the Media

A fourth perspective used to explain sexism in the media attributes sexism to the capitalist structure of media organizations. According to this approach, it is in the interests of sponsors to foster images that are consistent with the products they sell. Many of these products encourage particular values; for example, promoting obsessive cleanliness is necessary to sell the numerous household cleaning products placed on the market.

This perspective also claims that it is in the interests of a capitalist power elite to discourage images of reality that would foster discontent. Not only will sponsors promote any values that will sell, but they will also encourage traditional views that uphold the status quo, while discouraging and stereotyping those that challenge it. When the media respond to social criticism, they do so within the limits of existing institutions. For example, following the civil rights movement, when pressure was generated to increase the number of Black Americans in the media, more Black Americans appeared in advertisements and on television programs, but they were and continue to be primarily depicted in middle-class settings where they hold middle-class value systems and are not critical of U.S. society. Likewise, as noted previously, the feminist movement was depicted by the media as radical, trivial, and extremist. As the women's movement gained public support, the media selected its more moderate programs and leaders for public display.

An economic perspective of the media reminds us that the media are owned and controlled by the major corporations of U.S. society. From this perspective, Marx's idea is true that those who control economic production also control the manufacture and dissemination of ideas. The economic structure of the media explains much about why women continue to be shown as sex objects and household caretakers. These images are consistent with capitalist needs to maintain women's services in the home and to make commercial objects out of everything, including sexuality.

In itself, this explanation encourages a somewhat conspiratorial view of media owners and management who, although they are motivated by economic profit, may not have the specific intent of exploiting women. This perspective, along with the gender-inequality approach, gives us, however, a more complete understanding of sexism in the media. Observing the economic and social organization of the media causes us to ask who produces media images and how these images define legitimate forms of social reality.

Depictions in the media can also be seen as social myths by which the meaning of gender in society is established. Anthropologists study social myths to gain an insight into the culture and social organization of a people. Myths provide an interpretation of social truths, beliefs, and relationships that guide a society in its vision of the past, present, and future. They establish a "universe of discourse" that integrates and controls its members, gives them a common reality, and creates structures for what is said, done, and believed (Tuchman 1979). By creating a universe of discourse among their audience, the media act as powerful agents of social control. They engage people in passive fantasies, encourage dreams and visions that are consistent with the social structure, and establish a common basis for social interaction. In a fundamental way, the depiction of women, as well as men, in the media infiltrates our social consciousness and embeds itself in our imagination. Postmodernist theorists further explore this process.

Postmodernist Feminist Theory
Each of the preceding perspectives implicity assumes that the influence of the media is unidirectional—that is, there is little indication of how viewers (or readers) actually respond to these images. Also, these perspectives assume that, whatever the source of media images, they have a deleterious effect on those who watch or read them. This assumption is challenged by the arguments of postmodernist feminist theory—a theoretical perspective that assumes a more active perspective on the response of viewers to images perceived in various media outlets. **Postmodernism** views society as constructed through social meaning systems, which are highly fluid and changeable (see Chapter 13). From this perspective, symbols and representations are especially important to study because they reveal the meaning systems that shape society at any point in time. Postmodernist theory has generated renewed interest in cultural studies, since it is through culture that one sees the various representations that define modern life. From a postmodernist perspective, social

structures do not just determine gender identity, nor other forms of identity. Rather, identity is constructed through the subjective understandings that people bring to their reading of "social texts" (i.e., cultural images) (Currie 1997; Walters 1995).

Postmodernist theory tends to be highly abstract and has been criticized by some feminists for being so, since it is difficult for anyone but those highly trained in elite academic programs to understand it. But, an important point derived from postmodernist theory is that social actors are creative in constructing their identity, or, specifically, in the case of gender, what it means to be a woman or man.

In a concrete example of the study of cultural images from a postmodernist perspective, Dawn Currie (1997) has examined teen magazines and asked how young girls read them and the images of femininity they convey. Currie designed a study using small *focus groups* (i.e., discussion groups whose conversation is observed and recorded by the researcher). The focus groups of teen girls observed images taken from *Seventeen* magazine and discussed what they had seen. Currie found that the girls did not just passively accept the images as ideals; instead they selectively choose ads that they enjoyed and rejected the images conveyed in others. She argues that these young readers distinguished between fantasy and reality and were often quite critical of ads that they saw as making no sense or posing unrealistic images. Indeed, the girls were quick to reject images that they saw as inconsistent with their own identity.

This does not mean that the images in the magazines were completely without influence. In fact, when asked whom they most wanted to be like, many of the girls chose celebrities who had just been featured in *Seventeen*. Currie suggests that the formation of gender identity, as influenced by the media, is not a one-way process. Young women actively mediate what they see and what they think, thus emphasizing the role of human creativity in the formation of self, instead of seeing people as passive objects into whom cultural images are inserted.

We can see that postmodernist explanations of gender and culture go beyond theories of learned gender roles and gender differences by insisting on seeing agency (i.e., human creativity) in human behavior. This does not mean that domination by highly influential media industries is insignificant, nor does it mean that we should view the sexist images of gender in the media uncritically. Rather, postmodernism suggests that women and men view these images with an ability to shape the meanings of what they see, without necessarily completely internalizing such cultural ideals. Thus, postmodernist theory adds a strong social constructionist dimension to understanding how knowledge is created in society—a subject long studied in a field known as the sociology of knowledge.

❖ *The Sociology of Knowledge*

The preceding discussion underscores three essential sociological points: that knowledge in society is socially constructed, that knowledge emerges from the conditions of people's lives, and that knowledge is embedded in ideological systems. Knowledge is not just simple truth statements. Rather, knowledge is often generated from and tends to reinforce institutions that support existing social arrangements (i.e., the *status quo*). Whether reflected in language, the media, popular culture, or the arts, knowledge of gender is a powerful social construction.

In sociology, the study of the social construction of ideas is called the **sociology of knowledge.** The sociology of knowledge begins with the premise that ideas emerge from particular social and historical settings and that this social structural context shapes, although it does not determine, human consciousness and interpretations of reality. Studies in the sociology of knowledge relate ideas and consciousness to social structure and human culture. Intellectually, this perspective originates primarily in the works of Karl Marx and Karl Mannheim, both of whom, in distinct ways, grappled with the relationship between human knowledge and human existence. It was Mannheim who, in the early twentieth century, labeled the study of the sociology of knowledge and delineated its core ideas, but Marx's study of ideology and consciousness is the intellectual precursor of Mannheim's endeavor.

Marx and the Social Construction of Knowledge

Karl Marx (1818–1883) based his study of human ideas on the premise that the existence of living human beings—that is, their actual activities and material conditions—forms the basis for human history and the ideas generated in this history. Although Marx recognized that human beings live within particular physical settings (including climatic, geographical, and geological conditions), it is the social relationships formed in these settings that make up human society. In other words, human beings transform their environmental conditions through the activities in which they engage. Human society and history emerge as people use their labor to create their social environment. Marx argued that human beings are distinguished from animals by the fact of their consciousness. Although we now know that other animal species have linguistic ability and rudimentary systems of social organization, no other species has the capacity of humans for the elaboration of culture.

Marx's argument is that ideas follow from human behavior. In other words, thinking is derived from the actual activity in which human beings engage. Within Marx's framework, it is not the consciousness of persons that forms the bonds (and chains) of human society; rather, specific relationships among people shape human society and therefore people's ideas.

Marx is not denying that social relations involve an interpretive dimension. He is arguing, however, that ideas emerge from our material reality. This theory suggests that changes in consciousness alone do not generate social changes. Instead, the material conditions of society must be changed if we are to liberate people from oppression.

Marx goes one step further by arguing that within society, the dominant ideas of any period are the ideas of the ruling class. It is they who have the power to influence the intellectual production and distribution of ideas. You can see what he means by thinking about the vast power of media monopolies. Where do you get your news? the Internet? television? newspapers? books? radio? magazines? Whatever the source, the chances are that this outlet is owned by the same large corporation that owns several of the other media outlets. Moreover, given the concentration of media monopolies, there are only a few major corporations that own the various media outlets that provide you with information. Thus, the same company (Viacom) that owns the publisher of this book (Allyn and Bacon) also owns other publishers, the CBS television network, Paramount Television, Paramount Pictures, several television and radio stations, BET (Black Entertainment Television), Nickelodeon, MTV, TV Land, Nick at Nite, VH1, five theme parks, Blockbuster, over 1,700 movie theaters, and several Internet providers—all told a $26.6 billion industry.

The power of media monopolies over the images and ideas available to people is hard to overestimate. Marx thought that in capitalist societies, those who own the means of production also determine the ruling ideas of the period.

As Marx writes,

> *The ideas of the ruling class are in every epoch the ruling ideas: i.e., the class which is the ruling material force of society, is at the same time its ruling intellectual force. The class which has the means of material production at its disposal, has control at the same time over the means of mental production, so that thereby, generally speaking, the ideas of those who lack the means of mental production are subject to it* (The German Ideology, *in Tucker 1972:136).

From a Marxist perspective, under capitalism, what people think is shaped by the class system because, under capitalism, the ruling class controls the production of ideas. The ideas that are disseminated through communications systems, including the media, language, and other cultural institutions, authorize a reality that the ruling class would like us to believe. According to Marx, when subordinate groups accept the world view of dominant groups, they are engaged in **false consciousness.**

Feminists add to Marx's perspective on the social construction of ideas, arguing that in general men own the means of production (that is, capitalist industries) and therefore determine the ruling ideas of any given time. Sexist ideas justify the power of men over women and sanction male domination, just as racist ideas attempt to justify White supremacy. From a feminist perspective, ideas serve not only capitalist interests but also men's interests.

According to Canadian scholar Dorothy Smith (1990), in patriarchal societies men's ideas are also shaped by the gender-based division of labor. Men typically do not do the work that meets the physical and emotional needs of society's members. As a result, men's ideas (especially of those who engage primarily in intellectual work) assume a split, or bifurcation, between mind and body, and rational thought is accorded the highest value. This belief in the bifurcation of mind and body is made possible only because the labor of women provides for men's physical needs, mediates their social relations, and allows them to ignore bodily and emotional experience as an integral dimension of life.

Likewise, in racially stratified societies, the gender-based division of labor intersects with the racial division of labor. The ideas of White people, particularly those having the most privilege, are likely to take the labor of racial groups for granted, making it appear invisible or unimportant. Oddly enough, the ideology that supports racial inequality tends to define racial groups as "lazy" and "unwilling to work." This ideological belief does not reflect reality, but rather distorts the experiences of racial groups whose actual work affords certain Whites the privilege of not having to do menial labor. In addition, in societies structured by both race and gender privilege, the ideologies of sexism and racism intersect. Think, for example, of dominant cultural images of women on welfare (usually presumed to be women of color). The idea that they do not want to work pervades popular thinking, as if raising children on a meager income is not work.

Sexism as Ideology

Karl Mannheim (1893–1947) further developed the sociology of knowledge. Mannheim's sociology of knowledge relates ideas to the conditions under which they are produced. His work also provides a foundation for feminist scholarship because he develops the thought that ideas grow out of the relationship of knowledge to social structure.

Mannheim saw the task of the sociology of knowledge as discovering the relational character of thought. How are ideas embedded in the social experience of their producers and the social-historical milieu within which ideas are formed? All ideas must be evaluated within the context of their social making. This view is true not only for the grand ideas of intellectual history but also for the consciousness of human beings in their ordinary experience (Berger and Luckmann 1966).

Mannheim suggests that new ideas are most likely generated during periods of rapid social change. He explains this belief by suggesting that as long as group traditions remain stable, then traditional world views remain intact. New ideas appear when old traditions are breaking up, although the persistence of customary ways of thinking is also likely to make new ideas appear to be "curiosities, errors, ambiguities, or heresies" (1936:7).

Mannheim is best known for his study of ideology. **Ideology** refers to a system of beliefs about the world that involves distortions of reality at the same time it provides justification for the status quo. Following from Marx, Mannheim sees ideology as serving the interests of groups in the society who justify their position by distorting social definitions of reality. Ideologies serve the powerful by presenting us with a definition of reality that is false and yet orders our comprehension of the surrounding world. When ideas emerge from ideology, they operate as a form of social control by defining the status quo to be the proper state of affairs.

From Mannheim's work, we can understand **sexism** as an ideology that defends the traditional status of women and men in society. Although, as Mannheim says, no single idea constitutes an ideological belief system, the collective totality of an ideology (such as sexism) permeates our consciousness and our comprehension of the world in which we live. It is here that the sociology of knowledge merges with the political goals of feminism because in debunking sexist ideology, the social-historical origins of sexist thought are found and new definitions of reality can be forged. Although Mannheim is careful to distinguish political argument from academic thought, he recognizes that the unmasking of ideological systems is a function of sociological theory.

The sociology of knowledge helps us understand how ideas reproduce our definitions of social reality; who produces ideas; under what conditions ideas are made; and the consequences of ideas and beliefs that, in the case of sexism, systematically define women and men in stereotypical and distorted terms. It gives you a context for understanding the ideas and images of gender that this chapter has documented.

❖ *Chapter Summary and Themes*

The gendered images that we can observe throughout society generate cultural scripts that produce stereotypes about women and men.

The images of women and men that we see around us are pervasive and often taken for granted, despite their enormous influence. Although they change over time, they bombard us with images of women as thin, as sex objects, as tied to home. Such images create a concept of the proper roles for women and men, significantly influencing our self-esteem and our definition of others.

Language shapes our definition of reality, but can also transform how we think about gender.

Many think that feminist criticisms of sexist language are trivial, but language shapes our definition of reality. When language embeds sexist assumptions, it can shape how and what people think. Thus, changes in language both reflect and generate changes in people's consciousness.

Empirical observations of the media reveal numerous ways that gendered images define men and women in narrow and stereotypical ways.

Content analyses of various forms of culture document how different groups are depicted. Whether in television, magazines, the Internet, films, and other forms of popular culture, images of women in the media tend to restrict women to narrow roles. Images of men are similarly restricting. Furthermore, gendered images are compounded by race, class, sexual orientation, and age, among others. All of these images have a profound impact on our identities, our images of others, and our sense of social possibilities.

Theories about gender and the media analyze the relationship between images in the media and the social realities that they both reflect and create.

Images in the media to some extent reflect the values of a culture, but they also operate to create those values. Moreover, the images do not appear in a vacuum. Audiences are not just passive vessels, but actively respond to what they see—sometimes internalizing these ideals, other times critically responding to them. The capitalist structure of media industries influences how the media are organized and why the media promote the images and ideas that we observe.

The sociology of knowledge theorizes that all ideas are generated within a social context.

Understanding the social context in which ideas are generated—and believed—is a critical component of sociological thinking. What we think and the ideas made available to us are shaped by the social and historical context, including the influence of powerful organizations that produce the ideas of the time.

❖ *Key Terms*

content analysis	ideology	role-learning theory
controlling images	popular culture	sexism
essentialism	postmodernism	social constructionist theory
false consciousness	reflection hypothesis	sociology of knowledge

❖ *Discussion Questions/Projects for Thought*

1. Identify some aspect of popular culture (i.e., MTV videos, current children's films, television sitcoms) and develop a systematic way to observe the gender images portrayed. What do these images convey to the audience? Using the theoretical frameworks used to explain the depiction of women in the mass media, how would you explain the presence of these images? What do you suppose their effect is?

2. Compare the images of men to those of women in any of the following forms of popular culture: sports or hobby magazines, women's magazines versus men's magazines, television news programs and crime dramas, popular music from different time periods, etc. What do your observations tell you about the portrayal of men where there are different intended audiences? How does the historical time period affect these images? Whose interests are best served by these interests, and how does this illustrate the theoretical perspectives discussed in this chapter?

3. As a way of exploring the difference in essentialist and social constructionist theory, ask a group of women to observe advertisements in a women's magazine and talk about what they see in the images. Based on what they say, would you say that these women have internalized the ideal that these images suggest, do they resist it, or something in between? What does this tell you about social constructionist theory and essentialism?

❖ *Internet Resources*

About Face

http://www.about-face.org

This website challenges negative and sexist images of women in the media, with the goal of promoting women's positive self-esteem. The site includes resources, examples of positive media images, and a gallery of the "worst offenders." The point is to empower people to challenge such demeaning cultural messages. The site also includes links to other progressive media groups.

Jean Kilbourne

http://www.jeankilbourne.com

Jean Kilbourne is a nationally recognized expert and speaker, producer of the popular film, *Killing Us Softly*. Her website includes numerous links to organizations that advocate for change in the negative images found in the media. The site also includes synopses of her books and films, as well as films and other resources.

Television and News Research

http://www.missouri.edu/~jourvs

This website, maintained by Professor Vernon Stone, includes useful informatiom about the progress of women and minorities as workers in the television and radio industry.

Women's Educational Media

http://www.womedia.org/

This organization specializes in producing social documentaries that work to achieve economic and social justice. Their website includes a directory of their films and videos, as well as information about social issues.

❖ Suggested Readings

Collins, Patricia Hill. 1990. *Black Feminist Thought: Knowledge, Consciousness, and the Politics of Empowerment.* Boston: Unwin Hyman.
This important book connects race and gender in the sociology of knowledge by developing a framework for Black feminist thought. Collins uses this perspective to examine the controlling images that the dominant culture produces about Black women.

Craig, Maxine Leeds. 2002. *Ain't I a Beauty Queen? Black Women, Beauty, and the Politics of Race.* New York: Oxford.
Craig looks at Black women's racial identity, particularly as it is shaped by cultural changes relating to the politics of beauty. The book also shows how racial/gender politics change and affect Black women's lives.

Crawford, Mary. 1995. *Gender and Language.* Thousand Oaks, CA: Sage.
This basic text is a good review of the gendered character of language. The author places her analysis in the context of theoretical debates about sex differences, their origins, and their significance.

Dines, Gail, and Jean M. Humez, eds. 2003. *Gender, Race, and Class in Media,* 2nd ed. Thousand Oaks, CA: Sage.
This anthology explores the race, class, and gender images produced in the media, linking them to the perpetuation of cultural stereotypes. Some articles also explore the representation of gays and lesbians in the media, linking sexual stereotypes to other forms of cultural oppression.

hooks, bell. 1991. *Black Looks: Race and Representation.* Boston: South End Press.
A noted Black feminist scholar, hooks writes about the portrayal of African Americans in popular culture and the connection of these images to Black identity. Her powerful writing also discusses political resistance to racial and gender systems of domination.

Kilbourne, Jean. 2000. *Can't Buy My Love: How Advertising Changes How We Think and Feel.* New York: Touchstone.
Kilbourne's book shows the influence of advertising on gender meanings, as well as other subjects including violence, alcohol, and cigarettes.

Rodriquez, Clara E. 1997. *Latin Looks: Images of Latinas and Latinos in the U.S. Media.* Boulder, CO: Westview Press.
The articles in this anthology explore how Latinas and Latinos are depicted in the media, with a critical eye to changing cultural stereotypes.

Wolf, Naomi. 1991. *The Beauty Myth: How Images of Beauty Are Used against Women.* New York: William Morrow and Co.
Wolf's best-selling book shows how the beauty ideals promoted in popular culture harm women's self-esteem, as well as their physical health. As a cultural critic, she provides an accessible analysis grounded in sociological insight.

4

SEXUALITY AND INTIMATE RELATIONSHIPS

❖

The Social Construction
of Sexuality

The History of Sexuality
in the United States

Contemporary Sexual Attitudes
and Behavior

Race, Sexuality, and Power

Sexual Development over
the Life Cycle
  Menstruation
  Menopause

Love and Intimate Relationships

Interracial Relationships
Friendship

Lesbian, Gay, and
Bisexual Experiences

Chapter Summary and Themes

Key Terms

**Discussion Questions/
Projects for Thought**

Internet Resources

Suggested Readings

❖

❖ The Social Construction of Sexuality

Sexuality is an essential part of our identity and our relationship to others. It involves deep emotional feeling and intimacy as well as issues of power and vulnerability in relationships. Human sexual expression takes a variety of forms, although the expression of sexual behavior is influenced and constrained more by cultural definitions and prohibitions than by the physical possibilities for sexual arousal. In fact, what distinguishes human sexuality from sexual behavior among animals is that "human sexuality [is] uniquely characterized by its overwhelmingly symbolic, culturally constructed, non-procreative plasticity" (Caulfield 1985:344). Much of what we assume about sexuality, however, is distorted by assuming that sexuality is a "natural drive" or an internal state that is acted out or released in sexually exciting situations. But anthropologists and others have pointed out that what is seemingly natural about human sexuality is its being shaped by culture (Caulfield 1985). How sexuality is expressed and felt varies according to the cultural context.

Even though people like to think of sexuality as a private matter, social institutions direct and control sexuality. Some forms of sexual expression are seen and treated as more legitimate than others. Heterosexuality is a more privileged status in society than is homosexuality. Because of this, heterosexuals (or at least those presumed to be so) have more institutional privileges than do those defined as homosexual; thus, married heterosexual couples may legally marry, get employee health care benefits, and can file joint tax returns. In general, gay men and lesbian women are also more directly controlled by laws and institutional policies than are heterosexuals. That heterosexuality is institutional can be seen by the many laws, religious doctrines, and family and employment policies that explicitly and implicitly promote heterosexism.

One of the major social factors influencing sexual relationships is gender. We have already seen that beliefs about sexuality influence gender socialization. But gender also influences sexuality. The two (gender and sexuality) exist in a *dialectical* relationship—that is, each influences the other and the form they take emerges over time.

Across cultures and within our own, human sexual expression includes a wide range of behaviors and attitudes. Although we tend to think of our sexuality as internally situated, it involves a learned relationship to the world. The feminist movement has inspired among us a new openness about women's and men's sexuality and has helped free women's sexual behavior from its traditional constraints; yet, the persistent belief that heterosexuality is the only natural way of expressing sexual feeling continues to blind most people to other possibilities for human sexual feeling and practice. As we discard the notion that there is some single and unchanging way of expressing sexual feeling, we are much more likely to understand human sexuality and intimacy in all their variety and forms.

❖ The History of Sexuality in the United States

It is commonly thought that over time sexual behavior and attitudes have become less restrained and more uninhibited. Most people believe that sexuality was largely repressed in the past and that only recently have sexual ideas and practices become more liberated. Such a reading disregards the variability and change in sexual attitudes and behaviors and the differing historical ways in which sexuality has or has not been regulated. The history of sexuality is not a simple story of movement from repression to liberation or ignorance to wisdom (Freedman and D'Emilio 1988). Sexuality is constantly reshaped through cultural, economic, familial, and political relations, all of which are also conditioned through the prevailing social organization of gender, race, and class relationships at given points in time.

Historians of sexuality have argued that the dominant meaning and practice of sexuality have changed from their primary association with reproduction within families in the colonial period to their current association with relationships of emotional intimacy and physical pleasure for individuals (Freedman and D'Emilio 1988). The separation of sexuality from reproduction, because of the widespread availability of birth control, means that sex can be loosened from its traditional association with family. Additionally, sexuality has become more commercialized, and the tie between sexuality and reproduction has been loosened. Groups within society experience these broad-scale transformations in sexuality in different ways, however. For example, sexuality for women is still more closely linked to reproduction than it is for men; working-class and poor women are more likely to have to "sell" their sexuality than are middle-class or elite women. Gay men's and lesbian women's sexuality is more directly controlled by the state, and they are more subjected to continuing repressive attitudes than are heterosexual women and men.

You have to take care not to overgeneralize about sexual experience only from the experience of dominant groups. To say that sexuality in the colonial period and early nineteenth century was a family-centered, reproductive sexual system grossly distorts the sexual experiences of enslaved African American men and women. For them, family systems were neither recognized by the state nor respected by the dominant culture; sexual reproduction was often forced, not for purposes of a family-centered life, but for purposes of economic exploitation. Sexual exploitation was an integral part of the system of slavery. The images of African American men and women that emerged during that period to justify sexual exploitation continue to influence contemporary sexual stereotypes of African American women and men.

Three patterns recur in the history of sexuality (Freedman and D'Emilio 1988). First, political movements that attempt to change sexual ideas and practices thrive at times when an older system is undergoing rapid change and disintegration. For example, the movements of sexual liberation that emerged in the 1960s occurred while there were great transformations taking place in women's and men's roles, the definition and shape of family relationships, and the social behavior of young people. Even technological change played a part as the easy availability of birth control made possible the separation of sexuality and reproduction. Further transformations in broad-based gender relations (including women's increased labor force activity and their later marriage and increased likelihood of divorce) created a context in which movements for increased sexual tolerance and diverse forms of expression have flourished.

A second recurring pattern is the fact that sexual politics are integrally tied to the politics of race, class, and gender. Class and race hierarchies are often supported through claims that working-class people and people of color are sexually promiscuous and uncontrolled. These false images are then used to justify systems of social control; furthermore, gender inequality is maintained through controlling sexual images of women and men. The idea in the early twentieth century that professional women were "sexually inverted" (a veiled way of calling them lesbians) is a good illustration of how gender inequality is supported through manipulation of sexual ideas. Likewise, the contemporary belief that women who are raped must have "asked for it" maintains a fundamental injustice in the balance of power between men and women in the eyes of the state.

A third historical pattern is that the politics of sexuality is often linked to other social concerns, especially social movements and moral campaigns in which images of impurity and vice are used to stir public concern. For example, in the early twentieth century, nativist fears of immigration were often fueled by claims that immigrant women were wanton prostitutes. Rather than examining the economic needs of women immigrants, opponents incited moral outrage to further restrict immigration. In contemporary politics, those who have resisted programs on AIDS education in the public schools have based their position on the claim that distributing condoms will encourage promiscuous behavior.

The history of sexual attitudes and behaviors reveals much interconnection between sexual politics and other dimensions of race, class, and gender relations. Historically, systems of sexual regulation are highly correlated with other forms of social regulation. At the same time, historical analysis reveals the ever-changing nature of sexual meaning systems and sexual mores. Thus, reflection on the history of sexuality is a good way to see how sexuality is socially constructed and how it intersects with other features of the social structure.

❖ *Contemporary Sexual Attitudes and Behavior*

Changes in sexual attitudes and behaviors in the latter half of the twentieth century have been so extensive that they have been called a *sexual revolution.* This term is used to describe the greater freedom now found in sexual behavior, as well as the more liberal attitudes that many hold about sexuality. Surveys of sexual behavior and attitudes show that sex is more likely than in the past to take place outside of marriage, young people initiate sexual behavior at a younger age, people are more tolerant of diverse sexual practices, and more people—men and women—have sex with more than one partner in a lifetime. All of these and other changes associate the sexual revolution with greater sexual freedom.

The sexual revolution, however, has not necessarily separated the fusion between gender and sexuality. Some say that the sexual revolution has simply made women's sexual behavior more like men's—at least as indicated by the frequency of sex, number of sexual partners, and other measures of sexual behavior (Ehrenreich 1987; Laumann et al. 1994). Others say that traditional gender expectations still permeate sexual relationships, with women expected to be more passive and men expected to initiate and control sex. While there have been changes in women's sexual behavior, there are many ways that gender continues to influence sexuality.

Women's sexuality has traditionally been associated with passivity and men's with power. Although these definitions are loosening, they continue to influence how sexuality is understood. Men's sexuality is still associated with performance and achievement; in fact, the very term describing the absence of sexual arousal in power is a term that associates sex with power: impotence. Women's sexuality, on the other hand, is seen as something to be contained and controlled or as something dangerous and enticing. You can see this in the dichotomous labeling of women as either good girls or whores. Research in fact finds that women who are virgins in their young adult years perceive that they are rewarded for virginity; men of the same age, on the other hand, think they are stigmatized for virginity (Burgess et al. 2001).

In general, men are much more likely to be praised for being perceived as sexually very active. Of course, men have to negotiate the boundaries that gender and sexuality construct: Being a "stud" is a positive social identity for men (with no equivalent identity for a woman), but a man who is too casual in his sexual behavior may get labeled as a "player." It is hard to even imagine what a woman "player" would look like because women are not generally perceived as having the power in relationships that allows them to "play" men. What do you think a woman engaging in this behavior would be called, and what does this label suggest about gender, power, and sexuality? Although it has changed over time, the *double standard* that has differentiated women's and men's sexual behavior for years still casts them in different sex-gender roles (Fromme and Emohivich 1998). You can clearly see this connection by thinking about what produces stigma and praise for men and women in their sexual behavior.

The connection between gender and sexuality can also be seen in how women's sexuality has been defined as male-centered. We saw in the previous chapter how much sexual advice is given to women about how to please men sexually. Even the definition of sexual intercourse that most people think of as "having sex" is based on the centrality of the penis. Most people think that sexual intercourse specifically means penile-vaginal intercourse (Gallup Poll 1998). This was also apparent during the scandal involving President Clinton's affair with Monica Lewinsky, when he argued that, despite their sexual conduct, they had not had "sexual relations."

Phallocentric thinking is that which assumes that women need men for sexual arousal and satisfaction. Phallocentric thinking is historically revealed by Sigmund Freud's theory of the double orgasm, a sexual myth that long distorted the understanding of female sexuality. Freud's argument, and one that was widely believed, was that women have two kinds of orgasms—clitoral and vaginal. Clitoral orgasm, in Freud's view, was less "mature." He maintained that adult women should transfer their center of orgasm to the vagina, where male penetration made their sexual response complete. Freud's theory of the double orgasm has no basis in fact. The center of female sexuality is the clitoris; female orgasm is achieved through stimulation of the clitoris, whether or not accompanied by vaginal penetration (Masters and Johnson 1966). For nearly a century, the myth of the double orgasm led women to believe that they were frigid—unable to produce a supposedly mature sexual response.

Phallocentric thinking continues to appear in the assumption that women's primary sexual orientation is naturally directed toward men. If one is heterosexual, one may never question that claim, but if one views the claim from the perspective of a lesbian woman's experiences, one is likely to think otherwise. The belief that heterosexuality is the only natural form of sexual expression is rooted in a cultural framework that defines heterosexuality as compulsory and homosexuality as deviant or pathological (Rich 1980). **Compulsory heterosexuality** refers to the institutionalized practices that presume that women are innately sexually oriented toward men. In a social system structured on compulsory heterosexuality, women's sexual relationships with other women are not seen as a choice, but only as deviance from the social norm, unless they are eroticized in pornography for men. Although it may at first seem odd to think of heterosexuality as a compulsory institution, the social sanctions brought against women who are not identified as attached to men show how heterosexuality is maintained through social control. Even if women remain single and couple with no one, they are ridiculed and ostracized. If they love other women, they are seen as deviant. Lesbian women and gay men are subjected to legal sanctions that deny their basic civil rights, and they are often subjected to overt acts of violence and personal harm. The concept of compulsory heterosexuality indicates the degree to which sexual choices, relationships, and privileges are structured by social institutions. The belief that women need men to achieve a mature sexual response reflects the assumption that women are dependent on men for their sexual, emotional, social, and economic well-being. This assumption not only legitimates compulsory heterosexuality as an institution (Rich 1980) but also denigrates women's relationships with other women.

Cultural attitudes toward sexuality are strongly influenced by assumptions about gender. Men are stereotyped as having a stronger sex drive than women and as driven by their sexual impulses. Women are often blamed for their own victimization whether by rape or sexual abuse. These beliefs carry great force as cultural myths and reproduce the gender inequality on which they are based.

Contemporary sexual attitudes represent some loosening of rigid judgments about sexual behavior, but, predictably, these attitudes, too, are shaped by gender. For example, note the gender gap in sexual attitudes among entering college freshmen represented in Figure 4.1. More than half of the men (55 percent) agree that "it is all right for people who really like each other to have sex, even if they have only known each other a very short time"; only 31 percent of women think so. Such differences can lead to significant conflict between men and women, as shown in Figure 4.2.

Changes in sexual relationships are especially evident among young people and on college campuses. A relatively new form of sexual interaction, known among students as "hooking up," suggests that sex is more casual and more frequent than was true in the past. *Hooking up* refers to sexual behavior that includes no ongoing commitment to the other person. For some hooking up means kissing;

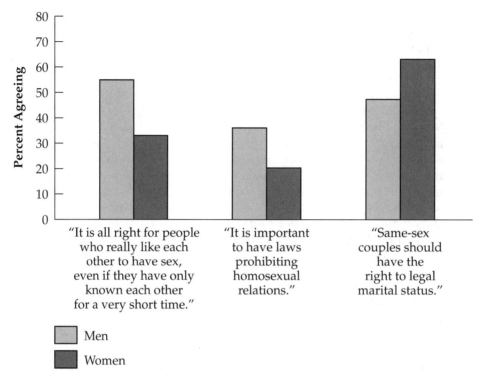

FIGURE 4.1   The Gender Gap in Sexual Attitudes

Source: American Council on Education and University of California at Los Angeles Higher Education Research Institute. 2000. "The American Freshman: National Norms for Fall 2000." Reprinted by permission.

for some it means sexual-genital play, but not intercourse; and for some, it means sexual intercourse. Although hooking up is associated with sexual freedom, studies find that students perceive others to be more comfortable with it than they are themselves. Men also express more comfort with these casual, noncommitted sexual of relationships than women do, and it seems that men still maintain the power in such relationships. Hooking up is also not as casual or risk-free as its cultural acceptance suggests. Women who are perceived as hooking up too frequently risk being considered overly promiscuous (although men do not), and college women who hook up frequently, especially in fraternities, have a much higher likelihood of experiencing rape and other forms of sexual violence (Paul et al. 2000; Lambert et al. 2003; Jordan-Simmons 2002; Bogle 2004).

Changes in sexual attitudes are also found in the fact that the public has become more liberal about topics such as homosexuality, with 52 percent of the public now saying that homosexual relations should be legal; women are more likely

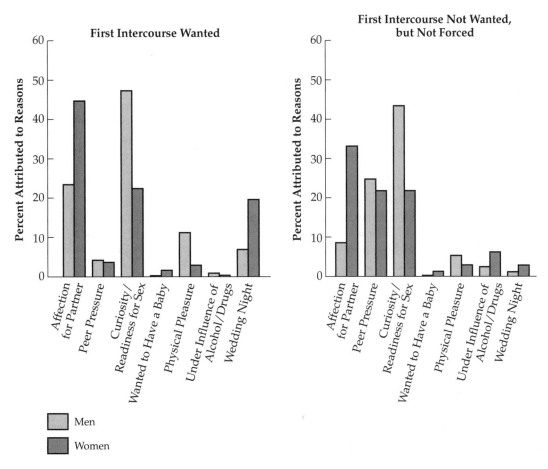

FIGURE 4.2   Reasons for Having First Sexual Intercourse

Source: Data from Robert T. Michael, John H. Gagnon, Edward D. Laumann, and Gina Kolata. 1994.
Sex in America: A Definitive Survey. Boston: Little, Brown, p. 93.

to think so than men; Whites are more likely to think so than Blacks and Latinos, although Black women are less homophobic than Black men (Lewis 2003; Battle and Lemelle 2002). Studies find that those with more traditional gender role attitudes are most inclined toward homophobia, and those with more authoritarian attitudes (that is, rigid in their beliefs) are more homophobic (Whitley 2001; Alden 2001). Not surprisingly, conservative Christians are also more homophobia than those with other religious beliefs (Finlay and Walther 2003). But it has also been found that the degree of contact one has with gay men and lesbian women significantly lessens homophobic attitudes (Basow and Johnson 2000; Cullen et al. 2002).

❖ *Race, Sexuality, and Power*

Although most people think of sexuality only in personal or individualistic terms, feminist perspectives examine sexuality within the context of power relationships. The term **sexual politics** refers to the link between sexuality and power (Collins 2004, 1990). Sexuality and power are linked through the intersections of race, class, and gender oppression. Within this system, sexual politics are marked by the domination and social control of White women and women and men of color. The particular forms of sexual oppression experienced by each group depend on the group's specific location in the race, class, and gender system.

Under a system of race, class, and gender oppression, sexuality is restricted and repressed. Sexual politics support and maintain oppression by race, as well as by class, which can be seen in the controlling images of subordinated groups and the degree of protection afforded dominant groups who engage in sexual deviance and crime. For example, Black men and women have been defined as sexually deviant and threatening; Latinas as "hot" or virginal; Latinos as "macho;" the working class and poor are defined as promiscuous and indiscriminate in their choice of sexual partners. Asian American women are stereotyped as sexually beguiling. At the same time, dominant groups are less likely to be stereotyped as sexually violent and, instead, as sexually "pure."

The sexual politics of race, class, and gender oppression are also apparent in the perpetration of sexual violence against women of color. Sexual violence has been a means of controlling and exploiting African American women (Collins 2004, 1990). During slavery, for example, African American women were used as sexual objects for the pleasure and economic benefit of White men. Marriage between African American women and men was not recognized. The rape of African American women by White slave owners both made African American women sexual objects for White men and added to the population of slave labor.

Both African American women and African American men are subjected to sexual violence, although the forms of sexual violence they have experienced are gender specific. Rape, pornography, and prostitution have been forms of sexual violence used to dominate and control Black women. Historically, lynching was a form of sexual violence used to control Black men. As Angela Davis (1981) argues, the myth of the Black rapist is one that was conjured up to justify the violence Whites directed against African American communities. Defining Black men and women as uncontrollably lustful and sexually uninhibited is a way of claiming the moral superiority of Whites and ideologically justifying social control and sexual violence (Collins 2004).

The sexual politics of race, class, and gender oppression are revealed not only in history but also in the current period. The same controlling images that were developed during slavery continue to permeate dominant images of Black men's and women's sexuality. Dominant images of Black men still depict them as sexually threatening and uncontrolled. Black women in pornography are depicted as sexual objects, frequently in bondage, wrapped in chains and ropes—reminding us of slavery and creating cultural images that continue to oppress Black women (Collins

1990; Tuan 1984). Frequently, images of Black women (both in pornography and in advertisements) sexualize them in the context of nature, as if to say that Black women are wild, uncontrolled, and animalistic. Depicting human beings as animals encourages their exploitation by implying that they can be bought and sold and need taming; even if seen with affection, they are treated condescendingly as pets. Either way, the image of Black women as associated with nature constrains and exploits their sexuality.

The intersections of race, class, and gender oppression are similarly revealed in the sexual politics shaping the experiences of all women of color. Asian American women, for example, are stereotyped as passive and subservient, willing to please and serve White men. The extensive use of Asian women as mail-order brides is evidence of this stereotype. In general, the stereotype of exotic Asian sexuality, centered on the pleasure of White Westerners, permeates notions of Asian American sexualities—both homosexuality and heterosexuality (Leong 1996; Espiritu 1997). Native American women are often depicted in pornography as being tortured. Cultural myths also portray Native American women as sexually free and as using their charms to negotiate treaties between White men and Native populations (Tuan 1984). Native American men appear frequently on the cover of romance novels as savage and lustful, with swooning blonde women in their arms (Nagel 2003). Dominant-group stereotypes of Latinas define them as virgins or whores, a dichotomy that restricts their sexual identity and expression. These stereotypes of Latinas are accentuated by the significance given to virginity within Latino communities. Not only is virginity revered within the Catholic Church, but, in addition, within Latino families honor is strongly tied to the sexual purity of women (Espin 1984).

Men are not excused from these racialized sexual images. In general, men are seen as unable to control their sexual urges and as needing sex all the time. But, as with women, this stereotype is mediated by racial images. Thus, while White men are seen as sexually aggressive, they are not demonized to the extent that men of color are. Race and gender stereotypes interconnect for men, too. Thus, Asian American men are stereotyped as asexual, Latinos as driven by machismo and as sexually "hot." Native American men are stereotyped as exotic, but fierce, and Black men as dangerous. Arab men are stereotyped as mysterious and dangerous.

All of these images distort the actuality of women's and men's sexual experiences and mask the extent to which power relationships shape the intersections of race, class, gender, and sexuality. Although sexuality is thought to be purely personal and private, examining it in the context of race, class, and gender relationships reveals the extent to which structural power relationships influence the experience of all groups of women and men.

❖ *Sexual Development over the Life Cycle*

Sexuality is not a fixed, biological event. Once we understand this, we can better understand how sexual identity is an emergent process—one that evolves both through history and in the course of individual development. Understanding that sexuality is socially constructed need not, however, ignore the influence of biological processes. Sociological analysis of sexuality includes discussion of the relationship between biology and culture, as already discussed in Chapter 2. Feminists add to this discussion the recognition that the understanding of biological processes has been distorted by the sexist assumptions permeating scientific discourse, a discussion also addressed previously in Chapter 3.

Menstruation and menopause—two aspects of women's experience that are both social and biological in nature—can be used as an example. Both are defined as key to women's sexual development, although their significance may well be overstated. For example, sexist myths define postmenopausal women as asexual, an assumption disproven by women's own accounts of their experiences. Likewise, menstruation has been depicted as disabling women, making them "unfit" for men's work, even though there is no supporting evidence for such a claim. How has feminist scholarship recast what is known about menopause and menstruation?

Menstruation

Menstruation is a universal phenomenon, yet, like menopause, it is one that takes on different meanings in different cultures. In many cultures, menstruation is symbolic of the strength of women, and elaborate rituals and rites of passage symbolize that power (Powers 1980). In other cultures, menstruation is seen as symbolic of defilement, and elaborate practices may be developed to isolate and restrict menstruating women. In the nineteenth century, for example, Southeast Asian women could not be employed in the opium industry, for it was believed that if a menstruating woman was nearby, the opium would turn bitter (Delaney et al. 1988). In contemporary U.S. culture, menstruation is depicted as secretive and invisible, as best seen in the advertising industry, which advises menstruating women to keep their "secret" protected, yet to feel confident, secure, and free.

As with menopause, most studies of menstruation associate it with disease. Exaggeration and alarm run throughout discussions of menstruation, probably showing more our culture's fear of women's reproductive processes than a genuine understanding of the menstrual cycle. Consider, for example, the apprehension generated by the so-called dangers of premenstrual syndrome (PMS). According to news tabloids, PMS is responsible for a wide range of deviant behaviors, including insanity, murder, and other criminal acts. When scientists declare that 25 to 100 percent of women experience PMS, what does that mean? It may simply mean that most women recognize bodily signs of oncoming menstruation, although it is possible that a small proportion of women do find the physical changes associated with menstruation to be incapacitating (Fausto-Sterling 1992).

Most certainly, many women do experience premenstrual tension, but the definition of PMS as a medical problem gives the medical profession, not women themselves, the authority to interpret and "treat" PMS (Markens 1996). The social construction of PMS as a disease or syndrome also means that any positive feelings and experiences associated with premenstrual cycles—such as enhanced feelings of sensuality, high energy states, or feelings of general well-being—are also ignored, since PMS becomes defined by medical authorities as a problem to be treated by them. Public attention to PMS also presumes that only women, not men, are regulated by bodily phenomena—reminiscent of traditional arguments of biological determinism.

These cultural attitudes can shape how young women experience menstruation. Studies show that most premenstrual girls (and boys of the same age) believe that menstruation is a physically and emotionally disruptive event. Associating menstruation with fear and repulsion encourages feelings of shame and can discourage young girls from discussing menstruation with each other, which would potentially provide them more information and support. Menstruation symbolizes the reproductive and sexual potential of women, and its onset occurs at the same time that young girls are developing their sexual identities. The meanings given to this experience are contextualized by a society that both devalues and trivializes women, by defining them as sexual objects. This is bound to affect women's experiences with menstruation and, in particular, to affect how young girls see their developing sexual selves (J. Lee 1996).

From a sociological point of view, menstruation is not just a physical process; it is laden with social and cultural meaning. Physiological conditions such as menstruation cannot be understood entirely without a consideration of the social context in which they occur. This can be seen as well with regard to the process of menopause.

Menopause

The biological process of aging is clearly one that is universal, inevitable, and based on human physiology. How long one lives is strongly influenced by one's gender. Life expectancy is shorter for men (74 years in 2000) than for women (79 years), and males have higher accidental death rates (in both childhood and adulthood) than do females (U.S. Census Bureau 2004). Men also have higher suicide and homicide rates than do women. The association of masculine roles with risk-taking makes many behaviors hazardous for men and results in higher rates of automobile accidents, death by firearms, heart disease—all likely leading to earlier death for men.

The physiological changes associated with aging are greatly affected by the social context in which aging occurs. Nutrition, for example, affects the biological health of aging persons, but social factors such as living alone or in an institution are known to affect dietary habits, as are factors such as income, cultural preferences for food, and exercise. Aging is also aggravated by stress—a condition generated by a variety of social and psychological difficulties.

For women, the aging process has its own strains. In a society in which women are valued for their youth and beauty, aging becomes a difficult social and psychological experience. Birthday cards that joke about women deteriorating after age 29 and commercials for creams that "hide your age spots" tell women that they should be ashamed of growing old. It should be no surprise, then, that a biological process such as menopause can become a difficult psychological experience. Menopause produces more anxiety and more depression in cultures that are less supportive of women as they age (Bart 1979; Clay 1977; Reitz 1977).

Cultural beliefs about biological events imbue these with significance and a character different from that produced by the physiology alone. In the case of menopause, the scientific and popular literature is replete with the metaphor of menopause as a disease—a fact that has severely biased both the scientific and popular understanding of menopause. The social context in which middle-aged women live, including their life histories and family relationships, is a more important predictor of emotional response to menopause than are the actual hormonal changes associated with menopause. Most women do not report menopause as a time of crisis, and there is no research to support the usually assumed association between menopause and serious depression (Fausto-Sterling 1992). Depression and mental illness among menopausal women are a function of other factors in their experience, not menopause per se.

Cross-cultural studies also show the extent to which menopause is shaped by cultural beliefs. In cultures where menopause is considered as a time of social—not just biological—changes, women subjectively experience menopause differently. In some cultures postmenopausal years are defined as a time of women's greater power and prestige (Lock 1998; Dickerson-Putnam 1996). Even within the United States, women's views of their sexuality are shaped by whether they emphasize the cultural and social basis of menopause, rather than just accepting the medical model of menopause (Winterich 2003).

Still, social myths portray the menopausal woman as prone to depression and anxiety, lacking sexual interest, and emotionally volatile; however, research indicates that when these problems exist, they stem from the social devaluation of aging women, not from the physiological process of aging itself (Defey et al. 1996). If society valued all women, not just those who are young, White, and middle class, the aging process would likely not be filled with the emotional and social difficulties some women experience (Stoller and Gibson 2000).

❖ Love and Intimate Relationships

Intimate relationships are an important context in which gender identity is created, re-created, and understood. Such relationships are an important source of love and caring; they provide many forms of social support and are critical to our social identity. Within intimate relationships, gender identity is continually reproduced. Sociologists do not see gender as a fixed individual trait; rather, they see gender as constantly reenacted and reinterpreted in the context of interpersonal relationships. This idea distinguishes sociological perspectives from individual perspectives on gender and interpersonal relationships.

To explain further, people tend to think of love and intimacy as individual choices. Intimate relationships do provide psychological support, and the psychological dynamics within intimate relationships are of interest to sociologists. Intimate relationships, like other social relationships, are conditioned by the cultural context, historical period, and institutional structures in which they occur.

Intimate relationships take many forms, each revealing different sociological dynamics. Intimate relationships may include a sexual relationship or may be based only on emotional intimacy, such as in close friendships. The sexual orientation of partners in an intimate relationship is important, however, because it locates the relationship in an institutional system that differently values and rewards intimacy based on heterosexual versus homosexual bonds. Understanding this helps us see how society structures and creates sexuality and intimacy.

Most people believe that relationships are formed simply because people like or are attracted to each other. But there is another sociological dimension to all relationships, including friendships, heterosexual love, and gay, lesbian, and bisexual relationships. All forms of these relationships are situated within relationships of power, social institutional structures, and systems of inequality based on the intersections of gender, race, and class. Although intimate relationships—whether sexual or not—are formed, in part, by the individual attitudes and attributes of those within them, they are significantly shaped by the institutional and historical context in which they develop. Thus, **patriarchy,** heterosexist institutions, the class structure, and racism all have a strong influence on the formation of intimacy, whether sexual or not.

First consider the dimension of power. **Power** is defined by sociologists as an individual's or a group's ability to influence another person or group. The exercise of power can take many forms, ranging from persuasion to physical force. Power is institutionalized in society—meaning that social institutions are structured in ways that give more power to some than to others. In a patriarchal society, men as a group have more power than do women. This institutionalized power, structured at the societal level, also influences the interpersonal and intimate relationships between women and men. Some research has shown that men's greater control of resources influences their power in relationships with women and that the greater a woman's contribution to household income is, the more power she exercises in family decision making. Even when wives earn more than their husbands, studies find that gender dynamics within the marriage reinforce the husband's power (Tichenor 1999; Spitze 1988; Pyke 1994).

At the institutional level, power is manifested in patriarchal institutions—the system that gives men systematic advantages over women. This can perhaps be most easily seen by looking at what happens when intimate relationships end, such as in divorce. What appears to be a private matter between two people terminating a marriage soon enters into a system of institutional advantage and disadvantage that overwhelmingly favors men. How can this be, when, theoretically at least, institutions are supposed to be based on equality before the law? Even without overt legal expressions of men's privilege, the law continues to operate in ways that are advantageous to men. First, men typically have access to more financial resources than do women. Thus, men can afford better legal representation when filing for divorce—a fact that provides a clear advantage. Second, seemingly gender-neutral laws, such as no-fault divorce, have been shown to be a disadvantage for women, who end up worse off financially after marriage than do men (Weitzman 1985, 1996; Peterson 1996a 1996b). Although most men experience some decline in their standard of living following divorce, their loss is not as great as women's (McManus and DiPrete 2001). In addition, without counting the value of child care and housework in the assets of a marriage, most women rarely see what they have contributed to a marriage actually valued in the division of marital property and assets. These illustrations show that institutions can still be patriarchal even when they are not explicitly identified as such.

Heterosexual institutions also structure intimate relationships. **Heterosexism** is the institutionalized set of behaviors and beliefs that presume heterosexuality to be the only acceptable form of sexual expression; a heterosexist system negatively sanctions those who act or are presumed to act otherwise. This context provides structural privileges for those in heterosexual relationships, while denying privileges and rights to those who do not assume a heterosexual identity. For example, although they may be in long-term, loving, and committed relationships, gays and lesbians do not receive the same insurance benefits that married couples might. Because gay partners are not considered a part of the immediate family, they might also be denied visiting rights if a partner is hospitalized and under critical care.

Heterosexism can also discourage the formation of relationships, particularly as heterosexism is manifested in homophobia. **Homophobia** is defined as the fear and hatred of homosexuality. Homophobia can discourage intimacy between same-sex friends if it makes them fear being labeled as gay or lesbian. This is especially, but not exclusively, apparent in relationships among men where homophobia establishes boundaries of intimacy between men. Despite cultural strictures that discourage gay relationships between men, much of men's interaction is in homosocial settings (i.e., segregated settings that include only men). Studies of interaction between men in such settings find that their interaction is based on emotional detachment, competitiveness, and the sexual objectification of women. Through these forms of interaction, social concepts of masculinity are re-created and reinforced, with boundaries created between men that separate them from identification with homosexuality even in these homosocial environments. At the same time, the men interact in ways that lead them to devalue qualities that are associated with women (S. Bird 1996b; Kimmel 2001; Messner 2001). Thus, homophobia not only limits the character of intimacy among men but it also reinforces sexist attitudes toward women.

Although most people think of homophobia as having a negative impact on gays and lesbians, this argument shows how damaging homophobia is to all kinds of relationships. By ridiculing and punishing affection between members of the same sex, homophobia shapes the expectations and expression of intimacy. Thus, heterosexual friends of gays and lesbians may find themselves "suspect" in the eyes of others, or heterosexual women who display intimacy in public may be ridiculed and accused of being lesbians. Heterosexual family members who accept and cherish relationships with gay and lesbian siblings may be chastised by other members of the family who do not. In these and other ways, homophobia and heterosexist institutions frame and shape the intimate relationships of many (see Table 4.1).

It is useful to think of heterosexism and homophobia in terms of the system of social control developed in Chapter 2. There is a continuum of social control mechanisms, ranging from peer pressure (such as ridicule and joking) through institutional mechanisms (manifested in law and social policy) to terrorism and violence (as in hate crimes) that punish homosexual behavior and distribute societal privi-

TABLE 4.1   Myths about Gays and Lesbians

Myth:	Reality:
There is a gay gene that causes homosexuality.	There is no scientific proof to this claim, even though the media typically use a medical model to frame news stories about research on gays and lesbians. Furthermore, scientists working on the human genome project have not identified a so-called "gay gene" (Horton 1995; Conrad 1998).
Homosexuality is biologically caused.	Although increasing numbers of people believe this (including gays and lesbians), there is not conclusive evidence that it is true. Also, sexual identity is socially constructed over the course of one's lifetime and emerges in the context of social relationships and social institutions (Simon and Gagnon 1998; Schwartz and Rutter 1998; Rust 2000).
Gays and lesbians are sexual deviants.	Most sexual deviance, such as child abuse, rape, incest, and other forms of sexual deviance, is committed by heterosexual men. Furthermore, a study of child molesters has found that although homosexuals are less likely than heterosexuals to commit such crimes, they are seven times more likely to be imprisoned, even controlling for prior record, admission of responsibility, and the seriousness of the crime (Walsh 1994; Freund and Watson 1992).
Children growing up in gay and lesbian families are psychologically harmed and are likely to become gay themselves.	Children growing up in gay and lesbian households are no more likely to become gay than are children raised in heterosexual households. The major harm that comes to such children is the stigma that they experience from the homophobic reactions of others (Stacey and Biblarz 2001).
Racial minorities are more tolerant of gays and lesbians than are Whites because of their greater sympathy with oppressed minorities.	Surveys show the reverse to be true—that is, African Americans hold more homophobic attitudes than Whites. At the same time, however, African Americans are more supportive than Whites of gay civil liberties and antidiscrimination policies (Lewis 2003).
Most gay men are rich.	It is difficult to compare the earnings of gay couples with heterosexual couples, since sexual orientation is not included as a variable in national census data; however, there is significant class variation among gay men, as there is among lesbians. Perceiving gays as all rich, White men also ignores those who are people of color and those who are poor, working class, and/or disabled (Gluckman and Reed 1997; Smith 1983).

(as in hate crimes) that punish homosexual behavior and distribute societal privileges based on the presumption of heterosexuality.

Interracial Relationships

Intimate relationships are also formed in the context of class and race inequality. Thus, research on friendship finds that working-class friendships have a high degree of reciprocity and interdependence with regard to material goods and services; middle-class friendships, on the other hand, tend to emphasize shared leisure, focus on networks of interesting friends, and place a high value on individualism (S. Walker 1995). Class and race also shape such basic facts as what relationships are formed, as data on the small number of racial intermarriages clearly show. Historically, racial intermarriage was prohibited by law. For example, California state law in 1880 prohibited Chinese Americans and White Americans from marrying. Later, California laws were written to prohibit marriage between Whites and Filipinos, Japanese, Hindus, American Indians, and Malaysians (Takaki 1989). Not until 1967 were such state laws, including those in the South prohibiting marriage between Whites and those defined as "Blacks," declared unconstitutional by the U.S. Supreme Court. Even now, intermarriage, although increasing, is still rare, with only 2 percent of all marriages being interracial (U.S. Census Bureau 2004).

The likelihood of interracial dating is greatly influenced by one's social context. Whether or not one's parents have a circle of diverse friends and whether young people have a diverse circle of friends are the strongest predictors of whether one will date interracially (Clark-Ibanez 1999). Patterns of racial segregation in society, however, mitigate against this since residential and school segregation shapes the likelihood of one's having friends from diverse racial backgrounds. For example, where high schools have greater racial diversity, cross-race friendships increase. In those schools with small numbers of racial minorities, minority students intensify a pattern of having friends only in their own group (Quillian and Campbell 2003). Surveys also find that people's willingness to date or marry a person of another race is also influenced by the race and gender of respondents. Black men are most likely to say they would date a person of another race (81 percent say they would), although, interestingly, along with White women, they are the least likely to say they would marry someone of another race. White women are least likely to say they would date someone of another race. Most people encounter significant resistance from their families for dating interracially—a pattern found among both Black and White families. Most families are not extremely hostile, but express strong enough feelings about this to put stress on the interracial couple (Majete 1999). And, although most Blacks and Whites express a color-blind stance toward interracial marriages, when pressed, they raise numerous qualifications and concerns about such pairings (Bonilla-Silva and Hovespan 2000). Generally speaking, among college students, racial minorities are more accepting of interracial dating than are White students; students in the Greek system on college campuses are less accepting than non-Greeks (Khanna et al. 1999).

In sum, systems of class, race, and gender shape all intimate relationships, whether they are platonic friendships (as you will see in the section below) or sexual relationships. Even something as abstract as the concept of love illustrates the significance of historical context in shaping intimacy. Popular images of love see it as unpredictable, uncontrollable, and never ending; yet, the specific meaning of love is one that has evolved over time. In ancient Greek society, for example, social norms defined love for elite Greek men as occurring between them and boys. With the ascendance of the Catholic Church in medieval Europe, love was defined as occurring only within marriage; sex was defined as sinful if it occurred outside the marital relationship. In the nineteenth century, during the Victorian period, strict moral codes regulating sexual behavior were established. Many have linked those strict moral codes to the evolving manufacturing system. The industrial revolution moved work from the home to the factory, requiring new forms of social control to encourage discipline among workers. Strict control of the emotions and sexuality was one way to enforce such discipline. At the same time, the move to a capitalist society in the West created new concepts of love.

The transition to a capitalist society polarized men's and women's roles and created new concepts of individualism. The separation of family from economic production (see Chapter 6) created separate spheres of activity in the home and in the factory. Relationships at work became more impersonal, while the family was increasingly defined as the place for intimacy and caring. The ideal woman was then one who devoted her life to her husband and children; men, on the other hand, were to be independent, disciplined, and emotionally restrained (Cancian 1987).

These transformations continue to influence our concepts of love and intimacy. Contemporary society emphasizes the significance of intimate bonds, even while human relationships are easily broken through workings of the economy. Intimacy is defined differently for men and for women; women are still defined as more other oriented and responsible for emotional ties, and men are defined as more isolated and individualistic.

In sum, intimate relationships are shaped by the same forces that structure other relationships. In fact, intimate relationships are one of the primary arenas where gender relationships are played out. Within intimate relationships, men and women create their identities and develop beliefs about appropriate gender roles. Gender is continually reenacted through and within intimate relationships. From a sociological perspective, understanding gender and intimacy requires the same analysis of social structures and institutionalized beliefs and behaviors that would be used to examine less personal social behavior.

Friendship

Gender plays an important role in structuring the intimate relationships between people—whether in same-sex relationships or relationships between women and men. This has been shown to be true in friendships as well as in relationships that include a sexual partnership. Research shows, for example, that men are more likely to be intimate with women than they are with other men, even though they report more same-sex friendships than do women. Within friendships, men tend to focus on shared activities, whereas women are more likely to emphasize talking and emotional sharing as the basis for friendship (McNelles and Connolly 1999).

However differently expressed, friendship is clearly important to both men and women. Despite long-held assumptions that women's primary identity was attached to men, research now shows the important role that friendships between women have, including women who live within stable heterosexual relationships. Studies of friendship indicate that friendships do not happen automatically, nor are they simply extensions of presumed natural capacities between the sexes. Making and keeping friends are complex processes, not just a matching of people with similar attitudes and social backgrounds. How one makes and keeps friends is intricately connected to the gender, race, and class relationships in which one lives. For example, professional women put great financial resources (in the form of travel, long-distance phone bills, dinners, and the like) into the making and keeping of good friends (Gouldner and Strong 1987). Less research has been done of friendships among working-class and poor women and among women of color; however, research done indicates the extent to which support from other women is a necessary part of women's ability to cope with the stress generated from class and race oppression (Sanchez-Ayendez 1986). Women's skills in keeping close ties with other women also help them in old age by giving them a sense of control over their lives (Powers 1996).

Comparing men and women, research finds that men and women place the same value on intimacy, but they have different ways of assessing it. Women are more likely than men to speak of the importance of being able to reveal themselves and be intimate in friendships. Women also engage in more diverse activities with their friends than men do (Baldwin and Keelan 1999; Yaughn and Nowicki 1999; Siwatu 2003). Other studies of friendship find that friendships involving at least one woman tend to be more satisfying and more intimate than those that do not. For example, men report their friendships with women as more satisfying and more intimate than their friendships with other men; women, on the other hand, find their friendships with other women and with men to be equally satisfying.

Intimacy between men is strongly influenced by the restrictive sanctions generated by homophobia. Fear of being called gay may makes men distance themselves from one another. Men who rate themselves as more "masculine" actually have fewer cross-sex friendships than men who identify with some "feminine" personality traits (Reeder 2003). Friendships between men are also influenced by the social settings in which the men work. As men grow older (for example, after their college years), the structures in which men find themselves become less conducive to friendship. Competition in the workplace, as well as time spent with family commitments, may discourage closer interaction with other men. One consequence is that men, different from women, have fewer close friends in older age and have less intimate interaction with people beyond the family as they grow older (Field 1999).

Cross-sex friendships are more common among younger people than among middle-aged and older adults. Except for friendships between couples, the norms of monogamous marriage seem to discourage friendships between men and women outside of marriage. Among middle-aged people, employed women have more cross-sex friendships than do women who work in the home only. Employment is not related to cross-sex friendships among men (Dickens and Perlman 1981).

In sum, research on friendship shows the significance of sociological factors in what friendships are formed, what they mean, and how they are experienced. Although friendship is idealized as what happens when two people "click," in actuality, friendship, like love, is culturally mediated.

❖ *Lesbian, Gay, and Bisexual Experiences*

Sociological and popular understanding of gay and lesbian relationships has been greatly distorted by the false presumption that only heterosexual relationships are normal ways of expressing sexual intimacy and love. We live in a culture that tends to categorize people into polar opposites: men and women, Black and White, gay and straight. On the subject of sexual desire, however, researchers conclude that such bipolar categories of sexual desire do not exist for most people (Schwartz and Rutter 1998). Rather, sexual desire is produced in the context of social relationships and identities; thus, "desire is created by its cultural context" (Blumstein and Schwartz 1983:122). In addition, culture creates understandings about how people are sexual; people adapt definitions of their own sexual identities depending on their experiences over the course of a lifetime.

It is not surprising that a majority of people assume the sexual identity prescribed by the dominant culture, but this fact should not be taken as evidence of normal or biological drive. For example, heterosexual identity is the result of scripts that boys and girls learn early in life, including the belief that men have an overpowering sex drive and that women link love, sex, and attachment. One result is that what is erotic to a woman may differ from what is erotic to a man, because men are taught to view women's passivity as erotic and stimulating.

Sociological views of sexuality examine the social and historical circumstances that create possibilities for sexual behavior. The explanation of sexual behaviors and identities is then based on social conditions, not fixed biological or cultural categories. Understanding the social organization of gender, both in personal life and in social institutions, is critical to understanding sexuality.

There is a long-standing assumption that sexual orientation is an "either/or" identity—that is, a person is either gay or straight. Recent scholarship on sexual identity, however, challenges this dichotomy. First, many argue that, by their nature, human beings are capable of bisexual attraction. John Money, one of the nation's foremost experts on sexual identity, argues that human beings are "psychosexually neutral" at birth (Money 1995). Throughout life, cultural proscriptions try to direct and channel people into socially legitimate sexual identities. Think, for example, of your childhood and teen experiences and the explicit and implicit messages you got to be heterosexual. Children's movies embed scripts about love between men and women; popular music extols the thrills of heterosexual love; adolescent jokes deride gays and lesbians. These and a myriad of other influences make it not surprising that most people become heterosexual, whatever their biological inclinations.

Second, studying the history of sexuality reveals that the categories of "homosexual," "gay," and "lesbian" have been created at specific historical points in time.

As much as people revile *homosexuality* and think of it as biologically based, the term was not invented until the nineteen century by Havelock Ellis, an early sexologist, who saw it as sexual inversion. Not until the early twentieth century, however, were the terms *homosexuality* and *heterosexuality* widely publicized—as the public became increasingly fascinated with the scientific study of sex. The contemporary meaning of the term *gay* is even more recent. Used in the first half of the twentieth century primarily as a self-satirizing and flippant adjective, in the 1960s, *gay* came to be used in a positive light to celebrate a community with a shared lifestyle. Specifically, *gay* was meant to shed the stigma that had come from the medicalization and criminalization of gay people (Money 1998). Associated with gay liberation, the term *gay* took on a positive and self-affirming meaning—the result of political activism (Fetner 2001; D'Emilio 1998).

Third, recent scholarship on transgender identities and bisexuality challenges the binary (i.e., "one way or the other") or dualistic thinking that is represented by the assumption that a person is either heterosexual or gay. The emergence of **queer theory** has underscored the idea that all sexual identities are socially constructed and that the categories of sexuality that we presume to be fixed can be disrupted and changed (Gamson 1995). Queer theory posits that institutional practices create sexual identities and that the boundaries that distinguish legitimate and illegitimate sex are politically constructed. Without questioning how sexual categories are constructed, theorists perpetuate the idea that only one form of sexuality is normal and all others are deviant, immoral, and wrong (Seidman 1994). Queer theory emerged from a criticism of gay and lesbian studies that these terms are not inclusive enough (Stein and Plummer 1994). That is, such studies do not incorporate the multiple sexual identities that people can assume, and in so doing, new light has been shed on studies of bisexuality, transgendered people, and gay and lesbian politics (Rust 1995; Firestein 1996; Califia 1997).

Thus, from a social constructionist view, as noted in the chapter opening, all forms of sexuality are socially constructed. Even if there is some biological basis to sexual orientation, what people become in their sexual identity and how they express it is as much the result of social experiences as it is a fixed biological fact. Cultural proscriptions, stigmas, and practices influence the construction of all people's sexual identities; moreover, sexual orientation is an ongoing process that occurs over the development of the life course. Gay, lesbian, and bisexual identities, like heterosexual identities, are constructed through an ongoing series of events and meaning systems (Rust 2000). For example, the *coming out* process rarely involves a single incident. Instead, someone in the process of coming out begins to see himself or herself in new ways and may develop new social contacts and reinterpret earlier experiences in a way that enables a new definition of self to emerge. Likewise, those who develop heterosexual identities are likely to support that identity through a system of consistent social supports and meaning systems that may even include denial or reinterpretation of experiences of being attracted to members of the same sex.

Current research shows that the development of sexual identity is not necessarily a linear or unidirectional process, with persons moving through a defined sequence of steps or phases. People do not move predictably through certain sequences in developing a sexual identity. While they may experience certain "milestones" in their identity development, many people move back and forth over a period of time between lesbian or gay identities and heterosexual identities. Some experience periods of ambivalence about their identities and may switch back and forth between a lesbian, heterosexual, and bisexual identity over a period of time. Studies of lesbian and bisexual women also find that some continue alternative identities even after defining themselves as lesbians; thus, some people defining themselves as gay may not necessarily keep that identity (Rust 1995). Some people may engage in lesbian or gay behavior but not adopt a formal definition of themselves as such. Certainly many gays and lesbians never adopt a public definition of themselves as gay or lesbian, instead remaining "closeted" for long periods of time, if not entire lifetimes.

This research shows the socially constructed basis of sexual identity and how sensitive sexual identity is to its societal context. Changing social contexts (including dominant group attitudes, laws, and systems of social control), relationships with others, and even changes in the language used to describe different sexual identities all affect people's self-definitions. As an example, political movements can encourage people to adopt a sexual identity that they previously had no context to understand, but there can be negative consequences to assuming a publicly gay identity. In just one example, a study of gay-and-lesbian–activist academics found that there were negative consequences for them in terms of discrimination in hiring, bias in promotion decisions, exclusion from professional networks, harassment, and devaluation of their work on gay and lesbian subjects (Taylor and Raeburn 1995). This context, where the stigma attached to gay identities is played out in power relations between dominant and subordinate groups, affects people's willingness to publicly claim a gay or lesbian identity.

Although sexual identity is socially constructed, individuals experience their sexual identities as stable. They perceive changes in their identities as part of the process of discovering their sexuality, often reinterpreting earlier life events as indications of some preexisting identity. From a sociological point of view, changing one's sexual identity is not a sign of immaturity, as if someone has missed a so-called normal phase of development; change is a normal outcome of the process of identity formation (Rust 1993).

Understanding the socially constructed basis of sexual identity is in stark contrast to ideas that sexual orientation is biologically determined. Such ideas are popular, not only among those who promote heterosexual orientation as "normal" but also among many lesbians and gays. What is the biological basis for homosexuality? Periodic reports appear in the media claiming to have found a "gay gene" or other scientific evidence for the biological basis of homosexuality. On close examination, however, such studies are typically based on very small research samples, without the scientific controls needed to prove a genetic or biological basis to homosexuality (Gagnon 1995; Hamer et al. 1993; Rist 1992). Although there may be some basis to such claims, a biological basis for sexual orientation has not been soundly established. There is far more evidence of social and cultural influences on sexual identity—studies that are rarely reported in the media. Even if there is some biological influence on sexual identity, we know that environmental influences interact with biological predisposition; therefore, trying to explain sexual orientation as a matter of biology alone is poor reasoning. The fact is that public belief in the biological basis of homosexuality, including among lesbians and gays, is stronger than the scientific evidence supports.

How extensive is the lesbian and gay experience? Here again is a matter for debate. Many claim that as much as 10 percent of the population is gay or lesbian (Janus and Janus 1993); others say the number is more like 4 percent (Laumann et al. 1994). In part, it depends on how this is measured (i.e., how the question is asked). The Kinsey Report of the 1940s first reported that a substantial number of people have some homosexual experience in their lifetimes. (Current surveys find that 22 percent of men and 17 percent of women do.) But this figure could refer to a single experience, not necessarily the adoption of a gay, lesbian, or bisexual identity. Surveys find that more men and women report having experienced desire for those of the same sex than will report being gay or lesbian (Laumann et al. 1994)—a fact that probably reflects the stigma associated with gay and lesbian identities.

Whatever the actual extent of gay, lesbian, and bisexual experience, the fact is that various social myths permeate our understanding of this experience. First among them is the idea that gays and lesbians are sexually perverted stems from reasoning similar to the previous argument. For example, fears that gays and lesbians are dangerous because they might make sexual advances toward strangers is a distortion of fact. Research consistently finds that it is heterosexual men who are the most frequent perpetrators of sexual abuse and other sexual crimes. Fears that gay and lesbian parents will have deleterious effects on their children are also unsupported by research. Research finds that there is little difference in outcomes for children raised in gay/lesbian households and those raised in heterosexual households. What differences exist are the result of other factors—not the sexual orientation of parents per se. The most significant differences found comparing children in these two groups is the homophobia and discrimination that is directed against children in lesbian and gay families, who are then more likely to be stigmatized by others. Children raised in gay and lesbian households are also less likely to develop stereotypical gender roles, and they are more tolerant and open-minded about sexual matters. They are no more likely to become gay themselves than are children raised in heterosexual households (Stacey and Bibliarz 2001).

Another social myth that is especially associated with gay men is that they are all rich and leading expensive lifestyles. Yet, studies find that workplace discrimination against lesbians, gay men, and bisexuals is extensive (Gluckman and Reed 1997). Data from national surveys report that gay and bisexual men earn 11 to 27 percent less than heterosexual men with the same experience, education, occupation, and region of residence. There is some evidence that lesbian and bisexual workers earn less than heterosexual women, but the difference is not so strong, probably because of the general depression of all women's wages (Badgett 1995). Many gays and lesbians remain closeted in the workplace to avoid the discrimination that comes from being "out" (Croteau 1996). There are well-documented risks to being "out" in the workplace, including discrimination in hiring, exclusion from social and professional networks, harassment and intimidation, and, for those doing research on gay and lesbian issues, a devaluation of their work (Taylor and Raeburn 1995).

The greatest difficulty that lesbian women and gay men face stems from the homophobia within society. Hateful harassment, physical violence, and insensitivity mar the everyday experience of lesbians and gays. Were as much time and energy invested in providing supportive social environments for all people, regardless of their sexual identities, as in telling homophobic jokes, bashing gays, and engaging in hate crimes, we would likely build a more caring society that embraced and sustained a diversity of loving relationships.

Gay and lesbian relationships lack the institutional support heterosexual relationships have. Gay and lesbian partners have no inheritance rights or tax subsidies, as do heterosexual married couples. Gay and lesbian relationships are not typically sanctioned by the legal community or the church, although in some places this is changing. Because of the absence of institutionalized support for gay men and lesbian women, they have to create their own forms of support and meaning within relationships and communities. As a result, researchers find that the maintenance of relationships among gays and lesbians is more dependent on the quality of the interpersonal relationship than on the institutional support the relationship receives (Meyer 1990).

Still, the vast majority of people (89 percent) support equal rights for gays and lesbians in the workplace (Moore 2004) and a growing number of corporations are developing nondiscriminatory policies, including adding sexual orientation to diversity training and extending employee benefits to domestic partners. Gays and lesbians also won a major victory in 1996 when the U.S. Supreme Court (in *Romer* vs. *Evans*) ruled that they cannot be denied equal protection of the law. This ordinance overturned local ordinances denying civil rights protections to gays and lesbians. Change is slow, however, and sometimes contradictory, as evidenced by the public resistance to gay marriage. The Defense of Marriage Act passed by the U.S. Congress allows states not to recognize same-sex marriages that might be legally legitimate in those states that have extended this right to same-sex partners (such as Massachusetts and Hawaii). Gay marriage is discussed further in Chapter 6.

In recent years, political activism has resulted in greater visibility and more acceptance of gays and lesbians, but homophobia and hate crimes are still rampant, as cruelly exemplified by the murder of Matthew Shepard, a young student in Wyoming who was beaten by two young men in 1998 and left to die in a remote field. After beating him and leaving him to die, the young men who killed him also beat up two Hispanic young men, yelling racial epithets at them as they did. This horrid incident shows how homophobia is linked to hatred stemming from racial prejudice and violence. It should teach us about the connections between forms of sexual, racial, and gender oppression (Jenness and Broad 1997; Ferber 2000; Jenness and Grattet 2001).

❖ *Chapter Summary and Themes*

Human sexuality is a socially constructed experience.

Although people think of sexual relationships as private and between two individuals, there are numerous social influences on how people create and experience sexual relationships. Gender is one of the most significant of such influences, resulting in different sexual experiences and identities for men and women.

The formation of sexual identity comes from social and cultural influences, not simply biology.

Social attitudes about heterosexuality and homosexuality shape how different sexual identities are judged and valued in society. Lesbian women, gay men, and bisexuals have fewer sexual rights and privileges because of the social structure of heterosexism and homophobia in society.

The history of sexuality reveals how it is shaped through cultural, economic, and political relations, including those of class, race, and gender.

Sexual ideas and practices tend to change the most when there are other transformations taking place in women's and men's roles. These changes have historically been generated by sexual and feminist social movements. Sexual politics are also significantly intertwined with the character of racial and class inequality in society.

Contemporary sexual attitudes and behaviors show greater tolerance for diverse sexual practices, although sexual attitudes and behaviors are also influenced by gender and other social factors, such as race, religion, age, and so forth.

Although there is evidence of greater tolerance for diverse sexual lifestyles, gender stereotypes and traditional attitudes still influence the degree of acceptance of sexual freedom. Homophobia is also common in society and is part of the mechanism of social control by which gender and sexual conformity is sought.

Sexual politics intersect with race and class politics.

Sexual stereotypes socially construct our images of different racial and class groups, with women and men of color being particularly stereotyped in sexual terms. These sexual politics are part of the system by which race, class, and gender inequalities are supported and sustained.

Human sexual development, though a physiological process, is also imbued with social and cultural meaning.

Life cycle events, such as menstruation and menopause, take on different social meanings in different cultural contexts. The meanings that are associated with these processes can shape how people actually experience them.

Gender identity is also constructed through the social character of intimate relationships.

Power shapes intimate relationships in ways that can be identified as gender-based, as well as class and race-based. Homophobia both directs hostility toward gays and lesbians and discourages intimacy among men. It is one of the mechanisms for reproducing gender inequality. Intimate relationships such as friendships are also shaped by the social context of race, gender, and class relations.

Gay and lesbian experience has been misunderstood by ideas that posit heterosexuality as the only socially legitimate way to express love and sexual desire.

New scholarship shows that gay, lesbian, and bisexual identity is socially constructed. Although gays and lesbians lack the social and institutional support given to heterosexual relationships, social attitudes about gays and lesbians are becoming more tolerant.

❖ *Key Terms*

compulsory heterosexuality	patriarchy	queer theory
heterosexism	phallocentric thinking	sexual politics
homophobia	power	

❖ *Discussion Questions/Projects for Thought*

1. How would you describe the sexual norms on your campus? How are people's sexual attitudes and behaviors linked to gender in this setting?

2. Over a period of one week, keep a written log of the homophobic comments and incidents that you observe. At the end of the week, review what you have seen and discuss what it means to say that compulsory heterosexuality is enforced through the social norms of everyday life. As you do this exercise, be aware that what you hear will be hurtful to many. You should keep this sensitivity in mind when discussing this project. How would you feel if such comments were directed toward someone you love?

3. Pick an area of popular culture (a TV series, greeting cards, popular songs, children's cartoons, etc.) and do a content analysis of the images of love depicted therein. Pay attention in your observations to how these images are linked to gender. How do your observations support the idea that the dominant culture promotes compulsory heterosexuality?

❖ *Internet Resources*

National Gay and Lesbian Task Force

http://www.ngltf.org

This national organization works for social policies on behalf of gays and lesbians and works for improved awareness about gay and lesbian issues. The website includes information on policy initiatives, as well as publications and information on organizing local chapters.

Alan Guttmacher Institute

http://www.agi-usa.org

This research institute is dedicated to understanding issues of family planning, contraception, and social issues such as teenage sexuality. The website includes a number of informative fact sheets, as well as information about current research and family planning services.

❖ *Suggested Readings*

Altman, Dennis. 2001. *Global Sex*. Chicago: University of Chicago Press.
   Altman looks at sexuality in a global context, showing how sex is linked to the international economy, including the sex traffic in women. His book enriches our understanding of sexuality by linking it to broader social and economic structures of gender, class, and international consumption.

Collins, Patricia Hill. 2004. *Black Sexual Politics: African Americans, Gender, and the New Racism*. New York: Routledge.
   Collins shows how the politics of both gender and race influence sexual relationships and, more generally, relationships between Black women and men. She shows the importance of understanding the ties between race, class, gender, and sexuality for social justice movements.

Freedman, Estelle B., and John D'Emilio. 1988. *Intimate Matters: A History of Sexuality in America*. New York: Harper and Row.
   An excellent history of sexuality in the United States, this book is also noted for its inclusion of the connections between sexuality, gender, race, and class.

Gold, Jodi, and Susan Villari, eds. 1999. *Just Sex: Students Rewrite the Rules on Sex, Violence, and Equality, and Activism*. Lanham, MD: Rowman and Littlefield.
   This is an anthology by students organized to stop sexual violence. It includes information on college policies against violence and personal testimony about sex and violence on college campuses.

Irvine, Janice M. 2002. *Talk about Sex: The Battles over Sex Education in the United States*. Berkeley, CA: University of California Press.

Irvine's work on the politics of sex education shows how the social structure of sexuality shapes public opinion. Her analysis reaches into the cultural definitions associated with gender, sexuality, and social change.

Michael, Robert T., John H. Gagnon, Edward O. Laumann, and Gina Kolata. 1994. *Sex in America: A Definitive Survey*. Boston: Little, Brown.
   Based on sociological surveys of sexual practices, this book provides an overview of sexual behavior in the 1990s.

Nagel, Joane. 2003. *Race, Ethnicity, and Sexuality: Intimate Intersections, Forbidden Frontiers*. New York: Oxford University Press.
   Nagel analyzes the belief systems that link gender, sexuality, race, and ethnicity. Her work provides important insights into how ideologies that support gender, race, and class inequality are linked to sexuality. She also puts her argument into an international context by showing linkages between nationalism and sexual beliefs.

Nardi, Peter M., and Beth Schneider. 1997. *Social Perspectives on Lesbian and Gay Studies*. New York: Routledge.
   This collection of articles provides a sociological perspective on new research on gay and lesbian issues. It includes classic readings with the work of young scholars who are redefining questions about sexual identity, community, and social change.

Schwartz, Pepper, and Virginia Rutter. 1998. *The Gender of Sexuality*. Thousand Oaks, CA: Pine Forge Press.
   This review of sociological perspectives on sexuality links the study of gender roles to sexuality.

Seidman, Steven. 2003. *The Social Construction of Sexuality*. New York: Oxford University Press.
Seidman questions the presumed "natural" basis of sexuality by examining the social basis of human sexuality. The book provides a good overview of the sociology of sex by examining different forms of sexual relationships, as well as social and historical changes in sexual values.

Stombler, Mindy, Dawn M. Baunach, Elisabeth O. Burgess, Denise Donnelly, and Wendy Simonds. 2004. *Sex Matters: The Sexuality and Society Reader*. Boston: Allyn and Bacon.
Developed by a team of sociologists, this anthology explores the various ways that society shapes our sexual attitudes, behaviors, and relationships. The book provides a comprehensive look at the social basis of sexuality.

GENDER, WORK, AND THE ECONOMY

5

Historical Perspectives on Women's Work

The Family-Based Economy
The Family-Wage Economy
The Family-Consumer Economy
Ideology and the History of Women's Work

What is Work?

Economic Restructuring, Class, and Gender Stratification

The Contemporary Status of Women

Labor Force Participation
Gender Segregation
Earnings
Promotions

Poverty and Welfare

Work Environments

Tokenism
Sexual Harassment
Workplace Culture

Intersections of Family and Work

The Second Shift
Housework and Care Work

Policies for Gender Equity

Chapter Summary and Themes

Key Terms

Discussion Questions/ Projects for Thought

Internet Resources

Suggested Readings

In 2003, women employed year–round and full–time earned $30,724; men employed year round and full time earned $40,668. Why after years of reform intended to reduce discrimination does this earnings gap persist? Women still earn only 75 percent of what men earn. Even with the same levels of education, women earn less than men. In 2003, women with a college degree earned $33,842; men, $54,069 (DeNavas-Walt et al. 2004; U.S. Census Bureau 2004). Why? What are the experiences of women at work and how does gender affect this fact of life for millions of women in the United States?

Gender shapes the experiences of all women at work, but exactly how this happens is also a matter of race, ethnicity, social class, age, and sexual orientation, among other things. How gender shapes the experience of a top woman executive, for example, will be drastically different from how it shapes the experience of her housekeeper, but, for both women, gender matters. But with increasing class polarization in our society—including among women—understanding how class intersects with gender and how race intersects with both is critical to understanding the topic of women and work.

The subject of women and work is not, however, just about money. Women's work is obscured by various social myths, many of which have persisted over time. These myths include that women, particularly women of color, are taking jobs away from men because of affirmative action; that women are achieving economic parity with men; that women's work is less valuable than men's; and that women who are at home with children are not working—the last myth being central in dominant group stereotypes of poor women. We examine these myths throughout this chapter.

❖ *Historical Perspectives on Women's Work*

The history of women's work shows the societal developments that result in women's economic inequality and the devaluation of women's labor both inside and outside the home. As this section shows, the history of gender inequality in the Western world is intertwined with the history of racial and class subordination. A full analysis of the history of women's work would examine the work experience of women of color and working-class women as an integral part of the history of women's labor; moreover, studying race, class, and gender inequality simultaneously furthers our understanding of women's work in the contemporary world—both in domestic and global terms.

A brief history of women's labor cannot possibly capture the diverse experiences of different groups of women, but it can reveal the broad patterns in the evolution of women's work and thereby elucidate the social organization of gender and work in the United States. Any single group, however, has a unique historical experience, one that is distorted by lumping different groups together under single labels, such as Hispanic or Asian American. Asian American women's history of work varies considerably, for example, among Chinese Americans, Japanese Americans, and Korean Americans. Moreover, the work experiences of contemporary Asian American immigrants is substantially different from that of Asian groups migrating to the United States earlier in the century and, indeed, is significantly different even among diverse Asian immigrants today. Similarly, Puerto Rican women have a more recent historical experience than Chicanas, whose families may predate many White settlers in the U.S. Southwest. Luckily, many new histories are beginning to document carefully the work experiences of these different groups (Amott and Matthaei 1996; Takaki 1989, 1993; Espiritu 1997).

At the broadest level, however, the historical transformation of women's work can best be described as falling in three basic periods: the family-based economy, the family-wage economy, and the family-consumer economy (Tilly and Scott 1978). Although these periods have been derived from studies of White European women's history, they do help organize the complex changes marking the development of the work system in the United States and the place of multiple groups of women within it.

The Family-Based Economy

The first period, the **family-based economy,** dates roughly from the seventeenth century to the early eighteenth century, although the time period shifts, depending on which group one considers. The family-based form of economic production was one where the household was the basic unit of the economy, since economic production was largely based on households, including small farms, large plantations, and haciendas. Although the specific form of different households would vary under this economic system, and different racial-ethnic groups were involved in different dimensions of this economy, the defining characteristic of this economic period was the household as the basic unit of production.

There would be little distinction during this period between economic and domestic life, since all household members (including nonblood kin, children, slaves, and other laborers) were all responsible for production. The typical household unit would largely have been agricultural, although, as cities developed, so did retailing; artisans' wives would also engage in household labor. In both rural and urban settings, the work of women and men was interdependent. Although the specific tasks done by each might vary, both women and men would be seen as contributing to the productivity of the whole.

White women's labor during this period was highly dependent on their class position and their marital status. Single women (unwed and widowed) might work in others' households doing traditional tasks such as spinning, weaving, and sewing (Kessler-Harris 1982). Women in these households would supervise much of the household work, especially the labor of children; White women might also supervise the labor of slaves. White women were also engaged in agricultural labor and the production of cloth and food, although elite women would not likely engage in such labor.

African American women in the family-based economy labored as slaves, although in many states, African American men and women worked as free laborers, doing a variety of jobs as skilled craft workers, farm laborers, and domestics. African Americans were forcibly brought to the United States by the slave trade, beginning in the early seventeenth century and persisting at least until 1807, when

England and the United States agreed, at least in law, to prohibit the trade. It is estimated that over 9.5 million Africans were transported to the United States, the Caribbean, and Brazil during this time, not counting the probably 20 million who died in passage (Genovese 1972).

Black women in slavery did most of the same jobs as men, although in addition, they worked in the masters' homes and on behalf of their own families (Jones 1985). The plantation economy functioned somewhat like the domestic economy because the plantation, like a household, functioned as the major unit of production. In the U.S. South, one-quarter of White families held slaves, although half of the slaves lived on farms with fewer than 20 slaves and three-quarters lived on farms with fewer than 50 slaves (Genovese 1972).

Under slavery, slaves provided most, if not all, of the productive labor, while White slave owners had total control and ownership of slave labor and the profits it generated. The plantation economy represented a transition between an agriculturally based society and an industrialized one because the population of slaves worked as a cheap and fully controlled labor force. After the abolition of slavery, African American women and men entered the labor market as free laborers, but even then, they could not compete equally for the same jobs available to White women and men.

The early history of Chicana labor was also influenced by a family-based economy. The United States annexed Mexican territory in the Southwest following the Mexican-American War in 1848. Before U.S. conquest, Mexican families in the Southwest worked primarily as agricultural units. A strong gender division of labor was maintained, with women's work located primarily in the home but contributing directly to the family-based production. As you will see in the following section, the transition to a wage-based economy upset existing patterns of Chicana labor and family life (Baca Zinn and Eitzen 2005; Dill 1988).

Similarly, labor patterns for Native American women were disrupted by U.S. conquest of Native American lands. Although particular forms of labor, its meaning, and its relationship to other social systems varied across Native American societies, in general Native American societies accorded great respect to women, even when there was a marked division of labor between women and men. Colonization by Whites radically disrupted this way of life, while also imposing external institutions onto Native American societies (Allen 1986; Amott and Matthaei 1996).

The Family-Wage Economy

In the second period of the transformation to advanced capitalism, called the **family-wage economy,** the center of labor moved out of the household and into the factory system. This shift was the result of industrialization that began in England in the mid-eighteenth century, followed in France and the United States somewhat later. In the family-wage economy, workers earned their living outside the home and the household became dependent on wages that the workers brought home. The shift to wage labor and the production of commodities outside the home had several influences on the character of women's work. It led to the development of dual roles for women as paid laborers and as unpaid housewives.

With industrialization, the household was no longer the primary center of production, although women's work in the home was still socially and economically necessary. As the focus of work moved beyond the home, the worth of all persons became measured in terms of their earned wage; therefore, the work of women in the home was devalued. In addition, with for-profit goods (not just for exchange or subsistence) being produced largely outside the home, international mercantilism developed, further eroding the position of women (Dobash and Dobash 1979).

In a wage system, producing, distributing, and purchasing goods requires cash. Although women and children worked for wages in the factory system, they received less pay than men did and, in fact, were chosen as workers because they were a cheap supply of labor. Male control of the wage-labor system, along with the capitalist pursuit of greater profits, weakened women's earning power (Hartmann 1976). Because cash resources were needed to survive in the new economy, women became more financially dependent on men (Tilly and Scott 1978).

African American women in the United States during this period worked primarily as domestic workers. Until 1940, as many as 60 percent of African American women labored as private domestic workers (Rollins 1985). African American men worked primarily in agriculture and as service workers, where seasonal unemployment and low wages prevented them from assuming the role of family breadwinner—the mark of masculinity and achievement in White, patriarchal societies.

The history of work for other groups in the United States shows similar patterns of the intersection of race, class, and gender oppression during industrialization and the move to a wage-based economy. In the Southwest, Chicanas were employed in the expanding agricultural market, which often forced whole families to migrate to find seasonal labor. The newly industrializing agricultural economy placed men in mining, railroad work, and agricultural field work as pickers; women were employed in canning and packing houses and in the textile industry; and Chicanas also continued to work as domestics—mainly as servants, laundresses, cooks, and dishwashers (Baca Zinn and Eitzen 2005).

The experience of Asian women in the United States has been one of exclusion. The Chinese Exclusion Act of 1882 prevented male Chinese laborers from bringing their wives to the United States. Other legislation restricted the entry of Asian immigrants and prohibited marriage between Asians and Whites. Those Chinese, Japanese, Filipino, and Korean women who were in the United States were stereotyped as cheap sex objects and worked in restricted occupations primarily as merchants' wives, domestics, laborers, or prostitutes (Chow 1987; Amott and Matthaei 1996).

In the Northeast, White immigrant women filled factory jobs in the textile and garment industries, where wages were low and working conditions hazardous. Other immigrant women worked as domestic workers. In fact, in 1870, one-half of all women wage earners in the United States were domestic workers. By 1920, the percentage of women working as paid domestics declined to 18.5 percent, reflecting employment changes for women as they moved into new fields as clerical workers, teachers, and nurses. Still, domestic work remained a major source of employment for Japanese and Chinese women immigrating to the United States in the first half of the twentieth century (Glenn 1986). Domestic work continues to be a major means of employment for contemporary immigrant women, particularly Latinas (Romero 1992; Hondagneu-Sotelo 2001) and new immigrants.

As production and commerce grew, management also become more complex, leading to vast increases in clerical and administrative occupations. The invention of the typewriter created a new concentration of women in the clerical labor force. The typewriter was introduced to the public in 1873 and, because there was a shortage of labor for the new jobs it created, women were recruited for typing jobs based on the ideological appeal that they were naturally more dextrous than men (Benet 1972). In other fields, too, women were recruited when labor shortages necessitated a new work force. As public education was expanded in the late nineteenth century, women were said to be naturally suited for a profession that required patience, nurturing, and the education of children. Similarly, when the middle class organized the public health movement of the early twentieth century to ward off the "contagions" of the poor, female nurses were recruited to serve doctors and to bring "feminine compassion" to the sick (Ehrenreich and English 1973a).

The Family-Consumer Economy

The third period of economic change is called the **family-consumer economy.** This period, also characteristic of the present, is really an extension of the family-wage system, as it developed through the twentieth century. In this period, technological change increased productivity, and the mass production of goods created households that specialized in consumption and reproduction (Tilly and Scott 1978). Although in the family-consumer economy economic production goes on outside the home, the labor of family members does contribute to their economic standing. As you have already seen, in this period women's work as housewives is often coupled with their participation in paid labor; in the family-consumer economy, women's economic productivity is even higher than it was in the past (Tilly and Scott 1978). Although women continue to do the same amount of housework they did in earlier periods (Vanek 1978), public institutions (such as schools, welfare systems, and the fast-food industry) also take over activities that were once located in the household. Women consequently become defined primarily as consumers, even though, in most cases, their wages are still necessary for household support, and most women of color continued to work for wages.

Throughout the twentieth century, women's labor force participation continued to rise. Much has been made about the dramatic influx of women into the paid labor force during World War II. Popular wisdom has it that because of the need for women's labor, women entered the labor force in unprecedented numbers, only to leave it and return to their homes at the end of the war. In fact, women did respond with enthusiasm to the appeals for wartime work, but three-quarters of those who were employed during the war had worked for wages before. Historians estimate that a sizable group of new women workers would have entered the labor force anyhow; thus, the influx of women to paid work during the war is not as dramatic as usually assumed. Women saw the emergency as an opportunity to get ahead; women of color, professional women, and older women took advantage of the reduction in discrimination to enter well-paying jobs (Kessler-Harris 1982). During the war, women were employed not so much in unprecedented numbers, but in unprecedented jobs—jobs that were well paid, were industrialized, and gave a new legitimacy and value to the work that women did (Sacks 1984).

At the conclusion of the war, many women did not leave the paid labor force, but took jobs in other areas—jobs that did not pay as well as those they had left. Women were laid off after the war at a rate double that of men and were shunted into jobs in the clerical and service sectors. Older women, married women, and racial-ethnic women had a hard time finding jobs after the war.

Since World War II, White women have dramatically increased their employment rates, resulting in convergence of the measures of labor force participation between White women and women of color. Women continue, however, to work in occupations highly segregated by race and gender (see Table 5.1).

In sum, the history of women's labor shows that women's work has been essential to economic productivity. Indeed, women's work, and particularly that of women of color, has been the foundation for the development of economic institutions in the United States. Women of color have always worked outside the home and thus have had to combine work and family in ways new to some White women. White women, at the same time, have been used as a reserve supply of labor, being kept out of the labor force unless there was a labor shortage or particular demand for cheap workers. As you will see, transitions in the role of women in the paid labor force have also been buttressed by belief systems that make women's labor patterns seem natural and to be expected.

Ideology and the History of Women's Work

In Chapter 3, *ideology* was defined as a belief system that seeks to explain and justify the status quo. The economic and technological changes that marked the transitions from the domestic economy to the consumer economy were historically accompanied by changes in the ideological definition of womanhood. The *cult of true womanhood* (Cott 1977), popularized in the nineteenth century, glorified women's ideal place as the home, where women were seen as having a moral calling to serve their families. The aristocratic lady of leisure became a model to be emulated and set the ideal, although not the reality, for women of the bourgeois class. At the same time, the Protestant ethic, which stressed individualism, success, and competition in the workplace, also encouraged White women to submerge their wills to piety, purity, and submissiveness (Kessler-Harris 1982). At least in White bourgeois families, women's destiny became defined as a separate sphere in which home, duty to the family, and religion would prevail.

Despite these ideals, working-class women and women of color continued to work both in the public labor force and in the home. The reality of their working lives in the early industrial period stands in contradiction to the myth of true womanhood. Only the most affluent families could maintain an idle woman; most women worked long hours in factories and then at home. While the cult of true womanhood was at its peak, African American women were working as slaves,

TABLE 5.1   Earnings in Selected Occupations: 2003

Occupation	Percent Women	Women's Median Weekly Earnings	Men's Median Weekly Earnings
Management	37.1%	849	1172
Architecture/ Engineering	14.1	827	1094
Teachers, college and university	44.9	878	1111
Teachers, preschool and kindergarten	97.8	493	n/a
Teachers, elementary and middle	81.7	757	843
Teachers, secondary	55.2	785	870
Librarians	84.4	789	n/a
Lawyers	27.6	1413	1619
Physicians	29.9	989	1577
Registered Nurses	92.1	887	1006
Social workers	79.5	685	735
Retail sales workers	50.4	382	599
Secretaries	96.6	531	573
Waitresses/waiters	74.3	318	385
Bartenders	57.7	361	466
Maids and housekeeping	88.4	317	371
Plumbers	1.0	n/a	466
Electricians	2.1	n/a	657
Bus drivers	48.4	470	536
Packagers (hand)	61.1	345	350
Electronic assembly	59.6	404	510

Source: Data from U.S. Department of Labor. 2004. *Employment and Earnings.* Washington, DC; U.S. Government Printing Office, pp. 209–214, 249–253.

n/a, Fewer than 50,000 workers in this category, too few for a meaningful figure.

and no ideal of femininity was bestowed on them. In fact, the myth of the ideal woman could be created only at the expense of other women because African American, immigrant, Latina, Asian, and poor women still performed the necessary household and factory tasks.

For example, around the turn of the twentieth century in the United States, the woman who stayed at home to do her own housework became a symbol of middle-class prosperity (Davis 1981). Consequently, women of color and immigrant women who had found employment as domestics were expelled from White middle-class homes and replaced by new technological devices that promised to make women's work easy. In fact, some of the advertising campaigns for new products in this period (such as irons) presented explicit images of these new products purging middle-class homes of the alleged germs and social diseases of Black and Chinese women (Cowan 1976). Homes became depicted during this period as bulwarks of defense against the rapid social changes occurring in the industrial workplace. The new ideology of domesticity portrayed women's place in the home as a moral alternative to the effects of the bustling, nervous organization of public labor. Because many of the industrial changes taking place involved the migration of African Americans, Asians, Chicanos, and immigrants to the cities, it can be said that the cult of domesticity was intertwined with the dynamics of racism. White, middle-class women were not only seen as pious and pure but they were also perceived as the moral antithesis of allegedly inferior women of color and poor women.

At the same time, by the early twentieth century, middle-class women were expected to apply the skills of rational professional men to the maintenance of their homes. Inspired by modern models of rational management, housework (under the guise of the domestic science movement) was to be efficient, sanitary, and technologically streamlined. Order, system, and efficiency were the goals of domestic science, and the housewife was to become an engineer who would keep accurate records, color-code her appliances, maintain an efficient schedule, and, in the modern sense of the word, manage her home (Andrews and Andrews 1974). Once again, clean houses and efficient management were seen as the antithesis of immigrant lives. Racism in this period depicted racial-ethnic groups as slovenly, diseased, and ridden with contagious germs (Higham 1965; Palmer 1989). Racist fears about the underclass propelled the middle classes to a new sense of themselves as both the moral agents of society and the social engineers of the future.

It is from this period that we have acquired many of our common household practices today. During the 1920s, many of the household designs that are now commonplace were introduced. Kitchens and bathrooms were to be pretty, as indicated in the following editorial:

> *Time was when kitchens were gloomy and dark, for keeping house was a gloomy business. . . . But now! gay colors are the order of the day. Red pots and pans! Blue gas stoves! . . . It is a rainbow, in which the cook sings at her work and never thinks of household tasks as drudgery.* (Ladies' Home Journal, *March 1928, cited in Cowan 1976:150–151).*

Old wooden furniture was painted pastel colors, new brides were advised to keep the gray out of their husbands' shirts, and protecting the family from germs became evidence of good maternal instincts (Cowan 1976). The ideology of domesticity added an emotional dimension to what had previously been the work of servants.

Women's roles in the home were further elaborated by the new importance placed on child care and the psychological life of infants and children. In the early twentieth century, the child became the leading figure in the family, and child psychology experts admonished mothers to turn their attention to their babies' emotional development and security (Ehrenreich and English 1978). In the end, the concepts of both housewife and motherhood emphasized new standards for women's services in the home. Although technological change created the potential for a reduction in household labor, ideological shifts in the concept of women's roles increased the social requirements for women's work. Whereas housework before had been necessary labor, it now carried ideological significance, as well. As contemporary ads imply, keeping a clean house is not just labor; it is also supposed to be an expression of love. These new standards of housework effectively raise the level of consumption by individual households, leading to the conclusion shared by many social scientists that consumption, not production, is one of the major functions of contemporary household units today.

The preceding discussion shows that an analysis of women's roles in economic production cannot be separated from their roles in family life. Although the family and the economy are usually perceived as separate institutions, they are, both in history and in the present, intertwined through the activities of production and reproduction. Women work both for wages and without wages. This discussion of women and work must be understood in this context; furthermore, understanding the history of women's work means knowing the history of race and class oppression.

❖ *What Is Work?*

There are different ways to think about the concept of work, including looking at the personal questions that individuals ask when thinking about work they do. These include questions like: What kind of work can I find? How can I earn a good income to support myself and those who depend on me? Will I be in a job that recognizes my abilities and promotes my accomplishments? Will I be treated fairly? How can I balance work and the other dimensions of my life—school, family commitments, personal life? All of these are important questions that individuals ask at varying points in their lives.

Sociological questions about work, however, have a different focus. Sociologists are concerned with the quality of individual experiences and the opportunities people have to find meaningful work, but they analyze the *social structure of work*, meaning how the societal patterns of gender, class, and race shape work experiences. From a sociological point of view, even the individual questions people ask about their jobs reflect gender, race, and class relations. To explain, any employed women might be concerned about balancing work and family, but exactly how these strains are felt and the resources women have to address the problem differ across social classes. A professional middle-class woman might solve part of this problem by paying someone else (most likely, a woman) to clean her house, but the woman who cleans it is not likely to have this option. For her, balancing work and family may mean holding down two or more jobs, finding friends or relatives to care for children, and worrying about having enough money to support her family. The point is that a sociological perspective on work has to analyze the gender, race, and class relations that shape the work experiences of different groups in society.

Studies of work have been much enriched by feminist studies that have sought to explain the specific experiences of women in the labor force. Inspired by many of the personal experiences women have had at work, feminist scholars have used sociological perspectives (and have drawn from fields such as economics, political science, history, anthropology, and psychology) to learn: What is women's role in the labor force? What historical changes have taken place for working women? What is the socioeconomic status of women workers, and how do they fare, relative to men? What factors influence the mobility of women workers? Why do women, on average, still earn less than men? These and other questions are the basis for feminist and sociological studies of gender and work.

Two other questions, however, have emerged from feminist studies of work: How do we define work and how has that definition had to change to recognize the work women do? Many people tend to think of work as that which people do for pay, but as the history of women's work shows, women (and sometimes men) often work without pay. Housewives work but do not get paid; Black women worked as slaves but did not get paid; volunteers work but do not get paid, and, in fact, many women have full-time careers as volunteers. Problems in the concept of work are not just a question of whether work is paid or unpaid, but are fundamental to the question of what constitutes work.

One consequence of feminist studies has been to question the traditional concept of work and its ability to include the full range of women's and men's productive activities. Feminists have pointed out that mothering is work, although it does not fit the criteria imposed by the traditional definition of work; moreover, if mothering is work, should fathering be considered work, as well? In considering the case of housework, feminist sociologists observe that there is an invisible dimension to the work, including not only the fact that it goes unnoticed but also the fact that part of doing housework is the work of "keeping in mind" various aspects of the tasks that constitute housework (DeVault 1991). Housework involves the physical work of doing tasks as well as the mental efforts of noticing and remembering the chores that need doing, mentally arranging the tasks that need doing, and keeping track of the work to be done. None of this mental work can be actually measured or observed; as a result, it is difficult to share, although it is an essential aspect of the work.

In addition, Hochschild (1983) developed the concept **emotional labor** to refer to the work people do in managing the emotions of others. Emotional labor, she argues, is work that is done for wages and that is meant to achieve a desired emotional effect in others. Emotional labor is done in jobs that require personal contact with the public, wherein creating a given state of mind in the client or user is part or all of the product being sold. Hochschild's research is a study of airline flight attendants, for whom emotional labor is a central part of job training, activity, and evaluation. Hochschild shows that as a result of the shift from a production-based to a service-based economy, and given the fact that women predominate in service-oriented jobs, emotional labor is a growing part of the work that women do. It is monitored by supervisors and is the basis for job rewards and reprimands. She concludes that doing emotional labor often requires putting on a false front; as a result, engaging in emotional labor is a source of workers' stress. Emotional labor is required in an increasing number of jobs and is therefore subject to the rules of mass production, resulting in what Hochschild calls "the commercialization of human feeling."

❖ Economic Restructuring, Class, and Gender Stratification

In most societies, gender is a category that organizes the social and economic relations between women and men. Most societies are also organized in a system of gender stratification, although in differing ways and to differing degrees. **Gender stratification** refers to the hierarchical distribution of economic and social resources along lines of gender. Gender stratification is a form of *social stratification*, the process by which groups or individuals in a society are arrayed in a hierarchy based on their differential access to the social and economic resources of a given society. There is nothing inherent in human nature or inevitable in social organization that requires unequal access to social and economic resources, although all societies are organized around a system for the production and distribution of goods and most are marked by some degree of stratification. But if inequality were an inevitable result of human nature, stratification patterns would not vary in societies to the extent that they do; moreover, we would not find egalitarian societies in the record of human history.

Many have noted that socioeconomic inequality emerges when there is a surplus of goods available in the society (Marx and Engels 1970). Simply put, a surplus of goods creates the possibility that one group of people can appropriate the surplus for themselves. This action forms the initial basis for class systems in which one class controls the resources of other groups in the society.

Women's access to societal resources is greatly influenced by the degree to which they control the means and forms of social and economic production. In virtually all societies, women's work sustains the economy, although in many societies (such as the United States), women's work is either invisible or devalued. Cross-cultural research shows that women tend to have the most egalitarian status in societies in which they directly contribute to the production of goods (Leacock 1978). In hunting-and-gathering societies, for example, women produce most of the food supply. Their status in these societies is relatively equal to that of men, even though a gender division of labor still exists. In agricultural societies, although women continue to be primary producers, their status deteriorates because land, economic surplus, and, subsequently, political power are concentrated in the hands of male rulers (O'Kelly and Carney 1986).

In preindustrialized societies, women's labor in the home is a vital part of the productive system because it is in the home that goods are produced; moreover, in these societies, women also have visible roles outside the home, as they distribute their goods in markets or even operate small businesses. As industrialization advances, though, economic production is shifted from the home to the factory, and although working-class and immigrant women hold factory jobs, women's domestic labor becomes both invisible and devalued. In U.S. history, the devaluation of household labor has not only resulted in a loss of status for middle-class women who work at home but has also created a class of the most severely underpaid and socially devalued laborers—child care and domestic workers (Hondagneu-Sotelo 2001).

Gender stratification has to be understood also in the context of **class stratification**—the institutionalized system by which some groups have more economic resources and power than do others. Class is one of the most important dimensions of women's and men's lives because it influences the access different groups have to economic, social, and political resources. Class standing determines how well social institutions serve you; thus, poor women have far less access to good health care, education, or other societal resources than do elite and middle-class women. The class system also places groups in different positions of privilege and disadvantage in society. Sociologists define and analyze class in different ways, but, simply put, class refers to the social structural position groups hold relative to the economic, social, political, and cultural resources of society. Members of a given class have relatively similar resources and tend to share a common way of life. Class matters, not just because of the different opportunities class privilege or disadvantage create for different people, but because society is structured in terms of class relationships. **Class** is not just a matter of individual resources; it involves the relationship between class groups and whole social systems. The class system is not simply the sum of individual opportunities; it is a structured (or institutionalized) system of privilege and inequality.

Class is indicated by who controls money, who controls the labor process, and who controls the production and distribution of goods and services. Those who have such control are dominant in the class system; those who do not are dominated. Class is more than an economic relationship; it involves power relationships as well as differential access to resources and control, domination, and power. Therefore, classes vary not only in terms of their access to economic resources but also in the degree of control they have over how things are produced, who produces them, and how work is organized and managed. The working class has little control over these things; the middle class, on the other hand, exercises greater control, and the elites have the most control of all. In sum, class is not just a matter of individual income and prestige; rather, class is part of a structured system involving control, power, and differential access to resources (Vanneman and Cannon 1987; Wright 1979).

Class can also be seen in terms of levels in a hierarchical system, typically using several common indicators to measure class standing: income, education, occupation, and place of residence. Although these indicators do not define class per se, they can be used to indicate a person's or group's class standing; these indicators also tend to be interrelated. Class is the common position groups hold in a social hierarchy (Wright 1979; Lucal 1994).

Class does not stand alone in shaping women's or men's experiences. As this book emphasizes throughout, class intersects both with gender and race in determining group standing in society. Systems of privilege and disadvantage cannot be described by either class, gender, or race alone. The next section reviews contemporary data about women's position in the labor market, with an eye toward understanding how the class system shapes women's economic standing.

The current system of gender, class, and racial stratification is being fundamentally changed by what has come to be called economic restructuring. **Economic**

restructuring is the term used to describe a multidimensional process of change in the nation's economy. This includes: (1) the transition from a manufacturing-based economy to a service-based economy; (2) increasing globalization; (3) technological change; and, (4) the increasing concentration of capital (i.e., economic resources) in the hands of a few. Economic restructuring is fundamentally altering the work people do, including who does it, how it is done, and what it is worth. Understanding economic restructuring is critical to understanding the position of women and men of all groups in the labor force.

First, the move from a manufacturing to a service-based economy has resulted in a massive decline of jobs within the United States in the manufacturing sector. These are goods-producing jobs—jobs that historically have been unionized with relatively good wages, job stability, and opportunities for some advancement. Although this sector of the economy was largely dominated by White men, it has been a route for upward mobility for women and minority workers. But with economic restructuring, such jobs have radically declined and manufacturing jobs have been relocated overseas in what is called a global assembly line—or the international division of labor. Furthermore, within the United States, many such jobs are now the work of recent immigrant groups. At the same time, job growth is in the service sector—where jobs involve the provision of services (such as food preparation and delivery, cleaning, or child care) or the processing of information (such as data entry jobs, banking, computer work, and clerical jobs). The majority of workers are now employed in the service sector. The service-delivery segment consists of many low-wage, semi- and unskilled forms of labor and employs high numbers of women and people of color, particularly in some of the least attractive jobs in this segment of the economy. This is a significant change in the labor market since jobs in the service sector, as we will see, are more often low-wage work with few opportunities for advancement and little job stability.

The growing global basis of the economy also means that jobs both in the manufacturing sector and the service sector can increasingly be located in countries where labor is cheap. Coupled with advances in technology, even jobs in the information sector can be performed in one country when the profit center for the industry is located in another. Thus, women—and often children—in poor nations might stitch the seams of sneakers sold at a huge profit margin to consumers in the more affluent nations. Or, women in a poor nation may key in the data for insurance claims being processed by a giant health care corporation whose profits are held by a few in a different part of the world. Economic restructuring also exacerbates the growing class division between affluent sectors of Western societies and the middle and working classes in those nations. At the same time, it is related to a system of global inequality whereby the resources (both natural resources and human labor) of one part of the world are exploited for the benefit of others.

Economic restructuring is having a major impact on women and men as workers within the United States. Many men who assumed they would be in the labor force until they retired are being pushed out of work. Young workers are finding it harder to find employment; those without education are facing massive unemployment. Furthermore, since economic restructuring is occurring at a time when the work force is becoming more diverse (i.e., more workers are women and members of racial minority groups), there are enormous consequences for white women and people of color (Fine and Weis 1998).

Economic restructuring means that for many groups, especially women and men in racial-ethnic minority groups and minority teens, there is not enough work; for others, it means there is too much work—long overtime hours, holding more than one job, and piecing together part-time and temporary work. The movement of labor out of the United States leaves many workers at home unemployed, since jobs they formerly held are now being done mostly by women workers in other parts of the world (e.g., Mexico, Asia, the Caribbean) where labor is cheaper, nonunionized, and without the job benefits U.S. workers would likely receive. At home, this has made many workers "disposable" (Sklar 1994).

Contingent workers have also grown as a share of the U.S. labor market. Contingent workers include those who are temporary employees, contract workers, and part-time workers. They are now one-third of the U.S. labor force (up from one-quarter in 1988). Although contingent work may be appealing to those who want more flexibility—or, in some cases, can work at home—data shows that contingent workers are less likely to receive job benefits (i.e., vacations, health insurance, unemployment insurance, pensions), are more vulnerable to harassment and health and safety hazards, have little job protection in the form of due process, are more likely to have to hold more than one job, and earn less than other workers. Moreover, the gap in earnings between contingent and noncontingent workers is greater for women than for men (a 30 percent difference for women; 20 percent for men). Contingent workers also typically spend much of their time looking for the next job, thus adding to worker stress. Perhaps not surprisingly, women are more likely to be contingent workers than men (Hipple 2001).

Economic restructuring has also resulted in a growth of low-income jobs. At the other end of the class spectrum, economic restructuring has also affected the jobs of those traditionally thought of as relatively protected from economic instability. Thus, companies have eliminated layers of management, "downsizing" their white-collar labor force to reduce costs and maintain business profits. Downsizing often eliminates the career ladders that have recently provided women and racial-ethnic groups (who are often clustered in middle-management positions) some opportunity for advancement. Those who are displaced workers, when they find new jobs, typically earn lower wages than before and, if rehired, tend to be hired into less-skilled work. Since older White men are those who have been most likely to be in such jobs, to date they are the workers most affected by economic downsizing. But, as seen in the aftermath of the terrorist attacks on September 11, 2001, many of the workers laid off in the economic downturn that followed were low-wage workers—men and women—often with little safety net to protect them from poverty.

In the future, women and racial-ethnic minorities are expected to comprise five-sixths of all new workers, meaning that their representation in the labor force will increase even more in the years ahead. Many in these groups will not, however, have the education and training necessary to compete in a technologically driven labor force, unless there are massive reforms in the educational system. New job opportunities are most likely to come in technological fields where education (and the scientific training that women often lack) are required. The transition from a predominantly goods-producing economy to one based on the provision of services, means that service-based industries, such as banking and finance, retail sales, or personal services, will predominate in the economy. As the process of economic restructuring unfolds, we will likely witness the increasing effects of this process on workers both in the United States and abroad.

❖ *The Contemporary Status of Women*

What is women's status in the labor market and how has it changed? More women are working than ever before, and many women now enter occupations that were previously held only by men. Women's earnings as a percentage of men's have improved, although a significant pay gap remains. At a glance, many might conclude that women's struggle for equality is over, yet on many measures women still lag behind. Although they are more likely to work, women remain highly segregated in certain jobs, their earnings are low, and they experience what has popularly been labeled the glass ceiling, referring to implicit limits on their ability to move up at work. What do we know about these trends and how can they be explained? We begin with a look at women's labor force participation.

Labor Force Participation

By 2000, 60 percent of all women were in the labor force, compared with 75 percent of men (see Figure 5.1); moreover, since 1960, married women with children have nearly tripled their labor force participation. Hispanic women are somewhat less likely than African American and White women to be employed, but these data are distorted by the clustering of different groups into one category as "Hispanic." Puerto Rican origin women have the highest employment rates among Hispanic women. Cuban American women have the lowest labor force participation rate (U.S. Department of Labor 2004). Asian American women are even more likely than other women to be in the labor force, but, like Latinas, Asian American women's work experiences vary significantly across different groups. Recent Asian American immigrant women from nations such as Laos, Vietnam, and Cambodia experience particularly high rates of poverty as the result of low wages.

In the future, the labor force is likely to include more women and minority groups. Among women, White and Black women are expected to have the highest labor force participation rate, followed by Asian women and Hispanic women. While women's labor force participation rate has been increasing, men's has been decreasing. In 1951, 87 percent of men were in the labor force, but by 2003, this had dropped to 73.5 percent. The decline of men's labor force participation is expected to continue, whereas that of women is expected to continue increasing (Fullerton 1997).

One of the developments influencing women's position in the labor force is the growth in immigration that the United States has witnessed in recent years. In

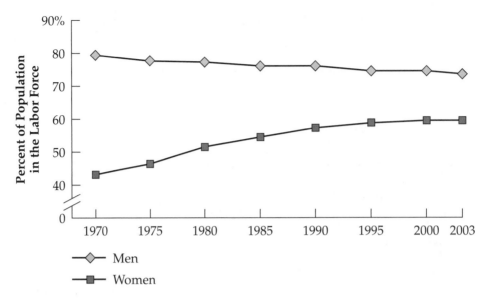

FIGURE 5.1   Labor Force Participation: 1970–2003

Source: Data from U.S. Department of Labor. 2004. *Employment and Earnings.* Washington, DC: U.S. Government Printing Office, p. 195.

the late 1990s, approximately three-quarter million immigrants were arriving each year—a rate of immigration not matched since the 1920s, when so many European immigrants arrived. Now, the largest number of immigrants come from Caribbean countries, Mexico, the former Soviet Union, China, and the Philippines. Other Asian and Latin American countries account for another large share of the total number of immigrants (U.S. Census Bureau 2004). For women, immigration has a number of consequences for labor force participation. Immigration is typically a family experience, as family units make decisions about who will migrate, who will work, and what impact immigration will have on family well-being. This means that women who may not have been in the labor force before will work for wages, often transforming gender roles within the family that existed prior to immigration (Hondagneu-Sotelo 1994; Grasmuck and Pessar 1996; Lim 1997; Pedraza 1991, 1996). Immigrant women can also find themselves "niched" in certain sectors of the labor market, such as domestic work or factory production, where wages are low and opportunities for advancement are poor (Repak 1994; Myers and Crawford 1998). Still, they may find that employment brings them more independence and more opportunity to exercise influence in family decisions.

Gender Segregation

One of the most significant factors influencing women's class position is gender segregation in the labor market. **Gender segregation** refers to the pattern whereby women and men are situated in different jobs throughout the labor force. Gender segregation is a particular form of *occupational distribution*—a term sociologists use to refer to the placement of workers in different occupations.

Most women work in gender-segregated jobs (see Figure 5.2). That is to say, women work in jobs where most of the other workers are women, and women constitute a numerical minority of workers in many of the jobs that have historically been identified as men's work. This is vividly seen in Figure 5.2, showing the distribution of women, African Americans, and Hispanics in selected occupations. Note that women constitute 97 percent of secretaries, 81 percent of elementary and middle school teachers, and 95 percent of child care workers, but only 30 percent of physicians and 28 percent of lawyers (a huge increase since the 1970s, when they were 8 percent of physicians and 12 percent of lawyers; Andersen 1983). Men are more broadly distributed across the labor market and are more likely located in the higher-paying professions, although this is mitigated by men's racial status.

Within occupational categories, women are concentrated in gender-segregated jobs. This is referred to as *internal gender segregation*. Take the example of teachers. Women are 77 percent of teachers (excluding college and university teaching), but they are 98 percent of preschool and kindergarten teachers and 82 percent of elementary school teachers. Likewise, in the category of production occupations where women are 31 percent of all workers, they are 79 percent of sewing machine operators and 56 percent of packaging operators (U.S. Department of Labor 2004). Women are internally segregated as professional workers, too. Although they make up half of professional workers (seeming equality), studies find that they are concentrated in lower status occupations within this category (Zimmerman 2000; Pierce 1995).

Gender segregation is further complicated by race. Chicanas, for example, are most heavily concentrated in secretarial, cashier, and janitorial jobs; Central American women in jobs as household cleaners, janitors, and textile machine operators; Filipinas as nurses, nurses' aides, and cashiers, and Black women as nursing aides, cashiers, and secretaries (Reskin 1999). As a result, the income of women of color is less than that of any other group. Like White women, women of color are most likely to work in jobs where most of the other workers are women and women of color, in particular. These numerical facts affect social relations at work, but they also affect women's income, since occupations with high concentrations of women of color are the worse paid of all jobs. In general, the larger the proportion of women in an occupation, the lower the pay (as shown in Figure 5.3)—a point we return to later in discussing reasons for the pay gap between women and men.

The data on gender and race segregation exposes the myth that women of color are entering the labor market and taking jobs away from White men. Although some individuals see this happen on occasion, the aggregate data reveal that this can be true only in a small number of cases. The general pattern is that women and people of color work in different occupations than do White men. You might ask why it has become such a big public issue when you consider the number of jobs over the years that have gone to White men and not to women and people of color. Criticisms of affirmative action hiring programs make it appear that women and minorities are flooding the labor market, taking jobs away from White men. The

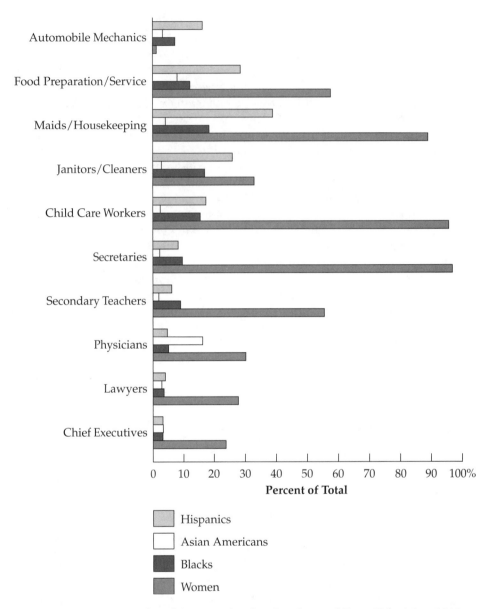

FIGURE 5.2   Occupational Segregation by Gender and Race-Ethnicity: 2003

Source: Data from U.S. Department of Labor. 2004. *Employment and Earnings.* Washington, DC: U.S. Department of Labor, pp. 209–214.

data show the contrary. Even with affirmative action policy and equal employment opportunity laws, White women, African American women and men, Hispanics, Asian Americans, and Native Americans are employed in a labor market divided by race and by gender (Browne 1999).

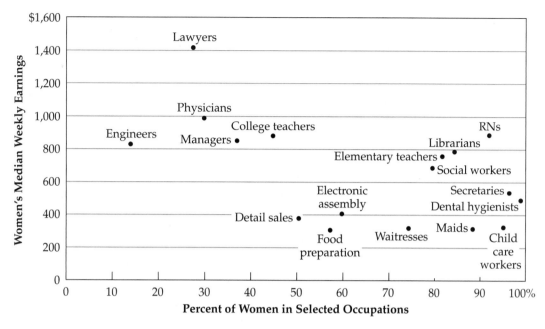

FIGURE 5.3   Income and Gender Segregation

Source: Data from U.S. Department of Labor. 2004. *Employment and Earnings.* Washington, DC: U.S. Department of Labor, pp. 209–214, 249–253.

Aggregate data on gender segregation provide a general view of where women work. To understand fully women's experiences in these different positions of work requires a closer view of women's experiences in various work settings. This gives us a picture drawn not just from government statistics but also drawn from the many studies of women and work that examine in detail the variety of circumstances where women are employed. Next, some of this work will be examined by looking in more detail at some of the broad categories of women's employment. This will also provide more analysis of the combined effects of gender, race, and class in the social and economic organization of work.

Women in the Professions

Women who work in the professions have the advantage of holding the most prestigious and highly paid jobs in the labor market. Women's presence in the professions has increased in recent years, although they are still a numerical minority in many of the most senior positions. Women constitute almost half of those in the Labor Department category "Management, Professional, and Related Occupations," but within this broad category are numerous different occupations with widely varying participation by women. Women represent 15 percent of chemical engineers, 30 percent of physicians, 24 percent of dentists, 14 percent of clergy, 28 percent of lawyers, and 39 percent of professional athletes. Where women predominate in the professions is in traditionally women's work; thus, they are 92 percent of nurses, 91 percent of dietitians, 92 percent of librarians, 80 percent of social workers, and 98 percent of dental hygienists (U.S. Department of Labor 2004).

It is in the professions where women have made some of the most dramatic numerical gains, yet they are still concentrated in the lower ranks and less prestigious specialties. In universities, although women constitute 38 percent of all college and university professors, they are only 23 percent of full professors (the top rank) and they are half of instructors and lecturers—positions that are often temporary, not well paid, and typically without the job benefits and rewards associated with other university appointments (*The Chronicle of Higher Education* 2004). Likewise, although it is changing, within medicine women are still more likely to specialize in pediatrics than are men (American Medical Association 2004). With the move to managed health care, women physicians are also more likely to work in university or hospital staff positions, not independent practice. Similarly, in law, although women are now more widely distributed across different specialties within law, they are still more likely to be found in certain areas (such as domestic law, real estate, trust, and general practice), and they are twice as likely as men to work in public service law (Epstein 1993). Moreover, studies of lawyers also find that women are significantly less satisfied than men with the level of responsibility they are given, their chances for advancement and salary, and the recognition they get for their work (Hull 1999).

Within the professions, patterns of sponsorship and mentoring are critical to upward mobility. Studies consistently find that men are more likely to get such sponsorship than are women. Professions are socially organized like communities and, as such, involve informal roles and practices and tend toward homogeneity and exclusionary relations. Social control in professional life, as well as access to rewards, typically operates through a sponsorship system that feminists have labeled the "old boy network." Within the network, social relations with one's peers and mentors can bring access to jobs, promotions, opportunities, and status. For women and men of color the lack of support and absence of mentoring can be especially burdensome and impede mobility in careers (Higginbotham 2001). Women and people of color excluded from the protégé system are likely to find themselves at a disadvantage when it comes to professional opportunities.The information and collegiality shared by those in the network are likely to give professional advantage to those who are "in the know." Whether by exclusion or personal choice, women and people of color who are not part of the old boy network are likely to find their careers detrimentally affected.

The climate in graduate and professional schools also influences women's subsequent career patterns. Studies show that the climate in these settings often reflects a male-dominated culture, which women encounter once they enter these professions. In law schools, race and gender dynamics in the classroom also discourage participation by women and people of color (Mertz et al. 1998; Pierce 1995). In addition, the clockwork of professional careers has been developed around male-centered models—that one should uproot one's family and move when opportunities are available, put in long hours independent of family and personal responsibilities, and be available whenever the profession calls for you, regardless of other commitments. Research on lawyers finds, for example, that women have poorer prospects for becoming partners than do men and that different gender expectations for men and women shape their perceived value as partners and thus the likelihood of their achieving partnership. Men are valued for maintaining traditional corporate family images, whereas women are valued for giving priority to work outside the home (Kay and Hagan 1998).

This professional culture has encouraged women professionals in most fields to establish alternative networks of support, both for professional advancement and for personal encouragement. Groups such as the Association for Women in Science, the Society of Women Engineers, Sociologists for Women in Society, and the American Medical Women's Association, to name only a few, have flourished. As both professional networks and local support groups for women professionals, these organizations encourage the development of alternative networks to promote the status of professional women.

Women as Clerical Workers

Women make up 76 percent of all administrative support workers, an occupational category of the U.S. census that includes clerical workers. Women are 96 percent of all secretaries and administrative assistants. Over the twentieth century, the number of clerical workers has drastically increased, but their prestige has declined—even though the technological skill required to do the job has increased.

Before the mechanization of office work by the invention of the typewriter in the late nineteenth century, skills such as shorthand and accounting were men's trades, and relatively prestigious trades at that. An 1888 book titled *How to Succeed as a Stenographer or Typewriter* was addressed to men, saying, "There are comparatively few verbatim reporters, and the young shorthand writer who has reached that distinction should consider that it gives him the rank of a scholar and a gentleman" (Baker 1888, cited in Benet 1972:39). The introduction of mechanized switchboards and typewriters and the corresponding need for new workers brought the rapid introduction of women workers to these jobs. Capitalist owners saved money by tapping the cheap, large, female labor market, and soon women workers experienced a decline in the wages and prestige associated with office work.

To this day, the median weekly earnings for women in administrative support work are low, especially compared with those of men. In 2003, full-time male administrative support workers earned $584 per week, compared to $513 per week for women (U.S. Department of Labor 2004). A huge supply of women clerical workers is also provided by temporary clerical services, where workers have low wages, little control of their work, minimal social relationships with co-workers, and highly alienated attitudes toward their jobs. Opportunities for advancement are greater for secretaries than for other clerical workers, but mobility for secretaries is often dependent on the promotion of their supervisor, not just their own performance.

Full-time secretaries, except those who work in large pools where work is heavily routinized, are tied to individual and patrimonial relationships with their bosses. Their status is then contingent on that of the boss, whose power may determine their own. Although studies find that secretaries most resent doing personal work for their bosses, bosses expect their secretaries to appreciate and provide nonmaterial rewards such as emotional intimacy, praise, and affection. Loyalty and devotion to their employers are often the bases for secretaries' rewards at work (Kanter 1977).

Clerical work, of course, varies in different settings, but in large companies where there is the most extensive automation and use of a secretarial pool, clerical work is becoming "proletarianized." That is, work is becoming organized more around manual than mental activities, tasks are externally structured and controlled, and relationships among workers more depersonalized. Automation in the form of electronic data processing and word processing means that computers now perform many clerical functions, decreasing the autonomy of workers and increasing fragmentation among clerical workers (Feldberg and Glenn 1979). The development of word processing increases productivity at the same time that it increases surveillance of clerical work (Machung 1984). The proletarianization of clerical work leaves workers with less control over the work itself, and makes relationships between workers and supervisors more impersonal. This process also has serious implications for the development of solidarity among clerical workers. As working groups become less interdependent and more physically separated, it is more difficult for workers to know if they share common conditions and occupy comparable positions in the office hierarchy. Although the strains associated with more mechanized work can create cooperation among the workers, the strains also increase workers' vulnerability, sometimes decreasing their desires for personal ties with others (Feldberg and Glenn 1979).

The increased use of computers has advantages and disadvantages for clerical workers. Computerized technology can eliminate some of the stress from routine, repetitive, and tedious aspects of one's job, but in occupations such as data entry, the work becomes more routinized. Increasingly, large numbers of women, especially women of color, work in "electronic sweatshops" entering keyboard data, with their work electronically monitored. Computer technology also brings new forms of fatigue, physical strain, and stress. Many researchers argue that the negative affects of computers are not the result of the technology per se, but of the way they are used in the workplace. Because clerical workers are seldom given any authority or responsibility for designing their workplace, it is little wonder that they suffer the consequences of poor workplace design and organization (Fox and Sugiman 1999).

Women in Blue-Collar Work

Among blue-collar workers, women have been entering the skilled trades at a rapid rate—faster, in fact, than men in recent years—although women still constitute only a small percentage of those in the more highly skilled trades. Women in blue-collar work are more likely to be employed as semiskilled machine operators than as skilled crafts workers; within the occupational categories in which they work, women earn less than men.

Women in blue-collar work also find gender segregation on the job. Even when women are employed in the same occupational category as men, they tend to be located in different industries. Women are more likely to be employed in the nondurable-goods sector, whereas men are more likely employed in manufacturing, where wages and job benefits have traditionally been higher. In fact, the largest majority of women in blue-collar work are employed in assembly work—jobs with little autonomy and often involving repetitive tasks. Depending on the region of the country, women in assembly work are a disproportionate number of assembly-line workers.

Blue-collar workers in the United States, both women and men, are also increasingly affected by global restructuring of the economy. Research and management are based in developed countries (e.g., the United States), while assembly-line work is relegated to underprivileged nations (especially in Latin America and Asia). In the global assembly line, women workers are relocated from their traditional work in home-based production and are employed in factories as assembly workers. This new work gives women somewhat greater independence from traditional patriarchal arrangements but introduces them to new forms of exploitation in the form of high job turnover, little mobility, low wages, and hazardous working conditions. Their work within these settings is often justified through crude sexist and racist ideologies defining them as "fit" for this demeaning work.

The global assembly line links the experiences of women in poor nations to the consumerism in the United States that "markets gender." Barbie dolls are a good example. Barbie is the "dream girl" of the United States, each version depicting a different fantasy life of beauty, fashion, romance, and play. But most Barbie dolls are manufactured by workers not much older than those who play with her in the United States. For these workers, it would take all of their monthly pay just to buy *one* of the dolls that many U.S. girls collect by the dozens. In China, where more toys are produced than in any other part of the world, workers molding Barbie dolls earn 25 cents an hour, and human rights organizations say violations of basic rights are flagrant. Moreover, this works to the advantage of corporate owners in the United States, such as the chief executive officer of Mattel (the company that produces Barbies), who, in 1995, earned $7 million and an additional $23 million in stock options—far more than the combined salaries of the 11,000 Mattel workers who produce Barbie dolls in China. Indonesian workers making Barbies earn the minimum wage of $2.25 a day; it would take such a worker a full month to earn the money to buy the Calvin Klein Barbie (Press 1996).

Similar analyses can be made of many products—action figures, jeans, and other gendered products—that are manufactured in the global assembly line for sale to an international gendered market. You do not have to look overseas to witness the conditions of women's labor in sweatshops. Within the United States, the largest number of sweatshop workers are immigrant women—many of whom work in the garment industry, although that is not the only industry that employs sweatshop labor. Sweatshops are often run by subcontractors who are selling labor to larger companies—such as the well-known brand names of men's and women's fashion. This method of subcontracting allows companies to cut labor costs, thereby increasing their profits.

The government defines a **sweatshop** as a workplace where an employer violates more than one law regarding safety and health, workers' compensation, or industry regulation. The government estimates that more than half of the laborers who work in garment production work in sweatshops where they are paid below minimum wage and work in unsafe and unhealthy workshops. Workers may also be reluctant to file complaints for fear of losing their jobs, or, if they are undocumented workers, they may fear deportation. Despite these fears many sweatshop workers have organized to campaign for workers' rights. A significant movement against the use of sweatshop labor to produce college logo products has also emerged on many college campuses (Bonacich and Applebaum 2000; Louie 2001; Applebaum and Dreier 1998).

Within the U.S. economy, women in blue-collar jobs are somewhat less likely than men to be protected by labor unions (12.9 percent of employed women are represented by unions compared to 15.6 percent of men). African American men and women are more likely to be represented by unions than are White men and women, but Hispanic men and women are less likely than White men and women to be unionized. Asian American men and women are comparable to Whites in union membership, although Asian American women are more likely to be unionized than Asian American men (U.S. Department of Labor 2004).

Despite low rates of union membership, being in a union has significant advantages for employed women and men. Not only does it increase the likelihood of due process and job protection, but median weekly earnings of those represented by unions exceed earnings of nonunion members. Despite declines in overall union membership, women, along with people of color, are increasingly important in trade unions. Given the declines in the manufacturing industry, union members are no longer centered primarily on factory labor, but include large numbers of organized service workers who, as we have seen, are more likely to be women and people of color. Women's activism within unions thus means that many unions now give greater attention to women's issues, including not only compensation and working conditions, but the development of family-friendly policies for workers. Union adoption of such issues has also been shown to depend on an increase in the membership of women in specific unions (Gerstel and Clawson 2001; Kirton 1999).

Within blue-collar labor, male supervisors' gender stereotypes and discomfort at the presence of women shape women's experiences at work. Supervisors may believe, for example, that women should be excluded from some jobs so they do not get hurt; paternalistic attitudes put supervisors in the position of gatekeepers who maintain the status quo by assigning women to gender-typed jobs. Often, the fact that supervisors' reservations about women are paternalistic rather than overt and hostile makes it difficult for women in such jobs to identify or document sexism, for it appears subtle or trivial; nonetheless, such attitudes and behaviors do create barriers to women's mobility. Supervisors' paternalistic attitudes also communicate to male co-workers that sexist behavior is acceptable (Reskin and Padavic 1988). Studies of desegregation in blue-collar work do show, however, that supervisors often lose their reservations about women's work after supervising more women. One mechanism for eliminating sexism in these occupations is to increase the number of women workers in these jobs (Padavic and Reskin 2002).

Some people assume that women do not choose to enter traditionally male blue-collar jobs as a result of their gender socialization not to prefer such work. Studies show, however, that although this plays some small part in women's choices about blue-collar work, economic need overrides any learned distaste women may have for such jobs (Padavic 1991).

Women and Service Work

Service work is the third largest category of women's employment, accounting for 20 percent of women in the labor force. Women in service work are among the lowest paid of employed women, yet this is the most rapidly expanding area of work—one where most new jobs are predicted to be found in the future. Included in service work are fast-food workers, waitresses, and health care assistants (e.g., nurses' aides, maids, and various personal service workers). This category of work employs large numbers of women of color, as well as older women workers returning to the labor force after years of working in the home. In 2004, the median weekly earnings for service workers (not including private and protective services) were $463 for men and $366 for women (U.S. Department of Labor 2004); those working in private households earned even less (see Table 5.1).

Service work is highly segregated by gender, even within specific occupational categories. For example, women constitute almost three-quarters of kitchen workers, but less than one-fifth of protective service workers (e.g., police, firefighters, and guards) where pay is better. High rates of turnover and part-time employment are also common in service work, further limiting women's chances for upward mobility in those occupations (Berheide 1988).

Service work can also be one of the most degrading forms of work for women. Women service workers are often supervised by men whose attitudes can be patronizing, impatient, and overtly hostile. Sexist expectations also shape women's experiences in these occupations. Waitresses, for example, are often expected to be young and sexy, to dress in provocative clothing, and to treat even the most obnoxious customer with grace and charm. Sometimes, sexist expectations for women service workers are very explicit, as in the old requirements of some airlines that flight attendants not exceed certain weight and height standards. Even when not written into explicit employment practices, these expectations often shape women's opportunities in service occupations. For women of color in these occupations, the combination of sexist and racist attitudes and behaviors can be doubly demeaning.

For many years, employment as a domestic worker was the only choice for women who needed to work, particularly women of color. Now, although other opportunities are available, large numbers of women still work in private households where their labor is unregulated and sometimes unreported. Although it pays poorly, domestic work is often the only work available for incoming groups of immigrant women, women with little education, and women with little choice of occupation. In recent years, refugees from Latin America have entered domestic work, receiving low wages and few, if any, benefits. Domestic workers seldom face opportunities for unionization and are rarely given employee benefits such as health care insurance, paid sick leave, retirement, or vacation. Although private-household workers sometimes have the benefit of negotiating their own work schedules and, thus, may have greater flexibility than workers in the public sector, they pay the price in terms of low wages and little job security (Repak 1994; Hondagneu-Sotelo 2001).

Women who work as domestic workers regard the independence and autonomy of the job as a positive feature of the work, but since domestic workers typically do not have co-workers, loneliness, especially for live-ins, is the most difficult part of the work (Rollins 1985). Rollins's study of Black domestic workers in the Boston area identifies maternalism as structuring the relationship between domestics and their employers. Rollins, who holds a Ph.D. in sociology, hired herself as a domestic worker as part of her research design. Through her own experiences and her interviews with Black domestic workers, she shows that because the domestic work is based on personal relations, it is both psychologically and economically belittling. Although employers may act caring and protective, the job is still structured as a power relationship. Patterns of deferential behavior, such as referring to the domestic as "girl" and treating the domestic as if she is invisible, reveal the subordination and exploitation in this work.

Farm and Migrant Labor

Farming, forestry, and fishing employ a very small proportion (.8 percent) of the total labor force and an even smaller proportion of women workers (.4 percent), yet it is significant because of the large number of workers in this category who are Hispanic and because of the importance of migrant labor in the contemporary economy. Migrant farm workers are at the very bottom of the occupational ladder, where they face physically demanding jobs, poor working conditions, and extremely low wages. Of farm workers, 40 percent are Hispanic men and women, 22 percent, African American (U.S. Department of Labor 2004).

Research on migrant workers shows the effect that the structure of this work has on gender roles. Men's and women's roles in families change as the result of the migration experience. Frequently, men move first, living in labor camps of mostly other men, where they have to cook, wash dishes, and manage other household duties. At the same time, separated from their husbands, women act more assertively and autonomously. As a result, when the family is reunited, both find that they have moved in a more egalitarian direction (Hondagneu-Sotelo 1992, 1994).

A similar pattern has been observed historically among Chinese people who migrate to the United States. Although Chinese women traditionally had low rates of labor force participation in China, the necessity of finding employment after migration challenged traditional beliefs that "a woman's place is in the home." Chinese women's work experiences in the United States instead produced a new attitude that married women have an obligation to work to help support their families (Geschwender 1992).

In sum, research on women and work shows how deeply structured the labor market is along lines of gender, race, and class. Moreover, as the brief portraits shown on these pages have revealed, patterns of segregation in the labor market (by gender and by race) have enormous consequences for all workers. As you will see next, one of the major consequences is in the earnings associated with gender-segregated jobs.

Earnings

Perhaps we would not care if women and men worked in gender- and racial-ethnic-segregated jobs if that fact did not have such enormous consequences for women's earnings (see Figure 5.4). In 2004, women working full time and year round earned 75 percent of what men earned (DeNavas-Walt et al. 2004). Women's concentration in gender- and racial-ethnic-segregated occupations is clearly related to this inequality, as shown in Table 5.1 and Figure 5.3. These low earnings have serious consequences for women. Those who head their own families are in an especially precarious position, since they are so likely to be poor (see Figure 5.5).

Why do these earning differentials persist? One explanation is overt discrimination. **Discrimination** refers to practices that systematically disadvantage one or more groups; it can be overt or covert. Overt discrimination occurs when someone treats someone differently simply because of some characteristic of the person (e.g., gender, age, sexual orientation, race, religion, or national origin, to name a few). Paying someone a different wage *because* she is a woman is discrimination, as is not hiring someone presumed to be gay or lesbian. Overt discrimination because of someone's sex, race, or age is illegal. The trick to understanding discrimination is that it is often not overt or conscious, even though, to the receiver, it may seem obvious and apparent. Discrimination is institutionalized, and so it can occur even in the context of individual good will and a seeming absence of overt prejudice or intent to discriminate. For example, there may not be someone in an employment office telling women they cannot apply for certain jobs, but the structural patterns whereby women historically have been denied access to those jobs or whereby women do not receive the education and training needed to qualify for such jobs is a form of institutionalized discrimination. It can be harder to see, because it is not represented by some person making a sexist comment or deliberately blocking access to a job, but it is real, nonetheless.

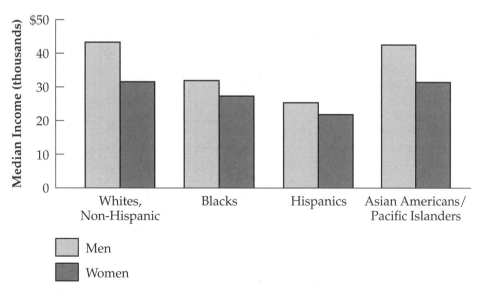

FIGURE 5.4   The Pay Gap: 2001 (Year-round, full-time workers)

Sources: Data from U.S. Census Bureau. 2001. *Historical Income Tables–People,* Tables p. 36A–E. http://www.census.gov

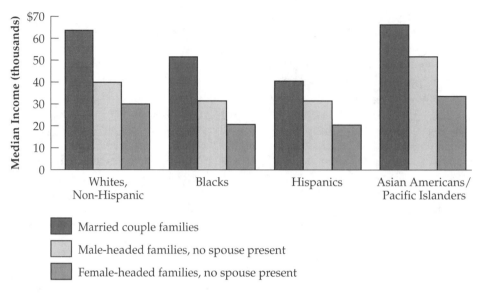

FIGURE 5.5   Gender, Race-Ethnicity, and Family Income: 2001

Sources: Data from U.S. Census Bureau. 2001. *Historical Income Tables,* Tables F-7B-E. http://www
.census.gov.

Although most people think overt discrimination has disappeared—or certainly diminished—research shows that it continues to influence work opportunities for women. Employer stereotypes about who are the most valuable workers influence who is hired (Neckerman and Kirschenman 1991, 1999; Moss and Tilly 2001). Studies also find that successful managers are still imagined to be men (Willemsen 2002) and employers still tend to rank White men as more valuable employees than either White or Black women; employers are therefore more likely to invest in their success (McGuire 2002). Numerous studies have also found that the stereotypes employers hold about women—and women of color in particular—continue to disadvantage women in sometimes subtle, but nonetheless, significant ways (Kennelly 1999). As sociologist Barbara Reskin has pointed out, sometimes men will organize as a group to block women from entering formerly male-dominated organizations. Historically, for example, men in labor unions developed policies excluding women and minorities from union membership, thereby excluding them from better-paying union-based jobs (Reskin 1988). One could interpret the contemporary backlash against affirmative action policies in a similar vein—the mobilization of dominant groups to preserve their historic privilege in the workplace.

Much of what happens to women in the labor market is not, however, caused by overt discrimination. Scholars have looked to other structural causes to explain the underlying reasons for continuing inequities in women's and men's earnings. Two primary explanations have emerged: human capital theory and dual labor market theory.

Human Capital Theory

Human capital theory explains wage differentials as a result of different characteristics of workers. Human capital consists of worker characteristics, such as level of education, marital status, prior experience, training, and so forth—individual level variables. Human capital theory assumes that, in a competitive economic system, wage differences reflect differences in human capital. According to this perspective, the quality of labor supplied by men and women varies because of characteristics of workers themselves. Presumably, high turnover rates, interrupted careers, and shorter participation in the labor force among women lead to lesser productivity and therefore lower wages.

There is some evidence that human capital theory explains some of the difference in women's and men's wages. Statistical studies of earnings in various occupations typically find that human capital variables explain a portion of the earnings gap, but studies also find a significant portion of the earnings gap unexplained by human capital theory (Firestone et al. 1998; Avalos 1996). As an example, a study of workers in higher education finds that, controlling for the effects of human capital variables, the gender composition of the occupational category also influences salary differential between women and men (Bellas 1997; Colker 1997). Although some studies find a strong effect of human capital variables (Tam 1997), more consistent is the finding that a high percentage of women in a given occupation depresses wages (Kilbourne et al. 1994). Thus, even though human capital theory explains some of the gender gap in earnings, it does not explain the full gap. Dual labor market theory is another explanation.

Dual Labor Market Theory

Dual labor market theory is a second explanation of gender inequality in wages. This perspective sees the labor market as organized around both a primary and a secondary market. Jobs in the primary labor market have more stability, higher wages, better working conditions, chances for advancement, and due process in the administration of work roles. The primary labor market restricts entry to a relatively few low-level entry jobs but is organized around long promotion ladders, worker stability, good working conditions, and job security.

Disadvantaged groups, including women and people of color, are employed primarily in the secondary market, which internally is less structured than the primary market and is characterized by numerous points of entry, short or nonexistent promotion ladders, less worker stability, little job security, and arbitrary work rules. The secondary labor market has jobs with low wages, few or no fringe benefits, poor working conditions, high turnover, few chances for advancement, and often arbitrary and capricious supervision.

Within the secondary labor market, the firms where women are employed have lower capital investments, low profit margins, irregular personnel practices, higher turnover, and lower pay, leaving women more at the mercy of economic fluctuations. Even in the less marginal industries where blue-collar women work, the jobs that women hold tend to have the characteristics of the secondary labor market (e.g., poor wages, poor fringe benefits, and unstable employment). The steady supply of women workers, however, discourages employers from paying better wages. The dual labor market perspective causes us to look at occupational distribution by gender as a major factor in the earnings gap between men and women and leads us to conclude that *where* people work, not *what* their individual characteristics are, is a better predictor of income.

Dual labor market theory points to gender segregation as a major cause of wage inequality. Also, studies find that as occupations become more populated by women, wages tend to decline—both for women and men. Such studies suggest that occupations become "feminized" when they are no longer attractive careers (Reskin and Roos 1990, 1992), as may be currently happening for physicians.

Unlike human capital theory, which looks at characteristics of individuals to explain wage differences among groups, dual labor market theory looks at social structural characteristics to explain the same thing. Thus, such societal level factors as the gender composition of an occupation, economic decline or prosperity, and historical effects are structural explanations of the wage gap. As you will see in a later section, such societal processes have strong effects on the status of women and men—independent (or at least intersecting with) of individual level differences.

Structural perspectives caution us against relying too heavily on "differences" as the framework from which to study wage equity, since differences in men's and women's earnings could be substantially reduced through deterioration in the economic status of men and no improvement in the status of women. There is evidence that, indeed, this is happening, as sociologists and economists are reporting that the decreasing wage gap between men and women occurring in recent years is significantly influenced by a decline in male earnings. Measured in constant dollars, White men in the bottom 20 percent of the labor market (measured by holding the value of the dollar constant) have seen a decline in wages since 1980. The gender wage gap has thus closed, both due to some improvement in women's wages and a decline for men. At the same time, women in the best paid occupations, like men, have seen large increases in their wages, resulting in increased class differentiation within gender groups (Mishel et al. 2003). This focuses attention on the need for economic justice to be at the forefront of feminist organizing.

Promotions

Research on women and work has tended to focus on why women are segregated in the labor market and why they earn less than men. A third important question, though, is whether women advance in work organizations. Studies of employed women, for example, find that when women are asked about their greatest frustrations at work, the problems most likely pointed to are obstacles to being promoted and the sexist perceptions that men at work have of them (Weber and Higginbotham 1995). The obstacles that women encounter at work have popularly come to be known as the **glass ceiling.** This phrase is meant to convey the fact that, even though most formal barriers to women's advancement have been removed, there are invisible mechanisms that prevent women from advancing. These mechanisms are "invisible" because they are built into the social structure of organizations, and they are not as obvious as formal restrictions and rules that discriminate against women. Still, they are such powerful barriers that, as late as 1995, a federal panel, the Glass Ceiling Commission, appointed by then Senate Majority Leader Robert Dole, issued a report concluding that, despite three decades of policies meant to address inequality in the labor market, women and minorities are still substantially blocked from senior management positions (Glass Ceiling Commission 1995; Naff and Thomas 1995).

What evidence, or lack thereof, is there of women's advancement in the workplace? Most studies find that women are actually promoted more often than men—that is, if promotion means moving from one job classification to another. However, for women, promotions are most likely to be lateral (i.e., from one location in an occupational system to another of similar rank and status), whereas men's promotions are more likely to be vertical (i.e., upward in the job ranks). Even when men and women have the same qualifications (i.e., education and prior experience), they seldom receive similar promotions. One source of the problem is that men and women may begin in different entry-level positions in an organization, with the positions men enter being those that are more likely to lead to upward mobility in the organization (DiPrete 1989; H. Smith 1998).

Researchers also find that the gender composition of an occupation affects the likelihood of women being hired and promoted in this occupation. Specifically, women are more likely hired and promoted into jobs with a high proportion of women. This is not just a statistical effect, since women are also more likely to be promoted in an occupation when there is a substantial minority of women in the level above. This indicates that women are more likely to be promoted when other women have gone before them (Cohen et al. 1998). The glass ceiling is even more of a barrier for women of color. Women of color are the most underrepresented group in senior management positions, and they are most frequently excluded from the most powerful positions in work organizations. Institutionalized practices that identify White men as leaders and others as just workers continue to disadvantage women and people of color who then get "niched" in parts of the organization where career ladders are nonexistent. Even when White women and men and women of color are promoted, they generally have to wait longer than White men (Ridgeway 2001; Cotter et al. 2001; Maume 1999; Baxter and Wright 2000; Durbin 2002; Porter 2003).

Job ladders in organizations reveal the organization's hierarchy as well as the chances for ongoing promotions in certain positions. This concept of job ladders reflects the fact that some jobs are more likely to be those that lead to mobility than others. Jobs where men predominate are less likely to be dead-end jobs (Baron et al. 1986). Unlike men, women tend to be stuck in jobs with fewer chances for continuing upward mobility. Secretarial work provides a good example. In most organizations, there is a top limit to the "grade" of the highest secretaries in the organization. Beyond that, it is rare for secretaries to move into higher positions where there are additional career ladders. As a result, a secretary might move from being a clerk-typist to an office supervisor, but will seldom move out of this job classification to a job defined as more professional and with more chances for advancement (such as an administrative assistant or manager), even though the skills in these jobs may be the same. This has led observers to say that not only is there is a glass ceiling for women in work organizations but there is also a "sticky floor" (Berheide 1992).

Whether looking at pay, location, or promotions, research on women and work consistently finds that, despite much change over recent years, structural obstacles to women's advancement in the labor force persist. Moreover, gender patterns in the labor market are compounded by race. Thus, Black women are more likely to be laid off than White women (Reid 2002). Although structural barriers of gender and race are not the same formal barriers of the past, they have similar effects. The point is that these barriers are structured into the character of the workplace, not just in the intentions of individual women and men. Although many women choose to work in historically women's work or some choose to put their priorities on personal and family matters rather than career mobility, even more women than in the past perceive that there is discrimination against women in the workplace. Only 32 percent of women in the United States think women and men have equal job opportunities, although a majority of men (53 percent) think so. One-quarter of women say they experience discrimination on a frequent basis (Saad 2001b).

❖ Poverty and Welfare

One of the consequences of women's status in the labor market is the high rate of poverty among women and their children (see Figure 5.6). The **poverty line** is an index developed by the Social Security Administration. It is based on the lowest cost for a nutritionally adequate food plan (as developed by the Department of Agriculture). The poverty line (based also on family size) is calculated by multiplying the cost of this food plan by three (assuming that a family spends one-third of its budget on food), adjusted by the Consumer Price Index. In 2004, the official poverty line for a family of four was $18,725.

Gender differences in poverty have increased in recent years, partially because of the fact that women now, unlike in the past, are more likely to be financially responsible for their children. This trend toward more of the poor being women and children is called the **feminization of poverty.** In 2003, the median family income for all families was $53,991, but in family households headed by women (with no husband present) median income was $29,307, with significant differences by race (see Figure 5.5). The most prosperous families are White families with both husband and wife present and both working. As you will see in the next chapter, although these families in some ways define the cultural ideal, they are by no means the statistical norm in contemporary U.S. society.

In 2003, 30 percent of all female-headed households (no husband present) lived below the official poverty line; 39 percent of Black and Hispanic female-headed households and 24 percent of Asian American families headed by women lived below the poverty line, compared with 21 percent of White, non-Hispanic female-headed households. One consequence of increasing poverty among women who head families is an ever-growing number of children who are poor. Thirty percent of Black and Hispanic children, 12.5 percent of Asian American children, and 9.5 percent of White, non-Hispanic children lived in poverty (see Figure 5.7). Note that

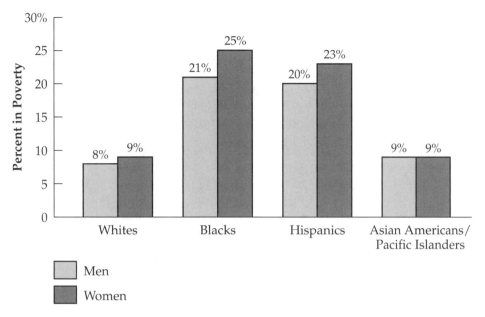

FIGURE 5.6   People in Poverty

Sources: Data from U.S. Census Bureau, 2004. *Poverty in the United States: 2003, Detailed Tables.* Table POV02. http://www.census.gov

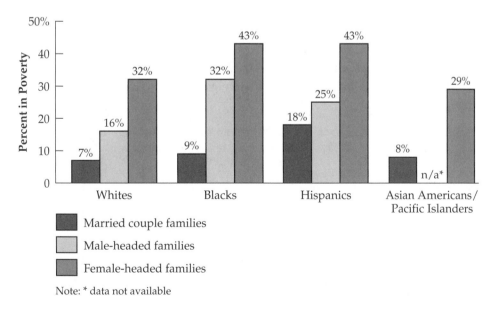

Note: * data not available

FIGURE 5.7   Poverty Status of Families with Children under 18 by Race and Household Type

Source: Data from U.S. Census Bureau. 2004. *Detailed Poverty Tables 2003.* Table POV04. http://www.census.gov

despite images of being the "model minority," poverty rates among Asian Americans are higher than among Whites; among Asian Americans poverty is highest among the most recent Asian immigrants and varies dramatically across Asian Americans of different national origins (Lee 1994; DeNavas-Walt 2004).

Limited opportunities for women in the labor market are a major cause of poverty. In addition to their secondary employment status, women's continuing responsibilities for child rearing, in the absence of adequate day care and other social supports, tend to leave them poor.

Women in poverty have been the focus of much public debate in recent years, particularly with regard to welfare. Welfare reform has been based on the assumption that welfare recipients need to work, with new welfare laws stipulating work requirements and time limits to welfare receipt. Until 1996, the major national welfare program was Aid to Families with Dependent Children (AFDC). This program was eliminated in 1996 with the passage of the **Personal Responsibility and Work Reconciliation Act,** generally known as "welfare reform." The new law places a lifetime limit of 5 years on receiving welfare and requires all welfare recipients to find work within 2 years—a policy known as *workfare.*

The new law gives block grants to states to administer their own welfare programs—now called **Temporary Assistance to Needy Families (TANF).** Under the new law, states can impose stricter time limits and work requirements than the federal law requires. The federal law also requires teen mothers to continue residing with their families if they are to receive welfare and also requires them to identify the father of their child. Many states have also refused to increase support payments for women who have additional children—a policy based on the erroneous assumption that women only have more children to increase the size of their support checks.

The work requirements of the new welfare policies have had mixed results. Many former welfare recipients did find jobs, although studies show that the jobs they get are poorly paid and do not allow them to get the education and training needed to improve their status in the labor market (Ntiri 2000; Cancian and Meyer 2000; Institute for Women's Policy Research 2001). The bureaucratic entanglements of TANF have also frustrated both welfare clients and workers in welfare offices (Hays 2003).

At the heart of public debate about welfare is the idea that poor people do not want to work and that providing public assistance encourages dependency. Studies show, however, that the low-wage work the poor may find is simply not enough to lift them out of poverty (McCrate and Smith 1998). Most poor women have to combine low-wage work with public assistance and support from family and friends to make ends meet. Even then, most poor and low-income women find a wide gap between what they need to support their family and what they have available through welfare support. Contrary to public myths, poor women have aspirations to find better work, move to better neighborhoods, buy their children good clothes, and have a nest egg for emergencies. They just find it impossible to do so on the limited resources available to them (Edin and Lein 1997; Hays 2003).

Moreover, much of the public seems to misunderstand other facts about poor women. Most women work. Even prior to welfare reform, poor women often left welfare for work, but found themselves in even more difficulty. The jobs poor women find tend to be low paying and unattractive, and child care is hard to come by (and to afford). Given the nature of the jobs most likely available to them, many find that they lose health insurance when they work or may experience violence from boyfriends and husbands who feel threatened by their becoming more independent by working. Sociologists have actually found that the exit from poverty is actually hastened when welfare benefits are higher, since higher payments give recipients the support they need to find job training and child care so that they can make the transition to a decent job (Butler 1996).

The connection made in the public eye between welfare, work, and poverty also ignores the vast numbers of people (women and men) who are employed and are nonetheless poor—a group known as the *working poor.* The poverty rate among employed women is higher than for men, obviously because of the lower wages women are paid. And, 9 percent of female-headed households where the female head worked full-time and year round were still poor (U.S. Census Bureau 2003).

Still, the myth abounds that welfare has nothing but negative consequences for women. In one sense, it does, since the stigma associated with welfare makes welfare recipients more secretive about how they put resources together to survive. It tends to affect their self-esteem, making it more difficult for them to act on their own behalf. Most often, people go on welfare because of life events over which they have little control (unemployment, divorce, poor health, racism, battering, etc.). Constructing a support system that enables people to survive such problems seems a far more humane way to build society than the victim-blaming reforms that have dominated social policy in recent years (Abramovitz 1996; Dujon and Withorn 1996).

Many have argued that the poverty rate among female-headed households is high because the male provider role has become "optional," but the preceding analysis suggests something quite different: Only policies specifically designed to improve women's status, not just return men to families or women to the labor force as is, are likely to alleviate the problem of poverty among women and their children.

❖ Work Environments

Women's experiences at work are not just a function of earnings, promotions, and placement in the labor force. Within a work organization, one's ability to succeed, to be influential, and to be satisfied with work are also shaped by the organizational climate. Factors such as tokenism, sexual harassment, and negative workplace cultures are characteristics of many of the work organizations.

Tokenism

The experience of women in organizations is influenced by the proportions in which they find themselves. Rosabeth Moss Kanter (1977) has identified four types of groups in work organizations, based on the numerical proportions in which different kinds of people are represented. The first is the *uniform group,* which has only one kind of person (e.g., all men or all White). *Skewed groups* are those in which there is a great preponderance of one type of person over another (e.g., a group that is 85 percent men and 15 percent women). In skewed groups, those in the numerical minority are identified as tokens. Third are *tilted groups,* in which there are less exaggerated differences, but in which one group still forms a clear majority (e.g., a group in which men constitute 65 percent of the group population and women 35 percent). Kanter argues that in tilted groups, minority members have the opportunity to form alliances with each other and can form coalitions and can begin to affect the culture of the group. Finally is the *balanced group,* one close to a fifty-fifty proportion of social types. Kanter suggests that only in balanced groups will organizational outcomes for individuals depend more on structural and personal factors than on the dynamics established by the group itself.

Most women entering traditionally male-dominated occupations find themselves in skewed groups where they are tokens; the same is true for people of color in predominantly White organizations. In such groups, tokens stand out in contrast to other members of the group; group dynamics will usually reflect these contrasts. The presence of tokens heightens the boundaries between different groups. For instance, members of the dominant group become more self-conscious of what they have in common, and they might "test" tokens to see how they respond to, for example, male culture. This means that in skewed groups, the contrast between tokens and the majority becomes exaggerated in social interaction. In skewed groups, tokens also receive extra attention and are more easily stereotyped than are those found in greater proportions in social groups. Kanter argues that these perceptual tendencies—visibility, contrast, and assimilation—put more performance pressures on tokens, because they live life in the limelight. At the same time, tokens may be more closely supervised, given "silent" treatment, or not be given the training and direction required in a job (Yoder and Aniakudo 1997).

Tokens respond to these performance pressures in a variety of ways. One response is overachievement, in which tokens try to gain more control over the extra attention given to their actions; this may, however, be difficult to accomplish, especially for those who are new to organizations. It also involves creating a delicate balance between doing well and not causing too much resentment among the majority. Tokens may also try to turn the notoriety of their uniqueness to advantage—for example, by flaunting their "only woman manager in the company" status. Kanter argues, however, that this strategy of response reinforces the dynamics of tokenism and disadvantages other women. Third, she says that tokens may respond to performance pressures by trying to become socially invisible, perhaps through dressing "like a man," keeping a very low social profile, working at home, or avoiding risks.

Kanter's research shows that a mere shift in numbers has the potential to transform the working experience of all members of an organization. Her work also shows, in a unique way, how the structure of groups themselves influences the organizational structure and climate of occupational settings. Some researchers have argued that by focusing on numbers alone, Kanter's work underestimates the backlash that men direct against women upon women's desegregation of traditionally male jobs. Research has shown that the negative consequences of tokenism are far more acute for members of groups who enter occupations defined as inappropriate for them and who have lower social status than the dominant group. Upper-status tokens (such as men who enter traditionally female occupations) actually experience rapid upward mobility and are more likely to be seen as innovators than are women in similar token positions (Yoder 1991). Such findings do not discount Kanter's analysis but show how the interplay of numbers, dominant group behavior, and social-structural context affect the experience of minorities in the workplace.

Sexual Harassment

Sexual harassment is defined as the unwanted imposition of sexual requirements in the context of a relationship of unequal power. Sexual harassment was first defined as constituting illegal discrimination by Title VII of the Civil Rights Bill of 1964. A landmark Supreme Court decision in 1986, ***Meritor Savings Bank* v. *Vinson,*** ruled that sexual harassment violates federal laws against discrimination. This decision makes sexual harassment unconstitutional.

There are a number of social myths about sexual harassment, including the myths that it affects only a few, that women ask for it, and that charges of sexual harassment are usually false. As a result of these myths, a woman may find it hard to speak out against sexual harassment because the myths establish the tendency for others to blame her. Often when women have spoken out about harassment, they have been ignored, discredited, or accused of misunderstanding the intentions of the other parties. The unveiling of sexual harassment as a serious issue affecting work environments for women has forced employers to create policies designed to deal with sexual harassment. The Supreme Court has made it clear that sexual harassment is a violation of the law, and public scandals have called attention to the seriousness of the problem.

Accurate counts of the extent of sexual harassment in the workplace are difficult to establish. Sexual harassment occurs in every kind of work setting and results in a number of problems, including stress, job turnover, depression, and physical illness (O'Connell and Korabik 2000). Researchers also find that the experience of sexual harassment varies, depending on whether it occurs in an area of traditional women's work or in areas where women are entering traditionally male occupations. In traditional women's occupations, sexual harassment is characterized by the threat of losing a job for failing to comply with sexual demands; the harasser in those settings is typically a supervisor. On the other hand, women entering traditionally male occupations encounter more sexual harassment, making it seem that harassment is a form of retaliation directed against women for threatening male economic and social status (Mansfield et al. 1991). In these settings, harassment expresses men's resentment of the presence of women. It can be more difficult for women workers in these jobs to bring charges of harassment, because their harassers are more likely to be co-workers.

Sexual harassment is fundamentally a matter of the misuse of power and it is deeply linked to gender attitudes. Men are more tolerant of sexual harassment than are women and women are more likely to see things such as sexist comments, verbal sexual advances, invitations for dates, and sexual propositions as sexual harassment than are men (McKinney and Crittenden 1992).

Workplace Culture

In addition to having interest in the social-structural characteristics of women's work on the employed labor force, feminist scholars are also interested in the cultures in work organizations. Work environments shape the experience of women (and men) at work, just as objective rewards can shape the work experience. Studies of gay and lesbian work experiences show that many fear they will suffer adverse career consequences if co-workers know they are lesbian, bisexual, or gay. This leads many to pass as heterosexual at work or keep their private lives secret, but being closeted at work puts workers at a disadvantage, since it isolates them from social networks in the workplace. Having to "manage" one's identity at work is stressful (Schmidt 2003; Chrobot-Mason et al. 2001). Studies show, however, that gay employees' relationships with co-workers are less stressful when the employee is "out," since gay workers no longer fear and anticipate rejection. When closeted, gays and lesbians are likely to be distant and avoid interpersonal contact to shield themselves from antagonism, resulting in potentially low performance reviews because they appear to be unfriendly, boring, and withdrawn (Schneider 1984; Badgett and King 1997).

Studies of work culture have found that women employ a variety of strategies to resist the male-dominated culture of organizations. Women's work culture is the ideology, rituals, and practices through which women forge a relatively autonomous sphere on the job. By sharing photographs, celebrating birthdays, elaborating informal norms among themselves about office procedures and norms, and developing other forms of women's culture at work, women exercise some control over the meaning and character of their work (Melosh 1982; Benson 1978).

Women's culture in the workplace can be the basis for political organization, resistance to oppression, and the creation of solidarity among workers. Recognizing and studying women's culture in the workplace shows how groups that lack power collectively define their positions and use their informal relations to adapt to or resist powerlessness. Although these informal relations may soften exploitative work conditions by humanizing the work force (Lamphere 1984), they can also be the basis for militant job actions (Costello 1985). As Zavella's (1985) research on Chicana cannery workers shows, in a labor market where workers are divided along race and sex lines, women's culture can create both ethnic and racial solidarity while also generating gender consciousness within exploitative work conditions.

❖ Intersections of Family and Work

For many years, studies of work presumed that work was separate from family life—as if work and family were separate spheres of life. This assumption reflected the sexist idea that men's place was in the work world and women's place was in the family. New studies of women and work (and, now, men and work) have shown this not to be the case. Quite the contrary is true: Work and family are strongly intertwined (Moen 2004). You will see this further in the following chapter on families, but this relationship is apparent in studying work, especially when considering the amount of work that people do (counting both paid, unpaid, labor force, and household work), and by reconceptualizing housework as work, not just as family activity.

The Second Shift

Studies of employed women have all concluded that women work a double day. That is, if they are employed for wages in the labor market, when they are home, they work a **second shift** (Hochschild 1989). This term refers to the work women do at home in addition to time spent in paid employment. Economists estimate that even middle-class women are working longer hours—an estimated increase of 12 weeks per year since 1979 (Mishel et al. 2003). Adding this to the number of hours women spend doing housework and child care has resulted in a substantial speedup in the amount of work that women are doing.

Contemporary sociologist Arlie Hochschild has studied the effect of speed-up on families. Based on extensive interviews with women and men in dual-career families, Hochschild found that women develop a variety of strategies for coping with these demands of the second shift. Some feign helplessness over certain tasks as a way to get men to do them. Others avoid conflict by taking on the work themselves. Some cut back on their expectations about what is necessary in the home or reduce their working hours. Often, women turn to women friends and family members for help or, if they have the economic ability, pay other women to work for them. Some try to be "supermoms;" those who do report feeling "numb" and out of touch with their feelings. In any case, women typically pay the greater price of this added household stress (Hochschild 1989).

Hochschild (1997) has also shown that, as more women have entered the paid labor force, life for most people centers more and more on work. The tensions then created at home mean that many women and men run their families like efficiency experts, having to manage time spent in child care, leisure activity, and household chores as if they were managers of their personal lives. Ironically, Hochschild's research also finds that, even in corporations with "family-friendly" policies (flextime, child care facilities, etc.), workers underutilize these benefits. Instead, people work more and more, often not using vacation benefits, even when they feel there is a time deficit in their lives. Why? Based on her research, Hochschild concludes that the "time bind" and stress that people feel at home means that they find more satisfaction and pleasure at work than they do at home. In her words, the social worlds of work and home have been reversed, with people feeling more "at home" at work and "at work" when home.

Housework and Care Work

The second shift shows that not all women's labor is paid labor, but, because the concept of work has been tied to paid employment, housework has long gone unrecognized as work, even though it is socially and economically necessary. The work that housewives do not only takes care of people's basic needs—food, shelter, and clothing—but also socializes new members of the society. Housework benefits employers, too, because housework sustains workers, making it possible for them to return to the labor force. Social myths about housework show us the contradictions that pervade our images of the work women do in the home. On the one hand, to be a housewife is idealized as a desirable goal for women; at the same time, however, housework is depicted as drudgery and menial labor. Both images obscure the fact that, for most women, housework is time consuming as well as physically and psychologically demanding, even though it can also be a source of satisfaction.

In advertisements women are surrounded by happy families and a wealth of material goods. The housewife in these ads is usually cheerful, buoyant, and smiling, although pathologically obsessed with cleanliness and food. Although housework is seen as glamorous, housewives are also ridiculed as scatterbrained, lazy, and disorganized. Anyone who has seen comic strip and greeting card depictions of a housewife standing bedraggled with an apron around her waist, a broom in her hand, and a cigarette dangling from her mouth has seen one facet of the contemporary myth about housework.

More recently, traditional images of housewives are being replaced by proclamations of the virtues of being a "stay-at-home mom." Numerous media reports have featured vignettes of women, once employed, who have decided to stay home to take care of their children full–time. Popular news outlets have also frequently featured stories and advice about women escaping the stress of combining work and family by becoming full-time mothers and wives.

Women who make this choice say they are largely satisfied with this arrangement (Riday 2003). Only time will tell if these marriages remain intact, if the women are later able to return to work at the same level at which they left, or women's economic dependence on men produces other problems, as historically happened for well-educated, economically dependent women in the 1950s.

Although feminists would say there is nothing inherently wrong with the choice to stay at home, it is not a choice for most women who must work to support their families—either as single heads-of-household or because the family needs their income to make ends meet. It is, in fact, telling that the women most often featured in the media as choosing to stay at home have considerable financial resources—most often through being married to economically successful men.

However the media idealizes stay-at-home moms, the reality is that most women simply cannot do this. Income data show that there is a 58 percent income gap between married-couple families where the wife is in the paid labor force—and the gap is even wider for African American families. Moreover, married-couple families where the wife is not employed fall below the national median income level (U.S. Census Bureau 2003). Put simply, families need women's incomes to make ends meet, so the idealized stay-at-home mom is a choice available only to those of certain socioeconomic classes.

Care work refers to all the forms of labor (including unpaid work) that is needed to nurture, reproduce, and sustain people—in other words, work that is critical to the maintenance of social life. This includes child care and housework, but also care for older family members, those with disabilities, and the mental work required to manage a household. When you consider all these forms of work, much of it unpaid, you see how essential women's work is to the maintenance of society. Despite changes in gender attitudes and roles in recent years, women continue to do the vast majority of such work, whether they are employed outside the home or not.

Studies show a strong gender division of labor in care work. This is conditioned, to some extent, by women's and men's employment patterns, as well as by the presence of children, men's and women's attitudes, and learned patterns of who does care work. Men married to women who work full time tend to do more housework (Stier and Lewin-Epstein 2000). Men also tend to reduce the time they have previously spent in housework when they enter a coupled relationship with a woman (Gupta 1999) Studies also find that men tend to overestimate the time they spend in housework, but women do not (Kamo 2000). Women's housework also increases when they marry, compared to when they were single. Even among children, there is a gender gap in the amount of housework that boys and girls do—a gap that increases in the high school years (Gager et al. 1999).

Some studies find that people spend somewhat less time in domestic labor now than in the past, although time spent in child care and shopping has remained stable (Bianchi 2000; Bianchi et al. 2000; Bianchi and Mattingly 2004). Also, the expansion of paid domestic work has occurred alongside the increased labor force participation of middle- class women; at the same time, that work has become strongly racialized—that is, most likely to be performed by women of color (Hondagneu-Sotelo 2001).

Tensions over who does the housework are a significant source of conflict within relationships between men and women (Stohs 1995). Both men and women tend to regard housework as "women's work," but men who have a more subordinated place in the workplace seem most likely to think this, leading scholars to conclude that doing housework is connected to men's gendered identities at work as well as at home (Arrighi and Maume 2000). Patterns of time spent in housework are also related to mental health. There is a clear relationship between time spent in housework and depression, with depression increasing with more time spent in housework (Glass and Fujimoto 1994; Bird and Fremont 1999; Strazdins and Broom 2004; Riley and Keith 2003). Also, when men increase the time they spend doing housework, their level of stress also increases—a pattern long noted for women (Marshall and Barnett 1995). Differences in the amount of housework men and women do also mean that men have more leisure than women, as well as more time to invest in careers (Sirianni and Negrey 2000).

Studies of care work also show that the amount of work men do is strongly influenced by the social structure of the family in which they were raised. Sociologists Naomi Gertsel and Sally Gallagher studied whether men's participation in care work is influenced most by their attitudes about gender equality or the structure of their families. They found that the characteristics of the men's families were the strongest influence on their engagement in care work. Men with more sisters spent less time helping with elder parents than men with fewer sisters. Furthermore, men's employment (hours employed, job flexibility, or job stability) had no effect on their involvement in care work. Gerstel and Gallagher concluded that, "It is primarily the women in men's lives who shape the amount and types of care men provide" (2001: 211).

Care work in this society is organized and conceived primarily as a private service. Of course, as we saw in the previous chapter, some care work is paid labor, although it is among the least compensated forms of work. Hospital orderlies, food service workers, child care workers, and other paid care workers typically labor in some of the most devalued jobs in society.

The history of housework also shows that how this work is organized changes over time and with transformation in gender relations in society more broadly. The earliest information on housework was gathered in the 1920s under the guise of the new science of home economics and its emphasis on rational management (Vanek 1978). In 1900, most U.S. homes had no electricity and no running water; in 1920, one-third of U.S. families still lived on farms. By the 1920s, a variety of canned and processed foods had become available, reducing the time a housewife spent producing and preparing food. By the 1930s, approximately 60 percent of homes in the United States had electricity, opening the way for mechanical refrigerators and washing machines and gas and electric ranges. By 1940, 70 percent of U.S. homes had indoor plumbing; in the 1950s, automatic washers replaced wringers; and in the 1960s, women's laundry work was changed by the introduction of dryers and wash-and-wear fabrics (Cowan 1976; Vanek 1978). In the 1970s, the fast-food industry offered to take the work of the housewife out of the home, although microwave ovens, food processors, and computerized home management systems increased the expectations of women's laboring within the home.

Although these technological and commercial developments created the potential for reducing women's work as housewives, ideological changes as well as actual changes in the requirements of housework have contributed to the demands on the housewife's time. For instance, the amount of time spent on food preparation, cleaning, and sewing and mending has decreased. The introduction of cheaper clothing and linens means, however, that there is more clothing and linen per household; consequently, the time spent doing laundry has increased. The invention of the automobile and the development of suburbs means that housewives spend more time transporting family members and shopping. Housewives' managerial tasks in the household have increased as financial and medical records, grocery lists, deliveries, and repairs have become routine work (Vanek 1978). As child care has become more the work of individuals, not extended families, the amount of time spent on child care has remained stable, even though people now have fewer children (Bianchi 2000).

The evolution of changes in household labor is part of the more general changes that have occurred in the relationship of the household to the economy and is also related to changes in the economic structure of life. The isolation of women's work in the home is not inevitable; indeed, anthropological evidence reveals the extraordinarily complex and varied structure of women's lives in different cultures. Not always is the domestic sphere separate from the so-called public world of work (Lamphere 2001). Women's lives at work and in domestic life are also often recognized and valued. Anthropological evidence also indicates that women have more egalitarian roles in those societies where individuals are directly dependent on the well-being of the society as a whole, where there is no structural dichotomy between the public and domestic worlds, and where those who make decisions also carry them out (Leacock 1978).

❖ *Policies for Gender Equity*

The social changes witnessed in gender relations in recent history have been the result of many groups mobilizing for change. As a result, specific policies form a framework by which some greater gender equity has been achieved, even though more needs to be done.

The **Equal Pay Act of 1963** was the first federal legislation enacted requiring equal pay for equal work; it has been extended by various executive orders and civil rights acts to forbid discrimination on the basis of sex. Title VI of the Civil Rights Act of 1964 forbids discrimination against students on the basis of race, color, or national origin in all federally assisted programs. **Title VII of the Civil Rights Bill of 1964,** amended by the Equal Employment Opportunity Act of 1972, forbids discrimination on the basis of race, color, national origin, religion, or sex in any term, condition, or privilege of employment. This law was amended in 1972 to cover all private and public educational institutions, as well as state and local governments. Title VII was a path-breaking law for women, as it established the principle of equal rights in federal law and opened the door for women's participation in education, employment, and athletics, to name some of its major areas of impact.

Title IX of the Educational Amendments of 1972 has been especially significant in opening up athletic opportunities for women and girls. Title IX forbids gender discrimination in any educational institution receiving federal funds, thus prohibiting schools, colleges, and universities from receiving federal funds if they discriminate against women in any program, including athletics. Adoption of this legislation radically altered the opportunities available to women in sports and has transformed the face of student athletics. Indeed, this legislation laid the foundation for many of the coeducational programs that are now an ordinary part of student life.

Now, however, Title IX is under significant threat from those who see it as having taken away opportunities for men—a perception not well supported by evidence. Some college sports for men have been eliminated, though most argue that this has been the result of budget pressures on schools, not the direct result of Title IX. Proponents of maintaining strong enforcement of Title IX have argued that men still dominate in school and college sports, especially when you consider the resources provided to football—a sport that, to date, still largely excludes women.

Although federal laws do forbid discrimination in employment, feminists have argued that because women tend to be located in different occupations than men, equal pay for equal work will by itself be adequate to eliminate wage inequities in the paid labor force. **Comparable worth** is the principle of paying women and men equivalent wages for jobs involving comparable levels of skill. Assessing comparable worth requires measuring the skill levels of comparable jobs and developing correlated pay scales, regardless of the sex of the job occupants. Comparable worth is an important concept for women workers and one that organizes workers for collective action against wage discrimination (Blum 1986).

Comparable worth goes beyond the concept of equal pay for equal work by creating job evaluation systems that assess the degree of similarity between different kinds of jobs. In places where comparable worth has been used as a method for evaluating women's and men's work, it has improved women's wages (Steinberg 1992; Jacobs and Steinberg 1990), but it has also been resisted by businesses, probably because they recognize the economic cost that would come from reassessing and increasing the worth of the work that women do.

Another public policy that has proven of great importance in bringing new opportunities to women and racial minority groups in the labor market is **affirmative action.** Affirmative action has now become one of the most controversial policies for creating better opportunities for members of historically disadvantaged groups. Affirmative action developed as a policy referring to positive efforts taken to open new areas of opportunity to groups who had previously been excluded from such jobs. Typically, an affirmative action program would identify the potential pool of eligible (i.e., qualified) workers in a given occupational category and then require employers to develop recruitment mechanisms to ensure fair opportunities to members of these groups. It includes such actions as advertising for jobs in places where women and minorities are likely to see job postings, instead of relying on word of mouth and "White men's networks" to recruit able applicants. Affirmative action policies have forced organizations to develop fair rules and uniform recruitment procedures so that some groups do not have an advantage over others.

Contrary to popular opinion, affirmative action does not set rigid quotas for jobs, although it does set goals or targets for different jobs, depending on the number of qualified women and minorities in the available pool. Affirmative action has also forced employers to think carefully about what the term *qualified* means; perhaps this is what has been most controversial. For example, in some jobs, performance on a written test is an important part of the application procedure, but affirmative action can mean that someone with a somewhat lower score on the test may, for other reasons, be seen as more qualified than someone whose test scores are slightly higher. If the person with the lower score is hired, it does not mean that person is not qualified (since he or she would not be hired with a significantly lower score), only that additional factors constitute the qualifications for the job. Affirmative action has also meant that diversifying the work force is itself a desirable goal.

Affirmative action has been under sharp attack from groups who perceive it as taking away opportunities from Whites and men. The fact remains, however, that it has been critical to the success of women and people of color. The fact that it is now being so vigorously opposed by various groups shows that it has had a strong effect in opening opportunities to groups that historically have been disadvantaged because they were not White or male. Affirmative action was also upheld as constitutional by an important Supreme Court decision in 2004 involving college admissions programs (see also Chapter 11). Critics of affirmative action argue that race-blind and gender-blind policies are the only fair way to proceed, but most feminists and civil rights advocates would argue that, as the evidence in this chapter would support, as long as the society is structured (even in less-visible ways) along gender-, class-, and race-stratified lines, seemingly "neutral" or color-blind policies cannot transform the institutional structures that have developed specifically out of gender and race inequities.

❖ *Chapter Summary and Themes*

The history of women's work shows that gender is linked to transformations in the structure of labor and its relationship to household, including the social structures of race and class.

The historic move to a cash-based economy created the family wage system, based on the presumption that men were the primary breadwinners and that women worked at home. This is despite the fact that working-class women and women of color have long worked for wages. The specific histories of women of color also show that their labor has been exploited for the gain of others.

Women's status in the economy is typically buttressed by ideologies that define their work as less significant than that of men.

Historically, the cult of domesticity for White, bourgeois women defined their role as in the home. Contemporary definitions of work continue to show how women's labor is often considered a "labor of love" and thus unpaid and devalued.

Economic restructuring is producing new forms of gender stratification.

Economic restructuring includes the transition to a service-based economy, increasing globalization, enhanced use of technology, and concentration of economic resources in the hands of a few. These changes in the social organization of work have specific consequences for gender stratification, particularly in increasing the proportion of low-paying, service sector jobs—jobs that are generally filled by women and people of color.

Gender stratification is reflected in the status of women in diverse occupational categories.

Gender segregation persists throughout the labor market resulting in a concentration of women in certain occupational categories. Gender segregation is one major source for the gender gap in earnings.

Multiple factors explain the persistent gap in earnings between women and men.

The most significant explanations of the pay gap include overt discrimination, human capital theory (that is, the characteristics that workers bring to the labor market), and the presence of a dual labor market in which gender and race and class segregation persist.

Women's status in the economy is resulting in high rates of poverty among women and their children.

Poverty has been increasing in recent years and is concentrated among women and their children. Welfare reform has attempted to reduce poverty by requiring recipients to work, but studies are showing that welfare recipients continue to be blamed for their own situation, despite the lack of social supports provided to lift people out of poverty.

Work environments for women are generally marked by male-dominated cultures that affect women's well-being and opportunities for advancement.

Patterns of tokenism plague women and minority groups in the labor market, producing social stresses that affect physical and mental health, as well as opportunities for promotion. Sexual harassment, though illegal, also permeates workplaces, especially where women are entering occupations traditionally dominated by men.

Work and families are social institutions that are deeply intertwined in ways that are manifested in the second shift of work that women provide in the home.

Even with more women working in the paid labor force, a gender division of labor persists in household and other forms of care work. Women continue to provide more of this work that, even though sometimes glamorized, is generally devalued and rarely equally shared.

❖ *Key Terms*

affirmative action	family-consumer economy	second shift
care work	family-wage economy	sexual harassment
class	feminization of poverty	sweatshop
class stratification	gender segregation	Temporary Assistance to Needy
comparable worth	gender stratification	Families (TANF)
contingent workers	glass ceiling	Title VII of the Civil Rights Bill
discrimination	human capital theory	of 1964
dual labor market theory	*Meritor Savings Bank* v. *Vinson*	Title IX of the Educational
economic restructuring	Personal Responsibility and	Amendments of 1972
emotional labor	Work Reconciliation Act,	
Equal Pay Act of 1963	1996	
family-based economy	poverty line	

❖ *Discussion Questions/Projects for Thought*

1. Using the Table 5.1 on page 111, calculate women's median weekly earnings in each occupational category as a percentage of men's earnings. In which occupations do women more closely approximate men's earnings? In which is there is the largest gap? Do the gaps appear to be related to the percentage of women in the occupation? (Note that these are selected occupations; if you want to see the full list, go to the library and look in the

January edition of *Employment and Earnings* under Annual Averages, as published by the U.S. Department of Labor.)

2. Give yourself a monthly budget of $1,560 (approximately the monthly amount that you would have if you lived at the federal poverty line). Imagine that you head your own household, with three children. Using prices from the area where you live, develop a monthly budget to account for everything you have to spend to get by. What would your life be like, and what would your children's lives be like?

What does this exercise teach you about contemporary images of people from low-income families?

3. Ask several young men and women how they expect to balance work and family commitments in the future. Then interview several people who are currently employed about how they balance these commitments. What do your interviews about expectations and current realities suggest for future social policies to support families and workers?

❖ *Internet Resources*

U.S. Census Bureau

http://www.census.gov

The Census Bureau Website includes numerous reports from the Current Population Survey that provides data on men's and women's median income, which was also surveyed according to an array of variables, such as educational level, family status, occupation, age, and race, among other factors.

U.S. Department of Labor

http://www.dol.gov

This website provides much information about the U.S. labor force, including such topics as employment, unemployment, job benefits, and occupational outlook data.

Institute for Women's Policy Research

http://www.iwpr.org

The Institute for Women's Policy Research is a nonprofit research organization that analyzes policy issues of importance to women. Their website includes data and information on policy initiatives involving work/family issues, the economic and social aspects of health care and domestic violence, and women's civic and political participation.

The Women's Bureau of the U.S. Department of Labor

http://www.dol.gov/wb

This division of the Department of Labor was created in 1920 with the purpose of promoting the interests of women at work. The website includes numerous resources, including data on employed women, as well as policy initiatives.

❖ *Suggested Readings*

Amott, Teresa L., and Julie A. Matthaei. 1996. *Race, Gender, and Work: A Multicultural History of Women in the United States*, 2nd ed. Boston: South End Press.
Based on an analysis of the intersections of race, class, and gender in the labor market, this book presents the histories of the work of women of color and White women

workers. It is an excellent introduction to the experiences of different women in the United States.
Ehrenreich, Barbara. 2001. *Nickel and Dimed: On "Not" Getting By in America.* New York: Metropolitan Books.
Ehrenreich, a noted feminist journalist, worked for six months as a low-wage

worker in several different jobs and writes about the experience "from the inside." Her book, which became a national bestseller, exposes the hard work and degrading conditions that characterizes the labor of millions of women.

Hays, Sharon. 2003. *Flat Broke with Children: Women in the Age of Welfare Reform.* New York: Oxford University Press.
This award-winning book is based on close observation of two welfare offices following the implementation of welfare reform. It is a poignant and revealing study of the impact of welfare reform on the women who receive it, as well as those who work in welfare offices.

Higginbotham, Elizabeth. 2001. *Too Much To Ask: Black Women in the Era of Integration.* Chapel Hill: University of North Carolina Press.
Based on interviews with African American women who were among the first to be college-educated professionals, Higginbotham's research explores how race and gender shape the context of African American women's experiences and how they cope with conditions that assault their dignity as human beings.

Hochschild, Arlie Russell. 1997. *The Time Bind: When Work Becomes Home and Home Becomes Work.* New York: Metropolitan Books.
Wondering why workers in the corporation she studied seldom took advantage of so-called family-friendly policies, Hochschild argues that people have to structure family life like efficiency experts and act devoted to work—an emotional commitment historically more associated with family life.

Hondagneu-Sotelo, Pierrette. 2001. *Doméstica: Immigrant Workers Cleaning and Caring in the Shadows of Affluence.* Berkeley: University of California Press.
This study of Latina domestics analyzes the complex class and race relations between domestic workers and their employers. The analysis also locates domestic workers within the context of global economic restructuring and the new dynamics of family and work that this creates.

Padavic, Irene, and Barbara Reskin. 2002. *Women and Men at Work,* 2nd ed. Thousand Oaks, CA: Pine Forge Press.
This comprehensive book provides a rich overview of the data and analyses that inform the sociology of gender and work.

Williams, Christine. 1995. *Still a Man's World: Men Who Do Women's Work.* Berkeley: University of California Press.
Based on interviews with men in the fields of nursing, elementary school teaching, social work, and librarianship, Williams shows how jobs become gendered. She also documents how men experience greater upward mobility in these jobs than women.

GENDER AND FAMILIES

Historical Perspectives
on Modern Families

Feminist Perspectives on Families
The Social Construction of Families
Family Diversity
*The Influence of Class, Race,
and Gender*
*Linking Social Structure
and Human Action*
The Family Ideal

The Diversity of
Contemporary Families
Measuring Family Status
Divorce
Balancing Family and Work
Cohabitation
Gay and Lesbian Families
Motherhood
Fatherhood

Race, Gender, and Families

Families and Social Problems
Family Violence
Teen Pregnancy
Child Care

Chapter Summary and Themes

Key Terms

**Discussion Questions/
Projects for Thought**

Internet Resources

Suggested Readings

Our boys are, in another score of years, to make the laws, heal the soul and bodies, for-mulate the science, and control the commerce of their generation. Fathers who, recog-nizing this great truth, do not prepare their sons to do their part toward accomplishing this work, are despised, and justly, by the community in which they live. Our girls are, in another score of years, to make the homes which are to make laws, heal souls and bodies, formulate science, and control the commerce of their generation (Harland 1889:202).

The home is woman's place, so the historical legacy tells us. In the period when the above housewive's guide was published (over 100 years ago), the glorification of the home and family was at its historical peak. The home was considered a moral sanctuary, and morality, which flourished in the home, was considered the work of women. It was women who would shape future generations. Although their place was ideally limited to the domestic sphere, within that sphere women were charged with preserving and creating the moral fiber of society.

Today's families may seem quite different from this ideal because the family is one of our most rapidly changing social institutions. Today, for example, only 24 percent of U.S. households are married couple families living with their own chil-dren (Fields and Casper 2001). The vast majority of families in the United States are now either two-earner families, female-headed or single-parent households, postchildbearing couples, or those who have no children. If we consider families to include more alternative forms of household organization, then cohabitors, gay and lesbian couples, singles, and various kinds of communal or cooperative living arrangements have to be included in our picture of contemporary families. In ad-dition, 30 percent of all children live in households with only one parent or with other relatives or nonrelatives (Fields 2003).

Still, the social ideal of the family remains quite different from the realities of contemporary households. The family is still idealized as a private world—one in which family members are nurtured and prepared for their roles in the outside world. The family is also a place where, even if women are employed in the public sphere, they still tend to provide primary care for children and manage the everyday affairs of the household, even with the increased efforts of men. The realities of con-temporary households and the persistence of the family ideal create a series of con-tradictions, especially for women. On the one hand, the family is idealized as women's world. It is glorified, isolated, and assumed to be detached from public life; it is also seen as an enclave for the development of family members' personalities and for the gratification of their physical and emotional needs. At the same time, families have been undergoing rapid social changes, making it clear that families are situated within the larger context of political, economic, and social conditions—all of which are structured in accordance with the gender relations of society.

Indeed, families have been the focus of public policy debates in recent years. What forms are deemed to be legitimate? Should same-sex marriage be legal? What family benefits should we expect from business and government? These and other questions are part of a cultural debate about family values—a debate that embeds within it many assumptions about gender and family life, even when such as-sumptions are not explicitly stated.

Although people experience their families in terms of personal, intimate relationships, those relationships are conditioned by events that extend far beyond immediate family life. Families take on great significance in the development of our individual lives. They are where we first encounter social expectations, where our physical needs are met, where our primary emotional bonds are first established, and where we first encounter systems of authority, power, and social conflict. Although the family seems to be a personal experience, many of the strains associated with family life can be seen as stemming from the conflicts posed by the family's relationship to other social institutions. For example, unemployment, divorce, and violence are all experienced within the family, although they are a part of broader social conditions.

The relationship of the family to other social institutions is also seen by the importance we give to the family as central to all other social institutions. Pleas for strengthening the family signify the threat that contemporary transformations in families pose to traditional ways of life in this society. Although appeals to family values at times stem from genuine concern about troubled families, they also represent a conservative view that regards many new family forms as symbolic of all that has gone wrong with the society. Although most people accept the reality that most women will work outside the home, many see this reality as damaging to children, and as we have seen, some advocate the return of women to the home. Contemporary politics surrounding families reveal the extent to which families are not isolated from other social realities.

❖ *Historical Perspectives on Modern Families*

Families in the Western world today are characterized by an emphasis on child rearing, an assumed separation of home from work, and the idealization of the home as women's world. In addition, the family is also idealized as a private world—one where conflicts are supposed to be self-contained, without the intervention of the state. In reality, of course, the family is heavily entangled with economic institutions and with the political state and its various social agencies.

The history of the Western family reveals the events that have molded contemporary families. Without historical analysis, we tend to see the family as an abstract form, void of its real context and social changes. Knowing the history of a contemporary institution is like knowing the biography of a good friend—it helps you understand the present.

It is impossible to pinpoint the exact time in history when the modern family first emerged. One could trace it to the patriarchal household in the early Roman family, one of the strongest patriarchal systems known. *Patriarchal households*—defined as those where men rule over women—are found throughout Western history. One could also look to the medieval period as an era when courtly love and chivalry marked gender and class relations between men and women.

The modern household in Western society, however, is generally depicted as having its origins (in the Western world) in the transformations of economic and political life found in the postmedieval period, roughly beginning in the fourteenth century. Philip Aries (1962) locates the origins of the modern Western family in a series of gradual transformations that began in the fourteenth century and culminated in the seventeenth and eighteenth centuries. Starting in the fourteenth century, the wife's position in the household deteriorated as she lost the right to replace her husband in the management of household affairs in the event of his death or insanity. By the sixteenth century, the wife was placed totally under the authority of her husband—any acts she performed without the authority of her husband or the law were considered null and void. At the end of the sixteenth century, the Church recognized the possibility of sanctification outside of the religious vocation. In other words, it became possible for institutions outside the Church to be seen as sacred at this point, and the family became an object of common piety. The marriage ceremony itself, in the seventeenth century, took on a religious form by becoming like a christening in which families gathered around the bride and groom.

Also in the sixteenth and seventeenth centuries, new importance was placed on the family, as attitudes toward children changed. Greater intimacy between parents and children established a new moral climate and, although the extension of school education made education increasingly a matter for the school, the family began to center its emotional life on that of the child. By the eighteenth century, the family began to hold society at a distance, thereby initiating the idea of the family as an enclave of private life. Even the physical character of the household changed. Homes became less open; instead of being organized around large communal spaces, they became characterized by several rooms, each specialized by function (Aries 1962). This change is explained as a result of homes becoming more organized around domestic work as commerce and production became increasingly located in the public workplace.

It is important to note that this evolution of family life was specific to the noble and middle classes and wealthy artisans and laborers. Even as late as the nineteenth century, the vast majority of the European population was still poor and lived like the medieval family, with children separated from their parents and the idea of the home and the family, as just described, nonexistent. Beginning in the nineteenth century, however, and continuing through the present, the concept of the family, as it originated in the well-to-do classes, extended through other strata of society. Still, the concept of the family as we know it today—a privatized, emotional, and patriarchal sphere—has its origins in the aristocratic and bourgeois classes.

By the late eighteenth and early nineteenth centuries, these historical transformations led to what U.S. historians have labeled the **cult of domesticity** (Cott 1977). The ideology of domesticity gave women a limited and gender-specific role to play—namely, that of the person responsible for the moral and everyday affairs of the home. This ideal, coupled with economic transformations in family life, limited women's idealized experiences to the private world of the family. In actuality, of course, large numbers of women, especially women of color and working-class women, also performed wage labor. The definition of womanhood as idealized femininity, however, stemmed from the bourgeois origins of the cult of domesticity. The cult of domesticity did provide the conditions for women's involvement in moral reform movements and, ultimately, feminism, because it encouraged women's nurturance to be turned toward social improvement (Cott 1977). In the context of the family, however, the cult of true womanhood limited women's experiences to affairs of the heart, not the mind. This ideal glorified a woman's role as homemaker at the same time that it fragmented the experience of women and men.

The idealized domestic role of women followed the transformations in women's labor (described in the preceding chapter). To review briefly, before the seventeenth century, the work role of women was not marginal to the economy or the household. In fact, as late as the seventeenth century, the household and the economy were one, the household being the basic unit of production. Domestic life in the earlier period was not splintered from public life, and households, as the basic units of economic production, consisted not only of individuals related through marriage but also of individuals with economic relationships, particularly servants and apprentices. In such a setting, women's labor, as well as that of children, was publicly visible, equally valued, and known to be economically necessary.

The emergence of capitalism, with the related rise of mercantilism, industrialization, and a cash-based economy, eroded the position of women by shifting the center of production from the domestic unit to the public workplace. This separation not only devalued women's labor in the home but it also made women more economically dependent on men (Tilly and Scott 1978). The emergence of a family-wage economy, as distinct from a family-based economy, transformed not only women's work but, equally important, the family and women's role within it (see Chapter 5).

When the workplace became separated from the home, the family, although still economically productive, became a vehicle largely for the physical and social reproduction of workers and for the consumption of goods. As more goods were produced outside the home, the value of workers became perceived in terms of their earned wages. The social value of women, especially those left unpaid as housewives, was diminished.

In addition, the status of women in the family was radically altered not only by changes in the economic organization of the household but also by political changes in the relationship of the family to the state. The displacement of large feudal households by the modern state enhanced the power of the husband over his wife. For example, in sixteenth-century England, the state assumed the powers of justice, punishment, military protection, and regulation of property originally assumed by feudal estates. At the same time, a massive propaganda campaign was initiated in support of the nuclear family. Family members were required to be loyal, subservient, and obedient to both the king and the husband (Dobash and Dobash 1979). The patriarchal family became the cornerstone—the basic social unit—for the emergence of the modern patriarchal state (Aries 1962; Foucault 1965). As capitalism developed further, there was a shift from private patriarchy within the family to public patriarchy centered in industry and government (Brown 1981). Although individual men may still hold power in families where they are present, the patriarchal state ensures that all women are subject to a patriarchal order. In contemporary society, social welfare systems, family courts, and reproductive policies are dominated by men and patriarchal values, even though their primary effect is on women and children.

Historically, the patriarchal family (and, ultimately, the state) was hierarchically structured around the power of men and morally sanctioned by the patriarchal church. With the Protestant Reformation, an ever-increasing amount of religious socialization occurred within the home. Whereas Catholicism had reluctantly sanctioned family life (and thus forbade it to the clergy), the Puritans embraced the family as an exalted and natural (God-given) order. The Protestant ethic, as it emerged, blessed the family as a unit of material labor. The ideal that one could do God's work in secular vocations encouraged a view of the family as sacred and as the place for spiritual life (Zaretsky 1976). In the end, the self-consciousness and individualism encouraged by the Protestant ethic helped ensure the subjective importance of the family. With the rise of capitalism, women's lower status in economic production was counterbalanced by their exalted status in the family as God's moral agents.

The split between work and home established by capitalism is related to a second schism—that between personal and public life. Modern capitalism depends on individual consumerism; thus, it encourages modern families to emphasize individualism, self-consciousness, and the search for personal identity. When personal identity is viewed as detached from objective material conditions, one can come to believe that personal liberation can occur without a change in the objective conditions of economic relations. The "plunge into subjectivity" (Zaretsky 1976:119) and its emphasis on lifestyle, consumerism, and personal awareness is a form of consciousness specific to, and consistent with, the ideological and economic needs of capitalist economies.

Modern families are also regulated by the patriarchal authority of the state and its various agencies. Especially in poor and working-class families, state agencies and reformers seeking to eliminate deviance regulate personal and family life through the work of professional experts. Even in the middle class, professional experts claim to know more about personal life, thereby defining individual and family needs and the character of contemporary social problems (Ehrenreich and English 1978; Illich 1977).

The development of specific family structures varies, depending on the specific historical experiences of given groups in the society. Working-class, ethnic, African American, Asian American, Latino, and Native American families did not develop in exactly the same fashion as did White, middle-class households, as you will see in a later section on racism and families. Transformations in White, middle-class households do, however, set the ideals by which other groups have been judged; the historical development of racial and ethnic families and working-class families has also been shaped by the same transformations in economic and family systems. This historical account of transformations in family life paints only a broad picture of the emergence of family life over time. Specific family histories, like other social experiences, are nested within the class, race, and gender relations of any given historical period.

The history of families shows that the family is an institution that is interconnected with economic and political institutions of society. Although we tend to think of families and personal life within them as relatively autonomous social forms, we cannot understand the sociological character of families without studying the interrelationships among families, the state, the economy, and gender, race, and class relations.

❖ *Feminist Perspectives on Families*

All societies are organized around some form of kinship system, although the definition of family changes in different cultural and historical contexts. Certain common characteristics of the family have been used to define the family. These include economic cooperation, common residence, socially approved sexual relations, reproduction, and child rearing. Anthropologists also add that, in most kinship systems, "marriage exists as a socially recognized, durable, although not necessarily life-long relationship, between individual men and women" (Gough 1975). It also appears that, in most societies, men have higher status and authority in the family than women (Gough 1975). Commonsense definitions of the family define the family to mean blood ties, although as discussed in the following section, many contemporary families do not meet this criterion. In addition, many contemporary families do not meet the criteria of common residence, socially approved sexual relations, reproduction, child rearing, or marriage, as the standard definition implies.

Feminist scholarship on families has transformed how we think about them, with family experts now using a framework of structural diversity to understand contemporary families. The **structural diversity model** is centered on several themes regarding how families form and operate (Baca Zinn and Eitzen 2005). These include the following:

- Family forms are socially constructed and historically changing.
- Family diversity is produced by the same structures that organize society as a whole.
- Families are embedded in and shaped by the intersecting hierarchies of class, race, and gender.
- Family diversity is constructed through social structure as well as the actions of family members.
- Understanding families means challenging monolithic ideas that conceive of the family in idealistic ways.

The Social Construction of Families

From a sociological point of view, the family is a social, not a natural, phenomenon. The assumption that families are natural or biological units prejudices our conceptions of the family by presuming families to be universal and detached from the influence of other social institutions. The idea that the family is "natural" is strongly held by some groups—especially conservative, religious groups. This ideal is often used to argue that women should remain in the family under the authority of men.

In fact, the meaning and character of family systems vary widely (see Figure 6.1). Both historically and in contemporary families, persons designated as kin may extend beyond blood relations; adoption is a case in point. Blood relations may sometimes even be excluded from the social network of the family. The traditional assumption that family relations are natural also stems from the ethnocentric attitude that the ideals of our own culture are universally the most appropriate social form.

Even a cursory look at cross-cultural studies of kinship systems reveals a great variety of family forms. For example, traditionally, in poor rural villages of the Dominican Republic, although single-mate patterns were the dominant ideal, women

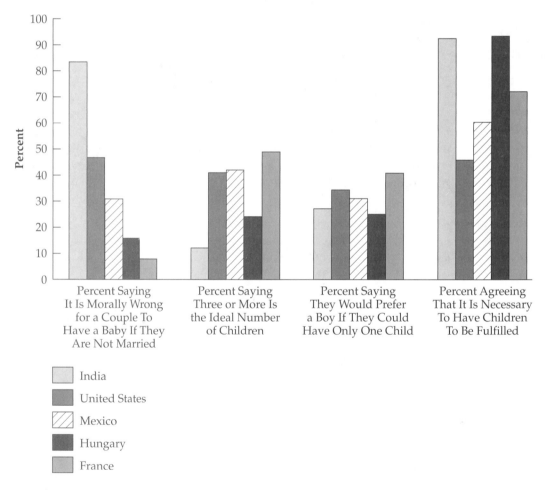

FIGURE 6.1   Family Values: A Global View

Source: Data from Gallup Organization. 2001. *The Gallup Poll.* Princeton, NJ: The Gallup Organization, http://www.gallup.com

usually had multiple partners, lived on or near the land of their own families, and had their children tended by maternal kin. Traditionally, among the Taiwanese, women marry into their husband's household where she must obey her husband and her mother-in-law and pay homage to her husband's ancestors, but, once she bears a son, her status in the family improves; when she becomes a mother-in-law herself, she achieves the greatest family power (Wolf 1972). In many parts of the world, families are women-centered, including in some societies where men must leave to find work (Brettell and Sargent 2001). In Afghanistan, under the rule of the Taliban, which began in 1996, women were excluded from public life—locked within their homes where windows were painted black so that no one could see them. Women were completely under the control of men and could not appear in public without them or without the *burqa* that completely covers them, except for a small net opening for their eyes. Women who even accidentally glanced at a man other than their husband or whose burqa might slip, revealing an ankle, were whipped and stoned to death in public. This extreme form of *gender apartheid*—the extreme segregation and exclusion of women from public life—completely restricts women to the family and, at that, restricts domestic life to the private world of the home.

These different examples show how family forms vary among different groups and also over time. An important point to understand is that the forms families take develop in the context of broader social and economic structures. Thus, families often develop kin networks that work as systems of social and economic exchange, such as is shown in Carol Stack's (1974) work on poor African American families in the United States. Kin in this context become recognized as those who share and meet socioeconomic obligations, regardless of blood ties. Among some Native American groups, traditionally, ancestry would be traced through maternal descent; young couples would reside with the woman's parent; and, wherever they lived, the women would assume control of the household—including the distribution of game that her husband caught (Axtell 1981). In another example, the system of *compadrazgo* among Latinos exemplifies an extended kinship network that extends beyond blood ties. *Compadrazgo* is a family system whereby those defined as kin have very strong connections to the family; in this system, kin includes not only blood relatives but also godparents (Baca Zinn and Eitzen 2005). The point is that these different family forms show that what seems natural about the Western **nuclear family**—families in which married couples live together with their children—is only that which dominant groups have defined as the ideal and that many have come to take for granted as the only, or best, family form.

Family Diversity

As we will see as we examine different forms of family, class, race, and gender all influence the social structures of families. Thus, the resources that families have available to them—or not—have a tremendous impact on how the family operates. Families are, in fact, deeply linked to the economic and political structures found in society at large, even though popular conceptions of the family define it as a refuge from the public world. This belief, however, hides the fact that families are organized around economic purposes, as well as reproductive and emotional ones.

You can see this by looking at the importance of family networks to the economic adaptations groups have to make. Studies of Vietnamese immigrant families show, for example, that such families patch together a wide array of resources, based on the belief in family collectivism (i.e., the belief emphasizing collective sharing and exchange, in contrast to individualism). This collectivist attitude encourages households to share economic and social resources as a way of coping with the economic difficulties that immigrant groups face (Kibria 1994; Zhou and Bankston 1998). The family, then, is an important source of economic adaptation, and this example shows how intertwined the family and economy are as social institutions.

Family organization both reflects and reproduces the class system of society. The availability of work for different family members will affect the family's form, pattern relationships within the family, and shape the family's lifestyle. The economic resources available to family members will also determine much about their experience in the family, in schools, at work, and at play. Just as class arrangements influence families, so do families influence class arrangements. In the family, people learn values and personality characteristics that make them suitable as workers; families shape our understanding of class systems and our aspirations and definitions of ourselves within them.

The role of the state in shaping family life also cannot be underestimated. Particularly for the poor, state intervention in family life is an everyday reality, just as economic policies (e.g., through the tax system) can shape the type of family one creates.

Family diversity is not only across different families, but can also be seen within families. Men and women, for example, experience the family in different ways. Jessie Bernard (1972), one of the foremothers of feminist scholarship in sociology, first wrote about how marriage was experienced differently by women and men within the family. Research on families has since shown that not only do women and men experience the family in different ways but they also hold different expectations for marital roles, with men tending to have more traditional expectations than women do. Furthermore, single women have more expectation of egalitarian marriage roles than do married women, suggesting that people's expectations change once in a marriage (Bartling and Broussard 1999; Wilkie 1993).

You can also see the internal diversity of families by observing the power that men and women have within families. For many years, sociologists have been able to show that the amount of power men and women have within families is highly dependent on their relative material resources (Blood and Wolfe 1960). Wives who are not employed or who do not bring material resources to a marriage are less likely to be able to influence family decision making, although this also depends on the extent to which men consider women's employment a threat or a contribution to the marriage (Pyke 1994).

The Influence of Class, Race, and Gender

It follows from the point above that families are shaped by the racial, class, and gender structures in society. Race and gender, along with class, organize the social structure of families and create experiences within families that are connected to the family's location in the system of race, gender, and class relations. This is true for all families—not just so-called minority families, but White families as well. White families, for example, benefit from some degree of racial privilege in a society that is marked by racial inequality; that privilege, however, is also influenced by the class position of the family. A working-class White family will not have the same access to resources as an African American middle-class family; nonetheless, the African American middle-class family will likely teach family members how to deal with the racism they are likely to experience, even given their class location. Strong sociological analyses of the family thus take race, class, and gender into account in considering how families are organized, how they change, and what different members within families experience.

In the past, studies of racial-ethnic families have been biased by the assumption that families should conform to dominant group norms (Baca Zinn and Eitzen 2005). As scholars and the public have realized that this ideal no longer reflects reality, there has been a greater willingness and ability to understand all families without judging them by some dominant ideal. Scholarship on African American, Latino, Asian American, and Native American families has also transformed many of the assumptions earlier built into family studies. New scholarship on families is also critical to understanding many current social issues—including welfare reform, teen pregnancy, and violence—since these problems are often miscast as the fault of families of color.

For example, federal policy under the Bush administration has advocated marriage as a solution to women's poverty. No doubt, two-income households are financially better off, and female-headed households are those most likely to be poor. But suggesting that marriage will alleviate poverty among women ignores the problems that marriage itself can pose for women. To begin with, given the rates of male unemployment, incarceration, and even early death in poor communities, there is a shortage of marriageable men. But, in addition, as poor women themselves will say, marriage can put them at risk of violence, provides no guarantees of a stable male income, and can make women dependent on men (Butler 1996). Thus, the idea that marriage would lift women out of poverty ignores the actual conditions in which poor women live.

Promoting marriage as a solution to poverty can be traced to the cultural belief that there is something wrong with women-headed households and to beliefs that women who stay home to care for their children are not working. Thus, rather than looking at the social structural conditions that poor women—both White and women of color—live within, such cultural beliefs instead blame families of color for their own situation.

Linking Social Structure and Human Action

It would be a mistake to think of family forms only in abstract terms, as if the behavior of people within families had no influence on family life. Sociologists use the term *human agency* to describe the intentional actions that people take in adapting to and sometimes changing the conditions they face in life. Human agency is an important part of all of social life, not just families, and it reminds us that human beings—despite the social structural influences on their lives, are not merely passive creatures who simply accept whatever society expects of them.

Throughout this chapter you can see the influence of agency in families, as people make decisions about how to respond to the conditions they face. Yes, families are social structures, influenced by a wide variety of social forces that exist for any given individual, but individuals also make choices, adjust their attitudes, develop new values, and change their lives. All of these factors influence how families work and how they change.

The Family Ideal

Feminist scholars have argued that the label the *family* has a specific and ideological meaning—in particular, "the family" implies a monolithic and unchanging entity. The family ideal portrays the family as a haven where people can seek refuge from an impersonal, heartless world; yet, such an image distorts the actual character of life within families (Baca Zinn and Eitzen 2005). Although families can be a source of love, care, and support, they can also be sources of trouble, conflict, and sorrow. Likewise, the image of family as equally fulfilling to all within it can mask the work and inequities that occur within families where, despite some changes, women continue to provide the greatest share of family labor. Furthermore, the myth that families are harmonious and stable is contradicted by the high rate of family divorce and the diversity of family forms in contemporary life (see Figure 6.2). The family ideal is an *ideology*—one that assumes that all people should live in nuclear families, that women have husbands to support them, and that motherhood is women's major role. This ideology mystifies women's work in families and, as a result, reinforces their economic exploitation (Thorne 1992).

Feminist scholars suggest instead that we think of the family as distinct from actual households, because each word, *family* and *household*, has a different and distinct connotation. We tend to think of families as involving blood ties; households, on the other hand, imply the existence of a material (or economic) unit. Households are residential units that cannot be analyzed apart from their socioeconomic context. As Rapp, Ross, and Bridenthal describe them, "Households are material units within which people pool resources and perform certain tasks. It is within households that people enter into relations of production, reproduction, and consumption with one another, and on one another's account" (1979:176).

This concept leads to the final point in feminist perspectives on the family. *Family* connotes a particular social ideal, and, because of its singular form, the word implies that there is one dominant form of family life. *Household* underscores the connection between residential units and the economic structure of society, but *family* carries ideological significance, as well (Rapp, Ross, and Bridenthal 1979). Distinguishing households from families allows us to recognize the diversity in people's lived experiences and frees the discussion of household life from the traditional assumptions that have biased our study of families. Because most households no longer meet the family ideal, it seems appropriate to think of new language and concepts to describe this change. Old traditions die slowly, however, and it

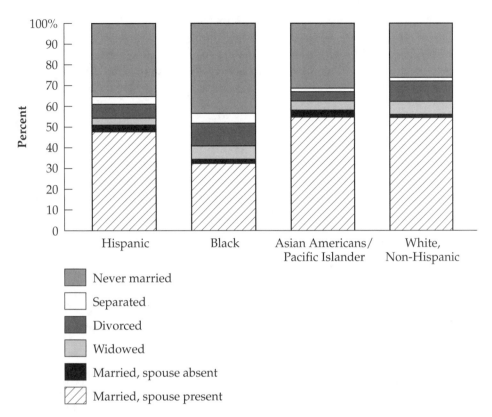

FIGURE 6.2   Diversity in U.S. Families/Households

Source: Data from U.S. Census Bureau. 2003. *America's Families and Living Arrangements,* Detailed Tables. Washington, DC: U.S. Department of Commerce. www.census.gov

seems likely that the word *family* will remain in our consciousness and our analysis. The preceding discussion should point out the importance of recognizing that traditional concepts of the family are no longer adequate to describe the social facts of most people's family experience. At least, the plural form, *families,* is more descriptive of the diverse realities in contemporary U.S. households (Baca Zinn and Eitzen 2005).

❖ *The Diversity of Contemporary Families*

What do contemporary families in the United States look like? First, among Western industrial nations, the United States has the highest rate of marriage, despite the fact that the rate of divorce is also high. In 2000, 54.2 percent of the population (over age 15) was married. Single persons make up 29 percent of the population; 9.6 percent are divorced; 2.1 percent, separated; and, 6.2 percent, widowed (see Figure 6.3; U.S. Census Bureau 2003). More children are now being born outside of marriage and will spend at least part of their childhood in a single-parent household. Changes are so widespread that both children and adults are likely to experience multiple changes in the composition of their families during their lifetimes (Teachman et al. 2000).

The changing character of families is especially visible in divorce statistics and the increase in single female-headed households (which includes both divorced mothers and women with children who have never been married). With regard to divorce, the United States has one of the highest divorce rates of any country in the world; annually, there are 1.2 million divorces (about 4 for every 1,000 people), although the rate of divorce has been declining in recent years (U.S. Census Bureau 2004).

Measuring Family Status

Changes in family experiences are reflected in the difficulty the U.S. Census Bureau has in counting and categorizing families and households. Before 1980, the national census routinely classified the husband as the head of the family if he and his wife were living together. Now, because of how families have changed, the Census Bureau defines **household** as a living unit containing one or more people—in other words everyone living in a housing unit makes up a household. The person who owns or rents the household is the **householder.** The Census Bureau then goes on to distinguish family households from nonfamily households. **Family households** are those where at least two members are related by blood, marriage, or adoption. A **nonfamily household** includes those living alone and households where people live together who are not related to the householder (such as roommates or boarders). Complex as these definitions may be, they reflect the diversity of household and family forms in contemporary society and they allow the Census Bureau to track and enumerate the characteristics of diverse living arrangements in society.

The overall picture that the Census Bureau provides includes these facts:

- Nonfamily households are more common and family household less common now than was true in 1970;
- 14.8 percent of households are women living alone;
- 30 percent of all households and 18 percent of all family households have female heads;
- Among Black Americans, 44 percent of family households have female heads; Hispanics, 23.3 percent, Whites (non-Hispanic), 12.6 percent; Asian/Pacific Islanders, 13.2 percent (see Figure 6.3; Fields and Casper 2001; U.S. Census Bureau 2004).

These facts point not only to the variety of family and household forms now common in the United States, but also to the significant trend toward more women heading their own households than was true in the past. This is accounted for by a number of factors, including later age at first marriage, high rates of divorce, less

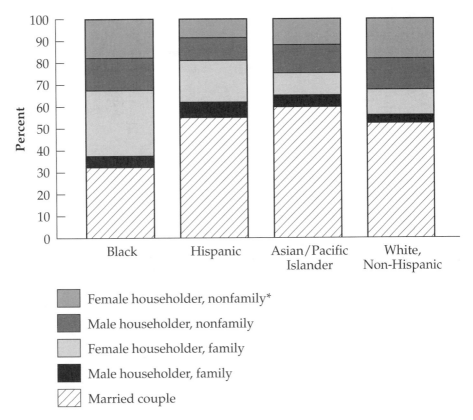

FIGURE 6.3   Households by Type and Race

Source: Data from U.S. Census Bureau. 2003. *America's Families and Living Arrangements:* 2003; Detailed Tables. Washington, DC: U.S. Department of Commerce. http://www.census.gov

*Nonfamily households are either persons living alone or sharing the housing unit with nonrelatives only. Family refers to a household with at least two members related by blood, marriage, or adoption.

likelihood that pregnant teens will marry, and, in some communities, the high rates of incarceration of young men.

Divorce

It is well known that marriages do not endure, as the ideal implies. The divorce rate in 2001 was 4 per 1,000 persons in the population, compared with 2.2 in 1960. Perhaps this divorce figure does not seem so large until you consider that each year there is one divorce for every two marriages made that year. Keep in mind that this does *not* mean that half of all marriages end in divorce—only that there are half as many divorces in a year as there are marriages, many of those marriages endure, but the average marriage lasts only 7 years—not exactly the lifelong commitment implied by the ideal.

Following divorce, women are far more likely than men to obtain custody of children. Eighty-five percent of custodial parents are mothers. Mothers who are custodial parents are somewhat less likely to be working full time than custodial fathers, making them also more dependent on child support and/or public assistance. Close to one-third of custodial mothers live below the poverty line, compared with 10 percent of custodial fathers. Only 45 percent of mothers entitled to child support actually received the full amount due; 28 percent received partial payments, and 20 percent receive no payment at all (U.S. Census Bureau 2004). Obtaining child support is a major problem for women following a divorce, resulting not only in financial hardship, but also the additional burden of coping with the legal system, including repeated visits to the courts and social services to try to receive payments.

Following divorce, both women and men have to redefine relationships with friends and families, come to terms with a changed identity, and build a new personal life. For those who are custodial mothers, this also has to happen while they carry the major burden of child rearing and parenting. Many mothers nonetheless report better relationships with their children following a divorce because they have had to redefine their relationships and their new, shared situation. Both women and men report exclusion from their married friends after divorce, but for women the exclusion is exacerbated by the change in their social-class status (Grella 1990). Women also find it difficult to have a social life outside of their family (Arendell 1992). Separated and divorced women, however, tend to be better able than men to rebuild and maintain old social bonds. Men are more likely to drop their old ties, whereas divorced women's social ties reproduce their home-centered lives.

Despite the problems faced by those who divorce, for many it can be a better option than remaining in a troubled marriage. One such study focusing on women in the aftermath of divorce has found that, although divorce is emotionally stressful and financially risky, many women report it as a positive option (Kurz 1995), especially if they are in abusive relationships or where their husbands have left them for other women. Changes in women's roles also mean that women are less financially dependent on husbands than in the past. Even though most women are financially less well off without the benefit of a man's income, the economic interdependence that once bound women and men together in marriage is no longer as strong as it once was.

Balancing Family and Work

Changes in family structure are also reflected in the beliefs and practices of people about balancing work and family life. Thirty-eight percent of women say it is ideal for one parent to stay at home; 45 percent of men say so. These attitudes vary by age group, however, with younger people (aged 18–29) less likely to think it is ideal for one parent to stay at home (McComb 2001). Men are now more likely than in the past to want marriages where they share work, housekeeping, and child care.

These changes in attitudes also reflect the reality faced by most couples that it is more difficult to support a family based on one person's income.

Studies find that younger men are now more skeptical about definitions of themselves that focus solely on work, although women hold even more flexible attitudes about gender, work, and family. What this will mean in the long run is not clear, but it surely means that men and women, regardless of the form of family relationship they make for themselves, have to negotiate gender options at home and at work more consciously, instead of following more rigid social roles (Gerson 2002).

Although men's and women's attitudes about sharing family work have changed over the years, actually balancing work and family demands is difficult. Integrating family and work is a balancing act for all employed women and men, but sociologists have found that the ability to do so varies by class, gender, and marital status. Working-class women are more likely to give their families priority over their work, whereas professional/managerial women see work as more central to their lives. Single mothers or mothers with children who have special problems have the greatest difficulty integrating work and family (Burris 1991). As we saw in the previous chapter, the fact that women still do most of the housework and child care means that the demands of balancing family and work are especially difficult for women.

Women and men develop a number of strategies for coping with the demands of work and family. At the heart of these demands, however, are deep-seated conflicts about gender ideology—conflicts that are brought on by time pressures felt within relationships, most particularly marriage (Hochschild 1997). Women respond by trying to redefine their roles, choosing men to marry who plan to share work at home or, following marriage, trying to change the husband's understanding of his role at home. Some women force men's greater involvement in work at home by feigning helplessness over certain kinds of tasks; other women cope by trying not to impose change on their husbands, thereby avoiding conflict. Some women attempt to be "supermoms," but, as Hochschild found in her research on dual-earner families, supermoms pay the price, seeming "out of touch" with their feelings and reporting being "numb" (Hochschild 1989:196). Others respond by cutting back on work or, very often, redefining what is necessary in the home. Women also respond by seeking outside help, either other female relatives or friends, or, for those with economic privilege, paying other women to do the work at home (Hochschild 1989).

Other studies of dual-earner families find that couples try to cope with the dual demands of work and family by scaling back on some activities. This can include husbands and wives trading responsibilities over the life course, for example with husbands taking on greater responsibility for family and wives' carrying the major responsibility for family income. But the most common form of "scaling back" is for women to reduce their working time or limit their careers. This is especially likely following the birth of a child (Becker and Moen 1999). The ability to do so, however, depends on one's social class.

Balancing work and family is complicated by the power differences between men and women in families. Those power differences, in turn, influence marital satisfaction. Wives are much more likely than husbands to desire change in the areas of domestic labor, children, sexuality, leisure activities, and finance. Power differences within marriage tend to confirm gender roles, with women desiring more change than men. Some have suggested that marital power dynamics shift when the wife earns more money, particularly when she earns more than her husband (still a rare event). Research on this issue however shows that wives' earnings per se do not alter power relations within marriage. More significant is gender—that is how the couple negotiate gender roles within the marriage (Tichenor 1999).

Despite the strains of balancing work and family, there are positive consequences. Men and women alike report some success in balancing work and family and, when they feel they have been able to achieve some balance, they do report greater happiness. It is when women perceive unfairness and when they have to make tradeoffs at work to meet family demands that unhappiness results (Milke and Peltola 1999; Voydanoff and Donnelly 1999).

Some dual-earner couples, both married and unmarried, find it necessary, because of their job locations, to maintain separate residences. One partner may have to leave the region of residence to find work or may be relocated for an extended period of time. Some may experience an extended geographical separation from the family; others may work out a commuting relationship with partners living in separate places. Such arrangements can occur in middle-class families, probably the most common image of a commuting couple, but they are also common among working-class couples who are vulnerable to job displacement. Commuter couples also experience problems posed by their long-distance arrangements, which can include the increased financial burden, but also the lack of daily companionship and emotional support.

Men and women in commuter marriages report high levels of satisfaction with the relationship and report being equally committed to their partners and careers (Skirboll and Taylor 1998; Groves and Horm-Wingerd 1991). Like commuting couples, couples who reside together but do shift work find that considerable strain is put on the marriage. Studies have found that shift work has a strong effect on the likelihood of divorce. Divorce in the first 5 years of a marriage is three times more likely when wives have to work the night shift and six times more likely when men do (Presser 2000). These patterns show how strongly work affects family dynamics.

Cohabitation

Recent trends among single persons include a profound increase in the numbers of persons who are cohabiting outside of marriage (Seltzer 2000). Since 1970, the number of unmarried persons living together has tripled, with researchers now estimating that soon a majority of persons will experience this lifestyle at some point in their lives (Sassler 2004).

In about three-quarters of cases, cohabitation leads to marriage (Peres 1998), even though delayed (Spain and Bianchi 1996). Researchers find that there are similar patterns of interaction among partners in cohabiting relationships and those who marry, and there are similar rates of happiness within these relationships

(Brown 1996). On the other hand, some also find higher rates of violence among co-habitors than among spouses, at least among those who have come from violent households (Jackson 1996). Those who cohabit prior to marriage also have higher divorce rates (Nock 1995). The likelihood of cohabitation is also related to factors such as educational status, gender-role attitudes, and political orientation, with those most likely to cohabit being more likely to have favorable attitudes toward gender equality and nontraditional gender roles. Cohabitors are also more likely to remain together when they establish an egalitarian relationship (Lye and Waldron 1997; Brines and Joyner 1999; Sanchez et al. 1998; Thornton et al., 1995; Barber and Axinn 1998).

Gay and Lesbian Families

Same-sex marriage has been much the subject of public debate in recent years, brought on both by the greater visibility of lesbian and gay relationships and the legal recognition that some states and municipalities have tried to give to same-sex marriages. The state of Massachusetts has recognized same-sex marriage—a decision also upheld by the Massachusetts Supreme Court. The city of San Francisco tried to legally recognize same-sex marriage, but was overruled by the California Supreme Court. Many businesses recognize the legitimacy of gay and lesbian relationship by extending employee benefits to domestic partners, and the majority of the U.S. public, though not supporting gay marriage, believes that lesbian and gay relationships should be recognized as legally civil unions (Moore and Carroll 2004).

Those who are opposed to same-sex marriage argue that it threatens the institution of marriage—as if changes in the marriage institution are the fault of gays and lesbians. Clearly this is not the case, as we have seen that transformations in contemporary families come from a variety of social forces, including the greater participation of women in the labor market, smaller family size, and the growth of single and female-headed households. Attributing changes in marriage to the alleged influence of gays and lesbians assumes that gays and lesbians have the power to change social institutions, when, in fact, as a minority group in society, though not without influence, it seems far-fetched to blame gays and lesbians for social changes that are otherwise underway.

The resistance to same-sex marriage has also been compared to the historical resistance to interracial marriage. In both cases, proponents argue, people are being deprived of their civil rights. But, when interracial marriage was illegal, people also argued that it was perverted and sexually deviant and threatened to undermine the racial and gender social order. By marginalizing and sexualizing relationships that differ from dominant group norms, people disempower social groups, such as gays and lesbians, forcing them to invent social support systems of their own (Ross 2002).

Gay and lesbian families are, in fact, creating new forms of social relationships, including adapting and creating rituals, such as marriages and commitment ceremonies, that affirm their commitment to each other, but also symbolizing the perceived legitimacy of these relationships (McQueeney 2003). Thus, lesbian women who have become mothers have to negotiate their identities in the context of mainstream definitions and their particular social networks (Hequembourg and Farrell 1999; Nelson 1999).

Research on lesbian experiences finds that lesbian women tend to form extended networks of support that operate at local and national levels. In a sense, these support networks function like a large family, except that, unlike patriarchal families, they tend to be nonauthoritarian and nonhierarchical. The increasing numbers of lesbians having children either through in vitro fertilization, surrogate fathers, or adoption means that lesbian mothers are reconstructing existing norms about family life. Studies of lesbian mothers are finding that these mothers actively construct new concepts of family relationships (Dalton and Bielby 2000).

Fewer children live in gay male households, both because of the association of parenting with women and because fewer fathers gain custody of their children following divorce. However, raising children is increasingly common by gay fathers, including gay fathers who adopt children. The small amount of research that has been done finds that compared with heterosexual fathers, gay fathers tend to be more nurturing, less traditional in their overall parenting practices, and less accepting of the idea that being an economic provider is the main ingredient of good fathering. Research also shows that gay fathers have very positive relationships with their children, that they try to create stable home lives, and that the fathers' sexual orientation is of little importance in the overall parent-child relationship (Bigner and Bozett 1989).

Studies of lesbian households also are an interesting context for studying the division of labor in household work. Generally speaking, lesbian couples tend to have more gender equality within their households than do heterosexual couples, so long as both partners are employed (Sullivan 1996). However, when one partner is the primary breadwinner and the other the primary caregiver for children, the partner staying at home becomes economically vulnerable, less able to negotiate with her partner about her needs, and more devalued as a person and a daily contributor—just like the traditional pattern where women stay home and men are the primary breadwinners.

Many have wondered what effect being raised in a lesbian or gay household has on children. Research on this question finds that there is little difference in outcomes for children raised in gay/lesbian households and those raised in heterosexual households. Although children raised in lesbian and gay households do have some difficulties, this is mostly the result of the ridicule and stigma that they experience as the result of others' homophobic attitudes. Thus, any adjustment problems they have are the result of society's disdain for lesbians and gays, not the sexual orientation of parents per se. Children raised in gay and lesbian households are less likely to develop stereotypical gender roles; they are no more likely than children of heterosexual parents to become gay themselves, but they are more tolerant and open-minded about sexual matters (Stacey and Biblarz 2001). Overall, gay and lesbian families tend to make quite positive adjustments under stressful societal conditions (Patterson 2000). If we lived in a society more tolerant of diversity, the differences that do emerge might be viewed as strengths, not deficits.

Motherhood

The child-centeredness of modern families has tended to distract us from thinking about mothers; yet, an examination of motherhood as a social institution reveals both the objective and the subjective dimensions of this experience. Women's roles as mothers are idealized in our culture as all-loving, kind, gentle, and selfless; however, the objective conditions of motherhood in this society fill the role with contradictions, conflicts, and pleasures. Motherhood is, in fact, a social institution—one that is controlled by the systems of patriarchy and the economic relations in which it is embedded (Rich 1976). Like other institutions, motherhood involves a complex set of social relations organized around specific functions. Once established, institutions also involve a system of power relations, a division of labor, and the distribution of resources (Glenn et al. 1993).

Viewing motherhood as an institution distinguishes motherhood as something more than a caring relationship between a woman and her children (Rich 1976). Mothering involves not just care for children but also situates women in various institutions. Viewing mothering only in the isolated context of the family misses its connections to other social institutions. As an example, research on Latina and African American mothering finds that low-income women define their mothering as an activist activity when they are engaged in community work that they see as an extension of their mothering role. For these mothers, activism is essential to providing the safety, health care, education, and other services that they know are necessary for their children's welfare (Naples 1992). Seen in this light, mothering is work that takes place not just within the family, but throughout social institutions. It is a socially constructed practice, one wherein mothers construct an understanding of themselves and their children in relationship to the society around them.

In U.S. society, motherhood is typically characterized by its isolation. Although most young girls are socialized to become mothers, they are seldom prepared for the solitary activity of actually caring for children in the home. Jessie Bernard (1975) suggests, in fact, that when women marry, their early socialization for dependency is reversed, because as wives and mothers they are expected to be responsible for both their husbands and their children. The experience of motherhood then becomes a mixture of satisfaction and pleasure, but this can be mixed with frustration and bitterness (Rich 1976).

Because motherhood is a role exclusively reserved for women, women's identities develop in ways that reproduce mothering qualities. Nancy Chodorow has explored this issue by asking how the psychological structures of gender emerge from the "asymmetrical organization of parenting" (1978:49; see also Chapter 2). Chodorow notes that the role of women as mothers is one of the few seemingly universal elements of the gender division of labor. Instead of relying on explanations that see motherhood as a natural fact, however, she asks why the psychological characteristics of motherhood are reproduced so that women, and not men, want to be mothers and develop the capacity of nurturing others. According to Chodorow, "Women, as mothers, produce daughters with mothering capacities and the desire to mother. These capacities and needs are built into and grow out of the mother-daughter relationship itself. By contrast, women as mothers (and men as not-mothers) produce sons whose nurturant capacities and needs have been curtailed and repressed" (1978:7).

Chodorow explains this process as the result of both the gender division of labor and the psychological processes it inspires. Both boys and girls, in order to become their own person, must separate—psychologically—from the parent. Because the parent most often present is a woman, the process of individuation is complicated by gender identity. Boys, who identify with the gender of the father, learn that their gender role is one of detachment and distance, because the father is seldom present in the home. Girls, on the other hand, identify with the gender of the mother; thus, their own psychological process of separation and individuation is less complete. Girls, then,

> *are more continuously embedded in and mediated by their ongoing relationship with their mother. They develop through and stress particularistic and affective relationships to others. A boy's identification processes are not likely to be so embedded in or mediated by a real affective relation to his father. At the same time, he tends to deny identification with and relationship to his mother and reject what he takes to be the feminine world; masculinity is defined as much negatively as possible. . . . Feminine identification processes are relational, whereas masculine identification processes tend to deny relationship (Chodorow 1978:176).*

As a consequence, gendered personalities both reflect and re-create the gender division of labor in the household. Women become mothers because this role is consistent with their acquired psychological being; the fact that they are mothers, then, re-creates similar personality structures of nurturance in their daughters. In sum, the social organization of parenting creates psychic structures that orient the person to his or her social behavior. To reverse this process, so that men as fathers become more nurturant, will require that men be placed in the household on an equal basis with women. Because the organization of parenthood is tied to the organization of economic production, both the family and the economy must be transformed, however, if we are to eliminate gender inequality.

Chodorow's analysis is psychoanalytic in its orientation; thus, the evidence for her argument is clinical evidence. As her critics point out, clinical evidence is weak because it rests on patients' accounts and psychoanalysts' interpretations of those accounts. Beyond these methodological criticisms, some sociologists are concerned that Chodorow overemphasizes psychological processes in lieu of social-structural conditions as the source of women's choice to become mothers. It is ideologically normal in our society for women to become mothers; furthermore, given the inequality in men's and women's incomes, it is reasonable for fathers, not mothers, to be the primary wage earners in families (Lorber et al. 1981:484).

Other questions about the class, race, and culture bias of Chodorow's explanation can also be raised, for she assumes that the mother in the gender division of labor is a devalued woman. Although this is true in many cultures, including the dominant U.S. culture, it is not universally true. An important test of her theory would involve the study of boys and girls who are raised by men or in cultures where women are not devalued and parenthood is more equally shared. Recall that in Chapter 2, Chodorow's work was discussed in the context of Chicano families where researchers have found it provides valuable insights to the women-centered households common among Chicanas (Segura and Pierce 1993).

The psychoanalytic perspective may not, however, account for variations in the actual practices and relationships of mothers who are raising children. The mother's own personality, as well as the child care arrangements she makes, may alter the degree to which her sons and daughters separate or do not separate themselves from her, and it certainly alters their relationship with her. Still, Chodorow's analysis gives us a provocative account of the formation of gender identity and its relationship to the social structure of the family.

Most importantly, Chodorow points out that the family is "a primary constituent of the male dominant social organization of gender and, as such, is as fundamental a constituent feature of society as a whole—of 'social structure'—as is the economy or the political organization" (Lorber et al. 1981:502). One is not dependent on or contained by the other; people live in families, just as they live in societies. Chodorow's analysis has led us to see the importance of understanding how cultural understandings of masculinity and femininity are linked to the social organization of families and to our gendered identities. In sum, Chodorow provides an insightful explanation of some of the effects of nuclear family relations, in which the woman's work as a mother is isolated from that of other persons.

Fatherhood

Fathers' roles in the family have traditionally been defined as instrumental. That is to say, fathers were to be the primary breadwinners and the source of authority in the family, while mothers were to fulfill the emotional needs of family members. Just as women have found their traditional roles to be limiting and one sided, many men have tried to redefine their roles as fathers to include more primary care of children (Silverstein and Auerbach 1999).

Research on fathers has traditionally been based on the assumption that fathers have a limited role in families (Robinson and Barret 1986), although as fathers have assumed more responsibilities in family life, fathers' roles are changing. Still, the research shows that following the birth of a baby, most fathers tend to "help out" rather than share child care, and they continue to view caring for the baby as the mother's work (Walzer 1996; Belsky and Kelly 1994). Fathers' involvement in family care is changing, however, and studies find that their increased involvement in childrearing is linked to greater stability in marriage, in part because wives are then happier (Kalmijn 1999).

Families headed by single fathers have also increased, although they are a small percentage of families. Despite the increase in the number of single and divorced fathers, as well as the greater involvement of many men in their roles as fathers, there are few social support networks for men. Many men continue to feel pressure to put their jobs and careers first, and, although employers give lip service to increased family involvement, workers perceive that choices have to be made between family and career. Single fathers also tend to use outside help, typically from women, and to use daughters as mother substitutes—to do child care, housework, and manage household affairs (Grief 1985). Single fathers feel competent about their skills as parents and demonstrate more mothering behaviors than do married fathers. Compared with men who are still married, single fathers spend more time with their children, report more sharing of feelings between father and child, are more likely to stay home with sick children, and take a more active interest in their children's out-of-home activities (Risman 1999).

Most single fathers are heading their own households as the result of divorce or widowhood, although new research on young unwed fathers adds to our understanding of the difficulties men face as fathers. Despite social stereotypes, many, if not most, young unwed fathers try to take some responsibility for their children, but their economic disadvantage is high. Most young unwed fathers are generally less well educated than other groups, have limited employment prospects, and are more likely to engage in crime. They also earn less, have less education, and are more likely to need public assistance; furthermore, the gap in socioeconomic status between single and married fathers has been increasing since the mid-1980s (Brown 2000). This gap is significant since studies of unmarried fathers also find increased involvement of these fathers with their children when their earnings are higher (Lerman and Sorenson 2000; Lerman and Ooms 1993; Marsiglio 1995). These conditions, particularly acute among African American men, make it difficult for these fathers to support their children, even though studies find that these men want to be good fathers and provide for their children (Hamer 2001).

Sociological perspectives on fatherhood see fathering, like mothering, as a role, not just a biological connection to one's offspring. Neither kinship nor household membership is always necessary for a man to perform the psychological and instrumental functions associated with a father. Men who have worked to include more expressive and caretaking work in their roles as fathers report considerable rewards in creating fuller relationships with their children, although they also note that society provides little emotional, practical, or financial support for men to spend time with their children. Societal support in the form of paternity leaves, new work arrangements for parents, and transformation in our attitudes about gender and parenting are as essential for fathers' roles as for mothers' roles. (See Table 6.1.)

❖ Race, Gender, and Families

We have seen in the structural diversity model of families how significant the racial organization of society is in shaping family experience. Examining diverse families in more detail underscores this point.

Both the historical and contemporary forms of racial-ethnic families stem from the conditions of oppression that they have experienced—conditions that, although differing from group to group, nonetheless reveal a history of structural exploitation from which women and men had to try to forge strong family ties (Dill 1988).

TABLE 6.1   Maternity Leave Benefits: A Comparative Perspective

Country	Length of Maternity Leave	Percentage of Wages Paid in Covered Period	Provider of Coverage
Zimbabwe	90 days	6–75%	Employer
Cuba	18 weeks	100%	Social Security
Iran	90 days	66.7% for 16 weeks	Social Security
China	90 days	100%	Employer
Saudi Arabia	10 weeks	50 or 100%	Employer
Canada	17–18 weeks	55% for 15 weeks	Unemployment insurance
Germany	14 weeks	100%	Social Security to a ceiling; employer pays difference
France	16–26 weeks	100%	Social Security
Italy	5 months	80%	Social Security
Japan	14 weeks	60%	Social Security or health insurance
Russian Federation	140 days	100%	Social Security
Sweden	14 weeks	450 days, 100% paid	Social Security
United Kingdom	14–18 weeks	90% for 6 weeks; flat rate thereafter	Social Security
United States	**12 weeks**	**0**	**n/a**

Source: Data from United Nations. 2000. *The World's Women 2000: Trends and Statistics.* New York: United Nations, pp. 140–143.

Consider first the history of African American families. Some have argued that the high rate of female-headed families among African Americans is a holdover from slavery where African American men and women could not form legally recognized marriages. Although they formed families on their own outside of the formal recognition of marriage, families were separated by slave sales and disrupted by the practice of slave breeding, as well as the intense racism experienced by the Black slave community (Frazier 1948). Although the study of families under slavery is important and reveals the conditions under which African American women and men have had to live, it is just as important to locate the analysis of family life within contemporary economic and social structures.

This was shown in an important and classic study of African American families in slavery and in the twentieth century. Historian Herbert Gutman argues that if slavery were the source of Black family structures, we would expect the family to be less stable as we move backward in time. To test this assumption, Gutman traced five generations of kin as they adapted to the changes of postslavery society in the United States. Part of his research is based on 1925 census data from New York City that show that 85 percent of kin-related Black households at that time were headed by both parents; 32 of the 13,924 families had no father present; and five in six children under age six lived with both parents (Gutman 1976: xix). Based on this information, he concluded that female-headed households are a contemporary phenomenon, not just remnants of the past. His historical research is complemented by that of Genovese (1972), who shows that slaveowners used the family as a form of social control. Genovese recognizes that separation of families occurred, but he suggests that it was often to the benefit of slave owners to maintain stable families as a way of preventing slave revolts. The slave family, according to Genovese, was subordinated to the economic interests of the owner. If it benefited him, he would break up families for sale; in fact, most slave owners broke up families when owners were under economic pressure (Genovese 1972:453).

Both Genovese's and Gutman's analyses indicate that slave families faced oppressive conditions that tested the adaptive capacities of men and women. Within slave communities, a subculture of resistance emerged in which family relations and women's role fostered resistance to dominant White institutions (Davis, 1971, 1981). As a result of the gender division of labor, Black women in slavery provided domestic labor not only in the White households but also in their own. The labor they provided for their own family was the only labor not claimed by the ruling class; it was for the benefit of the slave community. As a result, Black women's labor in the slave community "la[id] the foundation for some degree of autonomy" (Davis 1971:5), and the Black woman became essential to the survival of the slave community. Because of her indispensable labor in the household of the oppressor, she developed a practical awareness of the oppressor's dependence on her. As Davis says, "The master needs the slave far more than the slave needs the master" (1971:6). Black women's consciousness of their oppression benefited the slave community, because women were responsible for the socialization of future generations. Thus, the women in their roles in the family and community passed on a culture of resistance to oppressed kin (Caulfield 1974).

The picture of the African American family emerging from these studies is one of resistance to conditions of oppression. Instead of explaining patterns in Black families as the result of slavery or individual pathology, it makes sense to analyze the origins of African American family life in terms of the patterns of urbanization, industrialization, and poverty in current society (Billingsley 1966; Frazier 1948; Staples 1971). In the early twentieth century, racial discrimination in the labor force denied African Americans employment using the skills they had acquired in slavery. As a result, men could find only unskilled, often seasonal, and always underpaid, employment; women were more likely to find steady, although also severely underpaid, employment in private domestic labor. In 1920, 41 percent of Black women worked as servants and 20 percent as laundresses (Katzman 1978:74). Black women's labor thus made them steady providers for their family. As the twentieth century developed, continuing patterns of unemployment, the elimination of Black men through war and imprisonment, and the conditions the social welfare system established for households encouraged the formation of female-centered households.

The contemporary structure of African American households must then also be understood in terms of both racism and sexism and the economic context in which they are embedded, not in conditions of the past. As we look at African American families without racist and sexist assumptions, we see that even in the poorest of families, systems of cooperation and social exchange characterize the organization of family life (Collins 1990; Stack 1974; Stack and Burton 1993). The social and community ties that people generate in the face of poverty and oppression, in fact, appear stronger than some of the ties of nuclear families. This fact shows us that African American families, like an increasing number of all families, are not always organized according to dominant group ideals. Seen in this way, the role of women in the African American family can be seen for the strength it creates, not the social destruction it allegedly causes. African American middle-class families promote among their children and through their community activities a strong sense of building a just and equitable society, whereas White middle-class families are likely to encourage family members to become individually better informed and enriched. (Willie and Reddick 2003; Hill and Sprague 1999).

These conclusions sensitize us to the different conditions that families face depending on their class and race location. Although certainly many African American families struggle with problems of poverty, unemployment, and violence, those problems stem from the social structural location of families in a race, class, and gender-stratified society, not from something inherently problematic in women's heading households or in African American values.

Similar transformations of thinking have come from new studies of Latino families. Like past studies of African American families, past studies of Latino families have been founded on the assumption of pathology. *Machismo* in Latino families has been assumed to encourage aggressive, violent, authoritarian behavior in men and saintly, virginal, submissive behavior in women (Staples and Mirandé 1980). Some researchers see machismo as a more benevolent feature of Latino families, encouraging honor, respect, and dignity among family members (Mirandé 1979; Murillo 1971). Research shows that Latino families are more egalitarian than the ideal of machismo suggests and that the Latino family is more woman centered than prevailing stereotypes suggest (Baca Zinn 1976).

Chicano families have been characterized as close-knit kinship systems, typically explained as a consequence of Chicano culture. Scholars now recognize that these family patterns represent adaptation to a hostile society that excludes Chicanos from full participation and keeps them socioeconomically marginal (Baca Zinn and Eitzen 2005; Dill 1994). Especially for women, close kinship networks provide social exchanges and support that are not available elsewhere. Studies of Latino families show considerable differences in family experiences, depending on the different social histories and contemporary status of particular groups categorized as "Latino." Thus, Chicanas (women of Mexican descent born and raised in the United States) are more likely to hold the ideal of stay-at-home motherhood than Mexicanas (Mexican women immigrants residing in the United States). Because Mexicanas are more likely to have mixed family and employment, they are less likely to dichotomize family and work in their understandings of motherhood (Segura 1998).

For all groups, family experience is bound by the broader systems of race, class, and gender inequality. So, for example, Puerto Rican families have experienced one of the most rapid rises in female-headed households, largely due to the decline of industrial employment for men in the regions where Puerto Ricans tend to be concentrated. As a result, although Puerto Rican families are traditionally headed by men, the rate of families headed by females among Puerto Ricans has nearly converged with that of African Americans. This trend is further evidence that societal conditions, not just cultural preferences, shape family structure (Baca Zinn and Eitzen 2005).

New patterns of family life in the context of widespread immigration illustrate this point well. High rates of immigration in recent years—especially from Central America, the Caribbean, and Southeast Asia—are creating a new classification of family life: **transnational families.** In these families, family members live in different countries, usually at considerable distance from one another, but with a pattern of moving back and forth across national boundaries. Thus, as in Hondagneu-Sotelo's (1997) study of transnational mothers, women may work as domestic workers in Los Angeles, while their children reside in Mexico, El Salvador, or Guatemala. The very structure of the work they do may discourage having children physically present in their new home, thus challenging strong beliefs that mothers should raise their own children. Yet, transnational mothers do not see themselves as abandoning their children; rather, they redefine motherhood to include mothers' obligations to financially support their children and to value the contributions of other caregivers (e.g., grandmothers, aunts, and friends) to the well-being of their children. As Hondagneu-Sotelo concludes, "Transnational mothering radically rearranges mother-child interactions and requires a concomitant radical reshaping of the meanings and definitions of appropriate mothering" (1997:557). Other studies of transnational families show that women negotiate and sustain relationships across national borders because this is how they forge their identity and maintain a sense of security in their homeland in the face of racial oppression and class disadvantage in their new location (Das Gupta 1997; Alicea 1997).

Research on Asian American and Native American families is less extensive, but, as with African American and Latino families, family experience in these groups should be seen in the context of the racist policies that discourage strong and cohesive families and in the specific class locations of racial-ethnic groups (Dill 1988; Baca Zinn and Eitzen 2005). Asian Americans, for example, are typically stereotyped as the "model minority"—meaning that they have been depicted as highly successful in comparison to other immigrant groups, presumably as a result of their hard work, education, and thrift (and, by implication, the absence of these qualities among other racial-ethnic groups). This simplistic view ignores the barriers to mobility that Asian Americans have encountered and is based on the myth that hard work always reaps commensurate rewards (Woo 1992). In addition, it overlooks the diversity within Asian American groups.

U.S. policies regarding Asians have encouraged the use of Asians in specific cheap forms of labor, at the same time that they have explicitly discouraged family unity (Lai 1992). So, for example, in the nineteenth century, young Asian men were seen as desirable workers in agriculture, mining, and railroads; women were not. The Page Law, passed in 1875, intended to exclude Chinese women as prostitutes, was so strictly enforced that it functionally excluded Chinese women from coming to the United States. The Chinese Exclusion Act of 1882 prohibited the entry of Chinese laborers (men or women) and forbade wives of resident laborers from entering the United States (Takaki 1989). Later, the Immigration Act of 1924 prohibited the entry of any Chinese women to the United States, making it impossible for families of Chinese men to join them.

In addition to explicit laws restricting immigration, many Asian immigrants believed that their work in the United States would be temporary; so, in accordance with tradition, wives remained at home. In the elite classes, the practice of footbinding also limited women's ability to travel. As a result, the large number of men in Chinese communities in the United States made them bachelor societies. Only in Hawaii, where sugar planters thought Chinese women could control Chinese laborers through their taming influence, were women encouraged to immigrate.

Before 1868, as part of its isolationist policy, the Japanese government forbade its citizens to leave; however, with a new emperor in 1868, Japan encouraged select classes to seek education abroad. Economic depression in the 1880s encouraged many small farmers to seek opportunities in the United States, where wages were high compared with those in Japan and hard work held the promise of enabling workers to return to Japan as wealthy people—a promise that rarely came true. Japanese immigrants to the United States tended to come from middle-class backgrounds and, on the whole, were better off economically than other Asian and European immigrants to the United States. Like the Chinese, the earliest immigrants were mostly men who worked in unskilled labor in agriculture, mining, railroads, and lumber. They, too, believed their work in the United States was temporary (Glenn 1986).

Japanese women were allowed to come to the United States under the terms of the Gentlemen's Agreement of 1908. This law restricted the entry of Japanese laborers but allowed parents, wives, and children of those already in America to settle here. This law also encouraged the practice of "picture brides," particularly among Japanese and Korean immigrants. Consistent with the traditional practice of arranged marriage, Asian men in the United States would marry women who, hopeful of upward mobility, applied and were displayed in offices in many of the port cities (Takaki 1989). Until ruled unconstitutional in 1967, **antimiscegenation** laws barred marriages between Whites and "Mongolians," or laborers of Asian origins (Chow 1987). Such policies made it difficult, if not impossible, for stable Asian American families to form. This history reveals that family stability is as much a result of policies and practices that promote family life as it is of the culture and characteristics of different groups.

Among Native Americans, family lifestyles vary widely, because diversity among groups is a key element of culture. The attempt to impose Western family forms on these people complicates the picture of Native American family life. Interference in these cultures by social workers, the federal government, and other outsiders might have done more to promote family and cultural disorganization than to assist these groups. Among Native American families, urbanization contributes to high rates of unemployment and dependence on public welfare (Miller 1975). Left to their own culture, Native American families tend to rely on extended family networks to fulfill family functions (Redhorse et al. 1979; Rousey and Longie 2001). The imposition of Western standards on these traditional forms creates stress for the community and the family, because adapting to both traditional and dominant societal values poses difficulties for both individuals and families.

The problems faced by diverse families underscore the point that families do not exist in a cultural and economic vacuum. Economic changes, racial and cultural conflicts, and gender relations interact to produce family systems. In sum, we can see that no single model of family life characterizes *the* American family, despite ideological beliefs to the contrary. Even the feminist perspective that family life is debilitating for women seems questionable when we consider the role of the family in the cultural resistance of minority groups. Sociological perspectives on family life should be sensitive to the interaction of the family with other social institutions and should keep in mind that the ideology of the family often, if not always, departs from the actual structure of both dominant- and subordinate-group family systems. Understanding family experiences for all groups requires an understanding of the intersections of race, class, and gender oppression in the structuring of family life.

❖ Families and Social Problems

Family Violence

The tensions experienced within families are evident by the extent of violence that occurs within families. These once-hidden problems now seem disturbingly common. Although accurate measures of the extent of family violence are difficult to establish, researchers estimate that the problem is widespread across families in all classes and races. With regard to wife battering and child abuse, indirect evidence of their extent also comes from police records of domestic disturbances, hospital emergency room files, family court records, homicide rates of women killed by husbands and lovers, and the great number of divorces that cite violence as the primary reason for ending the marriage. Information on incest is even harder to obtain because social taboos against it make incest one of the most hidden of social problems. As victims of incest have spoken out, we have begun to see its high incidence across class and race. Although we have tended to think of violence as most prevalent in lower classes and among minority groups, it is important to point out that it occurs in all groups, although the middle and upper classes have more ability to keep violence hidden.

Partner Violence
Studies indicate that the overwhelming amount of domestic violence is directed against women. Coupled with the idea that violence is purposeful behavior, this fact leads to the conclusion that violence against women in families is a form of social control—one that emerges directly from the patriarchal structure and ideology of the family. Historically, wife beating has been a legitimate way to express male authority. Scholars contend that the transformation from the feudal patriarchal household to the nuclear family had the effect of strengthening the husband's power over his wife by placing systems of authority directly in the hands of individual men, not in the indirect rule of the state. Throughout the seventeenth, eighteenth, and nineteenth centuries, men could, within the law, beat their wives, and there was little community objection to their doing so as long as the method and

extent of violence remained within certain tacit, and sometimes formally documented, limits. For example, eighteenth-century French law restricted violence against wives to "blows, thumps, kicks, or punches on the back if they leave no traces" and did not allow the use of "sharp edged or crushing instruments" (Castan 1976, cited in Dobash and Dobash 1979:56–57). One ancient code, from which we get the phrase *rule of thumb*, allowed a man to beat his wife with a stick no thicker than his thumb (Dobash and Dobash 1977).

Researchers estimate that approximately one-quarter of women and 7.6 percent of men have been physically assaulted or raped by a current or former spouse, cohabiting partner, or date at some point in their lifetime (see Table 6.2). A number of risk factors contribute to the likelihood of violence in any relationship, especially power imbalances that occur between partners, with the least powerful and most dependent partner being most at risk. Thus, a pattern has been found that violence is more likely to occur in relationships when a woman's educational level is higher than that of her partner, another indication of how power operates within relationships. Physical disability is also linked to violence, with partners who are disabled more likely to be victims of violence. In addition, patterns such as a prior history of violence (including within one's family of origin), substance abuse, and attempts to end a relationship (separation and divorce) are linked to the likelihood of violence (Tjaden and Thoennes 2000; Kantor and Jasinksi 1998).

TABLE 6.2   Intimate Partner Violence: Percent of Persons Victimized by Intimate Partner Violence

	Women	Men
In Lifetime:		
Rape	7.7	0.3
Physical assault	22.1	7.4
Rape and/or physical assault	24.8	7.6
Stalking	4.8	0.6
Total	25.5	7.9
In Previous 12 Months:		
Rape	0.2	n/a
Physical assault	1.3	0.9
Rape and/or physical assault	1.5	0.9
Stalking	0.5	0.2
Total	1.8	1.1

Source: Data from Patricia Tjaden and Nancy Thoennes. 2000. *Extent, Nature and Consequences of Intimate Partner Violence: Findings from the National Violence against Women Survey.* Washington, DC: National Institute of Justice.

A common pattern within violent relationships is the isolation that battered partners experience. When a pattern of violence emerges in a relationship, the batterer may work to isolate the partner from friends, families, and other support networks. Violence by intimates is often accompanied by emotionally abusive and controlling behavior. Thus, women whose partners are jealous, controlling, or verbally abusive are much more likely to report being raped, physically assaulted, or stalked by their partners (Tjaden and Thoennes 2000). Furthermore, being battered can produce psychological problems, including depression and anxiety, and can further isolate someone from potential support networks. This isolation then feeds on a cycle of violence such that battered women feel that they have no options other than continuing the relationship.

This cycle explains a common reaction of others to domestic violence: Why doesn't the battered woman leave? Studies of battered wives show that at some points in the relationship, most do in fact leave, but often only temporarily. Once a pattern of violence is established in a relationship, women may believe they have no options. Their feeling that they have no place to go is often a realistic assessment of their economic situation and their powerlessness to effect changes within the relationship. When women do stay in abusive relationships, they tend to rationalize the violence to themselves—perhaps thinking the violence will stop, the man will change, or they will find some way to change the relationship. Research finds that women who stay within violent relationships use these different types of rationalizations, including believing that the man can be "saved" or explaining the battering as the result of external forces that the batterer cannot control, thereby excusing the behavior and putting themselves in the traditional role of "helper" trying to save someone else, not themselves.

When women do decide to prosecute their batterers, they are faced with the problem of having to prosecute a man who is both their partner and, possibly, the father of their children. Even if the wife brings charges, when the husband is released, he returns to the home—probably more angry than when the violence began. If the husband was employed, but jailed, she will also experience a decline in family income. Thus, despite good intentions, policies that remove violent men from the home may actually impose different forms of hardship on women who depend on their earnings (S Miller 1997).

The movement to establish refuges for battered women has assisted many victims. Such centers have proliferated in communities throughout the country. Battered women's shelters are an important part of the support network for women and their children, although they are usually strained to meet the demands of a larger population in need than they have funds to support.

Violence is not confined to marriage, nor to heterosexual couples. Unmarried, cohabiting couples actually have a higher risk of partner violence than married couples (Tjaden and Thoennes 2000). Although studies of violence within same-sex relationships are only beginning to emerge, these studies indicate that women living in intimate relationships with other women are the most likely to be victims of violence, but their assailants are men. It appears the least likely form of relationship to produce violence is an intimate relationship between women. That does not mean that violence does not occur in lesbian relationships—only that the rate appears to be lower than violence involving male-female intimates and male-male intimates (Tjaden and Thoennes 2000; West 1998; Renzetti 1997). Within same-sex relationships, homophobia plays a role in the perpetration of violence. It can be used as a psychological weapon if a partner threatens to expose the relationship to parents or employers. Internalized homophobia can also lead to patterns of violence (West 1998; Renzetti 1997).

The consequences of violence are many, ranging from psychological harm to death. Wives' risk of homicide from family violence is three times that of husbands' (Hampton and Coner-Edwards 1993), and women are far more likely to be injured through violence. Even when men are the victims of family violence—a phenomenon that has been exaggerated in the media, but does occur—men are less likely to be seriously injured than are women in violent relationships (Brush 1990). Studies also link numerous health problems to domestic violence (Fischbach and Herbert 1997). For children, witnessing family violence has a strong effect. Researchers estimate that 11 to 20 percent of children report having witnessed parental violence when they were young (Hennig et al. 1996). This can lead to emotional and physical distress, personality and adjustment problems, disciplinary problems, and educational underachievement, to say nothing of putting children in physical danger (Wolak and Finkelhor 1998).

Feminist scholars argue that violence is a weapon men use to control women and that gender-neutral explanations ignore the specific patriarchal relationships from which violence stems (Kurz 1989). This perspective puts the cause of domestic violence in the power dynamics existing between men and women in the family. According to this argument, men abuse their wives as an expression of their power. This has been investigated in a number of studies, particularly those that examine whether women's and men's contributions to family economic resources are related to violence against women. Some studies find that men are more likely to be violent when their financial power in the family is eroded (whether because of low income, unemployment, or a shift in the balance of what husbands and wives contribute to total family income). Violence becomes one way that men maintain their power over women, even when their economic power is diminished (McCloskey 1996).

Marital Rape

Marital rape is defined as "forced sexual activity demanded of a wife by her husband" (Frieze 1983). Legal definitions of marital rape vary from state to state, and in many states forced sex is still not considered a crime in marriage. Historically, the "right" to sex was fundamental to the legal definition of marriage (Ryan 1995). Many still view rape as something that cannot happen in marriage, as shown in studies of undergraduates who minimize the seriousness of rape by a husband compared to rape by a stranger (Monson et al., 2000).

Estimates of marital rape are hard to come by, but most studies find it occurring in 7 to 14 percent of married couples—more common than rape by a stranger. Most wives experiencing marital rape have experienced it multiple times in the marriage (Mahoney and Williams 1998; Tjaden and Thoennes 2000).

Marital rape is associated with other forms of violence in the relationship. Sometimes wives who have experienced sexual assault in marriage report being forced to engage in sex with their children, with other people, or in public. Sexual assault often occurs when the couple is in the process of separation or divorce or when the husband suspects sexual infidelity. Marital rape has also been found to be common when the wife is ill, pregnant, or has just given birth. Studies of offenders find that themes of power, control, dominance, and humiliation are common among these men and that they are likely to believe rape myths, such as that their wives enjoyed being forced to have sex. Male offenders also typically do not understand the harm they have caused as the result of their violence (Mahoney and Williams 1998).

Wives in these marriages have few resources of their own to draw on, exacerbating their powerlessness in this situation; moreover, the belief that sexual access is a right in marriage allows the idea that they have not been raped. The evidence on marital rape nonetheless shows the extent to which the definition of women as the property of men continues to affect marital relationships (Yllo 1999).

Incest and Sexual Abuse

Accurate estimates of the extent of incest and sexual abuse are very difficult to establish. Russell's (1986) study, the most widely cited, indicates that 16 percent of women have been sexually abused by a relative by the time they are 18 years old; other forms of incest range between 4 and 12 percent of the population. Girls are far more likely to be abused than boys and, when they are, to experience greater harm (Nelson and Oliver 1998).

Feminist clinicians who have studied incest have challenged traditional Freudian assumptions about incest, which presume that children lie or fantasize about incestuous sexual encounters. Those subjected to incest do try to stop the incest by seeking help or striking back, although often they are not believed. Research from feminist clinicians has shown that families in which incest occurs tend to share several characteristics, the most significant of which is the estrangement of mother and daughter.

Mothers may be aware of incestuous abuse, but they are typically powerless to stop it. A mother may become a silent bystander because her emotional and/or economic dependence on her husband prevents her from confronting the situation. Studies of different cultures where various forms of sexual abuse are inflicted on daughters (including genital mutilation, infanticide, footbinding, and other practices) explain mothers' participation in such harm in the context of power relations within the family and the culture at large (Candib 1999). Particularly in families where mothers are unusually powerless as a result of battering, disability, or mental illness there is an especially high risk of sexual abuse, especially among daughters who have taken on the household responsibilities. In such families, the daughter is often led to believe that she must comply with the father's demands if she is to hold the family together (Herman and Hirschman 1977). Molested daughters in this situation are still dependent on their fathers for care and, since this may be the only affection they receive, they often report warm feelings for their fathers, who make them feel special (Herman 1981).

This research finds that the father/assailant feels no contrition about his behavior. When mothers are incapacitated, fathers do not take on the nurturing functions, nor do they express nurturing feelings for the child or understand the destructiveness of the incest. Fathers typically blamed their wives or their daughters for the incest and, distressingly, Herman finds that daughters often reinforce this view, blaming the mothers and themselves, while exonerating the fathers (Herman 1981).

This portrait of incestuous behavior underscores that the intersection of power and gender relations in families is a contributing fact in incestuous behavior. Researchers also are only now beginning to see the multiple consequences of sexual abuse. For example, childhood abuse is linked to a variety of social problems, including delinquency, substance abuse, developmental problems, and later violence in relationships (Milner and Crouch 1993; Hernandez 1995; Conte 1993). These findings also suggest that sexual abuse is important for practitioners to consider when developing treatment programs for other social problems concerning women and young girls.

Feminists have pointed to violence as the logical result of both women's powerlessness in the family and a male culture that emphasizes aggression, domination, and violence. The modern form of the family leads women to be economically and emotionally dependent on men, and, as a result, the traditional family is a source of social conflict and a haven only for men (Hartmann 1981a). The phenomenon of violence in the family shows clearly the problems that traditional family structures create for women. Feminist criticism of the family rests, in part, on the psychological, physical, and economic threats families pose for women, and it is for those reasons that feminists argue for a change in traditional family structures. These changes, intended to empower women, would not necessarily abolish the family, but they would create new values regarding women's work in the family and new rewards for women in the family, regardless of whether they are also working in the public labor force.

Teen Pregnancy

The teen birth rate has actually been declining and is now 45.8 births per 1,000 women. Contrary to popular stereotypes, the decrease in the rate of teen births is less among White teens than Black teens. The most significant change has been in the rate of births to unmarried women—a phenomenon affecting all age groups, but most pronounced among White women, where the percent of births to unmarried women (of any age) increased from 27 percent in 1990 to 33 percent in 2001. Over the same period, the percentage of births to unmarried Black women was changed from 67 percent to 68 percent (U.S. Census Bureau 2004). In the same period the birth rate to teens declined among Blacks, American Indians, and Whites. (Hispanics were not separately counted.)

Teen mothers face higher medical risks in pregnancy as well as a greater risk of low-birth-weight babies and infant mortality. In addition to health problems, teenage parents face chronic unemployment or, when they work, low earnings and low-status jobs. In 2003, the unemployment rate for Black teenage males was 36 percent; for White teenage males, 17 percent. For teenage females, unemployment was 30 percent for Blacks and 13 percent for Whites. For Hispanic male teens, the rate was 22 percent; for Lantina teens, 18 percent. The figures for Asian teens are 20 percent for men and 14 percent for women. (U.S. Department of Labor 2004).

Such figures point to the chronic problems of teens finding work to support themselves and their children.

Approximately 85 percent of teenage mothers continue to live with their families, many of whom are themselves single-female heads of household who were also teenage mothers. One-third of teen mothers live in poverty, regardless of race; those who live on their own are more likely to be poor. Regardless of their race and class background, teen mothers do value marriage as an ideal, but they are not sure they will ever marry. Compared with teen mothers of the past, present-day teen mothers from all races and classes feel much less pressure to marry. Although they do regard childbearing as a marital event, they also see sex as separated from marriage. Many teens no longer think that marriage is necessary to legitimate a birth. They remain unmarried because they think fathers are unwilling or not ready to marry, because they are not ready for marriage, and because their families counsel them against marrying precipitously (Farber 1990).

Sociological studies of African American teen mothers show that, contrary to stereotypical views, the Black community does not condone teen pregnancy. Elaine Bell Kaplan (1997) has done detailed ethnographic research in two communities in the San Francisco Bay Area: East Oakland and Richmond, both communities with a large African American population. These neighborhoods are characterized by high rates of unemployment, poverty, inadequate schools, crime and drug-related violence and high numbers of single-parent households. Kaplan spent several months in the community, working as a volunteer in a community teen center, "hanging out" with a group of teen mothers. She interviewed the teen mothers and, when she could, their mothers and, sometimes, the fathers of their children. Kaplan found that, unlike what stereotypes would suggest, the teens were embarrassed by being pregnant and had numerous conflicts with their mothers, who saw their daughters' pregnancies as disrupting the hopes they had for their daughters' success. The teen mothers were also ashamed of having to go on welfare and, if they did, they tried to hide that they needed welfare to make ends meet. These conclusions are directly counter to the public image that such women do not value success and live in a culture that promotes welfare dependency.

The high rate of teenage pregnancy has caused much concern over the issue of birth control and the sexual behavior of young people. Since the early 1970s, birth control has become widely available, and evidence shows that an increasing number of women and men now engage in sexual intercourse before marriage. About four in five people have sexual intercourse while they are teenagers, most initiating sex in their mid to late teens. About two-thirds use a contraceptive during their first experience with intercourse—a number that has increased in recent years because of an increase in condom use among teens.

Promoting abstinence from sexual activity has been suggested as the best way to reduce teen pregnancy. How effective has this campaign been? The reduction in teen pregnancy in recent years might lead you to think that abstinence campaigns have been a success, but studies have found that sex education programs focusing exclusively on abstinence have shown no effect in delaying sexual activity among teens. Increased use of birth control by teens, in part because of the campaign for sex safe from AIDS, is far more effective in reducing teen pregnancy (Dailard 2003).

Among teens using birth control, the most frequent contraceptive is the pill (44 percent), followed by the condom (38 percent), injectable birth control (10 percent), withdrawal (4 percent), and the implant (3 percent). The number of teens using birth control has increased in recent years, perhaps due to widespread publicity about AIDS and safe sex, perhaps contributing to the recent decline in teen pregnancy. Ease of use, such as with "the shot" (injectable birth control), has likely increased effective use of contraceptives by younger women. Women under age 24 are the group most likely to use the injectable and the implant for birth control (Alan Guttmacher Institute 1998).

Still, a large number of young women have sex without birth control (35 percent). A sexually active teen who does not use contraception has a 90 percent chance of getting pregnant within one year (Alan Guttmacher Institute 1998). Many have argued that a sociological reason for young women not using birth control is that the regular use of contraceptives requires conscious recognition of oneself as sexually active (Luker 1975). Teenage sex tends to be episodic; for a young woman to make calculated plans for contraceptive protection requires her to see herself as a sexually active person. Cultural and legal proscriptions that encourage the denial of sexuality to young women seem likely only to exacerbate this situation.

Many also argue that sex education does not filter down to adolescents before they start having sex. Girls often have little or no information about their bodies and are often seriously misinformed about sex (for example, believing they cannot get pregnant if they are standing up during intercourse!). The fact that mothers, not fathers, talk to their children about sex also spreads the message that men have no responsibility in this area, discouraging young men from being responsible for birth control and resting the decision to avoid pregnancy only on young girls. Researchers find that pregnant teens romanticize the demands of motherhood, and many believe they can give their babies a better life than they received. Because adolescent pregnancy disproportionately affects poor and minority youth, having children may be their only way of achieving masculinity or femininity in a society that denies them the expression of these traits in adult roles (Ladner 1986; Horowitz 1995).

Adolescents who do get pregnant are more traditional in their gender-role orientation than other sexually active young teens. They perceive themselves as competent in highly gender-typed activities, have lower aspirations and grades, and have less sense of personal control. It has been demonstrated that more egalitarian gender-role attitudes are associated with the belief in contraceptive use; moreover, young men with egalitarian gender-role attitudes are more likely to use contraceptives in premarital intercourse than are young men with more sexist attitudes (MacCorquodale 1984). This should lead us to conclude that programs and policies designed to alleviate the problems of teenage pregnancy must recognize the importance of gender relations in understanding and reducing teen pregnancy.

Child Care

Child care in the United States is, by virtue of the character of the family, largely a system of private care. The parent-child unit is allegedly self-sufficient and, given the gender division of labor, the responsibility for child care falls heavily on individual women. The experience of mothers (or other caregivers) is based on the assumption that children are best cared for by their mother. Exceptions to this design do exist, although even then the arrangements for child care are usually managed by the mother, and it is other women who do the work. Although it is more and more impractical to do so, mothers usually have the major responsibility for the everyday care of their children.

The privatized and exclusive character of child care seems especially inappropriate when we consider the labor force participation rate of mothers. As already noted, increases in the labor force participation rate are highest among women with children, especially women with children of preschool age.

Women's access to child care can significantly influence their prospects for employment, because the cost of child care can be a significant deterrent to women seeking employment (see Figure 6.4). Many must rely on kin or other volunteers for child care. Extended kin networks can facilitate women's access to jobs, but show how parents must often rely on their own networks and families for child care support (Uttal 2002; Uttal and Tuominen 1999).

Employed women then use a variety of arrangements to care for their children, with most being cared for by another relative (see Figure 6.4). Two-thirds of non–school-aged children are cared for either in their homes or in another private home. Fewer than one-quarter are tended in organized child care facilities. Among children in school, relatives are the most common form of child care,

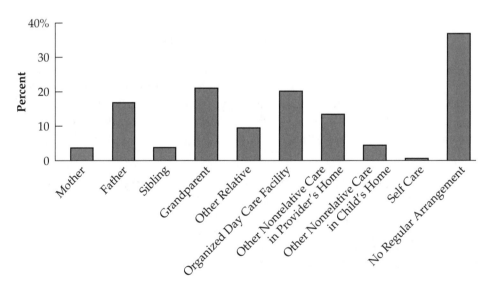

Note: Percentages exceed total of 100% because of multiple arrangements

FIGURE 6.4   Child Care Arrangements for Preschoolers

Source: Smith, Kristin. 2002. *Whose Minding the Kids: Child Care Arrangements: Spring 1997.* Washington, DC: U.S. Census Bureau, p. 3.

most often the other parent, a grandparent, or sibling (U.S. Census Bureau 2004). White children are more likely to use self care, whereas Black and Hispanic children are more likely to be in after-school programs.

The affordability of child care is a serious problem for many families—both low and middle income—and can consume a large portion of a family budget. As Figure 6.5 shows, nearly half of all working families (48 percent) with children incur child care expenses with an average cost of $286 per month—9 percent of the typical family's earnings. For low-income families, the cost of child care is actually a higher portion of family earnings than for middle-income families; this is both because the family budgets are lower, but also because low-income children spend more time in child care because of parents' working hours (Giannarelli and Barsimantov 2000; Capizzano et al. 2000). Families with disabled or chronically ill children have an even greater burden in paying for child care (Lukemeyer et al. 2000).

The Family and Medical Leave Act (FMLA) of 1993 provides some help for families since it requires employers to grant 12 weeks of leave to a parent to care for newborn or adopted children or to care for a sick child, spouse, or parent. But, the leave is unpaid and only applies to employers in companies with 50 or more workers. In addition, employees are required to first exhaust vacation and sick leave. The law also applies only to married, heterosexual couples, although some companies are more liberal in the implementation of this policy. Although the FMLA has made great improvement in the benefits to working people with family

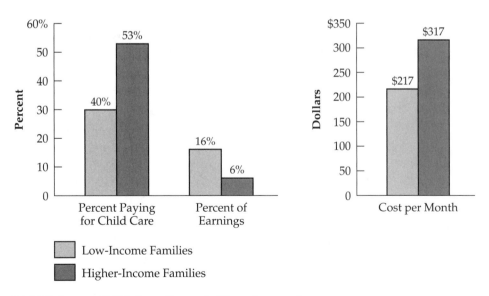

FIGURE 6.5   Child Care Costs: A Class Comparison

Source: Giannarelli, Linda, and James Barsimantov. 2000. "Child Care Expenses of America's Families." Washington, DC: The Urban Institute, p. 7.

responsibilities, more is needed to help people cope with the strains of balancing work and family. Currently, only 5 percent of companies provide any assistance for child care; 2 percent of these provide on-site child care to employees, 1 percent provide some accommodation for off-site care, and 2 percent provide some funds to employees for child care. Furthermore, whether employees get such support varies by their status in the organization. Eleven percent of professional/technical workers get such support, but only 5 percent of clerical and sales employees and only 2 percent of so-called "blue-collar" employees do—what you could consider a proxy for the working class (U.S. Department of Labor 2004).

These facts suggest the need to imagine new models and policies for child care in society (see Table 6.1). Historically, depression and war have provided the major impetus for establishing public child care facilities in the United States. Public child care in the United States first originated in the Works Progress Administration (WPA) of the New Deal. In the 1930s, WPA day care and nursery schools were designed to provide employment for needy teachers, child care workers, cooks, janitors, nutritionists, and clerical workers during the Depression. By the end of the Depression and the beginning of World War II, when jobs were no longer in short supply, the WPA nurseries were eliminated. In 1941, the Lanham Act (also known as the Community Facilities Act) was passed by Congress to meet the day care needs of mothers in wartime employment. The Lanham Act made matching federal funds available to states for the expansion of day care centers and nursery schools. Following World War II, when women were no longer needed in the labor force, Congress withdrew funds for day care, and most of the Lanham Act nurseries closed (Baxandall 1979).

Since World War II, federally funded day care programs have been established for the poor. For example, Project Head Start, funded through the Office of Economic Opportunity, was designed primarily for children from families below the poverty line. In the past, public attitudes toward funded child care were stigmatized by the association of federally supported child care with welfare services, but support for increased availability of child care services now runs high.

That women are still socially defined as primarily responsible for children is well illustrated by the now widely recognized phenomenon of *deadbeat dads*—those who, following a custody and support agreement, abandon financial support of their children. What kind of child support do women receive when they have custody of children following a divorce? As we have seen, less than half receive the full amount they are due; 20 percent receive none. In the rare cases where women owe men child support, men are actually less likely to receive it. Yet, women are more economically dependent on receiving support for their children. In these situations, women can feel stuck. They are unlikely to have the resources needed to pursue legally what they are owed. In many cases, particularly those involving young, uneducated men, the father may be unable to pay. State policies that have tried to enforce child support payments have helped, however, since the number of custodial parents actually receiving support has increased in recent years (Grall 2000).

With the number of young people increasing in society and the rate of poverty now being highest among young people, there is a compelling argument for more socially supported programs for child care and child support. Without this, a new generation of people will face economic hardship and the social disadvantage that follows. Simply leaving child care needs for individual women and men to handle on their own will not serve the overall needs of children and their society well. In general, U.S. society has a poor record of supporting the various forms of care work that sustain human life. Economically, if people and companies actually paid for the now unpaid work of caring for children and kin, the cost would be $196 billion dollars per year (Folbre 2001). Since women now provide most of that unpaid work, the hidden value of care work falls mostly on them. Only in a society where women's work—and women's worth—is systematically devalued, even while being romanticized as part of "family life," could such exploitation of human labor be allowed to continue.

❖ *Chapter Summary and Themes*

The historic evolution of family forms stems from the family's relationship to economic systems and to ideologies of the family that have glorified the home as women's place.

Processes such as the development of capitalism and the growth of industrialization have shaped the forms that families have taken. Ideals such as the cult of domesticity emerged to justify the role of women in families, even though the ideal is race- and class-specific. Racial-ethnic families also emerge in relationship to the specific forms of labor that different groups have provided in society.

Feminist perspectives on family emphasize a structural diversity that emphasizes the social construction of family forms in the context of the specific class, race, and gender arrangements in society.

Structural diversity is found in the different ways that families must respond to conditions of inequality. Diversity is also found within families, as women and men have different levels of power in familiar relationships. Despite this diversity, ideology about the family paints it as monolithic and idealized. Even with the social structural influences on families, human beings actively create and adapt to this social institution.

Diversity, not uniformity, characterizes contemporary family forms.

Contemporary U.S. households are characterized by high rates of divorce and a large increase in the number of households headed by women. Households now rarely conform to the family ideal and consist of many types, including married, heterosexual couples, cohabitors, dual-earner families, gay and lesbian families, and singles. Balancing work and family commitments is an increasing challenge for many forms of families.

The race and ethnic relations in society, intertwined with class and gender, organize the social structure of diverse families.

Racial-ethnic families face unique experiences both because of the dominant ideologies that distort the understanding of such families and because racial stratification results in different labor patterns that affect family experiences. Historical realities, such as slavery, immigration, and forced conquest, continue to shape the family experiences of different racial-ethnic groups.

Many of today's social problems directly affect people in families and result from the gender relations that, though seldom recognized in social policy discussions, shape such problems as family violence, teen pregnancy, and the affordability of child care.

Violence against women in families is common and results from the association of gender with power and social control. Teen pregnancy, though decreasing, remains a problem that reproduces poverty and disadvantages young women and their children. The absence of affordable child care reflects the cultural ideal that children are best cared for by women in the home. With more women in the labor force, the lack of affordable child care strains family budgets, especially for the most economically vulnerable families.

❖ *Key Terms*

antimiscegenation	householder	structural diversity model
cult of domesticity	marital rape	The Family and Medical
family household	nonfamily household	Leave Act
household	nuclear family	transnational family

❖ *Discussion Questions/Projects for Thought*

1. Identify two families that could be described as having different structural characteristics (i.e., married working couple, commuting marriage, divorced head of household, lesbian couple, single-parent household, etc.) and interview each family member (including any children) about who does what work in the family, including finances, child care, housework, managing social relations, and so on. What does your project tell you about gender and the household division of labor?

2. Identify a group of working mothers and/or fathers and interview them about their child care practices, including questions such as:

Who cares for the child when the parent(s) work? What happens when the child is sick? How much does the child care cost and who pays? When do problems arise and how are they solved? What does your research on this reveal about gender and child care? What new policies would you recommend to provide affordable child care to working parents?

3. Find out if there is a shelter for battered women in your community. If so, interview some of the workers there and ask them about the patterns they see among those who come to the shelter. What do they think would stop violence against women? Do you agree?

❖ Internet Resources

Family Research Library, University of New Hampshire

http://www.unh.edu/frl/

This independent research unit is devoted to the study of family problems. Their website includes information about their current research and other projects related to the study of families.

National Partnership for Women and Families

http://www.nationalpartnership.org

This non-profit organization is dedicated to promoting policies that help women and men balance work and family demands. The website includes information on internships as well as policy initiatives and data useful in understanding policies about family leave and related subjects.

U.S. Census Bureau

http://www.census.gov

The U.S. Census Bureau collects assorted data about families and living arrangements. The website gives information about family structures, including data on female heads of households, marital status, child support, and other information important to understanding family structures.

Violence Against Women and Family Violence

http://www.ojp.usdoj.gov/nij/vawprog/welcome.html

This website from the Department of Justice program on violence against women provides information on research, conferences, publications, and related links.

❖ Suggested Readings

Baca Zinn, Maxine, and Stanley D. Eitzen. 2005. *Diversity in Families,* 7th ed. Boston: Allyn and Bacon.
  This comprehensive text reviews all aspects of family life from a sociological perspective and with a focus on the importance of race, class, and gender in shaping different family experiences.

Calhoun, Cheshire. 2000. *Feminism, the Family, and the Politics of the Closet: Lesbian and Gay Displacement.* New York: Oxford University Press.
  Based in feminist theory, this book explores patterns of heterosexual dominance and how this pushes gays and lesbians into positions of invisible citizenship.

Garey, Anita Ilta. 1999. *Weaving Work and Motherhood.* Philadelphia: Temple University Press.
  This study of employed mothers challenges the common idea that women construct their identity by orienting either to work or to family. Garey shows how women weave both work and motherhood into their identities, while analyzing the conflicts that employed women experience.

Hamer, Jennifer. 2001. *What It Means to Be Daddy.* New York: Columbia University Press.
  This study of low-income, never married African American fathers shows that, despite stereotypes to the contrary, these fathers want to be involved with their children and want to be good fathers. What fatherhood means to them is conditioned by the social structures in which they find themselves.

Hansen, Karen V., and Anita Ilta Garey, eds. 1998. *Families in the U.S.: Kinship and Domestic Policies.* Philadelphia: Temple University Press.
  This anthology is a comprehensive review of research on diverse family forms and experiences. It is an excellent introduction to

social science research on families and also uses a historical perspective to frame an understanding of families in the United States.

Jasinski, Jana L., and Linda M. Williams, eds. 1998. *Partner Violence: A Comprehensive Review of 20 Years of Research.* Thousand Oaks, CA: Sage.
Reviewing the empirical and theoretical research on violence, the authors in this anthology document and analyze the violence that occurs in different kinds of relationships, including marriage, parent-child violence, and violence within gay and lesbian relationships.

Kaplan, Elaine Bell. 1997. *Not Our Kind of Girl: Unraveling the Myths of Black Teenage Motherhood.* Berkeley: University of California Press.
Kaplan's study of African American teenage mothers challenges social myths and stereotypes about these young women and their families. Her ethnographic study provides an empathetic portrait of the experience of these young women in confronting racism, sexism, and class disadvantage.

Kurz, Demi. 1995. *For Richer, For Poorer: Mothers Confront Divorce.* New York: Routledge.
This study of divorced mothers shows the economic and sociological impact of divorce on women. It provides a feminist framework for family policies that would be more supportive of women and children.

Lehmann, Jennifer M., ed. 2001. *The Gay and Lesbian Marriage and Family Reader: Analyses of Problems and Prospects for the 21st Century.* New York: Richard Altschuler and Assoc.
This collection is an excellent resource on issues facing lesbian and gay families, including same-sex marriage, child custody and adoption, parenting, and coming out to family members.

WOMEN, HEALTH, AND REPRODUCTION

7

The Social Structure of Health
Gender and Health
Race, Class, and Health
Reproduction and Protective
    Legislation

Gender, Health, and Social Problems
Gender and the Body: Weight,
    Food, and Body Image
Substance Abuse: Alcohol, Drugs,
    and Smoking
Women and AIDS
Disability
Health Insurance

The Politics of Reproduction
Birth Control
Abortion
Racism and Reproduction

The Politics of Birth: Pregnancy
    and Childbirth
New Reproductive Technologies

Gender and the Health Care System
Women as Health Care Workers
The Women's Health Movement

Chapter Summary and Themes

Key Terms

**Discussion Questions/
Projects for Thought**

Internet Resources

Suggested Readings

Almost any day on the news you hear reports about new medical research that gives new insight into some aspect of a disease or health problem. Have you ever stopped to ask who such studies represent and what the implications of this research are for women? If you did, you might very well find out that all of the subjects in the study were men and that the same insights or procedures that medical researchers are heralding as advancing medical science have not been at all considered for their implications for women's health. Gender is such a strong factor in studies of health that in the spring of 2001, the National Academy of Sciences issued a report advocating that biomedical researchers should study gender as a basic human variable in all areas of health-related research. By issuing this report, the Academy was noting the extraordinary paucity of biomedical knowledge that takes gender seriously—even as late as 2001 (Pear 2001).

Until the Office of Research on Women's Health was founded at the National Institute of Health (NIH) in 1990, women were routinely excluded from research sponsored by NIH—the major research organization from which scientific, health-related research comes. Women were excluded from drug trials, thus we know little about the effects of various drugs for women at different phases of the life cycle or with different diseases. The widely promoted claim that taking an aspirin a day can prevent some heart attacks was thus based on a study of 22,000 men—all of them physicians—a study that excluded women based on the claim that there were not enough women physicians to include in the research sample. As a result, we do not know what effect aspirin might have for women. Perhaps it wouldn't make any difference if we did because studies also show that doctors treat women less aggressively for heart disease than they do men. Heart disease is one of the most heavily studied areas of health, but women are less likely than men to have bypass surgery or angioplasty, even though women are as likely as men to die of heart disease, adjusting for age (National Center for Health Statistics 2003).

Consider the attention given to Viagra, the drug that treats male impotency and for which the scientists who did the basic research underlying its functioning were given the Nobel Prize. Would fewer women be dying from breast cancer if such resources were poured into its study? Why, in 2004, was Viagra more readily available than flu shots? Would women be healthier if more resources were directed toward battering, eating disorders, or the prevention of smoking? This bias in favor of men is not unique to the United States. In Japan, where women's use of the birth control pill was not approved until 1999—and only then after the approval process took more than ten years—Viagra was approved by the Ministry of Health and Welfare in a record six months.

Physical health is one of the most basic of life's privileges. Although we tend to think of our bodies as best cared for through personal hygiene and individual diet and health habits, in fact, physical health is heavily influenced by sociological factors. One of those factors, gender, plays a significant part in determining physical well-being and in influencing our bodily experience, as do race and class.

For instance, the likelihood that one will encounter stress, become overweight, experience hypertension, or die of certain diseases is significantly affected by one's gender. National health statistics show that hypertension is more common among men than women (at all ages). Data also show that women are more likely than men (at every age) to be at a healthy weight, despite the extraordinary fears women seem to feel about being overweight and the enormous resources put into the diet industry. At every age, men are actually more likely to be overweight than women, although women are more likely obese, as defined by government standards.

Along with gender and age, racial status is a complicating factor in predicting health. For example, African Americans are far more likely than Whites to experience disability, to develop hypertension, and to suffer from poor nutrition (National Center for Health Statistics 2003). Figure 7.1 shows how hypertension, as one indicator of the combined stresses of race and gender, affects different race-gender groups in the U.S. population.

Such data indicate that physical health is mediated by social and cultural organizations. For this reason, gender influences not only what we will become but also how long our lives will be and when we are likely to die. Gender, along with race and class, also affects access to health care. Men are less likely to be covered by medical insurance than are women, for example (National Center for Health Statistics 2003). Gender relations in the society are also reflected in institutional patterns of health care systems. Health care institutions in this society are dominated by men, even though healing and caring for others have traditionally been defined as the work of women. Because of the structure of health care in this society, women have had little control over their own reproductive lives. Throughout this chapter, you will see that gender relations are important in determining the character of health and reproduction in contemporary society.

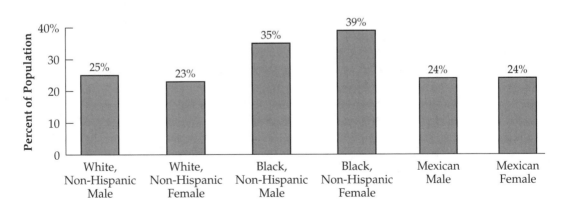

FIGURE 7.1   Hypertension by Race and Gender

Source: Data from National Center for Health Statistics. 2003. *Health United States 2003.* Washington, DC: Department of Health and Human Services.

❖ The Social Structure of Health

Gender and Health

Patterns of health change according to the social arrangements of the time. For instance, in the late nineteenth century, illness was quite fashionable for women—at least those of the upper-middle and upper classes. Women in these classes were expected to be idle and faint; consequently, retiring to bed because of "nerves" was not only acceptable but actually encouraged by medical practitioners (Ehrenreich and English 1973a).

Differences in life expectancy for men and women did not emerge in U.S. society until the beginning of the twentieth century. Even now, longer life expectancy for women occurs primarily in highly industrialized Western societies. Gender differences in mortality rates are because of a number of factors, most of which are culturally shaped by gender relations. Changes in women's roles mean that women now approximate men in the rate of death by heart disease, whereas as recently as 1980, men were far more likely to die by this cause (National Center for Health Statistics 2003). Mortality differences between men and women are determined by men's greater risk of death by accident, itself a function of men's engagement in risky behavior, violent activity, and alcohol consumption (see Figure 7.2).

Women's health, like men's, varies according to the sociological features of their lives. Studies have indicated, for example, that there are higher rates of reported illness among housewives than among women working outside the home, indicating that employment generally has positive effects on women's health. This effect, however, is mediated by other variables. For example, the characteristics of the work site (i.e., job demands, rewards and deprivations, physical environment, and social support) also influence the well-being of workers, regardless of gender, as does the division of labor in housework (Loscocco and Spitze 1990; Bird 1999).

There is little evidence that combining employment and motherhood has harmful health effects (Waldron et al. 1998). What is significant in predicting women's health and mental health are such factors as income, life satisfaction, and social contacts. Thus, women who at mid-life feel they have fallen short of their career aspirations experience higher levels of depression than women who feel more fulfilled (Carr 1997). Also, caring for ill, disabled, or elderly persons in the home increase women's psychological distress (Pavalko and Woodbury 2000). Financial strain for all groups is not only related to poor physical health but also to increased stress and depression. In one study examining mental health differences among married and unmarried mothers, researchers found that mothers who become employed experience little change in their levels of stress, since increases in the the stress of managing caregiving activities are offset by a decline in financial stress (Ali and Avison 1997). Generally speaking, whether a woman is employed or not, depression is associated with having to do routine things repeatedly and being responsible for things beyond one's control (Lennon 1994).

Women's health, both mental and physical, is also affected by the inequities they routinely face in the labor market. Studies find that, in general, inequality both within and across households is a strong predictor of health problems for different

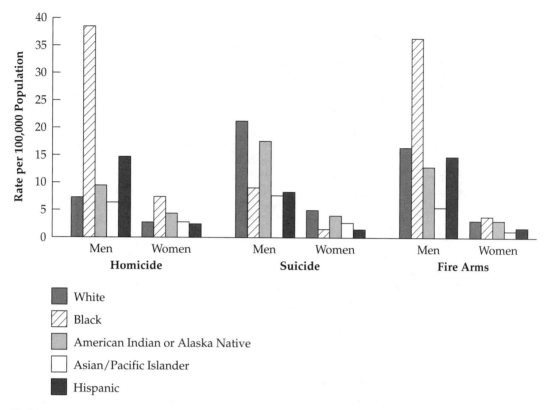

FIGURE 7.2   Death Rates by Homicide, Suicide, and Fire Arms

Source: Data from National Center for Health Statistics. 2003. *Health United States 2003.* Washington, DC: Department of Health and Human Services, pp. 146–150.

groups; but, more particularly, gender inequality in the work force produces a range of health consequences for women, including anxiety, depression, stress—all of which have negative consequences for physical health. Furthermore, simply being a minority in the workplace—a finding that holds for women and people of color—contributes to higher rates of health problems (Evans and Steptoe 2002; Griffin et al. 2002; O'Campo et al. 2004; Moss 2002). Together, these studies demonstrate the significance of gender in shaping life conditions, and therefore women's physical and mental health.

Mental health is also strongly associated with gender, race, and class status. Most studies indicate higher rates of mental illness for women than for men, at least as indicated by hospital admissions, clinical treatment, and the duration of treatment. Some explain this finding as a result of women's secondary status in society, which, because it produces stress, results in women becoming mentally ill more frequently than men. Others argue that high rates of mental illness among women reflect the fact that women are more likely to report mental problems, seek help, and think of themselves as emotional and lacking self-control. This explanation interprets women's higher mental-illness rate as the consequence of learned gender behavior. Both explanations are probably correct, underscoring the point that mental as well as physical health is connected to one's status in society.

Health is influenced by the social context in which people live. Sociological studies of health look to the environment in which people are located to understand the various health risks that different groups experience. Work environments are an important site for understanding the health risks faced by women and men; moreover, because work organizations are shaped by gender, work may have a different impact on health for women than for men.

The mythology of work in U.S. culture is that it provides an avenue for self-expression and the realization of personal goals. We have increasingly come to see, however, that work can be hazardous to physical and mental health. Toxic chemicals in the workplace produce risks for workers, although, typically, public attention to those risks for women has focused primarily on their reproductive health. Stress is also a significant health problem for workers in different environments; for women, this is more acute because of the double day employed women experience at work and at home. Studies of different occupational health hazards also reveal how these health risks are structured by the gender segregation that characterizes the workplace.

Race, Class, and Health

Racial-ethnic and class oppression in U.S. society further complicate patterns of health in men and women. Examination of health statistics by race shows significant differences in the patterns of health for different groups, with death rates by cerebrovascular disease, homicide, and diabetes, for example, significantly higher for Black Americans than for White Americans. As we have seen (Figure 7.1), women and men of color experience higher rates of hypertension than Whites; hypertension also increases with age. Although maternal death from the complications of pregnancy has decreased since 1960, Black women are four times as likely to die from causes related to pregnancy as White women. Black, American Indian, and Hispanic women are also less likely to receive prenatal care than White and Asian American women. And, although White women are more likely to get breast cancer than Black women, the rates of death from breast cancer are equal for both groups, suggesting that Black women are less likely to get effective treament (National Center for Health Statistics 2003).

The effects of racial inequality on health are dramatically shown by data on accidental deaths. As shown in Figure 7.2, death caused by accident is greater among Black men than White men. Note the very high rate of death by homicide among Black men. Suicide rates among Black men are lower than among White men, although suicide among Black men has been increasing in recent years. Suicide rates for Black women are half those for White women. It would appear that, although violent death is more common for Black Americans, cultural values and the economic dependence of families on Black women's work influence the lesser degree of suicide among them. Native Americans' health is also affected by the degree of oppression they experience. Their mortality rates are especially high among the young, particularly young men; moreover, Native Americans are twice as likely to die by homicide than are others in the general population (National Center for Health Statistics 2003).

Infant mortality, one of the major indices of the health of a population, is still almost twice as high for African Americans as for Whites. Although infant mortality rates have been decreasing over recent years, the rate of decline in infant mortality, especially among African Americans, has slowed. Black and Puerto Rican Americans are also more likely to have low-birth-weight babies, a fact that contributes to infant mortality and represents the health problems faced by these mothers.

Both historically and currently, women of color and poor women have been denied control over their reproductive lives. Studies indicate that very high percentages of poor and minority women have been sterilized, often without their consent. African American women are more likely than White and Hispanic women to have been sterilized (National Center for Health Statistics 2003). Although this may be voluntary, poor women are often coerced into sterilization. Studies indicate that among samples of welfare mothers, approximately half have been sterilized; the high sterilization rates of Black and poor women mean that feminist calls for "reproductive freedom" have particular meaning and resonance for women of color (Roberts 1997).

Much of the difference in health along lines of race is also attributable to social class. Social class has long been shown to have a strong influence on both physical and mental health, with poverty, in particular, having a strong influence on both access to health care and actual physical and mental well-being. Chronic illness is higher among less prosperous groups, as are disabilities, infectious diseases, and, as we have seen, infant mortality. There is little wonder that the higher one's social class, the better one's chance of a long and healthier life. The fact that racial inequality in this society results in higher rates of poverty for Native Americans, Latinos, and African Americans is a major factor in considering the health care of these diverse populations (Williams 1998; Council of Economic Advisors 1998).

Reproduction and Protective Legislation

Concern about women's work and health has almost exclusively focused on women's reproductive health (Novkov 1996; McCammon 1995; Crenshaw 1995). Interestingly, however, few ever consider how reproductive hazards for men are related to their work, leading to the erroneous conclusion, based on sexist premises, that only women reproduce. Clearly, occupational toxic agents and carcinogens can equally affect male sperm; yet **protective legislation** against reproductive hazards is almost always aimed at women workers (Daniels et al. 1990).

In the 1920s, the Women's League for Equal Opportunity staunchly opposed the protective legislation proposed by groups such as the Women's Trade Union League and the Consumer League of New York. They argued that consumer restrictions on the conditions of labor should be based on the nature of the industry, not on the sex of the worker (Stellman 1977:36); yet, history shows that protective laws apply specifically to women workers. The Supreme Court decision in *Muller v. Oregon,* for example, held in 1908 that it was constitutional to restrict the work day to 10 hours for women only. Protecting workers from long work days and unhealthy environments is a reasonable action, but when applied only to women, these laws exclude women from jobs under the benign guise of protection (Chavkin 1979).

Contemporary protective legislation has also been used to exclude women from work in trades in which the hazards seem no greater than those in some traditionally gender-segregated female occupations. For instance, Title VII of the 1964 Civil Rights Act prohibited employment discrimination on the basis of sex, race, color, religion, and national origin. It also provided for bona fide occupational qualification (BFOQ), which made it lawful to hire on the basis of sex when sex is a reasonable qualification for performance on the job (Hill 1979). For instance, the BFOQ clause allowed women to be excluded from jobs exceeding weight-lifting limitations set only for women. That weight restrictions on women's work are based on gender stereotypes is clearly shown by the fact that such restrictions do not appear in occupations that are typically female (such as waitressing) and that involve strenuous physical effort.

Subsequent court cases made it clear that the BFOQ clause could be applied only in a very restricted way. In both *Weeks v. Southern Bell Telephone and Telegraph Company* and *Rosenfeld v. Southern Pacific Company,* the courts ruled that individual women, like individual men, have to be given the opportunity to show that they are physically qualified for a job (Hill 1979). Overall, however, Title VII has been the basis for eliminating much protective legislation. In 1991, the Supreme Court ruled (in **Automobile Workers v. Johnson Controls**) that it was discriminatory to bar women from high-risk jobs in which there was potential harm to a fetus or reproductive system. Prior arguments for protective legislation assumed that pregnant women and fetuses are especially susceptible to toxic chemicals, radiation, and other risks. Although there is little doubt that these hazards do affect pregnant women and fetuses, they affect the reproductive health of men, as well. Legislation or company practices that apply to women only rest on the faulty assumption that only women reproduce. There is evidence of the damaging effects of lead poisoning on male sperm, the excess of chromosomal aberrations among male vinyl chloride workers, and of a causal relationship between the pesticide dibromochloropropane (DBCP) and male sterility (Wright 1979). Wives of male chloride workers also have excessive rates of stillbirths and miscarriages (Infante 1975). Removing only women from jobs in which they may be exposed to these substances clearly does not protect the reproductive health of the population.

Gender-biased assumptions in protective regulations are intricately bound to the gender-segregated character of the labor force. Concern for women's health has not caused companies to remove workers from jobs traditionally considered women's work—despite known risks from mutagens, teratogens, and toxic substances that are found in occupations employing mostly women. For example, women who work in health care are exposed to numerous chemical and toxic hazards, as well as infectious diseases, but no one has argued that women should be excluded from jobs as nurses, scrub personnel, and the like (Kemp and Jenkins 1992). Protective policies that restrict women from hazardous jobs seem to emerge only in higher-paying and traditionally male occupations into which women are moving (Chavkin 1979). Other occupations that pose equally serious hazards, yet are poorly paid and are filled by women, are usually excluded from protective legislation. Similarly, risks to the male reproductive system seldom are used to restrict their employment opportunities.

Limiting occupational health hazards solely to women or solely to reproductive effects is to overlook the complexities of work and the various health hazards it creates. All workers need protection from health hazards posed by their jobs. Included would be policies that protect the reproductive health of men and women and provide a good system of reproductive leave for both sexes. Toxic substances and radiation have a hazardous effect not only on workers in industrial plants but in surrounding communities, as well. As Supreme Court Justice Felix Frankfurter said in 1916:

> *Once we cease to look upon the regulation of women in industry as exceptional, as the law's graciousness to a disabled class, and shift the emphasis from the fact that they are* women *to the fact that it is* industry *and the relation of industry to the community which is regulated, the whole problem is seen from a totally different aspect. (1916:367, cited in Hill 1979)*

Discussion of women's health and work also cannot ignore the fact that despite real risks to health posed by contemporary jobs, employed women, as far as we can tell, are healthier on the average than women who are unemployed. Only the future will reveal the long-range effect of carcinogens, toxic substances, and radiation on human life, but current data indicate that employment has positive effects on women's health.

Although the specific hazards that workers face will vary depending on the type of work and the specific work conditions they face, there is a serious need for careful study of work-related health hazards. Policies that single out women as a restricted class do not solve this problem, nor does ignoring the complexities of gender relations in the workplace. In the end, safe workplaces, both in industry and in the home, must be constructed for men and women alike.

❖ Gender, Health, and Social Problems

Gender and the Body: Weight, Food, and Body Image

Do you like your body? If you are like most American women and men, your answer will likely be "No." Women and men obsess about their bodies, their weight, their appearance—at least if the size of the industries supporting diet products, food, and exercise is any indication. How many times have you gone on a diet? lifted weight to bulk up? looked at a beautiful person and thought, "I wish I looked like that"? How much money and time do you spend trying to look different than you do?

These questions cut to the heart of the cultural obsession with beauty, weight, and appearance—an obsession that is particularly strong among women and young girls, but from which men are not exempt. The obsession varies depending on one's race or class, but in the United States, although not everyone experiences angst over their body in the same way, we nonetheless live in a culture where we are bombarded with body and beauty ideals—ideals that few, if any, can actually achieve. Although physically real, bodies are also socially constructed. That is, our concepts of the body, how we define them, what we do to them, are deeply social, and therefore reflect the gender, race, and class relations that characterize society.

You can see this by observing popular culture, by noticing the dieting and eating patterns of those around you, or simply by asking people how they feel about their bodies. Popular culture is full of images that encourage us to associate food with desire at the same time that we are constantly sold various diet products. Advertisements also encourage women to associate beauty with thinness, so much so that eating disorders are strikingly common. Women, and men as well, are taught to dislike their bodies. No matter what their shape, size, or form, women's bodies seem never to meet the ideal promulgated by the advertising and modeling industries. Thus, research finds that, regardless of race or ethnicity, women are more dissatisfied with their bodies than are men. Furthermore, both women and men misjudge the body shapes that they think the other sex will find attractive, with women thinking that men like thinner bodies than men say they like (Demarest and Allen 2000). Such findings indicate the extent to which women's images of themselves—and their subsequent behaviors—can be driven by what they believe men will think of them.

One consequence of the cultural obsession with weight and thinness is the high rate of anorexia nervosa, bulimia, and compulsive eating among women and, increasingly, men. Although anorexia nervosa generally occurs among White, adolescent females, men and minorities are increasingly being affected. Black and Hispanic women, however, are more likely than White women to be overweight, especially those near poverty (National Center for Health Statistics 2003; see Figure 7.3). **Anorexia nervosa** is characterized by severe weight loss; anorexics also have delusions about their body images, thinking of themselves as fat when they are, in actuality, dangerously thin. They typically do not recognize signs of nutritional need and may, literally, starve themselves to death. Seen in the context of a whole array of practices designed to reduce women's body size—such as stomach stapling, diet fads, breast reduction surgery, and other extreme procedures—anorexia is even to be expected in a culture so obsessed with thinness (Chernin 1981, 1985).

Other eating problems, such as bulimia and compulsive overeating, also stem from the culture's definition of idealized womanhood. **Bulimia** is the syndrome in which women (typically) binge on huge amounts of food and then purge themselves by vomiting, using laxatives, or extreme fasting. Both anorexia and bulimia are strongly linked to gender roles. Both forms of eating disorder are linked to gender roles, with those who most internalize cultural definitions of femininity being most likely to engage in disordered eating. Eating disorders and the associated dissatisfaction with one's body are also most common among heterosexual women and least common among heterosexual men, with lesbian women and gay men falling in between. Eating disorders have additionally been linked to a sense among women of hypercompetition with regard to appearance—that is, women

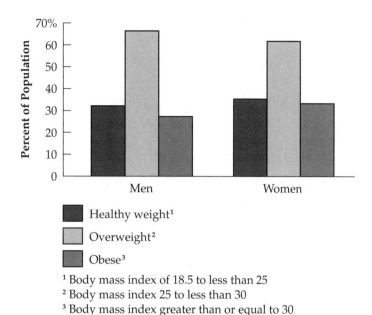

Healthy weight[1]

Overweight[2]

Obese[3]

[1] Body mass index of 18.5 to less than 25
[2] Body mass index 25 to less than 30
[3] Body mass index greater than or equal to 30

FIGURE 7.3   Body Weight by Race and Gender

Source: Data from National Center for Health Statistics 2003. *Health United States 2003.* Washington, DC: Department of Health and Human Services, p. 230–232.

who "overvalue" beauty are most likely to develop eating disorders (Strong et al. 2000; Burckle et al. 1999; Lakkis et al. 1999).

Women's concern with weight and body image can affect self-esteem and academic performance. Research finds that the less attractive a woman perceives herself to be and the more weight she wants to lose, the greater is her sense of academic, social, and psychological impairment (Hesse-Biber et al. 1987). Ironically, eating disorders, although contributing to poor academic performance and lowered self-esteem, are most common among women who value physical appearance, strive for success in multiple roles, and come from families where their daughters have insecure attachments to their parents (Hart and Kenny 1997).

Most studies of eating disorders have been based on the experiences of White women, and their conclusions should be judged accordingly. Latino, Native American, and African American women have never been portrayed as the "ideal woman"; their problems with weight are conditioned by the specific intersections of race, class, and gender in their experience. Thompson's (1994) research on compulsive eating among women of color finds, for example, that African American women with eating disorders tend to overeat to soothe the rage, fear, and disappointment in their lives. She also found that over two-thirds of the women in her study who were overeaters had also been sexually molested during childhood.

Thompson's work suggests that emphasis on the culture of thinness as the explanation for eating problems among women is race-specific. African American culture, for example, does not hold the same thin ideals for African American women that are found in the dominant culture. Quite the contrary, there are many positive images within the African American community of large women who enjoy food. As in other cultures of the society (such as Jewish culture), the preparation and enjoyment of food has a positive and valued place within the culture. A more multicultural approach to understanding the origins of women's eating problems, Thompson suggests, is one that directly links eating problems among women to the particular forms of oppression they experience. Thompson's study of African American, Latina, and White lesbian women found that compulsive eating, bulimia, and anorexia are not so much linked to women's obsession with appearance as they are responses the women have developed to soothe the distress they feel as the result of poverty, sexual abuse, racism, and/or homophobia. Although these women are not isolated from dominant cultural images of thinness, Thompson suggests that the origins of eating problems have to be seen in the broader context of class oppression, racism, homophobia, and the sexual abuse of women (Thompson 1994).

Beginning in the twentieth century, U.S. culture began to regard fleshiness as not sexy. Sexy bodies are now depicted as thin ones; in fact, cultural images of weight have projected an increasingly thin image, resulting in a very high rate of anorexia among models and actresses who portray these ideals. Being thin is also increasingly associated with wealth and class, because idealized sex objects also portray class images. In an odd sense, only rich women can "afford" to be thin, since poor women are much more likely to be overweight. Fat on women and men also violates gender roles, as we tend to think of overweight women as having improperly indulged themselves, and overweight men are derided for seeming passive, vulnerable, and soft (Millman 1980). Cultural constructions of the body thus create an increasingly narrow—and even dangerous—image of womanhood.

Even without developing the most serious forms of eating disorders, vast numbers of women struggle with issues about beauty, appearance, and weight. Even women who fall within the recommended ranges of weight and body fat typically consider themselves overweight, and estimates are that more than half of women between ages 10 and 30 are dieting. The weight-loss industry is at least a $33 billion industry, with new products (many of them harmful) appearing regularly and promising to make weight loss easy (often in the absence of a good diet and regular exercise). As the beauty ideal has increasingly promoted a "well-toned, but skinny robustness" (Zones 1997: 264), the exercise industry—and, for some, compulsive exercise—has also soared. The average person now uses more than 25 pounds of cosmetics, soaps, and toiletries each year, and plastic surgery has become a multi-billion dollar industry as women, the majority of plastic surgery clients, pay to shrink, expand, remove, and otherwise alter various parts of their bodies (Bordo 1995; Zones 1997). Think of how different your behavior and that of others around you might change were we to embrace a more diverse ideal of women's beauty—one that would encompass a full array of how women actually look.

Substance Abuse: Alcohol, Drugs, and Smoking

The problems associated with substance abuse are often understood as originating in personal problems that lead people to engage in behavior damaging to their health. An alternative way to understand these behaviors is to see them in light of gender relations in society. Patterns of substance abuse are clearly marked by gender differences. Thus, men are more likely to abuse drugs and alcohol, although women, especially young women, are more likely to smoke. But beyond noting differences is usage, how does gender shape the patterns of substance abuse—behavior that is known to be a hazard to health?

Alcohol

Men drink more frequently than women and drink more on any given occasion; men are more likely than women to be classified as problem drinkers (National Center for Health Statistics 2003; Wilsnack et al. 2000). Race also matters. African American and Hispanic women are more likely to abstain from drinking and are less likely to be heavy drinkers than White women; Asian American women have low rates of alcohol use, but Native American women have high rates of use, as reflected in high alcohol-related mortality among American Indian and Alaskan Native women (Horton 1995). Among women, drinking is heaviest among singles, those with high incomes, and employed women. Some have argued that women's employment makes them more likely to drink because it gives them greater independence and exposes them to cultural norms and expectations like those that men experience.

When women do drink, compared with men, they are more likely to drink alone, in private, or with a spouse. Women also tend to be introduced to alcohol by men and are encouraged by men to drink. The greatest amount of problem drinking occurs among women aged 18 to 20; moreover, drinking among young women has dramatically increased in recent years, nearly closing the gender gap between male and female drinkers (Wechsler 1995). This has been especially true on college campuses where binge drinking—defined as heavy, though episodic, drinking—has become a focal point for national concern. National surveys of college students find that although men are more likely to drink heavily than women, a large percentage of both women and men college students are binge drinkers (50 percent of men, 39 percent of women). Another 35 percent of men and 45 percent of women students drink, but not as binge drinkers (Wechsler 1995).

Gender plays a clear role in the drinking patterns of college men and women. For men, norms of masculinity permeate the drinking culture on campus. Studies find that men associate heavy drinking with "being a man." Furthermore, the men "perform" masculinity through drinking in that they use drinking to display competition, aggression, and, sometimes, violence. At the same time, drinking lets them excuse behaviors that would otherwise be associated with femininity, such as crying, being overly emotional, and being physically dependent. For women, gender norms also have a significant role in drinking behavior. Women perceive that drinking allows them to loosen the restrictions usually imposed on them because of gender. Unless programs designed to lessen the risks of alcohol abuse address the issue of gender, they are likely to fail, since some of the underlying dimensions of abuse stem as much from gender relations as they do alcohol per se (Peralta 2001).

Drugs

Although women are less likely than men to be drug abusers, there are significant health risks for women with substance abuse problems. Legal and illegal drugs, alcohol, tobacco, and caffeine are among the most prominent causes of health problems for premature death among both women and men. Substance abuse significantly increases the risks of pregnancy—both for women and infants (Blumenthal 1998).

Patterns of substance abuse are consistent with images of masculinity and femininity in the culture. According to traditional gender roles, women are not expected to drink and use drugs to the same extent as men. Indeed, women who become alcoholics tend to be perceived as more masculine and "hard" than other women, indicating that this behavior violates expected roles for women. Women heroin addicts are also seen as more deviant, more reprehensible, and less treatable than male addicts.

Research on drug abuse finds that the women most likely to abuse drugs are those whose other life options are significantly narrowed. Thus, women who are intravenous (IV) drugs users are likely to have experienced child sexual abuse, to have few options in the conventional world, and to become inundated with the drug culture (Ross-Durow and Boyd 2000; Mullings et al. 2001). Women are also likely to begin using illegal drugs in the content of heterosexual relationships where men introduce them into the drug subculture. Men, on the other hand, are more likely to enter this subculture through other male friends and associates (Henderson et al. 1994). Illegal drug use among women has also been connected to trying to cope with violence within relationships (Sales and Murphy 2000). Furthermore, a cycle of drug dependency often characterizes women's drug use. For example, when children are removed from a home because of the mother's addiction, the mother may increase her drug use to cope with the loss (Kearney et al. 1994).

The problem of drug abuse is, however, not just a problem with illegal drugs. Women are more likely than men to be prescribed tranquilizers, sedatives, and amphetamines. Three-fifths of people admitted to treatment facilities for addiction to tranquilizers and sedatives are women (Blumenthal 1998). In part, women are more often prescribed tranquilizing drugs because they are more likely to seek help for their problems than are men; others say that because of structured inequality, women's roles are more stressful and, as a result, women have more real complaints. Both are plausible explanations, but powerful economic and political interests also capitalize on women as a market for drugs that brings massive profits to their producers. Advertisements for legal drugs, including cigarettes, tends to associate certain product attributes with values women are known to hold, thus perpetuating women's abuse of these substances (Boyd et al. 1999–2000).

Smoking

Although tobacco has not been considered an addictive drug and therefore has not been regulated to the same extent as other substances, it has come under increasing public attention as an addictive health hazard. Ironically, although tobacco is significantly linked to multiple negative health consequences for all users, it has been manipulated by advertisers as a sign of women's independence.

Historically, men have been more likely to smoke than women. Although the rate of smoking for both women and men in the United States has declined in recent years, one in four men and and one in five women smoke. Once women start to smoke, they are also more likely than men to continue, making the initiation of smoking especially significant for women. Among high school seniors, 27 percent of men and 26 percent of women smoke, despite the known risks. An alarming 10.7 percent of eighth-graders (males and females) now smoke, although this has declined since 2000 (National Center for Health Statistics 2003; see Figure 7.4).

Smoking patterns among women and men seem significantly affected by gender roles. Researchers studying smoking behavior among adolescents have found, for example, that although peer pressure is significant for both boys and girls in the initiation of smoking, it is more significant for girls. Young men, on the other hand, are more influenced by "sensation seeking" (Martin and Robbins 1995). At the same time, girls (and later, women) are more likely to say that they smoke to control their weight (Logio 1998; Crisp et al. 1999). For both groups, appearance before others, whether it is to appear adultlike, to be slim, to be "tough," or to go along with the crowd, is a significant risk to health. Clearly, despite knowledge about the

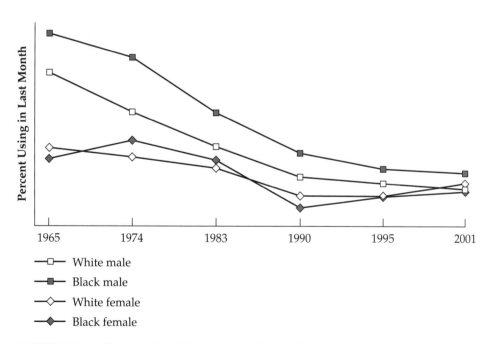

FIGURE 7.4 Cigarette Smoking (by gender and race, 1965–2001)

Source: Data from National Center for Health Statistics. 2003. *Health United States.* Washington, DC: Department of Health and Human Services, p. 212.

effects of smoking, gender and social status override rational decisions about health risks.

Women and AIDS

Originally identified as a disease affecting primarily gay men, AIDS (Acquired Immune Deficiency Syndrome) has taken on new dimensions. Although the majority of AIDS cases involve transmission between men having sex with other men, intravenous drug use is the second most common form of transmission. Among women, heterosexual contact and intravenous drug use are the most frequent forms of transmission, though heterosexual contact accounts for three-quarters of new cases among women. AIDS is no longer a disease only among men; now, one-third of new AIDS cases are women. Worldwide, the number of women with AIDS is predicted to soon equal the number of men, with 14.8 million women infected. AIDS is already the fourth leading cause of death for women worldwide and is the leading cause of death for women of reproductive age in several major U.S. cities (Blumenthal 1998; Schneider and Stoller 1995; National Center for Health Statistics 2003; Centers for Disease Control 2004). AIDS falls especially hard on women of color; 82 percent of all AIDS cases among women are among African American and Hispanic women.

These facts suggest the urgency of understanding AIDS in the context of a gender and race analysis (see Table 7.1). To begin with, women's social, sexual, and economic standing clearly influences their susceptibility to AIDS. Especially when seen in a global context, women's lack of access to education, medical care, and economic support makes them unable to protect themselves from this serious disease. Conditions of poverty among women of color in the United States contribute to the vulnerability of women to AIDS, because they turn to drugs for relief or have poor access to health and reproductive services that can provide some protection from

TABLE 7.1   Facts on AIDS: A Global Perspective

- Of the 33.6 million people living with HIV/AIDS, 14.8 million are women (44 percent).
- Women are nearly half of the newly affected adults (2.3 million out of 5 million).
- 2.1 million people died of AIDS in 1999; 1.1 million of these were women.
- There are half a million infections in children under age 15, most of which have been transmitted from mother to child.
- In sub-Saharan Africa, 55 percent of HIV/AIDS infections are women; in Southeast Asia, 30 percent, and in Europe and the United States, 20 percent.
- The majority of women contracting HIV/AIDS do so through heterosexual contact.

Source: World Health Organization. 2000. *Women and HIV/AIDS.* Website: www.who.int.

AIDS. In addition, women's position as sex workers and as vulnerable sexual partners enhances their risk of AIDS. As a consequence, women who have mobilized against AIDS have linked the prevention of AIDS to the necessity of improving women's status worldwide (Schneider and Stoller 1995; World Health Organization 2000).

Disability

Seeing disability through a gender lens reveals things about disability that one might not ordinarily see. The term *disability*, of course, carries multiple meanings—and, in fact, has been challenged by those who think that the term connotes inadequacies rather than the successes and achievements of those so labeled. In addition, the term has a broad range, including those who may be severely paralyzed as well as those with some limiting condition—perhaps even including the decreased abilities that come with aging. In reality, most of us will experience some form of disability at some point in our lives, a reality that advocates for the disabled (or differently abled or physically challenged) have used to invoke empathy for people who are otherwise treated as invisible and stigmatized.

Thinking about the meaning of disability shows how, like gender, it is as much a social construction as a physical reality (Zola 1989, 1993). Thus, physically limiting conditions need not be as "disabling" as society makes them. Note, for example, that in social interaction, people may look away from someone who is physically disabled or may treat them in a childlike fashion, thus diminishing their social presence and identifying them, even if unintentionally, as someone less of a social being. And, as with other "minority" groups in society, issues of access and rights of the disabled have been the basis for a strong and effective disability rights movement.

With regard to gender, you can see the connection between disability and social assumptions about gender by simply thinking about how manhood is associated with physical prowess and womanhood with sexuality. We read onto people's bodies gendered expectations that associate masculinity with strength and independence, not weakness or dependence. A physically disabled man is less likely to be seen as "masculine" (Gerschick and Miller 1994). Both men and women who are disabled are also perceived as asexual. These realities show the linkage that feminists have argued exists between social expectations about the conjunction of disability, gender, and sexuality (Smith and Hutchison 2004). It also reveals the extent to which our social expectations about bodies are framed by gender in society.

Gender also is reflected in the likelihood that one will become disabled. Aggregate data show that women are more likely to become disabled so that they need the help of others in handling routine needs; however, this is most likely because of women's longer life expectancy. But, regardless of life expectancy, African Americans are more likely to be disabled than are Whites and Latinos (National Center for Health Statistics 2003).

Some of the societal needs of the disabled have been supported through the passage of the **Americans with Disabilities Act of 1990.** This law protects disabled persons from discrimination and requires employers and other institutional providers (such as schools) to provide "reasonable accommodation" so that disabled people will have access to education, employment, and public facilities (such as transportation, bathrooms, hotel rooms, and so forth). It has been enormously important in extending basic rights to disabled people, as well as in transforming public awareness about disability.

Health Insurance

With so many known health risks for women, one would hope that national health care policy and health care systems would be able to meet the challenges of keeping women and men healthy. Especially in a nation known for its advanced health care system and in a nation that is affluent relative to other nations in the world, one would expect a health care system that works for the total population. Yet, data on health care coverage reveal that women are at risk of not being covered by health insurance, especially if they are poor, unmarried, and/or women of color.

In the aggregate, men are slightly more likely than women to have no health insurance, but looking in more detail, factors associated with gender make a difference. Unmarried women are two to three times less likely to be covered by health insurance than married women, who are often covered by the employment of their spouse (Meyer and Pavalko 1996). Women who are employed are also less likely to be covered by health insurance than are employed men, because of the structural patterns of gender segregation that place them in occupations with fewer health care benefits (Dewar 2000). Black and Hispanic Americans are also less likely to be covered by health care insurance than are Whites, making women of color especially vulnerable because of the combined effect of their race and gender (National Center for Health Statistics 2003). The lack of health insurance can be especially hard for young women, many of whom earn lower wages and are the group least likely to have health insurance. The high cost of giving birth means that many begin their lives as mothers already accumulating debt.

Even those with health insurance may find that their policies exclude some of the services that are essential to women's good health. Thus, screening for various forms of cancer varies according both to one's education and income level. Inclusion of mental health services varies in different insurance policies, often leaving those who are most in need of such services without a way to support the cost. And, as the population ages, long-term care is an increasing need. As people live longer, they run the risk of spending down all of their assets (if they have any to start with) should they acquire a long-term illness and disability. Yet, the cost of long-term care insurance is prohibitive for many. With national attention increasingly on the problems that people face because of health care, keeping a focus on the gender, class, and race dimensions of access to health care is an important priority (Ruzek et al. 1997).

❖ The Politics of Reproduction

The issues of abortion, birth control, and pregnancy are at the heart of feminist politics and are core issues around which feminist analysis has been built. Contemporary feminists see women's right to control their own bodies as essential to the realization of other rights and opportunities in society. As the Boston Women's Health Book Collective has written, "Unless we ourselves can decide whether and when to have children, it is difficult for us to control our lives or participate fully in society" (1984:291).

Whether individual women experience pregnancy, abortion, or birth control as stressful or traumatic is at least partially because of how they are socially organized. Women do not simply get pregnant and give birth in the physical sense alone; they do so within a definite set of social relations (Petchesky 1980). These social arrangements vary not only historically but also cross-culturally. Feminist arguments about the social control of reproduction clearly take this fact into account. Following her early study of seven Pacific Island cultures, Margaret Mead wrote:

> *Whether childbirth is seen as a situation in which one risks death, or out of which one acquires a baby, or social status, or a right to Heaven, is not a matter of the actual statistics of maternal mortality, but of the view that a society takes of childbearing. Any argument about women's instinctively maternal behavior which insists that in this respect a biological substratum is stronger than every other learning experience that a female child faces, from birth on, must reckon with this great variety in the handling of childbirth (Mead 1962:221).*

Female control of reproduction is cross-culturally and historically the dominant social arrangement (Oakley 1979); yet, in modern Western societies, reproduction is controlled by men. Traditional social theories have also largely ignored the question of reproduction, as if assuming that it is irrelevant in analyses of human experience and social organization.

Feminist perspectives on reproductive issues assert women's right to control their own bodies. Feminists see the medical profession as often unresponsive to women's needs. Not only are feminists distressed by the demeaning treatment women receive in medical institutions but they are also critical of the fact that it is usually men (either in medicine or in politics) who make decisions about reproductive issues (Ruzek et al. 1999). Feminists believe that it is women's right to choose their reproductive status. Not only do feminists believe in individual rights on reproductive issues but they also see that reproduction is embedded in systems of social power and social control (Petchesky 1980). The history of reproductive issues and their contemporary manifestations also show that reproduction is directly entangled with class and race relations, in addition to relations of gender. Changes in federal funding for abortion, a recurring history of sterilization abuse, and the manipulation of powerless women for medical experiments are all evidence of the powerlessness of women to control reproduction. This section reviews the politics of reproduction, focusing on three contemporary issues: birth control, abortion, and racism and reproduction.

Birth Control

Birth control, although a personal matter, is also controlled by decisions of the state, the social organization of scientific and medical institutions, and the normative system of public values and attitudes. Because birth control regulates sexual activity and population size, its significance extends beyond the individual relationships in which it is actually practiced. Moreover, the availability, form, and cultural significance of birth control bear directly on the role of women in society (Gordon 1977; Roberts 1997).

Many young women today probably take birth control for granted, although it was not long ago that the right to practice birth control was established in law, especially for the unmarried. A 1965 Supreme Court decision (***Griswold v. Connecticut***) established the first constitutional precedent that the use of birth control was a right, not a crime; however, this decision extended only to married persons. Not until 1972 (in ***Eisenstadt* v. *Baird***) were laws prohibiting the dispensing of contraceptives to any unmarried person, or by anyone other than a physician or pharmacist, held unconstitutional. This decision was introduced following an incident in which Bill Baird, a long-time birth control activist, handed a package of vaginal foam to an unmarried young woman during a lecture on contraception at Boston University. Baird, in violation of a Massachusetts law that prohibited the distribution of nonprescribed contraceptives, was arrested and convicted of a felony before the case reached the Supreme Court.

Before the establishment of the constitutional right to birth control, laws varied from state to state, and, even in those states where the distribution of birth control devices was legal, actual dispensing depended on the discretion of individual doctors. The effect was to shift the decision regarding birth control from women to men in the medical and judicial professions. Current policies on birth control are shaped by a political context that puts control over these issues into the hands of men and the government. For example, in 2001 the Bush administration barred the use of federal funds to overseas organizations that support abortion.

Adolescent reproductive rights have also been a recent area of judicial rulings. A series of court rulings has upheld the practice of requiring parental notification, as long as there is an adequate bypass when needed (such as allowing authorization by a judge). Although there is flexibility on the issue of a minor's rights to choose abortion, these decisions still place young women in the situation of needing the approval of parents or a court to proceed with an abortion (Goldstein 1988). Court delays make the timeliness of such decisions critical, but, more fundamentally, such decisions clearly take the control of the woman's body out of her hands.

Even with a more restrictive environment with regard to abortion, the use of birth control has increased substantially, including among young people. Estimates are that nine in ten sexually active women who do not want to become pregnant are practicing contraception; women who use no contraceptives account for nearly half of unintended pregnancies each year. Sterilization, the pill, and the condom are the most widely used forms of contraception. (Alan Guttmacher Institute 1999).

Among teen women, almost half (44 percent) of those using birth control use the pill; another 38 percent choose condoms as the primary method of birth control. Another 10 percent use the injectable form of birth control; 3 percent have implants and 4 percent count on withdrawal—a risky practice. The injectable and implants are most commonly used by women who are poor—these women are three times more likely to use injectables and the implant, in part because they are often forced to do so by social service providers (Alan Guttmacher Institute 1999; Roberts 1997).

Abortion

Women's rights to choose abortions were established by the 1973 Supreme Court decision in *Roe* **v.** *Wade*. This decision held laws that prohibited abortion unconstitutional, except where such laws are restricted to the last three months of pregnancy or to the stage of fetal viability. The Court's decision acknowledged that on the issue of abortion, separately legitimate social concerns collided: (1) the constitutional right to privacy, (2) the right of the state to protect maternal health, and (3) the right of the state to protect developing life. The Court thus divided the gestation period into thirds and argued that in the first trimester the woman's right to decide her future privately, without interference from the state, took precedence over the other two rights. In the second trimester, the state cannot deny an abortion, but it can insist on reasonable standards of medical procedure. In the third trimester, abortion may be performed to preserve the life or health of the mother.

In 1989, the Supreme Court (in *Webster* v. *Reproductive Health Services*) gave states the right to impose substantial restrictions on abortion (such as requiring fetus viability tests, restricting use of public funding for abortion, and refusing to allow public employees to perform abortions in public hospitals). Continued political pressure from antiabortion groups makes the future of abortion rights uncertain. Already analyses show that the various antiabortion activities have resulted in more scarce abortion services (Kahane 2000).

Despite the antiabortion movement, public support for abortion has remained steady, with 52 percent of the public identifying as prochoice and 41 percent as prolife. Although the public is evenly divided on how they define themselves with regard to abortion rights, support for the current law remains strong. Two-thirds of the U.S. public is opposed to any law that would make abortion illegal or any law stricter than under *Roe* v. *Wade*. One-quarter (24 percent) think abortion should be legal under any circumstances, more than half (56 percent) think it should be legal under certain circumstances; 19 percent say it should be illegal in all circumstances (Gallup Poll, October 2004).

In the United States, abortion was not viewed as morally wrong (if performed before quickening at four or five months) until the second half of the nineteenth century. Before that time, abortion was a common practice and was often performed using drugs, potions, techniques, and remedies made popular in home medical guides. Abortion was viewed as relatively safe and was commonly assisted by midwives, "irregular" physicians, and physicians of the period. The earliest laws governing abortion were not enacted until 1821 and 1841, but these laws placed guilt only on those who used particular methods feared unsafe for inducing abortion. None of these laws punished women for having abortions; they were intended as regulations to ensure safe methods (Mohr 1978).

In the mid-nineteenth century, abortion became a widespread phenomenon, especially among White, married, Protestant women. During this period, abortion also became increasingly commercialized. One noted woman entrepreneur,

Madame Restell, earned an enormous income from her abortion products and spent as much as $60,000 per year on advertising alone (Mohr 1978). As both the drug industry and the medical profession grew in the second half of the nineteenth century, more profits could be made by companies seizing control of the abortion market. In addition to eliminating midwives from the practice of abortion, the medical profession created laws and spread propaganda that altered the perception and practice of abortion.

These changes were additionally fueled by shifts in the class, racial, and ethnic structure of U.S. life. The emerging new class of physicians was not only incensed by the flagrant commercialization of abortion but also expressed the fear that the growing rate of abortion among the middle and upper classes would cause immigrants, Black Americans, and the poor to outbreed them. Spurred by the growth of social Darwinism and an increasing nativist movement, the antiabortion crusade appealed to racist fears and portrayed abortion as the work of criminals, backward medical practitioners, and immoral social agents (Mohr 1978). Beginning in the period between 1860 and 1880 and continuing through the first two-thirds of the twentieth century, antiabortion policies included strict criminal laws about abortion and put absolute control of abortion in the hands of the medical profession. By these laws, women seeking abortions—and their accomplices—were defined as guilty of murder, abortion was defined as a criminal act, and the distribution of abortion and birth control information was deemed illegal. The public moralizing about abortion seen in the late twentieth century emerged historically from new professional groups seeking to control abortion. Only very recently has abortion been seen as a moral issue stemming from religious beliefs.

Racism and Reproduction

The reproductive issues of abortion, birth control, and sterilization have particular significance for women of color. Although the majority of women of color support women's rights to abortion and birth control, history also shows that the birth control movement has been closely linked with racist movements for population control. For women of color, reproductive freedom thus means not just freedom of choice but the freedom to dismantle social arrangements that limit the choices women of color have (Roberts 1997).

In the early twentieth century, when Margaret Sanger was organizing the birth control movement, White birth control reformers were campaigning to prevent so-called racial suicide for themselves through their allowing the overpopulation of Black Americans, immigrants, the poor, and social misfits (Davis 1981; Gordon 1977). The campaign for birth control was interwoven with genocidal movements to eliminate racial groups, and appeals for birth control were clearly intended to limit what was perceived as overbreeding among the poor. Sanger herself made this appeal part of her campaign, and thus seemed to support the racist goals of the eugenics movement.

In the contemporary record, information on the sterilization of women of color and poor women confirms that birth control and population control are often linked. As we have already seen, sterilization rates are highest among African

American, Native American, and Puerto Rican women and female welfare recipients. These data raise the issue of the blurred distinction between forced and voluntary sterilization. Although forced sterilization is illegal, reports indicate that doctors and clinics do give misleading information to minority and poor clients. Although clients may technically agree to the procedure, they have frequently been misled or misinformed.

Federal investigations have revealed a high incidence of sterilization of minors in other government-sponsored clinics. High rates of sterilization, experimentation on Third World women and U.S. women of color for the development of contraceptives, and the inadequacy of health care for women of color all indicate the extent to which racism, coupled with sexism, is institutionalized in the health care system. White feminists have framed much of their discussion of reproductive health care in the context of individual choice, but for women of color and poor women, choice is restricted by the conditions of oppression they face in health care institutions. In fact, women of color have been sometimes reluctant to become involved in White feminists' movements for reproductive freedom. People of color have been wary about movements promoting abortion and birth control because historically these movements have been used as racist methods of population control. Women of color are also, however, the most frequent victims of restrictive reproductive policies because poor women and women of color are most dependent on public funding of reproductive services; they are also disproportionately most likely to suffer death and injury if abortion becomes illegal. This suggests that feminist analyses of reproductive freedom should be framed by a political perspective wider than individual choice; reproductive freedom should be framed by an understanding of the need for social justice for all women, not just those with the privilege to make free choices. Rights to privacy alone probably cannot achieve such freedom, because privacy itself is largely conditioned through the structured inequalities of race, class, and gender oppression (Petchesky 1990; Roberts 1997).

The Politics of Birth: Pregnancy and Childbirth

The emergence of modern medicine is usually seen as a conquest of ignorance and a triumph over superstition. Modern medical men are imbued with high status in U.S. society and are perceived as learned, rational, and wise. There was a time when healing was almost solely the province of women. Particularly in matters of birth and childrearing, women were perceived as the experts and birth was a female-centered, home affair (Dye 1980). Until the nineteenth century in this country, women presided over most births, in the presence of female friends and kin who provided comfort and aid to the childbearing woman (Wertz and Wertz 1977).

Because childbirth was originally placed in the hands of women as midwives, developments in the history of childbirth provide a case study in which what was once a female-oriented process has come to be dominated and controlled by men. Although this section focuses primarily on childbirth, it also reveals more general patterns in the emergence of modern medicine. In the end, you will see how particular characteristics of medicine as an institution still take control of reproduction away from women.

Childbirth has a distinctive social history and one that is tied to the emergence of medicine as a profession, as well as to changes in the ideology and structure of women's roles in society. In the colonial United States, childbirth occurred in the home and in the presence of female family members and friends (Dye 1980; Scholten 1977). During this period, six to eight pregnancies were typical for women, as was a fear of pain and the possibility of death in childbirth. Female midwives who attended births generally practiced noninterventionist methods of delivery and, along with the other females present, provided comfort and emotional support for the laboring mother. Records of the midwives' practices, successes, and failures are hard to find in this period, so it is difficult to know exactly how skilled or knowledgeable the midwives were. Information and experiences about childbirth were shared by women, and there is little indication in the historical record that midwives posed dangers for childbearing women. There are no recorded epidemics of puerperal fever, such as those that killed thousands of women when childbirth was moved to hospitals, and there are few recorded instances of midwives' incompetence in the colonial period. Without romanticizing midwives and the process of birth, it appears that, unlike images of midwives that appeared later with the advent of scientific medicine, "the stereotype of the midwife as a curse upon women seems unfitting for colonial midwives" (Wertz and Wertz 1977:13).

Certainly, the pain associated with childbirth was a significant factor in women's desire for alternative practices. New interventionist techniques promised by the male founders of medical science appealed to women who sought relief from long and difficult labors. Beginning in the mid-eighteenth century, a slow transition occurred in which birth was shifted from female to male control. Medical men in the United States took their lead from French and English physicians, who described the body as being like a machine and developed instruments or tools to intervene in natural bodily processes. Tools (such as forceps) promised to shorten labor and to make difficult labors more manageable, although such techniques were generally resisted by U.S. and English women midwives, who believed that these techniques introduced new dangers and unsafe procedures to the natural process of birth.

In the mid-eighteenth and early nineteenth centuries, there was an open market for both female midwives and the medical men who were developing new birth techniques. Advances in knowledge about the physiology of labor, as well as various birth techniques, were taught in medical colleges—most of which were located in England and France. Men from the United States learned from these colleges, but, because the government provided no financial support for medical education, women, with fewer financial resources than men, did not attend. Medical education during this period, however, was notoriously poor (Dye 1980), and many have argued that female midwives continued to have greater skills in birth, based on their practical experience, than did medically trained men (Ehrenreich and English 1978).

By the mid-nineteenth century, medical men had adopted an increasingly interventionist approach toward birth, whereas female midwives relied more on the normal course of delivery. Mary Wollstonecraft (1759–1797), an outspoken English feminist whom you will study in Chapter 12, deplored the takeover of childbirth by men and insisted that her daughter, Mary Shelley (author of *Frankenstein*), be born with a woman attendant. When the placenta was not delivered, a male midwife was called in, who, upon inserting his hand to withdraw it, caused Wollstonecraft to hemorrhage and later to die of puerperal fever (Flexner 1972; Wertz and Wertz 1977). Studies indicate that although physicians gained greater control of childbirth during this period, as late as the early twentieth century, midwives had high status in their communities (Litoff 1978), maintained their own apprenticeship systems (Mongeau et al. 1961), and had better mortality records than medical men (Dye 1980).

Transformations in childbirth that ultimately resulted in the medical model of contemporary birth were accelerated in the mid-nineteenth century, when obstetrics was first developed as a medical specialty and when Victorian cultural attitudes transformed bourgeois notions of female sexuality. During the Victorian period, pregnancy was treated with shame and concealment in the middle and upper classes. Because the Victorian period severely restricted women's sexuality and because pregnancy directly acknowledged their sexual activity, it became an event to be hidden and concealed. For example, it is reported that Susan B. Anthony's mother was embarrassed by her own pregnancy (Wertz and Wertz 1977). Like other bourgeois Victorian women, she disappeared from public view when she was pregnant.

At the same time, the emergence of the medical profession provided status to those who could afford new medical treatments. Families who could pay for it, especially in urban areas, began to go to medical specialists. Obstetrics was one of the first of these specialties, although most women continued to employ women midwives because they were more trusting of midwives' noninterventionist techniques and more comfortable in their modesty with other women (Bogdan 1978). Physicians themselves stated that medical midwifery was the key to a successful practice because, if they could eliminate midwives, physicians would have a dependable market; also, the uncharted knowledge of obstetrics provided a chance for the expansion of physicians' careers (Barker-Benfield 1976; Scholten 1977). In keeping with the Victorian sensibilities of the time, the typical obstetrician (so renamed from *male midwives* to symbolize their alleged professionalism) draped his client in cloth and avoided looking at her body; consequently, obstetrics with middle- and upper-class clients was commonly practiced by touch alone. Obstetricians thus gained little knowledge of their female patients and relied on experiments on poor and Black women to advance their field. Following the Civil War, maternity hospitals were established as charitable asylums for poor and unmarried pregnant women. Stating that such places would provide a more moral and sanitary environment than the patients' own homes, doctors provided free medical treatment for poor women (often servants of the upper classes) in return for using these patients as research subjects (Wertz and Wertz 1977). Because the physicians would have violated the "ladylike" codes of the period by actually examining an affluent woman's body, poor, Black, and immigrant women in the charity hospital became research subjects for medical treatment and observation.

One of the most outrageous cases of experimentation is found in the practice of J. Marion Sims, originator of gynecology and an early president of the American Medical Association. One of his early claims to fame was the discovery of ways to suture tears that occurred between the vagina and anus. He developed these techniques by purchasing Black female slaves, whom he kept in hospital quarters that he built in his own yard (Axelson 1985). Because he saw Black slaves as enduring, passive, and helpless, he performed countless experimental operations on them without anesthesia. The pain he inflicted on them had to create unimaginable agony, yet this seemed not to faze him in his obsessive search for techniques to build his own career (Barker-Benfield 1976). Nor did it seem to bother upper-class women, who later erected a statue to him in Central Park because of their gratitude for his surgical method! (They, of course, experienced it only after the development of anesthesia.)

Sims, like other medical men of his day, believed that women's psychology stemmed from their sex organs, and he was anxious to perform clitoridectomies and oophorectomies (removal of the clitoris and ovaries). His drastic use of the knife seemed intended not for the betterment of women but for the enhancement of his own career, for an aspiring specialist, then as now, made his name through the invention and publication of new techniques. Indeed, as one historian has noted, the operating rooms where female surgery was performed in the nineteenth century were essentially "an arena for an exchange between men" (Barker-Benfield 1976:101). Sims, in fact, developed gynecological procedures as if he were an explorer charting new frontiers; his own writings clearly show this to be his own metaphor about his work. He was the first to develop the speculum and says of it, "Introducing the bent handle of a spoon, I saw everything as no man had ever seen before. . . . I felt like an explorer in medicine who first views a new and important territory" (Barker-Benfield 1976:95). Other medical men, too, declared his "speculum to be to diseases of the womb . . . what the compass is to the mariner" (Barker-Benfield 1976:95).

The removal of childbirth from the home and the control of women contradicted the Victorian point of view that birth was a private matter, to be conducted in secrecy and within the domestic world. Initially, delivery by men was seen as a breakdown of moral standards and an offense to female delicacy (Donegan 1978). Over time, however, as doctors promised safer and less painful births, women began to desire the new techniques they were offered. Most women wanted less painful childbirth, although in the late nineteenth century, the absence of pain in childbirth was associated with supposedly precivilized women—especially Indians and Blacks. Racism in the middle and upper classes defined more "primitive" peoples as closer to nature and therefore unlikely to experience childbirth pain. From the racist perspective of the bourgeois class, to experience pain, and therefore to need relief from it, became a sign of one's civilized nature. Needing relief from childbirth pain was also an indication of the social distance of the upper and middle classes from other strata of the society. Pain, then, became a mark of the "truly feminine"—a fact with its own paradoxical truth because childbirth pain and complications were greatly increased by the "civilized" practices of tight corsets, lack of exercise, fashionable illness, and airless rooms (Wertz and Wertz 1977).

Rather than change their cultural habits, middle- and upper-class women sought relief from childbirth pain and thus became more interested in the promises of modern medicine. Promises were all many of these techniques gave, however, for although they might have alleviated extreme pain, there is little evidence that childbirth was made any safer by medical men of the early twentieth century. Puerperal fever, later found to be caused by infections generated by unsanitary hospital procedures and interventionist techniques, became a major cause of maternal death (Wertz and Wertz 1977). Epidemics of puerperal fever killed thousands of women who sought painless deliveries through hospital births.

The number of births occurring in hospitals increased rapidly after the 1930s. Before this time, hospital birth had been primarily an urban phenomenon and, even there, had occurred on a large scale beginning only in the twentieth century. In 1930, only about 25 percent of all births took place in hospitals; by 1990, over 95 percent of all births occurred in hospitals. Today, hospital births represent the ultimate transformation of birth from a female-centered, home activity to one that is male controlled and medically defined. The prevalence of hospital births followed a direct assault on women midwives in the second half of the nineteenth century, when propaganda to make women fear pregnancy and legislation to eliminate midwives combined to generate new definitions of women's place in childbirth and, more generally, in medicine (Barker-Benfield 1976). Legislation between 1900 and 1930 made licensing for midwives a necessity. To obtain a license, midwives were required to get vouchers of their moral character from a member of the medical profession, to have their homes and outfits inspected by a physician's nurse, and to have attended births under the supervision of a physician. Because few physicians would provide these credentials, the number of practicing midwives radically declined. In New York City, for example, the number of practicing midwives declined from 3,000 in 1908 to 270 in 1939, two in 1957, and one in 1963 (Barker-Benfield 1976). In most cases, women were excluded from medical schools and, if they wanted to enter the health care system, were relegated to secondary status as nurses (Ehrenreich and English 1978). Childbirth and, more generally, women's health had effectively been placed in the hands of male physicians.

The movement of childbirth to hospitals and medical men was further increased by popular racist fears of contagion and germs that were associated with poor, immigrant, and Black people. The fads of genetic science and social Darwinism of the 1920s and 1930s increased middle-class fears of associating with those from the lower strata of society. Coupled with the home economics movement of the 1920s that defined home environments as sources of germs and disease (see Chapter 6), popular opinions laced with racist and class ideologies further generated a social definition of childbirth as a scientific event to be placed under the authority of medical men.

Physicians now routinely define pregnancy and birth as medical events and, because of this model, they are more likely to prescribe drugs during pregnancy and birth, set strict limits on what is considered a "normal" pregnancy, and define medical intervention as essential during birth. Midwives, on the other hand, define pregnancy as a healthy and normal condition—one that is optimized not by intervention and technological management but by providing the best possible environment for the pregnant woman (Rothman 1982). Conflict between the medical and midwifery models of childbirth lies at the heart of struggles over the control of childbirth, including political conflicts over the licensing of midwives and the establishment of nonmedical birth settings (Sullivan and Weitz 1988).

The dominance of the medical model in controlling pregnancy and childbirth can be seen in how pregnancy and childbirth are routinely handled by the medical profession. Birth is most likely located in hospitals, where doctors and the staff, not the mother, have control and authority over the delivery procedures. Even in the birthing rooms, which some hospitals have established, ultimate authority lies with the physician, who may (and does) intervene in the birth process at any point. Reinharz (1988) has also shown how the medical model permeates physicians' treatment and women's understanding of miscarriage.

Interventionist practices characterizing the rise of male control over childbirth continue to dominate women's childbirth experiences. This fact is especially evident in the dramatic increase in the number of cesarean sections being performed in hospitals throughout the country. In an age when childbirth is supposed to be safer and less threatening than it was in previous years, how do we explain the high proportion of births using a process that clearly increases the risks to both mother and child?

Researchers cite the routine practices of technological monitoring of birth as contributing significantly to the increase in cesarean births. Although some also mention physicians' greed for higher compensation and their desire for predictable schedules as contributing to the incentives to perform cesareans, it seems most likely that the social organization of childbirth around technological intervention is responsible for the increase. Typically, the process of labor is now observed by an electronic fetal-monitoring device that not only replaces the monitoring originally performed by nurses but can keep the laboring woman passively strapped to the device and immobile throughout the course of labor. Even though changes in the baby's breathing and heartbeat are routine features of the birth process, the close detection of these changes by the electronic fetal monitor results in a high number of false indications of fetal distress (Corea 1980). As a result of this situation, which is complicated by doctors' fears of malpractice if an actually distressed fetus is missed, doctors seem to react quickly to the slightest indication of change in the fetal condition by performing a vast number of unnecessary cesarean sections.

As women, inspired by the feminist health movement, have become more critical of the medical management of childbirth, many changes have taken place in how birth is handled, even in hospitals. Mothers and newborn infants are no longer necessarily separated following the birth; fathers, friends, and family members are often welcome in the delivery room and actively participate in the process; birth centers are common in hospitals; and midwives often practice in conjunction with obstetricians. These changes, now common, can be directly attributed to the influence of the feminist health movement—one of the many ways that the feminist movement has transformed even some of life's most intimate and special moments.

New Reproductive Technologies

New reproductive technologies—including artificial insemination, in vitro fertilization, embryo transfer, cloning, and genetic engineering—raise new concerns and questions about women's control of their bodies. Feminists point out that while some of these technologies seem to offer liberating possibilities, at the same time they make women new targets for the manipulation of reproductive engineers (Roberts 1997).

Donor insemination, for example, means that lesbian women or women who merely want children without men can become pregnant. In vitro fertilization makes it possible for those who are infertile to have children. Amniocentesis and an array of other tests now allow for prenatal evaluation of the embryo, meaning that characteristics such as sex, disability, and disease can be determined before birth. Although these may appear to be laudable developments, they also raise disturbing questions. Why, for example, is biological parenthood so important that we would go to such lengths and costs to bear children? What are the implications of determining sex before birth, especially in cultures where female infants are less valued than males? What does it say about the oppression of people with disabilities and our prejudices against them if we screen for disabilities before birth?

The eugenics movement in the United States in the earlier part of the twentieth century, like that of Nazi Germany, sought to apply the principles of genetic selection to improve the offspring of the human race. In both Nazi Germany and the United States, the process was explicitly racist, including, for example, compulsory sterilization of those defined as "unfit" or "defective." Many feminists equate the contemporary development of reproductive technology with the possibility of a new eugenics movement—one that, although it may not appear blatantly racist, is still embedded in a racist, sexist, and homophobic culture. Would reproductive technology be used, for example, to control the fertility of those deemed unworthy? To whom are reproductive technology and choice over reproduction most likely made available?

Although new reproductive technologies appear to give women choices over how and when they will have children, these technologies do not affect all women equally. Some women may have "rights to choose," but the choices women have are structured by race, class, and gender inequality (Roberts 1997). Reproductive control can, in fact, become a façade for population control and, in the context of racism, population control is often a mechanism for more social and political control (Rothman 1982).

Such views make the question of power central to any discussion of reproductive technology. Feminists do not necessarily believe that reproductive technology should be eliminated altogether, but they argue that as long as it is controlled by men, women are still denied the rights to control their bodies. Only organized resistance to the control of women's bodies by men will ensure that these technologies do not become a new means for the oppression of women.

❖ Gender and the Health Care System

Like other social institutions, health care is a gendered institution. That is, its structure, organization, and ideology reflect gendered relationships and meanings. This is also an institution in transition with more women physicians than ever before and women as a growing proportion of medical school students. Within the health care system, women are more likely to be clients, since women exceed men in most measures of health care utilization, including number of physician visits, hospital admissions, and the prescription of drugs (National Center for Health Statistics 2003). Women's health care is intricately interwoven with gender, race, and class relations, all of which affect the quality of care received and the status of women workers within the health care system. Feminist criticism of medical institutions is a response to this gendered institution.

Women as Health Care Workers

Women constitute 74 percent of all health care workers, yet they are heavily segregated within the health care field—often found in the least prestigious and most poorly paid positions in this field.

Women now constitute 30 percent of physicians, and they have dramatically increased their representation in medical schools, now constituting close to half of medical school students. Because of the long period of training, internship, and residence in medical professions, the impact of women's increased enrollment on the composition of practicing physicians is only beginning to be felt.

These are major breakthroughs for women in medicine, but this generation is not the first to witness such changes. At the turn of the twentieth century, women were a significant proportion of all physicians, with some cities reporting almost 20 percent of all physicians to be women (Walsh 1977). The entry of women into medicine is historically closely aligned with feminism and the new opportunities it encourages for women. Although the feminist movement at the turn of the century was quite different from contemporary feminism, it did encourage women, at least of the upper and middle classes, to use their skills, especially in areas perceived as helping professions. Since the turn of the century women were excluded from medicine through overt discrimination (denied entrance to medical schools) and through informal practices whereby they received little encouragement or support, were channeled into nursing schools, encountered hostility from peers, and were excluded from the old boy network that placed persons in their careers.

Even now, the lack of sponsorship, tracking systems, nonsupportive peer environments, and overt ridicule can restrict opportunities for women in medicine, although women within medicine have created a number of organizations to counter such tendencies. The women's movement has helped create a climate of mutual support among women students and professionals, leading to the creation of an environment more conducive to women's success. But the historical record of women's decline in medical careers indicates that none of these gains can be taken for granted. Continual lobbying, network building among women, and federal support for women's medical education are all necessary for stabilizing the role of women in this profession.

Most women workers in the health care system are there as nurses, dietitians, health technicians, and aides. Ninety-three percent of registered nurses are women (U.S. Department of Labor 2004). African American and Hispanic women in health care are concentrated in the lowest paying of these occupations. Women who are nurses do not face the problem of existing in a male-dominated occupation, as women physicians do, but their position relative to that of male professionals creates its own set of problems. Women of color in these fields also face the problems of racism and discrimination, which hamper their career development. Nurses and other health care workers are put in the position in which male professionals hold authority over them, in addition to receiving greater material benefits. Moreover, men who enter nursing tend to progress to higher echelons than do women within the profession (compounding the problem of sexism that women in this field face).

Despite recent increases in their salaries, nurses face sexist attitudes that define their work as less valuable than that of men. On the job, nurses are subordinate to the doctors in authority; innumerable accounts have described the sexist put-downs, innuendoes, and insults that some doctors have directed toward the nursing staff. More generally, physicians maintain a monopoly over medical knowledge and medical practice, even though nurses have more actual contact with hospitalized patients (Ehrenreich and English 1973b). Such working conditions lead to a high sense of dissatisfaction among nurses and, as a result, high job turnover.

The subordination of the nursing profession to the authority of doctors has resulted in a split between the activities of curing and caring. Stereotypically, nurses are alleged to provide nurturing, whereas doctors maintain the expertise in healing. Such a myth not only belittles the professional knowledge of nurses but also creates an atmosphere that may not work in the best interest of patients. As alternative medical practices have shown, a patient's health involves a complex configuration of physiological, emotional, and social systems. It appears that a more useful system of medicine is one that integrates the process of healing with the complexities emerging from the interaction of these systems.

The Women's Health Movement

The women's health movement has suggested various alternatives to traditional medical care, ranging from more consumer information to feminist self-help clinics (Ruzek et al. 1997; Morgen 2002). As a social movement, the women's health movement has resulted from a reaction to the sexism of the medical profession and the criticism of traditional medical practices that deny women control of their own reproductive lives and physical health.

Numerous groups in the women's health movement are also organized to provide health care to women without the high-handed authority of traditional medical practitioners. Many of these organizations disseminate health care information, some offer direct services, and others work primarily as lobbying organizations, attempting to create changes in the health care system and its policies.

Altogether, the women's health movement has the goals of reducing differences in knowledge between patient and practitioner, challenging the mandate of physicians as the sole providers of health care, reducing the professional monopoly over goods and services, increasing the number of women practitioners, and organizing clients around health issues (Ruzek 1978). The emergence of the women's health movement is indicative of the dissatisfaction women have shown in health care institutions and over issues involving reproduction and health. As this chapter has shown, feminist perspectives on health and reproduction insist on women's right to control their own bodies. As long as the power to control women's bodies remains predominantly in the hands of men, feminists are likely to continue organizing on these issues.

❖ Chapter Summary and Themes

Physical and mental health is fundamentally shaped by social factors, most especially gender, race, and class.

The evidence shows that women's health, like men's, is shaped by their gender status, though this is compounded by race and class status. On measures such as life expectancy, likelihood of disease, and rates of mental health, significant gender differences emerge.

Because health is influenced by social context, the work that women (and men) do has an impact on their health.

Women's employment status affects their health, with women working solely in the home generally having higher rates of illness and depression that women in the labor force. Protective legislation has historically excluded women from jobs deemed risky to their reproductive health, even when the same risks have not excluded men from such work.

Social problems involving health are shaped by the gender expectations in society.

The cultural obsession with thinness means that women are especially likely to suffer from various eating disorders, although the form they take varies by race, class, and sexual orientation. Women are now the group most likely to be new AIDS cases, although they typically acquire AIDS from heterosexual men. Public issues regarding health insurance coverage also have a gender component; thus, analyzing gender is important to fully understanding the need for effective social policies.

Feminist perspectives on reproduction see this as an area where men have accumulated the power to control women's bodies, even though in earlier periods women have controlled reproduction.

Rights to birth control, abortion, and other forms of reproductive freedom have been achieved through feminist activism. Practices such as childbirth and reproduction are now largely managed through a medical model that places power in the hands of male-dominated professions. Race and class are also integrally linked to reproductive politics, with women of color having the least freedom to control their own bodies.

Health care is a gendered institution, meaning that it has taken on the characteristics that are associated with masculinity in this culture.
Within the health care system, women and people of color are typically in the lowest-status positions, and men have the power to control medical decisions and medical knowledge. The women's health care movement has resulted in many reforms in this system and continues to press for changes that give women more control over their own bodies.

❖ Key Terms

Americans with Disabilities Act of 1990	bulimia	protective legislation
anorexia nervosa	*Eisenstadt* v. *Baird*	*Roe* v. *Wade*
Automobile Workers v. *Johnson Controls*	*Griswold* v. *Connecticut*	
	infant mortality	
	Muller v. *Oregon*	

❖ Discussion Questions/Projects for Thought

1. Identify a group of women workers in the health care field (nurses, women physicians, medical technologists, radiologists, physicians' assistants, etc.) and interview them about their work. What opportunities are available to them? Are their jobs segregated by gender and race/ethnicity? How do they see themselves relative to men they work with? What happens to those who try to move up? Are they satisfied with their jobs? If not, why not; if so, why? What do your interviews tell you about the social structure of gender in the health care field?

2. Using a recent sampling of the magazines read most frequently by your peers, describe what the magazine conveys as the ideal image for women's bodies. How does this influence the eating behavior of those who read it? How extensive are eating disorders among women and men on your campus? What do you think are the origins of these problems?

3. Identify a group of women and men on your campus who smoke. Interview them about when they started smoking, why they do so, and what they perceive it as doing for them. Are they aware of the risks of smoking to their health? When you analyze the answers to your questions, ask yourself how gender influences the smoking patterns of people on your campus.

❖ Internet Resources

The Alan Guttmacher Institute

http://www.agi-usa.org

The Alan Guttmacher Institute is a nonprofit organization specializing in family planning and the provision of information about topics such as contraception, abortion, teen pregnancy, sexuality, and other reproductive health matters. The website includes many valuable reports and current information on these topics.

American Medical Women's Association

http://www.amwa-doc.org

This organization of women within the American Medical Association provides extensive information and a network of women physicians. This site details current legislative action, health information, and news updates on subjects pertinent to women's health.

The Center for Reproductive Law and Policy

http://www.crlp.org

This is an organization promoting women's reproductive rights as human rights. The website provides information on various international initiatives on reproductive rights and domestic policy initiatives on this topic.

National Women's Health Network

http://www.womenshealthnetwork.org

This network is organized to ensure that women's interests are not overlooked by current policy and research. The site includes information on women's health movement, as well as a bibliography of resources.

❖ *Suggested Readings*

Bordo, Susan. 1995. *Unbearable Weight: Feminism, Western Culture, and the Body.* Berkeley: University of California Press.
Bordo's book examines the depiction of women's bodies in Western history and culture. Bordo connects images of women's bodies with women's power (or lack thereof) in society, revealing how women's fears about their appearance are linked to their status in society.

Boston Women's Health Collective Staff. 1998. *Our Bodies, Ourselves for the New Century.* New York: Simon and Schuster.
Written by a feminist group of health care providers, this book includes sound medical information, as well as psychological and sociological insights about women's health and well-being. It is the single-most useful handbook about many health issues, including birth control, pregnancy, sexuality, menopause, and other topics.

Butler, Sandra, and Barbara Rosenblum. 1991. *Cancer in Two Voices.* San Francisco: Spinsters Book Company.
This book is a moving, firsthand account of the experience of two women lovers—a professional therapist and a sociologist—as one of them dies of cancer. The authors provide an intimate view of the relationship of the lovers, exploring how illness and death affect personal relationships and doing so with both a sociological eye and a strong feeling of love.

Clarke, Adele E., and Virginia L. Olesen. 1998. *Revisioning Women, Health, and Healing: Feminist, Cultural and Technoscience Perspectives.* New York: Routledge.
The authors provide a comprehensive review of feminist issues about women's health, with an eye to providing alternative perspectives to the dominant medical model.

Morgen, Sandra. 2002. *Into Our Own Hands: The Women's Health Movement in the United States, 1969–1990.* Piscataway, NJ: Rutgers University Press.
This book shows the influence of feminism on the development of the women's health movement, a movement that has challenged medical control—and male authority—over women's bodies.

Roberts, Dorothy. 1997. *Killing the Black Body: Race, Reproduction and the Meaning of Liberty.* New York: Vintage Books.
Roberts, a legal scholar, examines the various ways that reproductive policies have exploited Black women's and men's bodies. She argues for an expanded concept of reproductive freedom by incorporating the experience of women of color into reproductive feminist politics.

Rothman, Barbara Katz. 2000. *Recreating Motherhood: Ideology and Technology in a Patriarchal Society.* Boston: Beacon Press. This book examines the ideology of motherhood in a society characterized by sexism. It particularly looks at how technology has transformed the experience of motherhood in ways that disempower women.

Ruzek, Sheryl B., Virginia Olesen, and Adele E. Clarke, eds. 1997. *Women's Health: Complexities and Differences.* Columbus, OH: Ohio State University Press. This anthology provides an overview on topics about women's health, showing how gender, race, and class shape health care experiences and institutions.

Schneider, Beth E., and Nancy E. Stoller. 1995. *Women Resisting AIDS: Feminist Strategies of Empowerment.* Philadelphia: Temple University Press. This anthology studies various ways that women have organized on behalf of AIDS prevention and research. It not only provides valuable information about AIDs, with an emphasis on its effect on women, but it also explains how women are making a difference in AIDS education, prevention, and care.

Thompson, Becky W. 1994. *A Hunger So Wide and So Deep: American Women Speak Out on Eating Problems.* Minneapolis: University of Minnesota Press. Based on intensive interviewing with African American, Latina, and White lesbian women, Thompson's study challenges medical and psychological understandings of eating problems among women and revises feminist accounts that emphasize a "culture of thinness" as the primary origin for eating problems.

Weitz, Rose. 1998. *The Politics of Women's Bodies: Sexuality, Appearance and Behavior.* New York: Oxford University Press. This anthology looks at how ideas about women's bodies affect their lives. It examines diverse topics such as the effect of homophobia on women athletes, the fetal rights movements, sources of violence against women, and cultural definitions of how women should look.

WOMEN AND RELIGION

Sociological Perspectives
on Religion

Religion and Social Control

Religion and the Emergence of
Feminism in the United States

Women and Religiosity
Images of Women in Religion
Religious Texts as Interpretive
Documents
Gender and Religious Beliefs

Women's Status in
Religious Institutions
Gender and Religious Participation
Women as Clergy

Religion and Social Change
Race, Religion, and Social Justice

Religion and Antifeminism
Feminism and the Religious Right
in the United States
The Abortion Debate: A Conflict of
World Views
Faith, Feminism, and Spirituality

Chapter Summary and Themes

Key Terms

Discussion Questions/
Projects for Thought

Internet Resources

Suggested Readings

In 1895, Elizabeth Cady Stanton, a passionate feminist, close friend of Susan B. Anthony, and founder of equal rights and suffrage associations during the first wave of feminism in the nineteenth century, wrote:

> *From the inauguration of the movement for women's emancipation the Bible has been used to hold her in the "divinely ordained sphere," prescribed in the Old and New Testaments. The canon and civil law; church and state; priests and legislators; all political parties and religious denominations have alike taught that woman was made after man, of man, and for man, an inferior being, subject to man. Creeds, codes, Scriptures and statutes, are all based on this idea. The fashions, forms, ceremonies and customs of society, church ordinances and discipline all grow out of this idea (Stanton 1895/ 1974:7).*

More than 100 years later, Stanton's words still ring true. Religious beliefs have aroused conservative political movements that threaten many of the rights that women have won as the result of feminism, and in many religions, women continue to be excluded from positions of leadership. In those where they are now permitted to hold positions of leadership, they are still a small minority. Both in the United States and worldwide, some religious beliefs are the core of sexist ideologies that promote women's exclusion from the public world and that maintain women's subordination in the home.

Religion is a powerful source for the subordination of women in society; yet, across the years religion has also been an important source for the feminist movement and other movements for human liberation. This is evident particularly, but not exclusively, in the African American community, where religion has been a powerful instrument for social change and where women's roles in the church have provided African American women with opportunities for leadership, education, and the development of organizational skills. In addition, religious belief in the Black community rests on a strong faith in justice, fairness, and equality. The liberating effects of religion are also evident in Judaism—one of the most conservative religions in its doctrine about women—yet, its religious faith has spawned feminism and liberalism. There are many feminists who are also devout Christians, and there is a feminist movement among Islamic women (Fernea 1998; Mernissi and Lakeland 1992; Mir-Hosseini 1999).

Thus, although religion has been a repressive force in women's lives, it has also been a source of liberation. Bernice Johnson Reagon, Black feminist and performer, reflects on her religious experience in childhood, writing in her autobiography:

> *Everybody in church talked about/Miss Nana's relationship with God/People thought she had a sort of audacity/Everybody else would say/"Now, Lord, here comes me your meek and undone servant and you know me and you know my condition"/This was a way of saying/"Now Lord, I don't even need to go over my situation/Let us start now with where I am and what I need today"/ . . . /Miss Nana was grateful for what she got but she didn't let up on God for what she wanted/God had already given her a soul, right?/But then she'd say,/"That ain't all I need, Lord/You are not off the hook/I expect you to be here on time tomorrow night" (1982:90–91).*

Understanding of these dual tendencies of repression and liberation is best developed through exploring sociological and feminist perspectives on religion. The sections that follow explore several themes in the feminist critique of religion, including the historical relationship of women, religion, and feminism; women's religious beliefs and status within churches; the role of the church in minority communities; and, new perspectives inspired by feminist spirituality and theology.

❖ Sociological Perspectives on Religion

For most people, religion is something they hold dear, sometimes so much so that they see it as the only possible view of the world. Paul Tillich (1957), a liberal theologian, defines religion as the expression of humanity's ultimate concerns, the articulation of longing for a center of meaning and value and for connection with the power of being. Sociologists who study religion take another approach. They are not so much interested in the truth or falsity of a religious belief system but in how belief systems and religious institutions shape social behavior and reflect the collective experience of society's members.

From a sociological perspective, religion provides a culture with powerful symbols and conceptions that are deeply felt and shape a group's view of the world around them. Religious belief is often the basis for cultural and societal conflict and is frequently so strongly felt that people will fight and die for it. Religion is also the basis for in-group membership, sometimes strongly protected by sanctions against interfaith and same-sex marriages.

Sociological perspectives on religion also take the institutional structure of religion as significant in a variety of ways. Like other institutions in society, religious institutions socialize their members through enforcing group norms that dictate many aspects of everyday life, including what men and women wear; how life events (such as birth, puberty, marriage, and death) are defined and ritualized; and how men and women are defined in terms of home, work, child care, politics, and the law. Religious institutions also include power structures and, like other social institutions, are characterized by a system of stratification, which is clearly demarcated by gender, race, and class.

Religious belief is a particularly important part of many aspects of our experience. Religion, for example, influences how tolerant one is on sexual matters, with those who are most religious generally being less tolerant of premarital sex, homosexuality, and marital infidelity (Scott 1998; Hager 1996; Saguy 1999). However, this relationship is not as strong as one might think because secular (i.e., nonreligious) forces also influence people's beliefs. Thus, among evangelicals—those generally seen as sexual conservatives—there is diversity in opinions about sexual morality (Park 1999). Evangelicals have also generally been portrayed as antifeminist and conservative in views about women's roles. However, research finds that support for egalitarian gender roles (i.e., shared housework and childcare, leadership for women in the church, and women's employment) has declined among evangelical, conservative Protestants as they attempt to reconcile traditional beliefs about women's roles with the reality of a changing world (Gallagher 2003;

Hoffman 1997; Peterson and Donnenwerth 1998; Gallagher and Smith 1999). Nonetheless, fundamentalist religious groups have politically taken the position that the family should be morally autonomous, and thus the dominant political agenda of the religious right is one opposed to abortion and sex education and supportive of school prayer (Bendroth 1999). Religion has a strong influence on the political climate within which gender relations are being negotiated.

For feminist scholars, one of the beginning points of their analysis of religion is the fact that, as measured by a variety of indicators, women are more religious than men in U.S. society. Women are more likely to attend church than men are and to attend on a regular basis. Women express higher degrees of religiosity, but, as feminists have pointed out, despite the fact that women outnumber men in religious faith and in attendance at worship services, it is men, regardless of religious denomination, who maintain religious authority. In Christian churches it is men, for the most part, who are the priests and clergy, and they are typically backed up in the institution by men as deacons, elders, and vestry of the church. Orthodox Jews and Roman Catholics still deny ordination to women, and, although their numbers are growing, women are a numerical minority in seminaries of all faiths.

These patterns of gender inequality in religious institutions have raised the question of the extent to which religious traditions contribute to the subjugation of women. Religion is clearly one of the foremost forces in society to preserve traditions, conserve established social order, stabilize world views, and transmit values through generations, but religion is equally important in social transformation. Religious beliefs can and do frame new sources of human potential and possibility, and organized religious groups can release enormous bursts of political energy (Falk 1985). This is well demonstrated in the history of the civil rights movement, with its organizational center in African American churches. The civil rights movement demonstrates that religious institutions can provide liberation movements with the leadership, organizational structure, and values that provide both the support network for social movements and the visions for new futures that such movements need.

❖ *Religion and Social Control*

From a sociological perspective, religion is one of the forces that holds society together. Although it is also a source of conflict, both within and between different groups and societies, religion is an integrative force in that it shapes collective belief and therefore collective identity. Religious rituals—such as weddings, christenings, and bar and bat mitzvahs—promote group solidarity and symbolize group cohesion. Promoting identification with a religious group gives members a feeling of belonging; at the same time, it also promotes feelings of exclusionary or outsider status to those outside of the group. Jewish or Muslim people living in a predominantly Christian society therefore feel estranged from the dominant culture, yet, their religious faith creates their own awareness of group identity.

Because religion is such a powerful source of collective identity, it also is a form of social control. Religious sanctions, whether formal or informal, chastise those who violate religious norms. Religious beliefs, if internalized (i.e., learned and developed as part of one's self-concept and moral development), direct individual and group beliefs and behaviors. In this way, religion controls the development of self and group identity. At the societal level, religion also can be a form of social control. In the extreme, groups who deviate from religious proscriptions may be tortured, executed, or excommunicated; in more subtle ways, religious deviants may be ridiculed, shunned, or ostracized. In the history of Western religion, the persecution of witches is a good illustration of the connections between religion, social control, and gender.

During the Middle Ages in western Europe, it is estimated that between 30,000 and 9,000,000 women were killed or tortured as witches (Daly 1978). The breadth of this estimate indicates how difficult it is to pinpoint the number of witch persecutions. Toward the end of the seventeenth century in the United States, another 20 persons (seven of whom were men) were tried and executed as witches. Although the scope of this experience hardly matches that of the witch craze that swept Europe during the period of the Inquisition, the sociological impetus was the same. In both places, witches were believed to be women influenced by the devil, and they were perceived to be threats to social purity.

In western Europe, the *Malleus Maleficarum*, issued by the Catholic church in 1484, defined the church's position on witches. This document defined witchcraft, described the alleged practices of witches, and standardized trial procedures and sentencing for those persecuted as witches throughout Europe. The *Malleus Maleficarum* defined witchcraft as stemming from women's carnal lust; women were seen as instruments of Satan because of their insatiable desire. According to the *Malleus Maleficarum*, "All witchcraft comes from carnal lust, which is in women insatiable. Quoting Proverbs XXX: "There are three things that are never satisfied, yea, a fourth thing which says not, it is enough; that is, the mouth of the womb" (*Malleus Maleficarum*, cited in Dworkin 1974:133). People believed that witches collected male organs for use in satanic rituals and stole semen from sleeping men. They were also believed to cast spells over male organs so that the organs disappeared entirely!

Who were these women, and what was happening in history that there was such organized madness to eradicate them? Historians explain the witch hunts as stemming from the historical movement of the Catholic and Protestant churches to establish themselves as supreme authorities over sacred and secular matters. The period of the witch hunts in western Europe was a period of the solidification of church authority. Women who were singled out as witches were women who deviated from the religious norms of the time; they were healers, wise women, and midwives. Those who formed witch cults were women who had a strong sense of people as a part of nature and who, because of this belief, gave animals a prime place in some of their rituals. Such a belief system, with its integrated view of human life and nature, was anathema to the patriarchal and hierarchical structure of the church. As feminists have argued, because the church was the ultimate representation of male power, witchcraft also symbolized men's fears of female sexuality, its assumed relationship to nature, and its unbounded expression. Feminists describe the witch hunts as a means of men's desire to control women's sexuality

(Daly 1978; Dworkin 1974). Women defined as witches also were often widows and spinsters—in other words, single women who were living independently of men (Anderson and Gordon 1978; Szasz 1970). In sum, the witch hunts were a mechanism for ensuring the social control of women (and those who supported them), as represented in the emerging hegemony of organized patriarchal religion.

The persecution of women as witches is a historical case of the imposition of serious sanctions against women who lived outside the developing control of patriarchal religious bodies and outside the control of men. Modern sociologists see the persecution of witches as the persecution of sexual and religious deviants (Szasz 1970). Although, in retrospect, the treatment of women as witches may seem like an extreme case of religious persecution, there are contemporary equivalents. The treatment of women under Taliban rule in Afghanistan from 1996 to 2001 also illustrates the extreme to which some fundmentalist interpretations of religious belief can be taken. Under Taliban rule, women were banished from schools and workplaces, forbidden to leave their homes without a male relative escorting them, and could be beaten or stoned for the slightest infraction of Taliban rules. Sociologists who have analyzed the political, social, and economic subordination of Muslim women often see this as stemming from interpretations of Islamic theology to require the restriction of female sexuality (Mernissi 1987). As in all religions, different interpretations of religious texts lead to different conclusions about the treatment of women, but the point here is that religion often contributes to the subordination of women.

❖ *Religion and the Emergence of Feminism in the United States*

Discussion of religion as a form of social control may create an impression that religion is only a negative force in women's lives. Religion, however, is also a source of resistance to oppression. This duality is well illustrated by the history of feminism in the United States.

In the United States, the power of the Protestant and Catholic faiths was well established during the colonial period, and, although women outnumbered men in the churches, the church hierarchy was exclusively male (Cott 1977). Not until the nineteenth century in the United States do historians typically see the beginnings of significant social change in women's religious roles and the seeds of developing feminism. Two particular developments in the nineteenth century in the United States have major significance for the role of women in religion and the development of the feminist movement: the evangelical spirit of the Second Great Awakening and the widespread belief in the cult of womanhood that defined and restricted women's world to the world of domesticity (Hargrove et al. 1993).

The **Second Great Awakening** was a social movement in the early nineteenth century that emphasized a revivalist and egalitarian spirit in religion. During this period, ministers and laypersons began to see religion as a route to salvation on earth and they used this belief to teach the restraints they believed were necessary for an orderly society. Occurring in the aftermath of the French Revolution and in

the midst of worries about the destructive influence of growing urban populations and Catholic immigration, the Second Great Awakening had a democratic
impulse—reaching out to the urban poor and western frontier residents. The Second Great Awakening created a lay missionary spirit in which conversion and religious benevolence were seen as the solution to the social ills generated by
widespread social transformations affecting the fabric of American society (Cott
1977).

During this period, Christianity was softened (or "feminized"); rather than
stressing dogma, it instead exalted meekness. Christians also began to reinterpret
Christ as embodying these more gender-typed images of love, forgiveness, and hu-
mility. The "feminization" of American culture and religion meant that, among
other things, by the middle of the nineteenth century, women were the majority in
American religion (Douglas 1977; Welter 1976). During this time, women were defined as the keepers of the private refuge of the home—the place where piety and
religious spirit were to prosper. In this domestic refuge, women's purity and piety
were seen as vehicles for redemption; women were seen in opposition to the aggressiveness and competition of the public sphere that was identified with men. Although these images exalted the traditional status of women, many have suggested
that they also provided women with positive roles and images—at least ones that
did not degrade and denigrate women's culture. The exaltation of women's culture
encouraged women to speak in prayer meetings and congregations and encouraged them to participate in voluntary religious associations.

Women's religious societies were especially successful at fund-raising, and
these societies became the basis for a developing sense of sisterhood among
women. Local missionary activities trained women for what was defined as a life
of social usefulness, teaching them hygiene, citizenship, family values, and social
relationships and engaging them in fieldwork in the cities. As a consequence,
women's religious activities engaged them in other social reform movements.

During the nineteenth century, women—White women, at least—were considered to be more spiritual and more naturally prone to religious observance
and piety than were men. The belief that women were naturally good also influenced the development of the feminist movement in this period. Women's alleged moral superiority was perceived to have a potentially benevolent impact
on the more callous and harsh realities of the public world. Some feminists argued that extending the values of the domestic or private sphere to the public
would create a more compassionate public world—a theme now resounded
among some contemporary feminists, as well (Miller 1977). Throughout the
nineteenth-century women's movement, religious faith played an important
part in articulating feminist concerns. Women in the Women's Christian Temperance Union, one of the first feminist organizations, extolled the virtues of
women and blamed the impersonal and competitive culture of the male public
world for a variety of social ills.

Belief in the virtues of women's culture led early feminists to use the values
of the home as the basis for crusading in the public world and for demanding
women's rights. At the same time, as the suffrage movement developed, men
(and some women) also used arguments from the Bible against women's suffrage

and other changes in women's status. They maintained that scripture ordered a different and higher sphere of life apart from public life and that this "higher" sphere was the responsibility and, in fact, nature of women. As a result, many feminists eventually gave up on the traditional churches and turned to experimental religious societies, such as the Quakers, for more inner-directed spiritual experiences.

For most early feminists in the United States, religious faith was a significant part of their feminist ideology. Elizabeth Cady Stanton was herself relatively alone in seeing the domination of women as having religious roots. By the late nineteenth century, when Stanton first published *The Woman's Bible,* the influence of Darwin's thought was also paramount in U.S. culture. Stanton had likely been influenced by the more relativistic view of culture that Darwin's work inspired. Darwin's work had encouraged the development of anthropological relativism—a system of thought that saw ideas in society as emerging from culture. Such a belief made it possible to doubt that the Bible had been divinely inspired. While Stanton herself seemed to be influenced by this developing social consciousness, other feminists of the period did not share her perspective.

The first publication of *The Woman's Bible* in 1895 (reprinted in 1898) reflected Stanton's belief that domination of women had deep ideological and religious roots. Other feminists, however, did not share her sense of its importance. Members of the National American Women Suffrage Association, with the exception of Susan B. Anthony and a few others, repudiated any connection with this view (Hole and Levine 1971). Afterwards, *The Woman's Bible* went into obscurity, not to be rediscovered until the 1970s during the second wave of feminism in the United States.

Historians of religion have since asked why Christianity was a basis for women's progressive movements in the nineteenth century when in the twentieth century, Christianity is more often perceived as an enemy to feminists than a friend (Reuther and Keller 1986). The answer lies in observing the social transformations occurring in the nineteenth century. Throughout the nineteenth century, the process of industrialization meant that men had entered a new secular world. Even when women worked in the industrial sector, the cultural ideology of the time defined women's world as being in the home. Religion was defined as a part of women's culture, although, for women, religion was one of the few dimensions of public culture in which they were allowed to participate.

By the early twentieth century, White women's winning of the vote coincided with shifts in the boundaries between religious and secular domains. White women in the twentieth century entered the public world with men. Feminist social reformers of the 1920s and 1930s were more likely to use the language and philosophy of social science than they were to use theology to articulate their concerns. In the twentieth century, religion for women, if they believed it at all, had become more a private culture. At the same time, secularization resulted in the increasing conservatism of churches on women's issues. Churches, particularly Evangelical and Catholic churches, perceived secularism as having a pernicious influence on society. As a result, the churches politicized religious culture by using religious doctrine as a platform against women's equality—including their social, legal, and reproductive rights.

By the time of the emergence of the second wave of feminism in the 1970s, women's religious roles had changed dramatically. Although many feminists were still active in religious life, their critical distance from religious institutions and their understanding of religion's sexist roots created a new basis for feminist criticism of religion and a new basis for feminist transformation of religious thought.

❖ *Women and Religiosity*

Images of Women in Religion

Feminists have contended that the traditional view of women in most religious faiths idealizes and humiliates women (Daly 1978). Images of women in religious texts reflect and create stereotypical gender roles and legitimate social inequality between men and women. The New Testament of the Bible, for example, urges women to be subordinate to husbands, thereby fulfilling the assumed proper hierarchy of women as subordinate to men as men are subordinate to God. Jewish feminists have also repudiated the traditional Jewish morning prayer in which a man blesses God for not creating him as a woman, while a woman blesses God for creating her in accordance with His will.

The humiliation of women through religious texts is especially clear in religious depictions of female sexuality, defined by both Christianity and Judaism as a dangerous force to be feared, purified, and controlled by men. In Orthodox Judaism the myth that women are unclean during menstruation and seven days thereafter also reflects a negative view of female sexuality. Feminists see **misogyny,** meaning the hatred of women, depicted in the creation stories in male-dominated cultures that assign women responsibility for evil. In most of these legends women are seen as sexually alluring, curious, gullible, and insatiable. The biblical story of Adam and Eve is, of course, the classic example. Eve is depicted as cajoling Adam into eating the apple, thereby dooming them to live in a world of trouble and evil. Hebrew myth depicts Lilith, the first woman, as equal to Adam in all ways, but she refused to do what he wanted her to do. As this myth goes, in response to Adam's demands, the Lord created Eve from Adam's rib and made her inferior and dependent. One version of this legend in Hebrew tradition is that it was Lilith who persuaded Eve to eat the apple from the Tree of Knowledge. Feminists suggest that this creates dual stereotypes of woman—one as evil, the other as gullible. Either way, women are defined through these myths as bad (McGuire 2002).

Religious Texts as Interpretive Documents

Whether a group of religious believers accepts their religious tradition as literally true and divinely ordained by God or whether the group sees their religious text as subject to interpretation influences the group's acceptance of transformed religious roles for women. Sociologists see all religious texts, including the Bible, the Koran, and the Torah, as cultural and historical documents. That is to say, sociologists see these texts as not containing truth per se, but as cultural artifacts—records of particular cultural beliefs, historical practices, and societal legends. The legends and beliefs that the texts communicate are the basis for what Durkheim called the **collective consciousness** of a society—the system of beliefs in a society that create a sense of belonging to the community and the moral obligation to live up to the society's demands. Sociologists see these histories and texts as neither true nor false, but as symbols, powerful as they may be, of group belief and collective consciousness. Consequently, they are subject to interpretation and symbolic use by religious groups.

Seeing the Bible as a document to be interpreted, not just the literal word of God, is probably the most contentious point between sociologists of religion and those with strong and traditional commitments to religious world views. The use of Christianity to justify slavery shows, however, how Christianity and the Bible have been interpreted to support human oppression. European explorers who traveled to African cultures in the sixteenth century encountered societies having religious practices and beliefs quite unlike the Christian traditions of western Europe. Their response to such practices was to define African people as heathens and savages who worshipped pagan gods (Jordan 1968). Europeans' identification of Africans as heathens led them to believe that Black women and men were lustful, passionate, and sexually aggressive; this became the basis for racial and sexual stereotypes of Black men and women. White beliefs in Black men's sexual prowess created fears among White men that were the basis for extreme measures of social control—including lynching—throughout U.S. history. The identification of Black women as lustful also established White men's belief in their rights to sexual relations with Black women.

Christian beliefs played a central role in legitimating the exploitative treatment of African people. Slave traders and owners believed that Africans needed Christian salvation. Slaveowners saw their exploitation of slaves as the justifiable and necessary conversion of heathens, even going so far as to think that the slaves could not take care of themselves. Slaveowners reasoned it was their Christian duty, although a burden, to care for the slaves (Genovese 1972).

Although Christianity was a tool of the oppressing class, used to justify and legitimate the economic and cultural exploitation of millions of African American slaves, it also reinforced slaves' own belief in their rights as human beings. As a result, Christianity provided the basis for slaves' political resistance to exploitation. The slaves came to believe in the Christian values that slaveowners taught them, and therefore continued to believe in their own humanity and their rights to social justice. So, while Christianity was interpreted by slaveowners to justify slavery, for the slaves Christianity was also a source of salvation.

Understanding the relationship between Christianity, slavery, and emancipation also helps us understand why feminists who reject the misogynist traditions of religious beliefs and institutions sometimes see Christianity as providing the theological and philosophical basis for advocating women's liberation. In the sections that follow, we examine more carefully the role of women in religion and the new ways that feminist theologians have transformed traditional theology to generate new meaning systems intended for the liberation of human beings.

Gender and Religious Beliefs

As we have already seen, studies show that women are more religious than men, both in expressed religious faith and in women's participation in worship services (see Figures 8.1 and 8.2). This difference has persisted over time, despite the fact that church attendance has declined in U.S. society. Now, 48 percent of all Americans identified themselves as Protestant, 25 percent as Catholic, 3 percent as Jewish, 1 percent as Mormon, 1 percent as Greek or Russian Orthodox, 4 percent as other, and 7 percent said they had no religious preference. Women are also more likely than men to say they are religious (Carroll 2004; see Figure 8.3).

In the United States, 64 percent of the population say they are members of a church or synagogue, although considerably fewer (43 percent) say they attend church weekly (Carroll 2004). Because in polls more people report church membership than the churches themselves report to data-gathering agencies, poll data are not totally reliable. Nonetheless, the poll data indicate the public importance people attribute to religious affiliation, and polls are a sound measure of where people place their religious identification.

Despite the historical decline in religious faith and attendance at worship services, religion still plays a significant role in U.S. society. Religious belief influences a wide array of other social attitudes and behaviors. As previously discussed, this is especially evident on matters involving sexual attitudes and behaviors. Religious conservatism tends to engage traditional gender role attitudes (Hunt 2001; Ellison and Bartkowski 2002; Becker and Hofmeister 2001). One's religious affiliation is also related to one's politics, with those of Jewish faith typically being more socially and politically liberal than other religious groups.

Women's understandings of religion may differ from those of men and women may adopt those aspects of religious belief that speak best to their situations

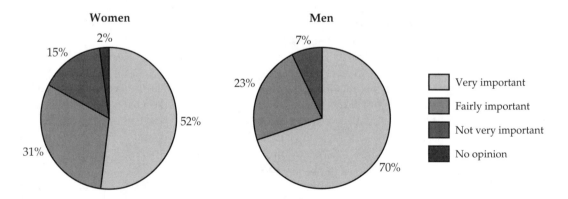

Question: How important would you say religion is in your life?

FIGURE 8.1   The Significance of Religion

Source: Data from Frank Newport and Lydia Saad. 1997. "Religious Faith Is Widespread But Many Skip Church." *The Gallup Poll Monthly* (March): 20–29.

Question: How often do you attend church or synagogue — at least once a week, almost every week, about once a month, seldom, or never?

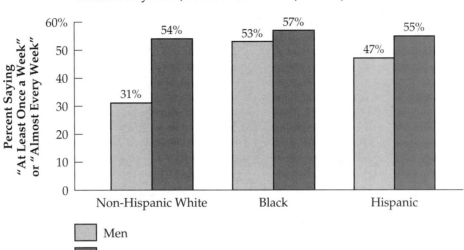

FIGURE 8.2   Frequent Church Attendance: Men vs. Women

Source: Data from Albert L. Winseman. 2004. "U.S. Churches Looking for a Few White Men." Princeton, NJ: The Gallup Organization.

(McGuire 2002). It is also questionable whether women see themselves as their religion sees them. Although the traditional image of women in religious texts is one that sees women as more passive, docile, and pious, women may be more active agents in the construction of their religious identity and beliefs than has typically been assumed. Although sexist images in religious thought remain, it may well be that women adapt them to their own circumstances, indicating that women's religious faith is not as passive or meek as the images in religious texts suggest.

This has been demonstrated in a study of contemporary, well-educated women who have returned to Orthodox Judaism. Lynn Davidman, a feminist sociologist, wondered how women who have the modern options of a career would turn to a traditional religious faith, one that professes very traditional roles for women. Such a conversion seems contrary to societal movement toward women's greater independence and new gender roles—transformations one would especially expect to see among well-educated women. Davidman found, however, that joining an orthodox religious community where women retreated from the public world was one way her respondents avoided the difficulties faced by other women who have to balance the competing definitions of womanhood generated by dual and competing roles for women in the family and at work. For the women she studied, religious orthodoxy provided meaning and a sense of self that was less fragmented than more modern and evolving definitions for career women. Davidman (1991) is careful to point out that the construction of women's identities, including their religious identities, is an active and conscious decision the women make. This perspective sees women not as

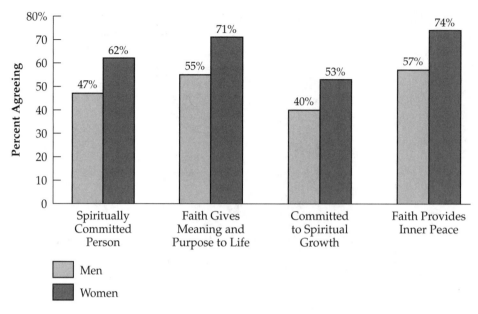

FIGURE 8.3   Religion and Spirituality: Does Gender Matter?

Source: Data from Albert L. Winseman. 2004a. "U.S. Churches Looking for a Few White Men." Princeton, NJ: The Gallup Organization.

mere victims of religious and gender roles but as active agents in the construction of their own identities and religious world views.

In recent years, there has been a dramatic resurgence of traditional evangelical Christianity. Evangelicals, popularly known as "born-again Christians," are those who claim to have been born again through conversion, who accept Jesus as a personal savior, who believe the scriptures are the authority for all doctrine, who feel urgency in spreading their faith, and who claim to have had a dramatic witnessing of the presence of a divine spirit (Flowers 1984; Pohli 1983). They also hold highly traditional views of womanhood. Forty-two percent of the U.S. population identifies themselves as "born again," an increase from 17 percent in 1981. The resurgence of this movement has created a consequent rise in the political power of this group. More women than men identify themselves as evangelical Christians (Winseman 2004b). Studies also find that among both young men and women a positive attitude toward Christianity is associated with belief in more traditional gender roles (Francis and Wilcox 1998).

❖ Women's Status in Religious Institutions

Gender and Religious Participation

Measures of church attendance and identification alone do not fully reveal the extent of women's religious participation. Although observers can easily document that women have been excluded from positions of religious leadership, nonetheless it is women who constitute the vast bulk of religious activity (Heyer-Gray 2000). Many of these activities are difficult to measure numerically, but observations of women's activities in religious organizations show that women run the church bake sales, dinners, and bazaars. Women also teach Sunday schools, babysit during religious services, visit the sick, join prayer circles, and arrange and staff religious social events. In fact, women have historically been those who raise funds for churches and temples. Although Orthodox Judaism defines women's religious role as centered in the home, women in Reform temples participate fully in the life of the temple and they engage in a wide array of volunteer religious, educational, and philanthropic activities (Hargrove et al. 1993).

These activities in different religious organizations make important social ties for women, but they also reflect a gender division of labor within religious institutions. In Protestant churches, women rarely preach, serve as trustees, control funds, or make decisions about the pastor, church, or church programs. In Roman Catholic churches, men have held all the positions of religious authority. This patriarchal structure is so pervasive that Roman Catholicism has even been described as a sexual caste system. This means that despite the greater participation and faith of Roman Catholic women, the organizational structure, beliefs, ritual expressions, and prescribed norms of the Catholic Church are patriarchal (McGuire 2002; Wallace 1992).

Within the African American community, as in other communities, it is the work of African American women that holds the church together. It is estimated that Black churches are 75 percent female. In the **sanctified church**—the term used to refer to Holiness and Pentecostal churches—women are 90 percent of the congregation. Women's activities are crucial to African American churches, and Gilkes (2000) contends that all African American churches have been influenced by the militancy of women in the sanctified church. Gilkes also points out that historically men have rarely matched the financial contributions of women in the sanctified church.

Gender segregation in religious institutions is also evident in various religious cults. These cults tend to be based on patriarchal authority systems in which women serve the men in exchange for the rewards of emotional gratification. The very intense nature of commitment in these nontraditional groups can lead to extremely repressive aspects. Women usually have domestic obligations required as demonstration of their religious commitment, and they are often expected to engage in sexual relations with male cult leaders. Whereas male devotees have access to positions of power as a means of bonding and sustaining their group affiliation, love and devotion are seen as leading to spiritual fulfillment for women in these movements. Women in these cults are also often subjected to psychological, physical, and sexual abuse, as they are expected to be devoted to the religious leaders. Those who have studied women who leave such movements have found that on leaving women tend to be depressed, spiritually confused, and alienated (Boeri 2002).

Despite the patriarchal structure of religious institutions, women develop organizational and leadership skills through their work in these institutions (Gilkes 2000). Although their contribution is often trivialized, there is a heavy dependence on women's labor in religious organizations; however, in most churches and temples, it seems that women are in the background. They play the support roles, but not the leadership roles. The Catholic church, for example, relies heavily on the work of nuns in the church, the schools, and the community, but, until the mid-1960s when Vatican II modernized the role of nuns by allowing them to discard their habits and take on a more public role, nuns were cloistered and were kept silent. Now they are among the active women within the church and are urging that women be ordained and given access to real power in the Catholic church.

Women as Clergy

The restriction of women to support positions in the church and their exclusion from making policies has led women to organize for the ordination of women in all the major denominations. Women now constitute 14 percent of all clergy, an increase from the past, but still a small proportion, especially considering that women are 56 percent of all religious workers. Even in the Catholic church, where women cannot be ordained, women serve as parish leaders in many places where there is no priest present (Wallace 1992; U.S. Department of Labor 2004).

The entry of women into the clergy is not entirely new, although its magnitude is certainly unprecedented. Throughout the nineteenth century, women were licensed as evangelists, and, beginning in the 1880s, African American women began to press for ordination in the mainline Protestant denominations. The African Methodist Episcopal Zion Church ordained women as early as 1884, and the African Methodist Episcopal Church began ordaining women in 1948, but Harvard Divinity School did not even open its doors to women until 1955.

African American women, like White women, seem to have greater participation in decision making in churches, especially in smaller congregations. Interviews with African American male ministers, however, reveal continuing prejudices against African American women in the ministry, resulting in unfair expectations and unjust treatment of women ministers whom they encounter (Grant 1982). Although African American women have played a central role in the church, they too have been excluded from many positions of authority and leadership. Holiness and Pentecostal denominations account for the largest share of all clergywomen. Gilkes's (2000) studies on the role of women in the sanctified church give us a detailed picture of African American women's participation in religious activity and institutions. The sanctified church elevates women to roles as heroines, both as spiritual and professional role models. Gilkes identifies a feminist infrastructure in the sanctified church that has its origins in women's racial uplift movements of the late nineteenth and early twentieth centuries. She also shows that the collectivist orientation of these churches has emerged from the relationship of African American culture and its churches to the dominant culture. They have rejected the patriarchal organization of major denominational churches, which has, in turn, encouraged a cooperative model of gender relations and pluralistic political practices within the church. In this sense, these churches can provide a feminist model of institutional organization and practice for the larger society. As these churches evolve into more traditional and bureaucratic organizations and away from more spiritual symbolic roles, the proportion of women in positions of clerical leadership decreases however (Barfoot and Sheppard 1980).

Evidence of the increasing role of women in the clergy is also seen by the substantial increases in their enrollments in divinity schools; Women now receive 32 percent of all Ph.D.s in theology, compared with 2.3 percent in 1970 (U.S. Census Bureau 2004).

More people now support having women in positions of religious leadership, with 75 percent of Lutherans, Methodists, Episcopalians, and Presbyterians supporting equality in church leadership. Half of Catholics now endorse this idea, but members of more conservative Christian denominations (e.g., Southern Baptists and Assemblies of God) are unlikely to support women's roles as leaders. Religious faiths that give a more priestly role to leadership and define women as supporters, rather than as leaders, are at least likely to support women as clergy (Hoffman 1997; Nason-Clark 1987; Jelen 1989). People are also more likely to endorse the idea of women's leadership in the church once they have experienced having a woman in this role. Women, young people, and those with more formal education are also most likely to support women's ordination (Dudley 1996). Generally, as the women's movement has changed the public perception of women's roles, resistance to women as clergy has declined over time (Chaves and Cavendish 1997). Because women are more liberal on critical issues facing religious organizations, such as abortion and the acceptance of gays and lesbians, an increase in women's leadership may well influence church positions on social issues in the future (Finlay 1997).

Those who advocate women's greater leadership in religious institutions often do so by asserting that women will bring a more woman-centered approach to these leadership roles (Lummis and Nesbitt 2000). Studies of women ministers and rabbis find that women in these roles do tend to have a more collaborative style than men and that there are gender-specific approaches to women's leadership roles. Women ministers also tend to be more open to a wide variety of service-oriented roles, whereas male clergy are more likely to want a high-status clientele (Finlay 1996). How women specifically define their roles depends somewhat on their faith. Women rabbis, for example, are more likely to emphasize the secular aspects of their leadership (as teacher, counselor, and community leader), whereas women ministers emphasize the more spiritual components of their role (saying they are a "moral voice" and emphasizing that they have been "called" to the ministry). In either case, women believe they carry out their role differently from male colleagues, saying they are more engaging, less formal, more people-oriented, and less concerned about power struggles (Lehman 1994; Wallace 1992; Simon et al. 1994).

❖ *Religion and Social Change*

The role of religion in social change movements, such as feminism and the civil rights movement, is a complex one. Many see religion as a force against progressive social change, but review of the development of feminism and civil rights shows the compelling role that religion plays in promoting, not just resisting, change. What is the relationship between religion and social justice?

Race, Religion, and Social Justice

For numerous racial and ethnic minority groups, religion is often a strong basis for one's political identity. For Jewish women and men, religious and ethnic identities are fused as a public and political culture. For Native Americans, Latinos, and African Americans, religion is one way to affirm one's ethnic subculture, while simultaneously creating a basis for political and social organizing. For African Americans, strong religious faith has buttressed and inspired activities for social justice. These facts reveal the complex relationship between religion, race and ethnic identity, and policies.

Among Latinas, although the Catholic Church has been seen as an oppressive social force, it also plays a positive role in relationships with friends, family, and community. Religion sustains ties to family and friends in the face of more industrialized and bureaucratic public life, although among both Catholic and Protestant Latinas, the influence of religion varies by social class, with the working class more committed to religious beliefs than the professional class (Williams 1990). The influence of religion is not monolithic, however—as is popularly imagined. Urbanization, education, and other social influences shape how Latinos interpret the meaning of religion in the context of their lives. Seen in this way, the influence of religion is not always one of resistance to social change; indeed in **liberation theology** throughout Latin America, religious belief has provided the foundation for movements for social change.

The role of religion among African Americans reveals a similarly complex relationship between religion, conservatism, and social justice movements. The role of African American churches is multidimensional and includes religious, as well as social and political, work. Because the central theme of Black theology is liberation (Flowers 1984), African American churches have been meeting places for political organizing and have been highly significant in the historical development of Black protest. The liberatory function of the African American church is evidenced by the fact that African Americans define the education of both oppressed people and oppressors as central tasks of Christian missions. Black spirituals and sermons are full of protest symbolism. The musical ministries of African American women have advanced and institutionalized their forms of creative expression (Dodson and Gilkes 1986). There is, in fact, enormous cultural significance to African American church music; almost every popularly recognized indigenous musical style in the United States has antecedents in the oral tradition of African American worship services.

Despite the liberatory functions of the African American church, sociologists have also shown that religion can serve as an "opiate" for social protest. In other words, sociologists use the term **religion as opiate** to describe the fact that religion can also suppress social protest by encouraging people to accept their social position. Some sociological research has shown that despite the connection of Black theology to movements for social justice, there is an inverse relationship between religious piety and political militancy (Marx 1967).

But, as in other minority communities, within African American communities the church has historically provided a buffer against segregation, discrimination, and bigotry. African American churches provide for the release of emotion that cannot be expressed in the dominant White racist society (Blackwell 1991). Most recognize that the church is, along with the family, the most important institution in African American society. It is the one institution over which African Americans have their own control (Frazier 1964), and it is an important source of social cohesion. African American churches are often described as the organizational and expressive core of African American culture and community, where the church performs a variety of social and community functions (Gilkes 2000).

African American churches are instruments for the development of Black leadership, and they provide a cohesive institutional structure within African American communities. They are also the basis for community action and act as charitable institutions on behalf of African American people. As a result of the churches' many functions, Black ministers (and, when the ministers are men, their wives) play roles as both social workers and political, personal, and religious advisors. The Black church has a function of supporting education and being an institution for the transmission of community values, historically stressing the value of the family, mutuality, and responsibility. The educational function of the African American church is illustrated by the fact that more than one-half of all historically Black colleges are funded by religious bodies. The church in African American communities can also be an agency for the development of business ventures, a situation especially well illustrated by the economic entrepreneurship of Black Muslims.

Religion and Antifeminism

As within racial justice movements, the feminist movement has a complex relationship to religion. Many simply associate religion with antifeminism, but doing so overlooks not only the feminist movement that has emerged within various religious faiths, but also ignores the way that some feminists interpret religious values as providing the basis for their feminism. Thus, a vast body of literature has emerged wherein feminists examine the relationship between their beliefs as feminists and the beliefs that emerge from their religious views.

One compelling example comes from examining the beliefs of the Islamic faith—an issue particularly compelling in the context of the U.S. war in Afghanistan following terrorist attacks on the United States on September 11, 2001. The subsequent interest in Islamic traditions—including the treatment of women—though it had long been on feminists' agenda, has captured more public curiosity. Under the rule of the Taliban regime in Afghanistan—a regime that had taken control of the nation in 1996 following the Afghani war with the Soviet Union—women were forcibly excluded from all public participation, including schools, health care facilities, work, even public baths. Women were forced to stay inside their homes and, if seen in public, had to be accompanied by a male relative and fully covered in the now widely recognized *burqa*—a covering that completely concealed women except for a narrow mesh slit over their eyes. When the Taliban were overthrown by other Afghani groups, with the support of the United States, many women jubilantly removed the burqa and returned to public life. Others remained veiled, although not always so fully covered as by the burqa. Is the Islamic faith inherently antifeminist or can it support movements for women's liberation?

This is a complex question, not easily answered without careful study of Islamic theology. But, like other religions, Islam is subject to interpretation and can be compatible with both antifeminist or feminist values. For some, the veiling of women in Islam stems from beliefs about women's sexuality—that women's sexuality is so compelling that they must be covered or men will lose control. But this is interpreted differently among different Islamic groups. Indeed, the whole subject of feminism and Islamic belief is much debated within Islam, with many arguing that Islamic beliefs are fully consistent with the liberation of women and others taking a more fundamentalist view that Islam requires the subordination of women (Mernissi 1987; Mernissi and Lakeland 1992; Fernea 1998). In this regard, Islam is no different from other faiths, although its practice has been dominated by extremist and patriarchal groups in many contemporary nations. But Islam is not the only religion that has been used to justify the oppression of various groups, as a review of the role of Christianity in supporting slavery clearly shows. Extremism emerges within every religious tradition, just as feminism has grown within the diverse religions of the world.

Feminism and the Religious Right in the United States

Within the United States, the rise of the **religious right**—the term used to refer to fundamentalist Christian groups that have politically mobilized on behalf of conservative causes—has generated a new period of religious activism. Conservative Christian groups have been strongly opposed to abortion rights, gay marriage, sex education in the schools, and other social changes. Many in the religious right see the church as the defender of public morality and perceive contemporary social changes associated with feminism and liberalism as threatening the values of family life and as violating the hierarchy of God to man to woman. Whether one believes in such antifeminist doctrine, however, depends on the extent to which one sees the Bible as a literal document or as one subject to interpretation. The most conservative and antifeminist evangelicals are those who take a more literalist position—that is the Bible is not subject to interpretation. Evangelicals with a more interpretive perspective tend to give women a stronger voice in church leadership and are more willing to challenge patriarchal structures of authority (Riesebrodt and Chong 1999).

In one of the most comprehensive studies of evangelical beliefs about feminism, sociologist Sally Gallagher found that religiously conservative Protestants are not as antifeminist as their image suggests. She found that 10 percent actually identify as feminists and 10 percent identify as distinctly antifeminist, but most find feminism to be a mixed blessing. In her sample, evangelical women were appreciative of the greater opportunities for women that feminism has generated, although they also believed that other aspects of feminism were opposed to their values, especially around the issue of abortion. She also found that evangelical Christians were critical of feminism for what they perceived as excessive individualism—a charge that, though false, they perceive as antithetical to their more family-centered values. One of Gallagher's major conclusions is that there is diversity among evangelical Christians with regard to their beliefs about feminism (Gallagher 2003, 2004).

Regardless of the diversity of beliefs found among those of deep religious faith, the religious right has been a politically effective force because of the strong organizational infrastructure it has established within Protestant and Catholic churches. Evangelical churches provide a massive communication network that has contributed to the mobilization of voters and has thus become a powerful source for conservative social changes. Although membership in Catholic or fundamentalist Protestant churches does not necessarily predict support for right-wing attitudes, there is a strong relationship between church attendance in these groups and conservative political attitudes.

One of the puzzling features of the religious and political right is that many of its activists are women. How can women be so numerous in a movement that to many seems opposed to women's interests? Studies show that women in the antifeminist movement tend to be White, middle-aged housewives (married or widowed), relatively new to politics, and focused usually on a single issue. But they are not monolithic in their beliefs. Some define their political activism in terms of gender roles, defending traditional roles in the family, which they see under siege by social changes that erode women's position. Others take the approach that individual lives should be free from government intrusion; their politics are not a defense of traditional gender arrangements per se, although many find themselves in coalition with socially conservative women (Klatch 1988).

The Abortion Debate: A Conflict of World Views

One of the most active programs of the religious right has been its organized opposition to abortion rights for women. Spurred by the 1973 Supreme Court case *Roe v. Wade* (see Chapter 7), many women who previously had not been politically active were prompted into antiabortion activism. Studies of women active in the prolife movement have found that they tend to be women who are married, with children, generally not employed, and with high school, and sometimes, some college education. The most thorough study of the abortion movement has come from sociologist Kristin Luker (1984), who analyzes the debate over abortion as a matter of conflicting world views—not just views on abortion, but fundamental differences in the gender location of different groups of women.

Luker based her study on two groups: those identified as prochoice and those identified as prolife. The prolife women were antiabortion activists who tended to believe that giving women control over their fertility (through abortion or birth control) breaks up the traditional relationships in families that have women caring for the home and children and men being responsible for the family's income. Prochoice women, on the other hand, saw women's control over reproduction as essential for them to have control over their lives. Prochoice women do not see reproduction as the primary purpose of sex; instead, they think of sex as a means of communication between partners and, if they think of it as sacred at all, it is because they see sex as a mystical experience that breaks down the boundaries between self and other. Women in the antiabortion movement, on the other hand, tended to see sex in more sacred terms, and they believed that the widespread availability of contraception encourages teens to have sex.

In Luker's research, prochoice and antiabortion activists also differed in their social characteristics. Generally speaking, prochoice activists are better educated and more likely to be single than are those organized against abortion. Prochoice activists are more likely to be employed with incomes of their own; if married, their husbands also usually have above-average incomes. Those active in the prolife movement were less likely to be employed and generally had lower family incomes than prochoice women. Luker found that the most dramatic difference between these two groups is in the role religion plays in their lives, a fact supported by other research (Himmelstein 1986). Three-quarters of the prochoice people in Luker's study say that formal religion is either unimportant or completely irrelevant to them. In contrast, over two-thirds (69 percent) of those opposed to abortion say that religion is important in their lives.

Luker interprets what she found as a struggle over very basic values—not just about abortion, but about religion, motherhood, and the direction of contemporary social changes. Those active in the antiabortion movement, she argued, tend to be concerned about a broad decline in religious commitment and a sense of common community. The struggle over abortion, in Luker's thinking, is also a struggle over the meaning of motherhood itself. She sees antiabortion activism as stemming from the status anxiety some women experience when social and economic changes in the society threaten their social and cultural status (Ehrenreich 1983; Luker 1984). Thus, antifeminism is not seen as just a function of socioeconomic variables like age, education, and class, but is explained by the fact that some groups see themselves as vulnerable to the very social, cultural, and economic changes that have also spawned feminism. Antifeminism, seen in this light, is then interpreted as the result of status anxieties that are produced for women who may interpret social changes as generating weakened commitments to family.

Faith, Feminism, and Spirituality

The connection between feminism and religion is not always one of opposition. Many feminists have developed their feminist politics through their religious faith. Although critical of patriarchal religion and its subordination of women, feminists have also developed a feminist view within diverse religious traditions. This concluding section examines the work of feminist theologians and activists who are working to construct new forms of faith and spirituality that will also support the liberation of women.

At the heart of the feminist critique of religion is a deep-felt sense of injustice (Christ and Plaskow 1992). This is particularly evident in the personal accounts some feminist scholars have written of their experiences in divinity school. Judith Plaskow, a noted feminist theologian, describes the reaction of her thesis advisor at Yale Divinity School when she said she wanted to do her thesis on theology and women's experience. "'Fine,' he told her; it was a good subject as long as she dropped all the references to women" (Christ and Plaskow 1992: i–ii). Both she and Carol Christ, another feminist theologian and scholar, were told by divinity faculty that the history of Christian attitudes toward women was not an important area for study (Christ and Plaskow 1992).

Theologians such as Christ and Plaskow nonetheless persisted in their studies of women and religion. The first feminist analyses of religion during feminism's second wave in the 1970s criticized the explicit statements of female inferiority found in religious texts, the subordination of women in the church, and the exclusion of women from ministry. Christian women, for example, rejected the biblical teaching that women must be subordinate to their husbands as indicated in, among other things, the passage in wedding ceremonies that women must obey their husbands. They also criticized the image of God as male and have developed new images for feminist worship. Feminists came to believe that the church and theology will transcend sexist ideologies only when women are granted full spiritual, theological, and ecclesiastical equality. They are not hesitant to acknowledge the interest-laden character of feminist theology, since they have openly declared the commitments out of which it emerges.

Beyond this reform position, however, lies a deepening analysis of the **androcentrism,** or male-centered view, of traditional theological views. This developing analysis is one that is critical of the theological world view of biblical faith and that sees sexism in religion as integrally tied to the dualistic and hierarchical mentality of traditional Christian theology (Reuther 1979). From this analytical perspective, feminist transformation of patriarchal religion will take more than eliminating or changing sexist images in religious thought and admitting women to positions of religious leadership. The more radical feminist critique suggests that the patriarchal models of patriarchal religions cannot be simply rehabilitated to include women. Instead, the radical perspective understands the exclusion and domination of women to be fundamental to the very nature of patriarchal systems of religious thinking. The radical view sees sexism as so deeply embedded in the theology of patriarchal religion that reforms alone could never create the postpatriarchal future that feminist theologians seek (Christ and Plaskow 1992).

This position in radical feminist theology sees the need for revolutionary changes in religious thought, practices, and organizations and refuses even to accept the possibility of the male messiahs of Christian tradition. Whereas many feminists believe that traditional religions can be reformed by identifying sexist language and symbols and giving women full status in places of worship, more radical feminist theologians say that women should simply discard patriarchal religious traditions and forge new visions of women's spirituality—ones that are distinctively based on women's experiences.

Several themes emerge from this radical theological stance: that patriarchal religions rest on and re-create the domination of women by men; that women, like nature, are degraded and seen as needing control; that patriarchal religion forms the basis for other patriarchal institutions; that patriarchal religion has emerged historically through the suppression of female power; and, finally, that spirituality based on women's experience is the only way of reclaiming a fully human faith and liberatory vision of the future.

Reuther (1979) early articulated the feminist view that Christian theology is centered on a domination model. She argues that traditional Christian theologies depict the soul and spirit as opposed to the human body—flesh, matter, and nature. This world view sees human beings as standing between God and nature and teaches human beings that they must subdue the irrational desires of the flesh to spiritual life. This creates a model for domination—one that sees human life as dominated by God, just as some human lives are dominated by others; furthermore, because Christianity depicts the desires of the flesh as needing suppression, the domination model of Christianity has justified the historical domination of those seen by Christians as more carnal (including Jews, African Americans, and Native Americans). Reuther contends that Christianity encourages a world view characterized by dualisms—such as the ethnocentric "we/they" view of the world that sees one group as superior and all others as inferior and in need of salvation and civilization. As a result, the missionary spirit of Christianity feeds the historical development of racism and the development of imperialistic power by seeking to create a monolithic empire.

Similarly, Daly argues that the "widespread conception of the 'Supreme Being' as an entity distinct from this world, but controlling it according to plan and keeping human beings in a state of infantile subjection, has been a not too subtle mask of the divine patriarch" (1979:56–57). Unmasking the patriarchal character of religious traditions causes us to see the powerful alliance between religion and oppressive social structures. Patriarchal theologies have in this way directly contributed to the oppression of women.

This more radical feminist critique of patriarchal religion leads to more fundamental changes in feminist visions of faith and spirituality—ones that are stimulated by asking what it would mean if women's experience were the basis for theological and religious world views. Experience is the key term in this developing feminist analysis. Feminist religious scholars take experience to mean the fabric of life as it is lived. In keeping with the feminist practice of consciousness-raising and defining the personal as political, they believe there is something unique about women's experience and that women's faith and spirituality should be centered on those experiences (Saiving 1979).

This has also led such thinkers to distinguish between religion and spirituality. They claim that religion is that which is historically associated with established and institutionalized structures and ideologies, whereas spirituality suggests a vital, active, and energizing interior perception of the power of being (Yates 1983). This vision of spirituality is exemplified in Ntozake Shange's play, *for colored girls who have considered suicide/when the rainbow is enuf:* "i found god in myself/& i loved her/i loved her fiercely" (1975:63).

Because religion has such a deep hold on the human psyche, radical feminist theologians believe one cannot afford to leave it in the hands of men. They see that men's control of religion emerged only with the suppression of female power and symbolism through the historical demise of goddess worship. They argue that there is nothing natural about patriarchal religion, pointing out that the introduction of male gods and messiahs occurs at specific historical points in the development of human experience and that before the introduction of male messiahs, goddess worship was a nearly universal phenomenon. The earliest artifacts of human culture, they suggest, are female statues and symbols, indicating the awe our ancestors felt for women and their bodily mysteries (Spretnak 1994).

The creation of new symbols, legends, myths, and rituals centered on women's experiences is central to new forms of feminist worship. Often, these rituals are explicitly linked to attempts by women to release anger and fear and to increase a sense of power and community. One study found that participation in such rituals helped women recover from sexual victimization and improved their mental health (Jacobs 1994). For contemporary women spiritualists, reclaiming the goddess has become symbolic of the affirmation of female power and the female body, the celebration of female will, and the recognition of women's bonds and heritage (Christ 1979). Positive attitudes about women's bodies are an essential dimension to this new feminist spirituality, and affirmation of the female body and the life cycle expressed in it have become the basis for new feminist rituals.

The positive value of female will is also expressed by newly celebrated practices such as women's spellcasting and witchcraft—forms of spirituality that have now come full circle from the persecution of women as witches to woman-centered forms of "new age" spirituality. The Wicca movement is a good example of some of new age and counter-cultural feminist movements. Founded in the 1950s by Englishman Gerald Gardner, a central concept in this movement is an ecological approach that links the health of the person to the health of the earth (Di Santo 2004). Based on ancient pagan rituals and other practices of witchcraft, those in the movement stress ancient belief systems and rituals. In such movements, spirituality and feminism often become merged as participants define spiritual healing as part of transforming their traditionally gendered identities (Foltz 2000). Some Wicca groups focus specifically on sexuality, blending pagan traditions with queer theory (Neitz 2000).

New religious movements, such as Wicca, often reclaim goddess imagery is a way of acknowledging female power as beneficent and independent. This is, of course, in radical contrast to the patriarchal perception of women's power as inferior and dangerous. The significance of the goddess for reevaluating women's bonds and heritage is that "as women struggle to create a new culture in which women's power, bodies, will, and bonds are celebrated, it seems natural that the Goddess would reemerge as symbol of the newfound beauty, strength, and power of women" (Christ 1979:285).

In sum, the emphasis in radical **feminist theology** is not just to point out the androcentric bias of traditional religious world views, but to fundamentally change theology and religion to represent women's experiences in all its forms. Some have criticized radical feminist theology as reflecting a White, middle-class, and Christian or post-Christian perspective. Jewish women have also criticized some feminist theology for its anti-Semitic framework (Hargrove et al. 1985). The many attempts to re-create systems of faith to acknowledge the presence and power of women are indicative of the far-reaching attempts of feminist thinkers to create new visions and world views that will provide the foundations for building a feminist society.

❖ *Chapter Summary and Themes*

Religion can be interpreted as both a powerful source of subordination for women and a powerful instrument for feminist social change.

Although many think of religion as repressive to women, there are numerous historical and current examples of religious faith inspiring feminist movements. From a sociological perspective, religion provides powerful symbols and beliefs that shape people's world view.

Historically the advent of patriarchal religion identified spiritual women as sexual and religious deviants.

Religion can be a system of social control, especially under conditions of intolerance and strongly patriarchal religious tenets. There are many historic examples of women resisting this form of religious oppression.

Images of women in religious texts tend to rely on stereotypical gender roles that subordinate women to men.

Women tend to be more religious than men, in both belief and practice, despite the fact that the interpretation of most traditional religious texts relegate women to subordinate positions relative to men. On various measures of religiosity and religious participation, women are seen to be more religious than men. Religion is a gendered institution in that women, although providing the majority of religious work, have been denied equal access to positions of religious leadership.

Religious beliefs are linked both to antifeminist values and movements for social justice.

Religion can be a source of liberating social change, such as in how religion inspired the civil rights movement. At the same time, religion has also been a source of the antifeminist movement in the contemporary United States. This is despite the fact that many women within evangelical Christianity see themselves as having benefited from the feminist movement.

New feminist forms of religion and spirituality are trying to create new theologies based on more woman-centered world views.

Feminist theologians and lay people have been interpreting religion in new ways that link spirituality and feminism. Some of these new theologies occur within mainstream churches, others in movements such as New Age spirituality, Wicca, and the like.

❖ *Key Terms*

androcentrism	liberation theology	religious right
collective consciousness	misogyny	sanctified church
feminist theology	religion as opiate	Second Great Awakening

❖ *Discussion Questions/Projects for Thought*

1. Talk with a group of people from different religious backgrounds (this could be a discussion group in class) and ask the men and women in the group what their religion taught them about women's roles. How did these ideas influence each person's self-concept?

2. Select a group of students who are opposed to abortion and another group who are prochoice. Interview people within each group, asking them about their religious beliefs and their attitudes toward women's roles. Do you find support for Luker's idea that those who are prochoice have less religious commitment and that those who are opposed to abortion are more traditional in their attitudes about women's roles?

3. Attend the religious services of a group with which you are unfamiliar. While there, observe who is in attendance and what they are doing and also observe the teachings of this religious group. What do your observations tell you about the role of women and men in this particular faith?

❖ *Internet Resources*

Catholic Network for Women's Equality

http://www.cnwe.org

This Canadian-based organization works to achieve equality for men and women within the Catholic church.

Muslim Women's League

http://www.mwlusa.org

This is a nonprofit organization of American Muslim women who connect the values of Islamic faith to promoting the status of women as free and equal in society. The web page includes discussion of topics related to women's status and Islamic faith, as well as publications and links to related news.

National Council of Jewish Women

http://www.ncjw.org

This organization promotes research, education, and community service on behalf of securing women's rights and advancing the well-being of women, children, and families. The website includes discussion of issues, publications, and links to other resources.

❖ *Suggested Readings*

Allen, Paula Gunn. 1986. *The Sacred Hoop: Recovering the Feminine in American Indian Traditions*. Boston: Beacon Press.
Allen's book examines the woman-centered perspectives of American Indian faith. Her work provides alternative visions of more feminist religious practices, not just within religion but in new forms of social organization.

Davidman, Lynn, and Shelly Tenenbaum. 1996. *Feminist Perspectives on Jewish Studies*. New Haven, CT: Yale University Press.
This book examines the development of feminist scholarship within the field of Jewish studies, including perspectives from sociology, anthropology, theology, literature, and other perspectives.

Gallagher, Sally. 2003. *Evangelical Identity and Family Life*. Piscataway, NJ: Rutgers University Press.
Based on a study of evangelical family advice literature, Gallagher examines how assumptions about gender made in traditional and evangelical Christian religion shape gender relations in the family.

Gilkes, Cheryl Townsend. 2000. *"If It Wasn't for the Women . . . ": Black Women's Experience and*

Womanist Culture in Church and Community.
Mary Knoll, NY: Orbis Books.
Gilkes examines the role of women in
African American churches, focusing
especially on women's work for social
justice, but also their leadership in Black
churches.

Haddad, Yvonne Yazbeck, and John L. Esposito,
eds. 1997. *Islam, Gender, and Social Change.*
New York: Oxford University Press.
The essays in this collection examine the
impact of the resurgence of Islamic
fundamentalism on the lives of women. It
provides a historical context for
understanding the present and challenges
images of Muslim women as passive and
subordinate.

Kaufman, Debra Renee. 1991. *Rachel's Daughters:
Newly Orthodox Jewish Women.* New
Brunswick, NJ: Rutgers University Press.

Based on interviews with 150 Orthodox
Jewish women, Kaufman explores the
meaning that religion has in the lives of
highly traditional women.

Mernissi, Fatima, and Mary Jo Lakeland. 1992.
*The Veil and the Male Elite: A Feminist
Interpretation of Women's Rights in Islam.* New
York: Addison Wesley.
This book examines Islamic religious beliefs
from a feminist perspective and is useful in
understanding the current role of women in
Islam.

Spretnak, Charlene, ed. 1994. *The Politics of
Women's Spirituality: Essays on the Rise of
Spiritual Power within the Feminist Movement,*
2nd ed., Garden City, NY: Anchor Books.
This anthology of writings by feminist
theologians provides a good overview of the
new analyses and questions feminism brings
to the study of religion.

9

WOMEN, CRIME, AND DEVIANCE

Sociological Perspectives
on Crime and Deviance

Early Traditions
Defining Deviance
Labeling and Social Deviance
Deviance, Power, and Social
*   Conflict*
Feminist Perspectives on Deviance

Women as Criminals

The Extent of Criminality
*   among Women*
Causes of Women's Crime
Defining Crime

Women as Victims of Crime

Rape
Causes of Rape

Women in the Criminal
Justice System

Gender and the Courts
Women and Prison

Chapter Summary and Themes

Key Terms

Discussion Questions/
Projects for Thought

Internet Resources

Suggested Readings

When you think of women and crime, what comes to mind? Chances are you imagine a widely publicized trial where a husband is being tried for the murder of his wife or girlfriend. You might think of a high-profile case of rape or sexual assault, where the woman was vilified for her sexual past. Or perhaps you imagine a serial killer, such as those frequently depicted on crime shows, where numerous women are brutally murdered, their bodies discarded, but the crime ultimately solved by clever and beautiful women scientists. You might have noticed that women are now highly visible as crime solvers in popular shows such as *CSI: Miami* or as professionals in the world of law and order, such as *Judging Amy* or even *Judge Judy*. Or maybe you remember the trial and imprisonment of Martha Stewart, convicted of insider trading and sentenced to a brief prison term in a minimum security prison.

Media depictions provide one way of looking at the world of women, crime, and deviance, though seldom are the actual crimes against women—or by women—as notorious and "glamorous" as high-profile cases. When women are victims of crime, it is usually not by a celebrity or serial killer, but by someone they are close to—a boyfriend, husband, or other known acquaintance. And, when women commit crime, it is usually an economic crime—selling drugs, passing bad checks, petty theft, and so forth.

This chapter examines the subject of women, crime, and deviance, using a perspective on gender and its relationship to race and class to understand not only the crime and deviance that women commit, but the patterns of victimization that we see when studying crime. We begin with some basic review of the sociological framework that informs the analysis of gender and crime.

❖ *Sociological Perspectives on Crime and Deviance*

Do women commit less crime than men and, if so, why? Are there distinctive characteristics of women as deviants and criminals? Why is women's deviance so frequently understood as based in their hormonal or biological states? How can we explain the high rates of violence against women in society? Why are men the vast majority of those who commit violent acts? These and other questions form the basis for the study of gender, crime, and deviance—a field that has been transformed through the development of feminist scholarship.

Feminists recognize, as do sociologists, that individual men or women may commit crimes or engage in deviant behavior, but they see these behaviors as related to the status of women in society—and more broadly, to how the social structure of gender is related to patterns of crime and deviance in society.

Still, the study of gender, crime and deviance is relatively new. The earliest studies of women's deviance reflected some of the highly sexist assumptions about women and, for a long time, distorted what was known about women either as victims or perpetrators of crime. A brief review of this history shows how much the assumptions made about gender at any given time in history can influence what is known, even within the social sciences.

Early Traditions

Early studies of women and deviance mostly depicted women's deviance as rooted in their biological and psychological predispositions. Lombroso's work in the 1920s, although by now discredited, was one of the earliest studies of female crime. His highly racist and sexist ideas depicted crime as based on biological differences between women and men, White and Black Americans, the fit and the unfit. Lombroso believed that crime represented the survival of primitive traits; his theory was explicitly linked to popular racist and sexist notions of the time (Higham 1965). He explained female crime by arguing that women are less highly evolved than White men and thus are more susceptible to primitive urges. He also depicted women as less varied in their mental capacities and, in general, more passive and sedentary than men (Klein 1980). As he said, "Even the female criminal is monotonous and uniform compared with her male companion, just as in general woman is inferior to man" (Lombroso 1920:122, cited in Klein 1980:78).

W. I. Thomas, an early sociologist, paid more attention to the role of social circumstances in producing crime. Thomas's work is of great importance to sociological thinking, although his work on female deviance is seriously flawed. Like Lombroso, he traced women's crime to biological differences between the sexes and to deep-seated psychological "wishes" that he defined as unique to young girls. In his early work, Thomas claimed that females are biologically "anabolic"—motionless and conservative—whereas males are "katabolic"—destructive of energy, yet creative because of the outward flow of this drive. (As an aside, Thomas also saw monogamy as an accommodation to these basic urges because he believed that through monogamy women became domesticated and men became leaders!)

Thomas's later work (*The Unadjusted Girl* 1923) contained an important sociological insight—that female delinquency is a normal response to certain social conditions. He still emphasized, however, that social behavior is a result of "primary wishes" that are derived from biological instincts. He identified these wishes as the desire for new experience, security, response, and recognition; for women, there is the added wish for maternalism. In Thomas's view, middle-class people are less likely to commit crimes because they are more likely to control their natural desires; delinquents are driven to crime because they long for new experiences. Girls, in particular, he says, engage in deviance in order to manipulate others, and their maternal instincts lead them to crimes such as prostitution, in which he claims they are seeking love and tenderness (Klein 1980).

Thomas did recognize differences in the attitudes of men and women and attempted to use these differences to explain patterns of delinquency and crime. His work, although seemingly crude now, has left an important message for more recent sociological work. He attempted to find a behavioral basis for sex differences in delinquency, and he tried, even if unsuccessfully, to relate those differences to attitudes that we now see as reflecting gender socialization. Whether patterns of women's crime can be properly attributed to gender socialization is an important question that is explored further in this chapter.

The major problem in Thomas's work—other than the crude gender stereotypes he used by seeing women as more manipulative, emotional, and desirous of love and tenderness than men are—was that he portrayed gender differences as internal to individuals, not as a product of their social environment. He had an important insight even on this point, however, because he thought that internal wishes and motivations could be directed by socialization and manipulation of the social environment. Thus, Thomas's work provided a foundation for seeing individual rehabilitation as the best solution to problems associated with deviant behavior.

Like Lombroso and Thomas, Otto Pollak (1950) traced women's deviance to their biological and psychological being. Pollak claimed that the basis for female crime is women's passive role in sexual intercourse. According to Pollak, women are able to conceal their sexual arousal from men and, because of this physiological manipulation, women become socially deceitful. His major concern with women's crime was the "masked" character of female criminality. He argued that the real extent of female crime is hidden from the public's view. Women, he argued, are deceitful and duplicitous; he saw them as the masterminds behind crime, manipulating men into committing offenses while they themselves remain immune from prosecution. Pollak saw women as liars and interpreted the hidden nature of their criminality as a reflection of their cunning behavior (Smart 1977). In Pollak's view, men have been so duped by women that they protect women through chivalry and thus fear to charge and convict them for their crimes.

Although the views of Lombroso, Thomas, and Pollak appear quite outlandish now, the issues they raised continue to be addressed in current research and theory. Many still assume that delinquency can be traced to different emotional states in men and women, and these theorists have looked to sexual character as the root of women's criminality. Some even continue to assert that biological differences between women and men explain differences in their criminal behavior. Thus, more contemporary analyists Wilson and Herrnstein argue that sex differences in crime among men and women must be understood as a function of aggression, which they see as rooted in the hormonal constitution of the sexes: "Knowledge has not yet advanced to the point where it can be said positively that human sex differences in aggression have been directly traced to differences in hormones. Yet, the evidence for some sort of connection is stronger than the . . . objections may suggest" (1985:119). Although Wilson and Herrnstein admit that social and cultural arrangements may have some influence on the gender gap in crime, they see biological differences as establishing differences that go deeper than social structure.

Wilson and Herrnstein's work has been soundly criticized by other scholars for its simplistic view of biology and culture as opposing systems, its misuse of scientific research, its confusion of correlates (such as gender, race, and crime) with genetic cause, and its omission of white-collar and corporate crime in their definition of crime (Kamin 1986). But, the popularity of recurring arguments about the biological basis for criminal behavior cannot be ignored. Even feminists have been known to make such arguments. Consider the case of Andrea Yates, the woman who confessed to murdering her five children in Texas in 2001. Many attributed her crime to the postpartum depression she developed following the birth of her fourth and fifth child. Although few excused her behavior, following her arrest and conviction a public debate ensued that centered on the role depression played in her behavior. The debate was further sparked when NOW (the National Organization for Women) attributed her crime to postpartum depression and established a legal defense fund for her. Although feminists did not argue that her depression was the result of innate sex differences, the association of postpartum depression with women's hormonal state conjures up biologically based arguments. Such reductionist arguments ignore the complex origins of various forms of behavior, including criminal and deviant behavior. It is important to remember that even biological conditions emerge in a social context. The social context is critical in explaining human behavior.

Now, sociological definitions of deviance (of which crime is a part) are based on three primary points: (1) deviance is social behavior that departs from conventional social norms; (2) deviance involves a process of social labeling; and, (3) deviance becomes recognized within the context of social institutions that reflect the power structure and gender, racial-ethnic, and class relations of society.

Defining Deviance

From a commonsense point of view, deviance is behavior that is bizarre, unconventional, and perhaps hard to understand. From a sociological perspective, however, this definition is inadequate and misleading. First of all, what is unusual in one situation may be quite ordinary in another; second, even the most extraordinary behavior can often be understood if we know the context in which it occurs. Sociologists define **deviance** as behavior that departs from conventional norms, noting that norms vary from one situation to another; consequently, sociologists see deviance as located in a social context. Knowing and understanding this context is essential to understanding deviant behavior.

Although deviance is defined as behavior that departs from conventional norms, deviant behavior, like conventional behavior, is often guided by norms and rules, both formal and informal. In fact, deviance may be practiced in subcultures in which the social norms of the group encourage members to engage in deviant acts. One example comes from the research on gang rape, which shows that violence escalates when there is peer pressure to show off one's "masculinity" through increased aggression and abuse of the victim. The "hypermasculinity" and group organization of young male gangs thus puts women involved with gang members at risk of sexual violence and abuse. (Brownmiller 1975; Knox 2004; Ullman 1999).

Another commonsense definition of deviance is that it is behavior of which people disapprove. This idea, too, is inaccurate because deviance is subject to social definition, and whether it is approved or disapproved depends on who is doing the defining. Because deviance is situationally specific, it is sometimes difficult to distinguish deviant behavior from conventional behavior. In fact, there is probably more overlap between deviant and conventional behavior than one might think. Most people engage in deviant behavior, sometimes on a regular basis. Whether they become identified as deviant may be a function of their social standing (including their gender, race, and class), the context of their deviant acts, and their ability to maintain a conventional identity.

For example, many would consider that the enjoyment of pornography is deviant behavior. It offends many people's moral sensibilities (including that of some feminists, who see it as portraying women in a degrading and dehumanizing way). The easy availability of pornography, its widespread consumption, and its appearance in even the most respectable settings, however, make it seem that pornography is a normal feature of everyday life. Whether one is perceived as deviant for reading or watching pornography depends on one's social standing and the social context in which pornography is viewed. This fact is evident when we consider the deviant label attached to a frequenter of peep shows or pornography houses, in contrast to the socially legitimate label afforded to the young man who rents pornographic videos for his faternity house. When we analyze pornography as an economic industry, we see that its social organization is very similar to (although perhaps more coercive than) that of other industries in which workers are exploited for profit and products are marketed by the use of women as sex objects.

Labeling and Social Deviance

This discussion brings us to the second major point that sociologists make about deviant behavior: Deviance involves a social labeling process (Becker 1963). One cannot be called deviant without being recognized as deviant, and sometimes persons become labeled as deviant regardless of whether they have actually engaged in deviant behavior. Becoming deviant involves societal reactions to one's behavior—or alleged behavior. **Labeling theory** emphasizes that some groups with the power to label deviance exercise control over what and who is considered deviant. Police, courts, school authorities, and other agents of the state thus wield a great amount of power through their control of institutions. For example, social workers, psychiatrists, or other agents of the state who define a woman as mentally ill can have a drastic effect on her behavior, identity, and life options.

Sociologists who work from the labeling perspective point out that in the absence of a deviant label, actual deviant behavior may have no consequences at all, but the process of being labeled as deviant may involve real changes in a person's self-image as well as his or her public identity. Sociologists note that once people are labeled deviant, they are likely to become deviant. This new identity, however, usually does not emerge suddenly or as the result of a single act. Instead, it involves a process of transformation wherein people adapt their self-images and behavior to the new identity being acquired (Lemert 1972). You can see the influence of the labeling process in thinking about how gender constructs different definitions for women and men who engage in the same behavior. Women are arrested as prostitutes; the men who pay them are not. Women who visibly have multiple sex partners are judged as deviants and "sluts"; men who do the same are praised for being "studs." Women who are raped are routinely thought to have done something to encourage it, as if being a rape victim is a stigmatized identity.

Deviance, Power, and Social Conflict

Labeling theory helps us see that deviance occurs in the context of social institutions. People in these institutions have the power to label some as deviant and others as not. This fact is especially true to the degree that the official agents of these institutions carry gender, race, and class stereotypes or biases that make them more likely to discover deviance in some groups than in others. These agents include the police, judges, lawyers, prison guards, and others who may enter the official process of labeling deviant behavior (e.g., psychologists, psychiatrists, counselors, social workers, and teachers). Because these official agents of social institutions have the power to label some groups and persons as deviant and others as not, and because these institutions reflect the power structure and the systems of race, class, and gender relations in the society, deviance tends to be a label that falls most frequently on less powerful people in the society. The labeling of deviant behavior can thus be seen as a form of social control.

Sociologists who focus on deviance have suggested that it be studied from the point of view of the deviant actor (Becker 1963). This method would allegedly prevent sociologists from seeing deviance only through official eyes and would create a more accurate portrayal of the deviant's social world. Many feminists studying deviance share this point of view, adding that, traditionally, women's deviance has been viewed through men's eyes.

Prostitution, for example, has traditionally been described in terms of men's demands for sexuality and women's supply of this "service." Although this is an apt description of the economic nature of prostitution, it also makes ideological assumptions about both men's and women's sexuality. Women are depicted as merely providing an outlet for male sexual needs and remaining sexually passive, while men are defined as having greater sexual urges than women. Prostitution is a gender-specific crime that punishes women, not men, for not subordinating their sexuality to monogamous marital relationships (Weatherall and Priestly 2001).

New studies of prostitution, informed by feminist scholarship, now take a very different approach, casting prostitution in the context of work, not just individual female deviance (Brewis and Linstead 2000a, 2000b). Examining prostitution in this way raises new questions and new insights, including that prostitution is part of a gender division of labor in a global network of work, colonization, and the commodification of women's bodies (Pyle and Ward 2003; West and Austrin 2002; Min 2003). People estimate that the global economy of human trafficking, most of which involves sex workers, is a $5 billion to $7 billion industry—one that builds on the economic needs of women, especially in poor countries (Schiffman et al. 2003). Sex tourism, a central part of this trafficking, draws men from the wealthier nations to places like Thailand, Amsterdam, and other places where women, often very young girls, work to support themselves and, frequently, their families (Wonders and Michalowski 2001). Reframing prostitution in this way focuses less on treating individual deviance and more on seeing prostitution in terms of women's rights to a safe life (West 2000).

Feminist Perspectives on Deviance

Feminist perspectives have added new dimensions to the understanding of deviant behavior. In the past, studies of women's deviance typically rested on stereotypes about women's sexual behavior and limited the study of women to sexual behavior, especially prostitution and promiscuity. Early studies of women's deviance often used a double standard of morality, marking some behaviors as deviant in women that were not considered deviant when done by men, such as teenage promiscuity. Teen boys are expected, if not encouraged, to be aggressive in their sexual encounters; girls who do the same thing may even now be labeled as "loose." Women's deviance has thus often been equated with sexual pathology.

Female deviance is often attributed to individual maladjustment or a poor family background. It is true that some deviance (including sexual deviance) involves psychosexual adjustment. Such experiences may provoke a woman to engage in deviant behavior, but events in her biography (which are by no means true for all female deviants) are not always the sole or the primary cause of deviant behavior. Feminist scholars argue that women's deviance, including that of girls and young women, is the result of the social context in which they live (Cepeda and Valdez 2003). The social context of gender, race, and class relations—as well as age—shapes both the causes and consequences of women's deviant behavior. Increasingly, scholars are also showing how social norms of masculinity also shape the deviant behavior of men (Messerschmidt 2000b). Whether studying violence against women, violence that women and men commit, or the treatment of women and men in the criminal justice system, gender has emerged as a significant factor.

As an example, we can now look at studies of gangs for what they reveal about gender and deviance. Studies of girls' gangs have shown that young women find in gangs the solidarity that they may not experience in their home environments (Joe and Chesney-Lind 1995). A good illustration comes from a study of Puerto Rican girls' gangs. Many young Puerto Rican girls live in a relatively confined social environment. They have little opportunity for educational or occupational advancement, and their community expects them to be "good girls" and to remain close to their families. Joining a gang is one way to reject the racial-ethnic, class, and gender role into which the girls have been cast (Campbell 1989). One can conclude that these young women are doing the best they can to adapt to their situation (Bloom et al. 2003). Others have also argued that gangs provide a haven for young girls to cope with the many problems they have because of the sexism, racism, and class inequality that they face. Studies of girls and boys in gangs reveal that girls tend to be more isolated in their families than are boys and they have lower levels of self-esteem (Esbensen et al. 1999; Joe and Chesney-Lind 1995).

Studies of juvenile delinquency also reveal the importance of gender in shaping girls' behavior and the response of the justice system to their behavior (Heimer and DeCoster 1999). Girls are still more likely to be held in the juvenile justice system for relatively minor offenses, although boys are more likely to be arrested for juvenile crimes (Chesney-Lind 1999). Much of the literature on juvenile justice has situated girls' delinquent behavior in the context of the sexism and racism that they experience in their lives (Holsinger 2000).

Many studies of girls' and women's deviance have also shown the great extent of sexual abuse in the life histories of women who engage in various forms of deviance, including gang activity, prostitution, drugs, and other forms of deviant behavior. Numerous studies document a strong association between deviant and criminal behavior and patterns of sexual abuse (Chesney-Lind 1999; Walker-Barnes and Mason 2001; Dembo et al. 1998)—so much so that one cannot help but wonder if stopping sexual abuse would be the most effective deterrent to deviant behavior.

Another major point of revision by feminist scholars of deviance has been in reconsidering what is considered deviant behavior. The deviant label often attached to lesbianism makes it appear that there is something perverted about loving persons of one's own sex. Instead of assuming that sexual preference is the result of individual maladjustment, being a lesbian can involve conscious resistance to conventional heterosexuality whereby women are defined as the adjuncts of men and female sexuality is seen as passive acquiescence to male demands. Feminist scholarship has thus rejected the deviance framework as a way of understanding gay and lesbian experience. It is the heterosexist structure of institutions that defines lesbians as deviant. Challenging such assumptions has created new knowledge about how gays and lesbians negotiate the worlds in which they live (Nardi and Schneider 1997).

Feminist research has produced new insights for understanding how gender shapes deviance and how the institutions that manage deviance are themselves gendered. The remainder of this chapter reviews the knowledge we have now accrued about crime and the victimization of women.

❖ Women as Criminals

In general, women commit much less crime than do men and women's crimes tend to be less serious than men's. Men are 78 percent of all persons arrested (Federal Bureau of Investigation 2003), thus comprising the majority of criminal offenders. However, women's participation in some crimes has increased in recent years. Central questions asked in the research on women and crime are: Has women's crime increased and, if so, for what types of crime? Is the amount of crime by women beginning to approximate the amount of male crime? How are women's crimes linked to gender relations, and have changes in gender roles created more opportunities for women to commit crimes?

The Extent of Criminality among Women

Available information on female crime comes primarily from official statistics (the FBI's **Uniform Crime Reports**), from self-report surveys, and from national victimization and crime surveys (see Table 9.1). Although each data source reveals different kinds of information, taken together they give a consistent picture of women's crime. Overall, crime (as measured by arrests) has decreased since the mid-1990s. But, although arrests of men have decreased (by 7 percent), for women they have increased (by 12 percent). Why?

First, arrest data must be interpreted with caution because arrest rates measure police activity as well as the actual commission of crime. Apparent increases and decreases in crime among different groups can reflect as much about police

TABLE 9.1   Arrests by Gender (2003)

	Percent of Persons Arrested		Percent of All Arrests (within gender group)[1]	
	Male	Female	Male	Female
Murder	89.7%	10.3%	0.1%	—[2]
Forcible Rape	98.7	1.3	0.2	—[2]
Robbery	89.6	10.4	−0.9	0.4
Aggravated Assault	79.3	20.7	3.4	2.9
Burglary	86.3	13.7	2.4	1.3
Larceny-Theft	62.9	37.1	7.0	13.6
Arson	82.2	17.8	0.1	0.1
Forgery	59.7	40.3	0.6	1.4
Fraud	55.4	44.6	2.2	4.2
Prostitution/ Commercial Vice	64.2	64.2	0.3	1.5
Drug Abuse Violations	81.7	18.3	13.0	9.7
Driving under the Influence	81.8	18.2	10.5	8.2

Source: Federal Bureau of Investigation. 2003. *Uniform Crime Reports.* Washington, DC: Federal Bureau of Investigation.

[1]Does not total 100% because not all crimes are included.

[2]Too small to be included.

activity as they do the actual behavior of various groups. Nonetheless, it is likely that women's crime has actually increased, reflecting not only changes in the likelihood that police will arrest women, but also changes in women's criminal activities.

Of the crimes considered part of the FBI's **crime index**—a measure of the overall volume and rate of crime, as indicated by offenses reported to the police (including murder, non-negligent manslaughter, rape, robbery, aggravated assault, larceny-theft, motor vehicle theft, and arson)—larceny-theft is the single greatest category of women's crime. These are crimes that include any form of theft without force of threat (which would define robbery) or breaking and entering (which defines burglary). In other words, larceny usually includes less serious theft, where there is no threat of violence to another person, or fraud; it includes shoplifting, pick-pocketing, bicycle theft, and the like. In other words, the highest arrest rates for women are for crimes that, although part of the FBI crime index, are relatively minor.

Causes of Women's Crime

Some criminologists suggest that patterns of crime among women represent extensions of their gender roles. Activities such as shoplifting, credit card fraud, and the passing of bad checks result from the opportunities women have as consumers. Likewise, the crimes that are less frequent for women (e.g., armed robbery, aggravated assault, and major embezzlement) involve either physical strength or economic opportunities more usually associated with men's gender roles.

These associations have led some to conclude that women's involvement in criminal behavior changes when there are changes in their social roles (Adler 1975). Some have, in fact, attributed increases in women's crime in recent years to the development of the women's movement. Adler argues that shifts in gender roles make women more willing to participate in crime and that this explains recent increases in crime among women. Others say that objective changes in women's situation, particularly their greater labor force participation, make more criminal opportunities available to women. Is either of these a valid explanation of increases in women's crime?

Even with increased economic opportunity for women in the labor force, the vast majority of women remain in low-paid, low-status jobs; thus, it is an exaggeration to say that women's opportunities for crime are related to women's rapid advancement in the labor force. Second, increases in women's crime that show up in the arrest statistics do not necessarily reflect an increase in the actual extent of crime; rather, these statistics may reflect an increase in the detection of women's crimes. This increased detection can occur in several ways.

Although the amount of crime may remain the same, the police may now be more likely to arrest women for offenses they commit, given a change in attitudes about women. A second possibility is that changes in the rate of women's crime do not result from changes in gender roles per se, but instead from broad structural changes in the economy, technology, legal systems, and law enforcement procedures. Greater reliance on electronic transactions, credit cards, and self-service markets have increased the opportunities for crime for all consumers. At the same time, detection systems (including national information systems, technological surveillance, and an expansion of private security forces) have increased the amount of social control and law enforcement.

Miller (1986) makes the most compelling and reliable argument about the causes of women's crime. She reminds us that increases in crime among women have been almost entirely in property crimes. Rather than attributing the causes of women's crime to the women's movement and the changes it engenders, she argues that the women's movement coincides with (and, in fact, stems from) other structural changes that best explain women's criminal behavior, as well. Those who have associated increases in women's crime with the rise of the women's movement do so because the women's movement and increases in women's crime can be marked in the same period of time; however, according to Miller, those who argue the association overlook important facts about women's employment status and high rates of poverty.

Miller notes that the increased labor force participation of women beginning in the mid-1960s was especially marked among better-educated women with children who had never worked. Occupational segregation also depresses the wages of all women workers and raises their unemployment rate; consequently, the entry of older, White, middle-class women into the labor force may disadvantage minority, poor, and younger women at the same time that the unskilled, domestic, and laborers' jobs these women might have held are becoming more scarce. The effect is to create an underclass of women, for whom criminal activity is the only means of supporting themselves and their children. This argument is also supported by historical evidence that there are significant increases in property crimes by women in periods of economic depression.

Women's crime, Miller argues, cannot be understood separately from the crime of the men for whom they often work. Her research on women hustlers shows that women's crime often benefits men—directly and indirectly. The street hustlers in Miller's study worked in the context of street networks, controlled by men having lengthy criminal records. Further encounters with the criminal justice system will likely lead to long prison sentences for these men, so their major source of income may be derived from the work of the women. The men create street networks in which women do the crime and they take the money, maintaining their criminal activity, without as great a risk of prosecution.

Miller's explanation of women's crime places the causes of women's crime in the context of women's social class status, thereby also supporting the long-standing association sociologists have seen between poverty, unemployment, and crime. This explanation of crime is particularly compelling because it explains women's and men's crime in the context of structural characteristics that involve class, race, and gender relations. Although the majority of the poor are certainly not criminals, poverty and blocked opportunity—and the economic need they create—are major underlying causes of crime.

Feminist scholars studying women's crime have also pointed to the strong connections between women's involvement in crime and women's victimization. What Daly (1994) calls the **reproduction of harm** means that women who have been emotionally and sexually abused, raised in families that are marginalized by poverty, and subjected to violence in relationships with men are more likely to become deviant or engage in criminal behavior. Engagement in deviant and criminal activity for some women and young girls may also be a strategy for coping with oppression—an argument that has been used to understand the deviance of young Black women. Arnold's (1994) research on African American women in prison, for example, found that African American women who are habitual criminals were abused as children, had few social networks to assist them in overcoming abuse, and grew up with a profound sense of powerlessness and isolation, feeling alienated both at home and school. Without what Arnold calls "structural supports" and with few skills, little education, and no occupational training, they turn to alcohol abuse, drug addiction, and criminal involvement as a form of rebellion against their marginal status.

Likewise, research by Richie (1996) suggests that many women are coerced into crime by their male partners. Her study of African American women in jail focuses on women who were battered by their male partners. Richie argues that women who are marginalized in the culture because of their race, ethnicity, class, and gender are vulnerable to abusive relationships. Although the women she studied aspired to "normal" family relationships, they were unable to establish these relationships, and instead became subjected to escalating violence—ultimately coerced into the patterns of crime resulting in their incarceration. Richie's analysis, like that of Arnold and Miller, locates the causes of women's crime in the societal factors that shape women's conduct, not simply in flawed character types or individual maladjustment.

Defining Crime

Feminist perspectives on crime define crime and the criminal justice system as systems of social control. What is considered crime is established by powerful persons in the society, who define some acts as criminal in order to protect their own interests (Messerschmidt 1986). Criminal acts, particularly crimes against property, are thus defined primarily as the crimes of the powerless. Laws defining crime are made by the rich and politically powerful; at the same time, laws are created that allow for the legal acquisition of money by the wealthy.

From this perspective, we might ask why some behaviors are considered crimes and others are not. For feminists, this question is also important. For instance, historical changes in the law sometimes defined abortion as criminal behavior and other times did not (see Chapter 7). These changes in abortion policy benefited medical doctors who sought to gain control of the abortion market (Mohr 1978). Those who define crime do so for their own interests, and these interests have often worked against the interests of women. Consider, for instance, who would be considered criminal if our definition of crime included the control of another person's body. From this perspective, some of the normal practices of the medical profession might be considered criminal (see Chapter 7), as would the acts of corporations whose products proved unsafe to women's health. The act of rape provides another case in point because, even now, in many states, rape within marriage is not legally defined as rape.

Feminist perspectives on crime and gender take a broadly based view of criminal behavior. Much criminological research generally asks who committed the crime and why; feminists see crime within a holistic context of social power, gender relations, and economic stratification. From a feminist perspective, it is inadequate to ask simply why women commit fewer crimes than men. Feminists have directed attention not only to the crimes committed by women, but even more to the crimes committed against women. A discussion of gender and crime is incomplete without an inquiry about women as victims of crime.

❖ *Women as Victims of Crime*

Statistics indicate that, overall, women are less likely to be victimized by crime than are men, although rates of violent crime victimization for men and women are getting closer (Bureau of Justice Statistics 2003). National data on victimization rates are taken from **victimization surveys** based on a national sample of households and businesses in which persons are asked to report crimes by which they were victimized in the preceding months. The fact that the surveys include crimes against businesses may distort the gap between male and female victimization because men are more likely to own businesses. Faulty recall among some research subjects and the fact that many crimes might not be reported to the survey interviewers also potentially distort these data. Particularly in the case of rape, it is quite possible that, if a woman never reported it to the police, she is also unlikely to report it to a researcher.

Given these qualifications in the data, how can we characterize the victimization of women by crime? As you can see from Figure 9.1, White women are less likely than men to be victimized by robbery and assault, and Black women are more likely victimized by any crime than are White women. In fact, they are three times more likely to be raped than White women. But, except for rape, men are more likely than women to be crime victims, especially Black men. Native American women and men experience higher rates of crime victimization than any other

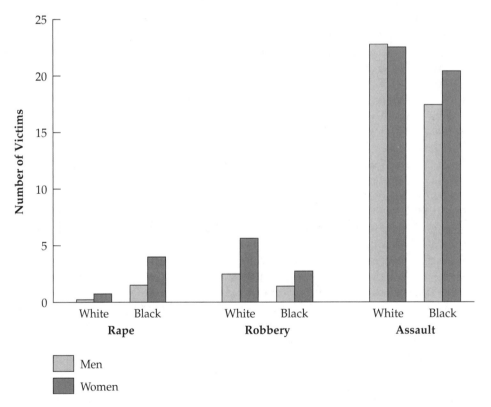

FIGURE 9.1   Crime Victimization (by gender and race)

Source: Bureau of Justice Statistics. 2003. *Sourcebook of Criminal Justice Statistics.* Washington, DC: U.S. Department of Justice.

group (Hispanics are not counted in a separate category and fall into either the "White" or "Black" category in the FBI data).

When violence is committed against women, it is most likely by someone they know (see Figure 9.2). Data from the Bureau of Justice Statistics show that two-thirds of all reported rapes are committed by someone the woman victim knows—either an intimate partner, a relative, or an acquaintance; in the rare cases when men are raped, it is more likely to be a stranger. And, when women are murdered, the odds are that she will have been murdered by a man, although when men murder, they are more likely to murder another man. When women murder, they, too, are most likely to murder a man—most likely a husband or boyfriend (Bureau of Justice Statistics 2003).

Studies have shown that women's fear of sexual victimization spills over into a more generalized fear of crime (Ferraro 1996; May 2001).Women's fear of crime also increased with age, even though older women are less likely to be crime victims. Sociologist Esther Madriz (1997) argues fear of rape is a mechanism of the

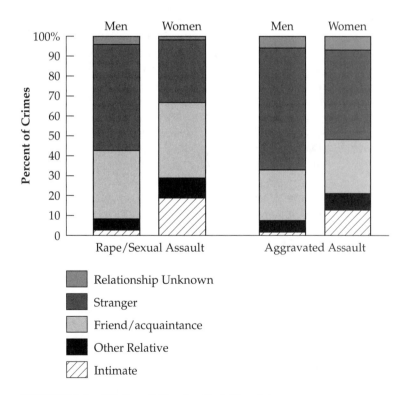

FIGURE 9.2   Victim-Offender Relationship for Violent Crimes

Source: Bureau of Justice Statistics. 2003. *Sourcebook of Criminal Justice Statistics.* Washington, DC: U.S. Department of Justice.

social control of women because it restricts their freedom to move about freely and without trepidation. Her studies show how fear of rape perpetuates stereotypes of women as powerless and vulnerable, limiting their public behavior, not men's. The frequent depiction of women in the media as victims of rapists, serial killers, and other violent men only exacerbates this problem.

Rape

The case of rape illustrates how isolation and powerlessness make women vulnerable to crime. Women report 93,000 rapes per year (a rate of 32 per 100,000 women in 2003), but this figure is the subject of debate. Because rape is underreported, the FBI has estimated that only one in four rapes actually shows up in the official statistics that are published in the *Uniform Crime Reports;* moreover, the *Uniform Crime Reports* do not includes rapes that end in death, because those are reported as homicides (Federal Bureau of Investigation 2003). Perhaps it is more important to understand how the official data on rape can be distorted by the different factors that result in underreporting than it is to know exactly how many rapes there are.

Specific data on which women are more likely to be raped show the connection of rape to women's status in society; women of the lowest status are the most vulnerable to rape. Victimization surveys show that African American and Hispanic women are more likely to be raped than White women and that divorced, separated, and never married women are much more likely to be raped than women who are married or widowed. For all women, the rape rate is higher for those with incomes under $7,500 per year. These data show the connection between rates of victimization and women's status in society.

Stereotypical images of rape associate it with strangers in public places. Yet, increasing attention has been given to **date rape**—or *acquaintance rape*—defined as forced, unwanted intercourse by a known aggressor. Date rape is the most underreported form of rape and thus is much more prevalent than official crime statistics show. Young women are the most likely victims of this form of rape.

National surveys find that among college women 1.7 percent are raped each year and 1.1 percent experience attempted rate. Adjusting for the short length of the academic year, this translates to a rate of 35 rapes or attempted rapes every 1,000 women students. Most of the victims knew the person who victimized them, as shown in Figure 9.3, and most incidents occurred in the student's living quarters. In more than three-quarters of the cases, the victim used some form of resistance against her assailant, although only 5 percent of the cases identified in this national survey had been reported to the police (Fisher et al. 2000).

Stalking on college campuses is even more common. Thirteen percent of women college students report having been stalked in the previous year (before the survey). Comparing by racial-ethnic identity, studies find that American Indian/Alaskan native women have the highest likelihood of any racial-ethnic group of being stalked (Tjaden and Thoennes 1998; Fisher et al. 2000). Women who have been stalked typically report psychological intimidation as the result of stalking, although some also experience physical injury. Stalking is also more likely to be reported to the police than is rape or attempted rape (Fisher et al. 2000; Davis et al. 2002).

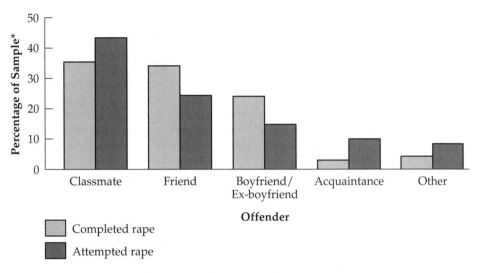

FIGURE 9.3   Victim-Offender Relationship for Rape Victimization among College Women

Source: Data from Bonnie S. Fisher, Francis T. Cullen, and Michael G. Turner. 2000. *The Sexual Victim- ization of College Women.* Washington, DC: U.S. Bureau of Justice Statistics, p. 19.

*Sample includes only victims, not all college women.

Stalking frequently occurs after the end of an intimate relationship. Studies have found that as many as 20 percent of women who have broken off relationships with men are stalked to the point where they fear for their safety (Haugaard and Seri 2003). Although fewer than half of stalking victims report being physically as- saulted, they do report intense psychological intimidation, and many also report financially controlling behaviors (such as having to change one's locks, change tele- phone numbers, or perhaps even lose control over one's finances). Stalking in- volves the use of power and social control to attempt to dominate—or even possess—women. And in many cases, such power and control was also a problem in the relationship prior to the breakup (Brewster 2003).

Sexual violence—on campus and elsewhere—has been shown to be more likely to occur in some organizational contexts than others. Some fraternities, for example, often have an organizational culture that is ripe for sexual violence. As social groups, fraternities are based on an ethic of masculinity. When masculinity is associated with competition, violence, and alcohol abuse and is further coupled with gender stereo- typing of women, sexual violence is likely to occur—sometimes on a group basis. Re- searchers argue that fraternities are conducive to violence against women when they define women as serving men or as sexual prey. Although certainly not all fraterni- ties are "rape-prone" environments, studies do find that fraternity members, along with male college athletes, are more likely to hold adversarial gender attitudes and to believe in various rape myths, such as that women bear responsibility for rape (Boswell and Spade 1996; Sanday 1996; Boeringer 1999). In a related vein, sorority women are more likely than other college women to be coerced into excessive use of drugs and alcohol and also to be victims of physical force (Tyler et al. 1998). Self-selection into fraternities by men with sexually aggressive attitudes may explain some of the organizational culture found in fraternities, and many campuses have initiated programs intended to reduce the violence and risk that women face in such settings (Koss and Cleveland 1996). Whenever rape occurs in a fraternity context, group loyalty, protection, and secrecy also make it difficult to prosecute the perpetrators because brothers' protection of each other can interfere with their willingness to cooperate with university, legal, and criminal justice officials (Martin and Hummer 1989).

Whereas all forms of rape are traumatic, some argue that rape by someone you know is particularly traumatic because it erodes a trusting relationship. Victims may also be part of a friendship circle that includes the assailant, making it even more difficult to talk about it with friends. As with other forms of rape, victims of date rape may fear being alone, become depressed, have sexual problems, or feel guilt and anxiety.

Causes of Rape

This information gives a compelling picture of women's experience and its relationship to violence as a system of social control. Explanations of violence against women have usually suggested that its cause lies within the personalities and social backgrounds of individuals who commit violence, but the empirical data on women as victims indicate that the causes of violence lie not in the characteristics of offenders but in the social status of their victims. This is not to say that women are responsible for the violence committed against them. Quite the opposite; it locates the causes of violence within the political and economic status of women in society. How one understands the causes of rape is significant—not just for understanding rape, but because different causal explanations have different implications for change. Rape crisis centers, for example, may see the causes of rape in individualist or social structural terms; this is significant in what they advocate and how they assist victims (Fried 1994; Schmitt and Martin 1999; Martin 1997). Theoretical explanations of rape can be broadly categorized into three categories: the subculture of violence theory, gender socialization theory, and political-economic theory (Andersen and Renzetti 1980).

Subculture of Violence
The first theory of the causes of rape comes from the **subculture of violence** perspective in criminology. This theory sees the social environment as the origin of violent behavior, but it is extremely biased by its differential emphasis on the behavior of African American, Hispanic, and working-class men. Although, as we have seen, some organizational contexts may be more conducive to violence, the subculture of violence theory tends to associate violence with working-class and minority communities, positing that violence becomes a routine feature of everyday life. In this perspective men's violence and aggression are explained as adaptations to poverty, but the emphasis is placed on the collective psychological

maladjustment of minority and working-class populations (Wolfgang and Feracuti 1967; Amir 1971). The problem with the subculture of violence thesis is not that violence in these communities is not a problem, but that this theory blames the culture of these communities for violent behavior.

Such a perspective begs the question of whether violence is more widespread in poor and working-class communities or whether it is just less hidden. Criminologists have frequently pointed out that the higher rape and violence rates found among minority and poor men largely reflect race and class discrimination in the criminal justice system. It is important to note that the most violent crimes (rape and homicide) show smaller race differences than the less violent crime of robbery (Bureau of Justice Statistics 2003). This fact seemingly discredits the subculture of violence theory. Critics of this perspective also point out that violence is equally extensive in the dominant culture; it is just more easily hidden or legitimized as appropriately masculine behavior. In the end, the subculture of violence theory gives us an inadequate explanation of violence against women because, in its focus on society's underclasses, it does not explain why violence is also symptomatic of the dominant culture.

Gender Socialization as a Cause of Rape

The second perspective used to explain rape comes from gender socialization theory. Feminists have suggested that the causes of rape can be traced to the dominant culture and its emphasis on masculinity as a learned pattern of aggression and domination. Unlike psychological and subcultural theories that emphasize deviations from the mainstream culture, feminist explanations show rape as an exaggeration of traditional gender roles. Gender socialization theory provides a perspective on rape that is sensitive to the variety of contexts in which it occurs. For example, a large proportion of rapes are committed by persons who are known to the victim. Many of these violent events occur in the context of a date or some other relationship between the person being raped and the rapist.

There is support in the research literature for this explanation. Men who rape are more likely to have attitudes that see sexual aggressiveness as legitimate (Scully 1990), and the presence of sexually aggressive friends is also the best predictor of whether a man will act sexually aggressive, indicating that men's image among other men is an important context for understanding their willingness to rape. This perspective also helps us understand the commonly reported finding that men who rape typically do not think they have done anything wrong. Convicted rapists typically justify rape in a variety of ways. They see the women as seductresses, think that women say no to sex when they really mean yes, think that those raped eventually relax and enjoy the rape, believe that nice girls do not get raped, or see what they did as only a minor wrongdoing. Scully's research on rapists also shows that men who rape see it as a means of revenge and punishment; those raped are thought to represent all women. Other rapists see rape as an afterthought, like a bonus after a burglary or robbery. Others define rape as recreational and say that it boosts their self-images (Scully 1990).

From the perspective of gender socialization theory, rape occurs because men have learned that forcing women to have sex is legitimate and normal behavior.

Understanding rape from this perspective helps us see how traditional gender re-actions encourage the high incidence of rape in this culture, but we cannot limit our understanding of rape only to socialization and interpersonal relations. Al-though it is correct to see rape as connected to learned patterns in the culture, this perspective is inadequate without an understanding of how the cultural concepts of masculinity and femininity emerge from the status of women and men in the society.

Rape and the Political-Economic Status of Women

Feminists suggest a third perspective on rape that explains violence against women as founded on the political and economic status of women in patriarchal and cap-italist societies. This political-economic theory states that women historically have been defined as the property of men in these societies. For example, the rape of African American women by White slaveowners is evidence of the relationship be-tween rape and the property status of women. Although women in contemporary society are no longer explicitly defined as the property of men, their use as sexual objects in advertising reduces their sexuality to a commodity. Images of violence against women in advertising and the popular media legitimate violent behavior against women and reiterate their status as sexual objects. To become an object is to become a piece of property, and this status, according to feminists, dehumanizes women and makes them an object for male violence.

The fact that most rapists do not believe they have done anything wrong shows that violence against women carries some degree of legitimacy within the society. Those women who are perceived as the least valuable in the society are apparently most likely to be raped. This fact explains why African American, Hispanic, poor, unemployed, and unmarried women are those most frequently raped. The evi-dence is that high rates of poverty and divorce have the strongest relationship to the likelihood of rape. This is a suggestive finding, since we have already seen the increasing linkage between divorce and poverty.

Cross-cultural evidence discloses that the level of violence against women is lowest in those societies where women have the most social, political, and eco-nomic autonomy (Friedl 1975; Sanday 1994). In patriarchal societies, where men rule women, women lose their autonomy and are encouraged to be dependent on men. Research on women who are raped shows that women who are not identified as belonging to a man (i.e., women who are alone in public, single, divorced, sep-arated, or living with nonfamily members) are raped most often. At the same time, increasing social isolation seems to be a pattern in the phenomenon of wife beat-ing (Dobash and Dobash 1979), and, in the case of incest, the isolation of women in the privacy of family life keeps that act a closely guarded secret.

Feminist research on rape has shattered the myths surrounding the crime. Still, women are told that they should not resist, that giving in is safer than fighting to avoid rape. Research refutes this. Women who confront rapists both physically and verbally and who resist in a variety of strategies are most likely to avoid rape. Sub-sequent research has confirmed that those who resist are much less likely to have rape completed; furthermore, most forms of resistance are not associated with higher rates of injury, as women may fear. The only forms of resistance associated with increased injury are unarmed forceful resistance and arguing with the rapist (Kleck and Sayles 1990).

Violence against women is based on the economic and political powerlessness of women living in patriarchal societies. Understanding violence against women requires an analysis that shows the relationship of violence to the structure of major social institutions. In this sense, stopping violence against women is intricately connected to the liberation of women from oppressive social and economic relations. In sum, violence against women is supported through the institutions of society. Cultural institutions ideologically promote violence against women; patriarchal social institutions encourage violence against women; criminal justice institutions minimize or cover up violence against women; and legal institutions resist radical change in policies to protect women from violence.

❖ Women in the Criminal Justice System

What happens to women when they enter the criminal justice system—either as victims or as defendants? Women in the criminal justice system are treated differently from men both as offenders and as victims. Is the symbol of justice—a blindfolded woman—representative of what happens to women in the criminal justice system?

Gender and the Courts

Even with much legal reform, research, particularly in the area of rape, shows that women victims are not equally credible before the law. In many rape trials, the victim's past sexual history may be introduced to discredit her testimony against her assailant. Many states have reformed their legal statutes to make a woman's past sexual history inadmissible as evidence in a rape trial, but, despite legal reforms, trial evidence indicates that lawyers' allegations about a woman's character are still used to discredit her testimony or to make her appear to have an illegitimate claim. Even before trial, police and prosecutors make judgments about the victim's credibility and the prosecutive merit of her case. If she had a prior relationship with her assailant; if she delayed reporting the crime; if she was under the influence of drugs or alcohol; or if she is a prostitute, a woman of color, a welfare recipient, or a hitchhiker—her case may be seen as unsubstantiated. How well a particular case fits prosecutors' preexisting ideas of what constitutes rape determines whether a case even goes to trial. Prosecutors' judgments about whether a case will hold up and result in conviction are an important predictor of whether a case goes to trial. (Frohmann 1991; Spohn et al. 2001).

Women's perceptions of the criminal justice system clearly influence their willingness to report and prosecute rape. They are much more likely to report rape when they see a high probability of conviction and when the rape fits prevailing definitions of a "classic" rape—that is, rape involving use of a weapon, rape by a stranger, rape in a public place, or rape with a break-in to the victim's home (Pino and Meier 1999).

Further research finds gender bias for women in the courts, in roles as both adjudicators and as defendants. The eighteenth-century legal scholar Blackstone, whose work provides the cornerstone for English and American law, thought women were rightfully prohibited from jury service because of the defect of sex. Although women are now being fairly represented on juries, until very recently they were severely underrepresented on juries and were often permitted exemptions from jury service simply because of their sex.

Gender bias in the courtroom also affects the disposition of jury cases, although not directly because of the gender of jurors. In cases of rape, jurors' beliefs about rape influence their willingness to convict or acquit. Men are more likely than women to believe in rape myths (Reilly et al. 1992). As a result, the greater representation of women on juries has resulted in a higher rape conviction rate in recent years. Women and men do however recommend similar punishments for defendants found guilty of rape (Hans and Vidmar 1986).

For women offenders brought before the criminal justice system, a number of factors influence the disposition of cases. Specifically, Daly (1989) early found that a defendant's work and family situations influenced sentencing of both men and women. Judges perceive men on a continuum, ranging from "good" men, who work and support dependents, to "irresponsible" men, who may or may not have a job and dependents but who do not contribute support. Men perceived as irresponsible, along with those who do not have jobs or dependents, are more likely to be sentenced. Similarly, women are judged along a similar continuum—the "good" woman being one who has dependents for whom she cares regularly (regardless of whether she holds a job) and the "irresponsible" woman being one who has dependents but does not care for them regularly. As with men, women judged to be irresponsible are more likely to be sentenced. This research concludes that judges seek to protect children and families, not women per se, as prior arguments about judicial paternalism and chivalry have implied.

This conclusion is further elaborated by subsequent research finding that women's family situations, such as whether there is someone who can care for her children, influence judges' sentencing of women. For men, this does not come into play as much as things such as their prior record and the seriousness of the offense (Flavin 2001; Koons-Witt 2002).

Women and Prison

The number of women in prison is a small percentage (6.6 percent) of all state and federal prisoners. Although both the rate of male and female imprisonment has increased over recent years, the female prison population has increased at a faster rate (see Figure 9.4). A disproportionate number of people in prison are members of racial minority groups. More than half of women prisoners are African American and Latinas, and almost two-thirds of men in prison are Black or Hispanic. The highest rates of imprisonment of women are for those between 25 and 39 years of age—years when they are also likely to be mothers (Harrison and Beck 2003).

FIGURE 9.4   The Growth of Imprisonment

Source: Data from Bureau of Justice Statistics. 2002. *Sourcebook of Criminal Justice Statistics.* Washington, DC: Department of Justice, Table 6.22.

Note: The *Y* axis, the number in prisons, is significantly different for men and women.

Two-thirds of women in prison have at least one child under age 18; about half of these children live with grandparents, and about one-fourth live with their fathers (Sharp and Marcus-Mendoza 2001; Enos 2001). Consistent with patterns of crime, a greater percentage of women are imprisoned for property and drug offenses than is the case for men (Mullings et al. 2002).

Once women are in prison, little attention is paid to their special needs. Some have argued that this is because, until recently, there have been so few women in prison that it is costly to develop special programs for them. Prisons are "gendered institutions," where organizational policies and practices are modeled on men's needs and interests, even while such practices (such as job training) are assumed to be gender neutral (Britton 1997). Gender stereotypes also shape the vocational training women get in prison; the prison experience typically leaves women marginalized upon their exit (Morash et al. 1994). Although men in prison may be trained in relatively well-paying trades (e.g., mechanics, carpentry, etc.), job training for women, to the extent that it exists, is for poorly paid, gender-segregated jobs that offer little hope for advancement (e.g., laundress, homemaker, or beautician). Women's prisons are smaller than men's prisons but have also become increasingly overcrowded. Increasingly, however, women in prison are being treated no differently than men—a mixed message, since this means that women are now subject to much of the same degradation as male prisoners (Chesney-Lind 1997).

Health care in women's prisons is also limited, particularly in meeting needs specific to women's medical and reproductive care. Many women enter prison with existing medical problems, including drug addiction, psychiatric illness, hypertension, and respiratory disease. One in four is pregnant or has recently given birth. If women become pregnant while in prison, they may have a long wait for medical care, making abortion a potentially high risk. Some facilities do not allow abortions at all. Should a woman prisoner carry through her pregnancy, she may not receive adequate prenatal care and, when she gives birth, is likely to be separated from her child (Ingram-Fogel 1991, 1993; McQuiade and Ehrenreich 1998; Young and Reviere 2001; Stoller 2003).

Women in prison say that separation from their children is the most difficult part of their sentence, and they see few alternatives for their children's care. They typically give them up for adoption, release them to foster care, or leave them with relatives (the choice most often selected). Studies find that women in prison are greatly concerned for their children and that this strain can be reduced by engaging them in mothering activities (Enos 2001; Forsyth 2003; Berry and Ergenberg 2003).

The conditions in women's prisons often lead them to fend for themselves. In the face of these conditions, research indicates that women's own social networks in prison are more supportive and affectionate than those formed in male prisons. This suggests that women actively construct a supportive subculture within prison, the characteristics of which vary in different institutional settings (Kruttschnitt et al. 2000). Although women in prison do not all come from similar cultural backgrounds, the subcultures they form in prison often exhibit resourcefulness, flexibility, and creativity in the social relations they develop. They are not merely passive victims of their situation; instead, they develop adaptive strategies to cope with the conditions they face.

Part of women's prison subculture is reflected in the lesbian relationships that emerge between some women prisoners. Women prisoners report forming sexual relationships with other women in prison, often for economic motivations, such as the exchange of favors or commercial goods. Compared to men, women are also more likely to form interracial relationships in prison, and women's relationship are generally less violent and involve less gang activity (Greer 2000). Still, coerced sex in women's prisons involves only about 4 percent of prisoners (Hensley et al. 2003). Little research has been done on the sexual abuse of women prisoners by prison staff, although women prisoners report that this abuse is common. The women clearly see sexual abuse as part of the power dynamics that exist between prison staff and the inmates (Calhoun and Coleman 2002).

Somewhat ironically, studies show that the number of women in prison is highest in those countries where women have advanced the most with regard to education, employment, and their overall social status (Heitfield and Simon 2002). Perhaps this reflects the diminution of protective attitudes toward women, as well as more opportunities for women to engage in crime. But it also shows the need for women's advancement to continue so that they will not experience the abusive relationships that can land them in prison, and women need better opportunities in the "outside" world to reduce the need to commit property crimes. Clearly, the increase in the number of women in prison calls for new social policies to deal with this growing population, including programs to help women readjust to a productive life once they are released (Kruttschnitt and Gartner 2003).

❖ Chapter Summary and Themes

Sociological perspectives on gender, crime, and deviance locate the origins of such behavior in the social structural conditions in which different groups live.

Early explanations of women's deviance were riddled with assumptions about women's maladjusted social-sexual identity,. Such thinking was also bounded by the racism of the time. As people began to think about the social origins of women's deviance, attention turned to such things as the labeling process and the role of social inequality in producing crime and deviance. Feminist perspectives have added the significance of women's location in power relationships and their economic status as causal factors in deviance and crime.

Although women are less likely to commit crime than men, you can trace the sources of women's crime to the status of women in society.

The kinds of crime that women commit are primarily property crimes— indicative of the poor economic status of women. Often, women's engagement in crime stems from a history of sexual abuse and/or their relationships with men.

Men are more likely to be victims of crime than women, but women's sexual victimization is a form of social control that can restrict women's freedom of movement.

Men are far more likely to be victims of crime than are women, except for rape. Among women, women of color and younger women are the most likely crime victims, although older women are more fearful of crime. Sociological studies of rape and other forms of sexual assault find that power dynamics between men and women are the best explanation of sexual victimization, even when people continue to blame victims for rape. Some organizational contexts—those based on highly masculine characteristics—are the most rape-prone environments.

Women have an increasing presence in the criminal justice system, both as workers and as prisoners.

Although the rate of men's imprisonment has begun to decline, the rate for women is increasing, although women remain a small proportion of prisoners overall. But a prison system that was designed primarily for men needs revision if it is to meet the health, labor, and family needs of women in prison.

❖ Key Terms

crime index	labeling theory	*Uniform Crime Reports*
date rape	reproduction of harm	victimization surveys
deviance	subculture of violence	

❖ *Discussion Questions/Projects for Thought*

1. Think of a time when you engaged in some activity that was considered deviant for someone of your gender. Alternatively, without putting yourself at risk, do something that violates the routine expectations associated with your gender. How do people react to you? How does this make you feel? What does your experiment tell you about the concepts of deviance, gender, and social control?

2. What services does your campus or community offer to assist women who are victims of violence? Contact some of those who work (or

volunteer) in one such organization and ask them what they have learned about violence against women. Based on these discussions, what links do you see between violence and women's status?

3. Follow the daily newspaper for one week, noting the stories involving criminal activity. What evidence of men's and women's crime do you see and how do your anecdotal observations support (or not) the data on gender and crime reported in this chapter?

❖ *Internet Resources*

Bureau of Justice Statistics

http://www.ojp.usdoj.gov/bjs/

This federal office, a division of the U.S. Department of Justice, maintains data on crime and crime victimization. The website includes many important publications of data involving gender and crime, including the victimization of women and intimate partner violence.

Federal Bureau of Investigation

http://www.fbi.gov

This website includes on-line publication of the *Uniform Crime Reports,* the best source of data on national measures of crime.

Violence Against Women Office

http://www.ojp.usdoj.gov/vawo/

The Violence Against Women Office of the U.S. Department of Justice was created in 1995 to implement the 1994 Violence Against Women Act. The website includes numerous useful reports with statistics about violence against women, federal regulations against violence against women, and numerous resources on issues including domestic violence, stalking, battering, child custody and protection, sexual assault, welfare reform, and interventionist programs.

❖ *Suggested Readings*

Belknap, Joanne. 2000. *The Invisible Woman: Gender, Crime, and Justice.* Belmont, CA: Wadsworth Publishing Co.
This anthology provides a thorough review of women as criminals, as crime victims, and as employees in the criminal justice system. Throughout, Belknap emphasizes how women are treated by the criminal justice system.

Madriz, Esther. 1997. *Nothing Bad Happens to Good Girls: Fear of Crime in Women's Lives.* Berkeley: University of California Press.
Madriz's research is based on focus groups and interviews with African American, Latina, and White women of different ages. She shows how fear of crime is a source of the social control of women, particularly for African American women and Latinas.

Messerschmidt, James W. 1999. *Nine Lives: Adolescent Masculinities, the Body, and Violence.* Boulder, CO: Westview Press.
Long established as a criminologist studying the connection between gender and crime, Messerschmidt here studies nine White, working-class teen boys to unravel some of the connections between masculinity and crime.

Miller, Susan L. 1999. *Crime Control and Women: Feminist Implications of Criminal Justice Policy.* Thousand Oaks, CA: Sage.
Miller's analysis of current criminal justice policies shows the consequences for women of such concepts as "three strikes, you're out" and mandatory sentencing for battering. Her analysis carefully links the consequences of social policy to patterns of racial, class, and gender inequality.

Price, Barbara Raffel, and Natalie J. Sokoloff, eds. 2003. *The Criminal Justice System and Women: Offenders, Prisoners, Victims, and Workers.* New York: McGraw Hill.
This comprehensive anthology includes current articles on various dimensions of women as criminals, as victims, and as workers in the criminal justice system.

Renzetti, Claire M., Jeffrey L. Edleson, and Raquel Bergen, eds. 2000. *Sourcebook on Violence against Women.* Thousand Oaks, CA: Sage Publications.
This comprehensive book covers many dimensions of the subject of violence against women and is useful for students, as well as those working with victims of violence.

Richie, Beth E. 1996. *Compelled to Crime: The Gender Entrapment of Battered Black Women.* New York: Routledge.
Based on extensive interviews with African American battered women in prison, Richie analyzes why women participate in crime. She argues that they become dependent on men who encourage their criminal activity because the women are both traditional in their gender ideology and trapped by the oppression of their race, class, and gender status. The life stories of the women she studies provide vivid evidence of the connection between women's criminality and social inequality.

Watterson, Kathyrn, and Meda Chesney-Lind. 1996. *Women in Prison: Inside the Concrete Womb.* Boston: Northeastern University Press.
This book analyzes the experiences of incarcerated women, particularly focusing on the psychological consequences of imprisonment.

GENDER, EDUCATION, AND SCIENCE

10

Women and the History
of Education

Gender and Educational Success
Gender and Schooling
Academic Achievement: Is There a
Gender Gap?
Gender and the Curriculum
Class and Race Inequality

Women in Higher Education

Gender, Science, and Society
The Status of Women in Science

Science, Feminism, and the Social
Construction of Knowledge

Chapter Summary and Themes

Key Terms

Discussion Questions/
Projects for Thought

Internet Resources

Suggested Readings

When Harvard University president, Lawrence Summers, stated (in 2005) that women were underrepresented in scientific fields perhaps because of innate (that is, inborn) differences or because women did not want to work as hard as successful scientific careers require, a national uproar followed. Summers made these remarks at a national conference of leading scholars on the subject of diversifying the scientific workplace. Numerous people and organizations issued statements criticizing Summers for ignoring the substantial evidence that differences in women's and men's achievements in science have social, not biological, causes (American Sociological Association 2005). Many also wondered why the president of such a prestigious university would harken back to biological determinism (see Chapter 2) to explain the status of women in science.

The national attention to issues about women in science is rooted in larger questions about the status of women in education more generally. Are there differences in women's and men's (or girls' and boys') educational experiences that lead to different educational outcomes? This debate also reflects the importance of education in predicting people's life chances. Without a good education, you are likely to have few skills and, thus, little job marketability, leaving you vulnerable to a lifetime of low-wage work. But education is not only about skill development. The experiences we have in school are also a significant part of our identity development, as we saw in Chapter 2. The interactions we have with peers and teachers provide one of the contexts in which our gender identity develops. Thus, our self-esteem, aspirations, and self concept are formed in part through our experiences in educational institutions. If the schools value the attributes and accomplishments of our gender (and race and class) group, then we are far more likely to grow up with identities that lead to achievement, not failure.

Education is thus a critical place in which to study the social construction of gender and the opportunities that are extended to women and men. In some societies, studying gender and education may be as basic as working to extend literacy to women. In contemporary Afghanistan, for example, like other poor nations, only 20 percent of women can read, compared with 49 percent of men (UNICEF 2003). In a society such as the United States, although 99 percent of the adult population is literate, there are also significant gaps in educational achievement—gaps that stem from gender inequities, along with race and class inequalities, in the schools. In a society so technologically advanced, not having a good education can leave you behind in access to good jobs and to other benefits of democratic citizenship. And, beyond a good education, people increasingly need the skills that scientific and technological literacy bring. In a society where technological and scientific skill is increasingly needed, anyone who lags behind in such skills is at a disadvantage. For that reason, closing the gender gap that persists in science and technology is an important part of achieving gender equity.

This chapter reviews the gender gap in education, including changes in the education of women over time. As we will see, much progress has been made in educating girls and women beyond the narrowly prescribed gender roles that characterized education in the past. But significant gender differences remain in the skills and identities that schools create. Furthermore, the growth of feminism has raised new questions about the social structure of science and how that structure works to minimize the role of women in science and to shape what is known in scientific thought.

❖ *Women and the History of Education*

The pursuit of knowledge has historically been considered the work of men. Either excluded by formal admissions policies or tracked into gender-typed fields and specialties, women have been seen as outsiders in education until only recently. Looking at the history of education reveals that the growth of mass public education is a phenomenon of the twentieth century. In the earliest part of the twentieth century, only a small proportion of the population completed even a high school education, and college was reserved for only the privileged few. Thus, in 1910 one-quarter of the population had less than five years of an elementary school education, only 14 percent completed high school, and 3 percent finished college. Now, only 3 percent have fewer than seven years of elementary school, 84 percent graduate from high school, and 26 percent complete college degrees (National Center for Education Statistics 2002).

In the early part of U.S. history, education was largely seen as a privilege for a few. Slaves, for example, were forbidden to read, although many learned to do so secretly by studying the Bible or the books of owners' children. The poor and working class seldom got much education since young people, including children, were needed as laborers. Among the advantaged classes, women's education was judged as important mostly because it was believed to make women better mothers. Not until 1918 was public education made compulsory. With the large-scale immigration that characterized the early twentieth century, public education expanded because schools were thought to "Americanize" the diverse ethnic groups that were entering the country. Many historians of education have argued that public education expanded as a way of keeping young immigrant men and women off the streets. Fears of crime, juvenile delinquency, and other forms of trouble that came with urbanization and immigration resulted in schools being a place where people believed the values of discipline and hard work would be inculcated in the nation's youth (Greene 1978; McMannon 1997).

From the start, then, schools reflected some of the other needs of society. Even today, the school calendar reflects the original needs of an agricultural-based society where young people were out of school during time periods when their labor was needed to bring in crops. With industrialization, schools became places where literacy was extended to masses who would occupy positions in a more bureaucratized society, where many would be employed in white-collar work. Today, with the growth of an information-based, highly scientific, and technological society, schools are needed to prepare students for the jobs that will characterize the twenty-first century.

Interestingly, as public education developed, women were somewhat more likely than men to complete high school. Thus, until as late as 1980, more women than men completed a high school education (although men were much more likely to attend college). The predominance of women in the public schools reflects the fact that men could find employment without necessarily completing high school. For women, through the 1940s and 1950s part of the curriculum was teaching them typing, shorthand, and other skills that were associated with women's presumed proper role. At the same time, however, women were the majority of high school teachers, although many states prohibited women from teaching once they were married.

With regard to college education, one of the most notable trends in recent years has been the vast expansion of college enrollment (see Figure 10.1) and, most recently, the fact that women now outnumber men as college students. College enrollment for both men and women expanded dramatically beginning in the 1970s and continued until the present. Now, the majority of college graduates are women, though, as we saw in Chapter 5, women college graduates still earn less than men. Moreover, women are more likely to graduate in certain fields—namely, education, the arts, humanities, social sciences, and law—whereas men more likely graduate in sciences, mathematics, and engineering (Bradley 2000). This pattern of gender segregation in the curriculum significantly affects the outcomes of education for both groups.

Because of its importance in shaping life chances, education has long been an area of feminist activism. In the nineteenth century, campaigns for women's educational rights were central to the growth of feminism. Early feminists, such as Emma Willard, who founded the Troy Female Seminary in 1821, understood the need for women to have an education that taught skills other than those associated with good mothering. Thus, Willard included algebra, geometry, and physiology in the curriculum of the seminary.

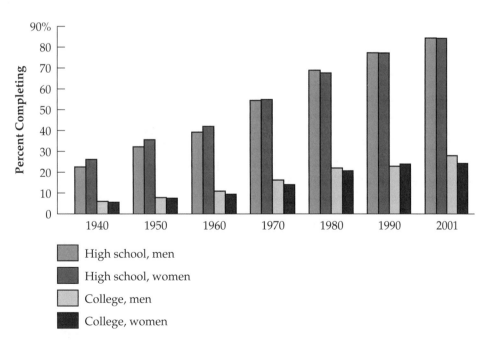

FIGURE 10.1   Men's and Women's Educational Attainment

Source: Data from National Center for Educational Statistics. 2002. *Digest of Education Statistics 2002.* Washington, DC: U.S. Department of Education. Website: http://www.nces.ed/gov.

In most schools, however, women's education was restricted by ideologies that depicted their minds as directed and limited by their bodies. Especially in the post-Civil War period, when major transformations were occurring in the traditional gender roles, leading educational reformers claimed that women's wombs dominated their mental life and thus they should not study or work vigorously! One such reformer, Dr. Edward Clarke, was a member of the Harvard Board of Overseers and a member of its medical faculty. He published several popular books in the late nineteenth century warning of the dangers that education and study posed for women. Clarke wrote, "A girl upon whom Nature, for a limited period and for a definite purpose, imposes so great a physiological task, will not have as much power left for the tasks of school, as the boy of whom Nature requires less at the corresponding epoch" (Clarke 1873:54, cited in Rosenberg 1982:10). Accordingly, he advised young women to study one-third as much as young men and not to study at all during menstruation.

Others agreed. Professor Charles Meigs admonished his class at Jefferson Medical College to think of the womb as a "great power and ask your own judgments whether such an organ can be of little influence on the constitution and how much!" (Meigs 1847:18, cited in Rosenberg 1982:6). The prominent gynecologist Thomas Emmet argued:

> To reach the highest point of physical development the young girl in the between classes of society should pass the year before puberty and some two years afterwards free from all exciting influences. She should be kept as a child as long as possible, and made to associate with children. . . . Her mind should be occupied by a very moderate amount of study, with frequent intervals of a few moments each, passed when possible in the recumbent position, until her system becomes accustomed to the new order of life (Emmet 1879:21, cited in Rosenberg 1982:10).

These admonitions reflect class biases of the time and also are consistent with racist arguments that defined Black Americans as biologically unfit for the same privileges accorded Whites. Such biological explanations of inequality are often used to justify oppression by race, class, and gender. Biological explanations of inequality seem to become especially popular during periods of rapid social change in class, race, and gender relations, because such beliefs develop as justifications for maintaining the status quo.

Women are no longer formally excluded from education, but research shows that even with the disappearance of such explicitly sexist forms of exclusion, gender bias in education persists. Beginning with preschool and extending through higher education, girls and women encounter perceptions and practices that can have long-term consequences for their life chances.

❖ Gender and Educational Success

When girls and boys begin school, they encounter a new world of gender expectations. Gender influences numerous facets of the experience boys and girls have in school, including their interactions with each other, relationships with teachers, and concepts of self. As a result, the outcomes of education reveal strong evidence of the influence of gender—in such things as achievement tests, course-taking patterns, curriculum content, and student interests. We have seen how schools work as agents of gender socialization (see Chapter 2), but what happens in schools that affects girls' and boys' opportunities?

Gender and Schooling

Remember your first day of school? Perhaps you were excited, maybe scared, and possibly feeling shy. Maybe you wondered what it would be like to meet new girls and boys, be away from home, and have a new teacher. But it is unlikely that you thought that your experience would be shaped by the simple fact of whether you were a girl or a boy. Yet, that fact does have significant consequences for your education—beginning from your first day and continuing through your last year of school—whether that is a year you drop out of high school, the year you complete a bachelor's degree, or when you go on to graduate or professional school.

Moreover, the gender gap in education exists despite many years of reform and policies that legally bind the nation to provide equal educational opportunities to women and men. **Title IX** of the Educational Amendments of 1972 is a federal law prohibiting sex discrimination in federally funded education programs and activities. This law has been critical in establishing equal educational opportunity for women, not just in schools, but also in state-sponsored athletics. Before Title IX, women in schools could be denied admission to various programs, often sat in sex-segregated classrooms, and had little access to the resources that supported school-sponsored athletics. Title IX mandated schools to open the doors of education to women on equal terms with men, and its implementation has been responsible for many of the successes and gains that women have seen in education in the years since its passage. Title IX has also been interpreted by the courts as prohibiting *sexual harassment* in schools, an issue discussed later in this chapter (see also Chapter 5).

Despite the gains that have come from the implementation of Title IX, gender inequities in education remain, and they are reflected in what students learn, how teachers interact with them, what teachers expect, and how students perceive themselves in school. As Myra and David Sadker write, "Sitting in the same classroom, reading the same textbook, listening to the same teacher, girls and boys get very different educations" (Sadker and Sadker 1994: 2). How does this happen? Girls and boys enter schools as equals, but over the years, the gender gap in education actually increases. Moreover, much of what happens is not consciously intended to discriminate against girls; rather, there is a hidden bias throughout education that may not even be visible to those who engage in it. Consequently, creating gender equity in education requires a conscious effort to overcome the gender bias that persists in education and that narrows the options that young women—and young men—will have later in life.

Observations of children in elementary school settings show how gender is given meaning through the ordinary interactions students have in school. Something as subtle as teachers always referring to boys first when referring to both girls and boys defines boys as more important, as the dominant group (Thorne 1993). Likewise, calling on boys more often, even if they are being singled out because of disruptive behavior, makes boys more noticeable, thereby communicating their greater sense of place. Gendered patterns in who talks more, who gets recognized, and who is rewarded for what kind of behavior all operate to produce a definition of gender that differentiates boys and girls (Sadker and Sadker 1994).

Teacher expectations also influence how boys and girls see themselves and are seen by others. The term **self-fulfilling prophecy** has been used to refer to the outcomes that occur as the result of teachers' and counselors' expectations. Thus, the counselor who thinks that girls are unlikely to become scientists is unlikely to encourage girls to pursue advanced science and math coursework. Consequently, fewer girls take such courses, possibly reinforcing the counselor's belief and producing a self-fulfilling prophecy. Research has clearly shown that what teachers expect of students has a strong effect on how students perform. Thus, the student labeled a high achiever is quite likely to live up to that expectation, just as the student labeled as deficient is likely to perform poorly.

Tracking systems in the schools, also known as streaming (where students are sorted into groups based on their presumed abilities), contribute to the self-fulfilling prophecy. Students placed in the higher academic tracks routinely get the better teachers, a more innovative curriculum, and greater access to educational advantages than do students placed in the lower tracks (Lucas 1999). Tracking has been shown to be strongly related to social class and race, but it is also related to gender, especially with regard to math placements (Ansalone 2001; Kubitschek and Hallinan 1996). Tracking also strongly affects women's and men's self-esteem and thus their educational performance. Studies also show that women placed in high tracks actually get more positive outcomes than men in high tracks, although the reverse is true for women and men placed in low tracks where women are more negatively affected than men (Catsambis et al. 1999).

Research on the self-fulfilling prophecy indicates that the stereotypes teachers (and others) have of students have a huge impact on student outcomes. Teachers who have high expectations for certain students will call on them more, praise them frequently, and give them more opportunities to demonstrate success. These stereotypes typically are based on gender, as well as on race and social class. Latinas and African American students risk being thought of as stupid; Asian Americans who are stereotyped as the "model minority," feel pressure to excel (Olsen 1997).

The influence of gender, race, and class stereotypes has been aptly demonstrated by the concept of **stereotype threat** (Steele and Aronson 1995). Steele and his associates have shown that negative stereotypes suppress academic performance. Developed first to explain differences in Black and White scores on standardized tests, stereotype threat means that when students (or others) perceive that they risk being judged by a negative stereotype, they do not perform as well as they otherwise might. Faced, for example, with the stereotype that women are worse at math than men, women's apprehension about the stereotype actually lessens their performance on math exams. Interestingly, this research has also shown that the higher the perceived threat, the lower the performance and, conversely, that *when* the threat of the stereotype is eliminated, women and men actually perform similarly on math tests. The strong implication is that the presence of stereotypes, not an actual difference in women's and men's abilities, is what produces differences in such things as math testing (Spencer et al. 1999).

You can see that the power of stereotypes is enormous. But stereotypes do not come only from teachers. Studies find that girls are actually more likely to blame their peers than teachers for discouraging school achievement (Haag 1999). Thus, girls who are smart report feeling tension between peer approval and academic performance. Similarly, African American and Latino students may be judged by peers as "acting White" or "selling out" if they excel in academics.

Thus, teachers and students construct the meanings of gender—and race and class—that permeate educational institutions. These patterns strongly mark girls' and boys' experiences in school. Seating patterns at lunchroom tables, lines where students stand, and playground activities all become constructed as gendered spaces. Although not strictly segregated by gender, such interactions reinforce gender as a primary social category—one that, as sociologist Barrie Thorne has analyzed it, "provides a continuously available line of difference that can be drawn on at any time in the ongoing life of schools" (1993: 35). Moreover, although gender segregation is present as early as the preschool and elementary levels, it becomes heightened over time, as students get older and move into higher grade levels.

Such gendered patterns have consequences, not only for how boys and girls define each other, but also for how they define themselves. **Self esteem**—that is, how well one thinks of oneself—is critical, not just because positive self-esteem is related to one's mental health, but because self-esteem is also linked to the aspirations one has for one's future. Studies show that by the middle years of school girls have lower self-esteem than boys (Phillips 1998; Haag 1999). Students who develop poor self-concepts are likely to lower their aspirations, thereby paying less attention to doing well and limiting their educational performance. Once they do so, teachers' come to expect less and label them as underachievers, thereby reinforcing their negative self-image and establishing a cycle of poor educational performance.

Schools are the places where many young people make the transition from childhood to adulthood. By the time young girls and boys enter middle school, gender has already taken a strong hold on their self-concepts and interactions with each other. But the transition into the middle school years magnifies the significance of gender. All of the studies, as well as casual observations, that examine young girls in their teens note the extraordinary concern with appearance, popularity, and image that emerges during these years. As one 13 year old puts it, "Girls struggle the most to fit in out of everything else in their lives. We try to wear the right clothes, be slim, and not say the wrong thing. Most girls would do anything to get a boyfriend. Girls also don't stay true to themselves. While trying to fit in, they becomes clones of each other. They need help finding themselves" (Haag 1999: 10). Girls in these years may spend more time worrying about their clothes, makeup, and other features of their attractiveness than they do focusing on their schoolwork. Furthermore, the preoccupation with appearance is supported not just by the fashion and cosmetic industries and the media that support them, it is bolstered by numerous institutional supports in the schools: Note the large number of school contests and activities that emphasize attractiveness for girls, including pompom teams, baton twirling, cheerleading, prom queen, homecoming queen, and so forth (Eder et al. 1995).

The enormous pressure to conform in school is one of the hallmarks of adolescent culture. Social cliques are a major feature of the landscape of schools. Ask any student to describe the different groups in schools. Although the names change over time, students are highly aware of the status rankings of different groups: "Preppies," "jocks," "geeks," "druggies" describe some of the various groups that fall into the status hierarchy in schools. The insecurities brought on by status hierarchies in the schools generate anxiety and insecurity, reactions that then accentuate the need to conform to group standards. The social cliques that emerge in schools also have a clear hierarchy—a social ranking system that is structured along lines of class, gender, and race. For example, cheerleading usually has high social status, but it is linked to a particular gender performance. Most students in this status hierarchy are generally unwilling to associate with groups perceived as lower status. Students in such low-status groups are usually ridiculed, teased, and generally looked down upon. Studies show that these patterns of the status rankings of different social groups are related to extracurricular activities, but are particularly marked by the social class background of students. Within the hierarchical structure of schools, the routine practices of interaction—talk, gossip, routines, and rituals—all reinforce gender beliefs (Eder et al. 1995).

It is not just girls in this context who become disadvantaged. In what has been called the "miseducation of boys" (Sadker and Sadker 1994; Ferguson 2001), educational researchers point out that schools are places where boys become labeled as problematic troublemakers. Moreover, the informal expectations that are communicated about gender track boys into certain areas, for example, putting pressure on them to be strong athletes. Boys and young men are also encouraged by gender norms to repress emotions, be tough, and display masculinity at all costs. Most important, boys and young men learn, above all, not to cross the gender line. For boys, being "tough" is an important part of the construction and display of masculinity in schools. The importance of toughness is constantly communicated through the insults boys give to each other: "Weenie," "wimp," "fag," "queer"— all are derogatory labels routinely directed against boys who show any sign of weakness that is associated with femininity or homosexuality. Such ritualized insulting has been shown to be especially common among male athletes. Thus homophobia reinforces the gender norms that force boys and girls into narrowly conscripted social roles (Eder et al. 1995).

Schools are thus the stage where society's roles—roles defined by gender, class, race, sexuality, and age—are played out. The entire context of school is one where educational achievement is strongly influenced by the personal issues that young girls and boys face. Issues about identity, sexuality, relationships, and family are all part of the context for student learning and development. Focusing solely on educational performance without an understanding of how gender, race, class, and other factors influence students' lives may leave teachers and school officials unable to fully understand the context in which students learn, or do not. In a national climate where school reform is on the national agenda, it is important that the underlying conditions in young people's lives be addressed if we are to understand what makes students succeed or fail.

Academic Achievement: Is There a Gender Gap?

Comparing the academic achievement of young women and men, girls and boys, is a complex topic of research. Moreover, whether or not researchers find gender differences depends on what and how they measure different indicators of ability and learning. For example, girls earn higher grades than boys in all subjects throughout schooling. And, on national tests of reading and writing, girls perform equally to boys. But on other standardized tests, differences emerge, although only depending on the subject matter. The most dramatic gender differences appear on the tests with the highest stakes, tests like the Preliminary Scholastic Aptitude Test (PSAT), Scholastic Aptitude Test (SAT), and Advanced Placement (AP) tests.

Because educational testing has such influence on decisions about student placement and educational opportunities, it has been the subject of much research. This research is highly detailed and therefore difficult to summarize. In general, it shows:

- Girls and boys show similar levels of achievement in many areas, though gaps exist in others. On closer examination, there are areas where girls exceed boys in academic achievement, while boys exceed girls in other areas.
- In some subject areas, although overall scores of girls and boys are similar, boys tend to outperform at the more advanced levels, such as in mathematics.
- Even when boys' and girls' overall performance is comparable, performance in particular skill areas can substantially diverge (such as in object rotation where boys exceed girls or writing where girls exceed boys).
- Gender differences in performance (at least as measured by standardized tests) are usually similar at lower grade levels, but diverge in later grades (Phillips 1998).

It is often thought that girls and boys differ significantly in their verbal and mathematical ability. Girls, the standard argument goes, excel in verbal skills, boys, in math. This is not entirely supported by research. Although earlier researchers could document differences in girls' and boys' scores on verbal ability tests, these differences have decreased over time. Girls' do tend to outperform boys on writing skills, although these results are inconsistent. In math and science skills, whether or not differences between boys and girls appear in standardized tests depends on the age of the sample, how academically selective the test is, and what cognitive level the test is measuring. The gender gaps that exist in math testing, however, tend to increase in the later grades (American Association of University Women, 1992, 1998). At earlier levels, namely fourth and eighth grade, gender differences on standardized math tests are minimal.

"High stakes" tests, such as the PSAT, the SAT, and AP tests show larger gender gaps than do standardized tests. This is important to understand because these tests have such a tremendous influence on entrance to college and, thus, students' futures. What does the gender gap mean?

Researchers have found that the construction of the test itself can advantage one group over another. Thus, boys tend to outperform girls on multiple choice sections of standardized tests, whereas free-response sections tend to favor girls. Also, sections that involve mechanical drawing or object rotation tend to favor boys. These conclusions indicate that the design of the test itself can generate a gender bias—one that has significant implications for students' educational outcomes (American Association of University Women 1998).

Understanding the gender bias that occurs in standardized testing will become even more important since national educational policy is moving toward more required testing at various grade levels. The massive effort in recent years to enhance the science and math skills of the nation's young women has resulted in a decline of gender differences in math and science testing. But, failure to pay attention to the sources of these differences, including in test design, could erode the progress that has been made.

Another source of the gender gap in test scores is the course-taking patterns of young women and men. In science, for example, girls are more likely to take biology and chemistry; boys, physics. Although the gap in science course-taking patterns has declined, it is still significant. In math, boys and girls tend to take the same number of math courses, but there are differences in what courses young boys and girls take. In high school, young women are more likely than boys to end their math studies after a second algebra course; in fact, girls now outnumber boys in taking algebra and geometry. But, young men are more likely to take trigonometry and calculus, thereby giving them an advantage on higher-level math skills (American Association of University Women 1998).

Science and math skills are increasingly important in a society where jobs are more technologically-based and where there is a strong division in the job market between those with good technological skills and those without such skills. Schools play an important role in what has been called the **digital divide,** referring to the gap that has opened between groups with strong computing skills and those without. Course-taking patterns in computer science, as well as advanced math, are important in generating the digital divide. Research finds that not only do boys and young men outnumber girls in computer science courses, but also that girls are more likely to cluster in lower-end computer science courses. Although girls will learn some computer skills in courses such as data entry and word processing, these are skills that limit them to less stimulating and less lucrative jobs. Courses like graphic arts and computer-aided design, which can lead to better jobs, attract significantly fewer girls (American Association of University Women 1998).

In sum, research on gender and academic achievement shows that efforts to reduce the gender gap have been successful in many regards, although much remains to be done. And since the research shows boys having an advantage on multiple choice tests, the increased reliance on student testing may magnify gender differences. Many educators suggest that relying on any single measure of assessment of student learning and ability will inevitably disadvantage some groups because students have different learning styles and different tests may measure different skills. If we use tests that only recognize a narrow range of skills, or that privilege certain skills over others, we build inequity into the assessment process. Developing educational programs—including educational assessment—that take the diversity of students into account seems to be the path most likely to produce favorable outcomes for both young women and young men.

Gender and the Curriculum

Educational reforms to enhance the status of women and girls in education have focused not just on school climate and academic achievement, but also on the content of what is learned in schools. Before the growth of feminism in the latter quarter of the twentieth century, women were almost absent in the content of the curriculum at all levels. The growth of women's studies in colleges and universities has been spawned largely through that recognition, and women's studies has made a significant difference in the extent to which women are included in the curriculum throughout education.

Nonetheless, research still finds that girls and women are often placed in stereotypical roles in student learning material. Although events like Women's History Month in March or Black History Month in February have highlighted the accomplishments of people long overlooked in school curricula, segregating this material into one part of the calendar can reproduce the marginalization of excluded groups.

Just as new materials were being revised to be more inclusive of gender, new technologies have emerged that have brought new material—and new forms of material—to the nation's classrooms. Computing technology is now considered the cutting edge of curricular materials, but it has the potential to exacerbate past gender differences. Girls do not necessarily have the same experiences with computing that boys do, and many of the technological materials now being used in computer classrooms are gender-biased. Thus, studies of technologically-based course materials find that women are depicted far less often than men, and, when women are found, they are typically in stereotypical roles, such as mother or princess. Although computing technology has the potential to eliminate gender bias, it may only play on existing stereotypes, especially because fewer women than men have entered this field as software designers and computer engineers (American Association of University Women 1998).

Beyond the formal curriculum, extracurricular activities also reproduce gender inequities in the curriculum. Boys are more likely to participate in team sports, especially in the upper years of school. On the other hand, girls are more likely to participate in the performing arts, school government and clubs, and literary activities. Each type of activity develops definite skills, but these choices tend to reinforce traditional areas of "gender competency" (American Association of University Women 1998).

Furthermore, sports receive the most attention of all of the extracurricular activities. Although girls and women have become much more active in sports (largely as the result of the Title IX legislation), boys' high profile teams—namely football and basketball—receive the most attention and, typically, the highest school budgets. You can see this simply given the newspaper coverage of different athletic activities. Research on the connection between students' athletic involvement and their academic work also reveals fascinating gender patterns. The graduation rates of male college athletes, particularly in those schools with the most prestigious football and sports programs, are notoriously low. Graduation rates for women athletes, on the other hand, are typically at or above the graduation rates for women who are not athletes. Different from boys, girls who participate in sports are consistently shown in the research literature to have stronger self-esteem, good physical and mental health, and strong academic performance (American Association of University Women 1998). However, an interesting caveat comes from studies of cheerleading. A recent study, based on a national sample of high school students, finds that participation in cheerleading is negatively associated with success in science (Hanson and Kraus 1998).

Class and Race Inequality

The gender gap in education is also conditioned by race and class inequalities that permeate educational institutions. Education is one area where much progress has been made in recent years. African Americans and Hispanics have improved their high school completion rates, although they still lag behind Whites. And the gender gap within racial ethnic groups is telling. Among African American women, 78.6 percent have completed high school, compared with 80.6 percent of African American men. Fifty-seven percent of Hispanic women have completed high school compared with 55.6 percent of Hispanic men. Nationally, the high school dropout rate for Hispanics is higher than for any other group; furthermore, the dropout rate has not declined over the past 25 years (Ginorio and Huston 2001; Adelman 1999; Secada et al. 1998). Latinas have higher rates of high school completion than boys, although they are less likely to graduate from high school than African American and white women and men (National Center for Educational Statistics 2002).

In looking at educational attainment data, it is important to look at diversity within groups—not only gender, but also class. Class and immigration patterns matter in predicting educational attainment. For example, by the year 2000, 75 percent of Asian school-age children were either foreign born or children of recent immigrants and, thus, more likely than other groups to be poor. Despite stereotypes of Asian Americans as high achievers, many live in poverty and are poorly educated. And there is a tendency to overlook Asian Americans, given the Black–White model that dominates the study of U.S. race relations (Olsen 1997). The diverse backgrounds of African American, Hispanic, Asian American, and Native American children make it important to examine race, class, and gender when studying educational achievement.

Even with the disadvantages that accrue to different groups by virtue of race, class, and gender, many succeed. Understanding how they do so is as important to building equitable educational policy as understanding the obstacles to success. One such study, a study of Latinas who have been successful in school (Barajas and Pierce 2001), reveals some of the factors that can encourage success. Latinos and

Latinas who have successful navigated the path from high school to college are shown to have maintained positive definitions of themselves, definitions that are often developed in the context of "safe spaces" where they develop positive relationships with other Latinas and where they have been carefully mentored by sponsors who look out for their well-being.

Research on student success has led many researchers to move away from the deficit model of education, in which women and people of color are seen as somehow lacking what White men have. Instead, scholars suggest seeing that different groups have their own educational needs. The point is not just to provide the same thing to everyone—or to postulate women and people of color as needing to catch up—but instead to shape education around the diverse needs of different groups of students.

Some suggest that with the increased attention given to improving educational equity for girls, boys are now at a disadvantage. The popular press has promoted many high-profile books touting the disadvantage produced for boys with the growth of educational equity programs for women. Is there a disadvantage for boys? This question cannot be answered without addressing issues of race and class. The data indicate that there are no differences in rates of high school completion or participation in college prep courses when comparing only by gender. But, if you introduce race and class, significant differences appear, as Table 10.1 shows.

Taking a college preparatory curriculum is also critical for students' ability to proceed to college. Here, significant class and race differences emerge. Among White students, there is no gender gap in having had college prep courses, regardless of social class background. But there are significant gender differences among Asian Americans at every class level in the likelihood that women will have taken such a curriculum. For African Americans, whether there is a gender gap depends entirely on social class (see Table 10.1). Furthermore, as we will see below, there are large differences within racial groups as to whether men and women will attend college, graduate, and go on for professional and postgraduate degrees.

TABLE 10.1 High School Graduates Taking "New Basics"* Curriculum

	Less than $25,000		$25,000–$75,000		More than $75,000	
	Men	Women	Men	Women	Men	Women
Asian American	24%	21%	29%	23%	32%	24%
Hispanic	12	13	22	19	N/A	N/A
African American	7	17	18	20	N/A	N/A
White	11	14	18	20	29	29

*Includes: 4 years English; 3 years social science; 2 years math and science; foreign language; and one semester computer science.

Source: Data from Jacqueline E. King. 2000. *Gender Equity in Higher Education: Are Male Students at a Disadvantage?* Washington, DC: American Council on Education, p. 5.

Those who have reviewed the patterns of gender, race, and class in educational achievement and opportunity thus conclude that "the gender gap is dwarfed by the educational chasms related to race/ethnicity and social class" (King 2000). This is not a reason to abandon efforts to build more gender equity, but it does emphasize the need to consider educational reforms in the full context of gender, race, and class inequality.

❖ *Women in Higher Education*

In higher education, women are no longer formally excluded as they were previously. In fact, women are now a majority of college students; but, as the educational pyramid represented in Figure 10.2 shows, the percentage of women in higher education declines as you move up the educational hierarchy. Women and men are equally likely to complete a high school education; then women are a ma-

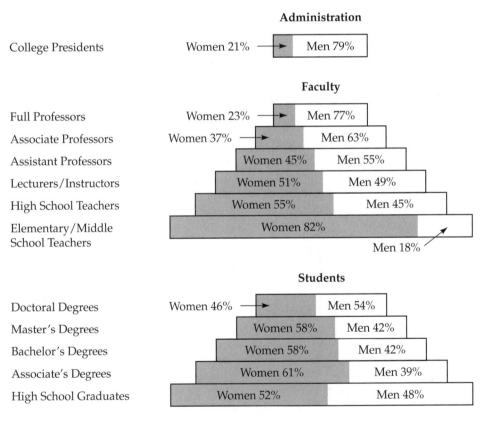

FIGURE 10.2   The Educational Pyramid

Source: The Chronicle of Higher Education, Almanac Issue, August 27, 2004, pp. 28–29; U.S. Department of Labor. 2004. *Employment and Earnings.* Washington, DC: U.S. Department of Labor, p. 210.

jority of entering college students and recipients of associate's, bachelor's, and master's degrees. They have gained as the percentage of those receiving doctorates and professional degrees (46 percent in 2002) and are expected to continue receiving the same percentage of such degrees into the foreseeable future (*The Chronicle of Higher Education Almanac* 2004).

As faculty, however, women are concentrated in the lower ranks. At the earliest levels of education, elementary and middle school, women are 82 percent of teachers, dropping to 55 percent of high school teachers. In colleges and universities, women are 38 percent of all faculty, but they are clustered in the lowest-status and lowest-paid faculty positions, as instructors and lecturers. At the highest rank, full professor, women drop to 23 percent of the faculty. And, to this day, the more elite and prestigious the institution, the smaller the likelihood that women will be found in the highest ranks of the faculty.

Race further complicates this picture, as shown in Table 10.1. As students, African Americans, Hispanics, and Native Americans are less likely to attend college than Whites, although all three groups have increased their college attendance quite substantially in recent years. Among both African Americans and Hispanics, however, women are more likely to attend college than men. Women of color thus earn more college degrees (at every level: associate, bachelor's, master's, and doctoral) than men of color. Oddly, this does not translate into women of color being more likely to be on the faculty, since among all minority groups—African American, Hispanic, Asian American, and Native American—men outnumber women as full-time faculty members, even though the percentage of both is quite small relative to White men and women. And, just as with the pattern by gender, the higher the academic rank, the smaller the proportion of men and women faculty of color (Harvey 2003).

The status of women and people of color in higher education is important not only because of the opportunity structure that gender, race, and class are embedded within, but also because the status of women and people of color in educational institutions has important ramifications for how academic knowledge is constructed. In Chapter 3 we studied how ideas are constructed within institutional contexts. Academic knowledge is no exception. Like popular culture, the creation of academic knowledge is shaped by the context in which it is developed. Because what is generated as knowledge is the basis of our understanding of the world and the source of new discoveries, understanding the setting in which research and scholarship is produced can teach you much about the assumptions built into what we know.

Because of the status of women in higher education—a status that is marked both by exclusion, invisibility, and segregation—women have often been either overlooked or distorted in the research that forms our society's body of knowledge. This inaccuracy has several consequences both for the personal experiences of women faculty and for the state of knowledge in general. At the personal level, women may find that their personalities (formed as they are through cultural expectations of femininity) are at odds with the values and behaviors surrounding them. This dilemma was expressed by Alice Rossi in 1970 and is still common today. Rossi wrote:

> *Women who are intellectually or politically brilliant are more readily accepted by men if they are also properly feminine in their style and deportment with men. This helps*

to assure that there will be few women of achievement for men to "exempt" from the general category of women, since the traits associated with traditional femininity—softness, compliance, sweetness—are rarely found together with the contradictory qualities of a vigorous and questioning intellect, and a willingness to persist on a problem against conventional assumptions (1970: 36).

Women's status in academic life (as in other organizations) creates a feeling of standing out, if only because women are different from men, long the majority (Kanter 1977). Moreover, women may find that their experience is translated into the concepts and categories that have been used to describe men's experience.

For students, the secondary status of women in education can also seriously affect their learning. Sexist attitudes about women students can discourage them from classroom participation or may even steer them away from particular courses and departments. Professors who fill their classes with sexist, racist, or homophobic comments can fill students with such anger that it is impossible for them to learn in that environment. Male students, too, are affected by such an environment because such an environment makes it difficult for men to see women as full peers and hampers men's ability to relate to women as equals in the worlds of work and families. For men with negative views about women, negative attitudes about women and sexist behavior in the classroom reinforce these views because these attitudes are confirmed by people with knowledge and high status (Hall 1982).

Of special concern is women's and young girls' risk of *sexual harassment* in schools. Large numbers of both girls and boys report being sexually harassed by their peers, including as early as grade school, although few studies have documented what sexual harassment actually means when students say it has happened. In surveys, 87 percent of girls and 79 percent of boys report being sexually harassed by peers, though girls experience overt forms of sexual harassment more than boys and boys are more likely to perpetrate it (Fineran and Bennett 1999; Murinen and Smolak 2000). Much of the harassment that occurs is between students, but not all. Studies also indicate that sexual harassment is most often directed against gay and lesbian students, who also feel more upset and threatened by harassment by peers than their heterosexual counterparts (Fineran 2001). Sexual harassment has serious consequences for students' well-being since it affects their mental and physical health, as well as having a negative effect on their academic work (Welsh 1999; Cortina et al. 1998). Although subject to change, current constitutional law does not make schools liable for sexual harassment by a teacher against a student unless a district official knows about it and does nothing.

The personal consequences of women's status in academia can result in the demise of many women's careers. As you saw in Chapter 1, women's status in the academic disciplines has influenced what is known about them. This has been the impetus for the development and growth of women's studies. Male domination of academic institutions influences the social production of knowledge because the existing schemes of understanding have been created within a particular setting, one in which men have authority over women. In sociology, for example, "how sociology is thought—its methods, conceptual schemes and theories—has been based on and built up within the male social universe, even when women have participated in its doing" (Smith 1974:7). Because the male-constituted world stands in authority over women (both inside and outside the academy), sociologists "impose the concepts and terms in which the world of men is thought as the concepts and terms in which women must think about their world" (Smith 1974:7). Women then become outsiders, not only because their status in universities is less than that of men but also because they are estranged from the dominant world view surrounding them in academic life.

Sociological theory provides insight in understanding how the status of outsiders influences their perspectives. Georg Simmel (1858–1918) described a stranger as one who is "fixed within a particular spatial group whose boundaries are similar to spatial boundaries. But his [sic] position in this group is determined, essentially, by the fact that he has not belonged to it from the beginning, that he imports qualities into it which do not and cannot stem from the group itself" (cited in Wolff 1950:402). The stranger (or the outsider) is both close to and distant from the group and its beliefs. The outsider is both involved with and indifferent to the shared perspectives of the group as a whole. This detachment creates critical distance, so that what is taken for granted by group members may be held in doubt by outsiders. As feminists have put it, "The outsider is denied the filtered vision that allows men to live without too troubling an insight" (Gornick 1971:126).

As we will see in a later section on women and scientific knowledge, women's status in academic fields can give them a unique form of knowledge. Thus, Marcia Westkott writes:

> When women realize that we are simultaneously immersed in and estranged from both our own particular discipline and the Western intellectual tradition generally, a personal tension develops that informs the critical dialogue. This tension, rooted in the contradiction of women's belonging and not belonging, provides the basis for knowing deeply and personally that which we criticize. A personally experienced, culturally-based contradiction means that in some fundamental way we as critics also oppose ourselves, or, at least, that part of us continues to sustain the very basis of our own estrangement. Hence, the personal struggle of being both an insider and outsider is not only a source of knowledge and insight, but also a source of self-criticism (1979: 422).

In the history of sociological thought, marginality and alienation, especially during periods of rapid social change, have produced many valuable insights. Scientific thinking, including sociological thinking, has flourished in periods of uncertainty because doubt and transformation foster the development of personal and collective creative thought. As C. Wright Mills suggests, personal and societal troubles that destroy the facades of conventional wisdom also form the scientific basis of the sociological and feminist imagination.

For outsiders, their paradoxical closeness to and remoteness from social groups may result in new perspectives on knowledge. It is the outsider who suspends belief in the taken-for-granted attitudes of institutions. As a result, the status of women as outsiders in intellectual life results in new methodologies and new perspectives in social and political thought. Women of color within the academy also stand as outsiders, or as what Patricia Hill Collins (1986, 1998) calls "outsiders within." Marginalized by both their race and gender, women of color have a unique standpoint in the academy and can therefore provide distinct and revealing analyses of race, class, and gender. Insiders to any group develop similar worldviews; as a result, it often takes the perspective of outsiders to challenge these taken-for-granted views. As outsiders within the academy, women of color are in a unique position to generate new knowledge. They are trained in the methods and theories of their disciplines, but do not necessarily share the privileges, patterns of belief, or historical experiences of insiders. Because they are outsiders within, women of color can generate new forms of insight and make visible those structures of oppression that are less apparent to members of more privileged groups.

❖ Gender, Science, and Society

Feminist criticism of women's outsider status in education has been especially important in studying women in science. As one of the areas where women have been most excluded, science has been a strongly gendered institution. In the remainder of this chapter, we look at the status of women in science with a particular eye to what this means for the social construction of knowledge in a society so strongly rooted in scientific thought and discovery.

The Status of Women in Science

Even a cursory look at the position of women in science shows the gender segregation and gender hierarchy of science as an institution. Beginning early in students' learning, boys and girls begin to depart in their expressed interest in math and science (see Figure 10.3). Furthermore, the gap is reflected in course-taking patterns. While more girls are taking science and math courses than before, boys are still more likely to take higher level courses, thus better preparing them for math and science careers. By the college years, gender segregation in the math and science curriculum is high, with women being a significant minority of majors in math and science (except biology). And, except for the social sciences, women are then a relatively small proportion of the scientific workforce (see Figure 10.4). On the positive side, the numbers of women receiving science and math degrees, and therefore being more likely to move into scientific careers, has increased substantially since the 1980s. But science continues to bear the imprint of the fact that most scientists have been men. Increasing the numbers of women in science is one thing, but scholars have also shown that the culture of scientific workplaces (including in industry, research, and academia) is marked by an organizational culture that values the attributes most often associated with men. Thus, women report that they are not often taken seriously and that scientific careers follow a male life course trajectory (such as in the fact that one is expected to do one's best work while still quite young—a time when many will be establishing families). For this reason, feminist scholars have argued that bringing more women into science is not just about num-

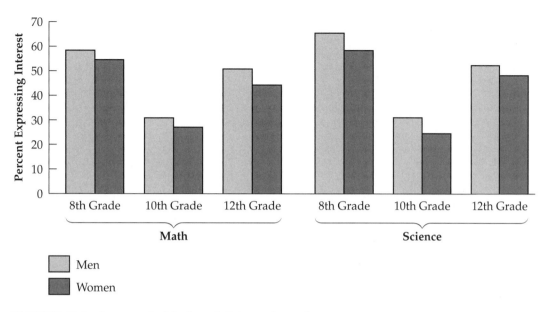

FIGURE 10.3   Interest in Math and Science Learning
(Percentage of 8th-, 10th-, and 12th-graders (1988 cohort in 1988, 1990, and 1992)
who expressed positive attitudes relating to math and science, by gender)

Source: Data from National Center for Education Statistics. 2000. *National Education Longitudinal Study of 1988 Entry and Persistence of Women and Minorities in College Science and Engineering Education.* Washington, DC: U.S. Department of Education.

bers, but also about transforming the culture that marks science as an institution (Fox 2001).

Women are not, of course, absent from science; they constitute a large proportion of the technical, clerical, domestic, teaching, and plant maintenance staffs required to do scientific work. Still, women, and especially women of color, appear as objects and "others" in science; they are exploited as research subjects, and their labor in the production of science remains invisible to the scientific elite. The decision makers in science—those who define scientific problems, set scientific agendas, fund scientific projects, and relate science to public policy—are overwhelmingly men.

Science is produced and applied within a distinctively masculine framework, one that values objective separation from the objects of research and, yet, is nonetheless gendered in the descriptions and explanations it offers of the natural and social worlds. Evelyn Fox Keller calls this a "science/gender" system, a network of associations between our concepts of masculinity and femininity and the construction of science. She argues that to examine the roots, dynamics, and consequences of the science/gender system, it is necessary to understand how ideologies of gender and science inform each other and how this affects social arrangements between men and women, science and nature (Keller 1985).

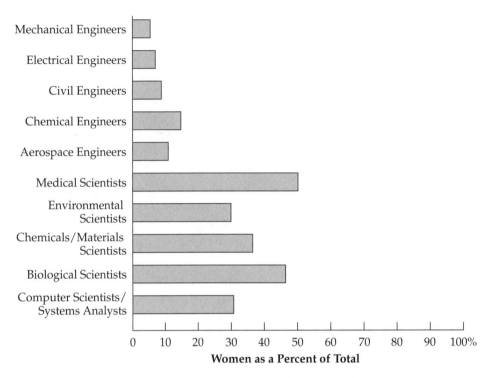

FIGURE 10.4   Women in Science and Engineering Professions

Source: U.S. Department of Labor. 2004. *Employment and Earnings.* Washington, DC: U.S. Department of Labor, p. 209–210.

Asking how and why women have been excluded from the practice of science is one way to reveal deeply embedded gender, race, and class patterns in the structure of scientific professions and consequently in the character of scientific thought. Rossiter's (1982) work on the history of women in science shows that the concept of a woman scientist is perceived as a contradiction in terms, since scientists are supposed to be tough, rigorous, rational, impersonal, unemotional, and competitive, which women are presumed not to be. Often, when women make major contributions to science, their work is ignored, belittled, or claimed by men. A classic example is the discovery of DNA. James Watson, one of the scientists who discovered DNA, tells the story of his and Francis Crick's (a man) discovery in a famous book, *The Double Helix* (1968). The book reviles a woman colleague, Rosalind Franklin, who, it is clear from other accounts, should have shared Watson's and Crick's credit (Sayre 1975).

Sometimes women's exclusion from science is not only as scientists but also as subjects of scientific research. In the early 1990s, for example, several reports published in medical journals and reported in the national press documented the exclusion of women from major national health studies of heart disease, lung cancer, and kidney disease. As a result, a federal law was passed requiring researchers using federal funds to analyze the effects of new drugs and treatments on women. But a report issued in 2000 indicated that researchers often skirt the law, thereby producing conclusions that cannot be generalized to the whole population (Pear 2001). Extrapolating from studies of men to the treatment of women leads to potentially faulty treatment. Men and women sometimes report different symptoms of the same disease, and some treatments may be more effective for one group than another. For example, although women suffer from depression more than do men, much of the research on antidepressant drugs has involved only male research subjects. Treating women based on the results of research from all male samples can be risky.

Science, Feminism, and the Social Construction of Knowledge

Understanding the relationship between the gendered structure of institutions (such as education) and how knowledge is constructed within these institutions is key to understanding the critique of science that has emerged from feminist studies. Scientific knowledge in our society is seen as a source of great authority. Scientific careers carry much prestige, and scientists have a great deal of power to influence the everyday experiences of our lives. Scientific explanations are generally thought to be objective accounts that are uninfluenced by the values and interests of scientific thinkers. Science thus has the image of being value neutral and true to the facts. Objectivity in science is depicted as stemming from the calculated distance between the observer and the observed. In the scientific framework, personal characteristics of scientific observers are not expected to influence their results.

Despite the strong claims of neutrality and objectivity by scientists, the fact is that science is closely tied to the centers of power in this society and interwoven with capitalist and patriarchal institutions. This has many implications for understanding the social structure of science as well as for understanding how the social structure of science influences the production of scientific knowledge. As you have already seen, allegedly scientific claims are often used to support sexist and racist beliefs. One could argue that such claims are simply a case of bad science, but feminist critiques of scientific knowledge go deeper, asking how the social structure of scientific professions is related to the scientific views and conclusions scientists make.

Many argue (Fee 1983; Harding 1986, 1991, 1993, 1998) that gender identity is at the very heart of the definition of science because scientific norms of detachment, distance, and rationality match those of masculine culture. Feminist critiques of science also reveal that scientific thought often reflects the patriarchal ideology of the culture. One way this happens is through the projection of patriarchal values onto scientific descriptions of the physical world. For example, kingdoms and orders are not intrinsic to the nature of organisms but have evolved in a patriarchal world that values hierarchy and patrilineage (Hubbard 1984). Note, also, the description of the experimental **scientific method** offered by Francis Bacon, one of the sixteenth-century founders of modern scientific thought:

> *For you have but to follow and as it were hound nature in her wanderings, and you will be able when you like to lead and drive her afterward to the same place again. . . . Neither ought a man to make scruple of entering and penetrating into those holes and*

corners, when the inquisition of truth is his whole object (cited in Harding 1986:116).

The emergence of modern science is founded on an image of rational man as conquering the passions of nature, which is depicted as female. Consider Machiavelli's famed quotation regarding fortune:

Fortune is a woman and it is necessary if you wish to master her to conquer her by force; and it can be seen that she lets herself be overcome by the bold rather than by those who proceed coldly, and therefore like a woman, she is always a friend to the young because they are less cautious, fiercer, and master her with greater audacity (from The Prince; cited in Harding 1986:115).

Such depictions of science and nature might be dismissed as old-fashioned ramblings of patriarchal days gone by, except for the fact that gendered descriptions of biological phenomena still influence the way we imagine physical events. Think, for example, of sperm, popularly depicted as lively and aggressive swimmers, rigorously pursuing the waiting egg. Alice Rossi describes this as a fantasy of male sexual power. She writes:

Ever since Leewenhoek first saw sperm under the microscope, great significance has been attached to the fact that sperm are equipped with motile flagella, and it was assumed that the locomotive ability of the sperm fully explained their journey from the vagina through the cervix and uterus to the oviduct for the encounter with the ovum. . . . Rorvik (1971) describes the seven-inch journey through the birth canal and womb to the waiting egg as equivalent to a 500-mile upstream swim for a salmon and comments with admiration that they often make the hazardous journey in under an hour, "more than earning their title as the most powerful and rapid living creatures on earth." The image is clear: powerful active sperm and a passive ovum awaiting its arrival and penetration, male sexual imagery structuring the very act of conception (1977: 16–17).

In fact, as Rossi points out, uterine contractions, stimulated by the release of the hormone oxytocin, propel the sperm through the female system so that "completely inert substances such as dead sperm and even particles of India ink reach the oviducts as rapidly as live sperm do" (Rossi 1977:17).

In her study analyzing the images of reproduction in contemporary biology textbooks, Emily Martin, an anthropologist, has found that sperm are still described as active, aggressive agents, while eggs are portrayed in passive terms. According to Martin, the texts stress that sperm are actively produced, while female ova "merely sit on the shelf, slowly degenerating and aging like an overstocked inventory" (1991:487). Citing text authors, Martin writes that texts liken the egg's role to that of Sleeping Beauty: "a dormant bride awaiting her mate's magic kiss, which instills the spirit that brings her to life." Sperm, by contrast, have a "mission," which is to "move through the female genital tract in quest of the ovum." One popular account has it that the sperm carry out a "perilous journey" into the "warm darkness," where some fall away "exhausted." "Survivors" "assault" the egg, the successful candidates "surrounding the prize" (1991: 490).

The fact is, sperm do not merely penetrate a passive egg; rather, the sperm and egg stick together because of adhesive molecules on the surface of each. Nor are sperm as mobile as their descriptions suggest. Despite knowledge to the contrary, metaphorical descriptions of the biological reproductive process make the event seem like a contemporary soap opera or moral fable. As Martin illustrates, the descriptions used by scientists have prevented them from seeing how eggs and sperm actually interact. Thus, cultural values influence the discovery of scientific facts (Bordo 1995).

The point is not to abandon science, but to understand that within scientific studies, bias can enter the scientist's choice of topic, choice of research subjects, definitions of concepts, method of observation, analysis and interpretation of data, and manner of reporting (Longino and Doell 1983; Messing 1983). Gendered assumptions infiltrate the scientific record; many of the "truths" alleged by scientific studies merely reflect the interests of a male-dominated society. Feminist revisions of science call for a more inclusive and reflective perspective by recognizing the interplay between scientific knowledge and the social systems in which science is produced. Feminist revisions of science also seek a more humanistic science, one in which science is used for human liberation from race, class, and gender oppression.

Social experience and consciousness are conditioned by the location of our existence. Because men and women have quite different life situations, their consciousness, culture, and ideas are also different. As Dorothy Smith (1987, 1990) argues, the activity of women (and, by implication, men) forms the basis for their ideas. Because sex/gender systems organize social relations and because intellectual thought is shaped by social relations, the sex/gender system shapes our perspectives as social thinkers and researchers.

Epistemology refers to the ways of knowing that form systems of social thought. This idea emphasizes that knowledge is socially constructed and that ways of thinking are embedded in a variety of assumptions, implicit and explicit, that guide their shape and form. Feminist epistemology, a relatively recent development in feminist theory, is the examination of how gender relations shape the production of thought, including feminist theory itself. Feminist epistemology raises new questions, both about the systems of thinking that have been derived from androcentric (i.e., male-centered) ways of knowing and about new ways of constructing knowledge to be more inclusive of and centered in women's experiences.

One major area of discussion in feminist epistemology is the social construction of science, a particularly important subject because of the deep and central ways that scientific knowledge shapes Western ways of knowing. In the seventeenth century, as modern science began, scientific inquiry was justified for its specific social value; moreover, the legitimacy of scientific inquiry rested on the same principles of reform that today sound like feminist social practices—antiauthoritarianism, progressiveness, antielitism, educational reform, humanitarianism, and the unity of experience and knowing (Van Den Daele 1977). Contemporary debates about the social and political application of scientific knowledge (such as the examples of nuclear energy and the atomic bomb) also indicate that even in scientific circles the question of scientific purpose is not separate from the practice of scientific inquiry.

Historically, the scientific movement also emerged in specific opposition to the canons of traditional belief, especially as a challenge to the state and the political authority of the church. As historians of science write, "The breakdown of older patterns of authority and traditionally-held dogmas or consensus positions allows much broader boundaries for exploration and the staking out of positions previously proscribed—either tacitly or implicitly" (Mendelsohn et al. 1977:10). By removing the blinders of earlier commitments, scientists have argued that more objective inquiry would provide the new facts and new perspectives needed to meet the needs of emerging social institutions.

Feminists argue that the neutral claims of traditional scholarship mask nonobjective interpretations of women's lives that have been produced. According to feminist inquiry, new perspectives on women's lives—specifically ones that challenge sexist assumptions—will result in more accurate explanations of women's experiences. Feminists still use scientific methods in their studies, but they claim that their work is more objective because it is more inclusive of all persons' experiences.

A central question in feminist scholarship is the issue of objectivity and its relationship to the process of knowing (Harding 1986, 1991, 1998). According to standard arguments about sociological research, rigorous observation and the use of the scientific method eliminate observer bias, but feminists argue that the observer is not a neutral party. Because knowledge is socially produced, the particular experiences and attitudes that observers bring to their work influence what they study, how they study it, and what they conclude about it. Untangling the relationship between the knower and the known is essential, according to feminist scientists. Smith (1990) and Hartsock (1983) note that all research is done from a particular standpoint or location in the social system. The world is known from the perspective of the researcher. In any given research project, we must know both the subjects' and the researcher's points of entry to the project. Most often, sociologists enter research projects through official institutions (e.g., schools, police, social welfare agencies, etc.); consequently, the work they do may support the status quo and be distorted by the view of official agencies. Smith suggests, then, that most objective inquiries can be produced only by those with the least interest in preserving the status quo.

She explains this idea by using an example from the German philosopher Hegel. Suppose we want to comprehend the world of a master and a slave. Both of them live in the same world, but their experience within that world is quite different. The master takes the slave's labor (in fact, the slave's very existence) for granted; thus, the master's needs are immediately satisfied through slave labor. The slave, on the other hand, conforms to the master's will; his or her labor is an object of the master's consciousness. The organization of this relationship is invisible to the master. If the master were describing the world they both inhabit, the master's account would be less objective because the structures of that world are invisible to him or her. The slave's description of the world, on the other hand, would include the master, plus the fact of his or her own labor and its transformation to the status of an object. As a result, the slave is more objective because his or her account is both more complete and more directly related to the empirical events within the relationship and the world in which it is located.

When we begin describing the world by examining women's experiences, the knowledge we create does not merely add to the already established constructs of sociological thought. The experience of women, like that of the slave, has been invisible. Women inhabit the same world as men; in fact, women's labor shapes men's experience in the world (through housework and the maintenance of social and bodily relations). Women's labor makes men's mode of operation, detached and rational, possible; yet, it remains invisible to men as the dominant class. An objective sociological account of reality must make sense of both women's and men's experiences and must therefore be constructed from the vantage point of both.

Smith (1987) also argues that sociological research and theory must situate social actors within their everyday worlds. In other words, unless research begins with the ordinary facts of lives, then the knowledge that sociologists construct will be both alienating and apart from the actual experiences of human actors. Sociological analysis begins with the immediate experience of social actors, but goes beyond that experience by discovering the social—institutional context of their lives. Although the institutional context of everyday experience is not immediately visible to those who live it, the sociological perspective makes this context available and thus is a powerful agent of social change. Like the perspective of C. Wright Mills, Smith's objective is to establish the relationship between social structure and everyday life. This relationship is especially important in comprehending women's experiences, because the affairs of everyday life are the specific area of women's expertise. Given the gender division of labor, women are charged with maintaining everyday life. To overlook that fact or to treat it as insignificant is to deny women's reality (Reinharz 1983; Smith 1987).

Feminist **standpoint theory** suggests that the specific social location of the knower shapes what is known and that not all perspectives are equally valid or complete. Again, think of the master and the slave. Because the master takes the slave's existence for granted, the master cannot see the world as the slave sees it—including the world that constructs the relationship of the master and the slave. The slave's view is not as partial, or as incomplete, as that of the master, and it is likely to produce a less distorted account of the world in which both the slave and the master live.

Likewise, feminist standpoint theory argues that women's specific location in patriarchal societies is actually a resource in the construction of new knowledge (Harding 1991, 1998; Collins 1998). This does not result from the biological fact of being a woman but from the unique experience of women as an oppressed group confronting a patriarchal society. Standpoint theory assumes that systems of privilege are least visible to those who benefit the most from them and who, at the same time, control the resources that define dominant belief systems. Whites, for example, are more likely to deny that racism exists; people of color both see the assaults racism produce and understand the nuances of racism in everyday life. Similarly, men can more easily deny the presence of patriarchy than can women, even when women do not fully grasp the workings of sexist oppression. It takes the standpoint of oppressed groups to see and recognize systems of race, class, and gender privilege. Dominant groups can, of course, learn to see how race, gender, and class privilege structure social relations, but they do so through analysis and observation, not simply from the conditions of their own experience.

Standpoint theory does not mean that we have to take the word of oppressed groups at face value to know how society is structured. Systems of oppression also shape the consciousness of the oppressed. Theory constructed from the observed experiences of dominant and subordinate groups yields the insight that produces liberating knowledge.

❖ Chapter Summary and Themes

Historically, education has been defined as the privilege of a few, but the growth of public education has, over time, been extended to diverse groups.

Initially public education was intended to inculcate dominant group values among immigrant groups. Denying women's education was justified by ideologies that promoted biologically determinist arguments about women's abilities to learn.

Although women are now a majority of students at virtually every level of public education, a gender gap persists in various dimensions of the schooling experiences.

A hidden curriculum in schools is part of the gender socialization that produces different educational outcomes for women and men. Women become segregated into particular fields of education and still fall behind in education that leads to careers in math and science.

Women in higher education, although a majority of the students, are segregated into particular fields and, as faculty, have not achieved equity with men.

An educational pyramid shows that the higher one goes in education, the less likely one will find women—as students or as faculty. Although women are making many gains, they are still marginalized within higher education. These patterns are exacerbated for women of color.

Scientific fields are still largely perceived as the world of men, although women have been making some inroads.

Patterns of gender exclusion in the sciences begin early in schooling and are reflected in the lower percentages of women, compared to men, who enter scientific careers.

Feminist scholars have identified scientific knowledge as socially constructed through masculine imagery, thus distorting what is scientifically known.

Feminist standpoint theory suggests that the social location of knowers shapes what is known, including in the sciences. This perspective suggests that only with the greater inclusion of those who have been excluded can objective scientific knowledge be created.

❖ Key Terms

digital divide	self-esteem	stereotype threat
epistemology	self-fulfilling prophecy	Title IX
scientific method	standpoint theory	tracking

❖ Discussion Questions/Projects for Thought

1. Find out what the proportion of women is compared with men in your school, as well as the areas of study that each group pursues. Do you see evidence of gender segregation in education? If so, what explains it, and do you think this is changing over time?

2. Interview a group of young girls in elementary school, junior high school, and high school and ask about their interests in science and math. Do you see evidence of change in scientific interests over time? What do you think explains this?

3. Identify one of the other courses you are taking and examine the textbook to see where women are included and/or excluded. What does this tell you about the construction of knowledge in that field?

❖ Internet Resources

National Women's Studies Association

http://www.nwsa.org

The National Women's Studies Association is dedicated to feminist teaching, learning, research, and service at all levels of education. They publish a journal, hold conferences, and award various scholarships, information about which can be found on their website.

Women's Educational Equity Association (WEEA) Equity Resource Center

http://www.edc.org/womensequity/

Established by the Women's Educational Equity Act of 1974, this resource center was created to support the education of girls and women in the United States. WEEA's mission focuses on gender equity and is centered in the belief that gender equity benefits all groups. They publish materials, offer training for educators, conduct research, and maintain a network of organizations committed to equity in education.

National Center for Educational Statistics

http://www.nces.ed.gov

This site includes the Digest of Educational Statistics and other national data on educational attainment at all levels. It is a useful source of national information about women, men, and education.

Association for Women in Science

http://www.awis.org

This is an organization that promotes equity for women in science, mathematics, engineering, and technology. The website includes various publications and statistics on women in science, as well as job listings, a mentor net, and other resources to promote women's scientific careers.

❖ Suggested Readings

Eder, Donna, Catherine Colleen Evans, and Stephen Parker. 1995. *School Talk: Gender and Adolescent Culture.* New Brunswick, NJ: Rutgers University Press.

These researchers examine how the informal relations within schools construct gender identities for adolescent girls and boys. The study emphasizes the significance of language in shaping young people's gender beliefs.

Ferguson, Ann Arnett. 2000. *Bad Boys: Public School in the Making of Black Masculinity.* Ann Arbor, MI: University of Michigan Press.
Ferguson examines how young Black boys construct their gender and race identity in the context of schools that fail them. She shows how interactions in school and the institutional practices of the school lead the boys into trouble as they construct a sense of self in an unjust world.

Harding, Sandra. 1998. *Is Science Multicultural? Postcolonialisms, Feminisms, and Epistemologies.* Bloomington, IN: Indiana University Press.
Harding's work is known for elaborating feminist standpoint theory and for challenging the patriarchal biases in Western science. This book explores the scientific knowledge emerging from different cultural traditions and proposes thinking about science in ways that will support the liberation of groups often distorted or abused by scientific work.

Lim, Shirley Geok-Lin, and María Herrera-Sobek, eds. 2000. *Power, Race, and Gender in Academe: Strangers in the Tower?* New York: Modern Language Association.
This book includes essays about the exclusion that women, particularly women of color, experience on the faculty of colleges and universities. The essays explore the organizational practices and cultures that perpetuate exclusionary practices within higher education.

Sadker, Myra, and David Sadker. 1994. *Failing at Fairness: How America's Schools Cheat Girls.* New York: Scribners.
This important book reviews the treatment of girls in school, their academic progress, and their representation in the curriculum.

Smith, Dorothy E. 1990. *The Conceptual Practices of Power.* Boston: Northeastern University Press.
Smith's work as a sociologist has defined feminist standpoint theory from a sociological point of view. She also analyzes how traditional sociological scholarship has developed from an androcentric perspective.

Thorne, Barrie. 1993. *Gender Play: Girls and Boys in School.* New Brunswick, NJ: Rutgers University Press.
Thorne's study, based on extensive observations of boys and girls in school, examines how children's interactions in school shape their thinking about gender and their gender identities. She includes useful information for teachers on practices that are likely to generate greater gender equity in the classroom.

Weis, Lois, and Michelle Fine, eds. 1993. *Beyond Silenced Voices: Class, Race, and Gender in U.S. Schools.* Albany: State University of New York Press.
The essays in this collection challenge the policies and practices that exclude women and racial ethnic groups from a good education. In some of the essays students write about the race, class, and gender relations that they encounter in schools.

WOMEN, POWER, AND POLITICS

Defining Power

Women and the State

Women and the Law

Women in Government
   The Gender Gap
   Do Women Make a Difference?

Women and the Military
   Lesbians and Gays in the Military
   Feminism and Militarism

Rethinking the Political

The Women's Movement
   American Feminism in the
   Nineteenth Century

The Emergence of the
   Contemporary Women's
   Movement
Feminism and Civil Rights
The Second Wave of Feminism
Feminism for the Twenty-First
   Century: A Third Wave?

Chapter Summary and Themes

Key Terms

**Discussion Questions/
Projects for Thought**

Internet Resources

Suggested Readings

If you want to learn about the presumed place for women in politics, all you have to do is think about the presumably proper role for the nation's First Lady. First Ladies (a term that is itself laden with sexist connotations) are generally adored when they take on a traditional helpmate role—supporting their man, staying in the background, and focusing on concerns traditionally identified for women (children, education, and mental health). Thus, Laura Bush, widely popular, is rarely in the foreground and is, instead, most often seen accompanying her husband and sweetly smiling at him; she is praised for her traditional behaviors.

And, if you want to see how the image of First Ladies in traditional terms is reinforced, think of what happens when presidents' or candidates' wives act otherwise. When Hillary Rodham Clinton was appointed to head a national task force to reform health care, she was vilified for trying to share power with her husband. During the presidential campaign of 2004, Judy Steinberg—a practicing physician and candidate Howard Dean's wife—was ridiculed for wearing flat shoes and little makeup, for wanting a rhododendron for her birthday, and, most especially, for wanting to maintain her career should her husband be elected. Because of her independence, she was actually defined as a liability in her husband's campaign. Likewise, Teresa Heinz Kerry, married to Senator John Kerry, was publicly scorned for presumably being too outspoken in her feminist beliefs and independent style.

Women have, of course, made extraordinary contributions in the realm of politics—both historically and now. So why does such intolerance of independent women persist? How do these traditional gender beliefs affect women's political behavior and their place in political institutions?

Since the 1990s, record numbers of women have been elected to national office, and women are increasingly visible in mainstream politics. More women serve in the U.S. Senate than at any time in history—14 of 100, but enough that in 1992 the Senate had to be remodeled because there was no bathroom for women near the Senate floor. Although women are reaching new heights of political power, old attitudes and stereotypes remain.

Feminist scholars have shown how deeply gender influences political behavior, political attitudes, and the structure of political institutions. Gender shapes power and politics, although the dominant construction of gender in politics has been resisted and fought by the many women who have organized politically to create social change. The feminist movement, also called the women's movement, has been one of the most powerful forces of social change in our times, and women have also been critical in the mobilization of other movements—the civil rights movement, the environmental movement, and antiwar movements. As you read about women, gender, and political behavior, you should keep this resistance in mind. It is evidence of the capacity of women—and men—to make change even in the face of what seems to be an intractable.

❖ *Defining Power*

Power has traditionally been believed to be the province of men. Indeed, judging by some indicators, this has changed very little—just notice how few women are heads of state, particularly in the major world powers. Women, instead, are seen as exercising power primarily at home (a myth exposed by considering men's power in the family; see Chapter 6). Women have also been stereotyped as holding the "power behind the throne," as if women's power comes primarily from their presumed manipulation of men and as if women's primary political role is to remain invisible and out of public view.

Sociologists define **power** as the ability to influence others. Power comes in many forms. It can be exercised by individuals or groups and within and outside of formal social institutions. Power can come through persuasion, charisma, law, political activism, and coercion. It is not just an individual attribute, even though some individuals may be more powerful than others. Power in society comes as the result of a social process and social relationships; the use of power cannot be understood without reference to this social context. To explain further, although an individual may have characteristics that make him or her more powerful (i.e., the person's race, gender, age, religion, social class, education, etc.), it is the value that society has placed on these characteristics that gives the person power. Moreover, exercising power means people have to be situated such that they can mobilize the resources needed to influence others.

Consider men's power. Feminists describe men's power as a system of **patriarchy,** meaning an organized social structure whereby men as a group hold more power than women. Patriarchal societies give men power and authority over women; this can be institutional and/or individual. Societies will differ in exactly how patriarchal power is structured. For example, in a monarchy, an individual man (e.g., as a king or an emperor) may have ultimate power and authority. In a democratic society, power is determined through law and the various regulatory institutions that uphold and enforce the law. If men control the law-making process and the institutions that implement the law, however, they hold institutional power. In this sense, patriarchy becomes part of the structure of the society, even if power is not held by a single or particular man. In such a system, patriarchy structures the many social institutions that regulate and determine the nature of women's lives. In this sense, the United States is a patriarchal society.

Men's power does not stem from the mere fact of their being biologically male, nor does having institutions that are patriarchal mean that every individual man is a patriarch. Patriarchy in an institutional sense means that social institutions have been organized over time to give men more advantage than women (recognizing that this advantage is also influenced by other factors, such as one's social class, religion, race, etc.). It is the structural supports given to men's power that constitute the institutional basis of patriarchy.

To understand this, think about the subject of marital violence. Feminists explain men's violence against women as an expression of men's power, a power manifested in the actual marital relationship where violence occurs. Beyond the relationship between these two people, feminists have pointed out, other institutions are organized to support men's power. Women who turn to these institutions for help often find that the system does not work on their behalf. Understanding violence against women, then, is a matter of understanding both individual power relationships and institutional power relationships.

Power is not all one-sided, however. People can mobilize to challenge existing power arrangements in society, and individuals can work to create more egalitarian relationships. Power does not come only from within existing institutions. People can mobilize to alter the structural supports that give power to some groups and not others; thus, social movements and other forms of political action are means of challenging and transforming the status quo. While the existing system may give certain power resources to certain groups, people can develop the resources to alter social institutions. Power can come through mobilization of vast numbers of people (such as in mass movements); through effective use of strategies such as boycotts, civil disobedience, or media campaigns; and through the exercise of law, including, if needed, legal reforms. Although groups can be described as more or less powerful than others, these forms of political action can change the circumstances even of those considered to be the most powerless. The women's movement, as an example, has mobilized women and men to make a number of changes that have altered the power that women hold both as a group and as individuals. Likewise, the civil rights movement involved the mass mobilization of African American people who were otherwise quite powerless—unable to vote, unable to use public accommodations, and without access to the best educational institutions. Although as a group Whites still hold more power than do people of color and men as a group hold more power than do women, these political movements have altered the power base of race and gender in the United States.

Sociologists also distinguish the concepts of power and authority. **Authority** is power that is perceived by others as legitimate and that is structured into specific social institutions. Authority comes not just because a person or group exercises power, but because their constituents believe their power is legitimate and because there are institutional supports in place that make this authority legitimate. The recognition of authority varies across societies, depending on the structure of that society. In a monarchy, for example, the king or queen has authority over all matters; in a totalitarian society, the dictator or emperor has total authority over all affairs. In a democratic society based on the rule of law, the law serves as the system of authority, with those who interpret and execute it as the primary agents of authority. One of the further consequences of patriarchy is the tendency to see men and men's activities as more authoritative in the areas deemed to be most important.

❖ *Women and the State*

The institution that embodies the official power system is the *state*. Sociologists use the term **state** to refer to the organized system of power and authority in society. This is different from the ordinary meaning of the term as a geographic area (e.g., California, Missouri, or Georgia). As a concept, the state refers to all of the institutions that represent official power and authority in society. The state regulates many societal relations, ranging from individual behavior and interpersonal conflicts to international affairs. Different institutions make up the state, including formal systems of government, the military, the courts and the law.

Feminist thinking about the state begins from the premise that an analysis of gender is critical to understanding the state. Feminists see the state as a *gendered institution*—that is, an institution that embeds within it the characteristics associated with a particular gender. Feminists conceive of the state as embodying the masculine characteristics of presumed rationality, detachment, power, forcefulness, and impersonality. As one of the most bureaucratic of all institutions, the state operates as if it were neutral, when, in fact, according to feminists, it is organized on quite gender-specific grounds. Not surprisingly, then, some of the specific institutions comprising the state (e.g., the military and the police) are the most masculine (in the cultural sense) and male-dominated of all social institutions.

Because the state represents the imposition of power and authority in society, it is characterized by feminists as representing men's interests more than women's. Furthermore, it is an imposing force in many women's lives. Women on welfare, for example, have the state intruding in their affairs more than happens for women with more class privilege. The state may regulate how one lives, whether one is forced to work, how one cares for children, and what kind of health care is available. For all women, the state is also a source for laws that govern many features of everyday life, ranging from reproductive rights to rights to work and rights for equal protection.

Two primary theoretical models have been used by social scientists to explain how the state operates. The first, the **pluralism** model, sees the state as representing the plural interests of different groups in society. According to this model, the state tries to balance the different interest groups in society. Interest groups are those that are organized around a specific cause or purpose, such as the National Gay and Lesbian Task Force, the National Women's Political Caucus, the National Abortion Rights Action League (NARAL), Planned Parenthood, and the National Organization for Women (NOW). This model interprets the state as representing the diverse interest groups in society. These groups mobilize to achieve political results and use their influence to achieve their political ends.

The other model of the state is known as the **power elite.** According to this perspective, a powerful ruling class controls the actions of the state. The power elite consists of those who hold power in the economy, the executive branch of the government, and the military. Elites in these institutions share common interests and shape the political agendas in the society. Since this powerful group is primarily men, the power elite model represents men's interests as shaping the major decisions in society. This model also sees a strong alliance between government and corporate business, since the power elite, through their role in government, shape decisions that protect the interests of big business. The power elite model sees the state as part of the structure of domination in society, including gender domination, racial domination, and class domination.

Feminists have supplemented these models of state theory with the argument that the state essentially reflects men's interests, not only because men are those most likely to be in the power elite but also because men control most of the major interest groups that influence the workings of the state. Feminist theory sees the state as fundamentally patriarchal—that is, representing the power of men over women. Some have concluded that despite the presence of some women in positions of authority in the state, on the whole, the state promotes men's interests. As Catharine MacKinnon, a noted feminist legal scholar, puts it, "the state is male" (1983:644).

The argument that "the state is male" can be vividly seen if you just looked at a photograph of national leadership. Although women are increasingly present in elected offices, if you took a group photo of the President and his cabinet, the Supreme Court, all of the Congress, and the nation's governors, you would mostly see White, middle-aged and older men in dark suits. And, if you also looked at a photograph of the world's leadership—all heads of state—you would also find surprisingly few women.

Ironically, although some feminists analyze the state as essentially oppressive to women because the state represents men's interests, feminists also see the state as the only institution to which disadvantaged groups can turn for redress. Both the women's movement and the civil rights movement have used state power to enforce existing laws or to work to change the law. While the state can (and does) support gender inequality—for example, by denying women the right to vote or, as was the case in the early history of this country, denying women the right to speak in public—the state is also the institution that guarantees women equal protection under the law. Legislation that has brought women civil rights, defined sexual harassment as illegal, and provided some degree of reproductive freedom has been developed through the state. It is important to point out, however, that this state action has come only as the result of political mobilization by feminist groups.

❖ Women and the Law

Law is the written system through which state authority is defined; thus, the study of law is extremely significant in feminist analysis. Like the state, the law is both a source for the denial of women's rights and one of the avenues to which feminists have turned to address the problems of women's inequality. Significant scholarship in women's studies has developed both to describe the changes in law that have stemmed from the women's movement and to understand the process by which the law has encoded men's interests. Feminist legal scholars have also developed the analysis of feminist jurisprudence—that is, they have developed studies of law that interpret the law as reflecting men's power but that try to revise legal doctrine to be consistent with feminist theory and practice. These studies have shown that although the law is a significant source of change for women, it is also limited in its ability to transform women's lives (Baer 1998; Crenshaw et al. 1996).

Since the 1960s, women's position relative to the law has changed dramatically. Whereas historically the law officially excluded women from full citizenship, now the law has taken a neutral position on gender. Early on, there was no protection for those women who departed from traditional roles in family. Laws overtly prohibited women from entering certain professions and treated men and women differently at every level. The Equal Pay Act of 1963, which required equal pay for equal work, was the first law to begin breaking this discriminatory framework. Strengthened by the Civil Rights Bill of 1964 and subsequent pieces of legislation, the law now, at least in theory, gives women equal civil rights to men.

As they are written, laws provide some basis for the equal treatment of men and women before the law. How the law is interpreted and implemented, however, may be another matter. Even with an equal rights framework in place, executing the law is a function of many sociological factors, including how police, lawyers, and judges interpret and execute the law and how the legal system is structured to give legal advantage to some groups and not others.

On the first point, feminists have pointed out that women are underrepresented among those who are responsible for interpreting and exercising the law. As lawyers, women have dramatically increased their representation in recent years, now comprising 28 percent of lawyers. Women lawyers are more likely to practice some areas of law than others, and although they are more widely distributed across legal specialties than in the past, they are more likely to work in the least prestigious area of public service law, where salaries are also lower (Epstein 1993; U.S. Department of Labor 2004).

Women are about 20 percent of judges. Judges, like lawyers, have considerable power in the interpretation of the law. The fact that women are underrepresented as judges means that in practice the law likely embodies men's perspectives and values—even though the law and its execution are allegedly neutral. This has been a major point in feminist analyses of the law, since it gets to the crux of how some feminists see the law as encoding men's power. Do women judges matter? Some think that women would bring a unique perspective to the bench as a result of their presumably different gender perspective (Coontz 2000). The evidence is mixed. While some studies actually find that women impose harsher sentences on criminal defendants (Steffensmeier and Hebert 1999), other research finds that gender of the judge is less important than such things as severity of the offense, the victim's gender and age, and the defendant's prior record (Bogoch 1999b; Neilson 2002). Women judges are less likely to support death penalty verdicts, and their presence on the bench also seems to influence male judges not to support death penalty verdicts (Songer and Crewes-Meyer 2000). Where women judges seem to make a great difference is in cases involving gender equality and battering and abuse (Martin et al. 2002). Studies find that judges now, regardless of their gender, are less likely to blame battered women for their own abuse, indicative of some of the progress made by the women's movement in the realm of judicial reasoning (Cassidy and Trafinow 2002). The rationale that women should serve on the bench because they bring a different perspective to the administration of justice may not hold up, but it is certainly the case that a judiciary that does not itself represent gender equality is suspect in a democratic society (Malleson 2003).

Feminist critique of the law has generated the question: Are equal rights enough? As you will see in Chapter 12 on liberal feminism, although many feminists take the position that creating equal rights for women is the best strategy for social change, others argue that this strategy neither recognizes the different conditions of women's lives that make unique solutions for women necessary nor addresses the fundamental ways that gender, race, and class structure the basic institutions of society, including courts and the law. Some feminists have also raised the question of whether treating everyone the same under the law is appropriate, given women's unique life experiences. For example, should women be given special treatment before the law for pregnancy and maternity? This is a source of debate within the feminist literature. Some feminists, for instance, have been opposed to protective legislation that has excluded pregnant women from certain occupations (see Chapter 7). Under current law, maternity has no special place; it is defined as a disability. Is this an adequate framework for the legal protection of pregnant women?

Beyond these questions of whether women should be treated the same or differently by the law are more radical questions. Some feminists have argued that the presumed neutrality of the law is problematic for women, because under the guise of legal neutrality, the law protects men's power.

As an example, consider rape law. First, most state laws define rape as occurring only when penetration has taken place—a definition that feminists would argue takes a phallocentric position, as if sexual intercourse has only taken place when a man inserts himself (or an object) into a woman. In addition, despite changes in actual law, women are still sexualized during rape trials; men are not. In rape cases, the law also makes consent the crux of whether the assailant is guilty, thereby making most rape trials as much a trial for the victim as for the rapist. In a society where women are defined as sexual objects, any number of factors can influence whether consent is perceived by the police, the defense attorney, the judge, or the jury. A woman is easily discredited on the issue of consent, particularly if she had been drinking or was under the influence of drugs at the time of the assault or if she had any prior relationship (including marriage) with the assailant. What the woman was wearing, where she was walking, how she earns her income, and any number of other factors influence people's judgments about consent.

What if a different standard existed in the law and woman's consent was not the most significant issue? For example, how would rape laws and trials be different if men's dominance was the major point to prove? This is the kind of thinking that feminist scholars consider when they argue that the law, presumably neutral, is masculine in its very framework.

Finally, feminists also argue that the legal method reflects masculinist culture. Legal interrogation is adversarial, based on rational argument, outdoing one's opponent, and arguing minute details. Think again of a rape trial; the method of interrogation is so masculine that rape victims report that the trial feels like a repetition of the rape. Some feminists have concluded that the legal method—debate and argument—is a masculine mode of thinking and acting. The reliance on former precedent and case law also replicates gender inequities, because this reliance gives weight to tradition without looking at the gendered context in which that tradition was constructed.

In sum, feminist studies of the law have both analyzed the legal reforms that have produced more equity for women and, as well, have criticized the gendered basis of the law. As you will see in the chapters to come, different theoretical and political positions underlie feminist arguments and form a substantive debate around the use of the law as a framework for liberating social change for women.

❖ Women in Government

One way to change women's standing before the law is to increase the number of women who are lawmakers; thus, one of the major feminist political strategies in recent years has been to expand the number of women serving in public political office. In the past, women were explicitly barred from political office. In the early history of the nation, political rights were based on birth, property, age, and religion. Basic political rights that have defined this nation as democratic were not originally extended to women; women were denied rights to free speech and property, and the right to assemble. They were effectively excluded from participating—not just as political officials, but in sharing the same political rights as White men. When the American Revolution gave universal suffrage to White men, women were officially denied the right to vote (Darcy et al. 1994:8).

With this history behind us, feminists now ask why there continue to be so few women elected to formal political office in the United States. Compared with most other democratic, industrialized nations, women in the United States are an amazingly small number of elected officials (see Figure 11.1), although women's representation in government has been increasing (see Figure 11.2). The number of women in the U.S. House of Representatives reached an all-time high in 2005 (65 women of 435 members); 14 women (the historic high) serve with 86 men in the Senate. Although these numbers have increased and reached record highs, women are still a small portion of the national Congress.

Women fare somewhat better in statewide offices; in 2005, 22 percent of state legislators and nine governors were women (Center for the American Woman and Politics 2004). This means that matters of greatest national importance are still determined mostly by men. Since holding a state office is also typically a route to mobility in the political system, being underrepresented there has consequences for women's likelihood of being elected to higher office.

Why are there so few women elected officials? Research offers a number of possible explanations. One explanation is that sheer prejudice has taught people to think that women are not well suited to politics. This is reflected in the attitude that women do not have the personality characteristics that suit them for politics. Although only a small minority of people in the United States explicitly believe this, the attitude persists in some people's minds.

As late as 2001, 20 percent of men and 14 percent of women said that the country would be governed worse if women were in charge. Those who identify as conservative and those who are Republican are less likely than liberals and Democrats to think having more women in politics would be beneficial for the country (see

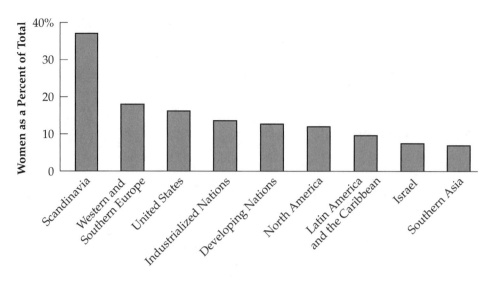

FIGURE 11.1   Women's Representation in National Legislatures

Source: The Waterglass, April 28, 2004. www.thewaterglass.net.

Figure 11.3). Still, attitudes are changing. Young people (those between age 18 and 49) are especially likely to think there would be benefits from electing more women to office (55 percent of men in this age group think so, compared with 70 percent of women). And, although neither of the two major parties has even nominated a woman for president, 87 percent of Americans say they would vote for a woman if she were nominated—an increase from 66 percent in 1971 and only 33 percent in 1937 when the question was first asked in a national survey. Among young people, support is even higher (Jones and Moore 2003).

A second explanation of the small number of women in politics is that gender-stereotyped socialization does not encourage women to see themselves as potential political candidates. A large number of people think that women do not enter politics because as girls growing up, they are not encouraged to do so. One-third of the public still think that men are emotionally better-suited for politics than most women (General Social Survey 1998).

Explaining women's underrepresentation in politics as a matter of prejudice and socialization, however, does not expose the social structural factors that discourage women's greater political participation. Being successful in politics requires, among other things, having the support of party leaders. If those leaders do not encourage women to run for office, there is little likelihood of women's success as politicians.

Other social structural factors also influence the likelihood of women winning political office. Being an incumbent, regardless of one's gender, carries a huge advantage in political elections. As new entrants to politics, women are at a disadvantage in challenging those who already hold office. As one example of the power

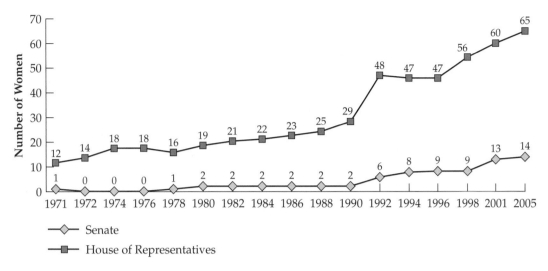

FIGURE 11.2   Women in the U.S. Congress

Source: Data from Center for the American Woman and American Politics. 2004. *Fact Sheet on Women's Political Progress.* New Brunswick, NJ: Rutgers University; Center for the American Woman and American Politics. 1998. *Women's Electoral Success: A Familiar Formula.* New Brunswick, NJ: Rutgers University. www.rci.rutgers.edu/~cawp/.

of incumbency, political scientists have found that 90 percent of political action committee contributions go to incumbents (Malcolm 1993).

One of the ways that people succeed in politics, as in other high-level careers, is through the use of social and political networks. These networks are important resources for people in positions of influence, since they provide systems of support for information, communication, and acquaintances where associates can be counted on for help. In any high-level job, networks are critical. Women, however, tend to have less extensive networks than do men and to be isolated from the male-centered networks where the most power lies. Having fewer women in political office also gives women fewer ties than men have, because people often form their networks based on gender similarities. On the other hand, having fewer women in these offices at least encourages more gender integration, since the low proportion of senior women ensures that women have to form networks with male co-workers (Moore 1990, 1992). If these men hold sexist attitudes, however, it cuts women off from the circles of power that are critical to political success.

Campaign financing is another area where women are at a structural disadvantage, relative to men. Political campaigns are notoriously expensive. Women, who as a group have lower incomes than men and fewer economic resources, are not likely to have the financial resources necessary to mount expensive political campaigns. One way that women have organized to counter this disadvantage is through groups like Emily's List. Emily is an acronym for "Early Money Is Like Yeast." Begun in 1985, Emily's List is a national organization whose purpose is to

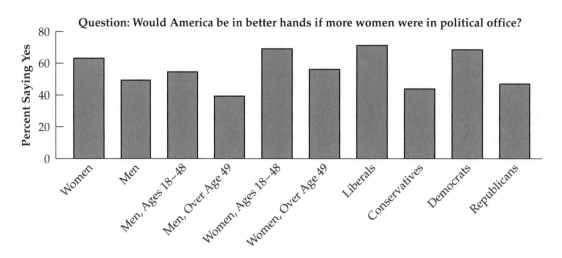

FIGURE 11.3   Women in Politics: Public Attitudes

Source: Data from Wendy Simmons. 2001. "Majority of Americans Say More
Women in Political Office Would Be Positive for the Country." Princeton, NJ:
The Gallup Organization. www.gallup.com.

raise funds that are used to support women's election campaigns. In 2004, Emily's
List raised $10.6 million to support prochoice, Democratic women running for of-
fice. Other groups are now engaging in similar fund-raising efforts on women's behalf, including Sisters United, a New Jersey organization that supports Black
Democratic women.

Finally, women's dual roles in work and the family may put them at a disadvantage in running for political office. As long as women hold the primary responsibility for family care, it is difficult for them to meet the time and energy
requirements of political office. Numerous studies have shown that women's family obligations, including the availability of child care, interfere with their ability to
take on political jobs. One study of women judges, however, found that 80 percent
of women judges report their spouses are very favorable toward their careers; male
judges are far less likely to say this. This may reflect the fact that strong spousal
support is prerequisite for women to seek public office. In the past, women were
more likely than men to feel conflict between their marriage and career aspirations;
now, parental roles are more likely to be a source of conflict than marital roles (Martin 1990).

Despite the structural barriers to women's increased role in politics, women
are making numerous inroads to political power. Their increased representation
in formal government is partially the result of a concerted effort by many groups
to increase women's political power in formal political systems. Without such political activism on behalf of more women in politics, one wonders if there would
have been much change at all.

The Gender Gap

Studying women and politics is not just a matter of studying women as elected officials. Gender is also a major social factor influencing political attitudes and behavior. The term **gender gap** refers to the differences in women's and men's political behavior and political attitudes. One indication of the gender gap is that women are more likely than men to hold and support liberal views—and to identify and vote as Democrats. The development of the gender gap is a recent phenomenon, however. For many decades, men were more likely to vote than women, and, when asked, women reported voting like their husbands or fathers. Now, this trend is reversing. In the 2004 national elections, men were more likely to vote Republican than women. Black men and women voters overwhelmingly vote for Democratic candidates.

Women are now equally likely to vote as men do, but there are significant differences between their political outlooks. The gender gap is widest on issues involving violence and the use of force. Women, for example, are more likely than men to be peace-seeking and to support gun control. The gender gap is also evident on so-called compassion issues. Women are more likely to support government spending for social service programs, and they are more liberal on issues such as abortion, gay and lesbian rights, and women's rights.

Do Women Make a Difference?

The other important question that feminists ask about women's representation as elected officials is whether women's political participation makes a difference. Some argue that women's increased representation in government will bring a more compassionate view to politics. Gender differences between women and men suggest that women might bring different interests and different values to their work as elected officials. Do women have a different view? Does their participation in politics differ from that of men?

Research on women politicians indicates that they tend to be most active in areas traditionally associated with women, including education, health, and welfare. Women state legislators are now equally active to men in public speaking and floor activity, and they are actually more likely to succeed in getting their priority legislation passed (Darcy et al. 1994). In general, women are also more liberal and more feminist than their male counterparts, even controlling for political party and age. On a variety of issues, women differ from men—for example, in being less likely to support the death penalty, not trusting the private sector to solve economic problems, and opposing laws requiring parental consent for minors to have an abortion. Women are also more likely than before to make women's issues a priority. In public opinion polls, women also are more pacifist than men and they hold less militaristic values. Some feminists argue that women's traditional roles as mothers and caregivers produce these different value systems. Carol Gilligan's work on women's moral values, for example, suggests that women have different moral values than men and make value judgments by different sets of criteria—using an ethic of caring rather than absolute judgments about moral right and wrong, which is more characteristic of men (Gilligan 1982).

These contrasts suggest that women will make a difference as they move further into the political area. Some feminists caution us about such an expectation, however, claiming that arguments about women's different ways of being are based in an *essentialist position*, meaning one that too easily assumes fixed differences between women and men. Although those who argue that women are different recognize the socially constructed nature of these differences, their critics argue that some too easily base women's differences from men in their reproductive roles and their psychosexual makeup. This ignores how women's distinctive consciousness is shaped by history and the specific politics of race, class, and gender that create diverse experiences for different groups of women.

Those who claim that there are basic differences between women and men tend to ignore or understate differences among women. Critics of the essentialist position suggest that the gender gap in women's attitudes and behaviors may be explained by other factors. For example, some of the largest differences in political opinion are those between middle-class and working-class women; since middle-class women are more likely to get elected to political office, this may confound some of the research results purporting to find a gender gap.

The fact is that having such a small number of women in elected office makes it difficult to tell if their presence makes a difference in political outcomes, since they are typically a numerical minority and can be treated like tokens. If the numbers of women in office truly represented women's proportion in the population, perhaps there would be a big difference in political agendas, but we also have to be cautious about using gender stereotypes to assume that women will inevitably be different from men once they enter dominant social institutions.

❖ Women and the Military

When the United States invaded Iraq in 2003, over 200,000 women were on active military duty. Women now serve in all branches of the military, and some have made it the very top ranks of military service. Still, it was only as recently as 1996 when the U.S. Supreme Court (in *United States* v. *Virginia*) ruled that women could not be excluded from state-supported military academies. This case involved The Citadel and the Virginia Military Institute (VMI), which had excluded women from admissions based on arguments that women were unfit for the required and rigorous physical training that the institutions required. The Supreme Court disagreed, saying that women were protected under the equal protection clause of the Fourteenth Amendment (Kimmel 2000).

Since then, women have played an active military role in the combat in Iraq, constituting one-seventh of all U.S. military personnel in Iraq. Over 2,000 women serve in Iraq, and they are closer to combat zones than they have been in the past. Twenty-seven women have died in the Iraq war (as of December 2005)—more women than have died in combat ever before. Women have been highly visible during the Iraq war, including being among those tried for prisoner abuses at Abu Ghraib prison.

It was only in 1976 that women were first allowed into any of the military academies. Since then, there have been profound changes in the presence of women in the military. The percentage of women has increased from a mere 1.6 percent in 1973 to 15 percent in 2005. There are an additional 209,000 women in the reserves, not including the Coast Guard and its reserves. Women, however, are underrepresented as military officers; 15 percent of officers are women, even though, in general, women in the military are better educated than their male counterparts. Nearly all women (99.8 percent) in the military are high school graduates (not much different from men, 98 percent of whom are high school graduates), but women are more likely than men to have attended college—27 percent of women versus 21 percent of men (U.S. Department of Defense 2003; Becraft 1990).

In the past, the exclusion of women from full participation in the military, especially combat, has been justified by the belief that women need protection by men and that they can best carry out their womanly duties as mothers and wives. The fear among many that women might have to serve in combat was also one of the major ideological reasons for defeat of the Equal Rights Amendment. Despite these public reservations, women are actively serving in combat-related roles in the military. The Defense Authorization Act of 1992 also allows women to fly combat aircraft, traditionally an option only for men. The public is somewhat divided on having women in combat. Forty-five percent think they should receive combat assignment only if they elect to; 38 percent think they should get combat assignments on the same terms as men. Sixteen percent think they should never receive combat assignments (Carlson 2003). Whether this will shift over time, for example, should a draft be reinstated, remains to be seen.

There are, nonetheless, significant racial and gender differences in support for women's roles in combat and other nontraditional military employment. African Americans are less supportive of women's roles in combat than are Whites, and women are more supportive than men. White men who have been in combat are the group least likely to support women's roles in combat. Attitudes toward other egalitarian gender roles are the best predictors of people's positions on roles for women in military service; those who support women's expanded roles in the military see the matter as one of equal opportunity (Wilcox 1992).

Currently, women are still barred by law from direct combat in the air force, navy, and the army; however, women are increasingly allowed in "combat-related" tasks. The United States is not the only country that bars women from combat, although numerous countries allow women in combat, and many nations have rescinded their laws restricting women from combat. Israeli women, like Israeli men, are subject to military conscription and are assigned to combat units; however, if the unit is deployed on a combat mission, the women are evacuated. The only NATO countries to exclude women from the military are Italy and Spain.

Gender relations in the military extend beyond looking at women who serve in the military. The experience of military wives, for example, is greatly affected by their husbands' employment as soldiers. Frequent moving means that military wives are less competitive in the labor market. And the presence of a military base in a given area seems to depress women's wages in the area (Booth 2003; Booth et al. 2000). At the same time, wives of military officers are expected not to pursue their own careers or risk their husbands' promotion (Harrell 2001).

Lesbians and Gays in the Military

Prejudices against women in the military pale beside the related prejudices that characterize gay and lesbian experiences in the military. There has been a long-standing policy to exclude gays and lesbians from the military, although gays and lesbians have made significant contributions to the nation's armed forces. Until recently, they have had to remain deeply closeted, however. Gays and lesbians have served in all branches of the U.S. armed forces for years. Now, military policy is a "Don't ask, don't tell" policy, first adopted by the Clinton administration. According to this policy, recruiting officers cannot ask about sexual preference and individuals should not reveal their sexual preference; those who reveal that they are gay or lesbian can be excluded from military service, based on their sexual orientation.

Critics of this policy have argued that it effectively keeps gays in the closet by forcing them to keep their sexual identities secret. Although the policy does not allow the explicit discharge of individuals because of homosexuality, nor does it allow the military to screen recruits based on being gay, neither does it fully acknowledge the civil rights of gays and lesbians. Gay soldiers and potential recruits have filed several lawsuits against the U.S. government to overturn these exclusionary rules. Whether they will win the right to full military inclusion remains to be seen.

Those who oppose gays in the military argue, among other things, that the presence of gays affects the morale of the troops and thereby makes them less effective. Supporters of a ban against gays and lesbians in the military argue that the morale of other soldiers will drop if they are forced to serve alongside gay men and lesbian women. They also claim it will "threaten national security" and that having *known* homosexuals serving in the military would upset the status quo. Citing the "tight quarters" where recruits live and work, opponents of gay rights seem to assume that gays and lesbians cannot control their sexuality when living so close to members of the same sex. Their assumption is that gays and lesbians are out to convert all others to their lifestyle. Fear and misunderstanding about AIDS has fueled these homophobic ideas (Belkin and Bateman 2003).

Ironically, there seems to be more cause for worry about sexual harassment, in general, in the military—particularly the harassment of heterosexual men toward military women. Various scandals and the exposure of widespread sexual harassment in the military have exposed this issue before the public. Unlike the homophobic arguments that gays should be excluded from the military because they cannot control their sexuality and might affect military morale, no one has argued that heterosexual men should be excluded. Indeed, a culture of masculinity permeates the military, making sexual harassment a systemic problem (Firestone and Harris 2003).

Ideas like those being used to exclude gays and lesbians from the military were also used earlier in history to exclude African Americans from military service. Opponents of desegregating the armed services argued that it would lower military morale and that it would be difficult for Whites and Blacks to live together in close quarters. In fact, when President Truman ordered the racial desegregation of the military by executive order in 1948, he showed that these arguments were not true. Although racial integration in the military has not been fully achieved, the military is one of the most desegregated institutions in the nation.

Feminism and Militarism

Feminists have criticized the military not just for its discriminatory treatment against women and gays and lesbians, but also for the masculine character of the institution as a whole. Earlier, the concept of a *gendered institution* was discussed— a gendered institution being one that embodies the characteristics of a specific gender. The military is a perfect example of a gendered institution in that it is characterized as a most masculine institution, one emphasizing hierarchy, force, violence, and aggression (Connell 1992). This can be seen in a variety of ways.

First, national involvement in war and military aggression is often justified in terms of a nation being "tough," "supreme," and "heroic"—all characteristics associated with men's gender role. Numerous examples throughout history also show how military propaganda uses images of threatened manhood to rationalize a nation's engagement in war. Aggression and the capacity for violence are seen as indicating national strength, just as they are seen as indicating the strength of individual men. While men's violence occurs in day-to-day interactions, in its most escalated form it results in war and terrorism.

Militaristic values also legitimate much violence and sexual aggression against women, especially that which accompanies war and military occupation. The large-scale rape of women by invading armies in the war-torn Sudan is an example of how military conquerors tend to see sexual violation of women as their right following a military victory. Rape is common in war, as is the widespread use of women sex workers in brothels and as prostitutes in occupied territories and war zones (Enloe 1989).

The strong association between militarism and masculinity is also evident in military training practices where homophobic socialization forces military recruits to be tough, aggressive, and strong as a way of proving their masculine heterosexuality. Labeling as "faggots" those perceived as weak is one way that military recruits are initiated into military roles.

❖ Rethinking the Political

Reviewing the workings of state institutions—including courts and the law, government, and the military—raises many new questions for feminist analysis. One of the primary questions to have emerged from feminist studies in this area is a rethinking of what *political* means. When most people think of something political, they likely think in terms of formal election politics and the workings of official government. In this sense, political behavior is only that which occurs within public political institutions. Feminist scholars, on the other hand, have defined the term *political* more broadly and have argued that traditional concepts of the political have been marked by an incorrect conceptual dichotomy between the public and private spheres of life. Assuming that the political is only that which occurs in the formal, public sphere overlooks significant political activity by women in other arenas, and limits our understanding of the political only to those institutions where men have predominated. In addition, feminist scholars argue that the conceptual separation of the public and private spheres leads to oversight of how the public and private spheres intersect, as, for example, in understanding how women's work in the private sphere supports public institutions, even when that work is devalued and ignored.

Redefining the political to include a broader spectrum of behavior encourages thinking of political behavior in new ways. Women's community activism is one such area that has long been overlooked by those studying politics, but which, on closer look, reveals the many ways that women engage in political behavior. As examples, Gilkes (1980) has shown how African American women who have careers as community workers use their work both to help their communities in everyday survival and to transform social institutions. Although these women are seldom recognized as "political women," their work in social service organizations, on the boards of local organizations, and as directors of agencies has important political ramifications for the African American community. Their political work stems not from their activity in dominant institutions but from their commitments to change and their mobilization of resources in service of the Black community. In a similar vein, Naples (1992) has studied low-income Latina and African American mothers, finding that they see their community work as stemming from their desire to improve the lives of their families and neighbors, the specific problems around which they organize include health care, housing, crime and safety, and sanitation. As activist mothers, their political action is part of the continuum of their caregiving activities.

These are but two examples of how women engage in political action, but from the grassroots (that is, the local level). This gives political activism a different meaning than that which is associated with mainstream politics. In both cases, the distinction between women's private work in their families and communities is blurred with their public work as political actors.

Although women's grassroots activism is rarely the substance of evening news headlines, as is the formal political work of men, it is nonetheless significant in women's contributions to political life. Feminists argue that the media have obscured much of women's political activism, thereby lending the impression that women are not interested in politics or are ineffective in mobilizing on behalf of their interests. Furthermore, redefining the political to include the work that women do sheds more light on the political activism of working-class women and women of color—groups whose political contributions are largely ignored in the dominant culture, despite the fact that working-class women and women of color have a rich history of political organizing. Women work politically in the contexts in which they are found—local communities, workplaces, churches, and social service organizations, to name a few.

Because women's political action has been understudied and misunderstood, theories of political behavior typically fail to deal with gender as a central concept (Bookman and Morgen 1988); moreover, political theory has only in rare cases made women major subjects for analysis. As a consequence, much political analysis has made women invisible as political actors and made politics appear to be gender neutral. As two feminist scholars note, "Politics is conventionally understood as the activities of elected officials and the workings of government, both out of the reach of ordinary people" (Bookman and Morgen 1988:4). Such portrayals also create, among many women, a sense of disenfranchisement and alienation from mainstream politics, especially the working-class and poor women who are most disaffected by dominant institutions. This means that working-class and poor women have to make gains outside of traditional electoral politics—in factory organizing, in churches, on the streets, and through other grassroots activities—areas of political life that have been largely ignored by academic scholars.

Within grassroots politics, women are much more likely to contend with the intersecting politics of race, class, and gender. Grassroots politics rest on individual resistance to the dominant culture and, sometimes, to mass political mobilization. Through such political behavior, women challenge the dominant power relations of society and recognize the systematic forces that oppress women. Often through grassroots politics, women also change their ideas about the sources of their powerlessness and act to change conditions of their lives.

In sum, women are not as peripheral to politics as they might appear in an analysis of women and politics in the electoral world alone. Understanding the full range of women's political behavior means also seeing how working-class women and women of color have a long history of political activism, despite their invisibility in recorded history. These groups have also had a very feminist analysis, supporting women's independence and activism, even when this kind of feminism differs from—and is sometimes in conflict with—the feminism of White, middle-class women (Hine 1995). For all women engaged in the feminist work, however, phrases like *the personal is political* and *sexual politics* show how women have linked their everyday lives to their political action and beliefs.

❖ The Women's Movement

Women's political activism can be found on any number of issues, particularly beyond the formal political system. Women have been important in the work of many political groups that are organized on social and political issues, including environmental-action groups, groups uniting to fight racism, gay and lesbian movements and organizations, abortion rights groups, and many others too numerous to mention. The women's movement, or the feminist movement, was one of the most significant and influential movements in the twentieth century. There are probably few women or men in this country who have not been touched by some aspect of the women's movement, and, although many are reluctant to call themselves feminists, opinion polls show that the majority of people in the United

States support the values and programs that the women's movement has encouraged and supported (Robison 2002; Saad 2003).

Sociologists define **social movements** as groups that act to promote or resist changes in society. Movements often emerge because of their members' perceived sense of injustice and their wish to effect changes that will redress such injustices (Turner and Killian 1972). Social movements involve the sustained activity of organized groups, and they often include a network of organizations that, although they may have different goals and members, have a shared sense of belonging to the movement. Sociologists who study social movements also try to identify the societal conditions that foster the development of the movements. In the case of the contemporary women's movement, the development of feminism can be traced to the development of the nineteenth-century women's movement.

American Feminism in the Nineteenth Century

In the United States, many of the early feminists were women who advocated the equal rights of women to acquire an education. One of the earliest advocates of education for women was Emma Willard, who campaigned actively for the establishment of colleges for women in the 1920s. Frances Wright also was an active spokeswoman for the establishment of equal educational training for women. Education for women, these women argued, would extend the "rights of man" to all persons and therefore make for general and human improvement. As the result of their efforts, Oberlin College was the first college to admit women in 1833. Mount Holyoke College opened in 1837; Vassar in 1865; both Smith and Wellesley in 1875; Radcliffe in 1879; and Bryn Mawr in 1885 (Flexner 1975). Although extending education primarily to women of the upper class, these institutions nonetheless created an educated class of women, many of whom worked on behalf of women's rights.

Feminism did not, however, have its origins only in the activism of educated White women. Its political origins also lie in the abolitionist movement of the 1830s and the efforts of African American and White women and men to struggle for the abolition of slavery and women's rights. Charlotte Forten (1784–1884), an African American woman reformer and abolitionist, was a founder of the Philadelphia Female Anti-Slavery Society. She tutored her three daughters, Margaretta, Harriet, and Sarah Louise, each of whom was also active in the abolitionist and feminist movements. The Grimke sisters, Sarah (1792–1873) and Angelina (1805–1879), were daughters of a slaveholding family who traveled and spoke out vigorously against slavery in the 1830s. Both the Grimke sisters and Sarah Forten were delegates to the first Anti-Slavery Convention of American Women held in 1837. The correspondence between Sarah Forten and Angelina Grimke records their friendship and their strong sentiments about both **abolitionism** and feminism (Sterling 1984).

Frederick Douglass, a former slave and ardent abolitionist, supported women's rights for many years and was a strong supporter of women's suffrage. He and other male abolitionists believed that women's suffrage was necessary for the full enfranchisement of all citizens, although racism among White women and men in the women's rights movement forced Douglass and other abolitionists to subordinate the issue of women's suffrage to that of Black suffrage (DuBois 1978). The abolitionists saw clear links between freedom for slaves and freedom for women, although as the women's rights movement developed, White women discriminated against Black women in the movement and used racist appeals to argue for the extension of voting rights to White women.

From their work in the abolitionist movement, women learned how to organize a political movement. They challenged the assumption of the natural superiority of men and understood that suffrage was an important source for self-respect and social power. Historian Ellen Carol DuBois has concluded that

> *abolitionism provided [American women] with a way to escape clerical authority, an egalitarian ideology, and a theory of social change, all of which permitted the leaders to transform the insights into the oppression of women which they shared with many of their contemporaries into the beginnings of the women's rights movement (1978:32).*

In 1840, a World Anti-Slavery Convention was held in London. The mere presence of women delegates at this convention generated excitement about the potential power of women, although women were relegated to the galleries and were prohibited from participating in the proceedings. Their exclusion from the proceedings generated an increased awareness among women of the need for a women's movement. When they returned to the United States, two of the women attending the convention, Lucretia Mott and Elizabeth Cady Stanton, continued to meet and discuss strategies for establishing women's rights. On July 14, 1848, they called for a Woman's Rights Convention to be held in Seneca Falls, New York, five days later. Despite such short notice, 300 men and women came to Seneca Falls and there approved a Declaration of Sentiments, modeled on the Declaration of Independence. The Declaration of Sentiments declared that "all men and women are created equal; that they are endowed by their Creator with certain inalienable rights; that among these are life, liberty, and the pursuit of happiness" (Hole and Levine 1971:6). Those attending the Seneca Falls Convention also passed 12 resolutions, one of which resolved to grant women the right to vote.

The Seneca Falls Convention has since been heralded as the official beginning of the women's suffrage movement in the United States. Other women's rights conventions were held throughout the United States, including one in 1851 in Akron, Ohio, where Sojourner Truth, a former slave, challenged the popular doctrine of women's delicacy and physical inferiority. She exhorted:

> *Nobody ever helps me into carriages or over puddles, or gives me the best place—and ain't I a woman? . . . Look at my arm! I have ploughed and planted and gathered into barns, and no man could head me—and ain't I a woman? I could work as much and eat as much as a man—when I could get it—and bear the lash as well! And ain't I a woman? I have born thirteen children, and seen most of 'em sold into slavery, and when I cried out with my mother's grief, none but Jesus heard me—and ain't I a woman? (Hole and Levine 1971:191)*

In the beginning, the women's movement was not just a single-issue movement. Feminists saw the issue of suffrage as one aspect of women's rights and advocated full equality for women. The momentum of the women's movement was stalled somewhat by the Civil War, but after the war, feminists worked hard to get the word *sex* added to the Fifteenth Amendment. The Fifteenth Amendment declares that the right to vote cannot be denied or abridged by race, color, or previous condition of servitude, but it did not extend to women—either White or African American. Although feminists' efforts to get the term *sex* added did not succeed, this setback furthered their resolve for suffrage; in 1869, Susan B. Anthony and Elizabeth Cady Stanton organized the National Woman Suffrage Association (NWSA), which embraced the broad cause of women's rights. A few months later, Lucy Stone and others organized the American Woman Suffrage Association. This organization restricted itself more narrowly to the suffrage issue, trying to avoid more controversial issues like marriage and the church.

Suffrage, however, was not the only issue for which early feminists fought. The **temperance movement** in the late nineteenth century was organized by women with a strong feminist consciousness. The motto of the Women's Christian Temperance Union (WCTU), under one of its early presidents, Frances Willard, was "Do everything!" Willard organized departments in the WCTU, each with its own programs of activity, including work in prisons, in kindergarten, and with the shut-in sick; other departments were concerned with physical culture and hygiene, prostitution, and motherhood. One department, the most effective, worked for suffrage. The temperance movement pressed for laws restricting the sale and consumption of alcohol; women were encouraged to join because their status as married women gave them no legal protection against abuse or abandonment by a drunken husband (Flexner 1975).

In 1890, the American and National Woman's Suffrage associations merged to become the National American Woman Suffrage Association (NAWSA). By this time, the women's movement had become a single-issue movement. Feminist efforts were devoted to gaining women's right to vote—a right they believed would open other opportunities and give women full rights as citizens. Shortly after the turn of the century, a second generation of U.S. feminists appeared, including women like Carrie Chapman Catt, president of NAWSA. Also, Alice Paul, a young militant woman, became active in the suffrage movement. She formed a small radical group, the Congressional Union, to work solely on federal suffrage for women. The Congressional Union used tactics such as parades, mass demonstrations, and hunger strikes to further their cause. The combined efforts of the Congressional Union, NAWSA, and local suffrage groups and activists were eventually successful. On August 26, 1920, the **Nineteenth Amendment,** guaranteeing women the right to vote, was adopted.

With the success of the suffrage movement, the women's movement lost much of its public momentum and, many say, lay dormant for the years between passage of the Nineteenth Amendment and the rebirth of feminism in the United States in the 1960s. Others have shown, though, that feminist activities through this period did not totally disappear. Many women continued to pursue feminist goals in a variety of organizations and contexts; their work provided continuity between the early women's movement and contemporary feminism. Although only a few organizations from the 1920s to the 1960s embraced explicitly feminist goals, the birth control and family planning movement, the settlement house movement, the establishment of organizations working to improve working conditions for employed women, and the founding of professional women's groups (including the National Federation of Business and Professional Women's Clubs, the League of Women Voters, and the American Association of University Women) set the stage for feminist developments in later years (Ferree and Hess 1997). Even in the post–World War II period, when cultural ideology strongly defended the idea that a woman's proper place was in the home, the National Women's Party, organized by Alice Paul, continued to fight for improving the status of women. The National Women's Party had one major plank in its platform—passage of the Equal Rights Amendment (ERA). Since 1923, when the ERA was first introduced in Congress, Paul and other members of this organization worked to garner support from other women's organizations, lobbied Congress, and sought publicity for the amendment. Most other women's organizations opposed passage of the ERA, believing it would legitimate protective legislation for women. Despite their differing goals and philosophies, all of these organizations provided strong support networks for women in the particularly hostile environment of post–World War II sexist ideology (Rupp and Taylor 1987).

The Emergence of the Contemporary Women's Movement

Several transformations in women's roles occurring during the 1950s and 1960s influenced the development of contemporary feminism. These included changes in women's labor force participation, a change in women's fertility patterns, increases in women's educational level, and ideological patterns that glamorized women's domestic life. In the 1950s, White women were idealized as happy housewives whose primary purpose was to care for their husbands and children. In that decade, women were marrying younger, but they were also having fewer children because widespread use of contraception gave women control over their fertility. At the same time, White, middle-class women were better educated and, although their education was intended to make them better wives and mothers, they were acquiring many of the same skills as men. For women in the home, technological changes in housework simplified physical tasks, but the increased consumption and new patterns of family life in automobile-based suburbs complicated the role of housewives. Although there was less physical labor associated with housework, housewives were supposed to be constantly available to their children. Whatever time was saved by labor-saving appliances was more than replaced by increased shopping, transporting of children, and nurturing of family members. The dominant ideology of housework and motherhood told middle-class women that their work in the home would bring them fulfillment and gratification, but, in fact, many found the experience to be depressing, isolating, and boring.

This situation created a crisis for White, middle-class family women that was brought to the widespread attention of the public by the appearance of Betty Friedan's best-seller, *The Feminine Mystique,* in 1963. Friedan identified "the problem that has no name"—the isolation in the family—as the source of women's discontent. Friedan's book critically assailed the establishment (including mass advertising, women's magazines, and Freudian psychology) as contributing to women's problems. The chord she struck was soon repeated by a number of critical assessments of women's roles that appeared in academic and popular literature (Evans 1979).

In addition to experiencing a crisis in domestic life, women were, at the same time, appearing in the labor force in greater numbers. Throughout the 1950s, women from middle-income families entered the labor force at a faster rate than any other group. They were working not just in the years before marriage but later, in addition to their marriage and family roles. Although married women's work experience was defined in terms of helping their families, it broadened their horizons at the same time that it made them conscious of discrimination in the workplace. The decade of the 1950s and the early 1960s created a self-conscious cohort of women who lived in the contradictions of a society that idealized their role and promised them opportunity and gratification while it devalued their labor and denied them self-expression.

Professional women working within established institutions began pressuring politicians to recognize the problems facing women in the United States. In 1961, although it was likely done for political reasons, President John F. Kennedy appointed a Presidential Commission on the Status of Women, chaired by Eleanor Roosevelt. The commission was charged with documenting "prejudices and outmoded customs that act as barriers to the full realization of women's basic rights" (Hole and Levine 1971:18) and with making recommendations designed to alleviate the problem. The commission report, *American Women,* was released in 1963, the same year that Friedan's *The Feminine Mystique* appeared.

The commission's report made a number of recommendations involving employment and labor discrimination. It was the basis for the Equal Pay Act of 1963, requiring that men and women receive equal pay for equal work performed under equal conditions (Hole and Levine 1971:28ff). Problems in enforcing this law and exemptions that were later attached to it prohibited the act from making the radical changes it implied; thus, the commission's work had only a moderate effect. The commission also held steadfastly to the idea that the nuclear family was the foundation of U.S. history and that women's role in the family was an invaluable and necessary resource. Although recognizing the contribution that women made to the home, the commission ignored the effects of home life on women that Friedan's book so strikingly portrayed.

These developments within both the government and the society provided the context for women to begin to question their traditional roles, but it remained for major social movements of the period to crystallize the vague discontent that women felt. The birth of contemporary feminism must be seen as also stemming from the civil rights movement and, later, the anti–Vietnam War and student movements.

Feminism and Civil Rights

The civil rights movement was initiated within African American communities of the South during the 1950s as a challenge to public racial segregation and White racial prejudice. Like the nineteenth-century U.S. feminists who had developed their feminist politics through participation in the abolitionist movement, women working in the civil rights movement soon saw their own oppression as similar to the racial injustices against which they were organizing. Women worked in the civil rights movement out of their felt need to remedy the inequities of racial injustice, which they saw as a moral issue calling for their humanitarian participation. For White women and men, joining the civil rights movement required a radical departure from the dominant beliefs and practices of White society. Their challenge to the status quo on racial issues was soon to influence the way they also interpreted other social issues (Evans 1979).

Between 1963 and 1965, White liberals from the North (especially male and female college students) went to the South in great numbers to assist in the civil rights struggle. The nonviolent direct-action projects in which they engaged (voter registration drives, protest marches, and sit-ins) forced them to encounter institutional racism and generated a new consciousness not only of racial issues but of the institutional structure of society in the United States (Rothschild 1979). Most important, the civil rights movement's emphasis on examining the roots of oppression caused many White people to look into their own experience so as to comprehend their relationship to dominant institutions. In so doing, White women in the movement began to see the origins of their own oppression—both as they had learned sexism in their own lives and as it was reflected in the public institutions of society.

Despite a growing feminist consciousness, sexual politics within the civil rights movement divided Black and White women for two reasons. First, White women in the movement sometimes tried to prove their social liberalism by having sexual relations with Black men. Although this action was encouraged by the permissive atmosphere in the movement, it discouraged solidarity between Black and White women (Rothschild 1979). Second, both White and Black women believed that the movement had failed to address the issue of sexual inequality. Black women in the Student Non-Violent Coordinating Committee (SNCC) wrote position papers protesting the fact that women in the movement were relegated to clerical work, were not given leadership and decision-making positions, and were belittlingly referred to as "girls." White women, supporting the idea that the movement should be led by Blacks, were reluctant to present their own analysis of sexism, and distrust between Black and White women prevented their alliance against male sexism (Evans 1979).

Throughout the summers of 1964 and 1965, the position of Whites in the civil rights movement became increasingly precarious. Black disillusionment with White liberals and the ideology of Black power eventually resulted in the exclusion of Whites from SNCC in 1965. As a result, at the very time that women were becoming more conscious of their ties to each other, both White and Black women ended up working in movements that were even more male dominated and less open to an examination of gender inequality. For Black women, the Black Power movement explicitly appealed to the power of Black men and the role of Black women as supporters of men. White women, after their exclusion from the Black Power Movement, organized around antiwar and student issues, but in groups that were typically male dominated. These movements once again relegated them to traditionally women's work and treated them as sexual objects for the pleasure of radical men. By applying the analysis of racial injustice they had learned in the civil rights movement to their own oppression as women, White feminists emerged from the ranks of other activist groups (Evans 1979).

The feminism of Black women emerged under similar conditions, although as in the nineteenth century, Black women's feminist politics are much more situated in their antiracist activities. Increasing educational levels and transformation of the employment status of Black women throughout the 1960s and 1970s, however, created the sociological conditions through which their evolving feminist consciousness can be seen.

Surveys of Black women show that they are more likely than White women to hold feminist values, although they do not necessarily identify with the feminist movement. Black women's political consciousness is often situated in the context of their community work, where they identify themselves as working to empower the African American community—through both professional and political work (Gilkes 1980). For African American women, the concept of sisterhood has not been the basis for a political identity, as it has been for White women. African American women's political identity has more likely been formed around the issue of race, and as a result, they see feminist issues in a different context than do White women (Dill 1983). Whereas White women tend to see themselves oppressed as a sexual group, African American women are more likely to see race, class, and gender exploitation as intersecting in their lives (Collins 1990).

The Second Wave of Feminism

By the late 1960s, feminism in the United States had developed as a full-fledged movement, with a variety of organizations, local consciousness-raising groups, and political strategies intended to advocate transformations in women's status in society. Referred to as "the second wave of feminism" (in contrast to the nineteenth century "first wave"), the women's movement in the 1960s and 1970s had diverse origins, philosophies, and strategies for change.

Two major branches of the feminist movement evolved: the *women's rights* branch and the *women's liberation* branch. The women's rights branch took an "equal rights" strategy—working to extend equal rights to women, particularly through legal reform and antidiscrimination policies. Important in this part of the feminist movement was the **Equal Rights Amendment** (ERA), the proposed amendment to the U.S. Constitution that states: "Equality of rights under the law shall not be denied or abridged by the United States or by any state on the basis of sex." Advocates of the ERA saw it as essential for providing a constitutional foundation to protect women from gender inequality; opponents feared it would force women into military combat. Trivial as it seems, much of the opposition voiced their opposition by worrying about it eliminating separate public bathrooms for men and women! To date, the Equal Rights Amendment—a simple statement of gender equality—has not been approved, though another movement is afoot to make this historic amendment to the Constitution.

The women's rights branch of the women's movement was centered in a philosophy of anti-discrimination; thus, the best remedies would be the creation of gender-blind institutions in which all persons, regardless of sex (or race, religious preference, sexual preference, or physical disability), are given equal privileges. The women's liberation branch of the feminist movement, on the other hand, took a more far-reaching analysis, seeing that transformation in women's status requires not just legal and political reform but radical transformation of basic social institutions, including, to name a few, the family, sexuality, religion, and education. Women's rights and women's liberation are not separate movements, but the analytical distinction between the two shows the different political and social theories on which feminism is built. As you will see, the women's rights approach is more centered in the context of liberal political theory, while women's liberation has its roots in more radical philosophical theory.

Each wing of the feminist movement attracted different constituencies and developed different strategies for change. The women's rights wing (identified as *liberal feminism*) tended to attract older, professional women. The organizational structure of equal rights groups also reflected the more traditional style of their politics. These feminist organizations, especially as they have evolved over time, are typically more formal, with hierarchical leadership and authority structures, and with more formal procedures and rules for membership (Freeman 1973).

The style and organization of women's liberation groups, on the other hand, reflected their more radical ideological base. Participants tended to be younger than their liberal counterparts, and the organization of these groups was deliberately nonhierarchical, mass based, and with informal procedures and networks (Freeman 1973). The looser, more flexible style of discussion in women's liberation groups encouraged analyses that were not only more critical of establishment systems but also more person oriented and more likely to engage individuals in examining their own experience and its relationship to institutionalized sexism. This more radical branch of feminism recognized that personal life was tied to the structure of public institutions and would be altered only as these institutions changed.

The more radical feminist groups often emerged from the New Left and drew their participants from women who were critical of the often sexist and patronizing behavior of radical men (Evans 1979). Their early political analysis was forged from the appeals to justice that the civil rights and leftist movements had articulated and that women felt were being denied to them. Women in the antiwar and student movements of the 1960s were radicalized not only by the philosophies of these movements but also by the sexist behavior of men within the movements. African American women whose leadership had been central in the civil rights movement were often relegated to secondary status in the Black power movement, as the movement became more influenced by Black nationalism. Women's participation in all of these movements had the effect of further radicalizing White and African American women's feminist perspectives.

Still, African American women did not fully embrace the feminist position of White women; White women were more likely to see all men as the problem and were less sensitive to the class and race differences among men that gave them differential access to power. The feminist alliance between White women feminists and women of color is still imperfect, in part because of this issue and also because of racism among White women.

Feminism for the Twenty-First Century: A Third Wave?

With the evolution of the feminist movement over time, early distinctions between the equal rights and women's liberation branches of feminism have blurred, although diverse political beliefs and strategies among feminists remain. Some of those who were radical feminists in the 1960s and 1970s—then younger women, students, and movement activists—now work in positions of some power and influence. At the same time, liberal feminist organizations, although they work within the existing political system, are influenced by more radical feminist thought. Race, class, *and* gender have also become more central to feminist politics and feminist analyses. Although tensions continue to exist between White women and women of color, the feminism of women of color has become more elaborated, and more White women have worked to challenge their own racism and to build analyses that are inclusive of race, class, and gender.

Starting in the 1990s, feminists faced two new challenges: the identification of a so-called postfeminist generation and a backlash against feminism, both from the mainstream media and from the rise of the new religious and political right. The dominant media generated a strong image of feminism as no longer necessary and a thing of the past (Faludi 1991). In addition, the media created a stereotype of feminism that stigmatized it in the eyes of many, especially younger women. This image of feminists as anti–male, lesbian, humorless, and politically correct ideologues made feminism seem unapproachable to many, including those who otherwise supported its values and goals (Whittier 1995).

The rise of the religious right also promotes values specifically opposed to the feminist agenda. The right's advocacy of "traditional family values" endorses an anti–feminist stance, one promoting a strong connection of women to the home, little tolerance of diverse family forms, and many extremely homophobic platforms directed against gays and lesbians (such as some of the ballot initiatives in different states to deny same-sex marriage). The influence of this significant conservative movement means that feminism has lost ground on important issues like abortion rights, gay and lesbian rights, and state or federal support for any number of social programs that support women and their children. This conservative movement also generated a climate far less tolerant of feminist modes of thinking. The right-wing attack on being "PC" (i.e., "politically correct") has thus been strongly directed at women's studies programs and scholars, as well as those who promote more democratic, anti–elitist, and multicultural education.

In this context, there is little wonder that younger women in the new century may find themselves confused by feminism. Although the media has portrayed this generation as a "postfeminist" one, a more careful look finds that young women and men are those most likely to support feminist values, even though they may be reluctant to call themselves feminists. When asked if they support the specific goals of feminism, the majority of young people say yes, with widespread support for such feminist issues as equal employment opportunities for women, more equality in family roles, support of reproductive freedom, agreement with affirmative action, and support for more women in public office (Schnittker et al. 2003; Hall and Rodriguez 2003). The most likely age groups to support feminism are younger women and women who are now middle-aged who became adults during the second wave of feminism in the 1960s and 1970s (Peltola et al. 2004; Aronson 2003).

Ironically, the image of young women and men as uninterested in feminism has been most prevalent at the same time that enrollments in women's studies courses have soared on most college campuses over the past 20 years. It is probably more accurate to say that young women are not so much anti–feminist as they are cautious about being identified with a movement so reviled in the media and that they see as stemming from the concerns of a different generation.

Young women growing up now have had very different experiences from those of their mothers' generation, many of whom were part of the second wave of feminism. Younger women have grown up in a period dominated by conservative, not progressive, values. They have also benefited from the gains made by the second wave of feminism, so they do not have to worry so much about access to birth control, rights to education and employment, or exclusion from formerly men-only occupations and organizations—some of the issues that activated the second wave of feminism. Still, issues about women's safety from violence, men's and women's sexual identities, work and family roles, and other opportunities are by no means resolved. Young people have also grown up in a context where the politics of personal identity—gender identity, racial-ethnic identity, and sexual identity—have been a vocal topic in the political world. The generational differences between young women and their feminist foremothers thus shape the reactions of many young women to feminist politics (Whittier 1995). At the same time, however, the shape of the third wave of feminism will be determined by the political action taken by younger women and men who define feminism in the context of their own life experiences and needs (Walker 1995; Hernández and Rehman 2002).

There has been no demise of the women's movement. Quite the contrary, the women's movement remains one of the most influential sources of social change, even though there is not a single national organization that is identified as representing feminism. Some of the most radical feminist activities occur at the grassroots level, where women struggle against poverty, violence, harassment, and exploitation. At the same time, more mainstream feminist organizations continue to work on behalf of women's health and welfare, safety and security, and educational and employment rights. Just as the feminist movement has ebbed and flowed with different emphases and different agendas over the past 100 years or more, so will its future be influenced by the needs of diverse women in their own times.

❖ *Chapter Summary and Themes*

Power is the ability to influence others; as an organized system of power, the state has operated as a gendered institution, excluding women from positions of leadership and operating within a masculinist framework.

One of the ironies of considering the state from a feminist perspective is that it has operated as a patriarchal institution—against women's interests—at the same time that the state has been an avenue by which feminists have sought to eliminate formal discrimination and others forms of gender inequity.

As women have moved into more professional roles within the legal system, many have wondered whether women will administer justice differently than men, based on presumed gender differences in women's values.

Evidence of gender differences in the administration of justice is mixed. Some studies show that women use a unique standpoint in judgments about sentencing and in their perspective on issues before the law, but one must be careful not to overstate such differences, given the empirical evidence.

Women continue to be underrepresented in all aspects of formal political institutions, even though their numbers are increasing in this arena.

Explanations of the underrepresentation of women as elected officials include such factors as gender socialization, persistent gender bias in attitudes about political skills, exclusion from political networks, women's lesser resources for financing campaigns, and the dual roles that women have in the family and at work.

A gender gap in men's and women's attitudes about political and social issues persists, with women generally being more liberal than men.

Although women are generally more likely to support values such as peace, government support for social services, feminist issues, and so forth, one has to be careful not to attribute this to *essential* differences between women and men. People's opinions vary by other factors, such as generational differences, race, social class, and other social factors. Also, changes in the society at large can result in changed public attitudes.

Although still a minority of those serving in active military duty, women have increased their representation within the military, even though the military is still well-described as a gendered institution.

Women's historic exclusion from the military was justified based on their need for men's protection. As that attitude has eroded, women have moved into diverse military roles, although they are still underrepresented as officers. Public support for women serving in combat has grown. The extent of sexual harassment in the military and the suspicion directed against gays and lesbians shows how the military is structured around a culture of masculinity.

Although women have historically been excluded from many roles in the major political institutions, they have nonetheless been politically active, often in grassroots movements organized to meet community needs.

Although women have not always been visible in public political roles, when you think about political behavior more broadly, you see that women have a long history of political activism, activism that shows women to be strong, independently minded, and attentive to the needs of diverse groups, including their own communities.

The feminist movement, which dates to the nineteenth century, appeared in a "second wave" beginning in the late 1960s. It has been one of the most influential social movements of recent history.

Studies find that a substantial majority of the U.S. public supports feminist issues, though many are reluctant to call themselves feminist given how the dominant culture stigmatizes that label. Still, younger generations, now constituting a third wave of feminism, support feminist issues and have actively engaged in actions intended to reduce violence against women, protect women's rights in education and employment, and to promote women's health and security.

❖ Key Terms

abolitionism	Nineteenth Amendment	power elite
authority	patriarchy	social movement
Equal Rights Amendment	pluralism	state
gender gap	power	temperance movement

❖ Discussion Questions/Projects for Thought

1. Watch the national evening news for one week, keeping notes on which stories are reported and when women are mentioned. How frequently do women appear in the news? When they do, what is being reported? Are women depicted as active political news makers or are they "on the sidelines" of the news? What does this tell you about gender and politics?

2. Contact the military base nearest to you and inquire about services for military wives. What services are provided? What does this teach you about the experiences of women

associated with the military? In what ways is the military a gendered institution?

3. Take a current piece of legislation being debated by your state legislature or the federal government, and ask yourself: What are the implications of this law for women? Are the implications being considered as part of this political debate? If so, in what terms? If not, why not?

❖ *Internet Resources*

Center for American Women and Politics

http://www.rci.rutgers.edu/~cawp/

This organization, affiliated with Rutgers University, promotes understanding women and politics. Their website includes useful information on women in political office, research on women candidates, and updates about current elections.

The White House Project

http://www.thewhitehouseproject.org

This organization supports increasing the number of women in elected position, including the U.S. presidency. The website includes numerous facts and action projects on women in politics.

❖ *Suggested Readings*

Bookman, Ann, and Sandra Morgan, eds. 1988. *Women and the Politics of Empowerment.* Philadelphia: Temple University Press. This anthology examines women's political activism and redefines political behavior to include work that women do outside of formal political institutions.

Enloe, Cynthia. 1989. *Bananas, Beaches, and Bases.* Berkeley: University of California Press. Enloe's book presents a feminist perspective on international relations. Her compelling analysis studies the role of gender in peace, war, international development, and the social structure of the military.

Freedman, Estelle B. 2002. *No Turning Back: The History of Feminism and the Future of Women.* New York: Ballantine Books. This account of the influence of second-wave feminism also provides a comprehensive analysis of multiple feminist issues.

MacKinnon, Catharine. 1989. *Toward a Feminist Theory of the State.* Cambridge, MA: Harvard University Press. MacKinnon defines the state as "male," meaning that it is based on, and represents, men's power. Her radical feminist analysis is a powerful critique of dominant political institutions.

Martin, Patricia Yancey, and Myra Marx Ferree. 1995. *Feminist Organizations: Harvest of the New Women's Movement.* Philadelphia: Temple University Press. This anthology explores the diverse organizations that are engaged in feminist activism. Written from a sociological perspective, the articles examine how feminist organizations are structured and how the feminist perspective of the members influences their action and work.

Rosen, Ruth. 2000. *The World Split Open: How the Modern Women's Movement Changed America.* New York: Viking. Rosen's book chronicles the rise of the second wave of feminism and the enormous influence it has had in transforming society over the last half of the twentieth century.

Shilts, Randy. 1993. *Conduct Unbecoming: Gays and Lesbians in the U.S. Military.* New York: St. Martin's Press. This book provides a historical overview of gays and lesbians in the military and analyzes public and government response to this issue.

Stiehm, Judith Hicks. 1996. *"It's Our Military, Too!": Women and the U.S. Military.* Philadelphia: Temple University Press. This anthology covers a wide range of issues about women and the military, centering on the premise that one should understand the structure of the military to engage in current issues about violence, sexual harassment, and women's roles in the military.

Williams, Patricia. 1991. *The Alchemy of Race and Rights.* Cambridge, MA: Harvard University Press. Using literature, legal scholarship, and an imaginative form of presentation, Williams's analysis of race and gender shows both the limitations and the possibilities of law as a vehicle for social change.

12

WOMEN AND SOCIAL REFORM
Liberal Feminism

Frameworks of
Feminist Theory

The Liberal Basis
of Modern Feminism

Liberalism as a Mode
of Social Thought

Early Liberal Feminists
   Mary Wollstonecraft
   Harriet Martineau
   John Stuart Mill and Harriet
      Taylor Mill

The Critique of
Liberal Feminism

Chapter Summary and Themes

Key Terms

**Discussion Questions/
Projects for Thought**

Internet Resources

Suggested Readings

As a social movement, feminism has brought many changes to society—not the least of which is change in intellectual life. Although perhaps to many in the public, intellectual life seems like a rarified thing—distant, aloof, disconnected from reality—intellectual thought guides and is guided by many of the changes that we see in the world around us. As policymakers debate reforms in labor relations, family policy, social welfare, education, or any other arena of life, they often draw on the knowledge of experts to guide their work as agents of change. These experts come from a variety of intellectual and political perspectives—thus, the great debates that characterize some of the more difficult and pressing issues of our times. In the absence of feminist theory, few of these changes are likely to be informed by an analysis that understands the implications of such change for women.

In addition, sometimes people advocate changes with an implicit, and perhaps even unconscious, set of assumptions built into their ideals for change. For example, liberalism is the dominant political philosophy in the United States. A basic premise of liberalism is that all people should be treated alike, with no formal barriers to opportunity and equal rights before the law. Consciously or not, liberalism guides many of the changes people advocate in contemporary times.

You will notice that the term *liberal* is being used differently here than the way it is bandied about in the press. Liberal is a label that conservatives often apply to those with whom they disagree on social and political issues. Thus, those who support social issues such as abortion rights, affirmative action, gay rights, and a myriad of other issues have been targeted as "liberal," even when the term is being misused.

In this chapter, note that liberalism has a very particular meaning in philosophical and social thought—ironically, one now adopted by conservatives who would never call themselves "liberals" even though the gender-blind and color-blind policies they tend to support actually derive from classical liberal theory. Understanding the philosophical origins and framework of liberalism is thus critical if you are to be fully informed about contemporary debates about social policy—especially as those policies affect women and people of color.

Should we create gender-blind social policies? Can such policies address the persistent inequities that women face? Where do men fit in such a picture? Should we just treat women and men the same, or must we somehow account for gender differences in social policies for gender justice? These questions lie at the heart of feminist discussions and are vitally important to the formulation of social policy. Although not everyone engaged in such discussions is consciously guided by a theoretical perspective, understanding theory helps you dissect the assumptions that undergird various perspectives on the possibilities for social change.

Feminist theory is the social and political thought that lies behind much of feminist politics. It forms the basis for social policies and social actions that have driven change in recent years. The development of feminist theory is not separated from the women's movement; indeed, the two are inextricably linked. Behind feminist politics lie modes of analysis (i.e., feminist theory) that guide and inform social and political action. These modes of thought are as diverse as the feminist movement itself, but they can be roughly grouped into broad categories, including liberal feminism and more radical forms of feminist thought.

As you will see in this chapter, throughout history feminist theory has been tied to broad intellectual and social changes in society. The social thought of influential European thinkers in the eighteenth and nineteenth centuries (Mary Wollstonecraft, John Stuart Mill, and Harriet Taylor Mill) laid the groundwork for contemporary liberal feminism. During the nineteenth century, Karl Marx, whose writings changed the course of world history, also influenced the development of feminist thought. Within the United States, social movements—including abolition, temperance, and the women's suffrage movement—have also influenced the development of feminist theory. At the same time, social changes taking place in society—including industrialization, geographic expansion, expanding educational opportunities for women, and the growth of social reform movements—have all influenced the development of feminist thought over time. In the chapters that follow, you will examine this thought with the goal of understanding the underlying assumptions in diverse theoretical perspectives, since these same assumptions shape the imaginations people have for envisioning social change.

❖ *Frameworks of Feminist Theory*

To many people, the idea of theory implies a way of thinking that is highly abstract and perhaps void of any connection to the "real" world. Many tend to think of theories as ideas that hold a certain degree of fascination for intellectuals but that are not particularly relevant for the ordinary person's understanding of life or the world. Most of us, however, do have ideas about the way society is organized. Although we may not think of ourselves as theorists, we hold many assumptions, unexamined as they may be, about the organization of society and the possibilities for social change.

Sociological theory attempts to explain the relationship between social facts, like many of those you have observed in preceding chapters, and the social structure of society and culture. Feminist theory similarly attempts to situate the everyday events of women's and men's lives in an analysis that links our personal and collective experience to an understanding of the structure of gender relationships in society and culture. Feminists also claim that what we know, both intellectually and practically, is thoroughly infused with gendered assumptions about the character of the social world, its problems, its inhabitants, and its meaning.

The purpose of **feminist theory** is to help us understand the conditions in society and to envision the possibilities for liberating social changes. Feminist theory is not written about and discussed just for its own sake but rather for what it suggests about political change, as well. While theoretical analyses may seem complex and sometimes abstract, their purpose is to help understand the character of social structure and therefore the possibilities for social change. As we can see by examining the various frameworks of feminist theory and their relationship to feminist politics, different political frameworks in the feminist movement rest on different theoretical assumptions. Although these assumptions are not always evident in political discourse, understanding them can sharpen political analyses and inform strategies for social change.

For example, since feminism has moved into the mainstream of life in the United States, many people identify themselves as feminists with little understanding of the liberal framework they assume (Eisenstein 1981; see Figure 12.1). Whether one assumes a liberal or a radical feminist stance, examining the intellectual roots of different feminist perspectives provides a more complete understanding of the assumptions of a given perspective, as well as the different programs for social change that given perspectives imply. Careful study of particular feminist frameworks enables us to more accurately answer questions about women's status in society and therefore allows for a better assessment of possible directions for social change.

The theoretical and political frameworks of feminist thought emerge from some of the classical traditions of social and political theory. As you will see, in considering issues about women's lives, feminists have revised some of these classical perspectives to better explain the position of women in society. Like the intellectual traditions from which feminist thought stems, feminist theory is organized around varying assumptions about social organization and social change.

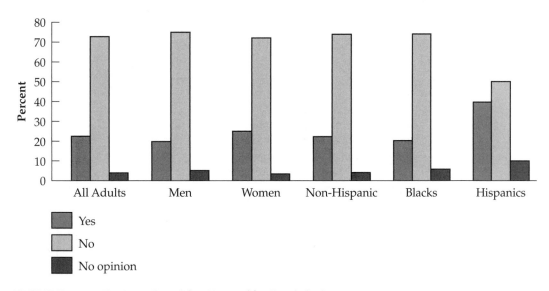

FIGURE 12.1   Do You Consider Yourself a Feminist?

Source: Data from Lydia Saad. 2001. "Women See Room for Improvement in Job Equity." *Gallup Poll Monthly* (June): 56–63.

These assumptions also guide how we interpret the empirical observations of social research, such as that reviewed in earlier chapters of this book. Depending on the theoretical position used to understand data, the data may take on a different meaning. Facts do not usually speak for themselves; they are interpreted within the context of assumptions made about their meaning and their relationship to other facts. Theories guide this interpretation and are therefore an integral part of the process of knowledge construction.

This chapter focuses on the framework of liberal feminism, a long-standing and far-reaching framework for feminist social change. Liberal feminism is rooted in the history of liberalism as a mode of political theory—one that developed particularly over the course of the nineteenth century—and it is centered on the premise of equality and the capacity for existing democratic social institutions to create equal rights and equal opportunity for all. Although rooted in thought over 200 years old, liberalism is the foundation for democracy; it promotes the removal of particularistic barriers—that is, practices that discriminate based on particular characteristics such as gender, race, and religion. Although to many this seems like an ideal solution for promoting gender equality, you will see that there are some fundamental limitations to this approach.

Liberal feminism emphasizes social and legal reform through policies designed to create equal opportunities for women. In addition, it emphasizes gender socialization as the origin of gender differences, thereby assuming that changes in socialization practices will result in more liberated and egalitarian gender relations.

Liberal feminism differs from other feminist theoretical perspectives in accepting the basic structure of democratic social institutions as conducive to social change. As you will see in the subsequent chapter, socialist feminism is a more radical perspective—one that interprets the origins of women's oppression in the systems of capitalism and patriarchy. Radical feminism analyzes patriarchy as the primary cause of women's oppression. Socialist feminism and radical feminism are examined in Chapter 13, along with other contemporary modes of feminist thought, including postmodernist feminist theory, multiracial feminism, and queer theory. As you will see, no single perspective provides the singularly most correct analysis of women's place in society. As these two chapters will show, each perspective has its own conceptual strengths and weaknesses and thus is able to answer some questions better than others. Together, these feminist theoretical perspectives provide a rich and engaging analysis of women in society.

The adequacy of each perspective should be assessed, in part, in terms of its ability to address several fundamental issues in feminist thought. Most important, because feminism purports to liberate *all* women, a sound feminist analysis must be able to address the interrelationship of race, class, and gender. The adequacy of a given theoretical and political framework must be judged according to the perspective it provides on these relationships.

In addition to explaining how race, class, and gender intersect in women's experiences, feminist perspectives must address some of the central issues that are encountered in thinking about women. These issues follow from the topics that have organized the preceding chapters of this book and include understanding the social contruction of gender; the status of women in different social institutions, and the possibilities and strategies for social change.

❖ *The Liberal Basis of Modern Feminism*

In political and sociological theory, *liberal* has a particular meaning quite different from its common usage to mean open-minded, tolerant, or socially nontraditional. The specific philosophical meaning of **liberalism** is characterized by an emphasis on individual rights and equal opportunity.

As was stated earlier, liberalism is the dominant political philosophy in the United States. Those who might never consider themselves liberal—in the sense the label has come to imply—nonetheless are likely to believe that the best society is one in which no group receives special treatment based on its race, color, religion, national origin, or gender. Indeed, this philosophy is the very foundation for modern civil rights legislation. It is a position that advocates a color-blind and gender-neutral society. Many take this position to the extreme, thinking that to even acknowledge another's gender or race is to be sexist or racist. This attitude stems from the underpinnings of liberal social thought, even when it is used by conservatives to support the status quo.

As a political and social theory, liberalism has generated quite specific programs for social change—notably, eliminating any practices or laws that either discriminate against particular groups and, as with the movement among current conservatives, trying to eliminate any programs that have race- or gender-specific components (such as affirmative action).

The liberal politics of the women's movement include a range of organizations and issues, perhaps best exemplified by the National Organization for Women (NOW), founded in 1966. As a national organization, NOW works within the established economic and political systems to advocate for social changes on behalf of women. Other liberal feminist organizations such as the National Women's Political Caucus and the National Abortion Rights Action League also work within the existing political system through extensive lobbying and agendas for legislative reform. The gains inspired by liberal feminism have made significant changes in women's lives. On issues ranging from equity in employment to reproductive rights, liberal reforms have resulted in increased opportunities for women and increased public consciousness of women's rights. The fact that liberal feminism works largely within existing institutions has, most likely, contributed to its broad-based support.

Because liberalism is such a popular strand of feminist thought and is fundamental to the assumptions of some feminist politics, it is important to carefully examine its intellectual roots. The origins of liberal philosophy lie in western Europe and the societal transitions of the eighteenth and nineteenth centuries. By examining this context and the social thought produced within it, you will see the theoretical tenets of the liberal perspective, as well as its connection to the evolution of feminist thought. Although you have already reviewed the growth of feminism in the United States in the nineteenth and twentieth centuries, this historical analysis of liberal thought will give a more detailed and analytical vision of the liberal basis of some feminist beliefs and politics.

❖ *Liberalism as a Mode of Social Thought*

The origins of contemporary liberal feminism reach back to the seventeenth- and eighteenth-century **Age of Enlightenment** in western Europe (also known as the *Age of Reason*). This period fostered an array of political, social, and intellectual movements, most of them characterized by an explicit faith in the capacity of human reason to generate social reform. As the setting for the early philosophies of feminism, the Age of Enlightenment is noted for its libertarian ideals, its pleas for humanitarian reform, and its conviction that "reason shall set us free" (Rossi 1973).

The philosophy of the period provided the theme for major changes in Western social organization (including the French and American revolutions), and it set the stage for the eventual development of social-scientific thought and the emergence of sociology as an academic field. The historical context of early feminist thought is found in conditions that inspired more general appeals to social reform through the application of human reason. This period provides the historical arena for the emergence of contemporary liberal feminism.

Two notable developments influenced broad-scale change in the West: the consolidation and expansion of a world system of capital (Wallerstein 1976) and a decline in the traditional sacred authority of religion (Nisbet 1970). The development of Western capitalism created new systems of inequality marked by the displacement of the poor from rural land and the concentration of wealth in the hands of the new capitalist class. The related developments of urbanization and industrialization also planted the seeds of the social problems that continue to confront us today: urban crowding and the development of slums, pollution and waste, poverty, crime, and new tensions in family life. In the Age of Enlightenment, political thinkers who observed these changes also delighted in the decline of the influence of the sacred authority of the church and the secular feudal state. Enlightenment thinkers fostered the hope that the human ability to reason would provide societies with reasonable solutions to the new problems they encountered.

One of the central tenets of Enlightenment philosophy and the political-social thought it inspired was that free, critical inquiry was to be the cornerstone for the future. At heart, the Enlightenment thinkers were optimists, and they seemed undaunted by the vast problems surrounding them. Although, in retrospect, they can be criticized for their naive faith in human rationality, their work emphasized open inquiry (Hughes 1958).

The Enlightenment libertarian ideals challenged the power of feudal elites and assumed that the future was in the hands of the masses. As they considered the development of history, they envisioned a decline in the brutal and "uncivilized" physical abuses of the past (de Tocqueville 1945). They believed that the church, identified by most Enlightenment thinkers as the villain of past repression, would continue to decline in its authoritarian influence; modern society would instead be regulated by the rational construction of democratic government.

The influence of the Enlightenment extends beyond the eighteenth century, laying the foundation for the development of social science in the nineteenth and twentieth centuries and influencing later thinkers such as *John Stuart Mill* in the nineteenth century. Sociology, in particular, is indebted to the Enlightenment for its emphasis on the application of reason and the scientific method to the solution of social problems. Early sociological thinkers such as *Auguste Comte* (1798–1857) and *Henry Saint-Simon* (1760–1825) believed that social knowledge would take the form of social laws, telling us how the social world operated and how we could therefore engineer positive changes. The simplicity of their faith in sociology as the ultimate science is now apparent, but their influence on the positivist methods of sociology is immeasurable. The positivism they inspired and that others have developed since assumes that the techniques of scientific observation in the physical sciences can be used in the discovery of social behavior. Their insistence on the application of sociological knowledge for engineering social change continues to influence the activities of modern social planners.

We are not sure what the Enlightenment was like for women, because its recorded history has been largely that of men's accomplishments. We do know that women's historical experience differs significantly from men's (Kelly-Gadol 1976), and feminist historians have suggested that the Enlightenment is no exception. They would argue that the Age of Reason is a reference only to the reason of certain men. During this same era, women's work was idealized as belonging in the emotional world of the home; nevertheless, women's labor (both in the home and outside of it) constituted a major part of the society's economic productivity. Most women still produced marketable goods in the home and, as factories became the sites for production, women and children were employed for long hours at low wages.

Seen in the context of women's lives, the period of Enlightenment takes on a somewhat different meaning. Both women and the working class seem to have been left out of the Age of Reason, because the intellectual movement of the Enlightenment was largely based on the thought of bourgeois White men. During this same period in the United States, most African American women and men were still enslaved, and, although slavery was one of the concerns of the men of the Enlightenment, histories of feminist thought rarely look to the thoughts of African American women, slave or free, as an origin for early feminist work. The development of feminist thought cannot be placed exclusively, though, in the Enlightenment. African American women such as Charlotte Forten, Maria Stewart, Sojourner Truth, and Ida Bell Wells articulated some of the early principles of feminist thought (Lerner 1973; Sterling 1984; Collins 1990). Maria Stewart, a former servant to a clergy family in New England, was the first woman in the United States to deliver a public lecture (in Boston on September 21, 1832). Although rarely recognized in the histories of feminism, her exhortations to women domestic workers and day laborers to improve their minds and talents, which she saw as thwarted by women's servitude, are clear and passionate feminist ideals. When she left Boston because of hostile public response to her work, she delivered a parting speech ardently defending the right of women to speak in public (Sterling 1984). To exclude women such as Stewart and the many other African American thinkers and activists of this early period from the history of feminist thought is to take White European and American philosophers as creating the history of feminism and to see African American women's feminist ideas only as secondary or as a reaction to White thought (Gilkes 1985).

This interpretation does not mean we should disregard the influence of Enlightenment thought on the history of feminism, but it does cast this history in a different light. The legacy of the Enlightenment as the triumph of man's reason is a celebration of the growing preeminence at this time of men's rational power. Women during this period were identified with the irrational and emotional side of life. The ascent of rationality, which the Enlightenment celebrates, can then be seen as the ascent of male rational power over the presumed emotionality and inferiority of women. This revision puts the thinkers of the Enlightenment period into a different context and also reveals different aspects of their work. Feminist historians who have studied the major Enlightenment philosophers (Rousseau, Diderot, and Condorcet, for example) conclude that although the Enlightenment philosophers had the potential to decry the sexist ideas of sacred traditions, most of the Enlightenment thinkers ignored the revolutionary potential of their ideas for change in women's lives (Kleinbaum 1977). Still, the thinkers of the Enlightenment did have a strong influence on the development of modern feminism.

Even with the caveat that most women did not experience the Enlightenment in the way men did, this period left a philosophical tradition in the dominant culture that lives on. The two central principles of this framework of thinking are: the concept of individual liberty and the emphasis on human reason as the basis for humanitarian social change. In liberal feminism, these philosophical ideals are the basis for the principle of equal opportunity and social reform. Much of the focus of social change among liberal feminist groups lies in the construction of legislation and in the regulation of employment practices. According to the liberal perspective, the obstacles to equal rights for women (as well as other groups) lie in traditional laws and practices that deny the same individual rights to women that men already have.

The liberal perspective assumes that persons can create humanitarian change through the use of human rationality. Injustice is viewed as the result of irrationality and ignorance. Reason and the pursuit of knowledge are believed to be the source of social change; consequently, liberal policies for change rely on a faith in the process of social reform. Liberal feminists' practical solutions to inequality include programs that prohibit **discrimination** (e.g., differential treatment). Given women's reports of continuing discrimination (see Figure 12.2) this is clearly an important goal. Liberal feminism also seeks the reform of individuals through, for example, the resocialization of children and the relearning of appropriate social roles for adults. A central emphasis of the liberal perspective is that all persons' abilities are culturally learned; therefore, egalitarian gender relations will follow from relearning traditional gender-role attitudes and behaviors.

The popularity of the liberal perspective makes it difficult to identify as a specific social and political philosophy. It is the philosophical backdrop to many contemporary programs for change, and it has been widely adopted by diverse groups working for legal and economic reform. Liberalism also encourages the acceptance of diverse lifestyles, because it sees lifestyle as a matter of individual choice. Within

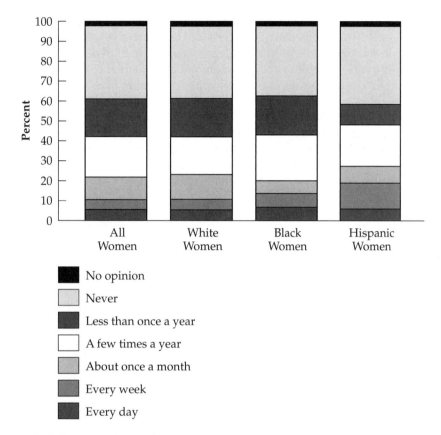

FIGURE 12.2   How Often Do You Feel Discriminated Against in Public Life or Employment?

Source: Data from Lydia Saad. 2001. "Women See Room for Improvement in Job Equity." *Gallup Poll Monthly* (June): 56–63.

the liberal perspective, persons and the societies they create should be tolerant and respectful of the choices persons make. Because persons have civil rights to exercise their freedom, societies should not erect barriers to individual liberties. The liberal perspective, like other feminist perspectives, rejects the conservative view that persons assume their status in life because of ascribed (biological) characteristics and attributes the different statuses that people acquire to social learning and the denial of opportunity. Liberal feminists (along with other feminists) thus reject the conservative belief that women are bound to particular roles and statuses because of their biological capacity to bear children.

In sum, liberal feminism assumes that the inequality of women stems both from the denial of equal rights and from women's learned reluctance to exercise their rights. The goal of liberal feminism is equality—the construction of a social world where all persons can exercise individual freedom. At its heart, the liberal perspective is a philosophy based on the principle of individual liberty. In the liberal framework, every person should be allowed to exercise freedom of choice, unfettered by either public opinion or law. In effect, all persons should be given equal opportunities, and civil rights should be extended to all. Liberal feminist philosophy lies behind the call for reforms such as the ERA (Equal Rights Amendment), which, if it had been enacted, would amend the Constitution to state: "Equality of rights under the law shall not be denied or abridged by the United States or by any state on the basis of sex." One indication of the nation's unwillingness to fully embrace liberal feminist ideals is the fact that such an amendment has never been ratified, so as to make it the law of the land.

❖ Early Liberal Feminists

Who were the early thinkers who developed the framework of liberal feminism? Mary Wollstonecraft is one of the first to provide the philosophical foundations of modern feminism. Harriet Martineau is another of the early women to analyze women's condition in society. And most political philosophers recognize John Stuart Mill as one of the founders of liberal political philosophy; feminists have added his life partner, Harriet Taylor Mill, to the history of liberal thought. Because of their importance in articulating the framework of liberal feminism, their works are detailed next.

Mary Wollstonecraft

Mary Wollstonecraft's (1759–1797) essay, *A Vindication of the Rights of Women*, first published in London in 1792, was so provocative that editions of it quickly appeared in Dublin, Paris, and New York (Poston 1975). So astutely did she outline the position of women that her essay was equally provocative to White, middleclass women who discussed it in consciousness-raising groups in the 1960s and 1970s. Her words continue to inspire women almost 200 years after the original edition was published—a testimony to the influence Wollstonecraft has had.

Wollstonecraft left her home as a teenager in 1778. Distressed by her father's excessive demands for obedience and her family's continued poverty, she wandered from town to town in the countryside of Wales and England (Rossi 1973). Her independence and self-sufficiency established a lifetime pattern of refusing to submit to authority—both in her life and in her writings. She later wrote:

> *I will venture to affirm, that a girl, whose spirits have not been damped by inactivity, or innocence tainted by false name, will always be a romp, and the doll will never excite attention unless confinement allows her no alternative. Girls and boys, in short, would play harmlessly together, if the distinction of sex was not inculcated long before nature makes any difference. I will go further and affirm, as an indisputable fact, that most of the women, in the circle of my observation, who have acted like rational creatures, or shown any vigour of intellect, have accidentally been allowed to run wild* (Wollstonecraft 1792/1975:43).

Her concern with subservience to authority recurs as a central theme in her work, and it is tied to her argument that learning and socialization are responsible for the formation of mind. Foretelling generations of feminists to come, Wollstonecraft argued that gender role characteristics were the result of education (used broadly in her work to mean all social learning). What appeared to be the natural weakness of women was the result of their lack of liberty and their dependence on men. She wrote, "All the differences that I can discern, arise from the superior advantage of liberty, which enables the former to see more of life" (Wollstonecraft 1792/1975:23). She went on to say:

It is vain to expect virtue from women till they are in some degree independent of men; nay, it is vain to expect that strength of natural affection which would make them good wives and mothers. Whilst they are absolutely dependent on their husbands they will be cunning, mean and selfish, and the men who can be gratified by the fawning fondness of spaniel-like affection have not much delicacy, for love is not to be bought; its silken wings are instantly shriveled up when anything besides a return in kind is sought (1792/1975:144).

Throughout her essay, Wollstonecraft emphasized that blind submission to authority not only limits social and political freedom but also inhibits the development of mental reasoning. Like others in the Enlightenment, she imagined that the downfall of tyranny would occur as society became organized around the principle of rational thought. She wrote, "Tyrants would have cause to tremble if reason were to become the rule of duty in any of the relations of life, for the light might spread till perfect day appeared" (1792/1975:150).

Wollstonecraft equated the life of a dutiful soldier to that of a well-socialized woman:

They both acquire manners before morals, and a knowledge of life before they have, from reflection, any acquaintance with the grand ideal outline of human nature. The consequence is natural; satisfied with common nature, they become a prey to prejudices, and taking all their opinions on credit, they submit blindly to authority. So that, if they have any sense, it is a kind of instinctive glance, that catches propositions, and decides with respect to manners but fails when arguments are to be pursued below the surface, or opinions analyzed (1792/1975:24).

More than other early White feminists, Wollstonecraft was sensitive to the issue of social class and the artificial distinctions among persons that she believed social class created. She directed her arguments especially to leisure-class women, for, she said, it is in that class that women are most dependent on men. She held in contempt the idleness of mind and attention to gentility that she believed wealth produced: "The education of the rich tends to render them vain and helpless, and the unfolding mind is not strengthened by the practice of those duties which dignify the human character" (1792/1975:9). "The preposterous distinctions of rank, which render civilization a curse by dividing the world between voluptuous tyrants and cunning envious dependents, corrupt, almost equally, every class of people, because respectability is not attached to the discharge of the relative duties of life, but to the station" (1792/1975:144). Although she recognized that her observations were of a particular social class, she gave little, if any, attention to women of other classes and cultures.

Wollstonecraft's outspoken portrayals of femininity, authority, and property relations earned her a lifetime of insults and insinuations about her bad character. Her contemporaries indexed articles written about her under the topic "prostitution" (Rossi 1973; Wardle 1951); more recently, her feminist beliefs have raised charges that she was "pitifully weak," "consumed with penis envy," and an "extreme neurotic" (Lundberg and Farnham 1947). These same critics wrote, "Out of her illness arose the ideology of feminism, which was to express the feelings of so many women in years to come" (Lundberg and Farnham 1947:145–159).

Wollstonecraft's work is a powerful criticism of women's role and its connection to power and social control. Her writing typifies the passion with which the Enlightenment thinkers pursued their condemnations of traditional authority, and it stands as one of the most persuasive accounts of the effects of women's subservience on their powers of thought, behavior, and self-concept. Her statement that more egalitarian education was needed to liberate women sounds as if it could have been written yesterday. It is a tribute to Wollstonecraft's own capacities for reason and her unchecked passion for justice that her words continue to inspire people more than two centuries after they were written.

Harriet Martineau

Not long after Wollstonecraft's death in 1797, another woman was born who could appropriately be called the mother of sociology. Little recognized in contemporary histories of sociological thought, English woman Harriet Martineau (1802–1876) was one of the first to use field observation as a method for the development of social knowledge. She was the translator of Auguste Comte's (the father of sociology) *Positive Philosophy*; and, like her counterpart, Alexis de Tocqueville, she traveled widely in the United States, producing a descriptive and analytic account of her observations in her book *Society in America* (1837). Her other book, *How to Observe Manners and Morals* (1838), was the first methodology book in sociology, for in it she detailed the method of participant observation as she developed it in her own work (Lipset 1962; Rossi 1973; Hill and Hoecker-Drysdale 2002).

Like many of the early feminists, Martineau matched her concern for women's emancipation with her support for the U.S. abolition movement. Her outspokenness on the slavery issue, coupled with her daring to travel as a single woman in the nineteenth century, generated threats against her life. She was eventually forced to restrict her travels to the northern section of the country, but in her analysis she insisted on the right of women to speak their conscience. She wrote:

> *The whole apparatus of opinion is brought to bear offensively upon individuals among women who exercise freedom of mind in deciding upon what duty is, and the methods by which it is to be pursued. . . . The reproach in all the many similar cases I know is, not that the ladies hold anti-slavery opinions, but that they act upon them. The inces-*

sant outcry about the retiring modesty of the sex proves the opinion of the censors to be that fidelity to conscience is inconsistent with retiring modesty. If it be so, let the modesty succumb (1837:158–159).

As Marx and Engels were also later to proclaim, she also wrote, "If a test of civilization be sought, none can be so sure as the condition of that half of society over which the other half has power" (1837:156).

The connection Martineau made between the abolition and feminist movements is indicative of the association that early feminists had with their antislavery movement in the United States. White women's dissatisfaction with their position likely led to their involvement in and appreciation for the abolitionist cause (DuBois 1978). Their involvement in the antislavery movement taught White feminists how to understand and change their situation.

African American women in the antislavery movement were more likely to put racial prejudice at the center of their feminist analyses. Sarah Forten, for example, writing in 1837, discussed the influence of prejudice on her life. She said:

It has often embittered my feelings, particularly when I recollect that we are innocent victims of it . . . and [I] consequently seek to avoid as much as possible mingling with those who exist under its influence. I must also own that it has often engendered feelings of discontent and mortification in my breast when I see that many were preferred before me, who by education—birth—or worldly circumstance were not better than myself—their sole claim to notice depending on the superior advantage of being white (Sterling 1984:124).

White women who worked in the abolition movement gained an understanding from African American women of the concept of institutional power and adopted the political conviction of natural rights for all individuals, regardless of race or sex. Their analysis of racial and sexual oppression, however, remained at the level of analogy. Early White feminists did not develop an understanding that took account of the historical specificity of the African American experience in the United States, nor did they ever make the kind of analysis that could adequately account for class and other cultural differences among women (DuBois 1978). As a result, the liberal tradition of feminism that was established by leaders such as Elizabeth Cady Stanton (1815–1902) and Susan B. Anthony (1820–1906) began and continued with an inadequate comprehension of race and class issues in women's experience.

Martineau's own analysis of race and class is filled with contradictions. She appealed to justice and freedom, yet maintained the ethnic stereotypes typical of her period. She wrote:

The English, soon find it impossible to get American domestic help at all, and they are consigned to the tender mercies of the low Irish; and everyone knows what kind of servants they commonly are. Some few of them are the best domestics in America; those who know how to value a respectable home, a steady sufficient income, the honour of being trusted, and the security of valuable friends for life; but too many of them are unsettled, reckless, slovenly; some dishonest, and some intemporate (1837: 171–172).

Martineau's work stands as an example of early White feminist thought, complete with its class and race contradictions. More generally, despite appeals to reason, free will, humanitarianism, and liberty, liberal feminism has never adequately addressed the issues of race and class inequality. In stating that racism and sexism are analogous forms of oppression, liberal feminism suggests an analysis that would take race, class, and gender into account, but, as the concluding section of this chapter shows, this analysis is not provided by liberal White feminists, leaving the theoretical and political task of comprehending race, class, and gender oppression to other thinkers.

John Stuart Mill and Harriet Taylor Mill

No thinkers have been more influential in the development of liberal feminism than John Stuart Mill (1806–1873) and Harriet Taylor Mill (1807–1858). *The Subjection of Women*, first published in 1851, was the philosophical inspiration for the British suffrage movement and, like Wollstonecraft's *A Vindication of the Rights of Women*, continues to be studied. Their essays relate women's oppression to a systematic critique of liberty and the relations between women and men.

From an early age, John Stuart Mill was steeped in the rigors of intellectual thought and disciplined study. Under his father's stern supervision, he began a course of study at age 3 that created his intellectual genius at the same time that it apparently robbed him of emotional gratification (Rossi 1970). His life was one of continuous intellectual production mixed with political activism and long struggles with emotional depression. His father's intense emphasis on rational thought left Mill with a long struggle to "cultivate the feelings," an accomplishment perhaps best made through his strong relationship with Harriet Taylor (later to become Harriet Taylor Mill).

The relationship between John Stuart Mill and Harriet Taylor is one that matches romantic commitment and intellectual collaboration with a fervor for individual liberty; so passionate and unusual was their life together that it is still the subject of discussion. Through their correspondence and conversation with each other, their published ideas were formed. Mill himself wrote that the ideas in *The Subjection of Women* (published after Harriet's death) belonged to his wife and had emerged from their vast discussions on a topic dear to them both. Over the years, scholars have seldom given Harriet Mill the recognition she deserves for her contribution to these works or, for that matter, to her own writing. The fact that Harriet Taylor Mill has so seldom been cited in the many detailed reviews of the Mills' work underscores the sexist character of philosophical criticism and points out how little credit has been given to women thinkers of the past. Alice Rossi has made a convincing case that the Mills' work was a joint effort, even though it was published under his name. She also argues that *Enfranchisement of Women* (published in 1851) was actually written by Harriet Mill (Rossi 1970).

Taken together, the Mills' essays provide the most comprehensive statement of the liberal perspective of feminist thought. The issues they raise can be grouped into several key areas—the logic of inquiry, gender differences, work and the family, and the process of modernization and social change.

The Logic of Inquiry

The logic of the Mills' arguments is typical of that inspired by the rational perspective of the Enlightenment thinkers. Convictions, the Mills claimed, fare poorly in argumentative debate, for the resistance of conviction to reason makes rational argument impossible. Strong feelings, they maintained, are impenetrable by rational debate; consequently, those who argue against almost universally held opinions will, most certainly, have a hard time being heard. In discussing the subordination of women, the Mills clearly argued that open inquiry—especially listening to women's voices—is a prerequisite to establishing knowledge of women's lives. They wrote:

> We may safely assert that the knowledge which men can acquire of women, even as they have been and are, without reference to what they might be, is wretchedly imperfect and superficial and always will be so, until women themselves have told all they have to tell. . . . Let us remember in what manner, up to a recent time, the expression, even by a male author, of uncustomary opinions, or what are deemed eccentric feelings, usually was, and in some degree still is, received; and we may form some faint conception under what impediments a woman, who is brought up to think custom and opinion her sovereign rule, attempts to express in books anything drawn from the depths of her own nature (cited in Rossi 1970:152–153).

The starting point of their argument, as well as the central concept in the liberal perspective, is that all persons have equal liberty, and therefore human institutions should treat all alike. Their words provide the philosophy behind the modern practice of equal employment opportunity and equality before the law. They wrote, "The law should be no respector of persons, but should treat all alike, save where dissimilarity of treatment is required by positive reasons, either justice or of policy" (Mill 1970:4). They defined human liberty as a natural right and one that should not be denied on the basis of any individual or group characteristics. As their writing shows, the rational style of their argument is coupled with a passionate emphasis on the necessity for liberating social changes.

The Social Construction of Gender

The Mills showed how social conditions create gender-specific attitudes and behaviors. By imagining new alternatives, the Mills showed how a change in the relationship between men and women would likely alter the characteristics usually thought to be natural differences. They argued that there is no reasonable defense for the current state of affairs and that the creation of liberty for women would benefit not just women but society as a whole. The social benefits of liberation would include "doubling the mass of mental faculties available for the higher service of humanity" (Mill 1970:153), overcoming the selfish attitudes and self-worshipping characteristics of humanity (1970:148), and enhancing the "softening influence" (1970:156) of women's moral tendencies.

What is considered to be natural is only what is taken for granted, they argued. Foretelling the thoughts of contemporary feminists, they wrote:

> *Was there ever any domination which did not appear natural to those who possessed it? There was a time when the division of mankind into two classes, a small one of masters and a numerous one of slaves, appeared, even to the most cultivated minds, to be a natural, and the only natural, condition of the human race. . . . Did not the slave owners of the Southern United States maintain the same doctrine, with all the fanaticism with which men cling to the theories that justify their passions and legitimate their personal interests (Mill 1970: 20–21)?*

Like contemporary social scientists, the Mills saw that what appears natural is primarily the result of social learning. Because women had been held in such an unnatural state of submission and domination, the Mills believed it was impossible to make claims about natural gender differences. All that we see as masculinity or femininity, they contended, is the result of learned, not actual, differences. They wrote, "Women have always hitherto been kept, as far as regards spontaneous development, in so unnatural a state, that their nature cannot but have been greatly distorted and disguised" (1970:104–105). They went on, "I deny that any one knows, or can know, the nature of the sexes, as long as they have only been seen in their present relation to one another" (1970:38), and said, "One thing we may be certain of—that what is contrary to women's nature to do, they will never be made to do by simply giving their nature free play" (1970:48).

The Mills made the case for liberty by identifying the detrimental effects of social learning or, in their words, education and custom, under a state of subjection. They assumed that persons construct their social arrangements and social identities, although some may have more power than others to do so. Human beings, they argued, are rational and creative. Only by removing constraints and obstacles to liberty can the free expression of rational choice and humane social development be encouraged. According to the Mills, human beings have a natural right to self-expression that unnatural systems of authority and rule take away.

The Mills' concept of liberty rests on the idea of voluntary contracts among human actors. Accordingly, they argued that marriage ties should be based on free and voluntary choice and that law, in marriage and other areas, should treat all alike—giving no unnatural advantage to one group or another. The purpose of *The Subjection of Women* is, in fact, to show the following:

> *The principle which regulates the existing social relations between the two sexes—and legal subordination of one sex to the other—is wrong in itself, and now one of the chief hindrances to human improvements; and that it ought to be replaced by a principle of perfect equality, admitting no power or privilege on the one side, nor disability on the other (Mill 1970:1).*

Harriet Taylor Mill, in her own essay, *Enfranchisement of Women,* argued, in addition, that: "We deny the right of any portion of the species to decide for another portion, or any individual for another individual, what is and what is not their proper sphere" (Rossi 1970:100). Although the Mills differed on their opinions about women's place in marriage, their attitude toward self-determination was clearly one that denies the right of any one group to restrain another. As they wrote, "The law which is to be observed by both should surely be made by both; yet, as hitherto, by the stronger only" (Rossi 1970:68). This premise in their work is also the foundation for their ideas on women's position in the workplace and the family.

Work and the Family
The Mills' belief in individual liberty is also seen in their arguments on women's occupations. They believed in the *laissez-faire* operation of the economic market, meaning that they favored a nonintervention approach to economic processes. Their assumption was that if persons are free to choose their occupations, then the best qualified will fill the positions most appropriate to their talents.

These assumptions are grounded in the earlier work of the British economist *Adam Smith.* Smith maintained that the economic market should be based on open competition and a lack of regulation or interference. According to Smith, this laissez-faire policy best suits the laws of the market. He identified the laws of the market as stemming from the self-interest of individuals and reasoned that open competition between individuals will establish a harmony of interests as individuals mutually compete to establish reasonable prices for the sale of goods. Because Smith believed this process to be the natural law of the market, he concluded that the most effective policy is a hands-off, or laissez-faire, approach.

Although the Mills did not speak so directly about the laws of the economy, they similarly assumed that free competition is the key to economic equity—at least in terms of occupational choice. In *The Subjection of Women,* they wrote:

It is not that all processes are supposed to be equally good, or all persons to be equally qualified for everything; but that freedom of individual choice is now known to be the only thing which procures the adoption of the best processes, and draws each operation into the hands of those who are best qualified for it. . . . In consonance with this doctrine, it is felt to be an overstepping of the proper bounds of authority to fix beforehand on some general presumption, that certain persons are not fit to do certain things (Mill 1970:32).

The Mills' arguments about an open choice of occupation have one important qualifier, however. Despite their general position on the emancipation of women, John Stuart Mill and Harriet Taylor Mill disagreed about women's preferred occupation. John Stuart Mill believed that the occupation women should (and would) choose is marriage. He argued that in marriage, women's work is to be the moral educators of children and to make life beautiful; thus, regardless of his advocacy of an open marketplace, in his correspondence with Harriet Taylor, he wrote:

It does not follow that a woman should actually support herself because she should be capable of doing so: in the natural course of events she will not. *It is not desirable to burden the labour market with a double number of competitors. In a healthy state of things, the husband would be able by his single exertions to earn all that is necessary for both: and there would be no need that the wife should take part in the mere providing of what is required to* support *life: it will be for the happiness of both that her occupation should rather be to adorn and beautify it (John Stuart Mill and Harriet Taylor Mill,* Early Essays on Marriage and Divorce, *in Rossi 1970:74–75).*

Later, in *The Subjection of Women*, Mill wrote:

In an otherwise just state of things, it is not, therefore, I think, a desirable custom that the wife should contribute by her labour to the income of the family. . . . Like a man when he chooses a profession, so, when a woman marries, it may in general be understood that she makes choice of the management of a household, and the bringing up of a family, as the first call upon her exertions, during as many years of her life as may be required for the purpose; and that she renounces, not all other objects and occupations, but all which are not consistent with the requirement of this (Mill 1970:88–89).

Despite his general arguments to the contrary, John Stuart Mill thought that women were more self-sacrificing than men and that they would by *nature* want marriage. Only a free market, however, will sort out which individuals have this nature and which do not. Still, he would prefer not to change the traditional activities of women in the family. He wrote, "The education which *does* belong to mothers to give . . . is the training of the affections. . . . The great occupation of women should be to beautify life" (Rossi 1970:76).

Harriet Taylor Mill disagreed with Mill on this subject, and her arguments show her to be the more radical of the two. In *The Enfranchisement of Women*, she argued, "To say that women must be excluded from active life because maternity disqualifies them for it, is in fact to say, that every other career should be forbidden them in order that maternity may be their only resource" (Rossi 1970:105). In the same essay, she said, "Let every occupation be open to all, without favour or discouragement to any, and employments will fall into the hands of those men or women who are found by experience to be most capable of worthily exercising them" (Rossi 1970:100–101).

The disagreement between John Stuart Mill and Harriet Taylor Mill indicates one of the shortcomings in liberal feminist philosophy. He stops short of advocating full equality for women, because he does not support major changes in family relations. Harriet Taylor Mill's analysis is more far-reaching because she argues for the unqualified equality of women with men. Both of them, however, fail to make a radical analysis of women's status because their assumptions ignore the limits to individual free choice that are created by structured inequality.

The Mills' analysis of occupation is characterized by meritocratic assumptions. A **meritocracy** is a system in which persons hold their positions allegedly on the basis of their individual talents and achievement. Although meritocracies supposedly allow anyone to succeed, regardless of their class, race, or gender, we know that these factors matter—and matter a lot—in shaping opportunities. The Mills' analysis ignores how social systems are marked by unequal power, privilege, and rewards. In short, their analysis does not overcome inequality.

Because the Mills do not develop a theory of social class or a perspective on racism, their view of the emancipation of women is also based primarily on the optimistic belief that social progress is marked by the increased liberty of the individual. As a central tenet in liberal philosophy, this concept of individual liberty leaves unanswered the question of how institutions are structured around inequality. At the same time, the liberal perspective implies that individual liberty will result in the social transformation of the whole society.

Modernization and Social Change

The picture of the future that liberalism portrays tends to be an optimistic one. Their view of history assumes that modern Western civilization is more progressive than past civilizations because, in the Mills' language, the modern, advanced state leaves behind the tyrannies and repressions of the past. The Mills conceptualized history in terms of progressive improvement, and they imagined the future as lacking the subjugation and repression of the past.

In keeping with the Enlightenment perspective, the Mills assumed that the historical rule of force would end with the development of modern rationalized institutions. History, they argued, replaces the use of force with the use of reason. Accordingly, social organization is no longer based on ascriptive roles, but rather on the achieved merit of individuals. The Mills wrote:

> *For what is the peculiar character of the modern world—the difference which chiefly distinguishes modern institutions, modern social ideas, modern life itself, from those of times long past? It is, that human beings are no longer born to their place in life, and chained down by an inexorable bond to the place they are born to, but are free to employ their faculties, and such favourable chances as offer, to achieve the lot which may appear to them most desirable (Mill 1970:29–30).*

The Mills' attitude toward this alleged change is consistent with their desire for equality of choice. Their plea for the enfranchisement of women was based on the argument that women are the only exception to an otherwise emancipated world. They wrote:

> *At present, in the more* improved *countries, the disabilities of women are the only case, save one, in which laws and institutions take persons at their birth, and ordain that they shall never in their lives be allowed to compete for certain things. The one exception is that of royalty. . . . The disabilities, therefore, to which women are subject from the mere fact of their birth, are the solitary examples of the kind in modern legislation (Mill 1970:35; emphasis added).*

Although this essay was published following the emancipation of the slaves in the United States, the Mills' arguments reveal naive optimism about the actual disenfranchisement of many social groups. Although broad-scale legislation had struck down many ascriptive barriers in the law, in practice a large majority of society remained oppressed. The Mills' naiveté in considering that inequality of rights was a "relic of the past" (1970:30) rests solely on their belief that rationality provides a new moral base for society. The Mills envisioned the Western world as the most advanced of all forms of civilization; yet this view is both **ethnocentric** (meaning that it regards one's own group as superior to all others) and is founded on class- and race-based assumptions about the desirability of present social arrangements. The Mills' commitment to rationality as a moral basis for society blinded them to the facts of continuing inequality and oppression of underprivileged peoples in the contemporary Western world.

The Mills' optimism about social change also led them to assume that women's status had necessarily improved over time. They wrote:

> *Experience does say, that every step in improvement has been so invariably accompanied by a step in raising the social position of women, that historians and philosophers have been led to adopt their elevation or disbasement as on the whole the surest test and most correct measure of the civilization of a people or an age. Through all the progressive period of human history, the condition of women has been approaching nearer to equality with men (Mill 1970:37).*

Feminist studies have shown that women's status has not necessarily improved with time (Kelly-Gadol 1976). In Western culture, women's status has fluctuated, depending on developments in industrialization, capitalism, the advent of technology, and transformations in patriarchal relations. The Mills' assumption that the position of women was necessarily improving is a reflection of their sincere commitment to bringing about that change. Because they did not study specific historical developments in women's roles created by capitalism and patriarchy, however, their analysis of social change has a hollow ring.

These criticisms aside, the Mills' arguments for the emancipation of women still stand as provocative, replete with insightful ideas on the relationship of gender inequality to other systems of unjust authority and to the repression of individual freedom. Their failures result from what they did not explain, not from the errors of their inquiry. It is uncanny how truthful the Mills' ideas seem today. Apart from the particular eloquence of their style, their words could be those of a contemporary feminist. This discovery is, in fact, rather disheartening, for it indicates how unchanged are many of the structures resulting in women's inequality, despite the many changes that have occurred.

❖ *The Critique of Liberal Feminism*

The strengths of the liberal feminist position are its insistence on individual freedom, its toleration for diverse lifestyles, and its support of economic, social, and political reform. These ideas reflect the bourgeois origins of liberal thought, which emphasize the importance and autonomy of the individual. Liberal philosophy reflects Western cultural values of individualism and personal achievement (Eisenstein 1981). But, liberalism's strengths are also its weaknesses, because each of these ideas has serious limitations that the liberal framework does not address.

Consider, for example, the theme of individual liberty and tolerance. Many probably agree that it is important to tolerate the individual's right to choose his or her lifestyle. The liberal perspective encourages us to say, for example, that gays and lesbians are entitled to live as they please. What liberalism does not do is to recognize that heterosexuality is institutionalized in this society and, thus, is made compulsory, with penalties for those who do not conform. From a liberal perspective, lesbianism is tolerated as a choice, but it is not seen as a positive alternative to the patriarchal control of female sexuality.

Similarly, the liberal perspective fails to explain the institutionalized basis for race and class oppression. By claiming that all persons—regardless of race, class, or gender—should have equal opportunities, liberals accept the existing system as valid, often without analyzing the structured inequality on which it is based. From a liberal feminist perspective, experiences of women of color are some among many. Explaining how White women's and White men's experience is also conditioned by racism is not part of the liberal program. Liberal feminism sees race as a barrier to individual freedom, but it does not see that the position of White women is structurally tied to that of women of color. This connection remains for other theoretical perspectives to make.

Liberal feminism's perspective on individual rights does remind us that social change must provide the basis for individual well-being; therefore, liberal feminism is premised on humanistic ethics for social change. Because liberal feminism is based on the premise that individuals are autonomous beings, it does recognize that women are independent of men. Early feminists (such as Wollstonecraft and the Mills) viewed women as having an independent and collective existence apart from men but left this point underdeveloped. The goal of liberal feminism is equality, but in saying that women should be equal to men, liberal feminism does not specify which men women want to be equal to. Thus, it glosses over the class and race structure of societal relations (Eisenstein 1981).

As a result, liberal feminism leaves much unanswered. It does not explain the emergence of gender inequality, nor can it account, other than by analogy, for effects of race and class stratification in women's lives. Its analysis for change tends to be limited to issues of equal opportunity and individual choice. As a political philosophy, it insists on individual liberty and challenges any social, political, and economic practice that discriminates against persons on the basis of group or individual characteristics. The major change advocated by liberal feminists is that more women should be admitted to the existing political and economic systems; consequently, discrimination is a key concept within the liberal framework, as is the conceptualization of women's oppression as the result of learned gender roles. The liberal perspective emphasizes gradual reform and assumes that progress can be accomplished within the structure of existing political, social, and economic institutions.

Understanding liberal feminism—its strengths and limitations—is important to understanding current discussions about **affirmative action** and other means of addressing gender inequality. Affirmative action was first developed as a program for social change by the Republican administration of Richard Nixon. The idea was that people had to act affirmatively to root out the effects of historic discrimination. Since the vestiges of discrimination from the past become rooted in the opportunity structure that people face in the present, affirmative action was developed to eliminate the favoritism accruing to those (i.e., White men) who, by virtue of gender and race discrimination, were in an advantaged position in the labor market relative to women and racial minorities. Affirmative action policies mean that employers have to take special note of the available pool of qualified women and minority applicants for a given job, thereby developing goals for employment that match the available pool of potential applicants.

Opponents of affirmative action now argue that it promotes race-specific and gender-specific policies. Affirmative action plans do recognize the race and gender characteristics of job applicants and student applicants as a factor to be considered, but not because the intent is to discriminate. Rather, the intent is to eliminate the influence of past discrimination (such as favoritism toward those with prior connections to the employer or, in the case of college admissions, so-called "legacy admissions"—meaning the favoritism given to children of alumni). Ironically, political conservatives have now implicitly adopted the philosophy of liberalism that no one should be treated differently because of their race, gender, or religion. This is, indeed, the cornerstone of a civil rights strategy to social change: the idea that no one's rights should be compromised because of gender, race, religion, nationality, age, sexual orientation, or other characteristics.

Affirmative action was upheld as a legal principle in a Supreme Court decision in 2004. Although opponents had filed two lawsuits based on an argument that affirmative action constituted "reverse discrimination," the Court ruled that race (thus, presumably gender as well) could be taken into account in affirmative action policies as long as they were narrowly tailored—that is, did not explicitly exclude people based on race. At the same time, however, the Court concluded that such policies would not be needed 25 years subsequent to their decision, leaving an optimistic footprint in the decision that race and gender discrimination would have disappeared by then. Time will tell.

The issue is how to change the cumulative and continuing privilege that accrues to some groups by virtue of their gender, race, and class while also creating a liberal, democratic society where—at least in the ideal—gender, race, and class no longer matter. Grappling with this question and with the fundamental injustices that are built into social institutions is the starting point for more radical feminist perspectives—examined in the following chapter.

❖ *Chapter Summary and Themes*

Feminist theory provides various frameworks for organizing the analysis of gender in society; each framework also underlies strategies for social change.

Liberal feminism is based on a reform framework, one that takes individual rights and neutrality in the law as the model for social change. Socialist feminism centers its analysis on the operation of the class system—and its relationship to the exploitation of women's work. Radical feminism analyzes patriarchy as the central cause of women's subordination. Each framework provides unique ways of analyzing women in society, and they can be used together for a comprehensive theoretical and political analysis.

Liberal feminism has its origins in the work of Enlightenment thinkers who valued human reason over traditional authority as the means to liberty and freedom for women.

Thinkers like Mary Wollstonecraft, John Stuart Mill, and Harriet Taylor Mill have left a legacy of analysis of the status of women that still informs us about women's role in society. Their work is founded on liberalism as a philosophical tradition that sees social tradition, not nature, as generating differences between men and women. They also argued passionately for women's rights, based on the liberal philosophy of equality before the law.

Even with its strengths, liberal feminism can be criticized for its focus on individual autonomy and the absence of an analysis of structured inequality.

Liberal feminism, like the liberal philosophy on which it is based, does not include an analysis of race or class differences and assumes that the basis for inequality lies mostly in past tradition, not in the continuing operation of systems of power and privilege.

❖ *Key Terms*

affirmative action	ethnocentric	liberalism
Age of Enlightenment	feminist theory	meritocracy
discrimination	liberal feminism	

❖ *Discussion Questions/Projects for Thought*

1. Identify a nineteenth-century African American woman whose works have been published. (See the collections by Anne Sterling, *We Are Your Sisters*, New York: Norton 1984, or Gerda Lerner, *Black Women in White America*, New York: Vintage 1973.) How would you describe the political theory of this thinker? How does her thinking compare to the feminism of White women during this period?

2. Identify one of the feminist organizations in your local community or state. Ask the organization for any material it has describing its goals and orientation. How would you describe the political orientation of this group? Is it based in liberal, socialist, or radical feminism? Identify the specific political ideals and actions that explain your answer.

3. Suppose that Mary Wollstonecraft were to return today and observe gender relations. How might she revise her feminist theory? What would she retain in her thinking?

❖ Internet Resources

National Organization for Women

http://www.now.org

Founded in 1966, the National Organization for Women (NOW) is one of the major feminist organizations. Although originating as a liberal feminist organization, NOW is an activist group that uses both traditional and nontraditional means to achieve justice for women. The website is rich with information about policies and activist projects to better women's lives.

The Gallup Organization

http://www.gallup.com

This organization conducts regular national opinion polls on a variety of subjects, including issues about women's rights, discrimination, and equal employment opportunities.

❖ Suggested Readings

Berry, Mary Frances. 1986. *Why ERA Failed: Politics, Women's Rights, and the Amending Process of the Constitution.* Bloomington: Indiana University Press.
This case study of the Equal Rights Amendment (ERA), written by the former director of the U.S. Civil Rights Commission, is an illustration of liberal politics, how they work, and why the passage of the ERA failed, despite its widespread support.

Eisenstein, Zillah. 1981. *The Radical Future of Liberal Feminism.* New York: Longman.
Although liberalism is typically criticized for its inability to make radical social change, Eisenstein shows the underlying radical philosophy of liberal feminism and its connection to fundamental social change.

Frye, Marilyn. 1983. *The Politics of Women's Reality.* Trumansburg, NY: The Crossing Press.
As a major feminist philosopher, Marilyn Frye illustrates the significance of feminist theory for analyzing society and women within society.

Jaggar, Alison M., and Paula S. Rothenberg, eds. 1993. *Feminist Frameworks: Alternative Theoretical Accounts of the Relations between Women and Men*, 3rd ed. New York: McGraw-Hill.
This collection of articles is organized around seven theoretical perspectives: conservatism, liberalism, classical Marxism, socialist feminism, radical feminism, multicultural feminism, and global feminism. It is one of the best anthologies to present the different theoretical positions of feminism and to do so by exploring how different theories explain certain issues in women's lives, including sexuality, work, and family.

Lorber, Judith. 1998. *Gender Inequality: Theories and Politics.* Los Angeles: Roxbury Publishing Co.
Lorber's book reviews diverse frameworks of feminist theory, especially as affecting sociological thinking.

Rossi, Alice, ed. 1970. *Essays on Sex Equality.* Chicago: University of Chicago Press.
This book includes reprints of the major essays on women by John Stuart Mill and Harriet Taylor Mill. Rossi's introduction provides the biographical and historical context for interpreting their work and their collaboration.

Sterling, Anne, ed. 1984. *We Are Your Sisters: Black Women in the Nineteenth Century.* New York: Norton.
This collection of writings is an outstanding sampler of the social and political thought of African American women in the nineteenth century. Although few of them have ever been formally recognized as major intellectuals, the anthology makes clear their major contributions to American thought.

13

CONTEMPORARY FRAMEWORKS IN FEMINIST THEORY

The Radical Origins of Feminist Theory: The Critique of Liberal Feminism

Historical Roots of Radical Feminism

Socialist Feminism: The Importance of Class and Capitalism

Karl Marx and Historical Materialism
Class and Capitalism
Ideology and Consciousness
The Woman Question
The Socialist Feminist Critique of Marx

Radical Feminism: The Power of Patriarchy

The Sex/Gender System
Sexuality and the State
Intersections of Capitalism and Patriarchy

Comparing Liberal, Socialist, and Radical Feminism

Multiracial Feminism

Postmodernist Feminism

Queer Theory and Sexualities

Continuing Questions for Feminist Theory

Chapter Summary and Themes

Key Terms

Discussion Questions/ Projects for Thought

Internet Resources

Suggested Readings

Feminist theory has its roots in the women's movement, a point important to remember as you learn about the different frameworks of feminist thought. As the women's movement has changed, so has feminist theorizing, because the evolution of feminism raises new questions for feminist analysis. It is important to remember that the women's movement has never been a unitary event. As we saw in Chapter 11, the women's movement emerged from multiple locations in society and embraces diverse perspectives and politics. Consequently, feminist theory arising from the women's movement is a mosaic of ideas, yet is one that is anchored in continuing questions about the structure of gender in society, its connection to other forms of oppression, and the gendered character of social institutions and beliefs.

In the previous chapter, we have already seen how liberal feminism grew from the movement to establish equal rights for women. In addition to liberal feminism, the women's movement has spawned other theoretical perspectives that raise different questions and have different implications for social activism and change. Feminist theory is not a static set of questions and perspectives; rather, it has evolved over a period of time, reflecting the concerns and assumptions of different historical moments in feminism. In the 1970s and 1980s, during the growth of the second wave of feminism, the major paradigms of feminist theory were liberal feminism, socialist feminism, and radical feminism—the latter two of which are examined in this chapter. Now, feminist theory is not so easily characterized within the bounds of these particular paradigms. Nonetheless, some of the questions that emerged from the radical critique of liberalism—as articulated by socialist and radical feminists—are still important.

Furthermore, feminist theory has also evolved into new paradigms that reflect the transformation of feminist thinking. Multiracial feminism, postmodernist feminism, and questions about sexuality now frame much of the scholarship feminists are producing. These new frameworks of thought stem from important contemporary questions about diversity among women, globalization and the international status of women, men's place in feminism, sexuality and gender, and the ongoing structure of power, as reflected in relations of gender, race, class, and power.

In this chapter, we review the emergence of more radical forms of feminism—namely socialist feminism and radical feminism—as frameworks that have guided the development of feminist theory. Following that review, we turn to contemporary perspectives in feminist theory and the new questions that such theorizing evokes.

❖ *The Radical Origins of Feminist Theory: The Critique of Liberal Feminism*

We have already seen that liberal feminism is grounded in some of the central principles of Western, democratic societies—particularly the focus on individual rights, freedom from discrimination, and equal access to social and political institutions. The work of the liberal feminist agenda is far from complete, given the barriers to equal opportunity that still exist. Liberal feminism is, nonetheless, theoretically congruent with dominant social institutions, even though women's rights are routinely compromised by these same institutions. Because liberal feminism is based on the concept of equal access to social institutions, it does not provide a criticism of the very structure of those institutions as a source of women's oppression. This has remained the task for more radical feminist perspectives.

In the early years of the second wave of the women's movement (beginning in the 1960s), socialist and radical feminism emerged as the major alternatives to liberal feminism. With their roots in more radical wings of the women's movement, these perspectives—along with the ongoing critique of feminism developed by women of color—provided alternative frameworks for the development of feminist theory. **Socialist feminism** located women's oppression in the structure of capitalism and its interrelationship with patriarchal gender relations. **Radical feminism** identifies patriarchal social relations as the primary cause of women's oppression. Since the origins of feminism, women of color have criticized the "whiteness" of the women's movement, seeing race and gender all along as intricately linked in women's experiences. As we will see later in the chapter, that criticism within feminism has now produced the rich body of theorizing known as **multiracial feminism.** Feminist studies have also been enriched by the development of **postmodernist feminism**—a perspective that emphasizes the socially constituted basis of gender in society. And, as feminists have sought to include sexuality in their analyses of gender, postmodernism and feminist theory have spawned **queer theory**—an analysis of sexualities that sees sexuality as highly fluid and subject to social definition. All of these forms of feminist theory are examined in this chapter, but first we examine socialist and radical feminism.

The radical analysis of socialist and radical feminism goes beyond the goal of liberal feminism to include women in existing societal institutions. Whereas the liberal framework emphasizes learned gender roles and discrimination as the primary causes of women's oppression, more radical feminists argue that dominant institutions are organized through gender, race, and class oppression. Radical feminists criticize liberal feminists for assuming that sexism is largely a remnant of traditional beliefs and practices—in other words, located in the past. As shown in the previous chapter, the liberal feminist perspective takes women's equality with men as its major political goal, and liberal feminists have documented the effects of discrimination and have identified the institutional practices and policies that foster continuing discrimination. In distinct contrast to this perspective, socialist and radical feminists argue that the success of liberal feminism only puts some women on a par with men without transforming the conditions of oppression that produce gender as well as class and race inequality. Thus, socialist and radical feminists have more thoroughly criticized the structure of Western, capitalist, patriarchal social institutions.

❖ *Historical Roots of Radical Feminism*

Just as liberal feminism has its roots in the historical frameworks of liberal thought, so do more radical feminist perspectives have earlier intellectual and political roots.

In the nineteenth century, the same political and economic changes that fostered the development of liberal political philosophy also stimulated the emergence of more radical perspectives, most notably the work of *Karl Marx* (1818–1883) and his collaborator, *Friedrich Engels* (1820–1895). Although working in the same period of time, the differences between the radical perspective of Marx and Engels and the liberal perspective of Mill point to the profound controversies over the analysis of social structure and social change that historical changes in the structure of Western society were generating at this time.

The middle and second half of the nineteenth century in western Europe and the United States were marked by the vast growth of capitalism and the rapid expansion of industrialization, along with widespread social and political changes inspired by the French Revolution and, in the United States, by the elimination of slavery, the expansion of western territories, and urbanization. The climate of social reform that began in this period set the stage for the British suffrage movement and the American feminist movement of the late nineteenth and early twentieth centuries. The political discourse that this period fostered created a diversity of political and social thought that fostered the growth of sociological theory (Bramson 1961; Zeitlin 1968).

Nineteenth-century feminism is characterized typically as a reform movement whose ideas are rooted in the liberal thought of persons such as John Stuart Mill and Harriet Taylor Mill, but the politics of this movement also emerged through debate and action between radical and reform leaders. Some groups in the nineteenth- and early twentieth-century feminist movement were as much influenced by class and union politics as they were by the spirit of moral reform characterizing the women's rights approach of nineteenth-century feminism. Case studies of both the suffrage movement (DuBois 1978) and the women's trade union movement (Dye 1975) in the United States reveal the complexities of the movements' attempts to grapple with the complexities of class, race, and gender politics. In the end, however, most nineteenth-century feminists were unable to transcend the class biases of their middle-class leadership. Some feminist leaders, such as Susan B. Anthony, also used prevailing racist and anti-immigrant sentiments to attract members and to articulate movement ideologies (DuBois 1978; Dye 1975). These failures to unite women across class, and race limited the effectiveness of nineteenth-century feminism, but some feminists in this period established a radical tradition for alliances with working-class women and articulated the beginnings of an analysis linking gender, race, and class oppression.

Many of the feminists of this period and the early twentieth century were also socialists who worked for radical causes, in addition to their feminist politics. *Charlotte Perkins Gilman* (1860–1935) developed a socialist feminist analysis in *Women and Economics* (published in 1898). She proposed that housework should be communally organized, particularly for working mothers, who were entering the paid labor force at this time. She suggested that apartment houses have one common kitchen where all families could be served and that cleaning, child care, nursing, and teaching should be paid professional work. The responsibility for this work should not fall on individual families, she thought, but instead on apartment house managers (Rossi 1973). Other radical thinkers of the time, such as *Emma Goldman*

(1869–1940) and *Agnes Smedley* (1892–1950), did not define feminism as their primary cause, but they clearly linked the oppression of women to other forms of economic and political oppression.

❖ Socialist Feminism: The Importance of Class and Capitalism

The stage for nineteenth century feminism was one where capitalist society was developing rapidly, bringing with it new forms of poverty, wage labor, and other changes that continue to mark our time. Slavery had just ended in the United States (following the end of the Civil War in 1865). Immigration from Europe to the United States was becoming more common. Women, although in many regards confined to families, were also moving into factory labor, as well as continuing their roles working in fields and in homes. Feminism was just emerging as a social and political force. This is the context for one of the most radical thinkers whose work continues to inspire both intellectual and political movements—Karl Marx.

Karl Marx and Historical Materialism

Marxist thought is one of the most influential and insightful analyses in modern intellectual history. Some argue that most sociological theory developed as a dialogue with the ideas that Karl Marx inspired (Zeitlin 1968). Certainly, for modern feminism, Marx's ideas are pivotal. Marx (1818–1883) began writing as a student; he was involved in some of the most politically and intellectually controversial movements of his time. He was active in a group known as the Young Hegelians, who based their studies and activities on the work of the German philosopher Georg Wilhelm Friedrich Hegel (1770–1832). Hegel's philosophy is based on the idea that persons create their world through reason; thus, rational ideas form the objective reality through which human beings construct their world. Hegel's philosophy, furthermore, sees the "real" as emanating from the "divine" (Giddens 1971:3), and Christian theology is an important foundation for his work. The Young Hegelians followed Hegel's concern with theology and adopted his philosophical perspective, until their outlook was radically transformed by the appearance of Ludwig Feuerbach's work *The Essence of Christianity* in 1841. Feuerbach (1804–1872) reversed the philosophy of ideas in Hegel's work by arguing that ideas follow the existence of human action. Feuerbach wrote, "Thought proceeds from being, not being from thought" (Giddens 1971:3). From Feuerbach's thesis, the divine is a construction of human thought; human activity, not ideas, provides the basis for social reality.

This philosophy led Marx's teacher and sponsor, Bruno Bauer (1809–1882), to assert that the Bible was a historical document and that Christian theology was a social and historical myth. Bauer was consequently dismissed from the university, because he was declared to be dangerous to the state. In a university system where one's future was dependent on academic sponsorship, Bauer's dismissal meant the end of Marx's academic career. Although Marx received his doctorate of philosophy from the University of Jena in 1841, he, who had once been predicted to be the most outstanding professor of his time, was never to hold a university post. The remainder of his life was spent in political exile and in poverty. He continued to write, working occasionally as a journalist, but he was forced to move from Germany to Paris and later to London because he was expelled by various governments.

In 1849, Marx moved to London, where he was to spend the last 34 years of his life. His family was extremely poor; several of his children died of malnutrition and disease. When his sixth child was born, he saw the birth as a catastrophe, because two of his children had already died and a third was gravely ill. He was scarcely consoled when the child was born a girl, Jenny Julia Eleanor, as he announced to his friend and collaborator Friedrich Engels that the child was "unfortunately of the sex par excellence" and "had it been a male the matter would be more acceptable" (Kapp 1972:21). Loans from Engels supported the family, along with Marx's occasional journalism jobs. Throughout this difficult time, Marx continued writing and studying, and he produced several works that would change the course of world history and the history of social thought.

The ideas Marx developed always reflected the early influences of Hegel and Feuerbach and resulted in a theoretical perspective often called **historical materialism** (also referred to as **dialectical materialism**). The central thesis of historical materialism is that the material conditions of people's lives shape their behavior and their beliefs. Human consciousness and behavior are formed by the interplay between persons as subjects and as objects in the world in which they live. Because human beings have the capacity to reflect on their actions, their ideas (and ideals) are reflections of their material world. People's relationship to their environment and what they think of it are mediated by the particular historical and social milieu of which they are a part. The possibilities for human existence are shaped by the choices and constraints imposed by material organization. Specifically, for Marx, the materialist thesis saw human production—what men and women actually do—as the basis for social structure. The cause of social change, for Marx, lay not in ideas and values that are abstracted from human experience. Instead, he saw societal change as emerging from the social relations and activities that themselves emerge through human labor (Giddens 1971).

The method of dialectical materialism, unlike that of many other sociological theories, is not deterministic. In other words, Marx did not see human history and experience as determined by particular features of social structure, but rather thought that social structure and social change are always emerging and reemerging according to the choices human beings make. In addition, Marx said there will always be contradictions within society and in the experience of human beings in society. That is to say, because social life is not simply determined, it will always involve inconsistencies and the tendency for conflict. Social change, according to Marx, arises from these contradictions and the action of human groups in trying to solve them.

According to Marx, human beings do more than merely exist; they reach their full human potential for creative living through social consciousness and their struggle against oppression. Capitalist social relations, he argued, distort human potential because, if human work is oppressive, then all social life is distorted. This must be changed—through a revolution against capitalism.

Marx saw systems of human production and reproduction as creating the conditions for everyday life. Marx and Engels defined *production* as the labor humans perform to satisfy their immediate needs and *reproduction* as the physical re-creation of both the species and the social systems in which human beings reproduce. In Engels's words, production and reproduction are the central features of human society:

> *According to the materialistic conception, the determining factor in history is, in the final instance, the production and reproduction of immediate life. This, again, is of a two-fold character: on the one side, the production of the means of existence, of food, clothing and shelter and the tools necessary for that production; on the other side, the production of human beings themselves, the propagation of the species. The social organization under which the people of a particular historical epoch and a particular country live is determined by both kinds of production: by the stage of development of labor on the one hand and of the family on the other (Engels 1884/ 1972:71–72).*

Class and Capitalism

The materialist perspective of Marx and Engels sees human activity (as it is engaged in productive relations) as the mainspring of social change and as the determining feature of social organization. In Marx's analysis, the economic mode of production forms the **infrastructure** of social organization; other institutions form the **superstructure,** meaning that they reflect the essential character of the economic system.

In the Western capitalist societies that Marx observed, the economic infrastructure was marked primarily by class struggle—the division of society into groups characterized by their relationship to the means of production. Under capitalism, two new major classes emerge: *capitalists,* who own the means of production, and the *proletariat* (or working class), who sell their labor to capitalist owners in exchange for wages. Two minor classes also exist: the *bourgeoisie* (merchants, managers, and artisans, for example), who become functionally dependent on capitalism, although they do not own the means of production; and the *lumpenproletariat,* who have no stable social location because they are individuals from a variety of classes and social locations. In Marx and Engels's words, they form "the 'dangerous class,' the social scum, that passive rotting mass thrown off by the lowest layers of old society" (Tucker 1972:25).

The Marxist concept of class differs significantly from that of non-Marxist social scientists, who use it to refer to stratified status or income hierarchies (see Chapter 5). **Class,** in the Marxist sense, refers specifically to the relationship of a group to the societal means of production; thus, it indicates a system of relationships, not a unit of like persons. Similarly, the concept of "ownership" refers not primarily to the accumulation of goods (which in Marxist theory may occur in any class), but to the actual ownership of a society's productive enterprises. To illustrate, a person in the proletariat class (working class) may own their shoes, but it is the capitalist class that owns the system of production that manufactures the shoes and profits from them.

Society emerges, according to Marxist thought, through class struggle. According to Marx and Engels, "The history of all hitherto society is the history of class struggles" (1970:16). Classes emerge as a society produces a surplus; as a division of labor emerges, thereby allowing for surplus production, the accumulation of a surplus can be appropriated by one group. As a result, this group stands in an exploitative relationship to the mass of producers, and class conflict is established (Giddens 1971). Marx and Engels point out that the first division of labor is the division of labor by sex for the purpose of propagating children and controlling women's labor in the household; gender thus provides the first class antagonism. They (and most subsequent Marxist thinkers), however, leave this point without further development.

As capitalism develops, the capitalist class appropriates the wealth produced by the subordinate classes because the capitalists have the power to control the conditions under which other classes work. The working class owns only its labor, which it must sell for wages; the capitalists, in turn, exercise the power to determine what wages they will pay and the conditions under which people work. As capitalists try to increase their profits, they do so at the increasing expense of laborers. Profit comes from the fact that workers produce more value than the wages they receive. The craft of distinctive workers becomes less important than the value of mass-produced commodities. Material objects, then, take on greater value than the workers who produce them. In effect, in Marxist analysis, the value of individual human activity decreases as the material value of the created products increases. You can see this process working today if you look at the use of labor in poor countries where workers (typically women and children) earn very low wages to make the goods that are consumed in wealthier nations. The capitalist class profits both at the expense of poor workers abroad and displaced workers in the United States.

Human beings, then, become alienated from the process, in the sense that they do not control or own the products of their labor; they choose neither the form nor the use of the products they make. Additionally, workers are alienated from each other, and they become alienated from themselves because they do not exercise the human ability to transform nature to their own design. Politically, according to Marx, workers must end the tyranny of private ownership of the means of production by reorganizing the means of production (and, feminists would add, reproduction); the accumulation of profit in the hands of a few must be eliminated. Marxists see that social changes that do not strike at the material basis of social life—capital accumulation by the owning class—will be insufficient because they will not change the underlying causes of social organization.

Ideology and Consciousness

The materialist thesis of Marx is also central to the perspective on consciousness and ideas that is developed throughout Marxist theory. Systems of knowledge take their historical form in response to the mode of production. Marx argued that the ideas of a period are a reflection of the interests of the ruling class (see also Chapter 3). Marx wrote:

> *The production of ideas, of conceptions, of consciousness, is at first directly interwoven with the material activity and the material intercourse of men, the language of real life. . . .We do not set out from what men say, imagine, conceive nor from men as narrated, thought of, imagined, conceived, in order to arrive at men in the flesh. We set out from real, active men, and on the basis of their real life-process we demonstrate the development of the ideological reflexes and echoes of this life process (Marx,* The German Ideology, *in Tucker 1972:118–119).*

Basic to this perspective on the sociology of knowledge is the proposition that "it is not the consciousness of men that determines their being, but, on the contrary, their social being that determines their consciousness" (Marx, *A Contribution to the Critique of Political Economy,* in Tucker 1972:4). Those who own the means of production also determine the ruling ideas of the period.

Consciousness is determined by class relations, for even though persons will normally try to identify what is in their best interest, under capitalism the ruling class controls the production of ideas. Also, even though humans create practical ideas from experience, most of their experience is determined by capitalist relations of production. The ideas that are disseminated through communication systems, including language, serve to authorize a reality that the ruling class creates. In this sense, ideas become **ideology**—understood to mean a system of beliefs that legitimate and maintain the status quo (see also Chapter 3).

For feminists, Marx's work on ideology is fundamental to understanding sexism. Sexism, as an ideology that justifies the power of men over women, emerges not in the best interest of women but as a defense of male domination. Like other ideologies, sexist ideology is a means by which one class rules a society and sanctions the society's social relations.

False consciousness emerges as the subordinate group accepts the world view of the dominant class. Because consciousness changes with historical change, at the time that workers see the nature of their exploitation, false consciousness is transformed into **class consciousness**—the understanding that groups get when they comprehend their material relationship to the capitalist system of production. At this point workers take the revolutionary struggle into their own hands.

Marx's theory is more than an academic analysis, because the idea that theory must be connected to social and political practice (*praxis,* in his words) is central to his work. Revolutionary theory is to be created by intellectuals who emerge from and are associated with the working class. Marx saw human beings as potentially revolutionary because their capabilities for creative work and social consciousness far exceed those allowed them under capitalist organization (Eisenstein 1979). This fact provides the basis for optimism in Marx's work, because it lays the foundation for radical change and the transformation from human oppression to human liberation.

The Woman Question

Marx and Engels's analysis of women's oppression is drawn mostly from their writing on the family, especially Engels's essay *The Origin of the Family, Private Property, and the State*, published in 1884 after Marx's death. Feminists who, in the beginning of the contemporary women's movement, were looking for alternative analyses to the liberal perspective began with this classical Marxist perspective.

Although Engels stated in the preface to *The Origin of the Family, Private Property, and the State* that production and reproduction together are the determining factors of history, he saw family relations as derived from the economic mode of production. From a Marxist perspective, in capitalist societies forms of the family change as class relations change, thus making family relations secondary to economic and class relations. In keeping with their perspective on the social origins of ideas, Marx and Engels would say, however, that the social image of the family is an idealized one that disguises the real economic structure of family relations.

They described the family under capitalism as a microcosm of the society's larger class relations; thus, particularly in bourgeois families, the wife is the proletariat. Engels wrote:

> *In the great majority of cases today, at least in the possessing classes, the husband is obliged to earn a living and support his family and that in itself gives him a position of supremacy, without any need for special legal ties and privileges. Within the family he is the bourgeois and the wife represents the proletariat (1884/1972: 137).*

Monogamous marriage, Marx and Engels argued, develops as part of the formation of private property. Particularly in the bourgeois family, the development of private property creates the need to determine lineage for the purpose of inheritance. Engels wrote:

> *Monogamy arose from the concentration of considerable wealth in the hands of a single individual—a man—and from the need to bequeath this wealth to the children of that man and of no other. For this purpose, the monogamy of the woman did not in any way interfere with open or concealed polygamy on the part of the man (1884/1972: 138).*

Engels did not explain how men and not women came to control property; therefore, feminists have criticized the Marxist perspective for not explaining the origins of patriarchy.

Marx and Engels discussed marriage as being, for women, a form of prostitution. Engels wrote:

> *Marriage is conditioned by the class position of the parties and is to that extent always a marriage of convenience. . . . This marriage of convenience turns often enough into crassest prostitution—sometimes of both partners, but far more commonly of the*

woman, who only differs from the ordinary courtesan in that she does not let out her body on piece-work as a wage-worker, but sells it once and for all into slavery (1884/1972:134).

Marx and Engels defined marriage as based on economic relations, although they made it clear that they would have preferred to see it based on individual sex-love. In marriage and the family, Marx and Engels recognized the woman's role is to be responsible for household management and child care. They argued that household work becomes a private service under advanced capitalism, because it loses the public character it has in earlier forms of economic life. In advanced capitalism, the work of the housewife is both a private service to the male head of the household and an unpaid economic service to the society as a whole. Marx and Engels concluded that "the modern individual family is founded on the open or concealed domestic slavery of the wife, and modern society is a mass composed of these individual families as its molecules" (Engels 1884/1972:137).

Based on their analysis of the family, Marx and Engels saw emancipatory social change in family relations as occurring only with the abolition of private property. Although they maintained a wish for monogamous relationships, they wanted monogamy to be the expression of a sexual commitment based on love, not property.

Because Marx and Engels saw male supremacy in the family as originating with the accumulation of property and the development of class relations, they suggested that the liberation of women will occur as the result of class struggle. Women's status is derived from the economic organization of society; therefore, the liberation of women will follow with the revolution of the workers and the abolition of private property. Although Marx and Engels noted that the gender division of labor is the first class oppression, their analysis assumes that women's oppression is secondary to oppression by class and that women will be liberated when class oppression is ended. It is on this point that socialist feminists begin their critique of Marx.

The Socialist Feminist Critique of Marx

When socialist feminism emerged in the 1970s, feminists argued that Marx and Engels had not considered seriously enough their own point that sexual division of labor is the first form of class antagonism. Socialist feminists concluded that women's oppression could not be reduced to capitalism alone, even though capitalism remains a highly significant source of women's oppression. Socialist feminists saw class relations as important in determining women's status, but also saw gender per se as equally important. Class and gender relations intersect in advanced capitalist societies (Hartmann 1976); class relations alone do not account for the location of women and men in social life. Therefore, eradicating social class inequality alone will not necessarily eliminate sexism as well. Socialist feminists thus agree in many ways with Marx, but disagree that the oppression of women is secondary to class oppression.

Family and Economy in Capitalist Society: Juliet Mitchell

One of the first socialist feminists to expand Marx's theory was the British scholar, Juliet Mitchell. Mitchell (1971), who analyzed the interrelationship between the economy and the family, placed the origins of the family in the dynamics established by the economics of capitalism.

Mitchell begins with the classical Marxist premise that the economic mode of production is the defining factor of social organization, but she argues that for Marx and Engels the liberation of women remains an abstract ideal, not a problem to be explained. Marx and Engels too easily assumed that the liberation of women would occur with the transition from capitalism to socialism, she argues. But, a specific theory of women's oppression is needed if the liberation of women is to occur. Mitchell links the subordination of women to the interplay of reproduction, sexuality, and gender socialization with the economic mode of production. She sees the economy as embracing the structure of the family, which, in turn, includes the structures of sexuality, reproduction, and socialization.

Mitchell argues that women were excluded from production in the past because of their presumed physical weakness and the involuntary character of childbearing. Now, however, technological developments have lessened the necessity for physical strength in labor, and the development of contraception makes childbearing a voluntary act. As a result, the ideological basis of family life as the unit of sexual and reproductive activity is destroyed. According to Mitchell, because women's exclusion of public work and their restriction to the private world of the family is the basis for their subordination, the right of women to earn a living wage must be a central goal of feminism.

Mitchell raised a number of issues that remain central to feminist theory. She opened the feminist discussion of the relationship of the family to the economy and noted that the family has changed from a unit of production to a unit of consumption. This has important material as well as ideological consequences. As she saw it, sexuality becomes intermixed with a consumption ethic. Although this can mean more sexual freedom for women, it also increases their use as sexual objects—a point that resonates in contemporary discussions of gender, sexuality, and postmodern culture, as we will see later in this chapter. Mitchell also saw that the family had both an economic and ideological role under capitalism. Its economic role lies not just in the work that is done within families, but it is in the family that workers are created and sustained—a point now being explored by feminists studying the "care work" that women, and especially women of color, do (see Chapter 6). Ideologically, it is in families where personalities are shaped with characteristics suitable for a capitalist labor force. Mitchell argues that the family promotes individualism and personal freedom at the same time that it encourages the accumulation of property. She writes, "The family is a stronghold of what capitalism needs to preserve but actually destroys: private property and individualism. The housewife-mother is the guardian and representative of these. She is a backward, conservative force—and this is what her oppression means" (1971:161). According to Mitchell, the one area of women's power—the socialization of children—becomes a mystique for their own oppression.

The Question of Separate Spheres

Mitchell's argument shows that women have traditionally been associated with the *private sphere* (the domestic world of home, children, reproduction, and sexuality) and men with the *public sphere* (paid work, institutionalized religion, political authority, and so forth). One of the accomplishments of feminist theory has been to make the activities of both men and women in the private sphere more visible. Because the private sphere has been identified with women, it has been perceived as inferior; the public sphere, superior.

The relationship of the public and private spheres is an important theme in the development of feminist theory. Women's relegation to the private, domestic sphere excludes them from public life and thus from equal access to social and economic resources, although the increasing entry of middle-aged, married women and mothers into the labor force makes it less true that women are confined to the home. Still, women's work in public labor is often said to mirror and extend the private services they provide in the home. Others have also argued that women's confinement to the private sphere is largely a White, middle-class phenomenon; the assumption of a public/private split is therefore a race- and class-bound argument. Without arguing that women's exclusion from the public sphere is the primary basis for their subordination, feminists point out that a theory of women's position must account for the relationship of the private, domestic realm to the public realm of social and economic life (Sacks 1975).

The question of separate spheres is one about both social structure and ideology. Structurally, the separation of public and private spheres is one that emerges with the rise of industrial capitalism in the nineteenth century. At that time, women's work was ideologically defined as taking place in the home, even though most working-class, poor, and minority women continued to work in factories, domestic service, agriculture, and other forms of public labor. Ideologically, the values associated with the public and private sphere become attached to assumptions about masculinity and femininity. Some Marxist-feminists argue that the alleged split between the public and private spheres obscures the economic role of the family (Zaretsky 1976). Moreover, the idea of separate spheres creates a new split: one between our "personal" life and our "public" life. This further obscures the forces of capitalism from political view, as people become more concerned with their own presumed uniqueness or style and are less conscious of the capitalist, material forces that shape their life conditions. As Zaretsky argues, personal life, emerging under capitalism, appears to be an autonomous process, and human relations become seen as an end in themselves, as if they are detached from the material world of economic fact. Individuals appear unique, and the subjective sphere of self and lifestyle take preeminence over the economic relations that define social organization. One consequence is that some men, for example, can pursue their own fulfillment through men's groups, but in the absence of a profeminist stance that is critical of patriarchal power (Messner 1997).

In sum, socialist feminism sees women's status as coming through the transformation of capitalist relations, along with efforts to transform gender as well. Socialist feminism shares with classical Marxism the idea that the oppression of women is primarily an economic fact, buttressed by ideological delusions. But, socialist feminism adds to Marxism that women's oppression must be related to their position in the private world of reproduction and the family. Extending this critique, radical feminists argued that patriarchy also had to be considered a historical force of its own. It is to the radical feminist perspective that we now turn.

❖ Radical Feminism: The Power of Patriarchy

Whereas socialist feminists argue that class and capitalism are the basis of women's oppression, radical feminists argue that male domination per se is the basis for women's oppression. Radical feminists define **patriarchy** as a "sexual system of power in which the male possesses superior power and economic privilege" (Eisenstein 1979:17). Radical feminism views patriarchy as being its own social, historical, and political force. Whereas socialist feminism emphasizes the economic basis of gender relations, radical feminism emphasizes male power and privilege as the bases of social relations. Radical feminism sees patriarchal relations as more fundamental than class relations in determining women's experiences. In fact, many radical feminists see class and racial-ethnic oppression as extensions of patriarchal inequality. Accordingly, radical feminists see the abolition of male supremacy as their primary political goal.

Since its inception, the radical feminist position has taken several different directions, some of them more explicitly tied to Marxism than others. Some radical feminist thought is totally apart from the materialist thesis in Marxist work, locating the causes of oppression solely within patriarchal culture and its control of women (Daly 1978). Much of radical feminism, however, has developed specifically because of the failure of Marxist perspectives to explain adequately the emergence and persistence of patriarchy. Some early radical feminists attempted to explain the origins of patriarchy by claiming that women controlled many of the early hunting and gathering societies, but men organized themselves to conquer women by force, thereby also gaining control of originally woman-centered forms of social organization.

Anthropological evidence would caution against such a sweeping claim since the arrangements between women and men vary so widely across different cultures and in different time periods. But, the important questions radical feminists raise are: How did men gain and maintain control of the systems of production and reproduction? What is the relationship of men's power to the structure of social institutions and how does it continue to oppress women?

Radical feminists argue that men's control of women cannot be explained simply based on class oppression. As the feminist anthropologist Gayle Rubin has written, "No analysis of the reproduction of labor can explain foot-binding, chastity belts, or any of the incredible array of Byzantine, fetishized indignities, let alone the more ordinary ones, which have been inflicted upon women in various times and places" (1975:163). One strength of the radical feminist perspective is its focus on men's violence against women and the many cultural practices designed to control female sexuality and reproduction. Indeed, the control of women's sexuality is central to many radical feminist analyses.

The Sex/Gender System

Gayle Rubin identified the **sex/gender system** as the "set of arrangements by which a society transforms biological sexuality into products of human activity and in which these transformed sexual needs are satisfied" (1975:159). Rubin argues that the oppression of women lies in social systems that create male solidarity, not simply in systems of economic production. Rubin writes that "the subordination of women can be seen as a product of the relationships by which sex and gender are organized and produced" (1975:177). According to Rubin, men "exchange" women through the marketplace. In fact, she was one of the first to introduce the idea of "the traffic in women," now commonly understood to refer to international marketing of women's sexuality. Rubin suggested that we find the location of women's oppression in men's control of women's sexuality.

In the radical feminist analysis, the production of gender also sets the preconditions for other forms of domination (Harding 1981). Men first learn to dominate women, setting a pattern for the domination of others. Economic systems may determine who these others are, but sex and gender systems establish the preconditions for domination to emerge. In the end, radical feminism sees systems of domination based on class, race, or nationality as extensions of the underlying politics of male supremacy (Bunch 1975).

Radical feminists also see patriarchal institutions as creating myths and forms of social organization that constrain women to exist in male-centered worlds (Daly 1978). One radical feminist solution to women's subordination is the establishment of women-centered beliefs and systems. For some, this movement has produced the separatist philosophy of radical lesbian feminism, whereby a woman-identified world is created through the attachments women have to each other, not to men.

Sexuality and the State

MacKinnon extended the radical feminist analysis to argue that men's control of women's sexuality is the central fact of the domination of women. As she writes, "Sexuality is to feminism what work is to Marxism" (1982:515). MacKinnon describes sexuality as a social process that creates, organizes, and directs desire; the process of directing the expression of desire creates the social beings we know as women and men, and their relations create society. She reminds us that through gender socialization, women and men come to identify themselves not just as social beings but also as sexual beings.

Sexuality is the primary sphere of men's power. Through rape, sexual harassment, incest, and violence against lesbians, men exercise their sexual power over women. Heterosexuality is the institution through which men's power is expressed; gender relations and the family are the specific forms of compulsory heterosexuality. Because this analysis sees heterosexuality as institutionalizing male dominance, radical feminism has also been critical to the development of new studies in sexuality, as we will see later in this chapter.

MacKinnon also interprets the **state** as embodying masculine authority. Liberals define the state as a form of disembodied reason; Marxists see the state primarily as a reflection of material interests. As a result, according to MacKinnon, liberal analyses of the state see women as simply another interest group and treat women as abstract persons with rights, but they do not see women as a specifically gendered group. In Marxist analyses, the state is a tool of dominance and a force that legitimates ideology; women in this analysis are relegated to just another subordinated group.

MacKinnon argues that the state—through the rule of law—defines and treats women in the same way that men see and treat women. Thus, the state is coercive and ensures men's control over women's sexuality. The implication of MacKinnon's analysis is that as long as the "state is male"—meaning that its meaning systems, its mode of operations, and its underlying assumptions are based on men's power—women cannot, as liberals would argue, overcome their subordination through actions of the state.

Intersections of Capitalism and Patriarchy

The assumption in radical feminist analyses that gender relations are more fundamental than class relations has posed important questions for feminist theory. The dialogue between radical feminists and socialist feminists thus raises new questions about the intersections between capitalism and patriarchy. Hartmann's (1981b) analysis of the interaction of patriarchal structures and the development of capitalism is one such work to make this synthesis. Hartmann, a socialist feminist theorist, argues that feminists must identify patriarchy as a social and historical structure if we are to understand Western capitalist societies. She says that Marxist analyses take the relationship of women to the economic system as their central question, but that feminist analyses must take their central question as the relationship of women to men. Understanding capitalism alone will not illuminate women's situation unless we recognize that capitalism is also a patriarchal system of social organization. Hartmann sees the partnership of patriarchy and capitalism as the critical starting point for feminist theory.

In precapitalist societies, Hartmann argues, men controlled the labor of women and children in the family: "In so doing men learned the techniques of hierarchical organization and control" (Hartmann 1976:138). As larger systems of exchange formed beyond local communities, men were faced with the problem of maintaining their control over women. Through patriarchy, men learned techniques of social control that, when capitalism emerged in Western societies, could be transformed from direct and personal systems of control to indirect and impersonal systems of social control. Thus Hartmann sees capitalism as emerging in interaction with—and reinforcing—patriarchy, but she does not see patriarchy as the sole cause of gender inequality.

Hartmann continues by arguing that "job segregation by sex . . . is the primary mechanism in capitalist society that maintains the superiority of men over women"

(1976:139), pointing out that the development of capitalism has had a more severe impact on women than on men. Not only was women's productive role in the family altered, but capitalism made women more economically dependent on men. The crux of Hartmann's research lies in her analysis of men's control of the wage-labor market, where she says the reason men excluded, rather than organized, women workers "is explained, not by capitalism, but by patriarchal relations between men and women: Men wanted to assure that women would continue to perform the appropriate tasks at home" (1976:155). Men both benefit from the higher wages they receive and from the household division of labor in which they receive women's services.

The synthesis of radical and socialist feminism shows how the gender division of labor is related to women's position in society as a whole, leading many to conclude that women's power in society is directly related to their contribution to production and the extent to which they control the resources they produce.

Comparing Liberal, Socialist, and Radical Feminism

Liberal, socialist, and radical feminism each make unique contributions to our understanding of the situation of women. Together, they suggest that we ground discussion of women's position in the dynamics of the gender division of labor, the emergence of class systems, the formation of patriarchal relations, and the social organization of the family. The point is that social change is informed by different premises about the social organization of society. Different feminist perspectives suggest different kinds of social change; therefore, for feminists to realize their goals for an egalitarian society requires careful examination of the underlying assumptions of given theoretical and political perspectives.

Of course, each of these perspectives is an *ideal type*—that is, they are not perfectly distinct from one another. In actuality, feminist organizations (and individual feminists) may use aspects of each framework to organize their thinking about women and gender in society. Moreover, organizations that are generally identified as working within the system and using the framework of liberalism might, on some issues or for some members, also embrace a more radical perspective. The point is that distinguishing different theoretical frameworks sharpens your thinking by helping you identify the underlying assumptions of each and, therefore, the implications of each one for social change.

In comparing them, we can see that liberal feminism emphasizes that social change should establish individual civil rights so that no one is denied access to the existing socioeconomic system based on sex, race, or class. Liberal feminism also tells us that sexism is the result of past traditions and learned identities. Consequently, it suggests reform in gender socialization practices. The political tactics of liberal feminism are primarily those of interest-group politics in which liberal feminists attempt to increase the political influence and power of women. Their political strategy involves building coalitions that align the issues of feminism with other political causes, thereby increasing the strength of the women's movement. This strategy also has its costs, however, because political compromises mean that only the most moderate feminist demands can gain the support necessary for a solid coalition.

Socialist and radical feminism, on the other hand, root the cause of sexism in the fundamental character of political and economic institutions. These perspectives challenge the very basis of social institutions, suggesting that revolutionary changes need to transform both capitalism and patriarchy. Socialist feminists make social class central to their analysis, arguing that classical Marxist theory has obscured the economic and social roles of women. Socialist feminism forces us to remember the significance of class.

Radical feminism locates sexism in the independent existence of patriarchy and the social relations that patriarchy generates. Radical feminism suggests that only the elimination of patriarchy will result in the liberation of women in society. Much of the strategy of radical feminist programs for change has been to redefine social relations by creating a women-centered culture. Radical feminists emphasize the positive capacities of women by focusing on the creative dimensions of women's experience. Radical feminists celebrate the creative dimension of women's lives, specifically because they see women's culture and experience as resisting patriarchal social relations.

The distinctions drawn here between these three feminist perspectives are in no way a perfect description of any. In theory and in practice, there are as many shared ideas and politics among feminists as there are differences. Discussion of the different feminist perspectives demonstrates that the questions that feminists raise have different answers and that they are as complex as the systems they seek to change. As you will see in the remainder of this chapter, the analyses of liberal, socialist, and radical feminism are themselves incomplete. It has remained for new feminist perspectives to raise and analyze questions that remain unaddressed in these historic modes of feminist theory.

❖ Multiracial Feminism

As the women's movement has developed, women of color have consistently stated the need for feminism to be inclusive of all women in its vision of change. Early on, Sojourner Truth, in her now well-known speech at the women's rights convention in Akron, Ohio in 1851, "Aint' I A Woman," articulated the need for feminist thinking to embrace the experiences of African American women in its actions and analysis (Collins 1998). With some of its roots in the activism of Black women in the civil rights movement, the women's movement could have from the start built feminist theory to include the experiences of women of color. However, much of the women's movement remained anchored primarily in the experience of White women. It has taken the work of women of color and some White women to build more inclusive feminist theory.

Just as theories that are exclusively centered in the lives of White men are distorted, so is feminist theory inadequate and incomplete, and sometimes just plain wrong, when it is not grounded in the experiences of women in different racial-ethnic and class contexts. Many of the earlier theories we have reviewed tried to build a "grand" theory of women to encompass women as a whole. But, in doing so, they sometimes falsely assumed that "woman" was a unitary category (Andersen et al. 2003; Baca Zinn and Dill 1996). For example, socialist feminism tends to see all women's experience as emerging from their class standing because socialist feminism sees the development of class relations under capitalism as the basis for the exploitation of both women and racial-ethnic groups. Socialist feminism reminds us of the importance of class in different women's experience. It also points to such facts as that the success of many middle-class and professional women rests on the labor of women of color who provide the domestic work (housework and child care) that many successful women no longer do (Dill 1980; Hondagneu-Sotelo 2001). But, because of its focus on class, socialist feminism tends to see both gender and race as secondary to class. As a result, socialist feminism understates the independent operation of race and gender relations.

Radical feminism assumes that gender is the primary form of oppression and that class and race are extensions of patriarchal domination (Daly 1978). In assuming that patriarchy is the central cause of all women's oppression, radical feminism provides little explanation of the powerlessness that people of color experience together. Radical feminism's insistence that eliminating sexism is the key to eliminating racism has a hollow ring to women of color, who face oppression on both counts and who experience racism as a more fundamental (or at least equally fundamental) fact of their lives. Radical women of color clearly recognize that sexism exists in their communities, but attributing the primary cause of their experience to patriarchy ignores the racism they encounter not only from men but also from White feminists (Moraga and Anzaldúa 1981).

Now, those working to incorporate race, class, and gender into feminist theory see that there can be no unitary analysis of "woman" as a category. Rather, the inclusion of women of color in feminist theory requires understanding multiple and overlapping forms of oppression. This insight, coming largely through the activism and scholarship of women of color, has now generated a new paradigm in feminist theory, labeled by some as multiracial feminism (Baca Zinn and Dill 1996). Grounded in the experiences of women of color, multiracial feminism provides a new starting point for feminist thought and action.

Multiracial feminism is not itself a unitary framework. Instead it is a perspective that incorporates the multiple systems of domination that shape the experiences of Latinas/Latinos, African American, Native American, Asian American, and White women and men. Thus, it is grounded in understanding the *intersections* of race, class, and gender in the shaping of people's experiences. A good way to think about this has been articulated by the concept of a "prism of difference." Maxine Baca Zinn, Pierrette Hondagneu-Sotelo, and Michael Messner—all feminist sociologists—state it this way:

> *Imagine a ray of light—which to the naked eye, appears to be only one color—refracted through a prism onto a white wall. To the eye, the result is not an infinite, disorganized scatter of individual colors. Rather, the refracted light displays an order, a structure of relationships among the different colors—a rainbow. Similarly, we propose to use the 'prism of difference' . . . to analyze a continuous spectrum of people, in order to*

show how gender is organized and experienced differently when refracted through the prism of sexual, racial/ethnic, social class, physical abilities, age and national citizenship differences" (2000:1).

Multiracial feminism can be described as organized around several themes. First, multiracial feminism interprets gender as socially constructed through interlocking systems of race, class, and other inequalities. Thus, women are not just gendered subjects, but are situated within an array of social factors, including class, race, sexual orientation, and other facets of their lived experience. Making any one of these dimensions of life visible—within an analysis that recognizes their interlocking character—is likely to make the others visible as well (Andersen and Collins 2004). Furthermore, people—both women and men—experience these interlocking systems *simultaneously*. Thus, women of color experience their race *and* their gender, not as separate categories, but as intricately linked in their experience. Although one factor may be more salient at a given moment than another, it is their linkage that shapes the experiences of women of color, not just one or the other added together (Moraga and Anzaldúa 1981; Combahee River Collective 1982; Collins 1990, 1998; Baca Zinn and Dill 1996; Andersen and Collins 2004).

Second, multiracial feminism sees the intersections of race, class, and gender operating at multiple levels of social life. Race, class, and gender are embedded in social institutions (what you might think of as the *macrostructural* level), but they are also part of our immediate social interactions, social identities, and social consciousness (the *microlevel*). This means that they are complex systems of social relationships in which different women and men are embedded. Thus, there are not simple divisions between those with privilege and those without, since the social factors of race, class, and gender cut in many directions. Thus, a Latino (man) may have some privileges associated with his gender, but may be disadvantaged by virtue of his racial-ethnic status and, perhaps, his social class. Multiracial feminism recognizes the complexity of these intersecting hierarchies—at all levels of experience (Baca Zinn and Dill 1996; Andersen and Collins 2004).

Third, multiracial feminism recognizes the socially constructed nature of both gender and race. Just as gender is a social construction, so is race socially constructed. Although many think of race as a biological category, its significance comes from its development as a socially created category of oppression and domination. Thus, the actual meaning of race changes over time, both as it is contested by oppressed racial groups and as the society changes regarding how race operates in social institutions and social relationships. Race is both a fluid category and one that has a concrete location in social institutions, such as in laws that define people in racial categories or in the income brackets that differentiate the class status of different racial-ethnic groups. Saying that race is socially constructed does not mean that it is not real, only that *it is the social reality of race that makes it meaningful in society.*

Fourth, multiracial feminism grows from, but is not limited to, the experiences of women of color. As feminist scholars have thought more inclusively about race, class, and gender as intersecting systems, they have interpreted the experiences of all groups, not just those of women of color, in new ways. Race, class, and gender affect the experience of all groups, not just those who are their victims. Thus, in studying race, Whites and people of color are included, just as studying gender brings new insights about men as well as women (Andersen and Collins 2004; Andersen 2003).

Fifth, multiracial feminism understands that there is an "interplay of social structure and women's agency" (Baca Zinn and Dill 1996: 328). This means that women (or other social groups) are not merely passive recipients of abstract forces of social structure. **Agency** refers to the active and creative way that human beings give meaning to their experience and act on their own behalf. People are not just empty vessels into whom social forces are poured. Even under oppressive conditions, people have a consciousness that they use to define their experience; they act in ways that construct a meaningful social existence. This may take the form of accomodating oneself to oppressive social forces, but it also takes the form of resisting oppression—or at the very least, adapting to the conditions one faces. The focus on human agency in multiracial feminism has highlighted the active and creative ways that groups resist oppression even at times when oppression seems overwhelming.

Scholarship that stems from a multiracial perspective has used a wide array of methodological techniques to examine the multiple facets of race, class, and gender in women's and men's lives (Baca Zinn and Dill 1996). But, fundamentally, this perspective requires shifting the starting point for the development of feminist thinking. As a result of centering knowledge in the experiences of those who have traditionally been excluded, multiracial feminism questions the assumptions of other, more singular and exclusionary modes of thinking.

As an example, Collins writes that if we want to know the thoughts and lives of African American women as intellectuals, we have to revise our way of thinking about who is an intellectual. African American women have historically been denied access to formal education; they have not had the privilege of finding publishers and public platforms for their ideas. To recover the work of African American women intellectuals, we must look to new sources and find intellectual thought in the everyday activities of Black women. Collins writes, "Reclaiming the Black female intellectual tradition also involves searching for its expression in alternative institutional locations and among women who are not commonly perceived as intellectuals" (1990:14).

Integrating race, class, and gender into feminist thinking requires a process of transformation in which we move from simply adding women of color into existing analyses to seeing race, class, and gender in relational ways. There are many rich empirical studies being produced within multiracial feminism, as well as historical and political analyses, that shed new light on social and historical processes. The challenge for feminist theorists in the coming years is to continue developing such work. Without it, feminists cannot hope to generate programs for social change designed for the liberation of *all* women and men.

❖ Postmodernist Feminism

Postmodernism is a form of contemporary social theory that explains all knowledge as stemming from the specific historical period and the conditions in which it is produced. But it goes beyond this to claim that communication in all its forms *is* reality. This theoretical framework interprets society not as an objective thing, but as a fluid and illusive construction of alternative meaning systems—although one external to our own consciousness. Thus, to postmodernists, society is only a series of stories that emerge from a variety of points of view and experiences; we can therefore only "know" something by deconstructing these stories or "texts." Linked to a theory known as *poststructuralism,* postmodernists think of social structure as a reified category that is real only because people believe it is and construct ideas to support that belief. To postmodernists, reality is simulated. Therefore, this perspective is particularly attractive in a world marked by highly technological forms of communication that increasingly penetrate everyday life.

Postmodernism recognizes that socially constructed assumptions are built into the knowledge frames that are characteristic of any given historical period or cultural context (Nicholson 1990). Postmodernist theory goes beyond simply understanding the influence of culture (a view common to all social sciences) by arguing that there is not a singular, monolithic social order (i.e., society); rather, society is a series of images and meaning systems over which people struggle (Fraser 1989). Postmodernists see reality as constituted through a broad range of **discourses,** that is, all that is written, spoken, or otherwise represented through language and communication systems. Whether it is science, the media, or other cultural artifacts, postmodernists see these discourses as framing knowledge and reality; in addition, these discourses are systems of social control. Gender ideology, as an example, is a form of social control represented in the discourses (science, language, cultural images) that embed specific representations of what it means to be male and female.

Postmodernism has arisen largely from the field of literary criticism and also from the critiques of science symbolized by feminist standpoint theory (see Chapter 10), but it has influenced many areas of feminist scholarship. Within literary criticism, the basic idea of postmodernism is that texts do not stand alone as objective entities apart from either the author's construction of the text or the reader's response to it. Because the focus of postmodernism is on alternative discourses and meaning systems, it emphasizes this idea of "texts." Texts may be actual literary texts, such as books, but the concept of a text in postmodernist theory is more than the literal text. It refers to the contested and constructed meaning systems that appear in all of social reality, whether that is books, media representations, or other cultural forms. A commercial, a conversation, or the nightly news is considered a text; indeed, from the postmodernist perspective, society itself is only a text in that it is constructed out of the interpretive processes that constitute it. The major method used in postmodernism is to examine texts as socially constructed objects. Because of this focus on texts, postmodernists are fascinated with the various artifacts of popular culture, as seen in the emergence of a new field of study, known as *cultural studies.*

In the social sciences, postmodernism emerges from criticisms of positivist science, that is, the idea that society can be known through systematic observation and generalization. Postmodernist theorists debunk this idea, because they assume it is impossible to reflect on something and see the world without presuppositions (Agger 1991). Postmodernists reject the scientific point of view that through detached measurement one can observe a world that is "out there." As we saw in Chapter 10, the scientific perspective is a specific world view, with its own assumptions about the world. Postmodernists see science, like everything else, as constructed; they do not see it as providing knowledge that is any more real or objective than literature. Instead, postmodernists see science, like literature, as needing to be "deconstructed," that is, analyzing the assumptions and meanings embedded in scientific works. Unlike other social scientists, postmodernists are wary about generalization, thinking instead that the world consists of diverse, multiple, and unique experiences.

There are serious challenges posed by postmodernist thought for feminists and social scientists who work within the scientific method—that is, thinking that one can use controlled observation and rigorous study to reveal the workings of something "real" known as social structure. Instead, postmodernism is founded on a distrust of some of the ways of thinking that are basic to the social scientific approach to understanding society and social life.

For feminists, postmodernism has had much appeal because of some commonly shared assumptions in both feminist and postmodernist theory. One of the basic premises of feminist thought is that gender is socially constructed; furthermore, one of the fundamental goals of feminist theory is to examine gender relations, see how they are constituted, and study how they are thought of or not thought of (Flax 1990). This critical attitude makes postmodernism appealing to feminists because feminism and postmodernism are fundamentally skeptical about existing knowledge. Each also recognizes the embedding of social assumptions in such things as language, cultural images, and the ideas of a given period. Because feminists see how ideas and images have been used to oppress women, they want to criticize these discourses, not take them for granted, and, like postmodernist theorists, they see gender and society as socially constituted (Fraser and Naples 2004).

Another basic insight of postmodernist feminism is the idea that there is nothing essentially male or female—an idea referred to as **essentialism.** Rather, there are socially constructed categories that emerge from specific cultural and historical contexts, not from anything fundamental about male or female biology. Postmodernists even challenge the idea that there are real biological categories to begin with, since they understand "male" and "female" only as constructed through human definition. In other words, postmodernists take the social construction of gender to its logical conclusion, arguing that our notion of biological differences between the sexes is itself a social construction. Thus, the body itself, from a postmodernist perspective, is something that is understood only through social interpretation (Bordo 1995; Fausto-Sterling 2000; Nicholson 1994). Some feminist postmodernists argue that the distinction other feminists make between sex and gender (see Chapter 2) is a false one because it still accepts biological differences as real. Instead, postmodernist feminists argue that biological sex differences are only a function of our knowledge, not necessarily objectively "real" categories of difference.

A good way to explain this point is to use the metaphor of a coat rack, suggested by Linda Nicholson, a postmodernist feminist. The coat rack metaphor assumes that the body is a rack upon which differing cultural artifacts are hung. In other words, the idea is that there is some constancy to nature but that culture elaborates this basic difference into different societal forms (Nicholson 1994). Postmodernists question whether the coat rack itself is anything other than a cultural construction. In other words, they deny that there is any essential difference in men and women other than those we construct as significant. As a result, postmodernist feminists challenge the very categories of "man" and "woman," seeing these instead as fluid, artificial, and malleable. Like other postmodernists, feminist postmodernists are skeptical about any categories, since they see all categories and definitions as humanly imposed (Bordo 1995).

Postmodern feminists have also focused on the social construction of language and understand language as not just a technical device for describing something "out there." Rather, they see language itself as actually constituting the thing it allegedly describes (Agger 1991). Postmodernist analyses of language rest on the idea that language, like other forms of knowledge, is not pure. Instead, language reflects the social categories and practices that characterize a given time and cultural period. For example, calling someone a man or a woman, just like calling someone White or Black, has a specific socially constituted meaning that makes no sense outside of its cultural time and place. Because this insight has been central to feminist thought (in that feminists have long deconstructed and exposed the sexist basis of language), many feminists find postmodernist arguments attractive.

In sum, postmodernist feminists see indeterminacy and construction, not determinism and fixedness, as characteristic of society. They emphasize diversity, not unity, in experience, and the unique, not the general. This perspective makes social science more subjective and tentative, since postmodernism is a more relativistic way of viewing the world. Some have argued that one of the reasons postmodernism is so appealing to contemporary intellectuals is that it reflects the disillusionment of the current generation (Rosenau 1992). Postmodernism causes people, including scholars, to examine their assumptions in constructing knowledge and formulating a worldview. Its theorists also deny that a singular voice defines all experience, as has been the case in androcentric and ethnocentric scholarship. Through their recognition that various disciplines encode value positions, such as standpoint theory, postmodernists helps us deconstruct the gendered basis of knowledge.

One of the criticisms of postmodernist theory is its very high level of abstraction—what one sociologist has called work that is "incredibly, extravagantly convoluted" (Agger 1991). Almost as a way of emphasizing the contextual nature of all that is known, postmodernists have often purposefully produced work that is obtuse and difficult to understand. As a consequence, the essence of postmodernism is typically inaccessible to those without a high degree of schooling in its interpretation. This fact has led some to charge that postmodernist theory is elitist, since it disallows one of the objectives of feminist theory—accessibility to wide audiences, particularly women who may not have access to the elite educational institutions in which postmodernism is produced.

Postmodernism makes it difficult ever to generalize about any characteristic or experience, as if all the world were merely individual discourses or voices. This is strikingly at odds with the basic principles of social sciences—that one can generalize through careful observation and analysis. Postmodernist thinkers are opposed to the concept of social structure as something that is "there." By criticizing an overly determinist view of gender, race, and class, they actually can "deconstruct gender right out of operation" (Bordo 1992:160), as if it hardly existed at all. Postmodernist theory has the advantage of emphasizing diversity and thus has added to new work on race, class, and gender, but it does so in a way that denies the reality of structurally based oppression. This makes it limited in its ability to explain structured inequality, whether by gender, race, class, or by all three (Collins 1998). It is as if studying race, class, and gender is just a matter of different voices, since it reduces the experience of oppression to cultural analysis texts and discourses alone. By denying the concept of social structure, postmodernism limits the framework through which one can understand oppression by gender, race, and class; furthermore, it makes social science only a matter of accounting for diverse social experiences (Agger 1991), instead of being committed to studying general principles of social structure and organization.

❖ Queer Theory and Sexualities

The influence of postmodernist theory has been especially strong in new feminist scholarship on sexuality. In part because feminists have wanted to break down taken-for-granted categories of sexual differentiation, postmodernist thought is consistent with the value placed on the fluidity of sexual categories. Postmodernist feminist theorists have thus found subjects like cross-dressing, transvestitism, and the crossing of sexual categories represented in some new forms of gay and lesbian studies to be fascinating and to provide new theoretical constructs for all feminist thought.

Queer theory is a new perspective emerging from studies of sexuality and from postmodernism. Queer theory understands sex and the body as purely social concepts. That is, the discourses and practices of popular and scientific thought construct sex and the body in particular ways. Therefore, interpreting sex and the body is a matter of challenging how sexual categories and understandings of the body are socially developed. As one sociologist writes, "Sex is viewed as fundamentally social: the categories of sex—especially heterosexuality and homosexuality, but also the whole regime of modern sexual types, classifications, and norms—are understood as social and historical facts" (Seidman 1994:171).

One of the arguments, from a postmodernist perspective, is that categories such as homosexual and heterosexual have emerged as particular social types only in modern Western societies. We have seen this in the studies of earlier work on sexual categories in other cultures (see Chapter 4). Beyond the recognition of cross-cultural differences in the social construction of sexuality, however, queer theorists make a more fundamental point: The categories of homosexual and heterosexual themselves have been constructed through particular scientific discourses—namely, the work of sexologists and others who have labeled sexual behaviors in dichotomous categories. Furthermore, these "discourses" have assumed an authoritative stance, with systems of power enforcing these labels. To postmodernists, sexual power is embodied in various aspects of social life (popular culture, scientific writings, literary texts, and daily conversations, to name a few). These discourses establish sexual boundaries that regulate sexual behavior and identities.

One of the major contributions of queer theory is its deconstruction of sexual categories. That is, it questions the presumed natural basis of sexual categories altogether, arguing instead, that all sexual identities are composites of socially defined distinctions (Stein and Plummer 1994; Seidman 1996). It is not that sexual categories and differences are not "there," only that the differences we think matter are the result of social constructions. Thus, the construction of a category such as *homosexual* imposes a particular construction of sex on its subjects and presumes the existence of some other normal and taken-for-granted category, that is, *heterosexual*.

Queer theory, like postmodernist feminism, criticizes traditional empirical studies of sexuality for being unreflective about the categories upon which such research is based. According to queer theory, studies of sexuality that compare men and women—or gays, bisexuals, transsexuals, and straights—presume that these different types have some fixed meaning. Instead, queer theory interprets these as highly fluid categories (Seidman 1994, 1996). This mode of thinking shifts the analysis of sexuality away from dualistic categories to a more fluid understanding of difference. At the same time, it challenges the assumption (one even made within the gay and lesbian community) that there is some natural basis to homosexuality. From this point of view, no one sexual identity is privileged over another; rather, sexual identity is all performance and meaning (Butler 1990).

There are important implications of postmodernist theory for political action by groups who want to challenge the oppression of gays and lesbians. Queer theorists are less inclined to support the civil rights strategy that has characterized the gay and lesbian political movement. The civil rights strategy is one that recognizes gays and lesbians as a minority group and contests that this group has rights, just as do other minority groups in society. Instead, the politics of a more postmodernist approach are to transgress and challenge sexual categories (Stein and Plummer 1994). Groups such as Act Up and Queer Nation use gender parodies as ways to subvert the dominant sexual order to resist and rebel against taken-for-granted sexual categories (Butler 1990). Their political strategy is to act in ways that challenge sexual categories, even when their behavior appears outrageous to others (e.g., by cross-dressing and having "kiss-ins"). The shock and outrage that such acts produce are deliberate ways of making people face the socially constructed assumptions about sex that they would normally take for granted. Often, such political behavior takes a playful and risqué attitude, again reflecting the postmodernist appeal to seeing sexual identities as scripts or performances.

Not all new feminist studies of sexuality use a postmodernist/queer theory framework. Indeed, as you have seen throughout this book, much of the new scholarship on sexuality has used both existing frameworks of sociological and feminist research and new theories to explore various questions about sexuality and its relationship to gender. Many feminists are, indeed, critical of the postmodernist approach to sexuality, arguing that it does not provide a political perspective that challenges the real structural basis of sexual oppression (Kitzinger and Wilkinson 1994). In their criticisms, feminists are arguing that structural systems of heterosexual privilege and power are real and cannot be reduced to texts, discourses, and performance. As in other areas of feminist thought, there are multiple frameworks for understanding sexuality; queer theory is only one such approach.

❖ Continuing Questions for Feminist Theory

The discussion of different modes of feminist theory reveals the richness that the women's movement has brought to intellectual life. But remember that one of the central tenets of feminist theory is that theory is not just for theory's sake. Rich as the intellectual discussions of feminist theorists are in intellectual life, their purpose is to improve the actual conditions in which women live.

Feminist theory, like the movements from which it stems, is also an evolving body of knowledge—one that, as we have seen, incorporates multiple questions and multiple ways of interpreting and thinking. Still, at different moments in time certain questions guide the development of feminist theory. Some of the questions currently being considered in feminist theory have been present from the beginning. For example, debates about essentialism have long characterized feminist scholarship and continue to do so as they are elaborated in postmodernist feminist thinking. Are men and women fundamentally different? Of course, many feminists reject an essentialist position that men and women are different, arguing instead that to the extent that differences exist, they are wholly socially constructed. But other feminists celebrate differences between women and men, seeing such differences as a strength, not a weakness. Questions about essentialism and difference will likely continue to foster debate within feminist studies.

Other questions have newly emerged, particularly as feminist theory has become more attentive to the diverse experiences among women. Thus, an important question now guiding feminist thought is how to explain the relations of power that exist between women and men when we know, based on multiracial feminism, that not all men are equally powerful. Indeed, many men exercise less power over others—even over their own lives—than some women exercise (Andersen et al. 2004). And, although socialist feminist theory has waned given the absence of a viable socialist movement in the United States, it is important to continue analyzing the significance of class, as well as race and gender, in feminist scholarship. New studies of feminism are also grappling with questions about the dialectical relationship between agency and social structure. That is, how will social structures that are organized around race, class, and gender emerge as the result of women's and men's actions and consciousness in the years ahead?

As feminist theory develops in the future, new generations of feminist thinkers will generate new discussions and raise new questions, although they will likely also elaborate some of the persistent issues that feminism addresses. But the gains made in feminist thinking—gains that reflect the diverse origins of feminist thought—will continue to emphasize the fundamental idea that knowledge about gender is socially constructed and must therefore be seen in the context of the so-cial relations in which knowledge is produced. As you have seen throughout this book, knowledge is incomplete without considering the multiple experiences of diverse groups in society and how their experiences are intertwined. This recogni-tion has brought increased attention within feminist thought to race, class, and gen-der and the interrelationships between these different axes of social experience. Future feminist studies will build on this and the insights of earlier thinkers to guide feminist research and action in the years ahead.

❖ *Chaper Summary and Themes*

While liberal feminism emphasizes equal rights, more radical feminist theories center their analysis on social class and its relationship to gender inequality and on men's power in patriarchal social systems.

More radical forms of feminist theory are critical of existing dominant institu-tions, criticizing liberal feminism for working within a system that holds gen-der, race, and class inequality at its core.

Socialist feminism, based on the work of Karl Marx, locates the cause of women's oppression in the workings of the system of capitalism and the inter-connection between productive and reproductive labor.

Marx and Engels's analysis of how capitalism worked emphasizes the owner-ship of systems of production and the exploitation of wage labor. Their work includes women only insofar as they are wage laborers, although socialist fem-inists added women's unpaid labor in the home to classical Marxist theory, thus analyzing women's role in production (as well as in reproductive labor) to socialist feminist theory.

Radical feminism locates the primary cause of women's oppression in the sys-tem of patriarchy in which men hold power over women.

Radical feminists see the power of men, as manifested in men's sexual vio-lence toward women, as a primary factor in the oppression of women. Some combine the insights of radical feminism and its emphasis on patriarchy to so-cialist feminism, thus theorizing the connections between capitalism and patriarchy.

Multiracial feminism studies gender by analyzing the interlocking relationships between race, class, and gender.

Multiracial feminism understands that race, class, and gender together influ-ence all aspects of people's lives and together construct dominant social insti-tutions. Thus, different from other forms of feminist theory, multiracial feminism sees gender as part of the systemic character of inequality, locating the oppression of different groups of women—and men—in the connections between race, class, and gender as structured forms of inequality.

Postmodernism interprets all forms of knowledge as constructed through discourses that are culturally and socially created.

Postmodernist feminist theory has thus emphasized the influence of cultural images and texts in the creation of meaning systems about gender that, though illusory, have real consequences for how people experience their social worlds.

Queer theory interprets sexualities as socially constructed forms, thus subject to transgression and challenge as people come to deconstruct—or challenge—presumed categories of sexual difference.

Although dominant cultural beliefs identify sexual categories in dichotomous terms (that is, either "gay" or "straight"), queer theory sees such categories as socially created and, thus, subject to change. In this sense, sexual identity is fluid and can be challenged through political activism and active transgression against fixed categories of presumed sexual difference.

Feminist theory hinges on actively thinking about social structures and their relationship to gender, as well as the understanding that human beings can think their way of out oppressive social relations.

Feminist theory emerges in relationship to the feminist movement and thus engages new questions over time, especially as feminist thinkers identify new questions for new generations. Nonetheless, the classic questions of feminist theory include understanding the relationship of gender to other forms of inequality and the ability of human beings—through human agency—to challenge existing social systems.

❖ Key Terms

agency	historical materialism	radical feminism
class	ideology	sex/gender system
class consciousness	infrastructure	socialist feminism
dialectical materialism	multiracial feminism	state
discourse	patriarchy	superstructure
essentialism	postmodernism	
false consciousness	queer theory	

❖ Discussion Questions/Projects for Thought

1. Imagine that Karl Marx has returned to the world as a woman. How might he revise his theory if he were analyzing capitalism and gender relations today?

2. Radical feminism has been vital to the growing awareness of violence against women

and the role that men's power plays in generating such violence. Do you think that patriarchy is a continuing feature of contemporary society? If so, what influence does it have on violence against women? If you think it is not as relevant as radical feminists do, what other framework might you use to explain the high rates of violence against women?

3. Using any one of the topics discussed in this book, identify the new questions that would be asked were you to use an analysis emphasizing the intersections of race, class, and gender versus one that only looked at gender.

❖ Internet Resources

Emma Goldman Papers

http://sunsite.berkeley.edu/Goldman/

This collection of documents by and about Emma Goldman provides an excellent overview of the work of this important socialist feminist leader.

Feminist Theory Website

http://www.cddc.vt.edu/feminism/

This site, developed at Virginia Tech University, is a useful resource with links to bibliographies on various themes in feminist theory and information about feminist thought in different nations and among different ethnic groups.

Women Make Movies

http://www.wmm.com

This nonprofit organization promotes multicultural and multicultural films by and about women. The website includes links to feminist film theory and criticism, as well as a film catalog and other commentary.

❖ Suggested Readings

Andersen, Margaret L., and Patricia Hill Collins. 2004. *Race, Class, and Gender: An Anthology*, 5th ed. Belmont, CA: Wadsworth. This anthology explores the diverse ways that race, class, and gender shape group experiences in the United States. Some of the articles also include personal narratives that help students empathize with those from backgrounds other than their own.

Collins, Patricia Hill. 1998. *Fighting Words: Black Women and the Search for Social Justice.* Minneapolis, MN: University of Minneapolis Press. Using Black women's standpoint as the point of orientation, Collins explores such topics as Afrocentrism, critical social theory, and postmodernist thought to ask how Black women's knowledge can inform analyses of social justice.

Crow, Barbara A., ed. 2000. *Radical Feminism: A Documentary Reader.* New York: New York University Press. This is a collection of the original documents and writings of radical feminists. It provides an excellent introduction to the analysis of the radical women's movement and reminds us of the significance of these early works of the second wave of feminism.

Engels, Friedrich. 1942/1972. *The Origin of the Family, Private Property, and the State.* New York: International Publishers. This statement of the relationship of the family, capitalism, and private property is the standard reference for interpreting classical Marxist perspectives on women's status under capitalism.

Hernández, Daisy, and Bushra Rehman, eds. 2002. *Colonize This! Young Women of Color on Today's Feminism.* New York: Seal Press. This anthology of writings by young feminists explores the implications of feminism for young women of color.

Mitchell, Juliet. 1971. *Woman's Estate.* New York: Pantheon. Juliet Mitchell's book was one of the first to use a classical Marxist perspective to interpret women's place in Western societies. Although it is old, it still stands as one of the strongest statements of Marxist feminism.

Rothenberg, Paula S. 2003. *Race, Class, and Gender in the United States,* 6th ed. New York: Worth. This anthology provides not only a contemporary perspective on the workings of race, class, and gender in the United States, but it also provides excerpts from important historical documents that have framed racial, gender, and class oppression.

Seidman, Steven, ed. 1996. *Queer Theory/Sociology.* Malden, MA: Blackwell Publishing. This collection of essays is a good introduction to new theorizing about sexualities. The contributors include some of the most innovative thinkers in contemporary feminist thought.

Glossary

abolitionism nineteenth-century movement organized to oppose slavery

affirmative action policy by which women and minorities are given extra consideration as a remedy against past discrimination

affirmative action referring to positive efforts taken to open new areas of opportunity to groups who have historically been disadvantaged in the labor market

Age of Enlightenment period in seventeenth- and eighteenth-century Europe marked by a belief in the ability of human reason to be used for humanitarian social change

agency a term referring to the active and creative way that human groups give meaning to their experience and act on their own behalf

Americans with Disabilities Act of 1990 (ADA) federal law requiring protecting disabled people from discrimination and requiring employers, schools, and other institutions to provide reasonable accommodations

androcentrism thought that is centered in men's experiences only

anorexia nervosa condition characterized by severe weight loss and delusions about one's body size

antimiscegenation the prohibition of marriage between different racial groups

authority power that is perceived by others to be legitimate and that is structured into specific social instituions

Automobile Workers v. *Johnson Controls* Supreme Court decision in 1991 holding that it is discriminatory to bar women from high-risk jobs in which there is potential harm to a fetus or reproductive system

biological determinism faulty reasoning assuming that a single condition inevitably determines a given outcome

biological reductionism faulty argument that reduces a complex phenomenon to a singular cause

bulimia eating disorder in which people, typically women, binge on huge amounts of food, followed by their purging through vomiting, laxatives, or extreme fasting

care work forms of labor (often unpaid) needed to nurture, reproduce, and sustain people

class the social position of group or individuals within the system of class stratification whereby some groups and individuals within these groups have greater access to resources and power than others

class consciousness in Marxist theory, understanding that develops as class groups comprehend their relationship to the system of production

class stratification the institutionalized system by which some groups have more economic resources and power than others

cognitive-developmental theory theory, based on the work of Jean Piaget, that explains children's development of the mental categories formed through interaction with others

collective consciousness system of beliefs, within a society, that create a sense of belonging to the community and convey the moral obligation to live up to the society's demands

comparable worth principle of paying women and men equivalent wages for performing jobs involving comparable levels of skill

compulsory heterosexuality institutionalized practices that presume women are innately sexually oriented toward men and that support privileges associated with heterosexuality

content analysis research method by which researchers analyze the content of documents or other artifacts

contingent workers those who are temporary employees, contract workers, and part-time workers

controlling images the concept used to refer to the power of media ideals to direct our concepts of ourselves and others

crime index a measure of the overall volume and rate of crime, as indicated by offenses reported to the police (including murder, non-negligent manslaughter, rape, robbery, aggravated assault, larceny-theft, motor vehicle theft, and arson)

cult of domesticity Victorian ideal that made women responsible for the moral and everyday affairs of the home

culture patterns of expectations, beliefs, values, ideas, and material objects that define the taken-for-granted way of life for a society or group

date rape sexual assault where the assailant is an acquaintance of the victim

deviance behavior that departs from conventional norms and is labeled and so recognized by groups with the power to do so

dialectical materialism *see historical materialism*

digital divide the gap that has opened between groups with strong computing skills and those without

discourse term used by postmodernist theorists to refer to all that is written or spoken and that requires analysis by social theorists

discrimination act or practice of systematically disadvantaging one or more groups

"doing gender" sociological perspective that sees gender as an activity accomplished through routine social interaction

dual labor market theory explanation of gender inequality as the result of a labor market organized into two segments: the primary and secondary market—where jobs in the primary labor market are more valued and more valuable than those in the secondary labor market

economic restructuring the term used to refer to a multidimensional process of change in the nation's economy, including the transition from a manufacturing-based economy to a service-based economy, increasing globalization, technological change, and the increasing concentration of capital in the hands of a few

Eisenstadt v. Baird Supreme Court decision (1972) extending unmarried persons the right to use birth control

emotional labor work people do to manage the emotions of others and which is part of one's work evaluation

epistemology term derived from the philosophy of science, referring to a theoretical way of knowing

Equal Pay Act of 1963 first federal legislation requiring equal pay for equal work

Equal Rights Amendment proposed amendment to the U.S. constitution that would prohibit the denial of rights based on sex (i.e., gender)

essentialism the idea that there are fundamental differences between women and men

ethnocentric seeing one's group as superior to all others; taking one's own group experience as the starting point for understanding all other experiences

false consciousness the beliefs that emerge when a subordinate group accepts and internalizes the world view of the dominant group

family a social ideal, generally referring to a unit of economic cooperation, typically thought to be related by blood, but revised by feminists to include those forming an economically cooperative, residential unit bound by feelings of common ties and strong emotion

Family and Medical Leave Act federal law enacted in 1993 that requires employers to grant 12 weeks of unpaid leave to a parent to care for newborn or adopted children or to care for a sick child, spouse, or parent

family household U.S. Census Bureau term for a household maintained with a family or unrelated persons residing together

family-based economy form of economic production wherein the household is the basic unit of the economy and the site for most economic production and distribution

family-consumer economy form of economic production in which mass production of goods leads to increased consumerism in families and households

family-wage economy form of economic production in which production moves out of the household into a factory system, where a wage-based system of labor is created

faulty generalization mode of thinking that takes knowledge from one group's or person's experiences and incorrectly extends it to another

feminism belief and action based in diverse political theories and principles, but advocating social changes intended to free women from oppressive social structures; also based on the idea that women's position in society is the result of social, not biological, factors

feminist theology new models of religious belief founded in feminist ethics

feminist theory analyses explaining the position of women in society, intended also to provoke the possibilities for liberating social changes

feminization of poverty trend by which a growing proportion of the poor are women and their children

gender the socially learned behaviors and expectations associated with men and women

gender display demonstrations of behavior that communicates gendered identity

gender gap differing political opinions and voting patterns between women and men

gender identity an individual's specific definition of self, based on that person's understanding of what it means to be a man or a woman

gender roles patterns of behavior in which women and men behave, based on the cultural expectations associated with their gender

gender segregation pattern whereby women and men are located in different categories of jobs throughout the labor force

gender socialization process by which gender roles are learned

gender stratification the hierarchical distribution of economic and social resources along lines of gender

gendered institution total pattern of gender relations embedded in societal institutions

glass ceiling popular phrase referring to the invisible mechanism that discourages women's advancement in organizations

global restructuring process by which research and management are based in developed nations, while assembly-line (or production) work is relegated to underprivileged nations

Griswold v. Connecticut first Supreme Court decision (1965) allowing married couples to use birth control

hermaphroditism *see intersexed persons*

heterosexism institutionalized set of behaviors and beliefs that presume heterosexuality to be the only acceptable form of sexual expression

historical materialism theoretical position postulating that the material organization of the world (i.e., economic systems) shapes people's behavior and beliefs; the basis for Marxist social theory

homophobia fear and hatred of homosexuals

household economic unit of those residing together, with a common economic base

householder term used by U.S. Census Bureau to refer to the person in whose name a household unit is owned or rented

human capital theory explanation of wage differentials as the result of different characteristics of workers

identification theory   theory of socialization that explains children's learning of gender-appropriate behaviors through identifying with the same-sex parent

ideology   system of beliefs that distorts reality at the same time that it provides justification for the status quo

infant mortality   the rate of infant death within a population

infrastructure   derived from Marxist theory, refers to the system of economic production as the determining feature of social organization

institutions   *see social institution*

intersexed persons   persons born with mixed sex characteristics

labeling theory   theoretical perspective in sociology, emphasizing that some groups with the power to label deviant behavior exercise control over who and what is considered deviant

liberal feminism   feminist theoretical position that interprets the origins of women's oppression as in blocked opportunities and legal obstacles to equal participation in society

liberalism   political philosophy characterized by an emphasis on individual rights and equal opportunity; the basis for liberal feminism

liberation theology   interpretations of religious belief that promote resistance to oppression; common in Latin American societies, but also significant in U.S. social movements against racial and ethnic oppression

marital rape   forced sexual activity demanded of a wife by her husband

matrix of domination   particular race, class, and gender configuration in society, which establishes a system of oppression

men's studies   a field of study focusing on men and challenging patriarchal biases in traditional scholarship

meritocracy   social systems in which persons hold their particular positions on the basis of individual talents and achievements

Meritor Savings Bank **v.** *Vinson*   Supreme Court decision in 1986 ruling that sexual harassment is a form of discrimination and, therefore, is unconstitutional

misogyny   hatred of women

Muller **v.** *Oregon*   Supreme Court decision in 1908 holding it constitutional to restrict the work-ing day to ten hours only for women

multiracial feminism   a perspective incorporating the multiple systems of domination that shape the experiences of Latinas, African American, Native American, Asian American and White women and men and that is grounded in understanding the intersections of race, class, and gender differences—and similarities—in the shaping of people's experiences

Nineteenth Amendment   the amendment to the U.S. Constitution that gives women the right to vote, passed in 1920

nonfamily household   a person living alone or one where a householder shares the unit with nonrelatives

nuclear family   family structure in which husband and wife reside together with their children

object relations theory   theory of psychological development that sees children as identifying with their same-sex parent but forming their own identities through detaching from the parents

patriarchy   institutionalized power relationships that give men power over women

Personal Responsibility and Work Reconciliation Act, 1996   the federal law passed that eliminated former welfare programs (AFDC) and placed lifetime limits on the receipt of welfare while also imposing work requirements

personal troubles   problematic events in the immediate experience of an individual

phallocentric thinking   thinking that assumes women need men for sexual arousal and satisfaction

pluralism   model of the state that interprets political action as the result of balancing the needs and actions of diverse interest groups

popular culture   beliefs, practices, and objects that are part of everyday traditions

postmodernism   form of contemporary social theory positing that society is not an objective entity and that all knowledge is situated in specific assumptions stemming from the historical period in which they develop; a theoretical perspective that sees society as not unitary, but instead composed of socially constituted and highly unstable images and selves

poverty line   index developed by the U.S. Social Security Administration that defines the official rate of poverty

power   individual or group ability to influence others

power elite   model of the state that sees power as stemming from the influence of a powerful ruling class

protective legislation   laws and policies prohibiting women from participating in certain jobs because of perceived risks to their reproductive health—generally thought to be discriminatory, since such protections have not been directed toward men as workers

public issues   events that originate beyond general immediate experience and that have their origin in the social structure of society

queer theory   an argument that interprets sexuality as socially constructed through institutional practices

radical feminism   feminist theoretical position positing that male power is the source of women's oppression

reflection hypothesis   explanation of the depiction of women in the mass media that assumes the mass media reflect the values of the population

religion as opiate   idea that religion is a form of social control that discourages social protest by oppressed groups

religious right   the term used to refer to fundamentalist Christian groups that have politically mobilized on behalf of conservative causes

reproduction of harm the idea that women who have been victims of sexual and emotional abuse, raised in poverty, and subjected to violent relationships are more likely to engage in deviant and/or criminal behavior

Roe v. *Wade* 1973 Supreme Court decision upholding women's right to abortion

role-learning theory explanation of media images of women and men that assumes that these images encourage role modeling by men and women observing the images

sanctified church term used to refer to Holiness and Pentecostal churches within the African American community

scientific method method of reasoning common to the practice of science, including systematic observation, analysis of data, and generalization

Second Great Awakening social movement in the early nineteenth century, emphasizing a revivalist and egalitarian spirit in religion

second shift work women do at home, in addition to paid labor

self-esteem how well one thinks of oneself

self-fulfilling prophecy term referring to the outcomes that occur as the result of others' expectations

sex biological identity of a person

sex chromosomes the chromosomal pairs determining the biological sex of an offspring

sex/gender system set of arrangements by which a society transforms biological sexuality into products of human activity

sexism beliefs that see women as inferior and defend their traditionally subordinated place in the world

sexual harassment unwanted imposition of sexual requirements in the context of a relationship of unequal power

sexual politics link between sexuality and power

sexually dimorphic traits differences appearing between males and females

social construction of gender the different processes by which expectations associated with being male or female are passed on through society

social constructionist theory perspective viewing people as constructing gender through their ongoing interaction with others

social institutions established patterns of behavior with a particular and recognized purpose; institutions include specific participants who share expectations and act in specific roles, with rights and duties attached to them

social learning theory theory of socialization emphasizing the significance of environment in explaining the socialization process

social movement work of groups organized to promote or resist change in society

social roles the culturally prescribed expectations, duties, and rights that define the relationship between a person in a particular position and the other people with whom she or he interacts

social structure concept referring to the organization of society that shapes social behavior

socialist feminism feminist theoretical position that interprets the origins of women's oppression in the system of capitalism; some socialist feminists also analyze the intersections of capitalism and patriarchy

socialization process by which social roles are learned

sociological imagination ability to conceptualize the relationship between individuals and the society in which they live

sociology of knowledge field of study within sociology that examines how ideas and knowledge are produced

standpoint theory feminist theoretical argument postulating that the specific social location of the knower shapes what is known and that not all perspectives on social life are valid or complete because of the different positions of knowers within systems of power and privilege

state organized and institutionalized system of power and authority in society, including the government, the police, law, and the military

stereotype threat a concept explaining the pattern whereby students (or others) perceive that they risk being judged by a negative stereotype and thus do not perform as well as they otherwise might

stratification process by which groups or individuals in a society are located in a hierarchical arrangement on the basis of their differential access to social and economic resources

subculture of violence idea that violence stems from the cultural attributes of particular groups

superstructure in Marxist theory, institutions of society as they reflect the economic system (law, family, and the like)

sweatshop a workplace where an employer violates more than one law regarding safety and health, workers' compensation, or industry regulation

symbolic interaction theory theoretical perspective in sociology that interprets social behavior as stemming from the meanings people attribute to things, including how they act

temperance movement a nineteenth-century social movement with feminist values, organized to oppose alcohol abuse

Temporary Assistance for Needy Families (TANF) state-based program providing limited economic support to poor families

Title VII of the Civil Rights Bill of 1964 federal law prohibiting discrimination on the basis of race, color, national origin, religion, or sex, in any terms, conditions, or privileges of employment

Title IX of the Educational Amendments of 1972 federal law prohibiting sex discrimination in federally funded education programs and activities; part of the Educational Amendments of 1972

tracking the practice whereby groups of students are sorted into groups in school based on their presumed abilities

transgender people who deviate from the binary system of gender as either male or female

transnational families families whose members live in different countries, usually at a considerable distance from one another, but with a pattern of moving back and forth across national boundaries

Uniform Crime Reports the official reports produced by the Federal Bureau of Investigation detailing the amount of reported crime and arrests

victimization surveys studies based on large, national samples that estimate the extent of crime victimization among particular groups

The Woman's Bible published in 1895 by Susan B. Anthony, the first attempt to rewrite the Bible, from a feminist perspective

women's studies field of study grounded in research and theory about women's lives that sees this knowledge as part of the process of changing women's lives for the better

Bibliography

Abramovitz, Mimi. 1996. "Dependent on the Kindness of Strangers: Issues Behind Welfare Reform." Pp. 287–294 in *For Crying Out Loud: Women's Poverty in the United States*, edited by Diane Dujon and Ann Withorn. Boston: South End Books.

Acker, Joan. 1992. "Gendered Institutions: From Sex Roles to Gendered Institutions." *Contemporary Sociology* 21 (September): 565–569.

Adelman, C. 1999. *Answers in the Tool Box: Academic Intensity, Attendance Patterns and Bachelor's Degree Attainment*. Washington, DC: Office of Educational Research and Improvement, U.S. Department of Education.

Adler, Freda. 1975. *Sisters in Crime*. New York: McGraw-Hill.

Agger, Ben. 1991. "Critical Theory, Poststructuralism, Postmodernism: Their Sociological Relevance." Pp. 105–131 in *Annual Review of Sociology*, Vol. 17, edited by W. Richard Scott and Judith Blake. Palo Alto, CA: Annual Reviews, Inc.

Alan Guttmacher Institute. 1998. "Facts in Brief." New York: Alan Guttmacher Institute. www.agi-use.org/pubs/

——. 1999. *Facts in Brief: Teen Sex and Pregnancy*. Website: www.agi-usa.org.

Albonetti, Celesta A. 1998. "The Role of Gender and Departures in the Sentencing of Defendants Convicted of a White-Collar Offense Under the Federal Sentencing Guidelines." *Sociology of Crime, Law, and Deviance* 1: 3–48.

Alden, Helena L. 2001. "Gender Role Ideology and Homophobia." Paper presented at the Annual Meetings of the Southern Sociological Society.

Ali, J., and W. R. Avison. 1997. "Employment Transitions and Psychological Distress: The Contrasting Experiences of Single and Married Mothers." *Journal of Health and Social Behavior* 38 (December): 345–362.

Alicea, Marixsa. 1997. " 'A Chambered Nautilus': The Contradictory Nature of Puerto Rican Women's Role in the Social Construction of a Transnational Community." *Gender & Society* 11 (October): 597–626.

Allen, Paula Gunn. 1986. *The Sacred Hoop*. Boston: Beacon Press.

Amadiume, Ifi. 1987. *Male Daughters, Female Husbands: Gender and Sex in an African Society*. London: Zed Books.

American Association of University Women. 1998. *Gender Gaps: Where Schools Still Fail Our Children*. Washington, DC: American Association of University Women.

——. 1992. *How Schools Shortchange Girls*. Washington, DC: American Association of University Women.

American Medical Association. 2004. "Women Physicians by Specialty." www.ama-assn.org.

American Sociological Association. 2005. "Statement of the American Sociological Association on the Causes of Gender Differences in Science and Math Career Advancement." Washington, D.C.: American Sociological Association. Website: www.asanet.org

Amir, M. 1971. *Patterns of Forcible Rape*. Chicago: University of Chicago Press.

Amott, Teresa L., and Julie A. Matthaei. 1996. *Race, Gender, and Work: A Multicultural History of Women in the United States*, rev. ed. Boston: South End Press.

Andersen, Margaret L. 1983. *Thinking About Women: Sociological and Feminist Perspectives*. New York: Macmillan.

——. 2003. "Whitewashing Race: A Critical Review." Pp. 21–34 in *Whiteout: The Continuing Significance of Racism*, edited by Eduardo Bonilla-Silva and Woody Doane. New York: Routledge.

——, Anne Bowler, and Michael Kimmel. 2004. "Do We Still Need Feminist Theory?" in *The Gender Kaleidoscope: Prisms, Patterns, and Possibilities*, edited by Catherine

Valentine and Joan Spade. Belmont, CA: Wadsworth.

——, and Patricia Hill Collins. 2004. *Race, Class, and Gender: An Anthology*, 4th ed. Belmont, CA: Wadsworth.

——, and Claire Renzetti. 1980. "Rape Crisis Counseling and the Culture of Individualism." *Contemporary Crises* 4: 323–339.

Anderson, A., and R. Gordon. 1978. "Witchcraft and the Status of Women—The Case of England." *British Journal of Sociology* 29: 171–184.

Anderson, Krisin J., and Campbell Leaper. 1998. "Meta-Analyses of Gender Effects on Conversational Interruption: Who, What, When, Where, and How." *Sex Roles* 38 (August): 225–252.

Andrews, W., and D.C. Andrews. 1974. "Technology and the Housewife in Nineteenth Century America." *Women's Studies* 2: 309–328.

Ansalone, George. 2001. "Schooling, Tracking, and Inequality." *Journal of Children and Poverty* 7 (March): 33–47.

Applebaum, Richard, and Peter Dreier. 1998. "The Campus Anti-Sweatshop Movement." *The American Prospect* 46 (September–October): 71.

Arendell, Terry. 1992. "After Divorce: Investigations into Father Absence." *Gender & Society* 6 (December): 562–586.

Aries, Philip. 1962. *Centuries of Childhood*. New York: Vintage.

Arnold, Regina. 1994. "Black Women in Prison: The Price of Resistance." Pp. 171–184 in *Women of Color in U.S. Society*, edited by Maxine Baca Zinn and Bonnie Thornton Dill. Philadelphia: Temple University Press.

Aronson, Pamela. 2003. "Feminists or 'Postfeminists?' Young Women's Attitudes toward Feminism and Gender Relations." *Gender & Society* 17 (December): 903–922.

Arrighi, Barbara A., and David J. Maume., Jr. 2000. "Workplace Subordination and Men's Avoidance of Housework." *Journal of Family Issues* 21 (May): 464–486.

Avalos, Manual. 1996. "Gender Inequality: Sorting out the Effects of Race/Ethnicity and Gender in the Anglo Male-Latino Female Earnings Gap." *Sociological Perspectives* 39 (Winter): 497–515.

Axtell, J. 1981. *The Indian Peoples of Eastern America: A Documentary History of the Sexes*. New York: Oxford University Press.

Baca Zinn, Maxine. 1976. "Chicanas: Power and Control in the Domestic Sphere." *DeColores* 2 (Fall): 19–31.

———. 1990. "Family, Feminism, and Race in America." *Gender & Society* 4 (March): 68–82.

———, and Bonnie Thornton Dill. 1996. "Theorizing Difference from Multiracial Feminism." *Feminist Studies* 22 (Summer): 321–331.

———, and D. Stanley Eitzen. 2005. *Diversity in Families*, 7th ed. Boston, MA: Allyn and Bacon.

———, Pierrette Hondagneu-Sotelo, and Michael A. Messner, eds, 2000. *Gender Through the Prism of Difference*, 2nd ed. Needham Heights, MA: Allyn and Bacon.

Badgett, M. V. Lee. 1995. "The Wage Effects of Sexual Orientation Discrimination." *Industrial and Labor Relations Review* 48 (July): 726–739.

———, and Mary C. King. 1997. Pp. 73–86 in *Homo Economics: Capitalism, Community, and Lesbian and Gay Life*, edited by Amy Gluckman and Betsy Reed. New York: Routledge.

Baer, Judith A. 1998. *Our Lives Before the Law: Constructing a Feminist Jurisprudence*. Princeton, NJ: Princeton University Press.

Baldwin, Mark W., and John Patrick Richard Keelan. 1999. "Interpersonal Expectations as a Function of Self-Esteem and Sex." *Journal of Social and Personal Relationships* 16 (December): 822–835.

Barajas, Heidi Lasley, and Jennifer Pierce. 2001. "The Significance of Race and Gender in School Success among Latinas and Latinos in College." *Gender & Society* 15 (December): 859–878.

Barber, Jennifer S., and William G. Axinn. 1998. "Gender Roles Attitudes and Marriage among Young Women." *Sociological Quarterly* 39 (Winter): 11–31.

Barfoot, C. H., and G. T. Sheppard. 1980. "Prophetic vs. Priestly Religion: The Changing Role of Women Clergy in Classical Pentecostal Churches." *Review of Religious Research* 22 (September): 2–17.

Barker-Benfield, G. J. 1976. *Horrors of the Half-Known Life*. New York: Harper & Row.

Baron, James, Allison Davis-Blake, and William Bielby. 1986. "The Structure of Opportunity: How Promotion Ladders Vary Within and Among Organizations." *Administrative Science Quarterly* 31: 248–273.

Barron, Martin, and Michael Kimmel. 2000. "Sexual Violence in Three Pornographic Media: Towards a Sociological Explanation." *Journal of Sex Research* 37: 161–168.

Bart, Pauline. 1979. "The Loneliness of the Long-Distance Mother." Pp. 245–261 in *Women: A Feminist Perspective*, edited by Jo Freeman. Palo Alto, CA: Mayfield.

Bartling, Carl, and Brenda Broussard. 1999. "Effects of Experimenter Gender, Testing Context and Marital Status upon Marital Role Expectations." *International Journal of Adolescence and Youth* 7: 317–325.

Basow, Susan A. 2003. " 'Troubles Talk': Effects of Gender and Gender-Typing." *Sex Roles* 48 (February): 183–187.

———. 1992. *Gender: Stereotypes and Roles*, 3rd ed. Belmont, CA: Brooks/Cole.

———, and Kelly Johnson. 2000. "Predictors of Homophobia in Female College Students." *Sex Roles* 42 (March): 391–404.

Battle, Juan, and Anthony J. Lemelle Jr. 2002. "Gender Differences in African American Attitudes toward Gay Males." *The Western Journal of Black Studies* 26: 134–9.

Baxandall, R. F. 1979. "Who Shall Care for Our Children? The History and Development of Day Care in the United States."

Pp. 134–149 in *Women: A Feminist Perspective*, edited by Jo Freeman. Palo Alto, CA: Mayfield.

Baxter, Janeen, and Eric Olin Wright. 2000. "The Glass Ceiling Hypothesis: A Comparative Study of the United States, Sweden, and Australia." *Gender & Society* 14 (April): 275–294.

Becker, Howard. 1963. *The Outsiders*. New York: Free Press.

Becker, Penny Edgell, and Heather Hofmeister. 2001. "Work, Family, and Religious Involvement for Men and Women." *Journal for the Scientific Study of Religion* 40: 707–22.

Becker, Penny Edgell, and Phyllis Moen. 1999. "Scaling Back" Dual-Earner Couples' Work-Family Strategies." *Journal of Marriage and the Family* 61 (November): 995–1007.

Belkin, Aaron, and Geoffrey Bateman. 2003. *Don't Ask, Don't Tell: Debating the Gay Ban in the Military*. Boulder, CO: Lynne Reinner Publishers.

Bellas, Marcia L. 1997. "Disciplinary Differences in Faculty Salaries: Does Gender Bias Play a Role?" *Journal of Higher Education* 68 (May–June): 299–321.

Belsky, Jay, and John Kelly. 1994. *The Transition to Parenthood*. New York: Delacorte Press.

Bendroth, Margaret Lamberts. 1999. "Fundamentalism and the Family" Gender, Culture, and the American Pro-Family Movement." *Journal of Women's History* 10 (Winter): 35–54.

Benet, M. K. 1972. *The Secretarial Ghetto*. New York: McGraw-Hill.

Benson, S. P. 1978. " 'The Clerking Sisterhood': Rationalization and the Work Culture of Saleswomen in American Department Stores, 1890–1960." *Radical America* 12 (March–April): 41–55.

Berger, Peter. 1963. *Invitation to Sociology*. Garden City, NY: Doubleday-Anchor.

Berger, Peter, and Thomas Luckmann. 1966. *The Social Construction of Reality*. Garden City, NY: Doubleday-Anchor.

Berheide, Catherine White. 1988. "Women in Sales and Service Occupations." Pp. 241–257 in *Women Working*, 2d ed., edited by Ann Helton Stromberg and Shirley Harkess. Mountain View, CA: Mayfield.

———. 1992. "Women Still 'Stuck' in Low-Level Jobs." *Women in Public Services: A Bulletin for the Center for Women in Government* 3 (Fall). Albany, NY: Center for Women in Government, State University of New York.

Bernard, Jessie. 1972. "Marriage: His and Hers." *Ms.* 1: 46ff.

———. 1975. *Women, Wives, Mothers: Values and Options.* Chicago: Aldine.

Berry, Phyllis E., and Helen M. Eigenberg. 2003. "Role Strain and Incarcerated Mothers: Understanding the Process of Mothering." *Women & Criminal Justice* 15: 101–119.

Bettie, Julie. 1995. "Class Dismissed? Roxanne and the Changing Face of Working-Class Iconography." *Social Text* 45 (Winter): 125–149.

Bianchi, Suzanne M. 2000. "Maternal Employment and Time with Children: Dramatic Change or Surprising Continuity? *Demography* 37 (November): 401–414.

———, and Marybeth J. Mattingly. 2004. "Time, Work, and Family in the United States." *Advances in Life Course Research* 8: 95–118.

———, Melissa A. Milkie, Liana C. Sayer, and John P. Robinson. 2000. "Is Anyone Doing the Housework?: Trends in the Gender Division of Household Labor." *Social Forces* 79 (September): 191–228.

Bigner, Jerry J., and Frederick W. Bozett. 1989. "Parenting by Gay Fathers." *Marriage and Family Review* 14: 155–175.

Billingsley, Andrew. 1966. *Black Families in White America.* Upper Saddle River, NJ: Prentice-Hall.

Bird, Chloe E., 1996. "Gender, Paid and Unpaid Work, and Depression." Paper given at the Annual Meetings of the Society for the Study of Social Problems.

———. 1999. "Gender, Household Labor, and Psychological Distress: The Impact of the Amount and Division of Housework."

Journal of Health and Social Behavior 40 (March): 32–45.

Bird, Chloe E., and Allen M. Fremont. 1999. "Are Sociological Models of the Effects of Gender, Paid Work, and Unpaid Work on Depression and Self-Rated Health Generalizable to Mental and Physical Health?" Paper presented at the Annual Meetings of the American Sociological Association, Washington, DC.

Bird, Sharon. 1996. "Welcome to the Men's Club: Homosociality and the Maintenance of Hegemonic Masculinity." *Gender & Society* 10 (April): 120–132.

Blackwell, James. 1991. *The Black Community: Diversity and Unity.* New York: HarperCollins.

Blackwood, Evelyn. 1984. "Sexuality and Gender in Certain Native American Tribes: The Case of Cross-Gender Females." *Signs* 10 (Autumn): 27–42.

Blake, C. Fred. 1994. "Footbinding in Neo-Confucian China and the Appropriation of Female Labor." *Signs* 19 (Spring): 676–712.

Blakemore, J. E. O. 1998. "The Influence of Gender and Parental Attitudes on Preschool Children's Interest in Babies: Observations in Natural Settings." *Sex Roles* 38 (January): 73–94.

Blane, D., L. Berney, and S. M. Montgomery. 2001. "Domestic Labour, Paid Employment and Women's Health: Analysis of Life Course Data." *Social Science and Medicine* 52 (2001): 959–965.

Blood, Robert, and Donald Wolfe. 1960. *Husbands and Wives: The Dynamics of Married Living.* New York: Free Press.

Bloom, Barbara, et al. 2003. "Focusing on Girls and Young Women: A Gendered Perspective on Female Delinquency." *Women and Criminal Justice* 14: 117–136.

———, Barbara Owen, and Stephanie Covington. 2004. "Women Offenders and the Gendered Effects of Public Policy." *The Review of Policy Research* 21: 31–48.

Blum, Linda. 1986. "Women and Advancement: Possibilities and Limits of the Comparable Worth Movement." Paper

presented at the Annual Meetings of the American Sociological Association, New York City, September.

Blumenthal, Susan J. 1998. "Women and Substance Abuse: A New National Focus." Pp. 13–32 in *Drug Addiction Research and the Health of Women,* edited by Cora Lee Wetherington and Adele B. Roman. Washington, DC: National Institute on Drug Abuse.

Blumstein, Philip, and Pepper Schwartz. 1983. *American Couples.* New York: William Morrow.

Boeri, Miriam Williams. 2002. "Women After the Utopia: The Gendered Lives of Former Cult Members." *Journal of Contemporary Ethnography* 31: 323–360.

Boeringer, Scot B. 1999. "Associations of Rape-Supportive Attitudes with Fraternal and Athletic Participation." *Violence against Women* 5: 81–90.

Bogdan, J. 1978. "Care or Cure? Childbirth Practices in Nineteenth-Century America." *Feminist Studies* 4: 92–99.

Bogle, Katie. 2004. *From Dating to Hooking Up: The Emergence of a New Sexual Script.* Ph.D. Dissertation, University of Delaware.

Bogoch, Bryna. 1999a. "Courtroom Discourse and the Gendered Construction of Professional Identity." *Law & Social Inquiry* 24: 329–375.

———. 1999b. "Judging in a 'Different Voice': Gender and the Sentencing of Violent Offences in Israel." *International Journal of the Sociology of Law* 27: 51–78.

Bonacich, Edna, and Richard P. Applebaum. 2000. *Behind the Label: Inequality in the Los Angeles Apparel Industry.* Berkeley: University of California Press.

Bonilla-Silva, Eduardo, and Mary Hovespan. 2000. "If Two People Are in Love: Deconstructing Whites' Views on Interracial Marriage with Blacks." Paper presented at the Annual meetings of the Southern Sociological Society.

Bookman, Ann, and Sandra Morgen. 1988. *Women and the Politics of Empowerment.* Philadelphia: Temple University Press.

Booth, Bradford. 2003. "Contextual Effects of Military Presence on Women's Earnings." *Armed Forces & Society* 30 (Fall): 25–51.

———, William Falk, David R. Segal, and Mady Wechsler Segal. 2000. "The Impact of Military Presence in Local Labor Markets on the Employment of Women." *Gender & Society* 14 (April): 318–332.

Bordo, Susan. 1992. "Feminist Skepticism and the 'Maleness' of Philosophy." Pp. 143–162 in *Women and Reason*, edited by Elizabeth D. Harvey and Kathleen Okruhlik. Ann Arbor: University of Michigan Press.

———. 1995. *Unbearable Weight: Feminism, Western Culture, and the Body*. Berkeley: University of California Press.

Boston Women's Health Book Collective. 1984. *The New Our Bodies, Ourselves*. New York: Simon and Schuster.

Boswell, A. Ayres, and Joan Z. Spade. 1996. "Fraternities and Collegiate Rape Culture: Why Are some Fraternities More Dangerous Places for Women?" *Gender & Society* 10: 133–47.

Bowen, Lawrence, and Jill Schmid. 1997. "Minority Presence and Portrayal in Mainstream Magazine Advertising: An Update." *Journalism and Mass Communication Quarterly* 74 (Spring): 134–146.

Boyd, Carol L., Thomas C. Boyd, and Jennifer L. Cash. 1999–2000. "Why is Virginia Slim? Women and Cigarette Advertising." *International Quarterly of Community Health Education* 19: 19–31.

Brabant, S., and L. A. Mooney. 1997. "Sex Role Stereotyping in the Sunday Comics: A Twenty Year Update." *Sex Roles* 37 (August): 269–281.

Bradford, J., Ryan, C., and E. D. Rothblum. 1994. "National Lesbian Health Care Survey: Implications for Mental Health Care." *Journal of Counseling and Clinical Psychology* 62: 228–242.

Bradley, Karen. 2000. "The Incorporation of Women in Higher Education: Paradoxical Outcomes?" *Sociology of Education* 73 (January): 1–18.

Bramson, Leon. 1961. *The Political Context of Sociology*. Princeton, NJ: Princeton University Press.

Brettell, Caroline B., and Carolyn F. Sargent, eds. 2001. *Gender in Cross-Cultural Perspective*, 3rd ed. Upper Saddle River, NJ: Prentice-Hall.

Brewis, Joanna, and Stephen Linstead. 2000a. " The Worst Thing is the Screwing' (1): Context and Career in Sex Work." *Gender, Work and Organization* 7 (July): 168–180.

Brewis, Joanna, and Stephen Linstead. 2000b. " The Worst Thing is the Screwing' (2): Consumption and the Management of Identity in Sex Work." *Gender, Work and Organization* 7 (April): 84–97.

Brewster, Mary. 2000. "Stalking by Former Intimates: Verbal Threats and Other Predictors of Physical Violence." *Violence and Victims* 15: 41–54.

———. 2002. "Trauma Symptoms of Former Intimate Stalking Victims." *Women and Criminal Justice* 13: 141–161.

———. 2003. "Power and Control Dynamics in Prestalking and Stalking Situations." *Journal of Family Violence* 18: 207–217.

Brines, Julie, and Kara Joyner. 1999. "The Ties That Bind: Principles of Cohesion in Cohabitation and Marriage." *American Sociological Review* 64 (June): 333–355.

Britton, Dana M. 1997. "Gendered Organizational Logic: Policy and Practice in Men's and Women's Prisons." *Gender & Society* 11 (December): 796–818.

Brown, Brett V. 2000. "The Single-Father Family: Demographic, Economic, and Public Transfer Use Characteristics." *Marriage and Family Review* 29: 203–220.

Brown, C. 1981. "Mothers, Fathers, and Children: From Private to Public Patriarchy." Pp. 239–267 in *Women and Revolution*, edited by Lydia Sargent. New York: South End Press.

Brown, Susan L. 1996. "Relationship Quality and the Transition to Marriage among Cohabitors." Paper presented at the Annual Meetings of the American Sociological Association.

Browne, Irene, ed. 1999. *Latinas and African American Women at Work: Race, Gender, and Economic Inequality*. New York: Russell Sage Foundation.

Browne, Malcolm W. 1998. "Can't Decide if That Centerfold Is Really a Perfect 10? Just Do the Math." *The New York Times,* October 20, p. D5.

Brownmiller, S. 1975. *Against Our Will*. New York: Simon and Schuster.

Brush, Lisa D. 1990. "Violent Acts and Injurious Outcomes in Married Couples: Methodological Issues in the National Survey of Families and Households." *Gender & Society* 4 (March): 56–67.

Bunch, Charlotte. 1975. "Lesbians in Revolt." Pp. 29–38 in *Lesbianism and the Women's Movement*, edited by N. Myron and C. Bunch. Oakland, CA: Diana Press.

Burckle, Michelle A., Richard M. Ryckman, Joel A. Gold, Bill Thornton, and Roberta J. Audesse. 1999. "Forms of Competitive Attitude and Achievement Orientation in Relation to Disordered Eating." *Sex Roles* 40 (June): 853–870.

Bureau of Justice Statistics. 2003a. Crime Victimization. Washington, DC: Bureau of Justice Statistics. www.ojp.usjod.gov/bjs/

Bureau of Justice Statistics. 2003b. *Sourcebook of Criminal Justice Statistics*. Washington, DC: Department of Justice.

Burgess, Samuel H. 2001. "Gender Ideology and Anti-Gay Opinion in the United States." Paper presented at the Annual Meetings of the Southern Sociological Society.

Burris, Beverly H. 1991. "Employed Mothers: The Impact of Class and Marital Status on the Prioritizing of Family and Work." *Social Science Quarterly* 72 (March): 50–66.

Butler, Amy C. 1996. "The Effect of Welfare Benefit Levels on Poverty among Single-Parent Families." *Social Problems* 43 (February): 94–115.

Butler, Judith. 1990. *Gender Trouble: Feminism and the Subversion of Identity*. New York: Routledge.

Buysse, Joann M., and Melissa Sherman Embser-Herbert. 2004.

"Constructions of Gender in Sport: An Analysis of Intercollegiate Media Guide Cover Photographs." *Gender & Society* 18 (February): 66–81.

Calasanti, Toni M., and Kathleen F. Slevin. 2001. *Gender, Social Inequalities, and Aging*. Walnut Creek, CA: AltaMira Press.

Caldera, Yvonne, and Mary A. Sciaraffa. 1998. "Parent-Toddler Play with Feminine Toys: Are All Dolls the Same?" *Sex Roles* 38 (November); 657–658.

Calhoun, Avery J., and Heather D. Coleman. 2002. "Female Inmates' Perspectives on Sexual Abuse by Correctional Personnel: An Exploratory Study." *Women and Criminal Justice* 13: 101–124.

Califia, Pat. 1997. *Sex Changes: The Politics of Transgenderism*. San Francisco: Cleis Books.

Cameron, Deborah. 1998. "Gender, Language, and Discourse: A Review Essay." *Signs* 23 (Summer): 945–974.

Campbell, Anne. 1989. *Girls in the Gang*. Cambridge: Basil Blackwell.

Campbell, Jacquelyn C., et al. 2003. "Intimate Partner Violence and Abuse among Active Duty Military Women." *Violence against Women* 9: 1072–1092.

Campenni, C. Estelle. 1999. "Gender Stereotyping of Children's Toys: A Comparison of Parents and Nonparents." *Sex Roles* 40 (January): 121–138.

Cancian, Francesca. 1987. *Love in America: Gender and Self-Development*. New York: Cambridge University Press.

Cancian, Maria, and Daniel R. Meyer. 2000. "Work after Welfare: Women's Work Effort, Occupation, and Economic Well-Being." *Social Work Research* 24 (June): 69–86.

Candib, Lucy M. 1999. "Incest and Other Harms to Daughters across Cultures: Maternal Complicity and Patriarchal Power." *Women's Studies International Forum* 22 (March-April): 185–201.

Carlson, Darren K. 2003. "Public OK With Gays, Women in Military." *The Gallup Poll*. Princeton, NJ: The Gallup Organization.

Carr, C. Lynn. 1999. "Tomboy Resistance and Comformity: Agency in Social Psychological Gender Theory." *Gender & Society* 12 (October): 643–664.

Carr, D. 1997. "The Fulfillment of Career Dreams at Midlife: Does It Matter for Women's Mental Health?" *Journal of Health and Social Behavior* 38 (December): 331–344.

Carroll, Joseph. 2004. "Religion is 'Very Important' to 6 in 10 Americans." *The Gallup Poll*. Princeton, NJ: Gallup Organization

Cassidy, Margery A., and David Trafimow. 2002. "The Influence of Patriarchal Ideology on Outcomes of Legal Decisions Involving Woman Battering Cases: An Analysis of Five Historical Eras." *The Social Science Journal* 39: 235–245.

Catsambis, Sophia, Lynn M. Mulkey, and Robert L. Crain. 1999. "To Track or Not to Track? The Social Effects of Gender and Middle School Tracking." *Research in Sociology of Education and Socialization* 12: 135–163.

Caulfield, Mina Davis. 1974. "Imperialism, the Family and Cultures of Resistance." *Socialist Revolution* 20: 67–85.

———. 1985. "Sexuality in Human Evolution: What is 'Natural' in Sex?" *Feminist Studies* 11 (Summer): 343–364.

Cavendar, Gray, Lisa Bond-Maupin, and Nancy C. Jurik. 1999. "The Construction of Gender in Reality Crime TV." *Gender & Society* 13 (October): 643–664.

Center for American Woman and American Politics. 2004. *Fact Sheet on Women's Political Progress*. New Brunswick, NJ: Rutgers University.

Centers for Disease Control. 2004. "A Glance at the HIV Epidemic." Website: www.cdc.gov.

Cepeda, Alice, and Avelardo Valdez. 2003. "Risk Behaviors among Young Mexican American Gang-Associated Females: Sexual Relations, Partying, Substance Use, and Crime." *Journal of Adolescent Research* 18: 90–106.

Chancer, Lynn. 1993. "Prostitution, Feminist Theory, and Ambivalence: Notes from the Sociological Underground." *Social Text* 37 (Winter): 143–171.

Chaves, Mark, and James Cavendish. 1997. "Recent Changes in Women's Ordination Conflicts: The Effect of a Social Movement on Intraorganizational Controversy." *Journal for the Scientific Study of Religion* 36 (December): 574–584.

Chavkin, W. 1979. "Occupational Hazards to Reproduction: A Review Essay and Annotated Bibliography." *Feminist Studies* 5 (Summer): 310–325.

Chen, Anthony S. 1999. "Lives at the Center of the Periphery, Lives at the Periphery of the Center: Chinese American Masculinities and Bargaining with Hegemony." *Gender & Society* 13 (October): 584–607.

Chernin, Kim. 1981. *The Obsession*. New York: Harper Colophon.

———. 1985. *The Hungry Self: Women, Eating, and Identity*. New York: Times Books.

Chesney-Lind, Meda. 1997. "Equity with a Vengeance." *The Women's Review of Books* 14 (July): 5.

———. 1999. "Challenging Girls' Invisibility in Juvenile Court." *Annals of the American Academy of Political and Social Science* 564 (July): 185–202.

Chodorow, Nancy. 1978. *The Reproduction of Mothering*. Berkeley: University of California Press.

Chow, Esther. 1987. "The Development of Feminist Consciousness Among Asian American Women." *Gender & Society* 1 (September): 284–299.

Christ, Carol. 1979. "Why Women Need the Goddess: Phenomenological, Psychological and Political Reflections." Pp. 273–287 in *Womanspirit Rising*, edited by C. P. Christ and J. Plaskow. New York: Harper and Row.

———, and Judith Plaskow, eds. 1992. *Womanspirit Rising*, 2nd ed. New York: Harper and Row.

Chrobot-Mason, Donna, Scott B. Button, and Jeannie D. DiClementi. 2001. "Sexual Identity Management Strategies: An Exploration of Antecedents and

Consequences." *Sex Roles* 45 (September): 321–336.

Chronicle of Higher Education. 2004. *Almanac Issue 2004–5* (August).

Clark, Roger, Rachel Lennon, and Leanna Morris. 1993. "Of Caldecotts and Kings: Gendered Images in Recent American Children's Books by Black and Non-Black Illustrators." *Gender & Society* 7 (June): 227–245.

Clark-Ibanez, Marisol Karina. 1999. "Gender, Race, and Friendships: Structural and Social Factors Leading to the Likelihood of Inter-Ethnic Dating." Paper presented at the Annual Meetings of the American Sociological Association, Washington, DC.

Clarke, E. 1873. *Sex in Education; Or, A Fair Chance for the Girls*. Boston: Osgood and Company.

Clay, V. S. 1977. *Women: Menopause and Middle Age*. Pittsburgh: Know, Inc.

Cohen, Lisa E., Joseph P. Broschak, and Heather A. Haveman. 1998. "Sex Composition and the Hiring/Promotion of Women Managers." *American Sociological Review* 63 (October): 711–727.

Colker, Brian D. 1997. "Wage Inequality in the Staff Workforce at UCLA." Paper presented at the Annual Meetings of the American Sociological Association, Toronto.

Collins, Patricia Hill. 1986. "Learning From the Outsider Within: The Sociological Significance of Black Feminist Thought." *Social Problems* 33 (December): 514–532.

———. 1987. "The Meaning of Motherhood in Black Culture and Black Mother-Daughter Relationships." *Sage* 4 (Fall): 3–10.

———. 1990. *Black Feminist Theory: Knowledge, Consciousness and the Politics of Empowerment*. Boston: Unwin Hyman.

———. 1998. *Fighting Words: Black Women and the Search for Social Justice*. Minneapolis: University of Minnesota Press.

———. 2004. *Black Sexual Politics: African Americans, Gender, and the New Racism*. New York: Routledge.

Coltrane, Scott, and Michele Adams. 1997. "Work-Family Imagery and Gender Stereotypes: Television and the Reproduction of Difference." *Journal of Vocational Behavior* 50 (April): 323–347.

Combahee River Collective. 1982. "A Black Feminist Statement." Pp. 13–22 in *But Some of Us Are Brave*, edited by Gloria T. Hull, Patricia Bell Scott, and Barbara Smith. Old Westbury, NY: The Feminist Press.

Connell, Bob. 1992. "Masculinity, Violence, and War." Pp. 176–183 in *Men's Lives*, 2nd ed., edited by Michael S. Kimmel and Michael A. Messner. New York: Macmillan.

Conrad, Peter. 1998. Constructing the 'Gay Gene' in the News: Optimism and Skepticism in the American, British, and Gay Press. Paper presented at the International Sociological Association.

Conte, Jon R. 1993. "Sexual Abuse of Children." Pp. 56–85 in *Family Violence: Prevention and Treatment*, edited by Robert L. Hampton, Thomas P. Gullotta, Gerald R. Adams, Earl H. Potter III., and Roger P. Weissberg. Newbury Park, CA: Sage.

Coontz, Phyllis. 2000. "Gender and Judicial Decisions: Do Female Judges Decide Cases Differently than Male Judges?" *Gender Issues* 18: 59–73.

Corea, Gena. 1980. "The Caesarian Epidemic." *Mother Jones* 5: 28ff.

Cortina, Lilia M., Suzanne Swan, Louise F. Fitzgerald, and Craig Waldo. 1998. "Sexual Harassment and Assault: Chilling the Climate for Women in Academia." *Psychology of Women Quarterly* 22 (September): 419–441.

Costello, C. B. 1985. " 'WEA're Worth It!' Work Culture and Conflict at the Wisconsin Education Association Insurance Trust." *Feminist Studies* 11 (Fall): 497–518.

Cott, Nancy. 1977. *The Bonds of Womanhood*. New Haven, CT: Yale University Press.

Cotter, David A., Joan M. Hermson, Seth Ovadia, and Reeve Vanneman, 2001. "The Glass Ceiling Effect." *Social Forces* 80 (December): 655–682.

Council of Economic Advisors. 1998. *Changing America: Indicators of Social and Economic Well-Being by Race and Hispanic Origin*. Washington, DC: U.S. Government Printing Office.

Cowan, R. S. 1976. "Two Washes in the Morning and a Bridge Party at Night: The American Housewife Between Wars." *Women's Studies* 3: 147–171.

Crabb, Peter B., and Dawn Bielawski. 1994. "The Social Representation of Material Culture and Gender in Children's Books." *Sex Roles* 30 (January): 69–80.

Crawford, Mary. 1995. *Talking Difference: On Gender and Language*. Thousand Oaks: Sage.

———, and M. Macleod. 1990. "Gender in the College Classroom: An Assessment of the 'Chilly Climate' for Women." *Sex Roles* 23: 101–122.

Crenshaw, Carrie. 1995. "The 'Protection' of 'Woman': A History of Legal Attitudes toward Women's Workplace Freedom." *Quarterly Journal of Speech* 81 (February): 63–82.

Crenshaw, Kimberle, Neil Gotanda, Garry Peller, Kendall Thomas, and Cornel West. 1996. *Critical Race Theory: The Key Writings That Formed the Movement*. New York: New Press.

Crisp, Arthur, Philip Sedgwick, Christine Halek, Neil Joughin, and Heather Humphrey. 1999. "Why May Teenage Girls Persist in Smoking?" *Journal of Adolescence* 22 (October): 657–672.

Croteau, James M. 1996. "Research on the Work Experiences of Lesbian, Gay, and Bisexual People: An Integrative Review of Methodology and Findings." *Journal of Vocational Behavior* 48 (April): 195–209.

Cullen, Jennifer M., Lester W. Wright Jr., and Michael Alessandri. 2002. "The Personality Variable Openness to Experience as it Relates to Homophobia." *Journal of Homosexuality* 42119–42134.

Currie, Dawn. 1997. "Decoding Femininity: Advertisements and

Their Teenage Readers." *Gender & Society* 11 (August): 453–477.

Dailard, Cynthia. 2003. " 'Understanding' Abstinence: Implications for Individuals, Programs, Policies." *The Guttmacher Report* 6. Website: www.agi-usa.org.

Dalton, Susan E., and Denise D. Bielby. 2000. " 'That's Our Kind of Constellation': Lesbian Mothers Negotiate Institutionalized Understandings of Gender within the Family." *Gender & Society* 14 (February): 36–61.

Daly, Kathleen. 1989. "Rethinking Judicial Paternalism: Gender, Work-Family Relations, and Sentencing," *Gender & Society* 3 (March): 9–36.

———, and Michael Tonry. 1977. "Gender, Race, and Sentencing." *Crime and Justice* 22: 201–52.

Daly, Mary. 1978. *Gyn/Ecology: The Meta-Ethics of Radical Feminism.* Boston: Beacon Press.

———. 1979. "After the Death of God the Father: Women's Liberation and the Transformation of Christian Consciousness." Pp. 53–62 in *Womanspirit Rising,* edited by C. P. Christ and J. Plaskow. New York: Harper and Row.

———. 1994. *Gender, Crime and Punishment.* New Haven, CT: Yale University Press.

Daniels, Cynthia R., Maureen Paul, and Robert Rosofsky. 1990. "Health, Equity, and Reproductive Risks in the Workplace." *Journal of Public Health Policy* 11 (Winter): 449–462.

Darcy, R., Susan Welch, and Janet Clark. 1994. *Women, Elections, and Representation.* Lincoln: University of Nebraska Press.

Data Essay. (2000). "Living Female." *The Public Perspective* 11(4): 20. Storrs, CT: The Roper Center for Public Opinion Research.

Davidman, Lynn. 1991. *Tradition in a Rootless World: Women Turn to Orthodox Judaism.* Berkeley: University of California Press.

Davies, Michelle, and Samantha McCartney. 2003. "Effects of Gender and Sexuality on Judgments of Victim Blame and Rape Myth Acceptance in a Depicted Male Rape." *Journal of Community &*

Applied Social Psychology 13: 391–398.

Davis, Angela. 1971. "Reflections on Black Women's Role in the Community of Slaves." *The Black Scholar* 3: 2–15.

———. 1981. *Women, Race and Class.* New York: Random House.

Davis, Keith E., and Irene Hanson Frieze. 2000. "Research on Stalking: What Do We Know and Where do We Go?" *Violence and Victims* 15: 473–487.

Davis, Keith E., Ann L. Coker, and Maureen Sanderson. 2002. "Physical and Mental Health Effects of Being Stalked for Men and Women." *Violence and Victims* 17 (August): 429–433.

Davis, Keith E., April Ace, and Michelle Andra. 2000. "Stalking Perpetrators and Psychological Maltreatment of Partners: Anger-Jealousy, Attachment Insecurity, Need for Control, and Break-Up Context." *Violence and Victims* 15: 407–425.

Davis, Shannon N. 2003. "Sex Stereotypes in TV Programs Aimed at the Preschool Audience: An Analysis of Teletubbies and Barney & Friends." *Sociological Spectrum* 23 (October-December): 407–424.

Defey, Denise, Eduardo Storch, Silvia Cardozo, Olga Diaz, and Graciela Fernandez. 1996. "The Menopause: Women's Psychology and Health Care." *Social Science and Medicine* 42: 1147–1156.

Deitz, S. R., K. T. Blackwell, P. C. Daley, and B. J. Bentley. 1982. "Measurement of Empathy Toward Rape Victims and Rapists." *Journal of Personality and Social Psychology* 43 (August): 372–384.

Delaney, J., M. J. Lupton, and E. Toth. 1988. *The Curse: A Cultural History of Menstruation.* Urbana: University of Illinois Press.

Dellinger, Kirsten, and Christine L. Williams. 1997. "Makeup at Work: Negotiating Appearance Rules in the Workplace." *Gender & Society* 11 (April): 151–177.

Demarest, Jack, and Rita Allen. 2000. "Body Image: Gender, Ethnic, and Age Differences." *Journal of Social Psychology* 140 (August): 465–472.

Dembo, Richard, Kimberly Pacheco, James Schmeidler, Gabrella Ramiresx-Garmica, Julie Guide, and Atiq Rahman. 1998. "A Further Study of Gender Differences in Service Needs among Youths Entering a Juvenile Assessment Center." *Journal of Child and Adolescent Substance Abuse* 7: 49–77.

D'Emilio, John. 1998. *Sexual Politics, Sexual Communities: The Making of a Homosexual Minority in the United States, 1940–1970.* Chicago: University of Chicago Press.

DeNavas-Walt, Carmen, Bernadette D. Proctor, and Robert J. Mills. 2004. *Income, Poverty, and Health Insurance Coverage in the United States: 2003.* Current Population Repots P-60–226. Washington, DC: U.S. Government Printing Office.

Dentinger, Emma, and Marin Clarkberg. 2002. "Informal Caregiving and Retirement Timing among Men and Women: Gender and Caregiving Relationships in Late Midlife." *Journal of Family Issues* 23 (October): 857–879.

Department of Defense. 2003. "Active Duty Military Personnel by Rank/Grade, September 20. Website: http://web1.whs.osd. mil/mmid/military/RG0402. pdf.

de Tocqueville, A. 1945. *Democracy in America.* New York: Knopf.

DeVault, Marjorie L. 1991. *Feeding the Family: The Social Organization of Caring as Gender Work.* Chicago: University of Chicago Press.

Dewar, Diane M. 2000. "Gender Impacts on Health Insurance Coverage: Findings for Unmarried Full-Time Employees." *Women's Health Issues* 10: 268–277.

De Welde, Kristine. 2003. " White Women Beware!': Whiteness, Fear of Crime, and Self-Defense." *Race, Gender & Class* 10: 75–91.

Diamond, Milton, and H. K. Sigmundson. 1997. "Sex Reassignment at Birth: Long-Term Review and Clinical Implications." *Archives of Pediatric and Adolescent Medicine* 151 (March): 298–304.

Dickens, W. J., and D. Perlman. 1981. "Friendship over the Life Cycle." Pp. 91–122 in *Personal*

Relationships, Vol. 2, Developing Personal Relationships, edited by S. Duck and R. Gilmour. New York: Academic Press.

Dickerson-Putnam, Jeannette. 1996. "From Pollution to Empowerment: Women, Age, and Power among the Bena Bena of the Eastern Highlands." *Pacific Studies* 19: 41–70.

Dietz, Noella Ann. 2003. "Women's Stalking Experiences: The Relationship between Stalking Practices, Perpetrators, and Violent Crime." Paper presented at the Annual Meetings of the Southern Sociological Society.

Dietz, T. L. 1998. "An Examination of Violence and Gender Role Portrayals in Video Games: Implications for Gender Socialization and Aggressive Behavior." *Sex Roles* 38 (March): 425–442.

Dill, Bonnie Thornton. 1980. " 'The Means to Put My Children Through': Childrearing Goals and Strategies Among Black Female Domestic Servants." Pp. 107–123 in *The Black Woman,* edited by L. F. Rodgers-Rose. Beverly Hills, CA: Sage.

———. 1983. "Race, Class, and Gender: Prospects for an All Inclusive Sisterhood." *Feminist Studies* 9 (Spring): 131–150.

———. 1988. "Our Mothers' Grief: Racial Ethnic Women and the Maintenance of Families." *Journal of Family History* 13: 415–431.

———. 1994. "Fictive Kin, Paper Sons, and *Compadrazgo.*" Pp. 149–170 in *Women of Color in U.S. Society,* edited by Maxine Baca Zinn and Bonnie Thornton Dill. Philadelphia: Temple University Press.

DiPrete, Thomas. 1989. *The Bureaucratic Labor Market: The Case of the Federal Civil Service.* New York: Plenum Press.

Di Santo, Annamaria. 2004. "Witch Healing. the Neo-Pagan Wicca Movement." *Religioni e Societa* 19: 106–10.

Dobash, R. E., and R. Dobash. 1977. "Love, Honor, and Obey: Institutional Ideologies and the Struggle for Battered Women." *Contemporary Crises* 1: 403–415.

———. 1979. *Violence Against Wives.* New York: Free Press.

Dodson, J. E., and C. T. Gilkes. 1986. "Something Within: Social Change and Collective Endurance in the Sacred World of Black Christian Women." Pp. 80–130 in *Women and Religion in America, Volume 3: 1900–1968,* edited by R. Reuther and R. Keller. New York: Harper and Row.

Donegan, J. 1978. *Women and Men Midwives: Medicine, Morality and Misogyny in Early America.* Westport, CT: Greenwood Press.

Donnerstein, Edward, and Daniel Linz. 1986. "Mass Media, Sexual Violence, and Male Viewers: Current Theory and Research." *American Behavioral Scientist* 29: 601–618.

Douglas, A. 1977. *The Feminization of American Culture.* New York: Knopf.

DuBois, Ellen Carol. 1978. *Feminism and Suffrage.* Ithaca, NY: Cornell University Press.

Dudley, Roger L. 1996. "How Seventh-Day Adventists Lay Members View Women Pastors." *Review of Religious Research* 38 (December): 133–141.

Dugger, Karen. 1988. "The Social Location of Black and White Women's Attitudes." *Gender & Society* 2 (December): 425–448.

Dujon, Diane, and Ann Withorn, eds. 1996. *For Crying Out Loud: Women's Poverty in the United States.* Boston: South End Books.

Durbin, Susan. 2002. "Women, Power, and the Glass Ceiling: Current Research Perspectives." *Work, Employment, and Society* 16 (December): 755–759.

Dworkin, Andrea. 1974. *Woman Hating.* New York: E. P. Dutton.

Dye, Nancy Schrom. 1975. "Creating a Feminist Alliance: Sisterhood an Class Conflict in the New York Women's Trade Union League, 1903–1914." *Feminist Studies* 2: 24–38.

———. 1980. "History of Childbirth in America." *Signs* 6: 97–108.

Eder, Donna, Catherine Colleen Evans, and Stephen Parker. 1995. *School Talk: Gender and Adolescent Culture.* New Brunswick, NJ: Rutgers University Press.

Edin, Kathryn, and Laura Lein. 1997. *Making Ends Meet: How Single Mothers Survive Welfare and Low-Wage Work.* New York: Russell Sage Foundation.

Ehrenreich, Barbara, and Deidre English. 1973a. *Complaints and Disorders.* Old Westbury, NY: Feminist Press.

———. 1973b. *Witches, Midwives, and Nurses: A History of Women Healers.* Old Westbury, NY: Feminist Press.

———. 1978. *For Her Own Good.* Garden City, NY: Anchor-Doubleday.

———. 1983. *Hearts of Men.* Garden City, NY: Anchor.

———. 1987. *Re-Making Love: The Feminization of Sex.* New York: Anchor.

Eisenstein, Zillah, ed. 1979. *Socialist Feminism and the Case for Capitalist Patriarchy.* New York: Monthly Review Press.

———. 1981. *The Radical Future of Liberal Feminism.* New York: Longmans.

Ellison, Christopher G., and John P. Bartkowski. 2002. "Conservative Protestantism and the Division of Household Labor among Married Couples." *Journal of Family Issues* 23 (November): 950–985.

Ellison, Louise. 2001. "Cyberstalking: Tackling Harassment on the Internet." Pp. 141–151 in *Crime and the Internet,* edited by David S. Wall. New York: Routledge.

Emerson, Rana A. 2002. " 'Where My Girls At': Negotiating Black Womanhood in Music Videos." *Gender & Society* 16 (February): 115–135.

Emmet, T. 1879. *Principles and Practices of Gynaecology.* Philadelphia: Lea.

Engels, Friedrich. 1884 [1972]. *The Origins of the Family, Private Property and the State,* edited by Eleanor Leacock. New York: International.

Enloe, Cynthia. 1989. *Bananas, Beaches, and Bases: Making Feminist Sense of International Politics.* Berkeley: University of California Press.

Enos, Sandra. 2001. *Mothering from the Inside: Parenting in a Women's Prison.* Albany, NY: State University of New York Press.

Epstein, C. 1993. *Women in Law.* Chicago: University of Chicago Press.

Esbensen, Finn-Aage, Elizabeth Piper Deschenes, and Thomas L. Winfree, Jr. 1999. "Differences between Gang Girls and Gang Boys: Result from a Multisite Survey." *Youth and Society* 31 (September): 27–53.

Espin, Oliva M. 1984. "Cultural and Historical Influences on Sexuality in Hispanic/Latin Women: Implications for Psychotherapy." Pp. 149–164 in *Pleasure and Danger,* edited by Carole Vance. Boston: Routledge & Kegan Paul.

Espiritu, Yen Le. 1997. *Asian American Women and Men.* Thousand Oaks, CA: Sage.

Evans, Lorraine, and Kimberly Davies. 2000. "No Sissy Boys Here: A Content Analysis of the Representation of Masculinity in Elementary School Reading Textbooks." *Sex Roles* 42 (February): 255–270.

Evans, Olga, and Andrew Steptoe. 2002. "The Contribution of Gender-Role Orientation, Work Factors and Home Stressors to Psychological Well-Being and Sickness Absence in Male- and Female-Dominated Occupational Groups." *Social Science and Medicine* 54: 481–492.

Evans, S. 1979. *Personal Politics: The Roots of Women's Liberation in the Civil Rights Movement and the New Left.* New York: Knopf.

Ex, Carine T. G. M., and Jan M. A. M. Janssens. 1998. "Maternal Influences on Daughters' Gender Roles Attitudes." *Sex Roles* 38 (February): 171–186.

Falk, N. 1985. "Introduction." Pp. xv–xxi in *Women, Religion and Social Change,* edited by Y. Y. Haddad and E. B. Findly. Albany: State University of New York Press.

Faludi, Susan. 1991. *Backlash: The Undeclared War on American Women.* New York: Crown.

Fausto-Sterling, Anne. 1992. *Myths of Gender,* 2nd ed. New York: Basic Books.

———. 2000. *Sexing the Body: Gender Politics and the Construction of Sexuality.* New York: Basic Books.

Federal Bureau of Investigation. 2003. *Uniform Crime Reports.* Washington, DC: Federal Bureau of Investigation.

Fee, Elizabeth. 1983. "Woman's Nature and Scientific Objectivity." Pp. 9–28 in *Woman's Nature,* edited by Marion Lowe and Ruth Hubbard. New York: Pergamon Press.

Feldberg, Roslyn L., and Evelyn Nakano Glenn. 1979. "Job vs. Gender Models in the Sociology of Work." *Social Problems* 26 (June): 524–538.

Ferber, Abby L. 2000. *Hate Crime in America: What Do We Know?* Washington, DC: American Sociological Association.

Fernea, Elizabeth Warnock. 1998. *In Search of Islamic Feminism.* New York: Doubleday.

Ferraro, Kenneth F. 1996. "Women's Fear of Victimization: Shadow of Sexual Assault?" *Social Forces* 75: 667–690.

Ferree, Myra Marx, and Beth Hess. 1997. *Controversy and Coalition: The New Feminist Movement,* rev. ed. Boston: Twayne Publishers.

Fetner, Tina. 2001. "Working Anita Bryant: The Impact of Christian Anti-Gay Activism on Lesbian and Gay Movement Claims." *Social Problems* 48 (August): 411–428.

Field, Dorothy. 1999. "Continuity and Change in Friendships in Advanced Old-Age: Findings from the Berkeley Older Generation Study." *International Journal of Aging and Human Development* 48: 325–346.

Fields, Jason. 2003. *Children's Living Arrangements and Characteristics: March 2002.* Washington, DC: U.S. Census Bureau.

Fields, Jason, and Lynne M. Casper. 2000. *America's Families and Living Arrangements.* Washington, DC: U.S. Department of Commerce.

Fine, Michelle, and Lois Weis. 1998. *The Unknown City: The Lives of Poor and Working-Class Young Adults.* Boston: Beacon Press.

Fineran, Susan. 2001. "Sexual Minority Students and Peer Sexual Harassment in High School." *Journal of School Social Work* 11 (Spring): 50–69.

———, and Larry Bennett. 1999. "Gender and Power Issues of Peer Sexual Harassment among Teenagers." *Journal of Interpersonal Violence* 14 (June): 626–641.

Finlay, Barbara. 1996. "Do Men and Women Have Different Goals for Ministry? Evidence from Seminarians." *Sociology of Religion* 57 (Fall): 311–318.

———. 1997. "Future Ministers and Legal Abortion: Gender Comparisons among Protestant Seminary Students." *Women and Politics* 17: 1–15.

———, and Carol S. Walther. 2003. "The Relation of Religious Affiliation, Service Attendance, and Other Factors to Homophobic Attitudes among University Students." *Review of Religious Research* 44: 370–93.

Firestein, Beth, ed. 1996. *Bisexuality: The Psychology and Politics of an Invisible Minority.* Thousand Oaks, CA: Sage.

Firestone, Juanita M., and Richard J. Harris. 2003. "Perceptions of Effectiveness of Responses to Sexual Harassment in the US Military, 1988 and 1995." *Gender, Work and Organization* 10: 42–64.

———, Richard J. Harris, and Linda C. Lambert. 1998. "Gender Role Ideology and the Gender Based Differences in Earnings" Paper presented at the Annual Meetings of the American Sociological Association, San Francisco.

Fischbach, Ruth L., and Barbara Herbert. 1997. "Domestic Violence and Mental Health: Correlated and Conundrums within and across Cultures." *Social Science and Medicine* 45 (October): 1161–1176.

Fisher, Bonnie S., Francis T. Cullen, and Michael G. Turner. 2000. *The Sexual Victimization of College Women.* Washington, DC: U.S. Bureau of Justice Statistics.

———, and John J. Sloan III. 2003. "Unraveling the Fear of Victimization among College Women: Is the "Shadow of Sexual Assault Hypothesis" Supported?" *Justice Quarterly* 20: 633–59.

Flavin, Jeanne. 2001. "Of Punishment and Parenthood: Family-Based Social Control and the Sentencing of Black Drug Offenders." *Gender & Society* 15 (August): 611–633.

Flax, Jane. 1990. "Postmodernism and Gender Relations in Feminist Theory." Pp. 39–62 in *Feminism and Postmodernism,* edited by Linda J. Nicholson. New York: Routledge.

Flexner, Eleanor. 1972. *Mary Wollstonecraft: A Biography.* New York: Coward, McCann, and Geoghegan.

———. 1975. *Century of Struggle: The Woman's Rights Movement in the United States.* Cambridge, MA: Harvard University Press.

Flowers, R. B. 1984. *Religion in Strange Times: The 1960s and 1970s.* Macon, GA: Mercer University Press.

Folbre, Nancy. 2001. *The Invisible Heart: Economics and Family Values.* New York: The Free Press.

Foltz, Tanice G. 2000. "Women's Spirituality Research: Doing Feminism." *Sociology of Religion* 61 (Winter): 409–418.

Forsyth, Craig J. 2003. "Pondering the Discourse of Prison Mamas: A Research Note." *Deviant Behavior* 24: 269–280.

Foucault, M. 1965. *Madness and Civilization: A History of Insanity in the Age of Reason.* New York: Vintage.

Fox, Bonnie, and Pamela Sugiman. 1999. "Flexible Work, Flexible Workers: The Restructuring of Clerical Work in a Large Telecommunications Company." *Studies in Political Economy* 60 (Autumn): 39–84.

Fox, Mary Frank. 2001. "Women, Science, and Academia: Graduate Education and Careers." *Gender & Society* 15 (October): 654–666.

Fraser, Nancy. 1989. *Unruly Practices: Power, Discourse, and Gender in Contemporary Social Theory.* Minneapolis: University of Minnesota Press.

———, and Nancy A. Naples. 2004. "To Interpret the World and to Change It: An Interview with Nancy Fraser." *Signs* 29 (Summer): 1103–1124.

Frazier, E. Franklin. 1948. *The Negro Family in the United States.* New York: Citadel Press.

———. 1964. *The Negro Church in America.* New York: Schocken.

Freedman, Estelle B., and Barrie Thorne. 1984. "Introduction to 'The Feminist Sexuality Debates.'" *Signs* 10 (Autumn): 102–105.

———, and John D'Emilio. 1988. *Intimate Matters: A History of Sexuality in America.* New York: Harper & Row.

Freeman, Jo. 1973. "The Origins of the Women's Liberation Movement." *American Journal of Sociology* 78: 792–811.

Freund, Kurt, and Robin J. Watson. 1992. "The Proportions of Heterosexual and Homosexual Pedophiles among Sex Offenders against Children: An Exploratory Study." *Journal of Sex and Marital Therapy* 18 (Spring): 34–43.

Fried, Amy. 1994. "'It's Hard to Change What We Want to Change': Rape Crisis Centers as Organizations." *Gender & Society* 8 (December): 562–584.

Friedl, E. 1975. *Women and Men.* New York: Holt, Rinehart and Winston.

Frieze, I. H. 1983. "Investigating the Causes and Consequences of Marital Rape." *Signs* 8 (Spring): 532–553.

Frohmann, Lisa. 1991. "Discrediting Victims' Allegations of Sexual Assault: Prosecutorial Accounts of Case Rejections." *Social Problems* 38 (May): 213–226.

Frye, Marilyn. 1983. *The Politics of Reality.* Trumansburg, NY: Crossing Press.

Fullerton, Howard N., Jr. 1997. "Labor Force 2006: Slowing Down and Changing Composition." *Monthly Labor Review* 120 (November): 23–38.

Fullerton, Jami A., and Alice Kendrick. 2000. "Portrayals of Men and Women in U.S. Spanish-Language Television." *Journalism and Mass Communication Quarterly* 77 (Spring): 128–142.

Furnham, A., and L. Gasson. 1998. "Sex Differences in Parental Estimates of Their Children's Intelligence." *Sex Roles* 38 (January): 151–162.

Furnham, Adrian, and Twiggy Mak. 1999. "Sex Role Stereotyping in Television Commercials: A Review and Comparison of Fourteen Studies Done on Five Continents over 25 Years." *Sex Roles* 41 (September): 413–437.

Gagne, Patricia, and Richard Tewksbury. 1998. "Conformity Pressures and Gender Resistance among Transgendered Individuals." *Social Problems* 45 (February): 81–101.

Gagnon, John. 1995. *Conceiving Sexuality: Approaches to Sex Research in a Postmodern World.* New York: Routledge.

Gallagher, Sally K. 2003. *Evangelical Identity and Family Life.* Piscataway, NJ: Rutgers University Press.

———. 2004. "Where are the Antifeminist Evangelicals? Evangelical Identity, Subcultural Location, and Attitudes toward Feminism." *Gender & Society* 18 (August) 451–472.

———, and Christian Smith. 1999. "Symbolic Traditionalism and Pragmatic Egalitarianism: Contemporary Evangelicals, Families, and Gender." *Gender & Society* 13 (April): 211–233.

Gallup, George, Jr. 1993. *The Gallup Poll: Public Opinion 1993.* Wilmington, DE: Scholarly Resources.

Gallup Poll. 2004 (October). "Abortion." Princeton, NJ: The Gallup Organization.

Gamson, Joshua. 1995. "Must Identity Movements Self-Destruct? A Queer Dilemma." *Social Problems* 42 (August): 390–407.

———. 1998. "Publicity Traps: Television Talk Shows and Lesbian, Gay, Bisexual, and Transgender Visibility." *Sexualities* 1 (February): 11–42.

Ganahl, Dennis J., Thomas J. Prinsen, and Sara Baker Netzley. 2003. "A Content Analysis of Prime Time Commercials: A Contextual Framework of Gender Representation." *Sex Roles* 49 (November): 545–551.

General Social Survey. 1998. Web page: http://webapp.icpsr. umich.edu/GSS/

Genovese, Eugene. 1972. *Roll, Jordan, Roll.* New York: Pantheon.

Gerschick, Thomas J., and Adam Stephen Miller. 1994. "Gender Identities at the Crossroads of Masculinity and Physical Disability." *Masculinities* 2 (Spring): 34–55.

Gerson, Kathleen. 2002. "Moral Dilemmas, Moral Strategies and the Transformation of Gender: Lessons from Two Generations of Work and Family Change." *Gender & Society* 16 (February): 8–28.

Gerstel, Naomi, and Dan Clawson. 2001. "Unions' Responses to Family Concerns." *Social Problems* 48 (May): 277–297.

———, and Sally K. Gallagher. 2001. "Men's Caregiving: Gender and the Contingent Character of Care." *Gender & Society* 15 (April): 197–217.

Geschwender, James. 1992. "Ethnicity and the Social Construction of Gender in the Chinese Diaspora." *Gender & Society* 6 (September): 480–507.

Giannarelli, Linda, and James Barsomantov. 2000. *Child Care Expenses of America's Families.* Washington, DC: The Urban Institute.

Gibson, Diane. 1996. "Broken Down by Age and Gender: 'The Problem of Old Women' Revisited." *Gender & Society* 10 (August): 443–448.

Giddens, Anthony. 1971. *Capitalism and Modern Social Theory: An Analysis of the Writings of Marx, Durkheim, and Max Weber.* Cambridge: Cambridge University Press.

Gilkes, Cheryl Townsend. 1980. " 'Holding Back the Ocean with a Broom:' Black Women and Community Work." Pp. 217–232 in *The Black Woman,* edited by L. F. Rodgers-Rose. Beverly Hills: Sage.

———. 1985. "Together and in Harness: Women's Traditions in the Sanctified Church." *Signs* 10 (Summer): 678–699.

———. 2000. *"If It Wasn't for the Women . . . ": Black Women's Experience and Womanist Culture in Church and Community.* Mary Knoll, NY: Orbis Books.

Gilligan, Carol. 1982. *In a Different Voice.* Cambridge, MA: Harvard University Press.

Ginorio, Angela, and Michelle Huston. 2001. *¡Si, Se Puede! Yes, We Can: Latinas in School.* Washington, DC: American Association of Women Educational Foundation.

Gitlin, Todd. 2001. *Media Unlimited: How the Torrent of Images and Sounds Overwhelms Our Lives.* New York: Metropolitan Books.

Glass Ceiling Commission. 1995. *Good for Business: Making Full Use of the Nation's Human Capital.* Washington, DC: U.S. Government Printing Office.

Glass, Jennifer, and Tetushi Fujimoto. 1994. "Housework, Paid Work, and Depression among Husbands and Wives." *Journal of Health and Social Behavior* 35 (June): 179–191.

Glenn, Evelyn Nakano. 1986. *Issei, Nisei, War Bride: Three Generations of Japanese-American Women in Domestic Service.* Philadelphia: Temple University Press.

———, Grace Chang, and Linda Rennie Forcey, eds. 1993. *Mothering: Ideology, Experience, and Agency.* New York: Routledge.

Gluckman, Amy, and Betsy Reed. 1997. *Homo Economics: Capitalism, Community, and Lesbian and Gay Life.* New York: Routledge.

Gordon, L. 1977. *Woman's Body/ Woman's Right.* New York: Penguin Books.

Gordy, Laurie K. 2002. "Distorted Progress: Images of Women in Sports Magazines." Paper presented at the annual meetings of the Southern Sociological Society.

Gornick, V. 1971. "Woman as Outsider." Pp. 126–144 in *Woman in Sexist Society,* edited by V. Gornick and B. Moran. New York: Basic Books.

Gossett, Jennifer Lynn, and Sarah Byrne. 2002. " 'Click Here': A Content Analysis of Internet Rape Sites." *Gender & Society* 16 (October): 689–709.

Gough, Kathleen. 1975. "The Origin of the Family." Pp. 51–76 in *Toward an Anthropology of Women,* edited by Rayna Reiter. New York: Monthly Review Press.

Gouldner, Helen, and Mary Symons Strong. 1987. *Speaking of Friendship: Middle-Class Women and Their Friends.* Westport, CT: Greenwood Press.

Gow, Joe. 1996. "Reconsidering Gender Roles on MTV: Depictions in the Most Popular Music Videos of the Early 1990s." *Communication Reports* 9 (Summer): 151–161.

Grant, J. 1982. "Black Women and the Church." Pp. 141–152 in *All the Women are White, All the Blacks Are Men, But Some of Us Are Brave,* edited by Gloria Patricia Bell Scott and Barbara Smith. Old Westbury, NY: Feminist Press.

Grasmuck, Sherri, and Patricia Pessar. 1996. "Dominicans in the United States: First- and Second-Generation Settlement." Pp. 280–292 in *Origins and Destinies: Immigration, Race, and Ethnicity in America,* edited by Sylvia Pedraza and Rubén G. Rumbaut. Belmont, CA: Wadsworth.

Gray, John. 1994. *Men Are from Mars, Women Are from Venus.* New York: HarperCollins.

Greene, B. 1994. "Ethnic-Minority Lesbians and Gay Men: Mental Health and Treatment Issues." *Journal of Counseling and Clinical Psychology* 62: 243–251.

Greene, Maxine. 1978. *Landscapes of Learning.* New York: Teachers College Press.

Greene, Susan. 2004. "Mothering and Making it, in and Out of Prison." *Punishment & Society* 6: 229–233.

Greer, Kimberly R. 2000. "The Changing Nature of Interpersonal Relationships in a Women's Prison." *Prison Journal* 80: 442–468.

Gregoire, Thomas K., Keith Kilty, and Virginia Richardson. 2002. "Gender and Racial Inequities in Retirement Resources." *Journal of Women & Aging* 14: 25–39.

Greif, Geoffrey L. 1985. "Children and Housework in the Single Father Family." *Family Relations* 34 (July): 353–357.

Grella, Christine E. 1990. "Irreconcilable Differences: Women Defining Class After Divorce and

Downward Mobility." *Gender & Society* 4 (March): 41–55.

Griffin, Joan M., et al. 2002. "The Importance of Low Control at Work and Home on Depression and Anxiety: Do these Effects Vary by Gender and Social Class?" *Social Science and Medicine* 54: 783–798.

Groves, Melissa M., and Diane M. Horm-Wingerd. 1991. "Commuter Marriages: Personal, Family, and Career Issues." *Sociology and Social Research* 75 (July): 212–217.

Gutman, Herbert. 1976. *The Black Family in Slavery and Freedom.* New York: Vintage.

Haag, Pamela. 1999. *Voices of a Generation: Teenage Girls on Sex, School, and Self.* Washington, DC: American Association of Women Educational Foundation.

Hager, Mark A. 1996. "Education Level, Liberal Attitudes, and Sexual Behavior: A Reinterpretation." *Alberta Journal of Eductional Research* 42 (December): 400–405.

Hall, Elaine J., and Marnie Salupo Rodriguez. 2003. "The Myth of Postfeminism." *Gender & Society* 17 (December): 878–902.

Hall, R. M. 1982. "The Classroom Climate: A Chilly One for Women?" Washington, DC: Project on the Education and Status of Women, Association of American Colleges.

Hamer, Dean H., Stella Hu, Victoria L. Magnuson, Nan Hu, and Angela M. L. Pattatucci. 1993. "A Linkage Between DNA Markers on the X Chromosome and Male Sexual Identification." *Science* 261 (July): 321–327.

Hamer, Jennifer. 2001. *What It Means to be Daddy.* New York: Columbia University Press.

Hampton, Robert L., and Alice F. Washington Coner-Edwards. 1993. "Physical and Sexual Violence in Marriage." Pp. 113–141 in *Family Violence: Prevention and Treatment*, edited by Robert L. Hampton, Thomas P. Gullotta, Gerald R. Adams, Earl H. Potter III., and Roger P. Weissberg. Newbury Park, CA: Sage.

Hans, Valerie P., and Neil Vidmar. 1986. *Judging the Jury.* New York: Plenum Press.

Hanson, Sandra L., and Rebecca S. Kraus. 1998. "Women, Sports, and Science: Do Female Athletes Have an Advantage?" *Sociology of Education* 71 (April): 93–110.

Harding, Sandra. 1986. *The Science Question in Feminism.* Ithaca, NY: Cornell University Press.

———. 1991. *Whose Science? Whose Knowledge?: Thinking from Women's Lives.* Ithaca, NY: Cornell University Press.

———. 1993. *The Racial Economy of Science.* Bloomington: Indiana University Press.

———. 1998. *Is Science Multicultural? Postcolonialisms, Feminisms, and Epistemologies.* Bloomington, IN: Indiana University Press.

Hargrove, B., J. M. Schmidt, and S. G. Davaney. 1985. "Religion and the Changing Role of Women." *Annals of the American Academy of Political and Social Science* 480 (July): 117–131.

Harland, M. 1889. *House and Home: The Complete Housewives' Guide.* Philadelphia: Clawson.

Harrell, Margaret C. 2001. "Army Officers' Spouses: Have the White Gloves been Mothballed?" *Armed Forces & Society* 28: 55–75.

Harris, R. J., and J. M. Firestone. 1998. "Changes in Predictors of Gender Role Ideologies among Women: A Multivariate Analysis." *Sex Roles* 38 (February): 239–252.

Harrison, J. 1978. "Men's Roles and Men's Lives." *Signs* 4 (Winter): 324–336.

Harrison, Paige M., and Allen J. Beck. 2003. *Prisoners in 2001.* Washington, DC: U.S. Bureau of Justice Statistics.

Hart, K., and M. E. Kenny. 1997. "Adherence to the Super Woman Ideal and Eating Disorder Symptoms among College Women." *Sex Roles* 36 (April): 461–478.

Hartmann, Heidi. 1976. "Capitalism, Patriarchy, and Job Segregation by Sex." *Signs* 1: (Spring): 137–169.

———. 1981a. "The Family as the Locus of Gender, Class, and Political Struggle: The Example of Housework." *Signs* 6 (Spring): 366–394.

———. 1981b. "The Unhappy Marriage of Marxism and Feminism: Towards a More Progressive Union." Pp. 1–41 in *Women and Revolution*, edited by Lydia Sargent. New York: South End Press.

Hartsock, Nancy. 1983. "The Feminist Standpoint: Developing the Ground for a Specifically Feminist Historical Materialism." Pp. 231–251 in *Money, Sex and Power*, edited by Nancy Hartsock. New York: Longman.

Harvey, William B. 2003. *Minorities in Higher Education, 2002–2003.* Washington, DC: American Council on Education.

Haugaard, Jeffrey J., and Lisa G. Seri. 2003. "Stalking and Other Forms of Intrusive Contact After the Dissolution of Adolescent Dating Or Romantic Relationships." *Violence and Victims* 18: 279–97.

Hawkins, R. A., and R. E. Oakey. 1974. "Estimation of Oestrone Sulphate, Oestradiol-17B and Oestrone in Peripheral Plasma: Concentrations During the Menstrual Cycle and in Men." *Journal of Endocrinology* 60: 3–17.

Hays, Sharon. 2003. *Flat Broke with Children: Women in the Age of Welfare Reform.* New York: Oxford University Press.

Heimer, Karen, and Stacey DeCoster. 1999. "The Gendering of Violent Delinquency." *Criminology* 37 (May): 277–318.

Heitfield, Heather, and Rita J. Simon. 2002. "Women in Prison: A Comparative Assessment." *Gender Issues* 20: 53–75.

Helwig, A. A. 1998. "Gender-Role Stereotyping: Testing Theory with a Longitudinal Sample." *Sex Roles* 38 (March): 403–423.

Hemmens, Craig, Kristin Strom, and Elicia Schlegel. 1998. "Gender Bias in the Courts: A Review of the Literature." *Sociological Imagination* 35: 22–42.

Henderson, Dorothy J., Carol Boyd, and Thomas Mieczkowski. 1994. "Gender, Relationships, and Crack Cocaine: A Content Analysis." *Research in Nursing and Health* 17 (August): 265–272.

Henley, Nancy. 1989. "Molehill or Mountain? What We Know and

Don't Know about Sex Bias in Language." Pp. 59–78 in *Gender and Thought: Psychological Perspectives,* edited by M. Crawford and M. Gentry. New York: Springer-Verlag.

Hennig, K., H. Leitenberg, P. Coffey, T. Turner, and R. T. Bennett. 1996. "Long-term Psychological and Social Impact of Witnessing Physical Conflict between Parents." *Journal of Interpersonal Violence* 11: 35–51.

Hensley, Christopher, Tammy Castle, and Richard Tewksbury. 2003. "Inmate-to-Inmate Sexual Coercion in a Prison for Women." *Journal of Offender Rehabilitation* 37: 77–87.

Hequembourg, Amy L., and Michael P. Farrell. 1999. "Lesbian Motherhood: Negotiating Marginal-Mainstream Identities." *Gender & Society* 13: 540–557.

Herman, Judith. 1981. *Father-Daughter Incest.* Cambridge, MA: Harvard University Press.

Herman, Judith, and Hirschman, L. 1977. "Father-Daughter Incest." *Signs* 2 (Summer): 735–756.

Hernández, Daisy, and Bushra Rehman, es. 2002. *Colonize This! Young Women of Color on Today's Feminism.* New York: Seal Press.

Hernández, Jeanne. 1995. "The Concurrence of Eating Disorders with Histories of Child Abuse among Adolescents." *Journal of Child Sexual Abuse* 4: 73–85.

Herring, Cedric, Verna Keith, and Heyward Derrick Horton. 2003. *Skin Deep: How Race and Complexion Matter in the "Color-Blind" Era.* Champaign-Urbana, IL: University of Illinois Press.

Hesse-Biber, Sharlene, Alan Clayton-Matthews, and John A. Downey. 1987. "The Differential Importance of Weight and Body Image among College Men and Women." *Genetic, Social, and General Psychology Monographs* 113 (November): 509–528.

Heyer-Gray, Zoey A. 2000. "Gender and Religious Work." *Sociology of Religion* 61 (Winter): 467–471.

Higginbotham, Elizabeth. 2001. *Too Much to Ask: Black Women in the Era of Integration.* Chapel Hill, NC: University of North Carolina Press.

Higham, J. 1965. *Strangers in the Land.* New York: Atheneum.

Hill, A. C. 1979. "Protection of Women Workers and the Courts: A Legal Case History." *Feminist Studies* 5 (Summer): 247–273.

Hill, Michael, and Susan Hoecker-Drysdale. 2002. *Harriet Martineau: Theoretical and Methodological Perspectives.* New York: Routledge.

Hill, Shirley A., and Joey Sprague. 1999. "Parenting in Black and White Families: The Interaction of Gender with Race and Class." *Gender & Society* 13 (August): 480–502.

Himmelstein, J. L. 1986. "The Social Basis of Antifeminism: Religious Networks and Culture." *Journal for the Scientific Study of Religion* 25: 1–15.

Hipple, Jay. 2001. "Contingent Work in the Late-1990s." *Monthly Labor Review* 124 (March): 3–27.

Hochschild, Arlie Russell. 1983. *The Managed Heart: Commercialization of Human Feeling.* Berkeley: University of California Press.

———. 1989. *The Second Shift: Working Parents and the Revolution at Home.* New York: Viking.

———. 1997. *The Time Bind: When Home Becomes Work and Work Becomes Home.* New York: Metropolitan Books.

Hoffman, Thomas. 1997. "Women in Church Leadership: An Analysis of Religious Beliefs." *Free Inquiry in Creative Sociology* 25 (November): 137–143.

Hoffnung, Michele. 2004. "Wanting It All: Career, Marriage, and Motherhood during College-Educated Women's 20s." *Sex Roles* 50(May): 711–723.

Hole, J., and Levine, E., eds. 1971. *Rebirth of Feminism.* New York: Quadrangle Books.

Holsinger, Kristi. 2000. "Feminist Perspectives on Female Offending: Examining Real Girls' Lives." *Women and Criminal Justice* 12: 23–51.

Hondagneu-Sotelo, Pierrette. 1992. "Overcoming Patriarchal Constraints: The Reconstruction of Gender Relations Among Mexican Immigrant Women and

Men." *Gender & Society* 6 (September): 393–415.

———. 1994. *Gendered Transitions: the Mexican Experience of Immigration.* Berkeley: University of California Press.

———. 1997. "'I'm Here, but I'm There': The Meanings of Latina Transnational Motherhood." *Gender & Society* 11 (October): 548–571.

———. 2001. *Doméstica: Immigrant Workers Cleaning and Caring in the Shadows of Affluence.* Berkeley: University of California Press.

Horowitz, Ruth. 1995. *Teen Mothers: Citizens or Dependents?* Chicago: University of Chicago Press.

Horton, Richard. 1995. "Is Homosexuality Inherited?" *New York Review of Books* 42 (July 13): 36–41

Hosken, F. P. 1979. *The Hosken Report: Genital and Sexual Mutilation of Females.* Lexington, MA: Women's International Network News.

Hoyenga, K. B., and K. Hoyenga. 1979. *The Question of Sex Differences; Psychological, Cultural, and Biological Issues.* Boston: Little, Brown.

Hubbard, Ruth. 1984. "Feminist Science: A Meaningful Concept?" Paper presented at the Annual Meetings of the National Women's Studies Association, New Brunswick, NJ.

Hughes, H. S. 1958. *Consciousness and Society.* New York: Knopf.

Hull, Kathleen E. 1999. "The Paradox of the Contented Female Lawyer." *Law and Society Review* 33 (October): 687–702.

Hunt, Larry L. 2001. "Religion, Gender, and the Hispanic Experience in the United States: Catholic/Protestant Differences in Religious Involvement, Social Status, and Gender-Role Attitudes." *Review of Religious Research* 43: 139–160.

Illich, I. 1977. *Disabling Professions.* Salem, NH: Boyars.

Infante, P. 1975. "Genetic Risks of Vinyl Chloride." *Lancet* 3: 734–735.

Ingram-Fogel, Catherine. 1991. "Health Problems and Needs of Incarcerated Women." *Journal of Prison and Jail Health* 10 (Summer): 43–57.

———. 1993. "Hard Time: The Stressful Nature of Incarceration for Women." *Issues in Mental Health Nursing* 14 (October–December): 367–377.

Institute for Women's Policy Research. 2001. *Working First But Working Poor: The Need for Education and Training Following Welfare Reform.* Washington, DC: Institute for Women's Policy Research.

Jackson, Nicky-Ali. 1996. "Observational Experiences of Intrapersonal Conflict and Teenage Victimization: A Comparative Study among Spouses and Cohabitors." *Journal of Family Violence* 11 (September): 191–203.

Jacobs, Janet L. 1994. "The Effects of Ritual Healing on Female Victims of Abuse: A Study of Empowerment and Transformation." Pp. 127–142 in *Gender and Religion,* edited by William H. Swatos, Jr. New Brunswick, NJ: Transaction Publishers.

Jacobs, Jerry A., and Ronnie J. Steinberg. 1990. "Compensating Differentials and the Male-Female Wage Gap: Evidence from the New York State Comparable Worth Study." *Social Forces* 69 (December): 430–469.

Jacobson, D. 1974. "The Women of North and Central India: Goddesses and Wives." Pp. 99–175 in *Many Sisters,* edited by C. Matthiasson. New York: Free Press.

Janus, Samuel S., and Cynthia L. Janus. 1993. *The Janus Report on Sexual Behavior.* New York: Wiley and Sons.

Jelen, Ted G. 1989. "Gender Role Stereotypes and Attitudes Toward Female Ordination." *Social Science Quarterly* 7 (September): 579–585.

Jenness, Valerie, and Kendal Broad. 1997. *Hate Crimes: New Social Movements and the Politics of Violence.* New York: Aldine.

———, and Ryken Grattet. 2001. *Making Hate a Crime: From Social Movement to Law Enforcement.* New York: Russell Sage.

Joe, Karen A., and Meda Chesney-Lind. 1995. " 'Just Every Mother's Angel': An Analysis of Gender and Ethnic Variations in Youth Gang Membership." *Gender & Society* 9 (August): 408–431.

Jones, J. 1985. *Labor of Love, Labor of Sorrow: Black Women, Work, and the Family From Slavery to the Present.* New York: Basic Books.

Jones, Jeffrey M., and David W. Moore. 2003. "Generational Differences in Support for a Woman President." *The Gallup Poll.* Princeton, NJ: The Gallup Organization.

Jordan, Winthrop. 1968. *White Over Black.* Baltimore: Penguin Books.

Jordan-Simmons, Kym Michelle. 2002. *Sexual Violence on Campus: The Relationship between Sorority Membership, Fraternity Contact, and Alcohol Consumption.* Ph.D. Dissertation, UMI Dissertation Abstracts AAI3038246.

Kahane, Leo H. 2000. "Anti-Abortion Activities and the Market for Abortion Services." *American Journal of Economics and Sociology* 59 (July): 463–485.

Kalmijn, Matthijs. 1999. "Father Involvement in Childrearing and the Perceived Stability of Marriage." *Journal of Marriage and the Family* 61 (May): 409–421.

Kalof, Linda. 1999. "The Effects of Gender and Music Video Imagery on Sexual Attitudes." *Journal of Social Psychology* 139 (June): 378–385.

Kamin, L. J. 1986. "Is Crime in the Genes?" *Scientific American* 254 (February): 22–27.

Kanter, Rosabeth Moss. 1977. *Men and Women of the Corporation.* New York: Basic Books.

Kantor, Glenda Kaufman, and Jana L. Jasinksi. 1998. "Dynamics and Risk Factors in Partner Violence." Pp. 1–43 in *Partner Violence: A Comprehensive Review of 20 Years of Research,* edited by Jana L. Jasinkski and Linda M. Williams. Thousand Oaks, CA: Sage.

Kaplan, Elaine Bell. 1997. *Not Our Kind of Girl: Unraveling the Myths of Black Teenage Motherhood.* Berkeley: University of California Press.

Kapp, Yvonne. 1972. *Eleanor Marx, Volume One.* New York: Pantheon.

Katzman, David. 1978. *Seven Days A Week: Women and Domestic Service in Industrializing America.* New York: Oxford University Press.

Kaufman, Gayle. 1999. "The Portrayal of Men's Family Roles in Television Commercials." *Sex Roles* 41 (September): 439–458.

Kay, Fiona M., and John Hagan. 1998. "Gender Stratification in Law Firms." *American Sociological Review* 63 (October): 728–743.

Kearney, Margaret H., Sheigla Murphy, and Marsha Rosenbaum. 1994. "Mothering on Crack Cocaine: A Grounded Theory Analysis." *Social Science and Medicine* 38 (January): 351–361.

Keller, Evelyn Fox. 1985. *Reflections on Gender and Science.* New Haven, CT: Yale University Press.

Kelly-Gadol, J. 1976. "The Social Relations of the Sexes: Methodological Implications of Women's History." *Signs* 1 (Summer): 809–824.

Kemp, Alice Abel, and Pamela Jenkins. 1992. "Gender and Technological Hazards: Women at Risk in Hospital Settings." *Industrial Crisis Quarterly* 6: 137–152.

Kennedy, Randall. 2003. *Interracial Intimacies: Sex, Marriage, Identity and Adoption.* New York: Pantheon.

Kennelly, Ivy. 1999. " 'That Single-mother Element': How White Employers Typify Black Women." *Gender & Society* 13 (April): 168–192,

Kessler-Harris, Alice. 1982. *Out to Work: A History of Wage-Earning Women in the U.S.* New York: Oxford University Press.

Khanna, Nikki D., Cherise Harris, and Rana Cullers. 1999. "Attitudes toward Interracial Dating." Paper presented at the Annual Meetings of the Society for the Study of Social Problems, Washington, DC.

Kibria, Nazli. 1994. "Household Structure and Family Ideologies: The Dynamics of Immigrant Economic Adaptation Among Vietnamese Refugees." *Social Problems* 41 (February): 81–96.

Kilbourne, Barbara Stanek, George Farkas, Kurt Beron, Dorothea Weir, and Paula England. 1994. "Returns to Skill, Compensating Differentials, and Gender Bias: Effects of Occupational Characteristics on the Wages of White

Women and White Men." *American Journal of Sociology* 100 (November): 689–719.

Kimmel, Michael S. 2000. "Saving the Males: The Sociological Implications of the Virginia Military Institute and the Citadel." *Gender & Society* 14 (August): 494–516.

———. 2001. "Masculinity as Homophobia: Fear, Shame, and Silence in the Construction of Gender Identity." Pp. 266–287 in *The Masculinities Reader,* edited by Stephen M. Whitehead and Frank J. Barrett. Cambridge: Polity.

———, and Annulla Landers. 1996. "Does Censorship Make a Difference? An Aggregate Empirical Analysis of Pornography and Rape." *Journal of Psychology and Human Sexuality* 8: 1–20.

———, and Michael A. Messner, eds. 2000. *Men's Lives,* 5th ed. Boston: Allyn and Bacon.

King, Jacqueline E. 2000. *Gender Equity in Higher Education: Are Males Students at a Disadvantage?* Washington, DC: American Council on Education.

Kirschenman, Joleen, and Kathryn M. Neckerman. 1999. " 'We'd Love to Hire Them, But . . . ' The Meaning of Race for Employers." Pp. 152–161 in *Race and Ethnic Conflict: Contending Views on Prejudice, Discrimination, and Ethnoviolence,* edited by Fred L. Pincus and Howard J. Ehrlich. Boulder, CO: Westview.

Kirton, Gill. 1999. "Sustaining and Developing Women's Trade Union Activism: A Gendered Project." *Gender, Work, and Organization* 6 (October): 213–223.

Kitzinger, Celia A., and Sue Wilkinson. 1994. "Virgins and Queers: Rehabilitating Heterosexuality?" *Gender & Society* 8 (September): 444–462.

Klatch, Rebecca. 1988. "Coalition and Conflict Among Women of the New Right." *Signs* 13 (Summer): 671–694.

Kleck, Gary, and Susan Sayles. 1990. "Rape and Resistance." *Social Problems* 37 (May): 149–162.

Klein, D. 1980. "The Etiology of Female Crime: A Review of the Literature." Pp. 70–105 in *Women, Crime, and Justice,* edited by Susan K. Datesman and Frank R. Scarpitti. New York: Oxford University Press.

Kleinbaum, A. R. 1977. "Women in the Age of Light." Pp. 217–235 in *Becoming Visible: Women in European History,* edited by R. Bridenthal and C. Koonz. Boston: Houghton-Mifflin.

Klinger, Lori J., James A. Hamilton, Peggy J. Cantrell. 2001. "Children's Perceptions of Aggression and Gender-Specific Content in Toy Commercials." *Social Behavior and Personality* 29: 11–20.

Kluckhohn, C. 1962. *Culture and Behavior.* New York: Free Press.

Knox, George W. 2004. "Females and Gangs: Sexual Violence, Prostitution, and Exploitation." *Journal of Gang Research* 11: 1–15.

Kohlberg, Lawrence. 1966. "A Cognitive Developmental Analysis of Children's Sex Role Concepts and Attitudes." Pp. 82–166 in *The Development of Sex Differences,* edited by Eleanor Maccoby. Stanford, CA: Stanford University Press.

Koons-Witt, Barbara A. 2002. "The Effect of Gender on the Decision to Incarcerate before and After the Introduction of Sentencing Guidelines." *Criminology* 40: 297–327.

Koss, Mary P., and Hobart H. Cleveland III. 1996. "Athletic Participation, Fraternity Membership, and Date Rape: The Question Remains-Self-Selection or Different Causal Processes?" *Violence against Women* 2: 180–190.

Kruttschnitt, Candace, and Rosemary Gartner. 2003. "Women's Imprisonment." *Crime and Justice* 30: 1–81.

———, Rosemary Gartner, and Amy Miller. 2000. "Doing Her Own Time? Women's Responses to Prison in the Context of the Old and the New Penology." *Criminology* 28 (August): 681–718.

Kubitschek, Warren N., and Maureen T. Hallinan. 1996. "Race, Gender, and Inequity in Track Assignments." *Research in Sociology of Education and Socialization* 11: 121–146.

Kurtz, Steven P., et al. 2004. "Sex Work and 'Date' Violence." *Violence against Women* 10: 357–385.

Kurz, Demie. 1989. "Social Science Perspectives on Wife Abuse: Current Debates and Future Directions." *Gender & Society* 3 (December): 489–505.

———. 1995. *For Richer for Poorer: Mothers Confront Divorce.* New York: Routledge.

Ladner, Joyce A. 1986. "Teenage Pregnancy: The Implications for Black Americans." Pp. 65–85 in *The State of Black America 1986,* edited by James D. Williams. New York: National Urban League.

La France, Marianne. 2002. "Smile Boycotts and Other Body Politics." *Feminism and Psychology* 12 (August): 319–323.

Lai, Tracy. 1992. "Asian American Women: Not for Sale." Pp. 163–171 in *Race, Class, and Gender: An Anthology,* edited by Margaret L. Andersen and Patricia Hill Collins. Belmont CA: Wadsworth.

Lakkis, Jacqueline, Lina A. Ricciardelli, and Robert J. Williams. 1999. "Role of Sexual Orientation and Gender-Related Traits in Disordered Eating." *Sex Roles* 41 (July): 1–16.

Lambert, Tracy A., Arnold S. Kahn, and Kevin J. Apple. 2003. "Pluralistic Ignorance and Hooking Up." *Journal of Sex Research* 40: 129–33.

Lamphere, Louise. 1984. "On the Shop Floor: Multi-Ethnic Unity Against the Conglomerate." Pp. 247–262 in *My Troubles Are Going to Have Trouble With Me,* edited by Karen B. Sacks and Dorothy Remy. New Brunswick, NJ: Rutgers University Press.

———. 2001. "The Domestic Sphere of Women and the Public World of Men: The Strengths and Limitations of an Anthropological Dichotomy." Pp. 100–109 in *Gender in Cross-Cultural Perspective,* 3rd ed., edited by Caroline B. Brittell and Carolyn F. Sargent.Upper Saddle River, NJ: Prentice-Hall.

Langhinrichsen-Rohling, Jennifer, et al. 2000. "Breaking Up is Hard to Do: Unwanted Pursuit Behaviors Following the Dissolution of a Romantic Relationship." *Violence and Victims* 15: 73–90.

Larson, Mary Strom. 2003. "Gender, Race, and Aggression in Television Commercials That Feature Children." *Sex Roles* 48 (January): 67–75.

Laslett, Barbara, Johanna Brenner, and Yesim Arat. 1995. *Rethinking the Political: Gender, Resistance, and the State.* Chicago: University of Chicago Press.

Laumann, Edward O., John H. Gagnon, Robert T. Michael, and Stuart Michaels. 1994. *The Social Organization of Sexuality: Sexual Practices in the United States.* Chicago: University of Chicago Press.

Lee, Janet. 1994. "Menarche and the (Hetero)sexualization of the Female Body." *Gender & Society* 8 (September): 343–362.

———. 1996. *Blood Stories: Menarche and the Politics of the Female Body in the United States.* New York: Routledge.

Lehman, E. C., Jr. 1994. "Gender and Ministry Style: Things Not What They Seem." Pp. 3–14 in *Gender and Religion,* edited by William H. Swatos, Jr. New Brunswick, NJ: Transaction Publishers.

Lemert, E. 1972. *Human Deviance, Social Problems, and Social Control.* Upper Saddle River, NJ: Prentice-Hall.

Leong, Russell, ed. 1996. *Asian American Sexualities: Dimensions of the Gay and Lesbian Experience.* New York: Routledge.

Lerman, Robert, and Elaine Sorenson. 2000. "Father Involvement with Their Nonmarital Children: Patterns: Determinants, and Effects on Their Earnings." *Marriage and Family Review* 29: 137–158.

———, and Theodora J. Ooms. 1993. *Young Unwed Fathers: Changing Roles and Emerging Policies.* Philadelphia: Temple University Press.

Lerner, Gerda. 1973. *Black Women in White America: A Documentary History.* New York: Vintage.

———. 1976. "Placing Women in History: A 1975 Perspective." Pp. 357–367 in *Liberating Women's History,* edited by Berenice Carroll. Champaign–Urbana, IL: University of Illinois Press.

Lewis, Gregory B. 2003. "Black-White Differences in Attitudes Toward Homosexuality and Gay Rights." *The Public Opinion Quarterly* 67: 59–78.

Lim, In-Sook. 1997. "Korean Immigrant Women's Challenge to Gender Inequality at Home: The Interplay of Economic Resources, Gender, and Family." *Gender & Society* 11 (February): 31–51.

Limbaugh, H. Rush, III. 1992. *The Way Things Ought to Be.* New York: Pocket.

Lindsey, Eric W., and Jacquelyn Mize. 2001. "Contextual Differences in Parent-Child Play: Implications for Children's Gender Role Development." *Sex Roles* 44 (February): 155–176.

———, J. Mize, and G. S. Pettit. 1997. "Differential Play Patterns of Mothers and Fathers of Sons and Daughters: Implications for Children's Gender Role Development." *Sex Roles* 37 (November): 643–661.

Lipset, S. M. (ed.) 1962. *Harriet Martineau: Society in America.* New York: Doubleday.

Litoff, J. B. 1978. *American Midwives: 1860 to the Present.* Westport, CT: Greenwood Press.

Lock, Margaret. 1993. *Encounters with Aging: Mythologies of Menopause in Japan and North America.* Berkeley: University of California Press.

———. 1998. "Anomalous Aging: Managing the Postmenopausal Body." *Body and Society* 4 (March): 35–61.

Logan, T. K., Carl Leukefeld, and Bob Walker. 2000. "Stalking as a Variant of Intimate Violence: Implications from a Young Adult Sample." *Violence and Victims* 15: 91–111.

Logio, Kim. 1998. *Here's Looking at You, Kid: Gender, Race, Body Image and Adolescent Health.* Ph.D. Dissertation, University of Delaware.

Logue, Barbara, J. 1991. "Women at Risk: Predictors of Financial Stress for Retired Women Workers." *The Gerontologist* 31: 657–665.

Lombardo, William K., Gary A. Cretser, and Scott C. Roesch.

2001. "For Crying Out Loud—The Differences Persist into the '90s." *Sex Roles* 45 (December): 529–547.

Lombroso, N. 1920. *The Female Offender.* New York: Appleton.

Longino, Helene, and R. Doell. 1983. "Body, Bias, and Behavior: Comparative Analysis of Reasoning in Two Areas of Biological Science." *Signs* 9 (Winter): 206–227.

Lopata, Helene Z., and Barrie Thorne. 1978. "On the Term 'Sex Roles.' " *Signs* 3 (Spring): 718–721.

Lorber, Judith. 1994. *Paradoxes of Gender.* New Haven, CT: Yale University Press.

———, Rose L. Coser, Alice S. Rossi, and Nancy Chodorow. 1981. "On 'The Reproduction of Mothering': A Methodological Debate." *Signs* 6: 482–514.

Loscocco, Karyn A., and Glenna Spitze. 1990. "Working Conditions, Social Support and the Well-Being of Female and Male Factory Workers." *Journal of Health and Social Behavior* 31 (December): 313–327.

Lucal, Betsy. 1994. "Class Stratification in Introductory Textbooks: Relational or Distributional Models?" *Teaching Sociology* 22 (April): 139–150.

Lucas, Samuel R. 1999. *Tracking Inequality: Stratification and Mobility in American High Schools.* New York: Teachers College Press.

Lukemeyer, Anna, Marcia K. Meyers, and Timothy Smeeding. 2000. "Expensive Children in Poor Families: Out-of-Pocket Expenditures for the Care of Disabled and Chronically Ill Children in Welfare Families." *Journal of Marriage and the Family* 62 (May): 399–415.

Luker, Kristen. 1975. *Taking Chances.* Berkeley: University of California Press.

———. 1984. *Abortion and the Politics of Motherhood.* Berkeley: University of California Press.

Lummis, Adair T., and Paula D. Nesbitt. 2000. "Women Clergy Research and the Sociology of Religion." *Sociology of Religion* 61 (Winter): 443–453.

Lundberg, F., and M. Farnham. 1947. *Modern Woman: The Lost Sex*. New York: Harper.

Lye, Diane N., and Ingrid Waldron. 1997. "Attitudes toward Cohabitation, Family, and Gender Roles: Relationships to Values and Political Ideology." *Sociological Perspectives* 40 (Summer): 199–225.

MacCorquodale, P. L. 1984. "Gender Roles and Premarital Contraception." *Journal of Marriage and the Family* 46 (February): 57–62.

Machung, A. 1984. "Word Processing: Forward for Business, Backward for Women." Pp. 124–139 in *My Troubles Are Going to Have Trouble With Me*, edited by K. B. Sacks and D. Remy. New Brunswick, NJ: Rutgers University Press.

MacKinnon, Catharine. 1982. "Feminism, Marxism, Method, and the State: An Agenda for Theory." *Signs* 7 (Spring): 515–544.

———. 1983. "Feminism, Marxism, Method, and the State: Toward Feminist Jurisprudence." *Signs* 8 (Summer): 635–658.

Madriz, Esther. 1997. *Nothing Bad Happens to Good Girls: Fear of Crime in Women's Lives*. Berkeley: University of California Press.

Mahoney, Patricia, and Linda M. Williams. 1998. "Sexual Assault in Marriage: Prevalence, Consequences, and Treatment of Wife Rape." Pp. 113–162 in *Partner Violence: A Comprehensive Review of 20 Years of Research*, edited by Jana L. Jasinkski and Linda M. Williams. Thousand Oaks, CA: Sage.

Majete, Clayton A. 1999. "Family Relationships and the Interracial Marriage." Paper presented at the Annual Meetings of the American Sociological Association, Washington, DC.

Malat, Jennifer. 2000. "Racial Differences in Norplant Use in the United States." *Social Science and Medicine* 50: 1297–1308.

Malcolm, Ellen R. 1993. "Reining Big Givers." *The New York Times*, March 30, p. A23.

Malleson, Kate. 2003. "Justifying Gender Equality on the Bench: Why Difference Won't do." *Feminist Legal Studies* 11: 1–24.

Mannheim, K. 1936. *Ideology and Utopia*. New York: Harcourt, Brace, and World.

Mansfield, Phyllis Kernoff, Patricia Bartalow Koch, Julie Henderson, Judith R. Vicary, Margaret Cohn, and Elaine W. Young. 1991. "The Job Climate for Women in Traditionally Male Blue-Collar Occupations." *Sex Roles* 25 (July): 63–79.

Markens, Susan. 1996. "The Problematic of 'Experience': A Political and Cultural Critique of PMS." *Gender & Society* 10 (February): 42–58.

Markson, Elizabeth W., and Carol A. Taylor. 2000. "The Mirror Has Two Faces." *Ageing and Society* 20 (March): 137–160.

Marshall, Nancy L., and Rosalind C. Barnett. 1995. "Child Care, Division of Labor, and Parental Emotional Well-Being among Two-Earner Couples." Paper presented at the Annual Meetings of the American Sociological Asssociation.

Marsiglio, William. 1995. "Young Nonresident Biological Fathers." *Marriage and Family Review* 20: 325–348.

Martin, Elaine. 1990. "Men and Women on the Bench: Vive la Difference?" *Judicature* 73 (December–January): 204–208.

Martin, Emily. 1991. "The Egg and the Sperm: How Science Has Constructed a Romance Based on Stereotypical Male-Female Roles." *Signs* 16 (Spring): 485–501.

Martin, Patricia Yancey. 1997. "Gender, Accounts, and Rape Processing Work." *Social Problems* 44 (November): 464–483.

———. 2004. "Gender as Social Institution." *Social Forces* 82 (June): 1249–1273.

———, and Robert A. Hummer. 1989. "Fraternities and Rape on Campus." *Gender & Society* 3 (December 1989): 457–473.

———, John R. Reynolds, and Shelley Keith. 2002. "Gender Bias and Feminist Consciousness among Judges and Attorneys: A Standpoint Theory Analysis." *Signs* 27: 665–701.

Martin, Steven S., and Cynthia Robbins. 1995. "Personality, Social Control and Drug Use in Early Adolescence." Pp. 145–161 in *Drugs, Crime and Other Deviant Adaptations*, edited by Howard B. Kaplan. New York: Plenum.

Martineau, Harriet. 1837. *Society in America*. Paris: Baudry's European Library.

Marx, G. 1967. "Religion: Opiate or Inspiration of Civil Rights Militancy Among Negroes." *American Sociological Review* 32 (February): 64–72.

Marx, K., and F. Engels. 1970. *The Communist Manifesto*. New York: Pathfinder Press.

Massoni, Kelley. 2004. "Modeling Work: Occupational Messages in *Seventeen* Magazine." *Gender & Society* 18 (February): 47–55.

Mast, Marianne Schmid, and Judith A. Hall. 2004. "When Is Dominance Related to Smiling? Assigned Dominance, Dominance Preference, Trait Dominance, and Gender as Moderators." *Sex Roles* 50 (March): 387–399.

———. 2001. "Gender Differences and Similarities in Dominance Hierarchies in Same-Gender Groups Based on Speaking Time." *Sex Roles* 44 (May): 537–556.

Masters, W. H., and V. E. Johnson. 1966. *Human Sexual Response*. Boston: Little, Brown.

Maume, David J., Jr. 1999. "Glass Ceilings and Glass Escalators: Occupational Segregation and Race and Sex Differences in Managerial Promotions." *Work and Occupations* 26 (November): 483–509.

May, David C. 2001. "The Effect of Fear of Sexual Victimization on Adolescent Fear of Crime." *Sociological Spectrum* 21: 141–174.

McCammon, Holly J. 1995. "The Politics of Protection: State Minimum Wage and Maximum Hours Laws for Women in the United States, 1870–1930." *Sociological Quarterly* 36 (Spring): 217–249.

McCloskey, Laura Ann. 1996. "Socioeconomic and Coercive Power within the Family." *Gender & Society* 10 (August): 449–463.

McComb, Chris. 2001. "Few Say It's Ideal for Both Parents To Work Full Time Outside of Home" *The Gallup Poll.* Princeton, NJ: Gallup Organization.

McCrate, Elaine, and Joan Smith. 1998. "When Work Doesn't Work: The Failure of Current Welfare Reform." *Gender & Society* 12 (February): 61–80.

McFarlane, Judith, et al. 2000. "Intimate Partner Violence." *Journal of Interpersonal Violence* 15: 158–69.

McGuffey, C. Shawn, and B. Lindsay Rich. 1999. "Playing in the Gender Transgression Zone: Race, Class, and Hegemonic Masculinity in Middle Childhood." *Gender & Society* 12 (October): 608–627.

McGuire, Gail M. 2002. "Gender, Race, and the Shadow Structure: A Study of Informal Networks and Inequality in a Work Organization." *Gender & Society* 16 (June): 303–322.

McGuire, M. B. 2002. *Religion: The Social Context,* 5th ed. Belmont, CA: Wadsworth.

McIntosh, Peggy. 1983. "Interactive Phases of Curricular Re-Vision: A Feminist Perspective." Working Papers Series. Wellesley, MA: Wellesley Center for Research on Women.

McKinney, Kathleen, and Kelly Crittenden. 1992. "Contrapower Sexual Harassment: The Offender's Viewpoint." *Free Inquiry in Creative Sociology* 20 (May): 3–10.

McMannon, Timothy J. 1997. "The Changing Purposes of Education and Schooling." pp. 1–17 in *The Public Purpose of Education and Schooling,* edited by John I. Goodlad and Timothy J. McMannon. San Francisco: Jossey-Bass Publishing.

McManus, Patirica A., and Thomas A. DiPrete. 2001. "Losers and Winners: The Financial Consequences of Separation and Divorce for Men." *American Sociological Review* 66 (April): 246–268.

McNelles, Laurie R., and Jennifer A. Connolly. 1999. "Intimacy between Adolescent Friends: Age and Gender Differences in Intimate Affect and Intimate Behav-

iors." *Journal of Research on Adolescence* 9: 143–159.

McQueeney, Krista B. 2003. "The New Religious Rite: A Symbolic Interactionist Case Study of Lesbian Commitment Rituals." *Journal of Lesbian Studies* 7: 49–70.

McQuiade, Sharon, and John H. Ehrenreich. 1998. "Women in Prison: Approaches to Understanding the Lives of a Forgotten Population." *Affilia: Journal of Women and Social Work* 13 (Summer): 233–247.

Mead, Margaret. 1962. *Male and Female.* London: Penguin.

Mechanic, Mindy B., et al. 2000. "The Impact of Severe Stalking Experienced by Acutely Battered Women: An Examination of Violence, Psychological Symptoms and Strategic Responding." *Violence and Victims* 15: 443–458.

Mechanic, Mindy B., Terri L. Weaver, and Patricia A. Resick. 2000. "Intimate Partner Violence and Stalking Behavior: Exploration of Patterns and Correlates in a Sample of Acutely Battered Women." *Violence and Victims* 15: 55–72.

Meigs, C. D. 1847. *Lecture on Some of the Distinctive Characteristics of the Female: Delivered before the Class of the Jefferson Medical College.* Philadelphia: Collins.

Melosh, Barbara. 1982. *"The Physician's Hand": Work Culture and Conflict in American Nursing.* Philadelphia: Temple University Press.

Mendelsohn, E., P. Weingart, and R. Whitely, eds. 1977. *The Social Production of Scientific Knowledge.* Dordredcht, The Netherlands: Riedel.

Mernissi, Fatima. 1987. *Beyond the Veil: Male-Female Dynamics in Modern Muslim Society.* Bloomington: Indiana University Press.

———, and Mary Jo Lakeland. 1992. *The Veil and the Male Elite: A Feminist Interpretation of Women's Rights in Islam.* New York: Perseus.

Mertz, Elizabeth, W. Njogu, and S. Gooding. 1998. "What Difference Does Difference Make? The Challenge for Legal Education." *Jour-

nal of Legal Education* 48 (March): 1–87.

Messerschmidt, James. 1986. *Capitalism, Patriarchy, and Criminology: Toward a Feminist Criminology.* Totowa, NJ: Rowman and Littlefield.

———. 2000a. "Becoming 'Real Men': Adolescent Masculinity Challenges and Sexual Violence." *Men and Masculinities* 2: 286–307.

———. 2000b. *Nine Lives: Adolescent Masculinities, the Body, and Violence.* Boulder, CO: Westview.

Messing, K. 1983. "The Scientific Mystique: Can a White Lab Coat Guarantee Purity in the Search for Knowledge About the Nature of Women?" Pp. 75–88 in *Woman's Nature,* edited by M. Lowe and R. Hubbard. New York: Pergamon Press.

Messner, Michael A. 1997. *Politics of Masculinities: Men in Movements.* Thousand Oaks: Sage.

———. 1998. "The Limits of 'The Male Sex Role': An Analysis of the Men's Liberation and Men's Rights Movements' Discourse." *Gender & Society* 12 (June): 255–276.

———. 2000. "Barbie Girls versus Sea Monsters: Children Constructing Gender." *Gender & Society* 14 (December): 765–784.

———. 2001. "Friendship, Intimacy, and Sexuality." Pp. 253–265 in *The Masculinities Reader,* edited by Stephen M. Whitehead and Frank J. Barrett. Cambridge: Polity.

Meyer, Jan. 1990. "Guess Who's Coming to Dinner This Time? A Study of Gay Intimate Relationships and the Support for Those Relationships." *Marriage and Family Review* 14: 59–82.

Meyer, M. H., and E. K. Pavalko. 1996. "Family, Work, and Access to Health Insurance among Mature Women." *Journal of Health and Social Behavior* 37 (December): 311–325.

Middlebrook, Diane. 1998. *Suits Me: The Double Life of Billy Tipton.* Boston: Houghton Mifflin.

Milkie, Melissa A., and Pia Peltola. 1999. "Playing All the Roles: Gender and the Work-Family Balancing Act." *Journal of Marriage and the Family* 61 (May): 476–490.

Mill, J. S. 1970. *The Subjection of Women.* New York: Source Book Press.

Miller, D. 1975. *American Indian Socialization to Urban Life.* San Francisco: Institute for Scientific Analysis.

Miller, Eleanor. 1986. *Street Women.* Philadelphia: Temple University Press.

Miller, J. B. 1977. *Toward a New Psychology of Women.* Boston: Beacon Press.

Miller, Jody. 2002. "The Strengths and Limits of 'Doing Gender' for Understanding Street Crime." *Theoretical Criminology* 6: 433–460.

———, and Rod K. Brunson. 2000. "Gender Dynamics in Youth Gangs: A Comparison of Males' and Females' Accounts." *Justice Quarterly* 17: 419–448.

Miller, Susan. 1997. "The Unintended Consequences of Criminal Justice Policy." Talk presented at Research on Women Series, University of Delaware, Women's Studies Program.

Mills, C. Wright. 1959. *The Sociological Imagination.* New York: Oxford University Press.

Milner, Joel S., and Julie L. Crouch. 1993. "Physical Child Abuse." Pp. 25–55 in *Family Violence: Prevention and Treatment,* edited by Robert L. Hampton, Thomas P. Gullotta, Gerald R. Adams, Earl H. Potter, III, and Roger P. Weissberg. Newbury Park, CA: Sage.

Min, Pyong Gap. 2003. "Korean 'Comfort Women': The Intersection of Colonial Power, Gender, and Class." *Gender & Society* 17: 938–957.

Minnich, Elizabeth Kamarck. 1990. *Transforming Knowledge.* Philadelphia: Temple University Press.

Mir-Hosseini, Ziba. 1999. *Islam and Gender: The Religious Debate in Contemporary Iran.* Princeton, NJ: Princeton University Press.

Mirandé, A. 1979. "Machismo: A Reinterpretation of Male Dominance in the Chicano Family." *The Family Coordinator* 28: 447–479.

Mishel, Lawrence, Jared Bernstein, and John Schmitt. 2001. *The State of Working America.* Ithaca, NY: Cornell University Press.

Mishel, Lawrence, Jared Bernstein, and Heather Boushey. 2003. *The State of Working America: 2002/2003.* Washington, DC: Economic Policy Institute.

Misra, Joya, Stephanie Moller, and Marina Karides. 2003. "Envisioning Dependency: Changing Media Depictions of Welfare in the 20th Century." *Social Problems* 50 (November): 482–504.

Mitchell, G., Stephanie Obradovich, Fred Herring, Chris Tromborg, and Alyson L. Burns. 1992. "Reproducing Gender in Public Places: Adults' Attention to Toddlers in Three Public Locales." *Sex Roles* 26 (September): 323–330.

Mitchell, Juliet. 1971. *Woman's Estate.* New York: Pantheon.

Modleski, T. 1980. "The Disappearing Act: A Study of Harlequin Romances." *Signs* 5 (Spring): 435–448.

Moen, Phyllis. 2004. "The New 'Middle' Work Force." The Life Course Center, University of Minnesota, Minneapolis and the Bronfenbrenner Life Course Center (and Cornell Careers Institute) at Cornell University, Ithaca, New York.

———, Jungmeen E. Kim, and Heather Hofmeister. 2001. "Couples' Work/Retirement Transitions, Gender, and Marital Quality." *Social Psychology Quarterly* 64 (March): 55–71.

Mohr, J. 1978. *Abortion in America.* New York: Oxford University Press.

Money, John. 1988. *Gay, Straight, and In-Between: The Sexology of Erotic Orientation.* New York: Oxford University Press.

———. 1995. *Gendermaps: Social Constructionism, Feminism and Sexosophical History.* New York: Continuum.

———, and A. A. Ehrhardt. 1972. *Man, Woman, Boy and Girl: The Differentiation and Dimorphism of Gender Identity from Conception to Maturity.* Baltimore: Johns Hopkins University Press.

Mongeau, B., H. L. Smith, and A. C. Maney. 1961. "The 'Granny' Mid-

wife: Changing Roles and Functions of a Folk Practitioner." *American Journal of Sociology* 66: 497–505.

Monson, Candice M., Jennifer Langhinrichsen-Rohling, and Tisha Binderup. 2000. "Does 'No' Really Mean 'No' after You Say 'Yes'? Attributions about Date and Marital Rape." *Journal of Interpersonal Violence* 15 (November): 1156–1174.

———, Gary R. Byrd and Jennifer Langhinrichsen-Rohling. 1996. "To Have and to Hold: Perceptions of Marital Rape." *Journal of Interpersonal Violence* 11 (September): 410–424.

Moore, David. 2004. "Modest Rebound in Public Acceptance of Homosexuals." *The Gallup Poll.* Princeton, NJ: The Gallup Organization, May 20.

———, and Joseph Carroll. 2004. "Support for Gay Marriage/Civil Unions Edges Upward." *The Gallup Poll.* Princeton, NJ: The Gallup Organization, May 17.

Moore, Gwen. 1990. "Structural Determinants of Men's and Women's Personal Networks." *American Sociological Review* 55 (October): 726–735.

———. 1992. "Gender and Informal Networks in State Government." *Social Science Quarterly* 73 (March): 46–61.

Moore, Joan. 1988. "An Assessment of Hispanic Poverty: Does a Hispanic Underclass Exist?" *Tomas Rivera Center Report* 2: 8–9.

Moorti, Sujata. 2002. *The Color of Rape: Gender and Race in Television's Public Sphere.* Albany, NY: State University of New York Press.

Moraga, Cherríe, and Gloria Anzaldúa. 1981. *This Bridge Called My Back: Radical Writings by Women of Color.* Watertown, MA: Persephone Press.

Morgan, Leslie A. 2000. "The Continuing Gender Gap in Later Life Economic Security." *Journal of Aging and Social Policy* 11: 157–165.

Morgen, Sandra. 2002. *Into Our Own Hands: The Women's Health Movement in the United States, 1969–1990.* Piscataway, NJ: Rutgers University Press.

Morin, S. F., and E. M. Garfinkle. 1978. "Male Homophobia." *The Journal of Social Issues* 34 (Winter): 29–47.

Moss, Nancy E. 2002. "Gender Equity and Socioeconomic Inequality: A Framework for the Patterning of Women's Health." *Social Science and Medicine* 54: 649–661.

Moss, Philip, and Chris Tilly. 2001. *Stories Employers Tell: Race, Skill, and Hiring in America.* New York, NY: Russell Sage.

Mullings, Janet L., James W. Marquart, and Pamela M. Diamond. 2001. "Cumulative Continuity and Injection Drug Use among Women" A Test of the Downward Spiral Framework." *Deviant Behavior* 22 (May—June): 211–238.

———, Joycelyn Pollock, and Ben M. Crouch. 2002. "Drugs and Criminality: Results from the Texas Women Inmates Study." *Women and Criminal Justice* 13: 69–96.

Murinen, Sarah K., and Linda Smolak. 2000. "The Experience of Sexual Harassment among Grade-School Students: Early Socialization of Female Subordination?" *Sex Roles* 43 (July): 1–17.

———, Carrie Wright, and Gretchen Kaluzny. 2002. "If "Boys Will be Boys," then Girls Will Be Victims? A Meta-Analytic Review of the Research that Relates Masculine Ideology to Sexual Aggression." *Sex Roles* 46: 359–75.

Myers, Dowell, and Cynthia J. Crawford. 1998. "Occupational Mobility of Immigrant and Native-Born Latinas." *American Sociological Review* 63 (February): 68–93.

Nagel, Joanne. 2003. *Race, Ethnicity, and Sexuality. Intimate Intersections, Forbidden Frontiers.* New York: Oxford University Press.

Nanda, Serena. 1998. *Neither Man Nor Woman: The Hijras of India.* Belmont, CA: Wadsworth.

Naples, Nancy A. 1992. "Activist Mothering: Cross-Generational Continuity in the Community Work of Women from Low- Income Urban Neighborhoods." *Gender & Society* 6 (September): 441–464.

Nardi, Peter M., and Beth Schneider. 1997. *Social Perspectives on Lesbian and Gay Studies.* New York: Routledge.

Nason-Clark, Nancy. 1987. "Are Women Changing the Image of Ministry? A Comparison of British and American Realities." *Review of Religious Research* 28 (June): 330–340.

National Center for Education Statistics. 2000. *Digest of Education Statistics 2000.* Washington, DC: U.S. Department of Education.

National Center for Health Statistics. 2003. *Health United States 2003.* Washington, DC: Department of Health and Human Services.

Neckerman, Kathryn M., and Joleen Kirschenman. 1991. "Hiring Strategies, Racial Bias, and Inner-City Workers." *Social Problems* 38 (November): 433–447.

Neilson, Linda C. 2002. "Comparative Analysis of Law in Theory and Law in Action in Partner Abuse Cases: What do the Data Tell Us?" *Studies in Law, Politics, and Society* 26: 141–187.

Neitz, Mary Jo. 2000. "Queering the Dragonfest: Changing Sexuality in a Post-Patriarchal Religion." *Sociology of Religion* 61 (Winter): 369–391.

Nelson, Andrea, and Pamela Oliver. 1998. "Gender and the Construction of Consent in Child-Adult Sexual Contact: Beyond Gender Neutrality and Male Monopoly." *Gender & Society* 12 (October): 554–577.

Nelson, Fiona. 1999. "Lesbian Families: Achieving Motherhood." *Journal of Gay & Lesbian Social Services* 10: 27–46.

Nicholson, Linda E., ed. 1990. *Feminism and Postmodernism.* New York: Routledge.

———. 1994. "Interpreting Gender." *Signs* 20 (Autumn): 79–105.

Nisbet, Robert. 1970. *The Social Bond.* New York: Knopf.

Nock, Steven L. 1995. "A Comparison of Marriages and Cohabiting Relationships." *Journal of Family Issues* 16 (January): 53–76.

Novkov, Julie. 1996. "Liberty, Protection, and Women's Work: Investigating the Boundaries

between Public and Private." *Law and Social Inquiry* 21 (Fall): 857–899.

Ntiri, Daphne W. 2000. "The Transition of Female Family Heads of Household from Welfare to Work: Implications for Adult Education. *Western Journal of Black Studies* 24 (Spring): 34–42.

Oakley, A. 1974. *The Sociology of Housework.* London: Mertin Robertson.

O'Campo, Patricia, William W. Eaton, and Carles Muntaner. 2004. "Labor Market Experiences, Work Organization, Gender Inequalities and Health Status: Results from a Prospective Analysis of U.S. Employed Women." *Social Science and Medicine* 58: 585–594.

O'Connell, Colleen, and Karen Korabik. 2000. "Sexual Harassment: The Relationship of Personal Vulnerability, Work Context, Perpetrator Status, and Type of Harassment to Outcomes." *Journal of Vocational Behavior,* 56 (June): 299–329.

O'Kelly, C. G., and L. S. Carney. 1986. *Women and Men in Society,* 2nd ed. Belmont, CA: Wadsworth.

O'Rand, Angela M., and John C. Henretta. 1999. "Labor Markets and Occupational Welfare in the United States." Pp. 131–157 in *Age and Inequality: Diverse Pathways through Later Life,* edited by Angela O'Rand and John C. Henretta. Boulder, CO: Westview.

Olsen, Laurie. 1997. *An Invisible Crisis: The Educational Needs of Asian Pacific American Youth.* New York: Asian Americans/Pacific Islanders in Philanthropy.

Padavic, Irene. 1991. "Attractions in Male Blue-Collar Jobs for Black and White Women: Economic Need, Exposure, and Attitudes." *Social Science Quarterly* 72 (March): 33–49.

———, and Barbara Reskin. 2002. *Women and Men at Work,* 2nd ed. Thousand Oaks, CA: Pine Forge Press.

Palmer, Phyllis. 1989. *Domesticity and Dirt: Housewives and Domestic Servants in the United States, 1920–1945.* Philadelphia: Temple University Press.

Park, Jerry Z. 1999. "Empowering Chastity: Sexual Morality among American Evangelicals." Paper presented at the Annual Meetings of the American Sociological Association, Washington, DC.

Patterson, Charlotte J. 2000. "Family Relationships of Lesbians and Gay Men." *Journal of Marriage and the Family* 62 (November): 1052–1069.

Paul, Elizabeth L., Brian McManus, and Allison Hayes. 2000. " 'Hookups': Characteristics and Correlates of College Students' Spontaneous and Anonymous Sexual Experiences." *Journal of Sex Research* 37: 76–88.

Pavalko, Eliza K., and Shari Woodbury. 2000. "Social Roles as Process: Caregiving Careers and Women's Health." *Journal of Health and Social Behavior* 41 (March): 91–105.

Pear, Robert. 2000. "Research Neglects Women, Studies Find." *The New York Times*, April 30: 16.

———. 2001. "Sex Differences Called Key in Medical Studies." *The New York Times* (April 25: A14).

Pedraza, Sylvia. 1991. "Women and Migration: The Social Consequences of Gender." *Annual Review of Sociology* 17: 303–325.

———. 1996. "Origins and Destinies: Immigration, Race, and Ethnicity in American History." Pp. 1–20 in *Origins and Destinies: Immigration, Race, and Ethnicity in America,* edited by Sylvia Pedraza and Rubén G. Rumbaut. Belmont, CA: Wadsworth.

Peltola, Pia, Melissa Milkie, and Stanley Presser. 2004. "The 'Feminist' Mystique: Feminist Identity in Three Generations of Women." *Gender & Society* 18 (February): 122–144.

Peralta, Robert. 2001. "Getting Smashed: Gender and Drinking among College Students." Unpublished Ph.D. Dissertation, University of Delaware.

Peres, Yochanan. 1998. "Cohabitation: A Contemporary Alternative to Marriage?" Paper presented at the International Sociological Association.

Perry, Imani. 2003. "Who(se) Am I? The Identity and Image of Women in Hip-Hop." Pp. 136–148 in *Gender, Race, and Class in Media,* 2nd ed., edited by Gail Dines and Jean M. Humez. Thousand Oaks, CA: Sage.

Petchesky, Rosalind. 1980. "Reproductive Freedom: Beyond a Woman's Right to Choose." *Signs* 5 (Summer): 661–685.

———. 1990. "Giving Women a Real Choice." *The Nation* (May 28): 732–735.

Petersen, Larry R., and Gregory V. Donnenwerth. 1998. "Religion and Declining Support for Traditional Beliefs about Gender Roles." *Sociology of Religion* 59 (Winter): 353–371.

Peterson, Dana, Jody Miller, and Finn-Aage Esbensen. 2001. "The Impact of Sex Composition on Gangs and Gang Member Delinquency." *Criminology* 39: 411–439.

Peterson, Richard R. 1996a. "A Re-Evaluation of the Economic Consequences of Divorce." *American Sociological Review* 61 (June): 528–536.

———. 1996b. "A Re-Evaluation of the Economic Consequences of Divorce: Reply to Weitzman." *American Sociological Review* 61 (June): 539–540.

Pharr, Suzanne. 1999. *Homophobia: A Weapon of Sexism.* Little Rock, AR: Chardon Press.

Phillips, Lynn. 1998. *The Girls Report: What We Know and Need to Know About Growing Up Female.* New York: National Council for Research on Women.

Pino, Nathan W., and Ronert F. Meier. 1999. "Gender Differences in Rape Reporting." *Sex Roles* 11–12 (June): 979–990.

Pierce, Jennifer L. 1995. *Gender Trials: Emotional Lives in Contemporary Law Firms.* Berkeley: University of California Press.

Pohli, C. V. 1983. "Church Closets and Back Doors: A Feminist View of Moral Majority Women." *Feminist Studies* 9 (Fall): 529–558.

Pollak, Otto. 1950. *The Criminology of Women.* Philadelphia: University of Pennsylvania Press.

Porter, Jennie Lee. 2003. "An Investigation of the Glass Ceiling in Corporate America: The Perspective of African-American Women." Dissertation Abstracts International: A: The Humanities and Social Sciences, 297-A.

Poston, C., ed. 1975. *A Vindication on the Rights of Woman.* New York: Norton.

Powell, Kimberly, and Lori Abels. 2002. *Women and Language* 25 (Spring): 14–22.

Powers, Bethel-Ann. 1996. "Relationships among Older Women Living in a Nursing Home." *Journal of Women and Aging* 8: 179–198.

Powers, M. 1980. "Menstruation and Reproduction: An Oglala Case." *Signs* 6 (Autumn): 54–65.

Press, Eyal. 1996. "Barbie's Betrayal." *The Nation* (December 30): 11–16.

Presser, Harriet B. 2000. "Nonstandard Work Schedules and Marital Instability." *Journal of Marriage and the Family* 62 (February): 93–100.

Preves, Sharon E. 2003. *Intersex and Identity: The Contested Self.* New Brunswick, NJ: Rutgers University Press.

Pyke, Karen D. 1994. "Women's Employment as a Gift or Burden? Marital Power across Marriage, Divorce, and Remarriage." *Gender & Society* 8 (March): 73–91.

Pyle, Jean L., and Kathryn B. Ward. 2003. "Recasting our Understanding of Gender and Work during Global Restructuring." *International Sociology* 18: 461–489.

Quillian, Lincoln, and Mary E. Campbell. 2002. "Beyond Black and White: The Present and Future of Multiracial Friendship Segregation." *American Sociological Review* 68 (August): 540–566.

Raag, Tarja. 1999. "Influences of Social Expectations of Gender, Gender Stereotypes, and Situational Constraints on Children's Toy Choices." *Sex Roles* 41 (December): 80–831.

———, and C. L. Rackliff. 1998. "Preschoolers' Awareness of Social Expectations of Gender: Relationships to Toy Choices." *Sex Roles* 38 (May): 675–700.

Radway, Janice. 1984. *Reading the Romance: Women, Patriarchy, and*

Popular Literature. Chapel Hill: University of North Carolina Press.

Rapp, R., E. Ross, and R. Bridenthal. 1979. "Examining Family History." *Feminist Studies* 5 (Spring): 174–200.

Reagon, B. J. 1982. "My Black Mothers and Sisters or On Beginning a Cultural Autobiography." *Feminist Studies* 8 (Spring): 81–96.

Redhorse, J. G., R. Lewis, M. Feit, and J. Decker. 1979. "American Indian Elders: Needs and Aspirations in Institutional and Home Health Care." Manuscript, Arizona State University.

Reeder, Heidi M. 2003. "The Effect of Gender Role Orientation on Same- and Cross-sex Friendship Formation." *Sex Roles* 49 (August): 143–152.

Reid, Lesley Williams, and Miriam Konrad. 2004. "The Gender Gap in Fear: Assessing the Interactive Effects of Gender and Perceived Risk on Fear of Crime." *Sociological Spectrum* 24: 399–425.

Reid, Lori L. 2002. "Occupational Segregation, Human Capital, and Motherhood: Black Women's Higher Exit Rates from Full-time Employment." *Gender & Society* 16 (October): 728–747.

Reilly, Mary Ellen, Bernice Lott, Donna Caldwell, and Luisa DeLuca. 1992. "Tolerance for Sexual Harassment Related to Self-Reported Sexual Victimization." *Gender & Society* 6 (March): 122–138.

Reinharz, Shulamit. 1983. "Experiential Analysis: A Contribution to Feminist Research." Pp. 162–191 in *Theories of Women's Studies,* edited by G. Duelli-Klein and R. Duelli-Klein. Boston: Routledge & Kegan Paul.

———. 1988. "What's Missing in Miscarriage?" *Journal of Community Psychology* 16 (January): 84–103.

Reitz, R. 1977. *Menopause: A Positive Approach.* Radnor, PA: Chilton.

Renzetti, Claire M. 1997. "Violence in Lesbian and Gay Relationships." Pp. 285–293 in *Gender Violence: Interdisciplinary Perspectives,* edited by Laura L. O'Toole and Jessica R. Schiffman. New

York: New York University Press.

Repak, Terry A. 1994. "Labor Recruitment and the Lure of the Capital: Central American Migrants in Washington, DC." *Gender & Society* 8 (December): 507–524.

Reskin, Barbara. 1988. "Bringing the Men Back In: Sex Differentiation and the Devaluation of Women's Work." *Gender & Society* 2 (March): 58–81.

———. 1999. "Occupational Segregation by Race and Ethnicity among Women Workers," Pp. 183–204 in *Latinas and African American Women at Work: Race, Gender, and Economic Inequality,* edited by Irene Browne. New York: Russell Sage Foundation.

———, and Irene Padavic. 1988. "Supervisors as Gatekeepers: Male Supervisors' Response to Women's Integration in Plant Jobs." *Social Problems* 35 (December): 536–550.

———, and Patricia Roos. 1990. *Job Queues, Gender Queues: Explaining Women's Inroads into Male Occupations.* Philadelphia: Temple University Press.

———. 1992. "Occupational Desegregation in the 1970s: Integration and Economic Equity?" *Sociological Perspectives* 35 (Spring): 69–91.

Reuther, R. 1979. "Motherearth and the Megamachine: A Theology of Liberation in a Feminine, Somatic, and Ecological Perspective." Pp. 43–51 *Womanspirit Rising,* edited by C. P. Christ and J. Plaskow. New York: Harper and Row.

———, and R. S. Keller, eds. 1986. *Women and Religion in America, Volume 3: 1900–1968.* New York: Harper and Row.

Rich, Adrienne. 1976. *Of Woman Born: Motherhood as Experience and Institution.* New York: Norton.

———. 1980. "Compulsory Heterosexuality and Lesbian Existence." *Signs* 5 (Summer): 631–660.

Rich, Melissa K., and Thomas F. Cash. 1993. "The American Image of Beauty: Media Representations of Hair Color for Four Decades." *Sex Roles* 29 (July): 113–124.

Richardson, Virginia E. 1999. "Women and Retirement." *Journal of Women and Aging* 11: 49–66.

Richie, Beth E. 1996. *Compelled to Crime: The Gender Entrapment of Battered Black Women.* New York: Routledge.

Riday, Jennifer Dawn. 2003. " 'First and Foremost, I'm a Mom!': The Experience of Full-Time and Part-Time Stay-at-Home Mothering." *Dissertation Abstracts International A: The Humanities and Social Sciences* 1095-A.

Ridgeway, Cecilia L. 2001. Gender, Status, and Leadership." *The Journal of Social Issues* 57 (Winter): 637–655.

Riesebrodt, Martin, and Kelly H. Chong. 1999. "Fundamentalisms and Patriarchal Gender Politics." *Journal of Women's History* 10 (Winter): 55–77.

Riley, Anna L., and Verna M. Keith. 2003. "Work and Housework Conditions and Depressive Symptoms among Married Women: The Importance of Occupational Status." *Women & Health* 38: 1–17.

Risman, Barbara. 1999. *Gender Vertigo.* New Haven. CT: Yale University Press.

———. 2004. "Gender as a Social Structure: Theory Wrestling with Activism." *Gender & Society* 18 (August): 429–450.

Rist, Darrell Yates. 1992. "Are Homosexuals Born That Way?" *The Nation* 255 (October 14): 424–429.

Roberts, Dorothy. 1997. *Killing the Black Body: Race, Reproduction and the Meaning of Liberty.* New York: Vintage Books.

Robinson, Dawn T., and Lynn Smith-Lovin. 2001. "Getting a Laugh: Gender, Status, and Humor in Task Discussions." *Social Forces* 80 (September): 123–158.

Robison, Jennifer. 2002. "Feminism—What's in a Name?" *The Gallup Poll.* Princeton, NJ: The Gallup Organization.

Rollins, Judith. 1985. *Between Women: Domestics and Their Employers.* Philadelphia: Temple University Press.

Romero, Mary. 1992. *Maid in the U.S.A.* Philadelphia: Temple University Press.

Root, Maria. P. P. 2001. *Love's Revolution: Interracial Marriage.* Philadelphia: Temple.

Roper Organization. 1995. *The 1995 Virginia Slims Opinion Poll.* Storrs, CT: Roper Search Worldwide.

Rosenau, Pauline Marie. 1992. *Postmodernism and the Social Sciences: Insights, Inroads, and Intrusions.* Princeton, NJ: Princeton University Press.

Rosenberg, R. 1982. *Beyond Separate Spheres: Intellectual Roots of Modern Feminism.* New Haven, CT: Yale University Press.

Ross, Josephine. 2002. "The Sexualization of Difference: A Comparison of Mixed-Race and Same-Gender Marriage." *Harvard Civil Rights–Civil Liberties Law Review* 37 (Summer): 255–288.

Ross-Durow, Paula L., and Carol J. Boyd. 2000. "Sexual Abuse, Depression, and Eating Disorders in African American Women Who Smoke Cocaine." *Journal of Substance Abuse Treatment* 18 (January): 79–81.

Rossi, Alice. 1970. *Essays on Sex Equality.* Chicago: University of Chicago Press.

———. 1973. *The Feminist Papers.* New York: Columbia University Press.

———. 1977. "Toward a Biosocial Perspective on Parenting." *Daedalus* 106 (Spring): 1–31.

Rossiter, M. 1982. *Women Scientists in America.* Baltimore: Johns Hopkins University Press.

Rothman, Barbara Katz. 1982. *In Labor: Women and Power in the Birthplace.* New York: Norton.

Rothschild, M. A. 1979. "White Women Volunteers in the Freedom Summers." *Feminist Studies* 5 (Fall): 466–495.

Rousey, Annmaria, and Erich Longie. 2001. "The Tribal College as Family Support System." *American Behavioral Scientist* 44: 1492–1504.

Rubin, G. 1975. "The Traffic in Women." Pp. 157–211 in *Toward an Anthropology of Women*, edited by R. Reiter. New York: Monthly Review Press.

Rupp, Leila, and Verta Taylor. 1987. *Survival in the Doldrums: The American Women's Rights Movement, 1945 to the 1960's.* New York: Oxford University Press.

Russell, Diane E. H. 1986. *The Secret Trauma: Incest in the Lives of Girls and Women.* New York: Basic Books.

Rust, Paula. 1993. " 'Coming Out' in the Age of Social Constructionism: Social Identity Formation among Lesbian and Bisexual Women." *Gender & Society* 1 (March): 50–77.

———. 1995. *Bisexuality and the Challenge to Lesbian Politics: Sex. Loyalty, and Revolution.* New York: New York University Press.

———. 2000. *Bisexuality in the United States: A Social Science Reader.* New York: Columbia University Press.

Ruzek, Sheryl Burt. 1978. *The Women's Health Movement: Feminist Alternatives to Medical Control.* New York: Praeger.

———, Virginia L. Olesen, and Adele E. Clarke, eds. 1997. *Women's Health: Complexities and Differences.* Columbus, OH: Ohio State University Press.

Ryan, Rebecca. 1995. "The Sex Right: A Legal History of the Marital Rape Exemption." *Law and Social Inquiry* 4 (Fall): 941–1001.

Saad, Lydia. 2001. "Women See Room for Improvement in Job Equity." Princeton, NJ: The Gallup Organization. www.gallup.com

———. 2003. "Pondering 'Women's Issues,' Part II." *The Gallup Poll.* Princeton, NJ: The Gallup Organization.

Sacks, Karen. 1975. "Engels Revisited: Women, the Organization of Production, and Private Property." Pp. 211–234 in *Toward an Anthropology of Women*, edited by R. Reiter. New York: Monthly Review Press.

———. 1984. "Generations of Working Class Families." Pp. 15–38 in *My Troubles Are Going to Have Trouble With Me*, edited by K. B. Sacks and D. Remy. New Brunswick, NJ: Rutgers University Press.

Sadker, M., and D. Sadker. 1994. *Failing at Fairness: How America's Schools Cheat Girls.* New York: Charles Scribner's Sons.

Saiving, V. 1979. "The Human Situation: A Feminine View." Pp. 25–42 in *Womanspirit Rising*, edited by C. P. Christ and J. Plaskow. New York: Harper and Row.

Saguy, Abigail Cope. 1999. "Puritanism and Promiscuity? Sexual Attitudes in France and the United States." *Comparative Social Research* 18: 227–247.

Sales, Paloma, and Sheigla Murphy. 2000. "Surviving Violence: Pregnancy and Drug Use." *Journal of Drug Issues* 30 (Fall): 695–724.

Sanchez, Laura, Wendy D. Manning, and Pamela J. Smock. 1998. "Sex-Specialized or Collaborative Mate Selection? Union Transitions among Cohabitors." *Social Science Research* 27 (September): 280–304.

Sanchez-Ayendez, Melba, 1986. "Puerto Rican Elderly Women: Shared Meanings and Informal Supportive Networks." Pp. 172–186 in *All-American Women: Lines That Divide, Ties That Bind*, edited by Johnetta Cole. New York: Free Press.

Sanday, Peggy Reeves. 1994. *Many Mirrors: Body Image and Social Relations.* New Brunswick, NJ: Rutgers University Press.

———. 1996. "Rape-Prone Versus Rape-Free Campus Cultures." *Violence against Women* 2: 191–208.

Sandnabba, Kenneth N., and Christian Ahlberg. 1999. "Parent's Attitudes and Expectations about Children's Cross-Gender Behavior." *Sex Roles* 40 (February): 249–263.

Sassler, Sharon. 2004. "The Process of Entering Cohabiting Unions." *Journal of Marriage and the Family* 66 (May): 491–505.

Sayers, S. L., Baucom, D. H., and A. M. Tierney. 1993. "Sex Roles, Interpersonal Control, and Depression: Who Can Get Their Way." *Journal of Research in Personality* 27: 377–395.

Sayre, Anne. 1975. *Rosalind Franklin and DNA.* New York: Norton.

Schmidt, Kathyrn J. 2003. " 'I Didn't Say Anything, but Everybody Knew': Sexual Orientation Disclosure through Tacit Understandings and Silence." Paper presented at the annual meetings of the Southern Sociological Society.

Schmitt, Frederika E., and Patricia Yancey Martin. 1999. "Unobtrusive Mobilization by an Institutionalized Rape Crisis Center: 'It Comes from the Victims.'" *Gender & Society* 13: 364–384.

Schneider, Beth. 1984. "Perils and Promise: Lesbians' Workplace Participation." Pp. 211–230 in *Women-Identified Women,* edited by Trudy Darty and Sandee Potter. Palo Alto, CA: Mayfield.

———, and Nancy E. Stoller. 1995. *Women Resisting AIDS: Feminist Strategies of Empowerment.* Philadelphia: Temple University Press.

Schnittker, Jason, Jeremy Freese, and Brian Powell. 2003.: Who Are Feminists and What Do They Believe? The Role of Generations." *American Sociological Review* 68 (August): 607–622.

Scholten, C. M. 1977. "On the Importance of the Obstetric Art: Changing Customs of Childbirth in America." *The William and Mary Quarterly* 34: 426–445.

Schwartz, Martin D., and Carol A. Nogrady. 1996. "Fraternity Membership, Rape Myths, and Sexual Aggression on a College Campus." *Violence against Women* 2 (June): 148–162.

Schwartz, Pepper, and Virginia Rutter. 1998. *The Gender of Sexuality.* Thousand Oaks, CA: Pine Forge Press.

Scott, Jacqueline. 1998. "Changing Attitudes to Sexual Morality: A Cross-National Comparison." *Sociology* 32 (November): 815–845.

Scully, Diana. 1990. *Understanding Sexual Violence: A Story of Convicted Rapists.* Cambridge, MA: Unwin Hyman.

Secada, M. S., R. Chavez-Chavez, E. Garcia, C. Munoz, J. Oakes, I. Santiago-Santiaago, and R. Slavin. 1998. *No More Excuses: The Final Report of the Hispanic Dropout Project.* Washington, DC:

Office of Bilingual and Minority Languages Affairs, U.S. Department of Education.

Segura, Denise. 1998. "Working at Motherhood: Chicana and Mexican Immigrant Mothers and Employment." Pp. 727–744 in *Families in the U.S.: Kinship and Domestic Politics,* edited by Karen V. Hansen and Anita Ilta Garey. Philadelphia: Temple University Press.

———, and Jennifer L. Pierce. 1993. "Chicana/o Family Structure and Gender Personality: Chodorow, Familism, and Psychoanalytic Sociology Revisited." *Signs* 19 (Autumn): 62–91.

Seidman, Steven. 1994. "Symposium: Queer Theory/Sociology: A Dialogue." *Sociological Theory* 12 (July): 166–177.

———, ed. 1996. *Queer Theory/ Sociology.* Malden, MA: Blackwell Publishing.

Seltzer, Judith A. 2000. "Families Formed Outside of Marriage." *Journal of Marriage and the Family* 62 (November): 1247–1268.

Shange, Ntozake. 1975. *For colored girls who have considered suicide/ when the rainbow is enuf.* New York: Bantam Books.

Sharp, Susan F., and Susan T. Marcus-Mendoza. 2001. "It's a Family Affair: Incarcerated Women and Their Families." *Women and Criminal Justice* 12.: 21–49.

Shifman, Pamela, Esohe Aghatise, Colette De Troy, Ruchira Gupta, and Aida Santos. 2003. "Trafficking and Women's Human Rights in a Globalised World." *Gender and Development* 11: 125–132.

Signorielli, Nancy. 1989. "Television and Conceptions About Sex Roles: Maintaining Conventionality and the Status Quo." *Sex Roles* 21: 341–360.

———. 1991. *A Sourcebook on Children and Television.* New York: Greenwood Press.

Signorielli, Nancy, and Aaron Bacue. 1999. "Recognition and Respect: A Content Analysis of Prime-Time Television Characters across Three Decades." *Sex Roles* 40 (April): 527–544.

Silverstein, Louise B., and Carl F. Auerbach. 1999. "Deconstructing

the Essential Father." *American Psychologist* 54 (June): 397–407.

Simmons, Wendy W. 2001. "Majority of Americans Say More Women in Political Office Would Be Positive for the Country." Princeton, NJ: The Gallup Organization. www.gallup.org

Simon, R. 1981. "American Women and Crime." Pp. 18–39 in *Women and Crime in America,* edited by Lee Bowker. New York: Macmillan.

Simon, Rita J., Angela R. Scanlan, and Pamela S. Nadell. 1994. "Rabbis and Ministers: Women of the Book and the Cloth." Pp. 45–52 in *Gender and Religion,* edited by William H. Swatos. New Brunswick, NJ: Transaction Publishers.

Simon, William, and John H. Gagnon. 1998. "Homosexuality: The Formulation of a Sociological Perspective." Pp. 59–67 in *Social Perspectives in Lesbian and Gay Studies,* edited by Peter M. Nardi and Beth E. Schneider. New York: Routledge.

Sirianni, Carmen, and Cynthia Negrey. 2000. "Working Time as Gendered Time." *Feminist Economics* 6 (March): 59–76.

Siwatu, Mxolisi S. 2003. "Platonic Same-Sex Friendship Intimacy: The Effects of Sex and Gender." Paper presented at the Southern Sociological Society meetings, New Orleans.

Skirboll, Esther, and Rhoda Taylor. 1998. "Two Homes, Two Jobs, One Marriage: Commuter Spousal Relationships." Paper presented at the International Sociological Association meetings.

Sklar, Holly. 1994. "Disposable Workers." *Z Magazine* (January): 36–41.

Slashinski, Melody J., Ann L. Coker, and Keith E. Davis. 2003. "Physical Aggression, Forced Sex, and Stalking Victimization by a Dating Partner: An Analysis of the National Violence against Women Survey." *Violence and Victims* 18 (December): 595–617.

Slevin, Kathryn F., and C. Ray Wingrove. 1998. *From Stumbling Blocks to Stepping Stones: The Life Experiences of Fifty Professional*

African American Women. New York: New York University Press.

Sloat, Lisa J., 1998. "Incubus: Male Songwriters' Portrayal of Women's Sexuality in Pop Metal Music." Pp. 286–301 in *Youth Culture: Identity in a Postmodern World,* edited by Jonathan S. Epstein. Malden, MA: Blackwell.

Smart, C. 1977. *Women, Crime and Criminology: A Feminist Critique.* London: Routledge & Kegan Paul.

Smith, Barbara. 1983. "Homophobia: Why Bring It Up." *Interracial Books for Children Bulletin* 12: 112–113.

Smith, Bonnie G., and Beth Hutchison, eds. 2004. *Gendering Disability.* Piscataway, NJ: Rutgers University Press.

Smith, Dinitia. 1998. "One False Note in a Musician's Life." *The New York Times,* June 2, pp. B1, 4.

Smith, Dorothy E. 1974. "Women's Perspective as a Radical Critique of Sociology." *Sociological Inquiry* 44: 7–13.

———. 1987. *The Everyday World as Problematic: A Feminist Sociology.* Boston: Northeastern University Press.

———. 1990. *The Conceptual Practices of Power: A Feminist Sociology of Knowledge.* Boston: Northeastern University Press.

Smith, Heather. 1998. "Ladders, Ceilings, and Trap Doors: The Promotion of Women and Men." Ph.D. Dissertation, University of Delaware.

Smith, Kristin. 2002. *Whose Minding the Kids: Child Care Arrangements: Spring 1997.* Washington, DC: U.S. Census Bureau.

Smith-Rosenberg, C. 1975. "The Female World of Love and Ritual: Relations Between Women in Nineteenth Century America." *Signs* 1 (Fall): 1–29.

Songer, Donald R., and Kelley A. Crews-Meyer. 2000. "Does Judge Gender Matter? Decision Making in State Supreme Courts." *Social Science Quarterly* 81: 750–762.

Spain, Daphne, and Suzanne M. Bianchi. 1996. *Balancing Act: Motherhood, Marriage, and Employment among American*

Women. New York: Russell Sage Foundation.

Spencer, Steven J., Claude M. Steele, and Diane M. Quinn. 1999. "Stereotype Threat and Women's Math Performance." *Journal of Experimental Social Psychology* 35 (January): 4–28.

Spitze, Glenna. 1988. "Women's Employment and Family Relations: A Review," *Journal of Marriage and the Family* 50 (August): 595–618.

Spohn, Cassia, Dawn Beichner, and Erike Davis-Frenzel. 2001. "Prosecutorial Justifications for Sexual Assault Case Rejections: Guarding the 'Gateway to Justice.' " *Social Problems* 48 (May): 206–235.

———, and David Holleran. 2000. "The Imprisonment Penalty Paid by Young, Unemployed Black and Hispanic Male Offenders." *Criminology* 38: 281–306.

Spretnak, C., ed. 1994. *The Politics of Women's Spirituality: Essays on the Rise of Spiritual Power Within the Feminist Movement,* 2nd ed. Garden City, NY: Anchor Books.

Sprock, June, and Carol Y. Yoder. 1997. "Women and Depression: An Update on the Report of the APA Task Force." *Sex Roles* 36 (March): 269–303.

Stacey, Judith, and Timothy J. Bibliarz. 2001. (How) Does the Sexual Orientation of Parents Matter?" *American Sociological Review* 66 (April): 159–183.

Stack, Carol B. 1974. *All Our Kin: Strategies for Survival in a Black Community.* New York: Harper Colophon.

———, and Linda Burton. 1993. "Kinscripts." Pp. 405–417 in *Families in the U.S.: Kinship and Domestic Politics,* edited by Karen V. Hansen and Anita Ilta Garey. Philadelphia: Temple University Press.

Stanton, Elizabeth Cady. 1974. *The Woman's Bible.* New York: Arno Press.

Staples, R. 1971. *The Black Family.* Belmont, CA: Wadsworth.

Staples, R., and A. Mirandé. 1980. "Racial and Cultural Variations Among American Families." *Journal of Marriage and the Family* 42: 887–903.

Steele, Claude M., and Joshua Aronson. 1995. "Stereotype Threat and the Intellectual Performance of African Americans." *Journal of Personality and Social Psychology* 69 (November): 797–811.

Steffensmeier, Darrell, and Chris Hebert. 1999. "Women and Men Policymakers: Does the Judge's Gender Affect the Sentencing of Criminal Defendants?" *Social Forces* 77: 1163–1196.

Stein, Arlene, and Ken Plummer. 1994. " 'I Can't Even Think Straight': Queer Theory and the Missing Sexual Revolution in Sociology." *Sociological Theory* 12 (July): 178–187.

Stein, D. K. 1978. "Women to Burn: Suttee as a Normative Institution." *Signs* 4 (Winter): 253–268.

Steinberg, Ronnie. 1992. "Gendered Instructions: Cultural Lag and Gender Bias in the Hay System of Job Evaluation." *Work and Occupations* 19 (November): 387–424.

Stellman, J. M. 1977. *Women's Work, Women's Health: Myths and Realities.* New York: Pantheon.

Sterling, Anne. 1984. *We Are Your Sisters: Black Women in the Nineteenth Century.* New York: Norton.

Stohs, Joanne Hoven. 1995. "Predictors of Conflict over the Household Division of Labor among Women Employed Full-Time." *Sex Roles* 33 (August): 257–275.

Stoller, Eleanor Palo, and Rose Campbell Gibson. 2000. *Worlds of Difference: Inequality in the Aging Experience.* Thousand Oaks, CA: Pine Forge Press.

Stoller, Nancy. 2003. "Space, Place and Movement as Aspects of Health Care in Three Women's Prisons." *Social Science & Medicine* 56: 2263–2275.

Strazdins, Lyndall, and Dorothy H. Broom. 2004. "Acts of Love (and Work): Gender Imbalance in Emotional Work and Women's Psychological Distress." *Journal of Family Issues* 25: 356–378.

Strong, Scott M., Donald A. Williamson, Richard G. Netemeyer, and James H. Geer. 2000. "Eating Disorder Symptoms and Concerns about Body Differ as a Function of Gender and Sexual

Orientation." *Journal of Social and Clinical Psychology* 19 (Summer): 240–255.

Sullivan, Deborah A., and Rose Weitz. 1988. *Labor Pains: Modern Midwives and Home Birth.* New Haven, CT: Yale University Press.

Sullivan, Maureen. 1996. "Rozzie and Harriet? Gender and Family Patterns of Lesbian Coparents." *Gender & Society* 12 (December): 747–767.

Szasz, T. 1970. *Manufacture of Madness.* New York: Dell.

Takaki, Ronald. 1989. *Strangers From a Different Shore: A History of Asian Americans.* New York: Penguin.

———. 1993. *A Different Mirror: A History of Multicultural America.* Boston: Little, Brown.

Tam, Tony. 1997. "Sex Segregation and Occupational Gender Inequality in the United States: Devaluation of Specialized Training." *American Journal of Sociology* 102 (May): 1652–1692.

Taylor, Verta, and Nicole C. Raeburn. 1995. "Identity Politics as High-Risk Activism: Career Consequences for Lesbian, Gay, and Bisexual Sociologists." *Social Problems* 42 (May): 252–273.

Tea, N. T., M. Castanier, M. Roger, and R. Scholler. 1975. "Simultaneous Radioimmunoassay of Plasma Progesterone and 17-Hydroxyprogesterone in Men and Women Throughout the Menstrual Cycle and in Early Pregnancy." *Journal of Steroid Biochemistry* 6: 1509–1516.

Teachman, Jay, Lucky M. Tedrow, and Kyle D. Crowder. 2000. "The Changing Demography of America's Families." *Journal of Marriage and the Family* 62 (November): 1234–1246.

The Waterglass, April 28, 2004. Website: www.thewaterglass.net.

Thomas, Jennifer J., and Kimberly A. Daubman. 2001. "The Relationship between Friendship Quality and Self-Esteem in Adolescent Girls and Boys." *Sex Roles* 45 (July): 53–65.

Thompson, Becky W. 1994. *A Hunger So Wide and So Deep: American Women Speak Out on Eating Problems.* Minneapolis: University of Minnesota Press.

Thompson, T. L., and Zerbinos, E. 1997. "Television Cartoons: Do Children Notice It's a Boy's World?" *Sex Roles* 37 (September): 415–432.

Thorne, Barrie, ed., with Marilyn Yalom. 1992. *Re-thinking the Family: Some Feminist Questions*, 2nd ed. Boston: Northeastern University Press.

———. 1993. *Gender Play.* New Brunswick, NJ: Rutgers University Press.

Thornton, Arland, William G. Axinn, and Jay D. Teachman. 1995. "The Influence of School Enrollment and Accumulation on Cohabitation and Marriage in Early Adulthood." *American Sociological Review* 60 (October): 762–774.

Tichenor, Veronica Jaris. 1999. "Status and Income as Gendered Resources: The Case of Marital Power." *Journal of Marriage and the Family* 61 (August): 638–650.

Tillich, P. 1957. *The Dynamics of Faith.* New York: Harper and Row.

Tilly, L. A., and J. W. Scott. 1978. *Women, Work, and Family.* New York: Holt, Rinehart and Winston.

Tjaden, Patricia, and Nancy Thoennes. 1998. *Stalking in America: Findings from the National Violence against Women Survey.* Washington, DC: Bureau of Justice Statistics.

———. 2000a. *Extent, Nature and Consequences of Intimate Partner Violence: Findings from the National Violence Against Women Survey.* Washington, DC: National Institute of Justice.

———. 2000b. "Prevalence and Consequences of Male-to-Female and Female-to-Male Intimate Partner Violence as Measured by the National Violence Against Women Survey." *Violence against Women* 6: 142–161.

Tovée, M., J. S. Reinhardt, and J. L. Emery. 1998. "Optimum Body-Mass Index and Maximum Sexual Attractiveness." *Lancet* 352 (August 15): 548.

Tovée, M. J., S. M. Mason, J. L. Emery, S. E. McCluskey, and E. M. Tovée. 1997. "Supermodels: Stick Insects or Hourglasses?"

Lancet 350 (November 15): 1474–1475.

Tuan, Yi-Fu. 1984. *Dominance and Affection: The Making of Pets.* New Haven, CT: Yale University Press.

Tuchman, Gaye. 1979. "Women's Depiction by the Mass Media." *Signs* 4 (Spring): 528–542.

———, A. K. Daniels, and J. Benét. 1978. *Hearth and Home: Images of Women in the Mass Media.* New York: Oxford University Press.

Tucker, R., ed. 1972. *The Marx-Engels Reader.* New York: Norton.

Turner, Ralph, and Lewis M. Killian. 1972. *Collective Behavior.* Upper Saddle River, NJ: Prentice-Hall.

Tyler, Kimberly A., Danny R. Hoyt, and Les B. Whitbeck.1998. "Coercive Sexual Strategies." *Violence and Victims* 13: 47–61.

U.S. Census Bureau. 2001. *Historical Income Tables*, Table P-16. www.census.gov.

U.S. Census Bureau. 2003. *America's Families and Living Arrangements: 2003*, Detailed Tables. Washington, D.C.: U.S. Census Bureau. www.census.gov

U.S. Census Bureau. 2004. *Detailed Poverty Tables*, POV 14. www.census.gov.

U.S. Census Bureau. 2004. *Statistical Abstract of the United States: 2003.* Washington, DC: U.S. Government Printing Office.

U.S. Department of Defense. 2003. Website www.defenselink.mil.

U.S. Department of Health and Human Services. 1998. *Health United States 1998.* Hyattsville, MD: National Center for Health Statistics.

U.S. Department of Labor. 2003b. *National Compensation Survey: Employee Benefits in Private Industry in the United States, 2000.* Washington, DC: U.S. Department of Labor.

U.S. Department of Labor. 2004. *Employment and Earnings.* Washington, DC: U.S. Department of Labor.

Ullman, Sara E. "A Comparison of Gang and Individual Rape Incidents." *Violence and Victims* 14 (Summer): 123–130.

UNICEF. 2003. *The State of the World's Children 2003.* New York: United Nations Children's Fund.

Uttal, Lynet, and Mary Tuominen. 1999. "Tenuous Relationships: Exploitation, Emotion, and Racial Ethnic Significance in Paid Child Care Work." *Gender & Society* 13 (December): 758–780.

———. 2000. "Using Kin for Child Care: Embedment in the Socioeconomic Networks of Extended Families." *Journal of Marriage and the Family* 61 (November): 845–857.

———. 2002. *Making Care Work: Employed Mothers in the New Childcare Market.* New Brunswick, NJ: Rutgers University Press.

Van Den Daele, W. 1977. "The Social Construction of Science: Institutionalization and Definition of Positive Science in the Latter Half of the Seventeenth Century." Pp. 27–54 in *The Social Production of Scientific Knowledge,* edited by E. Mendelsohn, P. Weingart, and R. Whitley. Dordrecht, The Netherlands: Riedel.

Vanek, J. A. 1978. "Housewives as Workers." Pp. 392–414 in *Women Working,* edited by Anne H. Stromberg and Shirley Harkess. Palo Alto, CA: Mayfield.

Vanneman, Reeve, and Lynn Weber Cannon. 1987. *The American Perception of Class.* Philadelphia: Temple University Press.

Vigorito, Anthony J., and Timothy J. Curry. 1998. "Marketing Masculinity: Gender, Identity and Popular Magazines." *Sex Roles* 39 (July): 135–152.

Vogel, Dena Ann, Margaret A. Lake, Suzanne Evans, and Katherine Hildebrandt Karraker. 1991. "Children's and Adults' Sex-Stereotyped Perceptions of Infants." *Sex Roles* 21 (May): 605–616.

Voydanoff, Patricia, and Brenda W. Donnelly. 1999. "The Intersection of Time in Activities and Perceived Unfairness in Relation to Psychological Distress and Marital Quality." *Journal of Marriage and the Family* 61 (August): 739–751.

Waldron, I., C. C. Weiss, and M. E. Hughes. 1998. "Interacting Effects of Multiple Roles on Women's Health." *Journal of*

Health and Social Behavior 39 (September): 216–230.

Walker, Rebecca, ed. 1995. *To Be Real: Telling the Truth and Changing the Face of Feminism.* New York: Anchor.

Walker-Barnes, Chanequa J., and Craig A. Mason. 2001. "Perceptions of Risk Factors for Female Gang Involvement among African American and Hispanic Women." *Youth and Society* 32: 303–336.

Wallace, Ruth A. 1992. *They Call Her Pastor: A New Role for Catholic Women.* Albany, NY: State University of New York Press.

Wallerstein, I. 1976. *The Modern World System.* New York: Academic Press.

Walsh, Anthony. 1994. "Homosexual and Heterosexual Child Molestation: Case Characteristics and Sentencing Differentials." *International Journal of Offender Therapy and Comparative Criminology* 38 (Winter): 339–353.

Walters, Suzanna. 1995. *Material Girls: Making Sense of Feminist Cultural Theory.* Berkeley: University of California Press.

Walzer, Susan. 1996. "Thinking About the Baby: Gender and Divisions of Infant Care." *Social Problems* 43 (May): 219–234.

Wardle, R. M. 1951. *Mary Wollstonecraft: A Critical Biography.* Lawrence: University of Kansas Press.

Warren, Tracey, Karen Rowlingson, Claire Whyley. 2001. "Female Finances: Gender Wage Gaps and Gender Assets Gaps." *Work, Employment, and Society* 15 (September): 465–488.

Watson, James D. 1968. *The Double Helix.* New York: Atheneum.

Weatherall, Ann, and Anna Priestley. 2001. "A Feminist Discourse Analysis of Sex 'Work'." *Feminism & Psychology* 11: 323–340.

Weber, Lynn, and Elizabeth Higginbotham. 1995. "Perceptions of Workplace Discrimination Among Black and White Professional-Managerial Women." *Working Papers Series.* Memphis: Center for Research on Women, University of Memphis.

Wechsler, Henry. 1995. *Binge Drinking on College Campuses. A New Look at an Old Problem.* Boston: Harvard School of Public Health.

Weisner, Thomas S., Helen Garnier, and James Loucky. 1994. "Domestic Tasks, Gender Egalitarian Values and Children's Gender Typing in Conventional and Nonconventional Families." *Sex Roles* 30 (January): 23–54.

Weitzman, Lenore. 1985. *The Divorce Revolution: The Unexpected Consequences for Women and Children in America.* New York: Free Press.

———. 1996. "A Re-Evaluation of the Economic Consequences of Divorce: Reply to Peterson." *American Sociological Review* 61 (June): 537–538.

Welsh, Sandy. 1999. "Gender and Sexual Harassment." *Annual Review of Sociology* 25: 169–190.

Welter, B., ed. 1976. *Dimity Convictions.* Athens: Ohio University Press.

Wertz, R. W., and D. C. Wertz. 1977. *Lying In: A History of Childbirth in America.* New York: Free Press.

West, Candace, and Sarah Fenstermaker. 1995. "Doing Difference." *Gender & Society* 9 (February): 8–37.

———, and Don Zimmerman. 1987. "Doing Gender." *Gender & Society* 1 (June): 125–151.

———. 1998. "Leaving a Second Closet: Outing Partner Violence in Same-Sex Couples." Pp. 163–183 in *Partner Violence: A Comprehensive Review of 20 Years of Research,* edited by Jana L. Jasinkski and Linda M. Williams. Thousand Oaks, CA: Sage.

West, Jackie. 2000. "Prostitution: Collectives and the Politics of Regulation." *Gender, Work and Organization* 7: 106–118.

———, and Terry Austrin. 2002. "From Work as Sex to Sex as Work: Networks, 'Others' and Occupations in the Analysis of Work." *Gender, Work and Organization* 9: 482–503.

Westkott, Marcia. 1979. "Feminist Criticism of the Social Sciences." *Harvard Educational Review* 49: 422–430.

Whitley, Bernard E. 2001. "Gender-Role Variables and Attitudes toward Homosexuality." *Sex Roles* 45 (December): 691–721.

Whittier, Nancy. 1995. *Feminist Generations: The Persistence of the Radical Women's Movement.* Philadelphia: Temple University Press.

Wilcox, Clyde. 1992. "Race, Gender, and Support for Women in the Military." *Social Science Quarterly* 73 (June): 310–323.

Wilkie, Jane Riblett. 1993. "Changes in U.S. Men's Attitudes toward the Family Provider Role, 1972–1989." *Gender & Society* 7 (June): 261–280.

Willemsen, Tineke M. 2002. "Gender Typing of the Successful Manager: A Stereotype Reconsidered." *Sex Roles* 46 (June): 385–391.

Williams, David R. 1990. "Socioeconomic Differentials in Health: A Review and Redirection." *Social Psychology Quarterly* 53: 81–99.

Williams, David. 1998. "Racial Variations in Adult Health Status: Patterns, Paradoxes, and Prospects." Paper presented at the National Research Council Research Conference on Racial Trends, 1998: National Academy of Science, Washington, DC, October.

Willie, Charles Vert, and Richard Reddick. 2003. *A New Look at Black Families.* Walnut Creek, CA: AltaMira Press.

Willson, Pam, et al. 2000. "Severity of Violence against Women by Intimate Partners and Associated use of Alcohol and/or Illicit Drugs by the Perpetrator." *Journal of Interpersonal Violence* 15: 996–1008.

Wilsnack, Richard W., Nancy D. Vogeltanz, Sharon C. Wilsnack, and T. Robert Harris. 2000. "Gender Differences in Alcohol Consumption and Adverse Drinking Consequences: Cross-Cultural Patterns." *Addiction* 95 (February): 251–265.

Wilson, J. Q., and R. J. Herrnstein. 1985. *Crime and Human Nature.* New York: Simon and Schuster.

Wilson, William Julius. 1987. *When Work Disappears.* New York: Knopf.

Winseman, Albert L. 2004a. "U.S. Churches Looking for a Few White Men." *The Gallup Poll.* Princeton, NJ: The Gallup Organization.

———. 2004b. "Born Agains Wield Political/Economic Influence." *The Gallup Poll.* Princeton, NJ: The Gallup Organization.

Winterich, Julie A. 2003. "Sex, Menopause, and Culture: Sexual Orientation and the Meaning of Menopause for Women's Sex Lives." *Gender & Society* 17 (August): 627–642.

Wolak, Janis, and David Finkelhor. 1998. "Children Exposed to Partner Violence." Pp. 73–112 in *Partner Violence: A Comprehensive Review of 20 Years of Research,* edited by Jana L. Jasinkski and Linda M. Williams. Thousand Oaks, CA: Sage.

Wolf, Margery. 1972. *Women and the Family in Rural Taiwan.* Stanford: Stanford University Press.

Wolff, Kurt H. 1950. *The Sociology of Georg Simmel.* New York: Free Press.

Wolfgang, M., and F. Feracuti. 1967. *The Subculture of Violence: Toward an Integrated Theory in Criminology.* London: Tavistock.

Wollstonecraft, Mary. 1792 [1975]. *A Vindication of the Rights of Woman,* edited by C. Poston. New York: Norton.

Woo, Deborah. 1992. "The Gap Between Striving and Achieving: The Case of Asian American Women." Pp. 191–200 in *Race, Class and Gender: An Anthology,* edited by Margaret L. Andersen and Patricia Hill Collins. Belmont, CA: Wadsworth.

Wonders, Nancy A., and Raymond Michalowski. 2001. "Bodies, Borders, and Sex Tourism in a Globalized World: A Tale of Two Cities-Amsterdam and Havana." *Social Problems* 48: 545–571.

Wong, A. K. 1974. "Women in China: Past and Present." Pp. 220–260 in *Many Sisters,* edited by C. Matthiasson. New York: Free Press.

World Health Organization. 2000. *Women and HIV/AIDS.* Website: www.who.int.

Wright, M. J. 1979. "Reproductive Hazards and 'Protective' Discrimination." *Feminist Studies* 5 (Summer): 302–309.

Wrong, D. 1961. "The Oversocialized Conception of Man in Modern Sociology." *American Sociological Review* 26: 183–193.

Yates, G. G. 1983. "Spirituality and the American Feminist Experience." *Signs* 9 (Autumn): 59–72.

Yaughn, Elizabeth, and Stephen Nowicki, Jr. 1999. "Close Relationships and Complementary Interpersonal Styles among Men and Women." *Journal of Social Psychology* 139 (August): 473–478.

Yllo, Kersti. 1999. "Wife Rape: A Social Problem for the 21st Century." *Violence against Women* 5 (September): 1059–1063.

Yoder, Janice. 1991. "Rethinking Tokenism: Looking Beyond Numbers." *Gender & Society* 5 (June): 178–192.

———, and Patricia Aniakudo. 1997. " 'Outsider Within' the Firehouse: Subordination and Difference in the Social Interactions of African American Women Firefighters." *Gender & Society* 11 (June): 324–341.

Young, Vernetta D., and Rebecca Reviere. 2001. "Meeting the Health Care Needs of the New Woman Inmate: A National Survey of Prison Practices." *Journal of Offender Rehabilitation* 34: 31–48.

Zaretsky, E. 1976. *Capitalism, the Family, and Personal Life.* New York: Harper and Row.

Zavella, Patricia. 1985. " 'Abnormal Intimacy': The Varying Work Networks of Chicana Cannery Workers." *Feminist Studies* 11 (Fall): 541–558.

Zeitlin, I. 1968. *Ideology and the Development of Sociological Theory.* Upper Saddle River, NJ: Prentice-Hall.

Zhou, Min, and Carl L. Bankston. 1998. *Growing Up American:*

How Vietnamese Children Adapt to Life in the United States. New York: Russell Sage Foundation.

Zimmerman, Mary K. 2000. "Women's Health and Gender Bias in medical Education." *Research in the Sociology of Health Care* 17: 121–138.

Zola, Irving. 1989. "Toward the Necessary Universalizing of a Disability Policy." *The Milbank Quarterly* 67 (Supplement 2): 401–428.

———. 1993. "Self, Identity and the Naming Question: Reflections on the Language of Disability" *Social Science and Medicine* 36 (January): 167–173.

Zones, Jane Sprague. 1997. "Beauty Myths and Realities: Their Impact on Women's Health." Pp. 249–275 in *Women's Health: Complexities and Differences,* edited by Sheryl Burt Ruzek, Virginia L. Olesen, and Adele E. Clarke. Columbus, OH: Ohio State University Press.

❖ *Name Index*

Page references followed by *f* or *t* indicate figures or tables, respectively.

A

Abbott, F., 52
Abels, L., 61, 429
Abramovitz, M., 139, 409
Ace, A., 415
Acker, J., 31, 409
Adams, M., 60, 414
Adelman, C., 298, 409
Adler, F., 269, 409
Agger, B., 394, 396, 397, 409
Aghatise, E., 432
Ahlberg, C., 39, 431
Alan Guttmacher Institute, 189, 216, 217, 409
Albonetti, C. A., 409
Alden, H. L., 34, 83, 409
Alessandri, M., 414
Ali, J., 200, 409
Alicea, M., 180, 409
Allen, P. G., 107, 257, 409
Allen, R., 206, 415
Altman, D., 102
Amadiume, I., 28, 409
American Association of University Women, 41, 287, 295, 296, 297, 298, 409
American Council on Education, 82*f*
American Medical Association, 124, 409
Amir, M., 277, 409
Amott, T. L., 106, 107, 108, 151, 409
Andersen, M. L., 15, 121, 276, 391, 392, 393, 399, 402, 409
Anderson, A., 237, 409
Anderson, K. J., 29, 58, 409
Andra, M., 415
Andrews, D. C., 112, 409
Andrews, W., 112, 409
Aniakudo, P., 140, 436
Ansalone, G., 292, 409
Anzalda, G., 391, 392, 427
Apple, K. J., 423
Applebaum, R., 128, 409

Applebaum, R. P., 128, 411
Arat, Y., 424
Arendell, T., 168, 409
Aries, P., 156, 157, 409
Arnold, R., 270, 409
Aronson, J., 292, 433
Aronson, P., 343, 409
Arrighi, B. A., 145, 410
Atchley, R. C., 41
Audesse, R. J., 412
Auerbach, C. F., 175, 432
Austrin, T., 265, 435
Avalos, M., 133, 410
Avison, W. R., 200, 409
Axelson, D. E., 222
Axinn, W. G., 171, 410, 434
Axtell, J., 161, 410

B

Baca Zinn, M., 18, 44, 107, 108, 159, 161, 163, 164, 165, 179, 180, 195, 391–392, 392, 393, 410
Bacon, F., 307–308
Bacue, A., 60, 432
Badgett, M. V. L., 98, 142, 410
Baer, J. A., 125, 320, 410
Baldwin, M. W., 94, 410
Bankston, C. L., 162, 436
Barajas, H. L., 298, 410
Barber, J. S., 171, 410
Barfoot, C. H., 247, 410
Barker-Benfield, G. J., 221, 222, 223, 410
Barnett, R. C., 145, 425
Baron, J., 135, 410
Barret, R. L., 175
Barron, M., 63, 410
Barsimantov, J., 191, 191*f*, 419
Bart, P., 87, 410
Bartkowski, J. P., 242, 416
Bartling, C., 162, 410
Basow, S. A., 5, 29, 34, 83, 410
Bateman, G., 330, 410
Battle, J., 83, 410
Baucom, D. H., 432
Baumgardner, J., 18
Baunach, D. M., 103
Baxandall, R. F., 192, 410

Baxter, J., 135, 410
Beck, A. J., 280, 420
Becker, H., 264, 265, 410
Becker, P. E., 169, 242, 410
Becraft, C., 329
Beichner, D., 433
Belkin, A., 330, 410
Belknap, J., 284
Bellas, M. L., 133, 410
Belsky, J., 175, 410
Bendroth, M. L., 235, 410
Benèt, J., 434
Benet, M. K., 109, 125, 410
Bennett, L., 302, 417
Bennett, R. T., 421
Benson, S. P., 142, 410
Bentley, B. J., 415
Bergen, R., 285
Berger, P., 31, 33, 71, 410
Berheide, C. W., 129, 136, 411
Bernard, J., 162, 173, 411
Berney, L., 411
Bernstein, J., 427
Beron, K., 422
Berry, M. F., 372
Berry, P. E., 282, 411
Bettie, J., 62, 411
Bianchi, S. M., 145, 146, 170, 411, 433
Bibliarz, T. J., 91*t*, 98, 172, 433
Bielawski, D., 40, 414
Bielby, D. D., 172, 415
Bielby, W., 410
Bigner, J. J., 172, 411
Billingsley, A., 178, 411
Binderup, T., 427
Bird, C. E., 145, 200, 411
Bird, S., 90, 411
Blackwell, J., 249, 411
Blackwell, K. T., 415
Blackwood, E., 28, 411
Blake, C. F., 29, 411
Blakemore, J. E. O., 38, 411
Blane, D., 411
Blood, R., 162, 411
Bloom, B., 266, 411
Blum, L., 148, 411
Blumenthal, S. J., 210, 212, 411
Blumstein, P., 95, 411

Boeri, M. W., 245, 411
Boeringer, S. B., 275f, 411
Bogdan, J., 221, 411
Bogle, K., 82, 411
Bogoch, B., 321, 411
Bonacich, E., 128, 411
Bond-Maupin, L., 413
Bonilla-Silva, E., 92, 411
Bookman, A., 333, 346, 411
Booth, B., 329, 412
Bordo, S., 208, 230, 309, 395, 396, 397, 412
Boston Women's Health Book Collective, 215, 230, 412
Boswell, A. A., 275f, 412
Boushey, H., 427
Bowen, L., 55, 412
Bowler, A., 409
Boyd, C., 420
Boyd, C. J., 210, 431
Boyd, C. L., 412
Boyd, T. C., 412
Bozett, F. W., 172, 411
Brabant, S., 40, 412
Bradford, J., 35, 412
Bradley, K., 289, 412
Bramson, L., 376, 412
Brenner, J., 424
Brettell, C. B., 161, 412
Brewis, J., 265, 412
Brewster, M. P., 275f, 412
Bridenthal, R., 164, 430
Brines, J., 171, 412
Britton, D. M., 281, 412
Broad, K., 99, 422
Broom, D. H., 145, 434
Broschak, J. P., 414
Broussard, B., 162, 410
Brown, B. V., 176, 412
Brown, C., 157, 412
Brown, S. L., 171, 412
Browne, I., 122f, 412
Browne, M. W., 54, 412
Brownmiller, S., 263, 412
Brunson, R. K., 427
Brush, L. D., 185, 412
Bunch, C., 387, 412
Burckle, M. A., 206, 412
Bureau of Justice Statistics, 271, 272f, 273, 273f, 277, 281f, 412
Burgess, E. O., 103
Burgess, S. H., 34, 80, 412

Burns, A. L., 427
Burris, B. H., 169, 412
Burton, L., 179, 433
Butler, A. C., 139, 163, 412
Butler, J., 398, 413
Butler, S., 230
Button, S. B., 414
Buysse, J. M., 60, 413
Byrd, G. R., 427
Byrne, S., 63, 419

C

Calasanti, T. M., 52, 413
Caldera, Y., 38, 413
Caldwell, D., 430
Calhoun, A. J., 195, 282, 413
Califia, P., 96, 413
Cameron, D., 57, 413
Campbell, A., 266, 413
Campbell, J. C., 92, 413
Campbell, M. E., 429
Campenni, C. E., 39, 413
Cancian, F., 93, 413
Cancian, M., 138, 413
Candib, L. M., 186, 413
Cannon, L. W., 116, 435
Cantrell, P. J., 423
Capizzano, J., 191
Cardozo, S., 415
Carlson, D. K., 329, 413
Carney, L. S., 115, 428
Carr, C. L., 45, 413
Carr, D., 200, 413
Carroll, J., 171, 242, 413, 427
Cash, J. L., 412
Cash, T. F., 55, 430
Casper, L. M., 154, 166, 417
Cassidy, M. A., 321, 413
Castanier, M., 183, 434
Castle, T., 421
Catsambis, S., 292, 413
Caulfield, M. D., 77, 178, 413
Cavendar, G., 56, 413
Cavendish, J., 247, 413
Center for the American Woman and American Politics, 323, 325f, 413
Centers for Disease Control, 212, 413
Cepeda, A., 266, 413
Chancer, L., 413
Chang, G., 419

Chaves, M., 247, 413
Chavez-Chavez, R., 432
Chavkin, W., 204, 413
Chen, A. S., 36, 413
Chernin, K., 206, 413
Chesney-Lind, M., 266, 267, 281, 285, 413, 422
Chodorow, N., 43, 173, 174, 175, 413, 424
Chong, K. H., 250, 430
Chow, E., 36, 108, 181, 413
Christ, C. P., 252–253, 255, 413
Chrobot-Mason, D., 142, 414
Chronicle of Higher Education, 124, 300f, 301, 414
Clark, J., 415
Clark, R., 40, 414
Clarkberg, M., 42, 415
Clarke, A. E., 230, 231, 431
Clarke, E., 290, 414
Clark-Ibanez, M. K., 92, 414
Clawson, D., 128, 419
Clay, V. S., 87, 414
Clayton-Matthews, A., 421
Cleveland, H. H. III, 276, 423
Coffey, P., 421
Cohen, L. E., 135, 414
Cohn, M., 425
Coker, A. L., 415, 432
Coleman, H. D., 282, 413
Colker, B. D., 133, 414
Collins, P. H., 15, 35, 44, 62, 74, 84, 102, 179, 304, 311, 340, 355, 390, 392, 393, 397, 402, 409, 414
Coltrane, S., 60, 414
Combahee River Collective, 392, 414
Coner-Edwards, A. F. W., 185, 420
Connell, B., 331, 414
Connolly, J. A., 93, 426
Conrad, P., 91t, 414
Conte, J. R., 187, 414
Coontz, P., 321, 414
Corea, G., 224, 414
Cortina, L. M., 302, 414
Coser, R. L., 424
Costello, C. B., 142, 414
Cott, N., 110, 156, 157, 237, 238, 414
Cotter, D. A., 135, 414

Council of Economic Advisors, 203, 414
Covington, S., 411
Cowan, R. S., 112, 146, 414
Crabb, P. B., 40, 414
Craig, M. L., 74
Crain, R. L., 413
Crawford, C. J., 120, 428
Crawford, M., 57, 58, 74, 414
Crenshaw, C., 414
Crenshaw, K., 320, 414
Cretser, G. A., 424
Crews-Meyer, K. A., 321, 433
Crisp, A., 211, 414
Crittenden, K., 142, 426
Croteau, J. M., 99, 414
Crouch, B. M., 428
Crouch, J. L., 187, 427
Crow, B. A., 402
Crowder, K. D., 434
Cullen, F. T., 83, 275*f*, 417
Cullen, J. M., 414
Cullers, R., 422
Currie, D., 64, 68, 415
Curry, T. J., 60, 435

D

Dailard, C., 188, 415
Daley, P. C., 415
Dalton, S. E., 172, 415
Daly, K., 280, 415
Daly, M., 236, 237, 240, 254, 270, 386, 387, 391, 415
Daniels, A. K., 434
Daniels, C. R., 203, 415
Darcy, R., 323, 327, 415
Data Essay, 415
Daubman, K. A., 434
Davaney, S. G., 420
Davidman, L., 243*f*, 257, 415
Davies, K., 40, 417
Davies, M., 415
Davis, A., 84, 111*t*, 178, 218, 415
Davis, K. E., 274, 415, 432
Davis, S. N., 61, 415
Davis-Blake, A., 410
Davis-Frenzel, E., 433
Decker, J., 430
DeCoster, S., 266, 420
Defey, D., 88, 415
Deitz, S. R., 415
Delaney, J., 86, 415

Dellinger, K., 45, 415
DeLuca, L., 430
Demarest, J., 206, 415
Dembo, R., 267, 415
D'Emilio, J., 78, 96, 102, 415, 418
DeNavas-Walt, C., 3, 105, 131, 138, 415
Dentinger, E., 42, 415
Deschenes, E. P., 417
de Tocqueville, A., 354, 360, 415
De Troy, C., 432
DeVault, M. L., 114, 415
Dewar, D. M., 214, 415
De Welde, K., 415
Diamond, M., 23, 415
Diamond, P. M., 428
Diaz, O., 415
Dickens, W. J., 94, 416
Dickerson-Putnam, J., 88, 416
DiClementi, J. D., 414
Dietz, N. A., 416
Dietz, T. L., 40, 416
Dill, B. T., 107, 176, 179, 180, 340, 391, 392, 393, 410, 416
Dines, G., 62, 74
DiPrete, T., 89, 135, 416, 426
Di Santo, A., 255, 416
Dobash, R., 108, 157, 183, 278, 416
Dobash, R. E., 108, 157, 183, 278, 416
Dodson, J. E., 248, 416
Doell, R., 309, 424
Donegan, J., 222, 416
Donnelly, B. W., 170, 435
Donnelly, D., 103
Donnenwerth, G. V., 235, 429
Donnerstein, E., 63, 416
Douglas, A., 238, 416
Downey, J. A., 421
Dreier, P., 128, 409
DuBois, E. C., 335, 361, 376, 416
Dudley, R. L., 247, 416
Due, L., 52
Dugger, K., 32, 416
Dujon, D., 139, 416
Durbin, S., 135, 416
Dworkin, A., 236, 237, 416
Dye, N. S., 219, 220, 221, 376, 416

E

Eaton, W. W., 428
Eder, D., 294, 313, 416

Edin, K., 138, 416
Edleson, J. L., 285
Ehrenreich, B., 79, 109, 113, 151–152, 158, 200, 220, 223, 227, 252, 416
Ehrenreich, J. H., 282, 426
Ehrhardt, A. A., 23, 24, 427
Eigenberg, H. M., 282, 411
Eisenstein, Z., 351*f*, 368–369, 372, 381, 386, 416
Eitzen, D. S., 44, 107, 108, 159, 161, 163, 164, 165, 179, 180, 195, 410
Ellison, C. G., 242, 416
Ellison, L., 416
Embser-Herbert, M. S., 60, 413
Emerson, R. A., 64, 416
Emery, J. L., 434
Emmet, T., 290, 416
Emohivich, C., 80
Engels, F., 115, 379, 380, 382–383, 402, 416, 425
England, P., 422
English, D., 109, 113, 158, 200, 220, 223, 227, 416
Enloe, C., 331, 346, 416
Enos, S., 281, 282, 417
Epstein, C., 124, 321, 417
Esbensen, F-A., 266, 417, 429
Espin, O. M., 85, 417
Espiritu, Y. L., 85, 106, 417
Esposito, J. L., 258
Evans, C. C., 313, 416
Evans, L., 40, 417
Evans, O., 201, 417
Evans, S., 338, 339, 340, 341, 417, 435
Ex, C. T. G. M., 39, 417

F

Falk, N., 235, 417
Falk, W., 412
Faludi, S., 342, 417
Farber, N., 188
Farkas, G., 422
Farnham, M., 360, 425
Farrell, M. P., 172, 421
Fausto-Sterling, A., 24, 26, 30, 52, 86, 88, 395, 417
Federal Bureau of Investigation, 267, 268*t*, 274, 417
Fee, E., 307, 417

Feit, M., 430
Feldberg, R. L., 126, 417
Fenstermaker, S., 18, 45, 435
Feracuti, F., 277, 436
Ferber, A. L., 99, 417
Ferguson, A. A., 294, 314
Fernandez, G., 415
Fernea, E. W., 233, 250, 417
Ferraro, K. F., 273, 417
Ferree, M. M., 337, 346, 417
Fetner, T., 96, 417
Feuerbach, L., 377
Field, D., 94, 417
Fields, J., 154, 166, 417
Findlen, B., 52
Fine, M., 118, 314, 417
Fineran, S., 302, 417
Finkelhor, D., 185, 436
Finlay, B., 83, 247, 417
Firestein, B., 96, 417
Firestone, J. M., 39, 133, 330, 417,
  420
Fischbach, R. L., 185, 417
Fisher, B. S., 274, 275f, 417
Fitzgerald, L. F., 414
Flavin, J., 280, 418
Flax, J., 395, 418
Flexner, E., 221, 334, 336, 418
Flowers, R. B., 244, 248, 418
Folbre, N., 193, 418
Foltz, T. G., 255, 418
Forcey, L. R., 419
Forsythe, C. J., 282, 418
Foucault, M., 157, 418
Fox, B., 126, 418
Fox, M. F., 305, 418
Francis, L. J., 244
Frankfurter, F., 205
Fraser, N., 394, 395, 418
Frazier, E. F., 177, 178, 249, 418
Freedman, E. B., 78, 102, 346, 418
Freeman, J., 341, 418
Freese, J., 432
Fremont, A. M., 145, 411
Freund, K., 91t, 418
Fried, A., 276, 418
Friedan, B., 338
Friedl, E., 278, 418
Frieze, I. H., 185, 415, 418
Frohmann, L., 279, 418
Fromme, R. E., 80
Frye, M., 8, 9, 372, 418

Fujimoto, T., 145, 419
Fullerton, H. N., Jr., 119, 418
Fullerton, J. A., 60, 418
Furnham, A., 38, 60, 418

G
Gager, C. T., 145
Gagne, P., 24, 418
Gagnon, J., 97, 418
Gagnon, J. H., 83f, 91t, 102, 424,
  432
Gallagher, S. K., 145–146, 234,
  235, 250–251, 257, 418, 419
Gallup, G., Jr., 418
Gallup Organization, 160f
Gallup Poll, 80, 217, 418
Gamson, J., 63, 96, 418
Ganahl, D. J., 60, 63, 418
Garcia, E., 432
Garey, A. I., 195
Garfinkle, E. M., 34, 427
Garnier, H., 435
Gartner, R., 282, 423
Gasson, L., 38, 418
Geer, J. H., 434
General Social Survey, 324, 418
Genovese, E., 107, 178, 241, 419
Gerbner, G., 64
Gerschick, T. J., 213, 419
Gerson, K., 169, 419
Gerstel, N., 128, 145–146, 419
Geschwender, J., 37, 130, 419
Giannarelli, L., 191, 191f, 419
Gibson, D., 43, 419
Gibson, R. C., 43, 52, 88, 433
Giddens, A., 377, 378, 380, 419
Gilkes, C. T., 245, 246, 248, 249,
  257, 332, 340, 356, 416, 419
Gilligan, C., 12, 327–328, 419
Ginorio, A., 298, 419
Gitlin, T., 61, 419
Glass, J., 145, 419
Glass Ceiling Commission, 3,
  135, 419
Glenn, E. N., 109, 126, 173, 181,
  417, 419
Gluckman, A., 91t, 98, 419
Goetting, A., 18
Gold, J. A., 102, 412
Gooding, S., 426
Gordon, L., 216, 218, 419
Gordon, R., 237, 409

Gordy, L. K., 60, 419
Gornick, V., 303, 419
Gossett, J. L., 63, 419
Gotanda, N., 414
Gough, K., 159, 419
Gouldner, H., 94, 419
Gow, J., 55, 419
Grall, T., 192
Grant, J., 246, 419
Grasmuck, S., 120, 419
Grattet, R., 99, 422
Gray, J., 58, 419
Greene, B., 35, 419
Greene, M., 288, 419
Greene, S., 419
Greer, K. R., 282, 419
Gregoire, T. K., 42, 419
Greif, G. L., 176, 419
Grella, C. E., 168, 419
Griffin, J. M., 201, 420
Groves, M. M., 170, 420
Guide, J., 415
Gupta, R., 145, 180, 432
Gutman, H., 177, 420
Alan Guttmacher Institute, 189,
  216, 217

H
Haag, P., 293, 420
Haddad, Y. Y., 258
Hagan, J., 125, 422
Hager, M. A., 234, 420
Halek, C., 414
Hall, E. J., 343, 420
Hall, J. A., 425
Hall, R. M., 302, 420
Hallinan, M. T., 292, 423
Hamer, D. H., 97, 420
Hamer, J., 176, 195, 420
Hamilton, J. A., 423
Hampton, R. L., 185, 420
Hans, V. P., 280, 420
Hansen, K. V., 195
Hanson, S. L., 298, 420
Harding, S., 307–308, 310, 311,
  314, 387, 420
Hargrove, B., 237, 245, 255, 420
Harland, M., 154, 420
Harrell, M. C., 330, 420
Harris, C., 422
Harris, R. J., 39, 330, 417, 420
Harris, T. R., 436

Harrison, J., 22, 420
Harrison, P. M., 280, 420
Hart, K., 207, 420
Hartmann, H., 108, 187, 383, 388–389, 420
Hartsock, N., 310, 420
Harvey, W. B., 420
Haugaard, J. J., 275*f*, 420
Haveman, H. A., 414
Hawkins, R. A., 26, 420
Hayes, A., 429
Hays, S., 138, 152, 420
Hebert, C., 321, 433
Heimer, K., 266, 420
Heitfield, H., 282, 420
Helwig, A. A., 39, 420
Hemmens, C., 420
Henderson, D. J., 210, 420
Henderson, J., 425
Henley, N., 13, 420
Hennig, K., 185, 421
Henretta, J. C., 42, 428
Hensley, C., 282, 421
Hequembourg, A. L., 172, 421
Herbert, B., 185, 417
Herman, J., 186, 187, 421
Hermson, J. M., 414
Hernandez, D., 343, 402, 421
Hernandez, J., 187, 421
Herrera-Sobek, M., 314
Herring, C., 61, 421
Herring, F., 427
Herrnstein, R. J., 262, 436
Hess, B., 42, 337, 417
Hesse-Biber, S., 207, 421
Heyer-Gray, Z. A., 245, 421
Higginbotham, E., 124, 134, 152, 421, 435
Higham, J., 112, 261, 421
Higher Education Research Institute, University of California at Los Angeles, 82*f*
Hill, A. C., 204, 205, 421
Hill, M., 360, 421
Hill, S. A., 37, 179, 421
Himmelstein, J. L., 252, 421
Hine, D. C., 333
Hipple, J., 118, 421
Hirschman, L., 186, 421
Hochschild, A. R., 114, 115, 143, 152, 169, 421
Hoecker-Drysdale, S., 360, 421

Hoffman, T., 235, 247, 421
Hoffnung, M., 3, 421
Hofmeister, H., 242, 410, 427
Hole, J., 239, 335, 338, 421
Holleran, D., 433
Holsinger, K., 266, 421
Hondagneu-Sotelo, P., 18, 37, 109, 116, 120, 129, 130, 145, 152, 180, 391–392, 410, 421
hooks, b., 74
Horm-Wingerd, D. M., 170, 420
Horowitz, R., 189, 421
Horton, H. D., 421
Horton, R., 91*t*, 209, 421
Hosken, F. P., 29, 421
Hovespan, M., 92, 411
Hoyenga, K., 22, 26, 421
Hoyenga, K. B., 22, 26, 421
Hoyt, D. R., 434
Hu, N., 420
Hu, S., 420
Hubbard, R., 307, 421
Hughes, H. S., 354, 421
Hughes, M. E., 435
Hull, K. E., 124, 421
Humez, J. M., 62, 74
Hummer, R. A., 276, 425
Humphrey, H., 414
Hunt, L. L., 242, 421
Huston, M., 298, 419
Hutchison, B., 213, 433

I

Illich, I., 158, 421
Infante, P., 204, 421
Ingram-Fogel, C., 282, 421
Institute for Women's Policy Research, 138, 422
Irvine, J. M., 102

J

Jackson, N-A., 171, 422
Jacobs, J. A., 148, 422
Jacobs, J. L., 255, 422
Jacobson, D., 29, 422
Jaggar, A. M., 372
Janssens, J. M. A. M., 39, 417
Janus, C. L., 98, 422
Janus, S. S., 98, 422
Jasinksi, J. L., 183, 196, 422
Jelen, T. G., 247, 422
Jenkins, P., 204, 422

Jenness, V., 99, 422
Joe, K. A., 266, 422
Johnson, K., 34, 83, 410
Johnson, V. E., 81, 425
Jones, J., 107, 422
Jones, J. M., 324, 422
Jordan, W., 241, 422
Jordan-Simmons, K. M., 82, 422
Joughin, N., 414
Joyner, K., 171, 412
Jurik, N. C., 413

K

Kahane, L. H., 217, 422
Kahn, A. S., 423
Kalmijn, M., 175, 422
Kalof, L., 55, 64, 422
Kaluzny, G., 428
Kamin, L. J., 262, 422
Kamo, Y., 145
Kanter, R. M., 126, 139–141, 302, 422
Kantor, G. K., 183, 422
Kaplan, E. B., 188, 196, 422
Kapp, Y., 378, 422
Karides, M., 427
Karraker, K.H., 435
Katzman, D., 178, 422
Kaufman, D. R., 258
Kaufman, G., 60, 422
Kay, F. M., 125, 422
Kearney, M. H., 210, 422
Keelan, J. P. R., 94, 410
Keith, S., 425
Keith, V., 421
Keith, V. M., 145, 430
Keller, E. F., 305, 422
Keller, R. S., 239, 430
Kelly, J., 175, 410
Kelly-Gadol, J., 12, 355, 368, 422
Kemp, A. A., 204, 422
Kendrick, A., 60, 418
Kennedy, R., 422
Kennelly, I., 132, 422
Kenny, M. E., 207, 420
Kessler-Harris, A., 106, 110, 422
Khanna, N. D., 92, 422
Kibria, N., 162, 422
Kilbourne, B. S., 133, 422
Kilbourne, J., 74
Killian, L. M., 334, 434
Kilty, K., 419

Kim, J. E., 427
Kimmel, M. S., 13, 46, 63, 90, 328, 409, 410, 423
King, J. E., 299*t*, 300, 423
King, M. C., 142, 410
Kirschenman, J., 132, 423, 428
Kirton, G., 128, 423
Kitzinger, C. A., 399, 423
Klatch, R., 251, 423
Kleck, G., 279, 423
Klein, D., 261, 423
Kleinbaum, A. R., 356, 423
Klinger, L. J., 61, 423
Kluckhohn, C., 27, 423
Knox, G. W., 263, 423
Koch, P. B., 425
Kohlberg, L., 45, 423
Kolata, G., 83*f*, 102
Konrad, M., 430
Koons-Witt, B. A., 280, 423
Korabik, K., 141, 428
Koss, M. P., 276, 423
Kraus, R. S., 298, 420
Kruttschnitt, C., 282, 423
Kubitschek, W. N., 292, 423
Kurtz, S. P., 423
Kurz, D., 168, 185, 196, 423

L

Ladner, J. A., 35, 189, 423
La France, M., 29, 423
Lai, T., 180, 423
Lake, M. A., 435
Lakeland, M. J., 233, 250, 258, 426
Lakkis, J., 206, 423
Lambert, L. C., 417
Lambert, T. A., 82, 423
Lamphere, L., 142, 146, 423
Landers, A., 63, 423
Langhinrichsen-Rohling, J., 423, 427
Larson, M. S., 61, 424
Laslett, B., 424
Laumann, E. O., 79, 83*f*, 98, 102, 424
Leacock, E., 115, 147
Leaper, C., 29, 58, 409
Lee, J., 87, 138, 424
Lehman, E. C., Jr., 247, 424
Lehmann, J. M., 196
Lein, L., 138, 416

Leitenberg, H., 421
Lemelle, A. J., Jr., 83, 410
Lemert, E., 264, 424
Lennon, R., 200, 414
Leong, R., 85, 424
Lerman, R. I., 176, 424
Lerner, G., 12, 355, 424
Leukefeld, C., 424
Levine, E., 239, 335, 338, 421
Lewin-Epstein, N., 145
Lewis, G. B., 83, 91*t*, 424
Lewis, R., 430
Lim, I-S., 120, 424
Lim, S. G-L., 314
Limbaugh, H. R. III, 5, 424
Lin, C. A., 60
Lindsey, E. W., 21, 39, 424
Linstead, S., 265, 412
Linz, D., 63, 416
Lipset, S. M., 360, 424
Litoff, J. B., 221, 424
Lock, M., 30, 88, 424
Logan, T. K., 424
Logio, K., 35, 211, 424
Logue, B. J., 42, 424
Lombardo, W. K., 29, 424
Lombroso, N., 261, 424
Longie, E., 181, 431
Longino, H., 309, 424
Lopata, H. Z., 32, 424
Lorber, J., 28, 174, 175, 372, 424
Loscocco, K. A., 200, 424
Lott, B., 430
Loucky, J., 435
Louie, M. C. Y., 128
Lucal, B., 116, 424
Lucas, S. R., 292, 424
Luckmann, T., 31, 71, 410
Lukemeyer, A., 191, 424
Luker, K., 189, 251, 252, 424
Lummis, A. T., 247, 424
Lundberg, F., 360, 425
Lupton, M. J., 415
Lye, D. N., 171, 425

M

MacCorquodale, P. L., 189, 425
Machiavelli, N., 308
Machung, A., 126, 425
MacKinnon, C., 320, 346, 387, 425

MacLeod, M., 57, 414
Madriz, E., 273, 284, 425
Magnuson, V. L., 420
Mahoney, P., 185, 186, 425
Majete, C. A., 92, 425
Mak, T., 60, 418
Malat, J., 425
Malcolm, E. R., 325, 425
Malleson, K., 321, 425
Maney, A. C., 427
Mannheim, K., 425
Manning, W. D., 431
Mansfield, P. K., 141, 425
Marcus-Mendoza, S. T., 281, 432
Markens, S., 86, 425
Markson, E. W., 42, 63, 425
Marquart, J. W., 428
Marshall, N. L., 145, 425
Marsiglio, W., 176, 425
Martin, E., 308, 326, 425
Martin, P. Y., 32, 276, 321, 346, 425, 432
Martin, S. S., 211, 425
Martineau, H., 360–361, 361–362, 425
Marx, G., 248, 425
Marx, K., 115, 380, 381, 425
Mason, C. A., 267, 435
Mason, S. M., 434
Massoni, K., 61, 425
Mast, M. S., 425
Masters, W. H., 81, 425
Matthaei, J. A., 106, 107, 108, 151, 409
Mattingly, M. J., 145, 411
Maume, D. J., Jr., 135, 145, 410, 425
May, D. C., 273, 425
McCammon, H. J., 203, 425
McCartney, S., 415
McCloskey, L. A., 185, 426
McCluskey, S. E., 434
McComb, C., 168, 426
McCrate, E., 138, 426
McFarlane, J., 426
McGuffey, C. S., 39, 426
McGuire, G. M., 132, 426
McGuire, M. B., 240, 243*f*, 245, 426
McIntosh, P., 13, 426
McKinney, K., 142, 426

McMannon, T. J., 288, 426
McManus, B., 89, 429
McManus, P. A., 426
McNelles, L. R., 93, 426
McQueeney, K. B., 172, 426
McQuiade, S., 282, 426
Mead, M., 215, 426
Mechanic, M. B., 426
Meier, R. F., 279, 429
Meigs, C. D., 290, 426
Melosh, B., 142, 426
Mendelsohn, E., 310, 426
Mernissi, F., 233, 237, 250, 258, 426
Mertz, E., 124, 426
Messerschmidt, J. W., 266, 271, 285, 426
Messing, K., 309, 426
Messner, M. A., 13, 18, 32, 45, 90, 385, 391–392, 410, 423, 426
Meyer, D. R., 138, 413
Meyer, J., 99, 426
Meyer, M. H., 214, 426
Meyers, M. K., 424
Michael, R. T., 83f, 102, 424
Michaels, S., 424
Michalowski, R., 265, 436
Middlebrook, D., 45, 427
Mieczkowski, T., 420
Milkie, M. A., 64, 170, 411, 427, 429
Mill, H. T., 365–366
Mill, J. S., 363–364, 365–366, 367, 368, 427
Miller, A., 423
Miller, A. S., 213, 419
Miller, D., 181, 427
Miller, E., 269–270, 427
Miller, J., 427, 429
Miller, J. B., 238, 427
Miller, S., 184, 427
Miller, S. L., 285
Millman, M., 208
Mills, C. W., 7, 303, 427
Mills, R. J., 415
Milner, J. S., 187, 427
Min, P. G., 265, 427
Minnich, E. K., 14, 427
Mirandè, A., 179, 427, 433
Mir-Hosseini, Z., 233, 427
Mishel, L., 3, 134, 143, 427
Misra, J., 63, 427

Mitchell, G., 38, 427
Mitchell, J., 384, 402–403, 427
Mize, J., 21, 424
Modleski, T., 65, 427
Moen, P., 42, 143, 169, 410, 427
Mohr, J., 217, 218, 271, 427
Moller, S., 427
Money, J., 23, 24, 95, 96, 427
Mongeau, B., 221, 427
Monson, C. M., 185, 427
Montgomery, S. M., 411
Mooney, L. A., 40, 412
Moore, D. W., 99, 171, 324, 422, 427
Moore, G., 325, 427
Moore, J., 427
Moorti, S., 63, 427
Moraga, C., 391, 392, 427
Morash, M., 281
Morgan, L. A., 42, 428
Morgan, S., 346
Morgen, S., 227, 230, 333, 411, 428
Morin, S. F., 34, 427
Morris, L., 414
Moss, N. E., 201, 428
Moss, P., 132, 428
Mulkey, L. M., 413
Mullings, J. L., 210, 281, 428
Munoz, C., 432
Muntaner, C., 428
Murillo, N., 179
Murinen, S. K., 302, 428
Murphy, S., 210, 422, 431
Myers, D., 120, 428

N

Nadell, P. S., 432
Naff, K. C., 135
Nagel, J., 85, 102, 428
Nanda, S., 28, 29, 52, 428
Naples, N. A., 173, 332, 395, 418, 428
Nardi, P. M., 102, 267, 428
Nason-Clark, N., 247, 428
National Center for Education Statistics, 288, 289f, 298, 305f, 428
National Center for Health Statistics, 5, 198, 199, 199f, 200, 201f, 202, 203, 206, 207f, 209, 211, 211f, 212, 213, 214, 226, 428

Neckerman, K. M., 132, 423, 428
Negrey, C., 145, 432
Neilson, L. C., 321, 428
Neitz, M. J., 255, 428
Nelson, A., 186, 428
Nelson, F., 172, 428
Nesbitt, P. D., 247, 424
Netemeyer, R. G., 434
Netzley, S. B., 418
Newport, F., 28
Nicholson, L. E., 394, 395–396, 428
Nisbet, R., 354, 428
Njogu, W., 426
Nock, S. L., 171, 428
Nogrady, C. A., 432
Novkov, J., 203, 428
Nowicki, S., Jr., 94, 436
Ntiri, D. W., 138, 428

O

Oakes, J., 432
Oakey, R. E., 26, 420
Oakley, A., 215, 428
Obradovich, S., 427
O'Campo, P., 201, 428
O'Connell, C., 141, 428
O'Kelly, C. G., 115, 428
Olesen, V. L., 230, 231, 431
Oliver, P., 186, 428
Olsen, L., 292, 298, 428
Ooms, T. J., 176, 424
O'Rand, A. M., 42, 428
Ovadia, S., 414
Owen, B., 411

P

Pacheco, K., 415
Padavic, I., 4, 128, 129, 152, 428, 429, 430
Palmer, P., 112, 429
Park, J. Z., 234, 429
Parker, S., 313, 416
Pattatucci, A. M. L., 420
Patterson, C. J., 172, 429
Paul, E. L., 82, 429
Paul, M., 415
Pavalko, E. K., 200, 214, 426, 429
Pear, R., 198, 307, 429
Pedraza, S., 120, 429
Peller, G., 414
Peltola, P., 170, 343, 427, 429

Peralta, R., 210, 429
Peres, Y., 170, 429
Perlman, D., 94, 416
Perry, I., 62, 429
Pessar, P., 120, 419
Petchesky, R., 215, 219, 429
Petersen, L. R., 429
Peterson, D., 429
Peterson, R. D., 235
Peterson, R. R., 89, 429
Pettit, G. S., 424
Pharr, S., 34, 429
Phillips, L., 41, 293, 295, 429
Pierce, J., 298, 410
Pierce, J. L., 44, 124, 175, 429, 432
Pino, N. W., 279, 429
Plaskow, J., 252–253, 413
Plummer, K., 96, 398, 433
Pohli, C. V., 244, 429
Pollak, O., 262, 429
Pollock, J., 428
Porter, J. L., 135, 429
Poston, C., 358, 429
Powell, B., 432
Powell, K., 61, 429
Powers, B-A., 94, 429
Powers, M., 86, 429
Press, E., 127, 429
Presser, H. B., 170, 429
Presser, S., 429
Preves, S. E., 24, 429
Price, B. R., 285
Priestley, A., 265, 435
Prinsen, T. J., 418
Proctor, B. D., 415
Pyke, K. D., 89, 162, 429
Pyle, J. L., 265, 429

Q

Quillian, L., 92, 429
Quinn, D. M., 433

R

Raag, T., 39, 430
Rackliff, C. L., 39, 430
Radway, J., 59, 430
Raeburn, N. C., 97, 99, 434
Rahman, A., 415
Ramiresx-Garmica, G., 415
Rapp, R., 164, 430
Reagon, B. J., 233, 430
Reddick, R., 179, 436

Redhorse, J. G., 181, 430
Reed, B., 91*t*, 98, 419
Reeder, H. M., 94, 430
Rehman, B., 343, 402, 421
Reid, L. L., 136, 430
Reilly, M. E., 280, 430
Reinhardt, J. S., 434
Reinharz, S., 224, 311, 430
Reitz, R., 87, 430
Renzetti, C. M., 185, 276, 285, 409, 430
Repak, T. A., 120, 129, 430
Resick, P. A., 426
Reskin, B. F., 4, 121, 128, 132, 134, 152, 429, 430
Reuther, R. R., 239, 253, 254, 430
Reviere, R., 282, 436
Reynolds, J. R., 425
Ricciardelli, L. A., 423
Rich, A., 6, 81, 173, 430
Rich, B. L., 39, 426
Rich, M. K., 55, 430
Richards, A., 18
Richardson, V. E., 42, 419, 430
Richie, B. E., 270–271, 285, 430
Riday, J. D., 430
Ridgeway, C. L., 135, 430
Riesebrodt, M., 250, 430
Riley, A. L., 145, 430
Risman, B., 32, 176, 430
Rist, D. Y., 97, 430
Robbins, C., 211, 425
Roberts, D., 203, 216, 217, 218, 219, 225, 230, 430
Robinson, B. E., 175
Robinson, D. T., 29, 431
Robinson, J. P., 411
Robison, J., 334, 431
Rodriguez, M. S., 343, 420
Rodriquez, C. E., 74
Roesch, S. C., 424
Roger, M., 434
Rollins, J., 108, 130, 431
Romero, M., 109, 431
Roos, P., 134, 430
Root, M. P. P., 431
Roper Organization, 3, 35, 36*f*, 415, 431
Rorvik, D. M., 308

Rosen, R., 346
Rosenau, P. M., 396, 431
Rosenbaum, M., 422
Rosenberg, R., 290, 431
Rosenblum, B., 230
Rosofsky, R., 415
Ross, E., 164, 430
Ross, J., 171, 431
Ross-Durow, P. L., 210, 431
Rossi, A., 301–302, 308, 354, 358, 360, 362, 363, 365–366, 372, 376, 424, 431
Rossiter, M., 306, 431
Rothblum, E. D., 412
Rothenberg, P. S., 372, 403
Rothman, B. K., 52, 224, 225, 231, 431
Rothschild, M. A., 339, 431
Rousey, A., 181, 431
Rowlingson, K., 435
Rubin, G., 386, 387, 431
Rupp, L., 337, 431
Russell, D. E. H., 186, 431
Rust, P., 91*t*, 96, 97, 431
Rutter, V., 91*t*, 95, 102, 432
Ruzek, S. B., 214, 215, 227, 228, 231, 431
Ryan, C., 412
Ryan, R., 185, 431
Ryckman, R. M., 412

S

Saad, L., 4*f*, 8*f*, 136, 334, 351*f*, 357*f*, 431
Sacks, K., 110, 385, 431
Sadker, D., 40, 41, 57, 291, 292, 294, 314, 431
Sadker, M., 40, 41, 57, 291, 292, 294, 314, 431
Saguy, A. C., 234, 431
Saiving, V., 254, 431
Sales, P., 210, 431
Sanchez, L., 171, 431
Sanchez-Ayendez, M., 94, 431
Sanday, P. R., 275*f*, 278, 431
Sanderson, M., 415
Sandnabba, K. N., 39, 431
Santiago-Santiago, I., 432
Santos, A., 432
Sargent, C. F., 161, 412
Sassler, S., 170, 432

Sayer, L. C., 411
Sayers, S. L., 34, 432
Sayles, S., 279, 423
Sayre, A., 306, 432
Scanlan, A. R., 432
Schlegel, E., 420
Schmeidler, J., 415
Schmid, J., 55, 142, 412
Schmidt, J. M., 420
Schmidt, K. J., 432
Schmitt, F. E., 276, 432
Schmitt, J., 427
Schneider, B., 102, 142, 267, 428, 432
Schneider, B. E., 212, 213, 231, 432
Schnittker, J., 343, 432
Scholler, R., 434
Scholten, C. M., 220, 221, 432
Schwartz, M. D., 432
Schwartz, P., 91*t*, 95, 102, 411, 432
Sciaraffa, M. A., 38, 413
Scott, J., 234, 432
Scott, J. W., 106, 108, 109, 157, 434
Scully, D., 277, 432
Secada, M. S., 298, 432
Sedgwick, P., 414
Segal, D. R., 412
Segura, D. A., 44, 175, 179, 432
Seidman, S., 96, 103, 397, 398, 403, 432
Seltzer, J. A., 170, 432
Seri, L. G., 275*f*, 420
Shange, N., 254, 432
Sharp, S. F., 281, 432
Sheppard, G. T., 247, 410
Shifman, P., 265, 432
Shilts, R., 346
Sigmundson, H. K., 23, 415
Signorielli, N., 60, 61, 432
Silverstein, L. B., 175, 432
Simmons, W. W., 326*f*, 432
Simon, R. J., 247, 282, 420, 432
Simon, W., 91*t*, 432
Simonds, W., 103
Sirianni, C., 145, 432
Siwatu, M. S., 94, 432
Skirboll, E., 170, 432
Sklar, H., 118, 432
Slashinski, M. J., 432
Slavin, R., 432

Slevin, K. F., 42, 52, 413, 433
Sloan, J. J. III, 417
Sloat, L. J., 55, 433
Smart, C., 262, 433
Smeeding, T., 424
Smith, B., 91*t*, 433
Smith, B. G., 213, 433
Smith, C., 235, 418
Smith, D. E., 45, 70, 302–303, 309, 310, 311, 314, 433
Smith, H., 135, 138, 433
Smith, H. L., 427
Smith, J., 426
Smith, K., 190*f*, 433
Smith-Lovin, L., 29, 431
Smith-Rosenberg, C., 433
Smock, P. J., 431
Smolak, L., 302, 428
Sokoloff, N. J., 285
Songer, D. R., 321, 433
Sorenson, E., 176, 424
Spade, J. Z., 275*f*, 412
Spain, D., 170, 433
Spencer, S. J., 293, 433
Spitze, G., 89, 200, 424, 433
Spohn, C., 279, 433
Sprague, J., 37, 179, 421
Spretnak, C., 255, 258, 433
Sprock, J., 34, 433
Stacey, J., 91*t*, 98, 172, 433
Stack, C., 161, 179, 433
Stack, C. B., 433
Stanton, E. C., 233, 433
Staples, R., 178, 179, 433
Steele, C. M., 292, 433
Steffensmeier, D., 321, 433
Stein, A., 96, 398, 433
Stein, D. K., 29, 433
Steinberg, R. J., 148, 422, 433
Stellman, J. M., 203, 433
Steptoe, A., 201, 417
Sterling, A., 334, 355, 361, 371, 372, 433
Stiehm, J. H., 347
Stier, H., 145
Stohs, J. H., 145, 433
Stoller, E. P., 43, 52, 88, 433
Stoller, N. E., 212, 213, 231, 282, 432, 433
Stombler, M., 103
Stone, V., 66
Storch, E., 415

Strazdins, L., 145, 434
Strom, K., 420
Strong, S. M., 94, 206, 434
Sugiman, P., 126, 418
Sullivan, D. A., 224, 434
Sullivan, M., 172, 434
Summers, Lawrence, 287
Swan, S., 414
Symons, M., 419
Szasz, T., 237, 434

T
Takaki, R., 92, 106, 180, 181, 434
Tam, T., 133, 434
Taylor, C. A., 63, 425
Taylor, R., 170, 432
Taylor, V., 97, 99, 337, 431, 434
Tea, N. T., 26, 434
Teachman, J. D., 166, 434
Tedrow, L. M., 434
Tenenbaum, S., 257
Tewksbury, R., 24, 418, 421
The Waterglass, 324*f*, 434
Thoennes, N., 3, 183, 183*t*, 184, 185, 274, 434
Thomas, J. J., 434
Thomas, K., 414
Thomas, S., 135
Thomas, W. I., 261
Thompson, B. W., 35, 207, 208, 231, 434
Thompson, T. L., 40, 434
Thorne, B., 32, 40, 52, 164, 292, 293, 314, 418, 424, 434
Thornton, A., 171, 434
Thornton, B., 412
Tichenor, V. J., 89, 170, 434
Tierney, A. M., 432
Tillich, P., 234, 434
Tilly, C., 132, 428
Tilly, L. A., 106, 108, 109, 157, 434
Tjaden, P., 3, 183, 183*t*, 184, 185, 274, 434
Tonry, M., 415
Toth, E., 415
Tovèe, E. M., 434
Tovèe, M. J., 54, 434
Trafimow, D., 321, 413
Tromborg, C., 427
Truth, S., 335

Tuan, Y-F., 85, 434
Tuchman, G., 64, 65, 66, 67, 434
Tucker, R., 70, 379, 381, 434
Tuominen, M., 190, 435
Turner, M. G., 275*f*, 417
Turner, R., 334, 434
Turner, T., 421
Turner-Bowker, D. M., 40
Tyler, K. A., 276, 434

U

Ullman, S., 263
UNICEF, 287, 435
United Nations, 177*t*
University of California at Los
   Angeles Higher Education
   Research Institute, 82*f*
U.S. Census Bureau, 59, 87, 92,
   105, 120, 131*f*, 132*f*, 137*f*, 139,
   144, 165*f*, 166, 167*f*, 168, 187,
   191, 247, 434
U.S. Department of Defense,
   329, 415, 434
U.S. Department of Health and
   Human Services, 434
U.S. Department of Labor, 3,
   111*t*, 119, 120*f*, 121, 122*f*, 123*f*,
   124, 125, 128, 129, 130, 187,
   192, 227, 246, 306*f*, 321, 434
Uttal, L., 190, 435

V

Valdez, A., 266, 413
Van Den Daele, W., 309, 435
Vanek, J. A., 109, 146, 435
Vanneman, R., 116, 414, 435
Vicary, J. R., 425
Vidmar, N., 280, 420
Vigorito, A. J., 60, 435
Villari, S., 102
Virginia Slims, 36*f*
Vogel, D. A., 38, 435
Vogeltanz, N. D., 436
Voydanoff, P., 170, 435

W

Waldo, C., 414
Waldron, I., 171, 200, 425, 435
Walker, B., 424
Walker, R., 19, 343, 435
Walker, S., 92
Walker-Barnes, C. J., 267, 435

Wallace, R. A., 245, 246,
   247, 435
Wallerstein, I., 354, 435
Walsh, A., 91*t*, 226, 435
Walters, S., 68, 435
Walther, C. S., 83, 417
Walzer, S., 175, 435
Ward, K. B., 265, 429
Wardle, R. M., 360, 435
Warren, T., 42, 435
Watson, J. D., 435
Watson, R. J., 91*t*, 418
Watterson, K., 285
Weatherall, A., 265, 435
Weaver, T. L., 426
Weber, L., 134, 435
Wechsler, H., 209, 435
Weingart, P., 426
Weir, D., 422
Weis, L., 118, 314, 417
Weisner, T. S., 38, 435
Weiss, C. C., 435
Weitz, R., 224, 231, 434
Weitzman, L., 89, 435
Welch, S., 415
Welsh, S., 302, 435
Welter, B., 238, 435
Wertz, D. C., 219, 220, 221, 223,
   435
Wertz, R. W., 219, 220, 221, 223,
   435
West, C. M., 45, 185, 414, 435
West, J., 265, 435
Westkott, M., 303, 435
Whitbeck, L. B., 434
Whiteley, R., 426
Whitley, B. E., 83, 436
Whittier, N., 342, 343, 436
Whyley, C., 435
Wilcox, C., 244, 329, 436
Wilkie, J. R., 162, 436
Wilkinson, S., 399, 423
Willemsen, T. M., 132, 436
Williams, C., 152
Williams, C. L., 45, 415
Williams, D., 185, 186,
   203, 436
Williams, D. R., 248, 436
Williams, L. M., 196, 425
Williams, P., 347
Williams, R. J., 423
Williamson, D. A., 434

Willie, C. V., 179, 436
Willson, P., 436
Wilsnack, R. W., 209, 436
Wilsnack, S. C., 436
Wilson, J. Q., 262, 436
Wilson, W. J., 436
Winfree, T. L., Jr., 417
Wingrove, C. R., 42, 433
Winseman, A. L., 243*f*, 244,
   244*f*, 436
Winterich, J. A., 88, 436
Withorn, A., 139, 416
Wolak, J., 185, 436
Wolf, M., 161, 436
Wolf, N., 75
Wolfe, D., 162, 411
Wolff, K.H., 303, 436
Wolfgang, M., 277, 436
Wollstonecraft, M., 358, 359–360,
   436
Wonders, N. A., 265, 436
Wong, A. K., 29, 436
Woo, D., 180, 436
Woodbury, S., 200, 429
World Health Organization,
   212*t*, 213, 436
Wright, C., 428
Wright, E. O., 135, 410
Wright, L. W., Jr., 414
Wright, M. J., 116, 204, 436
Wrong, D., 33, 436

Y

Yalom, M., 434
Yates, G. G., 254, 436
Yaughn, E., 94, 436
Yllo, K., 186, 436
Yoder, C. Y., 34, 433
Yoder, J. D., 140, 436
Young, E. W., 425
Young, V. D., 282, 436

Z

Zaretsky, E., 158, 385, 436
Zavella, P., 142, 436
Zeitlin, I., 376, 377, 436
Zerbinos, E., 40, 434
Zhou, M., 162, 436
Zimmerman, D., 45, 435
Zimmerman, M. K., 121, 437
Zola, I., 213, 437
Zones, J. S., 208, 437

❖ Subject Index

Page references followed by *f* or *t* indicate figures or tables, respectively.

A

Abolitionism, 334, 335, 350, 404
Abortion, 217–218
  debate over, 251–252
  in women's prisons, 282
About Face, 73
Abstinence, 188–189
Abu Ghraib prison, 328
Abuse, sexual, 186–187
Academic achievement, 295–297
Acquaintance rape, 274, 275*f*
Acquired immunodeficiency syndrome (AIDS), 212–213, 212*t*
Act Up, 398
Activism:
  grassroots, 332, 333
  political, 326, 332, 333
ADA (Americans with Disabilities Act of 1990), 213–214, 404
Adolescents:
  juvenile delinquency, 266
  reproductive rights of, 216
  sterilization rates, 219
  teen pregnancy, 187–189
Adult socialization, 41–43
Advanced Placement (AP) test, 295
AFDC (Aid to Families with Dependent Children), 138
Affirmative action, 148–149, 369–370, 404
Afghanistan:
  contemporary, 287
  under Taliban, 161, 237, 249–250
Africa, 28, 29
African Americans:
  abolitionism, 334
  alcohol abuse, 209
  in blue-collar work, 128
  body image, 207, 208
  body weight, 206, 207*f*

books by, 40
child care, 190–191
church attendance, 242, 243*f*
churches, 248–249
cigarette smoking, 211*f*
civil rights movement, 339
  in civil rights movement, 318
clergy, 246
community workers, 332
"constant television households," 60–61
death rates, 200, 201*f*, 202
deviance, 270
disability, 213
discrimination against women, 356, 357*f*
domestic workers, 108, 130, 355
educational achievement of, 292–293, 298, 299, 301
elderly, 41
families, 36–37, 158, 161, 163, 165*f*, 177–178, 179
family households, 166, 167*f*
female-headed households, 136–137, 166, 178
feminist politics, 340
feminists, 342, 351, 351*f*, 355–356, 391
gender, race-ethnicity, and family income, 131, 132*f*
health care workers, 227
health status of, 199, 203
high school graduates taking "New Basics" curriculum, 299, 299*t*
hypertension in, 199, 199*f*
intellectuals, 393
interracial relationships, 92
in jail, 270–271
labor force participation, 106–107, 108, 110–111, 112, 119, 121, 122, 128
in magazines, 62
in the media, 62–63, 66–67
men, 15, 35–36
military service, 330
models, 61

in music videos, 64
occupational segregation, 121, 122*f*
overpopulation, 218
parents, 36–37
pay gap, 130–131, 131*f*
in poverty, 136–138, 137*f*
promotions for, 136
rape rates, 274, 278
religious belief, 233, 235, 241, 248
religious participation, 245, 246
retired professional women, 42
sexual attitudes, 82–83
sexual violence against, 84–85
sexuality of, 78
in slavery, 106–107, 110–111, 241, 355
stay-at-home moms, 144
stereotypes of, 55, 78, 84, 241, 292
sterilization rates, 203, 218–219
subculture of violence among, 276
teen pregnancy, 187, 188
on television, 62–63
victims of crime, 272–273, 272*f*
women in politics, 326
women in prison, 280
African Methodist Episcopal Church, 246
African Methodist Episcopal Zion Church, 246
Age of Enlightenment, 354–356, 404
Age of Reason, 354–356
Agency, 393
Aggravated assault:
  arrests, 268, 268*t*
  victim-offender relationship for, 273, 273*f*
Aggression, 262
Aging, 41–43

Aid to Families with Dependent Children (AFDC), 138
AIDS (acquired immuno-deficiency syndrome), 212–213, 212*t*
"Ain't I A Woman" (Truth), 390
Alan Guttmacher Institute, 102, 229
Alaska Natives:
    alcohol abuse, 209
    death rates, 200, 201*f*
    stalkings of, 274
Alcohol, 209–210
Allyn and Bacon, 70
Ambiguous sexual identity, 22–24
American Association of University Women, 51, 336
American Indians, 28. *see also* Native Americans
    alcohol abuse, 209
    death rates, 200, 201*f*, 202
    interracial relationships, 92
    stalkings of, 274
American Medical Association, 222
American Medical Women's Association, 125, 230
American Woman Suffrage Association, 336
American Women, 338
Americans with Disabilities Act of 1990 (ADA), 213–214, 404
Amsterdam, The Netherlands, 265
Anabolic females, 261
Ancient Greece, 93
Androcentrism, 253, 404
Anorexia nervosa, 206, 208, 404
Anthony, Susan B., 239, 336, 361, 376
    The Woman's Bible, 239, 408
Antiabortion movement, 252
Antifeminism, 249–250, 252
Antimiscegenation, 181, 404
Anti-Slavery Convention of American Women, 334
Antiwar movements, 316

AP (Advanced Placement) test, 295
Apartheid, gender, 161
Arabs, 85–86
Arrests, 267, 268*t*
Artificial insemination, 225
Asian Americans, 15
    alcohol abuse, 209
    in blue-collar work, 128
    death rates, 200, 201*f*, 202
    educational achievement of, 298, 301
    families, 158, 163, 165*f*, 180, 181
    female-headed households, 136–137, 166
    feminists, 391
    gender, race-ethnicity, and family income, 131, 132*f*
    high school graduates taking "New Basics" curriculum, 299, 299*t*
    households, 166, 167*f*
    labor force participation, 119, 120, 122
    labor participation, 108–109, 111, 112
    in magazines, 61
    men, 35–36
    as "model minority," 136–138, 180, 292
    occupational segregation, 121, 122*f*
    pay gap, 130–131, 131*f*
    in poverty, 136–138, 137*f*
    stereotypes of, 55, 63, 84, 85, 108, 292
    teen pregnancy, 187
    on television, 62
    women's work, 105–106
Assaults:
    aggravated assault, 268, 268*t*, 273, 273*f*
    physical assault, 183, 183*t*
    sexual assault, 273, 273*f*
    victimization by, 272–273, 272*f*
Assemblies of God, 247
Association for Women in Science, 125, 313
Attitudes:
    gender gap in, 8, 8*f*
    sexual, 81, 82*f*

Authority, 318, 404
Automobile Workers v. Johnson Controls, 204, 404

B

Baby Boomers, 30
Baird, Eisenstadt v., 216, 405
Balanced work groups, 140
Balancing family and work, 168–170
Bangladesh, 11
"Barbie," 55, 127
Barbie dolls, 55, 127
Bauer, Bruno, 377–378
Beauty, 206
Behavior, 79–83
Beliefs, 27, 28*f*
Berdaches, 27–28
BET (Black Entertainment Television), 70
BFOQ (bona fide occupational qualification), 204
Bible, 241, 377–378
    The Woman's Bible (Anthony), 239, 408
Biological determinism, 25–27, 290, 404
Biological reductionism, 25, 26–27, 404
Biology:
    basis of sex identity, 22
    gendered descriptions of, 308
    and society, 21–32
Birth control, 188–189, 215–217, 218
Birth politics, 219–225
Bisexual experiences, 95–99
Black Entertainment Television (BET), 70
Black History Month, 297
Black Muslims, 249
Black power movement, 340, 341–342
Black suffrage, 334–335
Blacks (*see* African Americans)
Blockbuster, 70
Blue-collar work, 126–129
Body image, 205–208
Body mass index, 207*f*
Body weight, 206, 207*f*
Bona fide occupational qualification (BFOQ), 204

Books, 40
"Born-again Christians,"
  244
Bourgeoisie, 379
Boys, 294
Bryn Mawr, 334
Bulimia, 206, 208, 404
Bureau of Justice Statistics,
  284
Burqa, 161, 249–250
Bush, Laura, 316

C

California, 92
Calvin Klein Barbie, 127
Cambodia, 119
Campaign financing, 325–326
Canada, 177*t*
Capitalism, 157, 379
  and class, 379–380
  economy in, 384
  family in, 382, 384
  importance of, 377–386
  and the media, 66–67
  and patriarchy, 388–389
  Western, 354
Care work, 143–147, 384, 404
Caribbean:
  transnational families, 180
  women's representation in
    legislature, 323, 324*f*
Cartoons, 40
Catholic Network for Women's
  Equality, 255
Catt, Carrie Chapman, 336
CBS, 70
Center for American Women
  and Politics, 343
Center for Reproductive Law
  and Policy, 230
Central Americans:
  labor participation, 121
  transnational families, 180
Cesarean section, 224
Chicana/o Americans:
  families, 44, 179
  labor participation, 107, 108,
    112, 121
Child care, 189–193
  arrangements for
    preschoolers, 190, 190*f*
  costs of, 191, 191*f*

Childbirth, 219–225
  definition of, 223–224
  racism and, 222–223
  in women's prison, 281–282
Children:
  play and games, 38–40
  poverty status of families
    with, 136–138, 137*f*
  socialization of, 384
Children's literature, 40
Children's television, 60–61
China, 29, 127, 177*t*
Chinese Americans:
  families, 180–181
  immigrants, 37
  interracial relationships, 92
  labor force participation, 108,
    112, 120, 130
  stereotypes of, 108
  women's work, 105
Chinese Exclusion Act, 108, 180
Christian theology, 253, 254, 377
Christianity, 233, 239, 241
  Evangelical, 234–235, 244,
    250–251
  feminization of, 238
  sexual attitudes of, 83
Chromosomes, sex, 407
Church attendance, 242, 243*f*
Cigarette smoking, 210–212, 211*f*
The Citadel, 48, 328
Civil rights, 339–340
Civil Rights Bill of 1964, 321
  Title VII, 141, 147, 204, 407
Civil rights movement, 235, 316,
  318, 339
Class, 115–119
  and capitalism, 379–380
  child care costs comparison,
    191, 191*f*
  definition of, 404
  and health, 202–203
  importance of, 377–386
  influence of, 162–163
  Marxist concept of, 379–380
  significance of, 14–15
Class consciousness, 381, 404
Class inequality, 298–300
Class roles, 32
Class stratification, 116, 404
Clergy, 246–247
Clerical workers, 125–126

Clinton, Bill, 80
Clinton, Hillary Rodham, 316
Clinton administration, 330
Clitoridectomy, 222
Cloning, 225
Coat rack metaphor, 395–396
Cognitive-developmental
  theory, 45, 404
Cohabitation, 170–171
Collective consciousness, 241,
  404
College women, 274, 275*f*
Coming out, 96
Community Facilities Act, 192
Community workers, 332
Compadrazgo, 161
Comparable worth, 147–148, 404
Compassion issues, 327
Compulsory heterosexuality, 81,
  404
Comte, Auguste, 355, 360
Congressional Union, 336
Connecticut, Griswold v., 216, 405
Consciousness:
  class, 381
  false, 70, 381, 405
  ideology and, 380–381
Conservatives, 323–324
Consumer League of New York,
  203
Consumer Price Index, 136
Consumerism, 127
Content analysis, 59–60, 404
Contingent workers, 118, 404
Controlling images, 62, 404
Cosmopolitan, 61
Courts, the, 279–280
Crick, Francis, 306
Crime, 259–285
  arrests, 267, 268*t*
  definition of, 271
  early studies of, 261–263
  sex differences in, 262
  sociological perspectives on,
    260–267
  violent, 272–273, 272*f*, 273*f*
  women as victims of, 271–279,
    272*f*, 273*f*
  women's, 261–263, 267, 268*t*,
    269–271
Crime index, 268, 404
Criminal justice system, 279–282

Criminality, 267–268
Criminals, 267–271
Cross-dressers, 29
CSI: Miami, 260
Cuba, 177*t*
Cuban Americans, 119
Cult of domesticity, 112,
    156–157, 404
Cult of womanhood, 110, 237
Cultural narratives, 62
Cultural stereotypes, 42
Cultural studies, 394
Culture, 27–30. *see also* Popular
    culture
    definition of, 27, 404
    of masculinity, 330
    and the media, 53–75
    and sex, 20–103
    and society, 21–32
    subculture of violence,
        276–277, 407
    of thinness, 208
    workplace, 142
Curriculum:
    gender and, 297–298
    "New Basics" curriculum,
        299, 299*t*

D

Darwinism, 223
Date rape, 274, 404
Day care, 192
DBCP (dibromochloropropane),
    204
Deadbeat dads, 192
Dean, Howard, 316
Death rates, 200, 201*f*, 202–203
Declaration of Sentiments, 335
Defense Authorization Act, 329
Defense of Marriage Act, 99
Delinquency:
    female, 261
    juvenile, 266
    sex differences in, 261–262
Democrats, 323–324, 326
Depression, postpartum,
    262–263
Deviance, 259–285
    definition of, 263–264, 404
    early studies of, 261–263
    feminist perspectives on,
        265–267

labeling and, 264
social, 264
sociological perspectives on,
    260–267
women's, 261–263
Dialectical materialism, 378
Dibromochloropropane (DBCP),
    204
Dietitians, 227
Digital divide, 296, 404
Disability, 213–214
Discourse, 67, 404
Discrimination, 131
    definition of, 404
    reverse, 370
    against women, 356, 357*f*
Diversity, 161–162, 164, 165–176,
    165*f*, 182
Divorce, 165, 166, 167–168
DNA, discovery of, 306
"Doing gender," 46–47, 58, 404
Dole, Robert, 135
Domestic violence, 184, 270–271
    partner violence, 183, 183*t*
Domestic work, 108–109, 129,
    130
    second shift, 14, 143, 407
Domesticity:
    cult of, 112, 156–157, 404
    ideology of, 112
Domination, matrix of, 15, 406
"Don't ask, don't tell" policy,
    330
Double jeopardy, 15
Double standards, 80
Douglass, Frederick, 334–335
Drinking patterns, 209–210
Drug abuse, 209, 210
    arrests, 268, 268*t*
Dual labor market theory,
    133–134, 404

E

Earnings, 130–134
    and gender segregation, 121,
        123*f*
    median family income, 136
    median weekly earnings in
        administrative support, 125
    in selected occupations, 110,
        111*t*
East Oakland, California, 188

Eating disorders, 206, 207
Eating problems, 206, 208
Economic restructuring, 115–119
    definition of, 405
    political-economic status,
        278–279
    process of, 116–117
Economy:
    in capitalist society, 384
    family-based, 106–107, 405
    family-consumer, 109–110, 405
    family-wage, 107–109
Education:
    attainment of, 289, 289*f*
    gender gap in, 286–314
    higher, 300–304, 300*f*
    history of, 288–290
    interest in math and science
        learning, 304–305, 305*f*
    medical, 220
    miseducation of boys, 294
Educational Amendments of
    1972, Title IX of, 147, 291,
    297, 407
Educational pyramid, 300, 300*f*
Eisenstadt v. Baird, 216, 405
Elderly, 41–43
Electronic sweatshops, 126
Elite, power, 319, 406
The Ellen Degeneres Show, 63
Embryo transfer, 225
Emily's List, 325–326
Emma Goldman Papers, 402
Emotional labor, 114–115, 405
Empirical studies, 16
Engels, Friedrich, 376, 378, 379
Engineering workforce, 304–305,
    306*f*
Enlightenment, Age of, 354–356,
    404
Environmental movement, 316
Episcopalians, 247
Epistemology, 309–310, 405
Equal Pay Act of 1963, 147, 321,
    338, 405
Equal Rights Amendment
    (ERA), 329, 336, 340–341,
    358, 405
Equity Resource Center, 313
ERA (Equal Rights
    Amendment), 329, 336,
    340–341, 358, 405

Essentialism, 58, 328, 395, 405
Ethnocentrism, 368, 405
Eugenics, 225
Europe, 29
  medieval, 93, 236
  women's representation in
    legislature, 323, 324*f*
Evangelical Christians, 234–235,
    244, 250–251
  Second Great Awakening,
    237–239, 407
Expectations, 33–35
  gender, 29, 41
Extended family networks, 181
Extremism:
  leftist, 5
  religious fundamentalism,
    237, 250

F

Faith, 252–255
False consciousness, 70, 381, 405
Families, 153–196
  in capitalism, 382, 384
  contemporary, 165–176
  definition of, 405
  diversity in, 161–162, 164,
    165*f*, 182
  extended family networks,
    181
  feminist perspectives on,
    159–165
  gay and lesbian, 171–173
  gender and, 176–182
  historical perspectives on,
    155–159
  ideology and, 164–165
  influence of class, race, and
    gender on, 162–163
  measurement of, 166–167
  nuclear family, 161, 406
  poverty status of, 136–138, 137*f*
  race and, 176–182
  social construction of, 159–161
  as social ideal, 164
  and social problems, 182–193
  structural diversity model of,
    159, 176
  terminology, 164–165
  transnational, 180, 408
  and work, 142–147, 168–170,
    365–367

Familism, 44
Family (term), 164–165
Family and Medical Leave Act
    (FMLA), 191–192, 405
Family households, 166, 167*f*,
    405
Family income:
  gender and, 131, 132*f*
  median family income, 136
  race-ethnicity and, 131, 132*f*
Family Research Library,
    University of New
    Hampshire, 195
Family values, 160, 160*f*, 342
Family violence, 182–187
Family-based economy, 106–107,
    405
Family-consumer economy,
    109–110, 405
Family-wage economy, 107–109,
    405
Farm labor, 130
Fatherhood, 175–176
  deadbeat dads, 192
Father's Day cards, 56
Faulkner, Shannon, 48
Faulty generalization, 14, 405
Federal Bureau of Investigation
    (FBI), 284
  crime index, 268
  Uniform Crime Reports, 267,
    274, 408
Female delinquency, 261
"Female men," 28
Female pseudohermaphrodites,
    30
Female-headed households,
    136–137, 178, 180
  median family income, 136
  poverty status of, 136–138,
    137*f*
The Feminine Mystique (Friedan),
    338
Feminism, 9–10, 349
  American, 334–337
  backlash against, 342
  and civil rights, 339–340
  definition of, 9–11, 405
  early liberal, 358–368
  emergence of, 237–240
  and faith, 252–255
  frameworks of, 348–403

as leftist extremism, 5
lesbian, 387
liberal, 341, 352, 356, 368–370,
    374–375, 389–390, 406
  liberal basis of, 353–354
  and militarism, 331
  modern, 353–354
  multiracial, 374, 375, 390–393,
    406
  nineteenth century, 334–337,
    376
  postmodernist, 374, 375,
    393–397
  radical, 352, 374, 375–377,
    386–390, 389–390, 406
  radical lesbian, 387
  and the religious right,
    250–251
  second wave of, 340–342
  and social construction of
    knowledge, 307–312
  socialist, 352, 374, 375,
    377–386, 383–386, 389–390,
    407
  and spirituality, 252–255
  stereotypes of, 342
  twenty-first century, 342–344
"Feminist" (label), 10–11
Feminist epistemology, 309–310
Feminist health movement,
    224–225
Feminist Majority, 18
Feminist movement, 233, 316,
    333–344
Feminist perspectives, 1–19
  on crime, 271
  on deviance, 265–267
  on families, 159–165
Feminist politics, 340
The Feminist Press, 51
Feminist theology, 255, 405
  radical, 253, 254–255, 255
Feminist theory, 349–350
  contemporary frameworks in,
    373–403
  continuing questions for,
    399–400
  definition of, 405
  frameworks of, 350–353
  postmodernist, 67–68
  purpose of, 350–351
  radical origins of, 374–375

Feminist Theory Website, 402
Feminists, 342, 351, 351*f*
Feminization:
    of Christianity, 238
    of occupations, 134
    of poverty, 136, 405
Fertilization, 308–309
Fetal sex differentiation, 22
Feuerbach, Ludwig, 377
Fifteenth Amendment, 336
Filipina Americans:
    labor force participation, 108, 120, 121
    stereotypes of, 108
Filipinos, 92
Fire arms, 200, 201*f*
FMLA (Family and Medical Leave Act), 191–192, 405
Focus groups, 68
Food, 205–208
Foot binding, 29
Forten, Charlotte, 334, 355
Forten, Harriet, 334
Forten, Margaretta, 334
Forten, Sarah Louise, 334, 361
Fortune, 308
Fourteenth Amendment, 328
France:
    family values, 160*f*
    maternity leave benefits, 177*t*
    violence against wives, 183
Frankfurter, Felix, 205
Franklin, Rosalind, 306
Fraternities, 92, 275
Friedan, Betty, 338
Friendship, 93–95
Fundamentalists, 237
    religious right, 250–251

G
Gallup Organization, 372
Games, 38–40
Gangs:
    girl, 266
    male, 263
Gardner, Gerald, 255
Gay (term), 96
Gay families, 171–173
"Gay gene," 91*t*, 97

Gays, 95–99. *see also* Homosexuality
    in the media, 63
    in the military, 330–331
    myths about, 90, 91*t*
    sexuality of, 78
Gender, 2, 29
    and body image, 205–208, 207*f*
    and cigarette smoking, 211, 211*f*
    concept of, 29, 32
    controlling images of, 62
    and the courts, 279–280
    and curriculum, 297–298
    definition of, 405
    differences between genders, 25
    "doing gender," 46–47, 58, 404
    and the economy, 104–152
    and families, 153–196, 176–182
    and family income, 131, 132*f*
    formation of, 43–47
    and health, 200–202
    and the health care system, 226–228
    influence of, 162–163
    institutional basis of, 30–32
    learning, 40
    and the media, 59–68
    and occupational segregation, 121, 122*f*
    and popular culture, 56–59
    and religious beliefs, 242–244, 244*f*
    and religious participation, 244–246
    and schooling, 291–295
    and science, 304–312
    science/gender system, 305
    and sex, 20–103
    sex/gender system, 387, 407
    and sexuality, 77
    significance of, 14–15
    and social change, 348–403
    social construction of, 20–52, 363–365, 407
    and social institutions, 104–347
    and social problems, 205–214
    and society, 304–312

and spirituality, 242, 244*f*
    stress caused by, 35, 36*f*
    variability within, 25
Gender apartheid, 161
"Gender bending," 29
Gender bias, 279–280
Gender competency, 297
Gender displays, 47
Gender equity policies, 147–149
Gender expectations, 29, 41
Gender gap, 327
    in academic achievement, 295–297
    in attitudes, 8, 8*f*
    definition of, 405
    in delinquency, 261–262
    in education, 286–314
    in labor, 383
    organizational theories of, 65–66
    in politics, 327
    in sexual attitudes, 81, 82*f*
    in wages, 134
Gender identity, 33
    definition of, 405
    formation of, 33–37
    race and, 35–37
Gender relations, 329–330
Gender roles, 32, 405
Gender segregation, 120–130, 122*f*
    definition of, 405
    income and, 121, 123*f*
    internal, 121
Gender socialization, 33–37
    as cause of rape, 277–278
    definition of, 405
Gender stereotypes, 27, 28*f*
Gender stratification, 115–119, 405
Gendered institutions:
    definition of, 31, 405
    the military, 331
    prisons as, 281
    the state, 319
Generalization, faulty, 14, 405
Genetic engineering, 225
Genital mutilation, 29
Genotype, 24
Gentlemen's Agreement, 181
Germany, 177*t*
Gilman, Charlotte Perkins, 376

Girl gangs, 266
Glass ceiling, 134–135, 405
Glass Ceiling Commission, 135
Global restructuring, 405
Goddess imagery, 255
Goldman, Emma, 376–377
Emma Goldman Papers, 402
Government, 323–328, 324f, 325f
Grassroots activism, 332, 333
Greece, ancient, 93
Greek Orthodox, 242
Grimke, Angelina, 334
Grimke, Sarah, 334
Griswold v. Connecticut, 216, 405
Alan Guttmacher Institute, 102, 229

H

Harassment, sexual, 407
Harm, reproduction of, 270, 406
Harvard, 290
Harvard Divinity School, 246
Hate crimes, 99
Hawaii, 99, 181
Head Start, 192
Health, 197–231
    and class, 202–203
    feminist health movement, 224–225
    and gender, 200–202
    mental, 201–202
    physical, 198–199
    and race, 202–203
    and social problems, 205–214
    social structure of, 200–205
    women's health movement, 227–228
Health care, 281–282
Health care system, 226–228
Health care workers, 226–227
Health insurance, 214
Health technicians, 227
Hegel, Georg Wilhelm Friedrich, 377
Hermaphroditism, 22–23. *see also* Intersexed persons
    pseudohermaphrodites, 30
    true hermaphrodites, 30
Heterosexism, 90, 405
Heterosexuality, 96, 387–388, 398
    compulsory, 81, 404

High school, 298
    interest in math and science learning, 304–305, 305f
    "New Basics" curriculum, 299, 299t
Higher education, 300–304, 300f
Hijras, 28, 29
Hindus, 92
Hip-hop, 62, 64
Hispanic Americans:
    alcohol abuse, 209
    in blue-collar work, 128
    body weight, 206, 207f
    child care, 190–191
    church attendance, 242, 243f
    "constant television households," 60–61
    death rates, 200, 201f, 202
    discrimination against women, 356, 357f
    educational achievement of, 298, 301
    families, 165f
    farm and migrant labor, 130
    female-headed households, 136–137, 166
    feminists, 351, 351f
    gender, race-ethnicity, and family income, 131, 132f
    health care workers, 227
    high school graduates taking "New Basics" curriculum, 299, 299t
    households, 166, 167f
    labor force participation, 119, 122, 130
    occupational segregation, 121, 122f
    pay gap, 130–131, 131f
    in poverty, 136–137, 136–138, 137f
    rape rates, 274, 278
    subculture of violence among, 276
    teen pregnancy, 187
    victims of crime, 272–273, 272f
    violence against, 99
    women in prison, 280
    women's work, 105
Historical materialism, 377–379, 405

Historical perspectives:
    Black History Month, 297
    on education, 288–290
    on families, 155–159
    roots of radical feminism, 375–377
    Women's History Month, 297
    on women's work, 105–113
Holiness church, 245, 246
Homicide rates, 200, 201f, 202–203
Homophobia, 34, 83, 90, 99, 330, 405
Homosexuality, 78, 96, 398
    coming out, 96
    as deviant, 267
    "Don't ask, don't tell" policy, 330
    lesbian, gay, and bisexual experiences, 95–99
    lesbians and gays in the military, 330–331
    in the media, 63
    myths about gays and lesbians, 90, 91t
    same-sex marriage, 99, 171
Hooking up, 81–82
Hospital births, 221–222, 223, 224
Hot Wheels, 55
Household labor, 146–147
Householders, 166, 405
Households, 164
    definition of, 166, 405
    diversity in, 164, 165f
    family, 166, 167f, 405
    nonfamily, 166, 167f, 406
    patriarchal, 155
    by type and race, 166, 167f
Housework, 111–113, 114, 143–147
    second shift, 14, 143, 407
    as "women's work," 145
Human agency, 163–164
Human capital theory, 133, 405
Human trafficking, 265
Humanists Net Project, 18
Hungary, 160f
Hypermasculinity, 47, 263
Hypertension, 199, 199f

I

"Ideal woman," 111, 207
Identification theory, 43–44,
    405–406
Identity:
    gender, 33–37, 405
    sexual, 22–24, 398
Ideology, 71, 381
    and consciousness, 380–381
    definition of, 110, 406
    of domesticity, 112
    and the family, 164–165
    and the history of women's
        work, 110–113
    sexism as, 71–72, 381
Immigrants, 120. *see also specific*
        ethnic groups
    families, 181
    female-headed households,
        180
    overpopulation of, 218
Immigration Act, 180
Imprisonment, 270–271, 280–282
    growth of, 280, 281*f*
In vitro fertilization, 225
Incarceration, 270–271, 280–282
    growth of, 280, 281*f*
Incest, 186–187
Inclusion of women, 11–13
Income:
    earnings, 110, 111*t*
    and gender segregation, 121,
        123*f*
    median family income, 136
India, 28, 29, 160*f*
Indonesia, 127
Industrial revolution, 93, 157
Infancy, 37–38
Infant mortality, 203, 406
Infrastructure, 379, 406
Inquiry, logic of, 363
Inquisition, 236
Institute for Women's Policy
        Research, 151
Institutions:
    gendered, 31, 405
    social, 30–31, 104–347, 407
Insurance, health, 214
Intellectuals, 393
Interest groups, 319
Internal gender segregation, 121
Internet pornography, 63

Interracial relationships, 92–93
Intersexed persons, 23, 406
Intimate partner violence,
        182–185, 183*t*
Intimate relationships, 88–95
Intravenous (IV) drug users,
        210
Iran, 177*t*
Iraq war, 328
Islam, 249–250
Islamic radicals, 11, 237
Islamic women, 233
Israel, 323, 324*f*
Italy, 177*t*, 329
IV (intravenous) drug users,
        210

J

Japan, 30, 177*t*, 198
Japanese Americans:
    families, 181
    interracial relationships, 92
    labor participation, 108–109
    "picture brides," 181
    stereotypes of, 108–109
    women's work, 105
Jefferson Medical College, 290
Jews, 208, 242, 248
    Orthodox, 235
    Reform, 245
Job segregation, 270, 388–389
Johnson Controls, Automobile
        Workers v., 204, 404
Judaism, 233, 243, 245
Judge Judy, 260
Judges, 321
Judging Amy, 260
Juvenile delinquency, 266

K

Katabolic males, 261
"Ken," 55
Kennedy, John F., 338
Kerry, John, 316
Kerry, Teresa Heinz, 316
Kilbourne, Jean, 73
Kinship networks, 161, 179
Kitchens, 112
Knowledge:
    social construction of, 53–75,
        69–71, 307–312
    sociology of, 68–72, 407

Korean Americans:
    labor participation, 108
    "picture brides," 181
    stereotypes of, 108
    women's work, 105

L

Labeling theory, 264, 406
Labor:
    dual labor market theory,
        133–134, 404
    emotional, 114–115, 405
    gender division of, 383
Labor force participation,
        119–120, 120*f*
Labor unions, 128, 132, 376
Ladies' Home Journal, 61, 112
Lancet, 54
Language:
    gender and, 56–59
    nonsexist, 57
Lanham Act, 192
Laos, 119
Latin America, 323, 324*f*
Latina/o Americans:
    body image, 207, 208
    community workers, 332
    disability among, 213
    in domestic work, 129
    educational achievement of,
        292–293, 298–299
    elderly, 41
    families, 158, 161, 163, 179
    feminists, 391
    health status of, 203
    labor force participation, 111,
        119, 120
    in magazines, 61
    in the media, 62
    men, 15, 35–36, 55
    religion, 248
    in service work, 129
    sexual attitudes of, 82–83
    stereotypes of, 55, 84, 85, 292
    teen pregnancy, 187
    women in prison, 280
Law(s), 320–323. *see also specific*
        acts
    protective legislation,
        203–205, 322, 406
Leadership, clerical, 246–247
League of Women Voters, 336

Learning:
  gender, 40
  math and science, 304–305,
    305*f*
  social, 407
Leftist extremism, 5
Legislation. *see also specific acts*
  protective, 203–205, 322, 406
Lesbian families, 171–173
Lesbian feminism, radical, 387
Lesbianism, 267
Lesbians, 35, 57. *See also*
    Homosexuality
  body image, 208
  as deviant, 267
  experiences of, 95–99
  in the media, 63
  in the military, 330–331
  myths about, 90, 91*t*
  sexuality of, 78
Lewinsky, Monica, 80
Liberal (term), 349
Liberal feminism, 341, 352, 356
  comparison with socialist and
    radical feminism, 389–390
  critique of, 368–370, 374–375
  definition of, 406
  early, 358–368
  goal of, 357
Liberalism, 349, 353
  definition of, 406
  as mode of social thought,
    354–358
Liberals, 323–324
Liberation theology, 241, 248,
  406
Liberty, 363, 364
Literature, 40
Logic of inquiry, 363
"Loose" women, 266
Love, 88–95
Lumpenproletariat, 379
Lutherans, 247

M

Machismo, 179
Malaysians, 92
Male gangs, 263
Male midwives, 221
Male pseudohermaphrodites, 30
Male sterility, 204

Malleus Maleficarum (Catholic
  Church), 236
Manly hearted women, 28
Mannheim, Karl, 69, 71–72
Marital rape, 406
Marital violence, 317–318
Marriage, 159, 165
  antimiscegenation laws, 181
  arranged, 181
  Defense of Marriage Act, 99
  definition of, 383
  early essays on, 365–366
  monogamous, 382
  "picture brides," 181
  as prostitution, 382–383
  same-sex, 99, 171
Martineau, Harriet, 358, 360–362
Marx, Jenny Julia Eleanor, 378
Marx, Karl, 69, 350, 376, 377
  concept of class, 379–380
  and historical materialism,
    377–379
  and social construction of
    knowledge, 69–71
  socialist feminist critique of,
    383–386
  woman question, 382–383
Masculinity, 213
  concept of, 35–36
  culture of, 330
  hypermasculinity, 263
Massachusetts, 99, 171
Materialism:
  dialectical, 378
  historical, 377–379, 405
Maternity, 322
Maternity hospitals, 221–222,
  223
Maternity leave benefits, 176,
  177*t*
Math interest, 304–305, 305*f*
Matrix of domination, 15, 406
Mattel, 127
Media:
  capitalism and, 66–67
  content analysis and, 59–64
  gender and, 53–75
  theories about influence of,
    64–68
Medical education, 220, 223, 290
Medical experimentation,
  221–222

Medieval Europe, 93, 236
Menopause, 30, 86, 87–88
Men's studies, 13–14, 406
Menstruation, 86–87
Mental health, 201–202
Mercantilism, 157
Meritocracy, 366–367, 406
Meritor Savings Bank v. Vinson,
  141, 406
Methodists, 247
Mexican Americans:
  families, 179
  in family-based economy, 107
  hypertension in, 199, 199*f*
  labor force participation, 120
  men, 37
  stereotypes of, 55
Mexico, 160*f*, 179
Midwives, 220, 223
  definition of pregnancy and
    childbirth, 224
  male, 221
Migrant labor, 130
Militarism, 331
Military, the, 328–331
  gender relations in, 329–330
  as gendered institution, 331
  lesbians and gays in, 330–331
  racial integration in, 330–331
  sexual harassment in, 330
  state-supported academies,
    328
  women in, 329
Mill, Harriet Taylor, 350, 358,
  362–368, 376
Mill, John Stuart, 350, 355, 358,
  362–368, 376
Mills, C. Wright, 6–7
Minority groups, 213
Miscarriage, 204
Miseducation of boys, 294
Misogyny, 241, 406
Mitchell, Juliet, 384
Modern feminism, 353–354
Modernization, 367–368
"Mongolians," 181
Monogamy, 261, 382
Moral values, 327–328
Mormons, 242
Mortality:
  death rates, 200, 201*f*, 202–203
  infant, 203

Motherhood, 173–175
  mothers-in-law, 161
  othermothers, 44
  stay-at-home moms, 144
  supermoms, 143, 169
  teen mothers, 187, 188
  transnational, 180
  as work, 114
Motor vehicle accidents, 200,
  201*f*
Mott, Lucretia, 335
Mount Holyoke College, 334
MTV, 70
Muller v. Oregon, 203–204, 406
Multiracial feminism, 374, 375,
  390–393, 406
Music videos, 55, 64
Muslim extremists, 11, 237
Muslim women, 233
Muslim Women's League, 255
Myths:
  about gays and lesbians, 90,
  91*t*
  of the ideal woman, 111, 207
  work, 202

N

NARAL (National Abortion
  Rights Action League), 319,
  353
Nasrin, Taslima, 11
National Abortion Rights Action
  League (NARAL), 319, 353
National Academy of Sciences,
  198
National American Women
  Suffrage Association
  (NAWSA), 239, 336
National Center for Education
  Statistics, 313
National Collegiate Athletic
  Association (NCAA), 60
National Council of Jewish
  Women, 255
National Federation of Business
  and Professional Women's
  Clubs, 336
National Gay and Lesbian Task
  Force, 101, 319
National Institutes of Health
  (NIH), 198
National legislatures, 323, 324*f*

National Organization for
  Women (NOW), 263, 319,
  353, 372
National Partnership for Women
  and Families, 195
National Woman Suffrage
  Association (NWSA), 336
National Women's Health
  Network, 230
National Women's Party, 336
National Women's Political
  Caucus, 319, 353
National Women's Studies
  Association, 313
Native Americans:
  alcohol abuse, 209
  body image, 207
  death rates, 202–203
  educational achievement of,
  301
  families, 158, 161, 163, 180, 181
  feminists, 391
  health status, 203
  interracial relationships, 92
  labor patterns, 107, 122
  men, 15
  religion, 248
  stereotypes of, 55, 85
  sterilization rates, 218–219
  on television, 62
  victims of crime, 272–273, 272*f*
Nature/nurture, 24–25
Navaho Indians, 27
NAWSA (National American
  Women Suffrage
  Association), 239, 336
NCAA (National Collegiate
  Athletic Association), 60
"New age" spirituality, 255
"New Basics" curriculum, 299,
  299*t*
New Deal, 192
New Left, 341
New York City, New York,
  177–178, 223
News shows, 63, 66
Nick at Nite, 70
Nickelodeon, 70
NIH (National Institutes of
  Health), 198
Nineteenth Amendment, 336,
  406

Nintendo games, 40
Nixon, Richard, 370
Norms, cultural, 27
NOW (National Organization
  for Women), 263, 319, 353,
  372
Nuclear family, 161, 406
Nuns, 246
Nurses, 223, 227
Nurturing (*see* Nature/nurture)
NWSA (National Woman
  Suffrage Association),
  336

O

Oberlin College, 334
Object relations theory, 43–44,
  406
Obstetrics, 221
Occupational distribution, 121,
  365
  blue-collar work, 126–129
  bona fide occupational
  qualification (BFOQ), 204
  care work, 143–147, 384
  clerical work, 125–126
  contingent workers, 118
  farm and migrant labor, 130
  feminization of occupations,
  134
  health care workers, 226–227
  job segregation, 270, 388–389
  migrant labor, 130
  service work, 129
Office of Research on Women's
  Health (NIH), 198
"Old boy networks," 124, 148
Oophorectomy, 222
Oregon, Muller v., 203–204, 406
Organizational theories of
  gender inequality, 65–66
Orthodox Jews, 235
Orthodox Judaism, 243, 245
Othermothers, 44
Ownership, 379–380

P

Pacific Islanders:
  death rates, 200, 201*f*
  families, 165*f*
  female-headed households,
  166

gender, race-ethnicity, and
family income, 131, 132*f*
households, 166, 167*f*
pay gap, 130–131, 131*f*
in poverty, 136–138, 137*f*
Page Law, 180
Pain of childbirth, 222–223
Paramount Pictures, 70
Paramount Television, 70
Parenting, 36–37, 173
Partner violence, 182–185, 183*t*
Patriarchal households, 155
Patriarchy, 89, 317
capitalism and, 388–389
definition of, 386, 406
power of, 386–390
Paul, Alice, 336
Pay gap, 130–131, 131*f*
"PC" ("politically correct"),
342
Penis envy, 360
Pentecostal church, 245, 246
Personal as political, 333
Personal life, 385
Personal Responsibility and
Work Reconciliation Act,
1996, 138, 406
Personal troubles, 7, 406
Phallocentric thinking:
definition of, 406
definition of rape, 322
definition of sexual
intercourse, 80–81
Phenotype, 24
Philadelphia Female Anti-
Slavery Society, 334
Philippines, 120
Physical assault, 183, 183*t*
Physical health, 198–199
"Picture brides," 181
Planned Parenthood, 319
Play and games, 38–40
Playboy, 54, 55
Pluralism, 319, 406
PMS (premenstrual syndrome),
86–87
Policies for gender equity,
147–149
Political (term), 331–333
Political activism, 326, 332, 333
Political correctness, 342
Political women, 332

Political-economic status,
278–279
Politics, 315–347
of birth, 219–225
gender gap in, 327
public attitudes toward
women in, 323–324, 326*f*
of reproduction, 214–225
sexual, 63, 79, 84, 333, 407
of sexuality, 79
women's participation in,
327–328
Popular culture, 54, 55, 58–59
definition of, 406
gender and, 56–59
language and, 56–59
Popular stereotypes, 58
Pornography, 63, 84–85
Postfeminist generation, 342, 343
Postmodernism, 67–68, 393–394,
406
Postmodernist feminism, 374,
375, 393–397
Postmodernist feminist theory,
67–68
Postmodernist theory, 394
Postpartum depression, 262–263
Poststructuralism, 394
Poverty, 136–139, 137*f*
feminization of, 136, 405
overpopulation of those in,
218
Poverty line, 136, 406
Power, 89, 315–347, 317
definition of, 317–318, 406
of patriarchy, 386–390
race and, 84–85
sexuality and, 84–85
and social conflict, 264–265
Power elite, 319, 406
Praxis, 381
Pregnancy, 219–225
definition of, 223–224
legal protection of, 322
teen, 187–189
in women's prison, 282
Preliminary Scholastic Aptitude
Test (PSAT), 295
Premenstrual syndrome (PMS),
86–87
Presbyterians, 247
Preschoolers, 190, 190*f*

Presidential Commission on the
Status of Women, 338
Prisons, 270–271, 280–282, 281*f*
Abu Ghraib prison, 328
as "gendered institutions," 281
women's prisons, 281
Private sphere, 385
Professional women, 78, 123–125
retired, 42
in science and engineering,
304–305, 306*f*
Project Head Start, 192
Proletarianization, 126
Proletariats, 379, 382
Promotions, 134–136
Prostitution, 265, 331
arrests, 268, 268*t*
marriage as, 382–383
Protective legislation, 322
definition of, 406
reproduction and, 203–205
Protestant churches, 245, 246,
248
fundamentalist, 251
Protestant ethic, 110, 158
Protestant Reformation, 158
Protestants, 217–218, 234–235,
242
religiously conservative,
250–251
PSAT (Preliminary Scholastic
Aptitude Test), 295
Pseudohermaphrodites, 30
Public attitudes:
gender gap in, 8, 8*f*
sexual, 81, 82*f*
toward women in politics,
323–324, 326*f*
Public issues, 7, 406
Public life, 385
Public sphere, 385
Puerperal fever, 221, 223
Puerto Ricans:
families, 179–180
girl gangs, 266
labor force participation, 119
sterilization rates, 218–219
Puritans, 158

Q

Queer Eye for the Straight Guy, 63
Queer Nation, 398

Queer theory, 96, 375, 397–399, 406
Question of separate spheres, 385

R
Race:
  and body weight, 206, 207f
  and cigarette smoking, 211, 211f
  and families, 176–182
  and family income, 131, 132f
  and gender identity, 35–37
  and health, 202–203
  influence of, 162–163
  integration in the military, 330–331
  interracial relationships, 92–93
  multiracial feminism, 374, 375, 390–393
  and occupational segregation, 121, 122f
  and power, 84–85
  significance of, 14–15
  and social justice, 248–249
Race inequality, 298–300
Race roles, 32
Racial suicide, 218
Racism:
  and childbirth, 222–223
  and reproduction, 218–219
Radcliffe College, 334
Radical feminism, 352, 374, 375, 386–390
  comparison with liberal and socialist feminism, 389–390
  definition of, 406
  historical roots of, 375–377
Radical feminist theology, 253, 254–255, 255
Radical lesbian feminism, 387
Radio news, 66
Rape, 62, 274–276
  acquaintance rape, 274, 275f
  arrests, 268, 268t
  causes of, 276–279
  "classic," 279
  of college women, 274, 275f
  conviction rates for, 280
  date rape, 274, 404
  legal definition of, 322
  marital rape, 185–186, 406

partner violence, 183, 183t
  and political-economic status, 278–279
  victimization by, 272–273, 272f
  victim-offender relationships, 273, 273f, 274, 275f
  in war, 331
Rape law, 322
Reflection hypothesis, 64–65, 406
Reform:
  social, 348–372
  welfare, 138
Reform Judaism, 245
Religion, 232–258
  and antifeminism, 249–250
  definition of, 239
  and emergence of feminism, 237–240
  and gender, 242, 244f
  images of women in, 240
  as opiate, 248, 406
  significance of, 242, 242f
  and social change, 247–255
  and social control, 235–237
  and social justice, 248–249
  sociological perspectives on, 234–235
  The Woman's Bible (Anthony), 239, 408
Religiosity, 240–244
Religious attendance, 242, 243f
Religious beliefs, 242–244, 244f
Religious extremism, 250
Religious fundamentalists, 237
Religious institutions, 244–247
Religious participation:
  gender and, 244–246
  women as clergy, 246–247
Religious right, 250–251, 406
Religious texts, 240–241
Renaissance, 12
Reproduction, 197–231
  politics of, 214–225
  and protective legislation, 203–205
  and racism, 218–219
Reproduction of harm, 270, 406
Reproductive freedom, 203
Reproductive rights, 216
Reproductive technology, 225

Reproductive Health Services, Webster v., 217
Republicans, 323–324, 370
Restell, Madame, 217–218
Retirement, 42
Reverse discrimination, 370
Richmond, California, 188
Rights:
  civil rights movement, 235, 316, 318, 339–340
  Equal Rights Amendment (ERA), 329, 336, 340–341, 358, 405
  inequality of, 367–368
  reproductive, 216
  women's, 340–341
Robbery, 272–273, 272f
Roe v. Wade, 217, 251, 407
Role-learning theory, 65, 407
Roles:
  class, 32
  gender, 32, 405
  race, 32
  social, 31–32, 407
Roman Catholic Church, 85, 93, 158, 235, 239, 242, 248
  fundamentalist, 251
  Malleus Maleficarum, 236
  participation in, 245, 246
  women as clergy, 247
Romer vs. Evans, 99
Roosevelt, Eleanor, 338
Rosenfeld v. Southern Pacific Company, 204
Rule of thumb, 183
Russian Federation, 177t
Russian Orthodox, 242

S
Saint-Simon, Henry, 355
Same-sex marriage, 99, 171
San Francisco, California, 171, 188
Sanctified church, 245, 246, 407
Sanctions, 33–35
Sanger, Margaret, 218
SAT (Scholastic Aptitude Test), 295
Saudi Arabia, 177t
Scandinavia, 323, 324f
Scholastic Aptitude Test (SAT), 295

Schools, 291–295. *See also*
    Education
    sexual harassment in, 302
    socialization and, 40–41
Science:
    gender and, 304–312
    interest in learning, 304–305,
        305f
    social construction of, 309–310
    women's status in, 304–307,
        306f
Science/gender system, 305
Scientific method, 307–308, 407
Scientific movement, 310
Second Great Awakening,
    237–239, 407
Second shift, 14, 143, 407
Sega Genesis games, 40
Segregation:
    gender, 405
    occupational, 270
    racial, 330–331
Self-esteem, 293, 407
Self-fulfilling prophecy, 292, 407
Seneca Falls Convention, 335
Sensation seeking, 211
Separate spheres, question of,
    385
Service work, 129
Seventeen magazine, 61, 68
Sex, 29
    culture and, 20–103
    definition of, 93, 407
    gender and, 20–103
Sex chromosomes, 22, 407
Sex differences:
    in aggression, 262
    in crime, 262
    in delinquency, 261–262
Sex differentiation, fetal, 22
Sex education programs,
    188–189
Sex reassignment, 23
Sex workers, 265, 331
Sex/gender system, 387, 407
Sexism, 128, 389, 390
    definition of, 407
    as ideology, 71–72, 381
Sexual abuse, 186–187, 266–267,
    270
    in women's prisons, 282
Sexual assault, 273, 273f

Sexual attitudes:
    contemporary, 79–83
    gender gap in, 81, 82f
Sexual development, 85–88
Sexual harassment, 141–142, 291
    definition of, 141, 407
    in the military, 330
    in schools, 302
Sexual identity, 398
    ambiguous, 22–24
    biological basis of, 22
Sexual intercourse:
    definition of, 80
    first, 81, 83f
Sexual inversion, 78
Sexual orientation, 95
Sexual politics, 79, 84, 333
    definition of, 407
    of pornography, 63
Sexual relations, 80
Sexual revolution, 79
Sexual stereotypes, 78
Sexual violence, 84–85, 275–276
Sexuality, 76–103, 397–399
    and gender, 77
    history of, 77–79
    politics of, 79
    and power, 84–85
    social construction of, 77
    as social process, 387
    and the state, 387–388
    in the United States, 77–79
Sexually dimorphic traits, 24–25
    definition of, 407
    nature/nurture and, 24–25
Shelley, Mary, 221
Shepard, Matthew, 99
Sims, J. Marion, 222
Sisters United, 326
Skewed work groups, 140
Slavery, 106–107, 241, 355
    families in, 178
"Sluts," 264
Smedley, Agnes, 377
Smith, Adam, 365
Smith College, 334
Smoking, 209, 210–212, 211f
SNCC (Student Nonviolent
    Coordinating Committee),
    339–340
Soap operas, 64–65
Social behavior, 261

Social change, 367–368
    gender and, 348–403
    religion and, 247–255
Social conflict, 264–265
Social construction:
    of families, 159–161
    of gender, 20–52, 363–365, 407
    of knowledge, 53–75, 69–71,
        307–312
    of science, 309–310
    of sexuality, 77
Social constructionist theory, 58,
    407
Social control, 235–237
Social deviance, 264
Social institutions, 30–31
    definition of, 407
    gender and, 104–347
Social justice, 248–249
Social learning theory, 407
Social movements, 334, 407
Social problems, 205–214
    families and, 182–193
Social reform, 348–372
Social roles, 31–32, 407
Social Security, 42
Social Security Administration,
    136
Social structure, 8
    definition of, 407
    of health, 200–205
    linking with human action,
        163–164
    of work, 113
Socialist feminism, 352, 374, 375,
    377–386
    comparison with liberal and
        radical feminism, 389–390
    critique of Marx, 383–386
    definition of, 407
    view of women's status,
        385–386
Socialization:
    adult, 41–43
    childhood, 38–40
    of children, 384
    definition of, 407
    game stage, 39
    gender, 33–37, 405
    imitation stage, 38–39
    in infancy, 37–38
    across the life course, 37–43

Socialization *(continued)*
  play stage, 39
  and schools, 40–41
Socialization perspective, 33
  limitations of, 48–49
Society of Women Engineers, 125
Sociological framework, 16
Sociological imagination, 6–9,
  407
Sociological perspectives:
  on crime and deviance,
    260–267
  on religion, 234–235
Sociologists for Women in
  Society, 125
Sociology, 302–303, 360
  as empirical, 16
  of knowledge, 68–72, 407
Sororities, 92, 275–276
Southeast Asians, 86, 180
Southern Baptists, 247
*Southern Bell Telephone and
  Telegraph Company,
  Weeks v.,* 204
*Southern Pacific Company,
  Rosenfeld v.,* 204
Spain, 329
Speculum, 222
Sperm, 308–309
Spirituality, 254
  feminism and, 252–255
  gender and, 242, 244f
  "new age," 255
Sports Illustrated, 60
Sports Illustrated for Women, 60
Stalking, 274, 275
  partner violence, 183, 183t
Standardized tests, 295
Standpoint theory, 311, 407
Stanton, Elizabeth Cady, 239,
  335, 336, 361
State, the, 318–320, 388
  definition of, 318–319, 407
  as gendered institution, 319
  as male, 320, 388
  sexuality and, 387–388
Stay-at-home moms, 144
Steinberg, Judy, 316
Stereotype threat, 292–293, 407
Stereotypes, 55
  cultural, 42
  of feminism, 342

gender, 27, 28f
  popular, 58
  sexual, 78
Sterility, male, 204
Sterilization rates, 203,
  218–219
Stewart, Maria, 355
Stewart, Martha, 260
"Sticky floor," 135–136
Stone, Lucy, 336
Stone, Vernon, 73
Stratification:
  class, 116, 404
  gender, 115–119, 405
  social, 407
Streaming, 292
Stress, 35, 36f
Structural diversity model, 159,
  176
Student Nonviolent
  Coordinating Committee
  (SNCC), 339–340
"Studs," 264
Subculture of violence, 276–277,
  407
Subjectivity, 158
Substance abuse, 209–212
Sudan, 331
Suffrage:
  Black, 334–335
  women's, 334–335, 336, 350
Suicide:
  death rates, 200, 201f, 202
  racial, 218
Supermoms, 143, 169
Superstereotypes, 58
Superstructure, 379, 407
Suttee, 29
Sweatshops, 127–128
  definition of, 407
  electronic, 126
Sweden, 177t
Symbolic interaction theory,
  46–47, 407

T

Taliban, 161, 237, 249–250
TANF (Temporary Assistance
  for Needy Families), 138,
  407
Taylor, Harriet, 362
Technology, reproductive, 225

Teen pregnancy, 187–189
Television, 60
  children's, 60–61
  "constant television
    households," 60–61
Television and News Research
  website, 73
Television cartoons, 40
Television news, 63, 66
Temperance movement, 336,
  350, 407
Temporary Assistance for Needy
  Families (TANF), 138, 407
Thailand, 265
Theology:
  Christian, 253, 254, 377
  feminist, 405
  liberation, 241, 248, 406
  radical feminist, 253, 254
Theoretical perspectives, 43–47,
  47–48
Tilted work groups, 140
Tipton, Billy, 46–47
Title IX, Educational
  Amendments of 1972, 147,
  291, 297, 407
Title VII, Civil Rights Bill of
  1964, 141, 147, 204, 407
Tokenism, 139–141
Tracking, 292, 407
Trade union movement, 376
Trade unions, 128, 132
Transgender, 24, 407
Transnational families, 180, 408
Transsexuals, 29
Transvestites, 29
Troy Female Seminary, 289
True womanhood, cult of, 110,
  237
Truth, Sojourner, 335, 355, 390
TV Land, 70

U

Uniform Crime Reports (FBI), 267,
  274, 408
Uniform work groups, 140
United Kingdom, 177t
United States v. Virginia, 328
Universe of discourse, 67
University of Maryland
  Women's Studies Database,
  52